CHRISTIAN SPIRITUALITY
Post-Reformation and Modern

World Spirituality

An Encyclopedic History of the Religious Quest

Board of Editors and Advisors

EWERT COUSINS, *General Editor*

Volume 18 of
World Spirituality:
An Encyclopedic History
of the Religious Quest

CHRISTIAN SPIRITUALITY

POST-REFORMATION AND MODERN

Edited by
Louis Dupré
and
Don E. Saliers

in collaboration with
John Meyendorff

CROSSROAD • NEW YORK

This printing: 1998

The Crossroad Publishing Company
370 Lexington Avenue, New York, NY 10017

World Spirituality, Volume 18
Diane Apostolos-Cappadona, Art Editor

Printed in the United States of America

Library of Congress Cataloging-in-Publication Data

Christian spirituality : post-reformation and modern / edited by Louis
Dupré and Don E. Saliers in collaboration with John Meyendorff.
    p.   cm. — (World spirituality ; v. 18)
            Bibliography: p.
            Includes indexes.
        ISBN 0-8245-0766-5; 0-8245-1144-1 (pbk.)
1. Spirituality — History of doctrines.   I. Dupré, Louis K., 1925–
II. Saliers, Don E., 1937–   .   III. Meyendorff, John, 1926–
                    IV. Series.
            BV4490.C49   1989
        248'.09'03 — dc 19   89-526
                                    CIP

Contents

Preface to the Series

T HE PRESENT VOLUME is part of a series entitled World Spirituality: An Encyclopedic History of the Religious Quest, which seeks to present the spiritual wisdom of the human race in its historical unfolding. Although each of the volumes can be read on its own terms, taken together they provide a comprehensive picture of the spiritual strivings of the human community as a whole—from prehistoric times, through the great religions, to the meeting of traditions at the present.

Drawing upon the highest level of scholarship around the world, the series gathers together and presents in a single collection the richness of the spiritual heritage of the human race. It is designed to reflect the autonomy of each tradition in its historical development, but at the same time to present the entire story of the human spiritual quest. The first five volumes deal with the spiritualities of archaic peoples in Asia, Europe, Africa, Oceania, and North and South America. Most of these have ceased to exist as living traditions, although some perdure among tribal peoples throughout the world. However, the archaic level of spirituality survives within the later traditions as a foundational stratum, preserved in ritual and myth. Individual volumes or combinations of volumes are devoted to the major traditions: Hindu, Buddhist, Taoist, Confucian, Jewish, Christian, and Islamic. Included within the series are the Jain, Sikh, and Zoroastrian traditions. In order to complete the story, the series includes traditions that have not survived but have exercised important influence on living traditions—such as Egyptian, Sumerian, classical Greek and Roman. A volume is devoted to modern esoteric movements and another to modern secular movements.

Having presented the history of the various traditions, the series devotes two volumes to the meeting of spiritualities. The first surveys the meeting of spiritualities from the past to the present, exploring common themes that

A longer version of this preface may be found in Christian Spirituality: Origins to the Twelfth Century, *the first published volume in the series.*

can provide the basis for a positive encounter, for example, symbols, rituals, techniques. The second deals with the meeting of spiritualities in the present and future. Finally, the series closes with a dictionary of world spirituality.

Each volume is edited by a specialist or a team of specialists who have gathered a number of contributors to write articles in their fields of specialization. As in this volume, the articles are not brief entries but substantial studies of an area of spirituality within a given tradition. An effort has been made to choose editors and contributors who have a cultural and religious grounding within the tradition studied and at the same time possess the scholarly objectivity to present the material to a larger forum of readers. For several years some five hundred scholars around the world have been working on the project.

In the planning of the project, no attempt was made to arrive at a common definition of spirituality that would be accepted by all in precisely the same way. The term "spirituality," or an equivalent, is not found in a number of the traditions. Yet from the outset, there was a consensus among the editors about what was in general intended by the term. It was left to each tradition to clarify its own understanding of this meaning and to the editors to express this in the introduction to their volumes. As a working hypothesis, the following description was used to launch the project:

> The series focuses on that inner dimension of the person called by certain traditions "the spirit." This spiritual core is the deepest center of the person. It is here that the person is open to the transcendent dimension; it is here that the person experiences ultimate reality. The series explores the discovery of this core, the dynamics of its development, and its journey to the ultimate goal. It deals with prayer, spiritual direction, the various maps of the spiritual journey, and the methods of advancement in the spiritual ascent.

By presenting the ancient spiritual wisdom in an academic perspective, the series can fulfill a number of needs. It can provide readers with a spiritual inventory of the richness of their own traditions, informing them at the same time of the richness of other traditions. It can give structure and order, meaning and direction to the vast amount of information with which we are often overwhelmed in the computer age. By drawing the material into the focus of world spirituality, it can provide a perspective for understanding one's place in the larger process. For it may well be that the meeting of spiritual paths—the assimilation not only of one's own spiritual heritage but of that of the human community as a whole—is the distinctive spiritual journey of our time.

EWERT COUSINS

Introduction

I

A SURPRISING FEATURE OF "modern" Christian spirituality is its continuity with the past. The same models (the soul as image of God inhabited by a divine presence), the same influences (mainly Neoplatonic) that directed late medieval piety still determine the devotion of the modern age. And yet some of the most fundamental changes of the new era occurred in the area of religion: a Christianity until then basically united in doctrine suddenly became divided. Even more remarkable, then, is it that the spiritual lives of those divided Christians remain so similar to one another and to those of an earlier period. No one would consider Martin Luther a remnant of the Middle Ages. Yet his spiritual outlook is often indistinguishable from such late medieval sources as the *Theologia Germanica* which he himself edited. Comprehensive epochal divisions have increasingly come under question in all areas of culture. What we call "the baroque" in music does not coincide with the baroque in sculpture or painting. More and more we wonder how adequate overall historical divisions that include all areas of culture are. Nowhere is such a question more appropriate than in the devotional movements of the modern age. But spiritual life has a history of its own which admits of epochal distinctions, such as the period beginning with the devotion to the humanity of Christ. Our question, then, should not be primarily which spiritual movements correspond respectively to the cultural movements of Renaissance, baroque, Enlightenment, and romanticism, but rather whether any specifically religious characteristics distinguish spiritual life in the modern age from that of an earlier period. The authors of the following essays believe that there are such characteristics. Despite an undeniable continuity with the past, especially in the Catholic and Orthodox traditions, modern devotion nevertheless strongly reflects the impact of the fundamental changes in outlook and attitude that mark the beginning of the modern age.

Part I of the Introduction was written by Louis Dupré; Part II by Don E. Saliers.

Suddenly in most civilized regions of Europe, first in the Mediterranean area but soon also in the north, men and women felt a need to assert their individual and national identities in a manner they had never felt before. The new impulse also affected their religious attitudes. The term "secularization," often used to describe the change, hardly seems appropriate, if that term implies that modern religion was more world-oriented and less God-oriented than the previous epoch. Few spiritual writers in previous times equalled the radical theocentrism of the ones presented here. Which earlier epoch saw an outburst of spiritual literature such as took place between the middle of the sixteenth and the second half of the seventeenth century? It was the time of the Carmelite school of Teresa and John of the Cross, of the origin of the Jesuits in Spain and Italy and their development in France, of the French school of Olier, Bérulle, and the "devout humanism" of Francis de Sales, of the stern piety of the early Jansenists and of the beginnings of Quietism, of an amazing and irresistible spread of popular Catholic devotions in all of southern and eastern Europe. Taken together these movements constitute an unprecedented explosion of genuine spiritual life.

Yet the flowering of mystical movements may contain a darker message as well. One author has described it as a proliferation around a loss. "It reveals an absence that increases desire. At the threshold of modernity we encounter an end and a beginning—a departure."[1] In what does the loss consist, and what is the new "departure"? However continuous with its Christian past, since the end of the Middle Ages spiritual life had increasingly moved toward a marginal position with respect to culture as a whole. No longer firmly rooted in the communal experience of the High Middle Ages it tended to develop into a specialized, highly private mode of religious expression. When traditional structures, both institutional and doctrinal, began to be shaken, a need arose to seek salvation within oneself or in limited groups of like-minded Christians somewhat apart from the main body. Now, those intensely pursuing the life of the spirit have always displayed a certain independence vis-à-vis the hierarchical church as a whole. Every religious order owes its origin to a communal drive toward some spiritual autonomy. But the chasm created by late medieval theology between universal concepts and singular reality invited a more radically different experience, less mediated by established doctrinal and social structures (some of which had lost much of their former security). An increasingly rigid clericalization, begun after the Councils of Constance and Basel and eventually resulting in a total rejection of the conciliar theory, drove many devout believers toward a more internal, hence more personal, religious practice. "Spiritual life" thus assumed an existence of its own, next to and occasionally in opposition with, the institutional church. Meanwhile the church itself had ceased to be the sole spiritual power of the new age. The political bodies of the emerging national states ever more strongly emphasized their distinctness with respect to that universal culture of which the church for such a long time had been the sole guardian and the main repository.

With this breakdown of the traditional link between religious meaning and social structures, the need for a new discourse arose. Being the depth dimension of the entire culture, spiritual life had previously not required a language of its own. In the religious disembodiment of the late Middle Ages the search for a separate space and for a distinct discourse became imperative. The space was the *inner* realm of the soul, the discourse the confessional language of the self. Modern treatises in "mystical theology" continued the earlier Christian traditions, but they were phrased in a different language. The new meaning of the term "mystical" was itself symptomatic of a novel attitude. In the sixteenth century, its specialized meaning came to include most of what the more comprehensive terms "contemplative" or "spiritual" had signified in an earlier, homogeneously religious culture. The significance of this development is not that "mystical contemplation" became a universal characteristic of all religion, but rather that it was taken out of the mainstream of religious life and transferred to a relatively independent province. The creation of the noun "mysticism" (or *mystique,* or *Mystik*) completed the separation of what had once been an integral part of a complex religious attitude. The term "mystical theology" conveyed a quasi-independent status to private religious experience, thereby sealing the compartmentalization. In the absence of a solid ontological basis and the disintegration of scholastic theology (both resulting from the nominalist crisis) the development of the new language attained overriding importance. Without a new "mystical" language, it would have been exceedingly difficult to distinguish a "modern" spirituality as such. The divide that separates the modern from the pre-modern takes on a decidedly linguistic quality.

Still, to describe religious life in the new era, especially in its more balanced expressions, as "marginal" would convey a distorted picture. Again and again at the threshold of the new era and, even more so, after the Council of Trent, the Catholic Church attempted to reattach the powerful but privatized centers of spiritual renewal to her own main body. Most of the following essays, especially the ones on Catholic popular devotions and early Jesuit spirituality, show the remarkable extent to which it succeeded. The discussion of Jansenism and Quietism indicates that, even where the church failed, the vital ties with the "mystical body" were not severed on either side. In baroque art, Tridentine devotion, even in the highest Spanish and French mysticism, the church continued to provide both the main inspiration and the strongest spiritual impulse. For the most part thoroughly sacramental, the new piety remained intimately bound to what its adepts continued to regard as the sole source of grace. Nonetheless, even in these orthodox, ecclesial expressions, a new, more reflective, and more deliberate disposition became apparent. For as the new age wore on, the meaningfulness of a spiritual life ceased to be linked to the culture itself. It was to be "chosen" or, at least, freely accepted. This, however, was certainly not yet the case in the sixteenth century. When the Christian churches had fully come to terms with the new situation, spiritual life regained much of the communal quality it had lost at the end of the Middle Ages. The exhilarating mood of spiritual expansion, of a socially integrated new piety that prevailed all through the seventeenth century found an exuberant expression in baroque art.

Must we not say then, that, at least until the great withdrawal of the eighteenth century, the church regained control over the more intense spiritual movements, which it had lost in the fifteenth and early sixteenth centuries? Had the richness, both internal and external, of baroque devotion not effectively responded to the challenges of theological nominalism, political secularization, and pagan humanism? Yes and no. Granted, the recession of spiritual life from the mainstream of culture and even from the ecclesiastical rule did not *appear* until the eighteenth century. Yet what emerged at that time had begun as early as the fifteenth century and the temporary successes of the church provide no sufficient grounds for assuming a total reversal of the tide. Even at the height of the baroque expansion, "spiritual life" in the narrower, modern sense retained its separate character. Neither the intensity nor the multiplicity of its manifestations could prevent it from existing on the side of common practice and belief, and largely separate from the main currents of philosophical and scientific culture. Yet once it became able to create new channels, a language, organizations, and doctrinal schools relatively autonomous with respect to traditional ecclesiastical structures, its tremendous religious energy suddenly became released.

In one area, however, Christian spirituality achieved a real and definitive new integration with modern culture at large, namely, in its attitude toward human nature. The new trust in human nature, characteristic of the Jesuit schools (both the earlier, Spanish-Italian and the later French), the "devout humanism" of Francis de Sales and his many followers, as well as of the new popular devotions, links modern piety to Renaissance humanism. Even where the pessimism of the late Middle Ages continues to prevail, as in the "French school" and in Jansenism, the humanist attitude remains unchallenged. A new reflection on the religious significance of that position distinguishes modern piety. All its schools teach that human nature surpasses itself, both cognitively and appetitively, in ascending toward that higher reality of which it bears the image. In a humanist such as Francis de Sales no unbridgeable chasm separates this "natural" drive from the order of grace: a human nature called to this high vocation possesses a certain self-sufficiency and demands a basic trust in its light and power. Christian humanism assumes that all human beings are called not only to salvation but also to the higher life of the spirit.

Francis de Sales and his direct and indirect followers (J.-P. Camus, Yves de Paris), as well as the Jesuit spiritual writers, considered human nature totally incapable of posing a single salvific act without the support of a grace indispensable even for fulfilling nature's own goals. But, contrary to Bérulle and the writers of the French school, they denied that nature is to be "annihilated" in order to attain its supernatural destiny. If human nature has, at least in its *basic* aspirations and powers, remained sound, the principal task of spiritual life consists in allowing God's grace to accomplish its work without putting up any resistance. Such also was the guiding thesis of Quietist spirituality, which, in spite of more hazardous assumptions, in this respect remains solidly linked to the theology of devout humanism. Even the idea of "pure love" preferring God's pleasure to its own salvation appears already in Francis de Sales.

The emphasis on the central position of human nature was accompanied by a more comprehensive shift in attitude toward all of nature and a new vision of God's immanence in creation. Neoplatonic and Jewish ideas played an important role in this shift. Using the traditional paradigm of the divine circle, the center of which is everywhere and the circumference nowhere, we may say that, at the beginning of the modern age God's presence, more than before, is regarded as extending to the entire circumference of the created world. In Marsilio Ficino's words: "The divine center is in every place, that is, the power (*virtù*) which God attributes to the [created] natures is present in every minimal particle of the universe."[2] While the idea of an omnipresent center precedes the modern age, this presence now appears as dynamically moving into the created world and actively operating in it. Within this God-filled nature, the human person functions as the *copula mundi*, the microcosmic center that unites the various parts of the created universe with one another and with their divine origin. Such a central position in creation links persons to God as much as the divine inhabitation in the soul does. Spiritual life gains a new complexity by this greater concern with creation. Next to the turn inward to the divine center, the devout mind also moves out to the created periphery in a breathing-like rhythm of expansion and contraction. Such a movement from periphery to center and back had, in some measure, been anticipated in the fourteenth century by Jan van Ruusbroec's perpetual alternation from "essential" to "operational" union.

Modern spirituality appears within a new space, as if it had discovered another dimension of God's presence. Both aesthetics and devotion endeavor to fill this space with a multitude of forms, all of which, in their own finite way, reveal different aspects of the inexhaustible divine plenitude. The exuberance of "baroque" spirituality derives from a deeply felt urge to find ever new *loci* of the divine presence. Spiritual life itself takes on a multi-tudinous character—a luxuriant growth of ever more saints, angels, shrines, and popular devotions, an explosion of new religious congregations and schools of spirituality. Its wasteful exuberance baffles us, until we perceive it as the first exploration of the newly discovered spiritual space.

Yet the new space also revealed a new emptiness. As the physical universe in the period from Copernicus to Galileo gradually unfolded its immense proportions, the created world itself appeared lost in an infinite void. The abyss of God's infinite fullness manifest in creation seemed paralleled by the abyss of an infinite emptiness that surrounded this creation. In Pascal we hear the first cry of terror of this unholy void: "Je vois ces effrayables espaces de l'univers qui m'enferment" (*Pensées* 418). Here, contrary to the expansive movement we have just described, appears a circumference that has no center. Instead of an infinitely expanding center we have, as George Poulet has so aptly expressed it, an infinitely retracting one. This movement once again forces the god-seeking soul to abandon the ambiguous space around itself and drives her back into her own internal realm. Yet there a similar abysmal void confronts her. For from the infinitely small space of the soul also the divine center has vanished. One finds oneself alone, a point between two empty infinities.

Pascal and the early Jansenists forcefully express the disproportion between the universe, both external and internal, and the divine reality. The sense of absence, here first felt, becomes increasingly poignant as the modern age advances. In Newman we hear this cry of distress:

> What strikes the mind so forcibly and so painfully, is His absence, (if I may so speak) from His own world. It is a silence that speaks. It is as if others had got possession of His work. Why does not He, our Maker and Ruler, give us some immediate knowledge of Himself!"[3]

Such feelings would seem incompatible with the awareness of a divine presence on which spiritual life is based. Yet here we witness the birth of spiritual consciousness that, in the sense of absence itself, attains a negative but immediate sense of God's presence. The joyful awareness of God's pres-ence in nature yields to a profound suspicion of the entire natural order and ends up taking refuge in divine grace. A spiritual outlook based on such a negative experience would not appear to be conducive to mystical intimacy. And, indeed, Nicole, one of the prominent Jansenist theologians, became the leading polemicist against mysticism. Even so, the awareness that God's grace, without any natural mediation and in spite of personal corruption, has elected me to be fully and intrinsically redeemed, attains a unique spiritual intensity. Here at least Jansenism meets those more mystical movements that seemed, and were in fact, its natural adversaries.

Starting from a wholly different idea of human nature, Quietism promoted a similar abandon to God's grace. Though rooted in traditional, wholly orthodox sources, Quietist piety was occasioned by the sixteenth- and seventeenth-century discussions on nature and grace, and, more than any other spiritual movement of the modern age, by that experience of a "void" characteristic of the later phase of that period. In that void only language remains. Thus, paradoxically, a movement inclined to silence depends, more than any other spiritual current, on verbal articulation. Being so thoroughly modern both in its experience of a void and in its need to fill that void with language, it continues to attract, as a feeling of divine absence has become more universal in our entire culture. In the annihilation of desire, it strives to attain a new awareness of God's immanence beyond a *sense* of presence or absence.

Still, Jansenism and Quietism, though perhaps the most typically "modern," are not the most representative movements of modern devotion. Most schools continued to live in the earlier awareness of God's presence in nature without insisting so radically either on the contrast between the natural and the supernatural or on the need to "abandon" nature. Contrary to appearances, the high peaks of Carmelite spirituality show more affinity with the lowly valleys of Jesuit asceticism or Capuchin popular devotion than with the emptiness of the Quietists. They all optimistically agree that human nature may be elevated by divine grace and within itself redeem the entire cosmos. Today both tendencies, the positive and the negative, continue to exist. The expansive one continues to prevail in the Eastern church as well as in Western spiritual theologies of creation—such as those of Teilhard de Chardin and Hans Urs von Balthasar. The tendency to find God in the void appears most strongly in some monastic orders (particularly Cistercians) and in many spiritual men and women who, overwhelmed by the desacralization of modern life, have sought refuge in negative theologies—not only the ones elaborated in modern schools, but also those of an earlier Christian tradition going back to Dionysius and Eckhart, or even those of the non-Christian East.

II

The broad themes portrayed thus far constitute the complex tapestry of religious and philosophical ideas which characterize "modern" Christian spirituality. While the preceding section has focused principally on Roman Catholic movements, these same themes may be discerned in relation to the post-Reformation Protestant and Anglican traditions as well. To more specific non-Roman developments we must now turn, but with an initial reminder that Orthodox spirituality displays a very different set of concerns — most especially, a concerted effort to return to the "canon" of spirituality of the Byzantine millennium. One of the noteworthy turns of the twentieth century is precisely the unexpected impact of this trajectory within Orthodoxy upon the patterns of theological reflection and spiritual life among the divided Western churches, now searching for deeper unity.

The forces unleashed by the sixteenth-century reformers on the Continent and in England were at once social-political and theological-religious. The external changes in the liturgy, for example, which were wrought in the first-generation Lutheran and Reformed congregations, began to reshape the way believers prayed and conceived of the Christian life. The replacement of Latin by the vernacular languages in Wittenberg, Geneva, Zurich, Strassbourg, and other centers where the reformers gained ascendancy shifted both the sound and the sense of prayer. More powerful still was the introduction of congregational singing, of freely composed hymns among Lutherans and of metrical psalmody among the Calvinists. Eventually the whole range of proliferating Protestant bodies could be differentiated by virtue of what the people sang and heard in the patterns of preaching and teaching. The shaping of experience and doctrine by hymns and songs based on biblical texts and images, which were reinforced in preaching and catechetical structures, was a singular hallmark of the Protestant Reformation. So true was this, that for most nonliturgical Free Church traditions we can say that their hymnody carried their theology and expressed their pattern of religious exerience — and still does so today.

An appreciation of the liturgical reforms and especially the emergence of distinctive scripturally based congregational song, coupled with powerful new forms of preaching and catechesis, is necessary to understand the distinctive characteristics of the proliferating forms of Protestant spirituality from the second generation of the Reformation forward. In important respects the ear replaced the eye as the principal organ of faith. It is remarkable, of course, that the use of classical Catholic manuals of piety and devotion (both directly and as models for Protestant books) is pervasive, especially among the various Puritan movements. This is seen most clearly in the essays by Richard Lovelace, Charles Hambrick-Stowe, and Glenn Hinson. The larger philosophical issues of activist and Quietist types of spirituality among Protestants and Catholics, along with the impact of humanism and the debates over the relation between nature and grace all surface in these concrete forms of specific practice.

Luther's conception of the Christian life took the form of being passive under the divine grace and active in love toward the neighbor. But there also emerged a volatility and an ambiguity in the Lutheran approach concerning the need to *experience* God's gracious and justifying action in the life of the believer. As Jill Raitt rightly suggests, this ambiguity with respect to the validity of experience was, in the subsequent generation of Lutherans, "resolved on the side of experience by the pietists and against experience on the part of the seventeenth-century Lutheran scholastics."[4] The role of experiencing God's presence and activity in the life of believers, both individual and communal, is a central issue in every Christian tradition. But the complex number of variables that go together to determine a specific way of resolving the question in practice as well as in theology makes generalization difficult. Thus, the tension between the rationalist orthodox and pietist developments in both Lutheran and Calvinist traditions provides a principle for interpreting the impact of the Enlightenment on Protestant spirituality, as the essays by Eric Lund and Albert Outler amply illustrate.

At the same time, questions of what kind and intensity of focus attend the cultivation of spiritual experience run through the Radical Reformation developments, as well as debates among Non-Conformists in England and their common protest of the distinctively Anglican ethos. Within the Church of England and its subsequent far-flung branches, the point/counterpoint between evangelicals and Anglo-Catholic forms of devotion and spiritual discipline—not to mention styles of liturgical celebration and predominant hymnody—continues on into the nineteenth and twentieth centuries. The Wesleyan evangelical reforms of the eighteenth century, portrayed in David Trickett's essay, and the Oxford Movement of the nineteenth century are but two significant historical moments in the point/counterpoint. As is evident in the essay on Anglican spirituality and the concluding essay on the twentieth-century ecumenical developments, these seeming polarities are not always incompatible.

The tensions within the various first-generation Protestant movements over the role of experience and the relation between nature and grace continue some of the classical tensions inherent in the Western Catholic tradition. Perhaps the most comprehensive way of understanding the analogies and conflicts between Protestant and Catholic traditions, at least until recent times, is to reflect on the question of mediation. How is God's self-giving in human history and in the created order mediated to the church and to individuals? For the traditions springing from the Church of England, with its essential resonance with the Roman Catholic and the Eastern churches, the amplitude of mediation was maintained. That is, spirituality honors the accumulation of cultural forms which can mediate God's revelation to the church. Experientially, we may observe, the saints, the cycles of time, and the honoring of venerable liturgical forms are the genius of prayerbook spirituality, bringing the treasures of monasticism and the early church to the laity's participation in common worship. The Reformed traditions, whether in Geneva, Zurich, or in Scotland, and later into American Calvinist and Puritan traditions, distrust the mediation of grace through saints and ceremony or through the sacramental life of the church. The heart of Puritan forms of communal life was personal religion, a "sense of the heart" in which one had access to the divine forgiveness and grace without mediation of churchly tradition. The more radical or "left-wing" the tradition, the more stress was placed on unmediated access to grace, *sola fide,* to "pure experience" and "pure doctrine," as it were.

The stress on the individual before God without mediation of saints, ceremony, sacramental system, and "works" was a central principle for Luther. Yet Luther's liturgical reforms were conservative, as, for example, in his keeping the sacrament of penance and maintaining the elevation of the Host at Mass. The Lutheran traditions themselves continued to struggle with the question, How may we speak of sanctification yet avoid antinomianism without at the same time falling back into works-righteousness? This is, of course, to cast the issue in the vocabulary of the sixteenth and seventeenth centuries, though many Protestant traditions—especially the heirs of scholasticism or rationalist orthodoxy—continue to address the issues of spirituality this way. The Protestant spiritual traditions may better be understood today as living out the long-standing debate about how much cultural mediation of the grace of God in Christ is theologically and experientially permissible.

The issue, reflected in the tensions implicit in Smith's essay on the Afro-American traditions as well as in the issues of emerging feminist visions of the spiritual life, is whether the minimalism inherent in the Lutheran and most Protestant traditions is there to protect the centrality of the person and work of Christ from impurities and distortions, not to say idolatries. Conversely, is the amplitude of mediation of God's grace through saints and sacraments and varieties of indigenous cultural modes of expression required to do justice to all that the Christ has accomplished for the redemption of the world? This is, of course, to put the issues christologically. We may also put the issue in terms of the whole life of God conceived of as trinitarian.

On the one hand, the spiritual sensibility that emphasizes the pure and singularly mediated saving grace of God through Christ avoids the confusion of cultural spirit with the revelation of God. On the other—and this is a more characteristically Catholic and Anglican stance, reflected in part in Methodist, pentecostal, and various holiness emphases on growth in grace and sanctification—one can note a more flexible posture toward the contributions of indigenous cultural forms to the mediation of God's activity. In some cases Christian spirituality is marked by a focus on God's whole work in the world "outside" the church, with which the church is called to identify. This comes through in David Tracy's final sections as well as in the concluding essays in the fourth section of this volume, which speak of liberationist themes.

The twentieth century has witnessed a remarkable convergence and mutual interanimation of diverse traditions of spiritual life. Not only have the ecumenical and liturgical movements created an unprecedented sharing among Roman Catholic, Orthodox, and Protestant communions, but the increased social contact of ordinary believers, especially in North America and where pentecostalism and charismatic movements in Africa and Latin America have cut across denominational lines, has made sharing of mutual approaches to spirituality more natural, less proscribed by historical traditions. The growing awareness and appreciation of ways of spirituality across traditions as well as within traditions which have historically at times been polarized have created an entirely new climate. At the same time, the most essential and most venerable of the strands of Christian spirituality, in practice and in theology, have emerged with more force precisely because of the new situation. It is no longer easy to associate pure continuity with the Catholic tradition and discontinuity with the Protestant varieties—though it is unwise to ignore the counterforces of sectarian and virulently reactionary forces working within both Protestant and Catholic circles in our age. The convergences and mutual awareness must also be seen, in part, as a function of how the lacerations and antireligious forces have impinged on the entire Christian community in the twentieth century.

The convergences of liturgical structures, the shared approaches, both scholarly and devotional, to Scripture, and the common search for classics in prayer are shaping the whole of the Christian family of church traditions in powerful and unpredictable ways. In the late twentieth century we find Christians in the Anglican as well as Lutheran, Reformed, and more Free Church traditions drawing increasingly on the witness of writings of such diverse figures as Bonhoeffer, Merton, Anthony Bloom, and the *Philokalia* as well as admiring Dag Hammarskjöld and Simone Weil. Various renewal movements have affected Catholics, Anglicans, and Protestants with equal force.

At the same time, the problems of modernity have permeated much of the Protestant tradition, especially with respect to the bearing of Scripture upon patterns of piety and belief. The essay by David Pacini provides an excursus on the travail of modern spirituality in the Western churches, which, he argues, may be located in a shift in our understanding of language and the conception of writing and "text" which is found in the seventeenth century. The rise of biblical fundamentalism in our own times is but one manifestation of modernity—a rationalist approach to Scripture which shapes a distinctive form of religious life and theology.

Yet a final word is needed to situate the Western traditions. Perhaps the most surprising development, and in some ways the most paradoxical, is the impact of the revival of Orthodoxy on Protestant and Catholic spiritualities. The turn to the Byzantine "canon" of spirituality—the writings of the fathers, the monastic doctrine and experience of prayer in all its forms, the divine liturgy (Eucharist), and the ascetical way of life, epitomized in the *Philokalia*—has influenced both theology and practical vision in the late twentieth century. This is most notable in the work and worship of the World Council of Churches and, in particular, the documents of the Faith and Order Commission, discussed in the concluding essay of the volume. Alexander Schmemann and others have spoken of the scholastic and Western captivity of the Orthodox.[5] The distinctiveness of Eastern spirituality emerges in the essays in Part 3, so aptly concluded by John Meyendorff.

Certainly Orthodoxy is facing a formidable task within its own panoply of cultural and nationalistic differences. Yet the vision of a truly eschatological orientation for the whole of the church and the spirituality of all believers is being recovered and offered to the churches of the West. Here the themes of a living reality of eschatological life in the world and the power of the mystery of God's self-giving to transfigure culture itself are at the heart of the cosmic dimensions of Orthodox spirituality. Whether a genuine sharing across Western and Eastern Christian traditions is possible, while respecting the profound cultural differenes in mediation of God's self-giving remains an open question. Within the lifetime of the writers in this volume we are bound to see further developments, but perhaps no ecclesial resolution of this matter short of the eschaton itself. Yet lessons for the development of deeper Christian life today and for generations yet unborn can be learned from our tangled and complex history of spirituality, even as it unfolds, by reading the volume attentively.

LOUIS DUPRÉ
DON E. SALIERS

Notes

1. Michel de Certeau, *La fable mystique* (Paris: Gallimard, 1983) 25.
2. *Tractatus de Deo et Anima Vulgaris* (1457) *Supplementum Ficinianum* 11:147.
3. John Henry Newman, *A Grammar of Assent* (Garden City, NY: Doubleday, 1955) 39.
4. Jill Raitt, "Saints and Sinners: Roman Catholic and Protestant Spirituality in the Sixteenth Century," in *Christian Spirituality: High Middle Ages and Reformation,* ed. Jill Raitt et al. (World Spirituality 17; New York: Crossroad, 1987) 462.
5. Alexander Schmemann, *Introduction to Liturgical Theology,* trans. Asheleigh Moorhouse (London: Faith Press, 1966) 9–27; and especially his *For the Life of the World* (New York: St. Vladimir's Press, 1973).

General Bibliography

Sources

Classics of Western Spirituality. Edited by Richard J. Payne and John Farina. New York: Paulist Press. 1978–. 50+ vols.

Migne, J. P. ed. *Patrologiae cursus completus. Series graeca*. Paris: J. P. Migne, 1857–66. 161 vols.

Migne, J. P., ed. *Patrologiae cursus completus. Series latina*. Paris: J. P. Migne, 1844–64. 221 vols. and 4 index vols.

Studies

Bouyer, Louis, Jean Leclercq, and François Vandenbroucke. *A History of Christian Spirituality*. 3 vols. New York: Seabury, 1982. Vol. 1, *The Spirituality of the New Testament and the Fathers*. Vol. 2, *The Spirituality of the Middle Ages*. Vol. 3, *Orthodox Spirituality and Protestant and Anglican Spirituality*. The original French edition of this series also included Louis Cognet, *La spiritualité moderne* as part 2 of vol. 3 (Paris: Aubier, 1966).

Cross, F. L., and E. A. Livingstone. *The Oxford Dictionary of the Christian Church*. 2nd ed. Oxford: Oxford University Press, 1974.

[*Dict. Sp.*] *Dictionnaire de spiritualité ascétique et mystique doctrine et histoire*. Edited by Marcel Viller, assisted by F. Cavallera, J. de Guibert. Paris: Beauchesne, 1937–. This is the most useful single work for the history of Christian spirituality. As of 1983 it had reached volume 12 (fascicles LXXVI-LXXVII) and the letter *P*. The richly detailed and lengthy articles, as well as the generally excellent bibliographies, make this an indispensable work.

Dizionario degli Istituti di Perfezione. Rome: Edizioni Paoline, 1974–. This work, devoted to the history of religious groups and orders, has thus far reached seven volumes, up to the letter *R*.

The Westminster Dictionary of Christian Spirituality. Edited by Gordon S. Wakefield. Philadelphia: Westminster, 1983.

Part One

ROMAN CATHOLIC
SCHOOLS AND MOVEMENTS

1

Early Jesuit Spirituality: Spain and Italy

JOHN O'MALLEY

HE STORY OF IGNATIUS LOYOLA is well known and only a brief resumé of it need be provided here. Born into a noble family at the castle of Loyola in northern Spain in 1491, he had the sparse and chivalric education of his class. His military career ended in 1521 with a severe wound in his right leg received during the siege of Pamplona. During his convalescence he underwent a profound religious conversion while reading two medieval works—Ludolph of Saxony's *Life of Christ* and Jacopo da Voragine's lives of the saints entitled the *Golden Legend*.

He then spent a year in prayer and mortification at Manresa (1522–1523), where he experienced temptations and desolation of spirit, but also deep and refreshing mystical insights. He probably composed the substance of his *Spiritual Exercises* at this time, a sort of objectified recording of his own religious journey for the help of others. The desire to engage in some form of spiritual ministry soon convinced him that he needed a formal education in theology. After studying in several cities in Spain from 1524 to 1528, he finally arrived at the University of Paris, where he remained for seven years (1528–1535).

During all these years of study he guided a number of devout students through the course of his *Spiritual Exercises;* in Paris, finally, he gathered around himself a group of companions who would form the nucleus of the new order he soon founded. In 1537 Loyola and his companions went to Italy, and in 1540 Pope Paul III recognized them as a religious order, the Society of Jesus, with Ignatius as the first superior general. The *Exercises* were approved by the same pope in 1548, thus establishing the text as it had by then evolved as the definitive edition. Meanwhile, Ignatius began to compose the *Constitutions* of his order, the most thorough and systematically designed such instrument known up to that time. Toward the end of his life he was persuaded to tell his "story" to one of his companions, Luís Gonçalves

3

da Câmara, but he got no farther than the events of 1538. Brief and jejune in details, the account nonetheless provides considerable information about "the pilgrim," as Ignatius referred to himself, and especially about his motivations and mystical experiences. These documents, along with segments of his spiritual diary and the over seven thousand letters that comprise his correspondence, are the principal basis upon which we reconstruct his religious message. He died in Rome on 31 July 1556.

Like the founders of other religious orders within the Roman Catholic Church, Loyola left an indelible imprint on the spiritual traditions of the Society of Jesus, and thence upon modern Catholicism. Loyola's imprint was intensified, however, beyond that of many other founders. While he was in Paris as a student, he had, in effect, already set the development of the Jesuit order in motion by persuading each of his companions to go through the *Spiritual Exercises* for a month or more under his guidance. This same experience was prescribed for all those who subsequently entered the order. Ignatius obviously hoped to induce in others a conversion and religious experience similar to his own during the early years of his religious quest. As H. Outram Evennett observed: "[The *Exercises*] were in a sense the systematised, de-mysticised quintessence of the process of Ignatius' own conversion and purposeful change of life, and they were intended to work a similar change in others."[1]

The book of the *Exercises,* intended as a manual for the person guiding others through the program it outlines, is divided into four "weeks" or major parts. The first week presents considerations about the purpose of life, the heinousness of sin, and the necessity and sweetness of repentance. The second week begins with a meditation on "the kingdom of Christ," which is followed by a series of meditations on Christ's incarnation and life up to his last days. The third week is dedicated to his suffering and death, and the final week to the apparitions of the risen Savior and related events. Besides these and other meditations, the book contains a number of directives for the director and the retreatant, some guidelines on fasting, almsgiving, and similar matters, and a number of other considerations. The book is not, in the first place, an exposition of a spiritual doctrine, but a detailed program, in outline form, for a month or more of reflection on one's life and on central mysteries of the Christian religion. It has been called with some accuracy "a recipe for conversion."[2] Among the more important appendixes to the book are several sets of "rules." One of them is for "the discernment of spirits" (313–36), in which the saint gives directives concerning the movement of spiritual consolation and desolation. This set of subtle directives has been the object of a number of studies and is generally considered to be one of the most perceptive parts of the book. It is here that we catch some slight glimpse of the author's own spiritual journey and the temptations and confirmations in spiritual growth that he underwent. Morever, the role of "consolation" in Jesuit spirituality and as a goal in the Jesuits' ministry can hardly be overestimated.

Another of these appendixes is a set of rules for "thinking with the Church" (352–70). Almost certainly inspired by Loyola's antipathy to certain ideas of Erasmus and of the Protestant reformers, it sets the *Exercises* firmly within an ecclesiological context. Here we see that for Loyola genuine spirituality had to be founded on a recognition of one's membership in a larger religious community and of the need to test one's inspirations against the objectified traditions of that community. Though often interpreted in a narrowly Roman Catholic sense, these "rules" are susceptible of a less rigoristic reading.

In its concepts, images, and directives, the book of the *Exercises* stands squarely within the Christian spiritual tradition, so much so that the search for its sources has consistently been frustrated by the very commonplace nature of its ideas. Most commentators are agreed, however, upon some direct relationship to the *devotio moderna,* and Ignatius in fact had a special fondness for the principal document of that late-medieval tradition, *The Imitation of Christ.* Aside from the text of the Gospels, the *Imitation* is the only book specifically recommended to the person following the course of the *Exercises* (100).

Despite the commonplace sources upon which the *Exercises* draws, two features of the book give it special force and have made it one of the most important documents in the history of Christian spirituality. The first such feature is its clear design, aimed at carrying out its stated purpose: "to conquer oneself and to order one's life without being influenced in one's decision by any inordinate affection" (21). That clarity of purpose provided the book with a psychological dynamism that, under an experienced director, proved to be extraordinarily powerful. Though the purpose as stated by Ignatius sounds stoic and rationalistic, it is promoted less by logic than by an activation of the affections, especially through the key meditations and considerations. Of special importance here are the meditation on the "Two Standards" (136–48)—that of Christ and that of Satan—and the reflections on "three classes of persons" (149–57) and on the "three kinds of humility" (165–68). In these exercises the aspirations of the retreatant to generosity and to a sense of *noblesse oblige* are particularly appealed to. Loyola's genius lay, therefore, in his sense of psychological organization. With a laconic, understated style and with a mass of seemingly disparate elements, he constructed a course in which generations have found themselves prepared to respond in a new way to an inner call for intimacy with the divine.

But what is especially remarkable about the course Loyola provides is its nonprescriptive character. This is the second feature of the book that deserves special attention. No line in it better expresses what Loyola expected to happen during the *Exercises* than his advice to the director to "permit the Creator to deal directly with the creature, and the creature directly with his Creator and Lord" (15). The saint had a profound confidence in the direct inspiration of God, which he felt he had himself experienced from the first moment of his conversion. The chief purpose of the *Exercises* was to facilitate the reception of such inspiration and make it effective for the future direction of the retreatant's life. Though Loyola's own experience was formally paradigmatic for the structure of the *Exercises,* he insisted that there was no greater error than to believe that God led all along the same path, and he tried to make ample room for such liberty of spirit in his rubrics and directives in the book.

In summary, I would stress that the book, and with it Jesuit spirituality, while being rationalistic in its language and arguments, is more profoundly concerned with right affectivity; while being logical in the organization of its parts, it is more profoundly psychological in its movement and design; and while being methodical in the aids it provides to prayer and spiritual discernment, it is more profoundly nonprescriptive in the outcome it foresees for the direct divine intervention that is its basic premise.

The book is, nonetheless, clear in the goal toward which it points: an "election," an ordering of life "for the greater service and praise" of God. Thus emerges another essential component in Ignatian spirituality. The single word that best expresses this fundamental element is "service." In the key meditation on "the kingdom of Christ" (91–99), the exercitant is urged to "distinguish himself in whatever concerns the service of the eternal king and Lord of all." The knightly imagery and context in which this meditation is enshrined do not essentially diminish the transcultural nature of its appeal. It is this consideration that led Joseph de Guibert to describe the Ignatian way as essentially a "spirituality of service," a phrase upon which it would be difficult to improve.[3]

From the first moment of his conversion, Loyola was attracted by the great deeds of saints like Dominic and Francis. "If they could so distinguish themselves in the service of the Lord, why cannot I?" was the question he repeatedly asked himself. Especially after the year of retreat at Manresa, Loyola specified the "great deeds" in some form of ministry of the Word for the help of others. At first this ministry of the Word was nothing more than informal conversation with devout persons about "the things of God." He soon began to preach to small groups that gathered around him, and then he began to guide individuals through his *Exercises*. The spiritual doctrine of the Jesuits was thereby from its origins intimately related to ministry, and to a certain extent even subordinated to it. With Ignatius we find one of the first strong expressions of this relationship in the history of Christian spirituality, and he provides us in his correspondence and legislation for the order with numerous practical interpretations of it. It is difficult for us, and perhaps it was difficult even for him, fully to realize what a dramatic break he effected with the monastic traditions of the early church and the Middle Ages. A significant influence on his new way of conceiving of religious life may have been that he had no experience of cloister or established monastic practice until he and his companions decided to found their own order.

The most dramatic symbol of what was involved was his adamant refusal to allow the Jesuits to chant the Divine Office in choir. In his day this practice was considered so central to life in a religious order that many considered that the Jesuits could not be a religious order without it. Eager though Ignatius was to conform himself and his followers to the Catholic tradition in the smallest detail, eager though he was for papal approval of the new order, he would not surrender this point. He doubtless saw it as symptomatic of his whole vision of how his spirituality was "ordered." It was ordered to "service," to ministry, and anything that interfered with that ordering, like the obligation to be present in choir several times a day, had to be excluded.

In several important instructions about the training of the younger members of the order, Ignatius insisted that their time for prayer and their ascetical practices be carefully moderated, so that these not interfere with their direct training for ministry. What he envisioned was a correlation of ministry and spirituality so that one was inconceivable for members of the order without the other. His most telling expression of this vision was in his exhortation (*Constitutions* 288) that Jesuits should "find God in all things" — not just in prayer, not only in the disciplined quiet of their houses, not simply in the solitude of their rooms.

Of all his disciples, Jerome Nadal (1507–1580) is the one who gave most powerful articulation of this idea with his celebrated phrase "contemplative in action."[4] Nadal's idea, genuinely reflecting Loyola's, implies the contemporaneity or at least reciprocity of contemplation and ministry. One of Nadal's effective illustrations of his point is his description of the habitation of the members of the order. Their "most perfect dwelling-place is in travel and pilgrimage from place to place, by which they seek to gain for Christ those lost sheep that are perishing."[5] There could hardly be a more dramatic contrast with the typically monastic vow of stability, by which the monk promised to spend his whole life within the confines of the monastery he had entered. This commentary by Nadal gives force to Ignatius's requirement in the *Constitutions* (588) that the members of his order be ready to travel from place to place for the sake of their ministry. The *Imitation of Christ*, one of Loyola's favorite books, warned that the person who traveled much could not expect to attain holiness. Ignatius turned this axiom around by insisting that it was only by engaging in the pilgrimage implied in ministry that the Jesuit could hope to attain the sanctification proper to his vocation.

Once again, it is the ideal of service that underlay this provision. Put in other terms, it was an ideal of availability for the needs of others. This ideal was institutionalized in the Society of Jesus by the famous "fourth vow" of obedience to the pope that professed members pronounced. As universal pastor, the pope had, in Loyola's understanding, the large vision of where the greatest pastoral needs prevailed. The Jesuits wanted to put themselves at his disposition to meet these needs. This was clearly the purpose of the vow as the original members of the order conceived it, and it fits perfectly with the ministerial intentionality with which Ignatian spirituality is imbued. In commenting on this vow, Nadal insists that the Jesuits are to be sent to minister where there are no ministers, where no one else wants to minister, and they are to do this without regard for their personal convenience or preference.[6] Thus a new asceticism begins to emerge that is not dependent for its practice on self-imposed austerities to curb one's own disordered tendencies, but on the rigors and hardship imposed by total dedication to an ideal of ministry in the world of ordinary people, with their often undisciplined needs and demands.

This brings us to the "world-affirming" quality of Ignatian piety. The expression is dangerous, for it can be interpreted as suggesting a compromise with the transcendent or a surrender to its opposite. That interpretation would utterly contradict everything that Loyola had experienced of the divine action within himself and that he hoped for in others. Nonetheless, the term does highlight an engagement with human reality, with all its contingencies, and a positive appreciation for human values that was characteristic of him and his piety.

It is, indeed, possible to trace a gradual evolution in Loyola's thinking on this issue from the days at Manresa, where a rigorous asceticism, a desire for eremitical seclusion, and a distaste for anything that might ingratiate him with his fellows—even cleanliness and a neat appearance—prevailed. This is quite different from the later Ignatius, who heartily recommended to his disciples that, while giving a preeminence to the "supernatural" means of serving God like prayer, they employ all the "natural" means that time and circumstances offered for the advancement of their ministry.

This reconciliation of the natural and the supernatural perhaps found its theological grounding in Loyola's study of Aquinas at Paris, for the great scholastic subscribed to the principle that "grace builds on nature" and fully articulated it in his system. Its true origins, however, relate to his earlier mystical experiences. Be that as it may, Loyola's most sublime expression of this sense of reconciliation was in his "Contemplation for Obtaining Divine Love" at the end of the "fourth week" of the *Exercises* (230–37). Here the exercitant sees "all things as creatures of the goodness of God and reflections of it." He is urged to relish this profound religious truth. Ignatius thus moves the Christian tradition of asceticism away from the ideal of the *contemptus mundi* that characterized much of the spirituality of the Middle Ages and was found in a marked degree even in the *devotio moderna,* from which he originally drew some of his own inspiration.

Although this theological insight can be correlated with the medieval system of Aquinas, it also corresponded in a general way with one aspect of the religious culture of the Italian Renaissance in which the early Jesuits moved. Especially at the papal court in the sixteenth century, a group of preachers influenced by the humanistic movement formulated a similar style of piety of "service" for persons whose lives were lived outside the cloister in the public life of church and state. This piety, too, was remarkably world-affirming. I have elaborated on this important development elsewhere,[7] but have discovered no clear evidence of influence one way or another between it and the first Jesuits. I call attention to the parallel here, however, because it provides further substantiation for the break with medieval spirituality that the Ignatian system, for all its medieval roots, suggests, and it also intimates why that system proved attractive to so many persons in the early years of the Society. It was attuned to the times.

Another correlation of Ignatian spirituality with the religious culture of the sixteenth century is possible; this time a line of influence can be unmistakably detected. The Lutheran doctrine of "justification by faith alone" caused Catholics to search their tradition on this issue more carefully than before. By the time the Council of Trent dealt with the matter in Session IV in 1547, Catholic theologians were aware of the dangers of Pelagianism and Semi-Pelagianism that the Lutherans accused Catholics of teaching. The Council tried to avoid any formulations that might seem to support the save-yourself tenets traditionally ascribed to the Pelagians, but at the same time it insisted on the necessity of human cooperation in the process of justification. As interpreted in a popular way, this meant an insistence on the role of "free will" in attaining salvation, while still maintaining the prevenient and constitutive role of grace.

Loyola raises this issue in the book of the *Exercises* where he counsels that grace should be spoken of only in such a way that "works and free will" are not slighted (369). The early Jesuits were involved in discussion on this issue within the Council of Trent and in polemics on it outside the Council. Since Lutherans "denied free will," the Jesuits especially emphasized it. There is a direct relationship between this Jesuit emphasis in the controversies with the Protestants in the sixteenth century and their position vis-à-vis the Dominicans over many of the same problems in the so-called *De Auxiliis* controversies a century later.

What this means for Jesuit spirituality is that it tended to have a decidedly activist character and helped promote the activist piety that Evennett found characteristic of the Counter-Reformation in general. Evennett's summary is worth quoting: "The spirituality of the Counter Reformation sprang from a triple alliance, as it were, between the Tridentine clarifications of the orthodox teaching on Grace and Justification, the practical urge of the day towards active works, and certain new developments in ascetical teaching and practice which promoted this outlook."[8] That last element—the "new developments"—was particularly characteristic of the spirituality developed by Loyola.

This activist character manifested itself in the varied and energetic ministries the early Jesuits undertook—in their works of mercy directed toward orphans, prostitutes, prisoners in jails, the sick in hospitals, and especially in their schools and their preaching. For all of Trent's emphasis on sacramental ministry and the Jesuits' promotion of it, especially the frequent reception of the Eucharist and penance that Jesuit preachers urged from the beginning, their real contribution lay, as I mentioned earlier, in some form of "ministry of the Word." This was typical of most Protestant ministry at the time and is generally recognized as such. It is not so clearly recognized how typical it was of the early Jesuits. The motivations for this general interest are complex and relate inextricably with the personal histories of the great leaders like Loyola, Luther, Calvin, and others, but certainly part of the impetus derives from the invention of printing, from the humanists' new concern with the recovery of ancient texts, and from their new interest in rhetoric and in other disciplines related to verbal communication in classroom, pulpit, and other public forums. The word—printed and oral, human and divine—emerged as a new focus for the intellectual and spiritual life of the day.

For the Jesuits the ministry of the Word took a number of forms, especially the most traditional one of preaching. But even in this form their ministry showed an energy and an imagination that were notable, if not altogether original. They not only preached from the pulpit of churches but also sought listeners in hospitals, piazzas, prisons, and even inns. Ignatius insisted that his men undertake this ministry wherever they went, and he followed their efforts with keen interest. Both Juan Ramírez and Francesco

Borgia—Jesuit contemporaries of Ignatius—composed treatises on how to preach.

Jerome Nadal left an important exhortation on this ministry of the Word in its various forms.[9] Peculiar to the Jesuits was the emphasis that Ignatius and Nadal placed on informal conversation, with individuals or groups, about "the things of God." In his exhortation Nadal gives sensible directives about how this practice could be made most effective.

We do not have as clear information as we would like about the content of the formal sermons the Jesuits preached. Loyola wanted "the errors of the heretics" to be refuted when occasion demanded it, but he tempered this advice with the warning that charity and good example would be more forceful means to winning them over than confrontation and controversy. His frequent instructions to the members of the Society were that they preach both by their words and by their example. This coupling of word and deed, almost a truism in the Christian tradition, was notably revived in the sixteenth century by the humanists. But it seems to have had a special significance for Ignatius in that he so consistently joined the two as almost to equate them. "Example" is a message to the affections and noble aspirations of persons rather than directly to their minds, as the humanists never tired of saying, and it looks to behavior as well. This is what concerned Loyola all his life, and this is the orientation that he expected all "ministry of the Word" to have.

The point I am making is that in an age so agitated by dogmatic differences that, on one level, controversy was its distinguishing intellectual characteristic, Loyola showed himself in practice singularly detached from that controversy. His interest, quite simply, lay elsewhere, and he conceived "doctrine" in a different way than did many other leading figures of his time. For him "Christian doctrine" dealt in the first place with virtue, prayer, repentance, and conversion, and then "consolation"—with reform of life. Luther proposed that right thinking and preaching about justification were essentially what the world needed. For Loyola the central issue was right living and loving, based on a general spirituality in which certain affectivities were fostered and sustained. This position coincides perfectly with the basic character and emphasis of the *Spiritual Exercises*, whose stated purpose was "the ordering of one's life" (21).

The most distinctive form of this Jesuit ministry of the Word was in fact the guiding of devout persons through the *Spiritual Exercises*. This task implied constant recourse to the text of Scripture, for most of the meditations in the book deal with some aspect of the life of Christ. In these meditations the retreatant confronted the *deeds* of the Savior and was then asked to respond in kind, for he did "all this for me" (116). The retreatant is urged "not to be deaf to His call, but prompt and diligent to accomplish His holy will" (91). What is induced is a sense of companionship with Christ in ministry, suffering, and, finally, glory—a companionship intimated by the name Loyola insisted on for his order, "Compagnia di Gesù."

Further questions are put to the retreatant: "What have I done for Christ, what am I doing, what ought I to do?" (53). These questions once again point inexorably to the activist, even dynamic, nature of Ignatian spirituality. This dynamism, a contrast with the repose of monastic contemplation, is indicated by Loyola in a number of ways, but particularly by his favorite expression, "the greater glory of God." The phrase occurs countless times in the *Constitutions* of the order. The comparative form—"greater"—suggests a questing, a restlessness, almost an insatiability. This is the Ignatian "más," "magis," "more" that commentators have often noted.

For Ignatius, this "more" was meant to translate itself most directly into an ever greater and more generous oblation to the divine will and divine grace. The prayer he composed for the retreatant at the end of the "Contemplation for Obtaining Divine Love" in the *Spiritual Exercises* encapsulates this deep yearning of the saint: "Take, Lord, and receive all my liberty, my memory, my understanding, and my entire will, all that I have and possess. Thou hast given all to me. To Thee, O Lord, I return it. Dispose of it wholly according to Thy will. Give me Thy love and Thy grace, for this is sufficient for me" (234).

Loyola himself achieved this surrender to the divine in an eminent degree. Throughout his adult life he experienced a deep sense of the divine presence that often produced tears of consolation and joy. His perception of God was specified by the Christian doctrine of the three divine persons of the Trinity, with a strong sense of their individuality—Father, Son, Spirit. The trinitarian aspect of his personal mysticism has been the subject of a number of studies. But what must be emphasized here is that in Ignatius the dynamism of his spirituality found its source in the divine action within his own being. It was not the result of a self-induced compulsion or of a drive for some merely extrinsic behavior modification. He was a saint, and he was revered even during his lifetime for a union with God that seemed to manifest itself clearly to those who had to deal with him.

Unfortunately, the same cannot always be said of the spirituality that the order fostered. The early companions of Ignatius were close enough to him to have understood the spirit of his directives. When Ignatius observed in the *Exercises* that "love ought to manifest itself in deeds" (230), they knew that this was not meant in some pedestrian sense. Nonetheless, the insistence on the practice of the virtues, the importance attached to sacramental confession of sins and the "reform of life," and the insistence in

1. Gian Lorenzo Bernini, *Cathedra Petri*, 1657-1666.

Ignatius's writings to his fellow Jesuits on the practice of obedience could easily lead, in less expansive minds, to a moralism and a behavioralism that were far from the true intent of the saint.

A graphic illustration of an eclectic and superficial grasp of the spirituality of the order is the book published in 1609 by the Spanish Jesuit Alonso Rodríguez (1526–1616) entitled *Ejercicio de perfección y virtutes cristianas.* (This author is not to be confused with the Jesuit lay brother St. Alfonso Rodríguez [1531–1617].) Rodríguez had been for a number of years master of novices, responsible for the first training in spirituality of new recruits to the order. The audience he originally had in mind for his ideas must be noted for an understanding of his book, but he in fact composed it out of a number of exhortations that he gave to Jesuit communities in various cities of Spain.

Divided into three parts, each containing three treatises, the book follows no systematic plan. It draws on the mainstream of Christian asceticism in a presentation of virtues and in practical recommendations about prayer, mortification, silence, and similar matters. Rodríguez illustrates his points with numerous anecdotes and *exempla* drawn from John Cassian, the *Vitae patrum,* and the lives of the saints. Often quaint, sometimes amusing, these illustrations betray the author's preoccupation with reducing spirituality to conventional practicality.

The book's success was immediate and enormous, probably because of the simplicity of its presentation, its avoidance of controversial matters, and its comprehensiveness. Like Alice's medicine, there were so many good things in it that there was something to suit everybody's needs. Joseph de Guibert commends also the "robust realism" of the book and finds in that quality another reason for its success.[10] It is quite true that the book is filled with precise and concrete counsels, though these are sometimes irreconcilable with each other and are never related to any clearly distinguishable theological foundation. By 1626, in any case, there were seven Spanish editions as well as translations into English (partial, 1612), French (1617), Italian (1617), Latin (1621), German (1623), and Dutch (1626). The book continued to be popular well into the present century and has run through over three hundred editions in twenty-three languages.

Is this book an authentic reflection of early Jesuit spirituality? Its favorable reception in the order immediately upon its publication and the continued commendation it received from Jesuit authorities through the centuries would seem to indicate that it is. There can be no doubt that it caught one important aspect of the spiritual message of St. Ignatius and the early Jesuits. While appreciative of the higher forms of prayer, it insists that every interior inspiration be tested against the deeds it produces. If the deeds are virtuous, the inspiration is holy. Even the highest gifts of prayer are suspect, ultimately unacceptable, if they fail in this regard. The avoidance of sin, the observance of the duties of one's state in life, adherence to the traditions of the church and respect for its authority—these were the Jesuit touchstones for authenticity from the very beginning. Rodríguez never lets his reader forget them.

Viewed in this perspective, Rodríguez's book has an authentically Jesuit character. Loyola, moreover, doubtless considered these qualities to be perennially valid foundations for a solid spiritual edifice. Yet there were historical circumstances of his era that gave them a particular incisiveness and led some of his followers in the order like Rodríguez to exaggerate them, especially toward the end of the sixteenth century.

These circumstances were not so much the presumed dangers of Protestantism, as we might first suspect, but rather the spiritualism of the indigenous mystical tradition in Spain whose adherents came to be known as the *Alumbrados*. Originating in the late fifteenth century, this movement was perceived by ecclesiastical authorities as a danger because it attributed an undue importance to visions, revelations, raptures, and similar phenomena. Loyola himself was charged at Salamanca in 1527 with being tainted by the movement, and he was careful for the rest of his life to make clear his distance from it. Moreover, he fought within the order a tendency, especially in Spain and Portugal, to subordinate ministry to contemplation and to multiply the hours spent each day in prayer.

These problems reached a point of crisis under the fourth general of the order, Everard Mercurian (1573-1581). Mercurian took a number of measures to meet the crisis. In his opinion he was not reforming a spirituality gone astray so much as forming one that was still in its infancy. He imposed a greater regimentation in prayer and religious observance within the order, but especially emphasized the practical, non-Illuminist character of the spirituality of the Jesuits. Somewhat forgetting the other styles of prayer allowed or suggested in the *Exercises*, he put great emphasis on examination of conscience and on the form of "meditation" described by Ignatius in the section of the book entitled "Three Methods of Prayer." Sober and methodical consideration of such matters as the Commandments, the duties of one's office, various virtues and vices—even if the purported subject matter of the prayer was the text of Scripture—seems to have been his ideal. He even forbade the reading, without special permission, of medieval mystics like John Tauler, Jan van Ruysbroeck, Henry Suso, and others.

Mercurian's measures against two Spanish Jesuits—Antonio Cordeses (1518-1601) and Balthasar Alvarez (1534-1580), confessor for six years to Teresa of Avila—indicate the narrowness with which he conceived the spirituality of the order and his misunderstanding of some of the central teachings of the saint who founded it. He forbade Cordeses to promote "affective prayer," and he judged Alvarez's style too contemplative.

Alvarez is particularly important. Although he published nothing in his lifetime, his Jesuit disciple, Venerable Luis de la Puente, wrote a remarkable biography of him (1615), admired even today for its comprehensive design, the accuracy of its narrative, and the grace of its style. The biography ranks as one of the great works of spiritual biography produced in Spain in its golden age. Most important of all, La Puente summarized the teachings of Alvarez and thereby transmitted them to his contemporaries and to subsequent generations. The biography in effect vindicated Alvarez and allowed him to influence masters like the English Benedictine Augustine Baker (1588–1685), the Jesuit Louis Lallemant (1587–1635), and, later, St. Alfonso Liguori (1696–1787). This recognition of him as one of the leading figures in Spanish spirituality in the sixteenth century eventually led to the publication in modern editions of his exhortations, meditations, letters, and treatises.

Alvarez advocated a prayer of quiet and silence, into which he himself had moved about 1567 from a more discursive style and after a long period of aridity. His descriptions of this form of prayer are surely influenced by St. Teresa, John of Avila, Francisco de Osuna, and other contemporaries. The prayer consists essentially in placing oneself in the presence of God and of keeping oneself in a state of repose before him. In Alvarez it resulted in an interior sense of the corporal presence of the humanity of Christ. This experiential and mystical sense of Christ's presence within was at the heart of his teaching.

Throughout his life Alvarez held positions of high responsibility in the Society of Jesus. He was, for instance, several times rector and master of novices, and at the very end of his life (1580) he was named superior of the province of Aragon of the Society. Nonetheless, from about 1573 on he was subjected to repeated scrutiny by his superiors in the Society because his teaching on prayer was suspected of fostering illusions and of deviating from the teaching of the *Exercises,* as interpreted by Mercurian and others. His explanations failed to give satisfaction, and in late 1577 he submitted to the decision against his teaching.

Mercurian's motivations were sincere. He wanted to consolidate a spirituality that still lacked a large corpus of literature to sustain it, and he wanted to preserve it from influences that would lead it back into an essentially monastic mode. Within the order, especially in the Iberian peninsula, there flourished a strongly contemplative tendency, a desire in some cases for eremitical withdrawal from the *saeculum* and sometimes a cultivation of the suspect phenomena associated with the *Alumbrados*. All this forms a background for understanding the success of an author like Rodríguez and the approbation he enjoyed.

Mercurian's vision, fortunately, did not altogether prevail even during his generalate, and his successor, Claudio Aquaviva (1581–1606), was a person of larger spirit, who encouraged a less rigid and narrow interpretation of the charism of the order. As early as 1582 he delivered an important exhortation in Rome on the gifts of the Holy Spirit—traditional in its doctrine, but indicative of a spirituality irreducible to moralism and external discipline. At about the same time in Rome and Naples, Roberto Bellarmino (1542–1621), a respected theologian and later a cardinal and canonized saint of the order, delivered a series of exhortations on the same subject and, more important, a series on "liberty of spirit."

There were, then, at least two general strains to "Jesuit spirituality" by the beginning of the seventeenth century. One was cautious and soberly ascetical, favorable almost exclusively to a methodical and even moralistic style of prayer, suspicious of contemplation and other higher forms of prayer as inimical to the active ministry to which the order was committed. It ran the danger of reducing Loyola to a small-minded master of hackneyed precepts. The other strain was more expansive, more syncretistic within the broad tradition of Christian spirituality, and intent on developing the implications of the affective and even mystical elements in the life of the founder of the order. It bordered at times on the Illuminism that Loyola had so emphatically eschewed and wanted to exclude among his followers. Most Jesuit writers on spirituality whose books were actually published during these decades tended to strike a balance between extreme expressions of these two tendencies and were able more or less to perpetuate the synthesis that Loyola represented.

Among the early associates of the saint, none had done this better than Jerome Nadal (1507–1580), already mentioned several times. Born at Palma de Majorca, he pursued courses of study at Alcalá and Paris and was present in the latter city while Loyola was there gathering his first companions. At that time he refused to have anything to do with the group and in 1537 went to Avignon, where he was eventually ordained a priest and promoted to doctor of theology.

Sometime after his return to Majorca, he felt an attraction to the new order, now confirmed by the Holy See, and in 1545 he journeyed to Rome to join it. He immediately won the special confidence of Ignatius and soon was constituted by him as his special envoy to promulgate and explain the *Constitutions* of the order in various parts of the Society. In the judgment of Juan de Polanco, Loyola's secretary, Nadal grasped Ignatius's ideas better than any other,[11] and therefore came to be considered an authentic inter-preter of them. In his many writings—dialogues, letters, and especially the exhortations and instructions to Jesuit communities—we have a secure elaboration of the central themes of early Jesuit spirituality. Moreover, most Jesuits of his day, especially in Spain during his three official visits there, actually heard him speak about the Society and its spirit. His impact was, therefore, direct and enormous.

Most characteristic of Nadal is the evident theological and biblical basis on which he contructed his interpretation, and he has been described as "the theologian of Ignatian spirituality."[12] He clearly depended on a theological tradition represented by Aquinas and Bonaventure. Distinctive of him was the doctrine of "contemplative in action." This was, as I have indicated, simply a fuller articulation of Loyola's exhortation to his followers "to find God in all things." God was the goodness active in the world from which all other good descended. God was the author of both nature and grace, who impressed his own good on all reality. Here is the source of the world-affirming spirituality that would continue to mark the spiritual vision of many Jesuits through the centuries and that helps explain how some Jesuit missioners like Matteo Ricci (1552–1610) in China and Roberto de Nobili (1577–1656) in India could so easily affirm the values of the indigenous cultures in which they labored. Any study of early Jesuit spirituality that ignores the enterprises and cultural magnanimity of missioners like these misses a central element of the tradition.

Nadal's rhetoric on issues like these is even bolder than Loyola's. On a number of occasions he affirmed straightforwardly that for the members of the order "the world" was their "house." Although he of course recognized that for many Jesuits the houses of the professed members of the order would be the place from which they would normally exercise their ministry, he returned again and again to the idea that the Society was essen-tially a group "on mission," ready at any moment to travel to any point where there was need for its ministry. In Nadal's writings we find the most emphatic statements in the early history of the Jesuits of their break with the more monastic tradition.

Nadal's balance is evident in the way he encouraged and exemplified affec-tive and even mystical prayer while at the same time insisting on its correla-tion with ministry and with the necessity of a balanced asceticism. He cau-tioned against the excesses of the *Alumbrados* and at the same time rejected a frigid moralism and intellectualism, which he also saw as dangers as well.

One of Nadal's most innovative teachings concerned the "grace of voca-tion," especially within the context of a religious order of the Catholic Church. According to him, the "grace" of each institute within the church was specific, somewhat like the specific grace conferred by each of the sacraments. The grace proper to each institute was articulated in the life and gifts of the founder and was meant to be transmitted to each member of the order. In his exhortations Nadal made extensive use of Ignatius's *Autobiography,* dictated to da Câmara, as encapsulating the grace of the Jesuit vocation. Thus, the teachings of Loyola were for Jesuits something more than the teachings of a holy man whom all revered. Nadal imbued them with an exemplarity that required their appropriation by all members of the order. These teachings were articulated in the *Spiritual Exercises* and the *Constitutions* of the order, which spelled out the ideal of "contemplative in action" in a way that made it, according to Nadal, accessible to all Jesuits.

For this ideal, Nadal seems to have seen the biblical base clearly as Pauline. In a suggestive statement in 1557, he indicated that "Paul signifies the ministry of our Society."[13] Cryptic though this statement is in itself, Nadal expands on its implications in his other writings. In them "the ministry of the Word"–in a wide variety of forms–has preeminence over all others. The Pauline ideal of evangelization–of "becoming all things to all men," of intimate and mystical identification with the Christ, and of total expenditure of oneself "to gain all" for Christ–is spelled out by Nadal in detail. This same affinity with the doctrine and ministry of the "Apostle to the Gentiles" is discernible, in fact, in Ignatius himself.

Here we see another correlation of Jesuit spirituality with a more general phenomenon of the sixteenth century, a renewed interest in St. Paul. There is evidence of this revived interest in the humanistic tradition that preceded Luther, but without doubt Luther's affirmation of the Pauline doctrine of "justification by faith alone" is its most powerful and best known expression. Luther extracted from Paul a theological or doctrinal maxim; Loyola and his followers saw in Paul a pattern for ministry and an exemplar for loving identification with the Savior. These positions may not be quite so distant from each other as they at first seem. It is important, however, to note the differences between them and also to recall that neither of the parties involved seemed to be aware of any affinity with the other.

Nadal's writings were not published in any coherent form until their critical editions in this century. Indeed, as I mentioned, the spirituality of the Society of Jesus had no corpus of published writings to support it except those of Ignatius himself until toward the end of the sixteenth century, and this fact makes Mercurian's apprehensions about its being dissipated through the assimilation of other traditions more comprehensible. Nonetheless, the teachings of masters like Cordeses and Balthasar Alvarez, despite Mercurian's misgivings, began to have effect, at least in a modified form.

In 1608 Jacobo (Diego) Alvarez de Paz (1560–1620) published his *De vita spirituali ejusque perfectione*. Rodríguez's *Ejercicio* was published the next year, but the two works were quite different in their approach. Alvarez de Paz was a theologian and a contemplative. His book, though dense in its details, rests on a coherent theological base and emphasizes affective prayer. Its most distinctive characteristic is the elaborate discussion of "infused contemplation," a technical category to describe an advanced form of prayer that transcends methodical meditation. For our purposes, the book is important for its clear validation of an ideal like this sort of contemplation within the larger Jesuit tradition.

Perhaps the most important Jesuit author in this regard is another Spanish Jesuit, Luis de la Puente (1554–1624), the disciple of Balthasar Alvarez. He was beatified by Pope Clement XIII in 1759. Besides several important works published posthumously, he saw into print five major treatises during his lifetime: two volumes of *Meditaciones de los mysterios de nuestra sancta fe* (1605); *Guía espiritual* (1609); four volumes of *De la perfección del christiano en todos sus estados* (1612–1616); *Vida del Padre Baltasar Alvarez* (1615); and *Expositio moralis et mystica in Canticum canticorum* (1622). The volume of *Meditaciones* was his best known work, frequently republished, translated, summarized, and adapted.

The sources on which La Puente draws are the Scriptures, the fathers, Aquinas, and the *Exercises* of Loyola, from which he continually takes his inspiration. With his discussion of infused contemplation, he obviously sees higher forms of prayer as part of the Jesuit tradition, and his subsequent beatification eventually gave official, even if indirect, ratification of this interpretation of Jesuit spirituality. Moreover, his preoccupation with grounding his teaching on theological doctrine is a good exemplification of the *docta pietas* that Ignatius tried to instill in the order with his insistence on a long and exacting course of studies for those who joined the Society.

La Puente nowhere showed himself a more faithful disciple of the founder of the order, however, than in his *De la perfección del christiano en todos sus estados*. This seems to be the first work of such breadth in the history of Christian spirituality that applies that spirituality to the different states of Christian life, including the laity. The very conception of the work reflects Loyola's own conviction that genuine piety was not restricted to the cloister and further articulates Loyola's efforts to make such piety available to all through the course of the *Spiritual Exercises*.

During the first half century of the order there were in Italy no masters of spirituality of the same stature as these Spaniards. However, some of the works of the Spaniards were originally written in Latin, and others were soon translated into Latin or Italian; thus the writings were made available to brethren in that part of the world. Roberto Bellarmino, already mentioned, was important, but his major interest lay more strictly in the fields of exegesis and in speculative and controversial theology.

Italy was, in fact, less agitated by controversies and extremes in these matters than was Spain. Symptomatic of this fact was the volume by Bernardino Rossignoli (1547–1613), rector of the Roman College, *De disciplina christianae perfectionis,* published at Ingolstadt in 1600. Rossignoli dedicated the book to the general of the order, Claudio Aquaviva, whose moderate views were in fact well exemplified in it.

Aquaviva's tenure as general was not altogether untroubled, however, by the issues that were so live for his predecessor, Mercurian. Achille Gagliardi (1537–1607), a Jesuit born in Padua, undertook in 1584 the spiritual direction of Elisabetta Berinzaga, a visionary and mystic in Milan. He soon helped write and edit several works inspired by Berinzaga. Gagliardi almost immediately found himself embroiled in controversies that eventually required the intervention of Aquaviva and even of Pope Clement VIII. The details of this complicated affair need not detain us, much less an attempt to do justice to all the parties involved. But it is important to note that Gagliardi was subjected to the now standard accusation of trying to introduce a monastic spirit within the Society. Certainly, the influence of the Rhineland mystics, whose reading was prohibited by Mercurian, is evident in the writings for which he was at least partly responsible, especially the most widely circulated of them, the *Breve compendio intorno alla perfezione cristiana,* first published in French translation in Paris in 1596 and in Italian in Brescia in 1611.

Influenced by Gagliardi was Giuseppe Blondo in his *Essercitii spirituali di P. Ignazio,* published in Milan in 1587. The work was variously received in Jesuit circles, but eventually the attacks on it became so violent that Aquaviva "for the sake of peace" ordered it retracted from circulation in 1589. In France it probably had, nonetheless, an influence on Pierre de Bérulle (1575–1629) and through him on others in the seventeenth century. It is certain, in any case, that Bérulle knew and esteemed the *Breve compendio,* of which his own first published work, *Bref discours de l'abnégation intérieure,* is an adaptation. The development of French spirituality in the late sixteenth and the seventeenth century, including that of the Society of Jesus, is treated in chapter 3 of this volume.

The instruments the Jesuits devised or characteristically promoted to inculcate their spiritual doctrines and to assist people in appropriating them are perhaps as important for understanding Jesuit spirituality as the doctrines themselves. Here we find a significant reciprocity of form and content, the one influencing and being influenced by the other.

The first such instrument developed by the Jesuits was the "retreat." Although the practice of spending a period of time alone in contemplation is older than Christianity itself, there existed no widely recognized codification of it until the *Spiritual Exercises* of Ignatius of Loyola. The book not merely contained some of the saint's most important ideas but also provided a new framework in which to spend a limited period of time in prayer and reflection. Structure, progression, rubrics, "methods," and clear purpose were harmonized in such a way that these "forms" influenced the shape of the spirituality that emerged, as I indicated above.

A Jesuit who was asked to direct someone in retreat knew what was expected of him, and he had a ready-made plan to follow. Thus was inaugurated a new era in Christian spirituality in which a periodic retreat became a regular feature in the pattern of piety followed by many religiously minded persons. To aid the Jesuit in guiding someone through the *Exercises,* moreover, the Jesuits composed a *Directorium,* first published in Rome in 1599. Although this official document relied on some preliminary versions, it was in effect the first book of its kind—an official set of instructions on how to lead people, under the inspiration of God, through a set of considerations leading to "reform of life."

In substance, the *Directory* does little more than paraphrase, expand, specify, and put into better order instructions that Loyola indicated in the book of the *Exercises* itself. A clear humanity characterizes the *Directory,* as when it states that the person who is to direct the *Exercises* should be "of sweet rather than of stern disposition" (V.2). The same care is operative as in the *Exercises* that "God be allowed to dispose of His own creature, according to the good pleasure of His divine Goodness" (V.5). In prayer, however, the safe and sure "Three Methods" receive the most explanation and commendation, although "other methods are [not] excluded, such as the Holy Ghost is wont to teach" (XXXVII.13). More significant, the *Directory* explicitly related the "weeks" of the *Exercises* to the three traditional "ways" of Christian spirituality—purgative, illuminative, and unitive. The *Directory* thereby suggests that the *Exercises* are more than a "recipe for conversion"; they are a recipe for *ongoing* conversion that leads to higher prayer and an ever more interiorized spirituality (XXXIX). It thus reflects the viewpoint of Claudio Aquaviva, the superior general of the Jesuits who authorized its publication.

"Spiritual direction" is a second instrument that the early Jesuits developed to a high degree. This practice is, again, older than Christianity itself. But there is no doubt that it emerged with a new prominence in Catholic Europe in the sixteenth and especially in the seventeenth century—and precisely as a formalized and continuing relationship between the two persons involved. The book of the *Exercises* and, with it, the later *Directory* were the most important factors in promoting this development. Furthermore, the *Constitutions* of the Society insisted on the practice of spiritual direction for members of the order; thus it easily became normative for those to whom the Jesuits ministered.

Aquaviva published an important instruction in 1599 on the formation of spiritual directors in the Society, and in the next year he composed a small treatise on the subject that deftly combines experience with traditional teaching. We should not be surprised, therefore, that Rossignoli also insists on the indispensability of a *magister idoneus*. Alvarez de Paz, Luis de la Puente, and others do the same. Spiritual direction had by now become an essential component of Jesuit doctrine and practice.

Sometimes given in the sacrament of penance, sometimes outside it, the practice of direction by the early Jesuits had a number of aims. It was meant to give comfort in time of temptation and to advise in cases of doubt. As we might expect in this period, it was also seen as a way to safeguard against illusion and against the suspect mysticism of the *Alumbrados* and their kind. But it was especially aimed at helping the individual "discern" what "movements" were taking place within him and whence they came. All this was directed in the Jesuit system to greater intimacy with "the divine Goodness," which in turn was somehow to be expressed in greater "service" of that same Goodness.

The third instrument that the Jesuits adopted, modified, and then widely propagated was confraternities of various kinds, which they sometimes called "sodalities." These associations had been an important part of late medieval life, so there were models available for Jesuits to use. In Italian cities like Florence, such confraternities seem particularly to have flourished in the fifteenth century; their members sometimes dedicated themselves to specific works of mercy like burying the dead or nursing the sick, and they met regularly for prayers and sermons. Many confraternities also sponsored banquets, festivals, and similar activities for their members, which played a part in the development of local culture.

In Rome in 1563 a young Belgian Jesuit, Jan Leunis, founded the first such sodality for students attending the Roman College, the original Jesuit educational institution in the city, later known as the Gregorian University. About two decades later, Pope Gregory XIII recognized this organization and empowered its Roman headquarters to affiliate other sodalities willing to adhere to the rules approved by the Holy See. Sodalities quickly sprang up in Jesuit schools, where they became almost an integral part of the education offered there. An impressive body of spiritual literature was produced for the members of this organization, who were principally young men of good families.

This development was consonant with what the Jesuits were doing out-side their schools. As early as 1547 Loyola had formed a group of devout and charitable men in Rome whom he brought together regularly and encouraged to engage in works of mercy. In Parma, the "Company of the Most Holy Name of Jesus" traced its beginnings back to the Jesuit Pierre Favre's stay in the city in 1540. We still possess the program drawn up by Favre for these laymen: daily meditation, daily examination of conscience, daily Mass, weekly reception of the Eucharist, and regular engagement in works of mercy. This is roughly equivalent to what was later prescribed for sodalists in the schools. As sodalities spread outside schools in the seven-teenth century, they generally drew their members from homogeneous groups, so that we find sodalities of students, of artisans, of nobles, of businessmen, of sailors, of clergy, and on occasion of doctors, of lawyers, of judges—and even of prisoners in jails!

Continuous though the Jesuits' confraternities and sodalities were with their medieval paradigms, they also manifested some noteworthy differences. In general, the later institutions were more exclusively religious in character, more codified in their practices of devotion and of works of mercy, more likely to be based in some larger institution like a school, more securely placed under the direction of a priest. These were changes that were self-consciously introduced, not changes that spontaneously happened. Were they, however, changes for the better, as they were certainly meant to be? This question leads into the historiographical problem of how to fit early Jesuit spirituality into the larger context of the Counter-Reformation and how to see it as both reflection of that period in the history of Roman Catholicism and an agent within it. And that contextualization leads, in its turn, into the problem of how to evaluate early Jesuit spirituality.

The problem is too complex to deal with here except in the broadest way. Some historians, in brief, judge that the Counter-Reformation tended to force religion into ever more codified and institutionalized forms that were deviations from an earlier, healthier tradition. These historians would see the strength of the older medieval confraternities, for instance, in their close relationship to family and local culture, whereas the new confraternities, in-cluding the Jesuits' sodalities, made piety more formalized and removed it from the context in which people actually lived their lives. The confrater-nities are for these historians, however, only one aspect of this larger pattern of institutionalization and centralization that began to dominate the religious practice of the Catholic Church in the last years of the sixteenth century, after the close of the Council of Trent. In this viewpoint, the Counter-Reformation, for all its vitality and creativity, had finally a dele-terious effect on religion and, therefore, on spirituality. Insofar as this criticism is justified and applied to the early Jesuits, it means that their efforts to create a spirituality that would enable persons to "find God in all things" became so structured, so institutionalized, and so transformed that it made those same persons strangers to their own culture and "natural kinships."

The problem raised by such criticisms of the Counter-Reformation is real, although we must recognize that most of the criticism has been directed against changes in popular forms of piety, especially among the rural poor, rather than against the more intellectualized, urban patterns of spiritual doctrine and practice that have been the subject of this article. Moreover, it is quite possible to admit that early Jesuit spirituality was susceptible of some of the bad effects attributed to the religious forms promoted by the Counter-Reformation without at the same time denying the many positive achievements of that spirituality. In fact, the formalizing elements in the spirituality of the Counter-Reformation simply reflected these same tendencies in society at large in the late sixteenth and early seventeenth centuries. It was an age fascinated with "method"–in science, politics, and philosophy. We should not wonder that spiritual writings and practices felt these same pressures and evinced these same tendencies.

Most important of all for assessing early Jesuit spirituality, however, is the fact that its primordial and most authoritative sources—the writings of Loyola and of his best interpreter, Nadal—do not give first rank to these formalistic tendencies. These two authors proposed, in fact, a spirituality that in its aims as well as in the strategies it proposed to achieve those aims tried to assure "liberty of spirit" and to foster in individuals an adaptation of divine inspiration to every condition of life. If Jesuit spirituality later in the century fell into more stylized modes of thought and presentation, this change was rather a product of the later culture in which it was immersed than an inevitable development of Ignatius of Loyola's original legacy.

Notes

1. H. Outram Evennett, *The Spirit of the Counter Reformation,* 45.
2. Ibid., 65.
3. Joseph de Guibert, *The Jesuits: Their Spiritual Doctrine and Practice,* 176–81.
4. *Monumenta Nadal* (Monumenta Historica Societatis Jesu [hereafter MHSJ]), IV, 651; V, 162, ". . . simul in actione contemplativus."
5. Ibid., V, 153–54.
6. Ibid.
7. J. O'Malley, *Praise and Blame in Renaissance Rome* (Durham, NC: Duke University Press, 1979).
8. H. O. Evennett, *The Spirit of the Counter Reformation,* 32.

9. *Monumenta Nadal* (MHSJ), V, 820–65.
10. J. de Guibert, *The Jesuits,* 264.
11. See *Ignatii Epistolae* (MHSJ), V, 109.
12. Miguel Nicolau, "Nadal," in *Dict. Sp.,* 11, col. 13.
13. *Orationis Observationes,* ed. Miguel Nicolau (Rome: Institutum Historicum Societatis Jesu, 1964) 151.

Bibliography

Sources

All the texts of Loyola are published in the MHSJ. The correspondence and some of the other documents relating to his first companions are also published in that series, but other important texts are published elsewhere; some still await publication. On these editions, as well as translations into languages other than the original, see L. Polgár, *Bibliographie.*

Studies

The following series and journals regularly present studies relating to Jesuit spirituality: *Archivum Historicum Societatis Jesu* (AHSJ), *Christus, Geist und Leben, Manresa, Review for Religious, Studies in the Spirituality of Jesuits* (St. Louis), *The Way.*

Bangert, William V. *A History of the Society of Jesus.* St. Louis: Institute of Jesuit Sources, 1972.

Brodrick, James. *Saint Ignatius Loyola: The Pilgrim Years.* New York: Farrar, Straus, & Cudahy, 1956.

———. *The Origin of the Jesuits.* London: Longmans, Green, 1940.

———. *The Progress of the Jesuits.* London: Longmans, Green, 1947.

Conwell, Joseph F. *Contemplation in Action: A Study of Ignatian Prayer.* Spokane, WA: Gonzaga University Press, 1957.

Donnelly, John Patrick. "Alonso Rodriguez' *Ejercicio:* A Neglected Classic." *The Sixteenth Century Journal* 11/2 (1980) 16–24.

Dudon, Paul. *St. Ignatius Loyola.* Translated by William J. Young. Milwaukee: Bruce, 1949.

Egan, Harvey D. *The Spiritual Exercises and the Ignatian Mystical Horizon.* St. Louis: Institute of Jesuit Sources, 1976.

Evennett, H. Outram. *The Spirit of the Counter Reformation.* Edited by John Bossy. Cambridge: University Press, 1968.

Fessard, Gaston. *La dialectique des Exercices Spirituels de Saint Ignace de Loyola.* 2 vols. Paris: Julliard, 1956, 1966.

Gilmont, Jean-François. *Les écrits spirituels des premiers jésuites: Inventaire commenté.* Rome: Institutum Historicum Societatis Jesu, 1961.

Guibert, Joseph de. *The Jesuits: Their Spiritual Doctrine and Practice.* Translated by William J. Young. Chicago: Loyola University Press, 1964.

Guichard, Alain. *Les jésuites: Spiritualité et activité*. Paris: B. Grosset, 1974.

Iparraguirre, Ignacio. *Orientaciones bibliográficas sobre San Ignacio de Loyola*. Rome: Institutum Historicum Societatis Jesu, 1957.

———. *Contemporary Trends in Studies on the Constitutions of the Society of Jesus*. Translated by Daniel F. X. Meenan. St. Louis: Institute of Jesuit Sources, 1974.

———. *Répertoire de spiritualité ignatienne (1556–1615)*. Rome: Institutum Historicum Societatis Jesu, 1961.

Nicolau, Miguel. "Espiritualidad de la Compañía de Jesús en la España del siglo XVI." *Manresa* 29 (1957) 217–36.

———. *Jeronimo Nadal, S.I. (1507–1580): Sus obras y doctrinas espirituales*. Madrid: Consejo Superior de Investigaciones Científicas, 1949.

O'Malley, John W. "De Guibert and Jesuit Authenticity." *Woodstock Letters* 95 (1966) 103–10.

———. "The Fourth Vow in Its Ignatian Context: A Historical Study." *Studies in the Spirituality of Jesuits* 15/1 (1983).

———. "The Jesuits, St. Ignatius, and the Counter Reformation: Some Recent Studies and Their Implications for Today." *Studies in the Spirituality of Jesuits* 14/1 (1982).

———. "To Travel to Any Part of the World: Jerome Nadal and the Jesuit Vocation." *Studies in the Spirituality of Jesuits* 15/5 (1983).

Polgár, László. *Bibliographie sur l'histoire de la Compagnie de Jésus*. Vol. 1. Rome: Institutum Historicum Societatis Jesu, 1981.

Rahner, Hugo. *Ignatius the Theologian*. Translated by Michael Barry. New York: Herder & Herder, 1968.

———. *The Spirituality of St. Ignatius Loyola*. Translated by F. J. Smith. Chicago: Loyola University Press, 1953.

Ravier, André. *Ignace de Loyola fonde la Compagnie de Jésus*. Paris: Desclée de Brouwer, 1973.

Ruiz Jurado, Manuel. "La espiritualidad de la Compañía de Jesús en sus Congregaciones Generales." AHSJ 45 (1976) 233–90.

Scaduto, Mario. *L'epoca di Giacomo Laínez*. 2 vols. Rome: Institutum Historicum Societatis Jesu, 1964, 1974.

———. "Il governo di s. Francisco Borgia 1565–1572." AHSJ 41 (1972) 136–75.

Schneider, Burkhart. "Die Kirchlichkeit des heiligen Ignatius von Loyola." In *Sentire Ecclesiam*, 268–300. Edited by Jean Daniélou and Herbert Vorgrimler. Freiburg i/Br.: Herder, 1961.

Toner, Jules. *A Commentary on St. Ignatius' Rules for the Discernment of Spirits*. St. Louis: Institute of Jesuit Sources, 1982.

Wulf, Friedrich, ed. *Ignatius of Loyola: His Personality and Spiritual Heritage, 1556–1956*. St. Louis: Institute of Jesuit Sources, 1977.

2

Seventeenth-Century French Spirituality: Three Figures

M ICHAEL J. B UCKLEY

B LESSED PEACE had finally come to France in those last years of the sixteenth century. Henry of Navarre had made his entrance into the church through the solemn abjuration of Protestantism at Saint-Denis on 25 July 1593. The hesitant Pope Clement VIII had accepted this conversion as authentic in 1595, and Henry himself extended religious toleration to his nation through the Edict of Nantes in 1598. That same year saw the Treaty of Vervins with Spain's Philip, and France free of invading armies and internecine civil wars. The new century opened to a stillness of those religious arms which had savaged the cities and countryside for some fifty years, leaving country villages black in their ruin and hordes of hungry peasants sweeping through the land seeking food and shelter. Now only Savoy remained to be halted in order to settle the kingdom in quiet, and this was accomplished through the agreements of January 1601. France was exhausted, but at peace.

That same year admitted another invasion: the works of Teresa of Avila were translated from the Spanish into French, some four years after those of Catherine of Genoa and preceding that other genius of the Carmelite reform, John of the Cross, by two decades. Henry had promised Clement that the reforms of the Council of Trent would be introduced into his nation, and Trent found a support in this bevy of books.[1] The year that brought Teresa into France also attended the delivery of two other books, writings that bore a very different mark and channeled other tributaries into the weakened nation. Louis Richeome, the first figure in Henri Bremond's gallery of "devout humanists," put out his celebrated *L'adieu de l'âme dévote laissant le corps,* and Pierre Charron, representing the skepticism of the Third Academy now newly synthesized with piety and apostolic mission, published *De la sagesse.* The three influences were to run deep in the century being born: the profound reaches of a mysticism explored both in its experiences and in its psychological structures; the exuberant delight in a many-splendored human existence bespeaking in countless analogies the richness of creation and the invitations of God; the sober flight from the arrogance of all human assertions into an abyss of faith which could alone justify the leap beyond all doubt. These three religious traditions do not admit of easy signatures—but they were all there and came to expression in this *annus mirabilis* of the new century.

In no sense did these works bear their religious heritage into a century barren of profound spiritual influences. The tragedy which was French history in the latter half of the sixteenth century also carried the themes and agents that would write a different drama in the decades that followed. There were, for example, the Capuchins, emergent from troubled beginnings, to permeate France during its bloody decades with their preaching, their liturgy, and the austere witness of their lives. They numbered remarkable personalities among their ranks: Ange de Joyeuse, Honoré Bochart de Champigny, Archange of Pembroke, and, towering above them all, William Finch, better known as Benoît de Canfeld. Only toward the end of his life did Benoît publish his masterpiece, *Règle de perfection réduite au seul point de la volonté divine* (1609), a work that wielded great authority during the rise of French mysticism and secured a high place in the talented circle forming around Madame Acarie, as it simplified the many movements of contemplative development into the progressive identification of the human will with that of God.

Benoît de Canfeld opens this great age of French spirituality as Jean Pierre de Caussade will bring it to completion in the next century: Christian perfection is realized as one becomes "almost wholly absorbed into God and His Absolute Will."[2] The three stages of the interior life correspond to the three circles of those who range themselves before the divine will, and the divine will itself is distinguished into three corresponding levels of self-communication. The external will of God corresponds to the historical aspects of human life, to the Christian's active life in the world, and it is revealed to the Christian through the normative constituents of this tangible universe: the revelation in Christ carried and interpreted by the church. Second, the interior will of God corresponds to human subjectivity in its conceptual and affective moments, to the Christian's contemplative existence, and it is revealed to the Christian through the interior movements, graces, enlightenments which call to contemplation. Here especially figure the twofold annihilations of Canfeld, a dispossession of all that is not of God—either as motive or as guide—which for all its resemblance to John of the Cross actually brings the Rhineland and Flemish mystics into France. Finally, there is the essential will of God:

This essential will is purely spirit and life, totally abstract, pure, and stripped of all forms and images of things created, corporeal or spiritual, temporal or eternal. It is not apprehended by the senses nor by the judgment of human beings nor by human reason, but it is beyond all capacity and above every understanding of human beings, because it is nothing else than God Himself.[3]

The essential divine will is God, and the soul is united with God in a love so total that this unity can be called absorption.

The crucial position of Benoît de Canfeld did not lie simply with his writings, but with the immediate influence of his presence and of his teaching within that extraordinary group which formed around Madame Barbe Acarie. For them, this forgotten Capuchin was, in Bremond's enthusiastic evaluation: the "master of the masters themselves."[4]

If Benoît de Canfeld commanded this quiet authority, it was because another person of exceptional quality had made it possible, Madame Acarie. In the sixth year of her marriage, her husband had surprised her reading novels such as *Amadis de Gotha*. As appalled by her taste as he was delighted at her skills, he substituted volumes of religious literature recommended by his confessor. The reading continued, though its substance had changed, and M. Roussel, the assiduous confessor, underscored one Augustinian line which was to revolutionize her life: "trop est avare à qui Dieu ne suffit." Her life changed as if God had touched her directly through these words. From this year began an interior life of intense and frequent ecstasies, a life which Benoît de Canfeld assured her and her dumbfounded husband was of God. The husband soon disappeared from the scene, banished from Paris for years by Henry IV because of financial and political indelicacies. The newly found independence of the wife allowed her to gather around herself the major figures of the dawning French spirituality.

There is something peculiarly and appropriately French in having even this mystical invasion launched in a salon, with the salonière putting both her husband's business affairs into order and the religious masters of her time into conversation: such persons as the great Capuchins; the Jesuits Etienne Binet and Pierre Coton, confessor to Henry IV and Louis XIII; André Duval, the Sorbonne theologian who would one day write her life; Pierre Cardinal de Bérulle, the founder of the French Oratory; Dom Beaucousin, the Carthusian, who "exercised an incontestable authority over that milieu in which many were under his spiritual direction" and Francis de Sales.[5] She assembled within this group all the energies vital to the rebirth of French spirituality. Here the Rhineland mystics would intersect the growing spirit of the Spanish Carmelite reform, a reform which the members of this circle would eventually introduce into France. Here the universal spirituality of Francis de Sales would confront in his occasional visits to France the lay spirituality of the chancellor Michel de Marillac and René Gaultier. Here finally the finest reaches of Catholic mysticism would engage the active social compassion which embodied itself in the foundations of charity now spreading throughout the nation. Madame Acarie had made this as possible as the salonières of the eighteenth-century Enlightenment would enable the genius of Denis Diderot to meet that of Jean le Rond d'Alembert and mingle into this same stream Bernard de Fontenelle and Claude Helvétius. Madame Acarie also nourished the life of conversation which both expressed the religious hunger of the nations and indicated something of the resources that lay within the experiences and reflections of men and women so different. These conversations with the spirituality they communicated and the projects which they envisaged were long under way when the century opened, while rising with the century was the gentle grave wisdom of Francis de Sales, newly consecrated bishop and soon to journey to Geneva and to his life's parish.

Three figures have been selected for this inquiry into the emergent spirituality of the seventeenth century, a choice among so brilliant a company and by no means always of the most distinguished or better known. Any attempt to include them all would have meant painting with brush strokes so quick and so superficial that the canvas would hardly have been touched. Spirituality means more than a list of names and a calculation of attainments.

Let me take a paragraph to say something about the method in such an introductory study as this: Every Christian spirituality is a statement about (1) God, about (2) what it means to be a human being, and about (3) the way or the means or the journey by which the human is united with the divine. A different definition or a different value will be given to each of these three "topics" as a single spirituality specifies its own uniqueness, and the constellation of the three will form the character or figure of each spiritual life and its subsequent reflective study. Even further: each of these three topics or variables will be given their value or assume their meaning by a complex of four interplaying influences. What is the *experience* out of which these values originate, the experiences critical to this spirituality? What is the *expression* through which these experiences are both shaped and articulated, the fundamental experiences reaching their own completion in their cognate expression? What is the *hermeneutics or the theology* through which this experience and its correlative expressions are explored and explained, the reflection which brings experience under concept? And finally, what are the ways, the instrumentalities, and the counsels by which this experience-expression-explanation are placed in *communication,* are made available to others? Without inquiry into these three variables and the four questions that disclose the process by which they are given their values, every spirituality can be reduced to clichés about the divine and the human and every unitive journey into a pastiche of acceptable aphorisms. Neither the *topics* of God, the human person, and the means toward unity nor the *questions* which deal with experience, expression, explanation, and communication form anything but a set that permits the discipline of spirituality to achieve some accuracy and depth of understanding. Not as a grid mechanically superimposed upon religious literature but as adjustments and fine tuning which allow a frequency to be received does such a matrix of topics and questions achieve its own purpose. In the following pages, these will dictate an inquiry into the spirituality of three major figures from the dawn of seventeenth-century France: Francis de Sales, Pierre de Bérulle, and Louis Lallemant. Other figures and other authors could equally well have been chosen, and certainly Vincent de Paul, Jean-Jacques Olier, and Jean Eudes commanded an influence greater than some. The former three were chosen because they embodied in their complexities something of the profound powers at work in that period, and embodied them in manners so diverse.

Francis de Sales

If Benoît de Canfeld nurtured the nascent mysticism of the dawning century and Madame Acarie gave it methods of interchange which allowed different traditions to be in communication one with another to their mutual enrichment, Francis de Sales led the entire century into the world of devotion and the love of God.[6] It was not that other tractates had not treated the same topics and espoused similar exercises of piety. Pierre Coton—"this angel in the midst of the distractions of Court"—had himself written in a vein similar to the early Francis in his small book *L'intérieure occupation d'une âme dévote.*[7] But no one could approach Francis both in the comprehension of the range of spiritual development and in the deep tenderness that touched everything he treated. Devotion and the love of God—these center his major works and characterize all of his spiritual direction. His *Introduction à la vie dévote* made its first appearance in 1609, and so profoundly did it catch the religious sensibilities of that age that edition tumbled upon edition to meet the seemingly insatiable demands, ascending to some early ecumenical apogee when the dowager queen of France made a gift of it in jeweled binding to England's James. Francis's magisterial *Traité de l'amour de Dieu* had been first mentioned as a project to Jeanne Françoise de Chantal in November of 1607, and it reached publication some nine years later in March of 1616. Like its more modest predecessor, the *Treatise* met with instant celebrity. Presses in Lyon and Douai tried to satisfy the requests with repeated printings, and the first English edition of 1630 was translated from the eighteenth French printing. Francis touched the heart of the seventeenth century.

It is not surprising that so many would take to Francis so enthusiastically, for the horizon of all his writings was the personal. His letters and his conferences and his lengthy books include a world of experience within themselves, and that world is profoundly personal. When Francis wrote, he wrote not only about something but to someone, and even his greatest works are but correspondence writ large. The *Introduction* was little more than instructions to Madame Marie de Charmoisy. A litany of heroes and heroines opens the *Treatise,* from the great doctors of the Middle Ages and the many women who had "worked wonders in it" to his contemporaries such as Louis Richeome, who "is so amiable both personally and in his splendid writings" and Jean-Pierre Camus, whom Francis would celebrate because of "the thousand ties of sincere friendship that bind us together" (*Treatise* I, preface, 39).[8] The emphasis on the personal is not just a charming detail of Salesian spirituality; it lies at its heart in a way that few spiritual classics could match. Francis's experience was a world in which admiration, affability, and a gentle understanding grew into friendships, and to know his friends is to understand his works and to know the major influences on them. The *Treatise* must be explained to its reader through the presence in Annecy of the newly formed Visitandines.

> I must explain to you that we have in this city a community of young women and widows who have retired from the world so as to live together with one mind in God's service under the protection of his most holy Mother. . . . Frequently I have tried to repay them by dispensing the holy word and I have delivered it to them both in public sermons and in spiritual conferences. . . . A large part of what I now share with you, I owe to this blessed community. (*Treatise* I, preface, 48)

Friendship and direction, letters and extended conferences all merge into the experience that was his, and its record lies with the religious orders he inspired and the writings that remain to later generations. Everything about Salesian experience bespeaks this matrix of human communication, personal commitments, and friendship.

This general experiential context lends its significance to the single experience that lies at the basis of Francis's life and of which his subsequent theology is both explanation and expansion. Francis cannot be understood without some attention to this moment. As Augustine's thought can only be comprehended as a theology of conversion and that of Luther as a theology of the gratuity of grace, so the theology of Francis de Sales is only intelligible in the context of the six-week experience of mental torment that terminated in the Lady-Chapel of St. Etienne-du-Grès. Francis was a young student at the Jesuit College of Clermont, reserved, diffident, unsure of himself, and haunted by the fear that he had antecedently been predestined by God to rejection. Jeanne Françoise de Chantal made this deposition at an early stage of his canonization process:

> To give me strength to bear a difficulty of my own, he told me that when he was at college in Paris, he was tried by a state of extreme mental anguish firmly believing that he was doomed to go to hell and had no hope of salvation. This made him go cold with fear. . . . However terrible his state of mind, he held fast in the depth of his soul to his resolution to love and serve God with his whole strength while life lasted, and all the more lovingly and faithfully in this life as he thought he would have no chance of doing it in the next. This state of anguish lasted . . . about six weeks . . . and it was so violent that he could hardly eat or sleep and went thin and yellow as wax. One day, however, divine providence mercifully delivered him. . . . Coming to a certain church . . . he went in to say his prayers. He knelt down in front of an altar of our Lady where he found a little wooden board on which was mounted a copy of the prayer beginning: "Remember, O most loving Virgin Mary, that no one ever turned to you and was left forsaken. . . ." He said it right through, rose from his knees and at that very moment felt entirely healed; his troubles, so it seemed to him, had fallen about his feet like a leper's scales.[9]

This experience, detailed by one who knew Francis perhaps better than any other human being, grounded what would later become the theological characteristic of Salesian spirituality. The theology of predestination *ante praevisa merita* had been personalized by the young student—as he would personalize everything else in his life—and he had applied it to himself with all the intractable terror inherent in that cruel theory. It has become too easy to dismiss Francis's theology as a period piece, charming if somewhat bourgeois in its quaintness. Jacques Maritain maintained that it was idle to expect from Francis the theological penetration of the depth of providence that one could read in St. Thomas.[10] Actually it would be more a period piece to write off Francis's theology too facilely. Absolutely central to it and in the face of much of the theology of his time, Francis de Sales placed the universal salvific will of God, a will extended to every person. As friendships spelled out the meaning of his own life and a divine rejection was its ultimate horror, so what was central to his understanding of God was the universal, emphatic call of God to all human beings and in every form of human life to that charity which was friendship and salvation: "This redemption, abundant, superabundant, magnificent, and excessive. For us it has gained and as it were reconquered all the means needed to attain glory, so that no man can ever complain as if God's mercy were lacking to anyone" (*Treatise* II, 4, 113). Even if the history of salvation exhibits Christ known by some while others do not know him, by those Christians whose villages have religious influences and a sacramental life that gives a tangibility and peculiar efficacy to the offers of grace—even in such differences of conditions "each of us has a sufficient, even an abundant, measure of all things required for salvation" (*Treatise* II, 7, 120). Rather than the horror of a theology of predestination that would arbitrarily save some and equally arbitrarily damn others—by far the more popular theology of the times—Francis insisted on the abundance of grace offered to all and that whatever damnation did occur happened only *post praevisa merita*. Francis was not alone, but he was in a minority.[11]

To have lined up with Leonard Lessius against the Augustinians, the Banezian Thomists, the majority of Scotists, and the two major Jesuit theologians of the period, Robert Bellarmine and Francis Suarez, was not just a profound act of theological courage. This emphasis on the universal salvific will of God was the theological foundation of Salesian piety, calling all human beings from every walk of life to live out their baptismal consecration in a deeply Christian holiness. Even more this repeated insistence of Francis and Lessius and the few that clustered around this banner would begin a series of Catholic retreats from the doctrines of predestination, whose negative reprobation, after all the distinctions had been made, was not so different from the theories of Calvin. The condemnations of Jansenism would in their turn continue this rethinking of providence, to be extended by the reflections of Alphonsus Mary Liguori and Matthias Scheeben and to culminate in the teachings of the magisterium in Vatican II and among the theologians in the supernatural existentialism of Karl Rahner. Behind this development over centuries stands the figure of Francis de Sales, and his integration of this theology with spirituality was made possible by the density of experience which came to issue in the church of St. Etienne-du-Grès.

The experiences which issued in his theology did not allow for a differentiation between spirituality and theology. What he had learned in those dark days would mark his counsel and his life: compassion. To someone who was similarly tortured by such divine judgments, he wrote: "My soul, which endured the like for six long weeks, is qualified to compassionate those thus afflicted." Those six weeks he could never forget, and from them he had been taught "to have compassion on the infirmities of others."[12] It was through his own compassion that he read God: the universal salvific will of God was the archetype which his own compassion would mirror. Both were a form of love, brought into interaction with the world of human desire and choice. Francis would understand what it meant to be a human being finally in terms of love, just as his progressive understanding of God was only a deepening of his grasp of this comprehensive principle. He understood human choice, the human will, according to the loves that dominated it, and he understood love itself in terms of the mystery of God's inexhaustible goodness and his providential care for human beings (*Treatise* I–II). Whatever Francis wrote—letters, conferences, counsels, or tractates—he wrote of love. And the major treatises detailed the journeys in which this love could be realized.

The earliest of these journeys was to a life of devotion. "Devotion" carried a specialized meaning in the *Introduction*. Devotion was magnanimity in love—a great-souled agility so that one can love frequently, and promptly. To live a Christian life, one must possess charity; when that charity issues in a "great ardor and readiness in performing charitable action," it has developed into devotion. Francis lightly works out the homologies to natural history which will stamp all of his writings: "Ostriches never fly; hens fly in a clumsy fashion, near the ground and only once in a while; but eagles, doves, and swallows fly aloft, swiftly and frequently." So the sinners do not mount toward God; good people without devotion do so infrequently and awkwardly; the devout are like the eagles in their loving, moving toward the heavens beautifully and swiftly. Francis uses the same analogy which John of the Cross had employed in the *Living Flame,* but its application is to devotion rather than to the moments of love in a state of union: "Charity and devotion differ no more from one another than does flame from the fire. Charity is spiritual fire and when it bursts into flame, it is called devotion" (*Introduction* I, 1, 39–41). The *Treatise* will recognize that this devotion in its turn so increases charity that it becomes all-pervasive as the devout life is being lived; so the *Treatise* proposes to continue the work of the *Introduction,* that is, "to address souls that are advanced in devotion" (*Treatise* I, preface, 48). The life of devotion provides the experiential basis for an extended treatment of the stages of life—from its initial stages until its final moments—by the *Treatise* in terms of love: "an account of the birth, progress, decay, operations, properties, benefits, and excellences of divine love" (*Treatise* I, preface, 40). In many ways, the *Introduction* bears a striking resemblance to the first week of the *Spiritual Exercises*—in its subjects for meditation, its explanation of simple methods for mental prayer, its treatments of confession and frequent communion, and its directions toward a life of growing virtue. They are by no means identical, but the parallels between them are continual and striking.

What the spirituality of Francis possessed in common with that of Ignatius and with any number of other Christian masters was the sense of ongoing quest. Philothea's desire for devotion must be changed into resolution. After a general confession, she "enters into holy love," and the habitual use of the sacraments and of mental prayer is introduced at this point "in order to lead her forward." In the third part, the virtues are treated which are "most needed for her progress," while in the subsequent section the deceptive stratagems of evil are examined so that she "may avoid them and press forward." Finally, in the last part, Philothea has a sense of temporary arrival: it is necessary "to retire apart for a while in order to refresh herself, get back her breath, and recover strength so that she may afterwards more successfully gain ground and advance in the devout life" (*Treatise* I, preface, 35). No one can read these repeated metaphors and fail to see that Francis has framed the *Introduction* as a pilgrim's progress toward a life of devotion. John of the Cross had used the figure of the ascent to name and to explain one of his major works (practically never to have it reappear again). Francis, in contrast, structures the *Introduction* quite literally as an *intro-ducere,* a leading-into a life of devotion by the successive stages of a journey, and only those who miss the strenuous requirements of the quietly given advice for this journey could summarize its spirituality as nosegays and charming stories from Pliny about partridges and almond trees. The renunciations which this gentle voice demands for the journey and the inquiry he mounts into human motivation have long since swept the field of a sentimentality which would substitute for the harsh and dreadful claims of love. Francis's manner is always compassionate and even delicate; his analyses and advice are a two-edged sword.

Devotion, the world as essentially an interpersonal unity, and the basic understanding of the interior life as one of journey and development—all of these figure into an integrity when one grasps the meaning of "God" in Francis's *Introduction*. It is safe to say that the key to any distinctive spirituality is its formulation of the meaning of God, whether conceptually or in image. It is not that these "names of God" in Catholic spirituality contradict one another. It is rather that the finite human intellect, speaking out of the peculiarities of its own limited experiences and theologies, formulates its conceptualizations and imaginations of God either in metaphor or in concept so as to unite within its limitations the infinite attributes of the incomprehensible mystery that we call God. How a spirituality "names" God, draws into a unity the divine predicates which it emphasizes or by which it is captured, gives a delicate character to all the other topics and questions it treats.[13] How, then, does the image of God emerge most dominantly in the *Introduction?* As the divine majesty. The first dedicatory line sounds what will be thematic throughout the work and what will explain the importance given to devotion as a prompt readiness to serve: "Ah sweet Jesus, my Lord, my Savior and my God, behold me here prostrate before Your Majesty." Devotion becomes the highest form of bonding between the courtier and his monarch. So the *Introduction* itself can open: "You wish to live a life of devotion, dearest Philothea, because you are a Christian and know that it is a virtue most pleasing to God's Majesty" (*Introduction* I, 1, 39). But each person, not just the courtier, will serve the divine majesty in different ways, and each is called to serve him. What is at critical issue is the analogous nature of this devotion—for solitude and fasting and preaching and indigence are all only particular forms of life, while devotion to the divine majesty must be realized in every form of human life. It is the divine command:

> In like manner, He commands Christians, the living plants of His Church, to bring forth the fruits of devotion, each according to his position and vocation. Devotion must be exercised in different ways by the gentleman, the worker, the servant, the prince, the widow, the young girl, and the married woman. Not only is this true, but the practice of devotion must also be adapted to the strength, activities, and duties of each particular person." (*Introduction* I, 3, 43)

The centrality of devotion follows upon the conceptualization of God as the divine majesty, and it explains something of the pivotal position among the saints in the *Introduction* of St. Louis IX, king of France. He embodies the destiny and the values of this journey, of a spirituality in which the hidden presence of God is likened to "blind men who do not see a prince who is present to them," and the invocation before every prayer is framed as the soul which "prostrates itself before Him with profound reverence. It acknowledges that it is most unworthy to appear before such sovereign Majesty" (*Introduction* II, 2, 85–86). The gentleness of God is the infinite condescension of the monarch, while the continual refocusing upon the crucified reminds human beings of the unspeakable kenosis of such a king. Even the oft-repeated invocation, so characteristic of Salesian piety, bespeaks the central name he gives to God: "Live, Jesus."

Commentator after commentator has noticed the development in Salesian spirituality in the *Treatise,* ascribing the depth and the trends of this growth to his direction of Jeanne Françoise de Chantal and their abiding friendship. It is hardly remarkable that one who saw life and the world as developing realities would have grown himself. Perhaps the most startling development, however, has passed unnoticed. It lies with his understanding of God. The divine majesty has given way to a God who is profoundly maternal. Over and over again in the *Treatise,* God is homologized with a mother nursing her child, and as the tractate reaches its completion, Jesus himself is drawn into the same metaphor:

> Thus within Christ's maternal breast, His divine heart foresaw, disposed, merited, and obtained all our benefits, not only in general for all human beings, but for each one in particular. His breasts of sweetness prepared for us that milk which is His movements, His attractions, His inspirations, and the dear delights by which he draws, leads, and nourishes our hearts into eternal life. (*Treatise* XII, 12, 280).

The maternal is not the only image of the divine in the *Treatise,* but it is a governing one, and it brings into imaginative strength the central theme which runs through the experience and the theology of Francis de Sales. For Francis, the mother embodies the deepest form of unconditioned and active love: "Maternal love is the most urgent, the most active, and the most ardent of all forms of love, since it is an indefatigable and insatiable love" (*Treatise* III, 8, 183). Francis had not forgotten his own experience in the Lady-Chapel when his life was reborn, and this figures not only in the dedication of the *Treatise* to the Mother of God, "the most lovable, the most loving, and the most beloved of all creatures," but in the revolution in his understanding of God that the maternal worked and which Mary imaged.

The development of Francis's treatment of love follows a more complicated pattern in the *Treatise* as it envelops all the lines of human life. Just as Descartes opened modern philosophy in those same decades by a "return to the subject," so Francis de Sales founds the *Treatise* on a similar consideration of what it means to be a human being. It is to be a multitude of instincts, activities, gifts, and potentialities reaching integrity and human harmony by the dominance of the will. The primacy of will in St. Francis determines his understanding of the human: "over the countless multitude and variety of acts, movements, feelings, and inclinations, habits, passions, faculties, and powers that are in a human being, God establishes a natural monarchy of the will. It commands and dominates everything found in this little world" (*Treatise* I, 1, 55). In different ways, the human will controls external movement and the powers of memory, intellect, and imagination; but while "the will governs all other faculties of the human soul, . . . [it] is itself governed by its own love, and this causes it to be the same in character as that love" (*Treatise* I, 6, 65). The human manifold is governed by the will, and the will is governed by its loves, and all of the natural longings of the will are to love God above all things, longing now frustrated by a history of alienation and of sin. Crucial in Francis's anthropology is that the love of God defines human nature. Sin may make the realization of this love impossible, may have weakened the human will far more than it has darkened the human intellect, but the inclination to love God above all things remains definitionally present in human nature as does the natural light of reason.

This radical though impotent desire that marks the human is caught up by the universal desire of God and his reach into creation through providence. The whole of the spirituality of Francis falls within these two movements: the surge that is the human being and the outpouring that is the divine providence—the desire and the love of God to transform human beings into his friends, the universal salvific will: "God willed with a true will that even after Adam's sin, all human beings should be saved, but in a way and by means proper to their natural condition, which is endowed with free will" (*Treatise* III, 5, 177). Choice, then, figures as critically important: the choice of a human being in whom love builds to an integrity; the choice that is divine providence with which a person is graced. The unity of these two is charity, the fulfillment of every human desire and the divine will for human salvation.

Everything else in the spiritual journey of the *Treatise* is examined within that context. The immediate possibilities for such a life are either growth or decline, and both must be realistically assessed as possibilities. Further, love itself can be distinguished from complacence and benevolence as components of perfect charity. Growth demands prayer as the highest affective realization of human love for God, and Francis actually identifies prayer with that "mystical theology" which is a loving conversation with God, comprehending all the acts of contemplation (*Treatise* VI, 1, 267–69). Francis follows the classic pattern of discursive meditation gradually and organically giving way to the simple gaze of contemplation: "Contemplation is simply the mind's loving, unmixed, permanent attention to the things of God" (*Treatise* VI, 3, 275). The special grace of God can intervene here with such an experience of his love that the soul is drawn into the prayer of recollection, which Francis equates with Teresa of Avila's prayer of quiet and which possesses its own developmental process: "Sometimes this repose goes so deep in its tranquility that the whole soul and all its powers remain as if sunk in sleep" (*Treatise* VI, 8, 290). In such a repose the soul has no further need of memory, for it has its lover present with it. It has no need of imagination. "Why need we represent in an image, whether exterior or interior, him in whose presence we rejoice? Therefore, to conclude, it is the will alone, as if drawing gently at the breast, that sweetly takes in the milk of this sweet presence. All the rest of the soul remains in quiet by reason of the dear pleasure it has found" (*Treatise* VI, 9, 293). Yet this form of mystical theology has different interior degrees, dependent upon the manner in which one is united to God and the activity of the other human powers. This experience of love can rise to ecstasy. Here again the profound influence of Carmelite spirituality tells upon the *Treatise:* "The Blessed Mother Teresa effectively says that when union attains this perfection of keeping us held and fastened to our Lord, it is the same as spiritual rapture, transport, or suspension of spirit; it is called union, suspension or transport only when it is brief, whereas when prolonged, it is called ecstasy or rapture" (*Treatise* VII, 3, 23).

Effective love, on the other hand, and the love of benevolence move human beings to accomplish the divine will in all of their actions, a will that is signified to human consciousness by the divine commandments, counsels, and inspirations. This movement to perfect conformity between the human will and the divine advances beyond resignation into an "indifference" in which the love of God becomes the determinant of all that finds its place in human choice and human desire: "Indifference goes beyond resignation, for it loves nothing except for love of God's will, so that nothing touches the indifferent heart in the presence of God's will" (*Treatise* IX, 4, 105). Louis Cognet maintains that Francis may have "denied himself the chance of thoroughly analyzing certain elements of the problem: passivity, purifying trials, the theopathic state."[14] But in his treatment of union and indifference, Francis dealt with the purifications that deepen the soul's charity as a human life is plunged into that of Christ: "In the sea of sufferings that overwhelmed our Lord, all the faculties of his soul were swallowed up and buried as it were in a maelstrom of fearful pain" (*Treatise* IX, 5, 109). Francis's is the task of sketching the journey of human love from its very beginnings to its completion, a task that includes both the *Introduction* and the *Treatise,* a task that will leave any one aspect of the developmental constituents only as a moment of the whole and necessarily to be explored in greater depth by those conferences and letters that detail a more specific treatment. For all of these instructions and analyses are but various stages in the realization of the first and greatest of the commandments. From the natural orientations that defined the human person to the ecstatic possession of God in endless charity, human life develops in a providential order known finally only to God and imaged perfectly only in the Christ of the passion.

Pierre de Bérulle

If Francis de Sales brought to the formation of seventeenth-century spirituality a sensitive blending of the pastoral and the mystical, Pierre de Bérulle associated the mystical with great enterprises and with religious and secular politics.[15] The founder of the Oratory in France, the great reformer of the secular clergy, the pioneer of the establishment of the Carmelites within France—one of whose superiors he was to become—Bérulle has stamped such a mark on the soul of his nation that with justice is he called the Father of the French School. But polemics dogged his steps: battles with Richelieu prevented the publication of his *Oeuvres complètes* until that formidable cardinal had breathed his last, disagreements with the university and with the Jesuits about education, profound hostilities to Protestant national establishments against whom he attempted to forge a Catholic alliance, and finally quarrels with his beloved Carmelites upon whom he urged the piety embodied in his "vow of servitude to Jesus and Mary." Created cardinal in the last years of his life, Bérulle's multivalent figure stands central to much of the France that was emerging under Henry IV and Louis XIII.

Bérulle's own spiritual development can be calibrated from his earliest writing, the *Bref discours de l'abnégation intérieure* (1597), a tract composed while he was still a student at the Jesuit College of Clermont, under the direction of his confessor, the Carthusian Dom Beaucousin. "Composed" is an accurate designation, for the *Bref discours* is often little more than a translation or transposition of Isabella Bellinzaga's *Breve compendio intorno alla perfezione cristiana*. Isabella's director was the Jesuit Gagliardi, one of the first to write a commentary on the *Spiritual Exercises* and now generally credited with the real authorship of the *Breve compendio*. Bérulle's work proposes to guide the soul by way of successive deprivations to the annihilation of the human self and the transforming union with God. The stages of privation are but a preparation for the divine action upon the soul, a transcendence over that self-love which is religious narcissism and which inhibits passivity under the influence of God. Much of this work is standard fare for the times: the focus is on the human person and the counsels necessary for cooperation with the work of God. But that is exactly what makes the work so striking: its emphasis will change radically before one comes upon the spirituality that will characterize Bérulle. Even more striking: While Gagliardi/Bellinzaga had given serious attention to the person of Christ, Bérulle's transposition suppresses most of these places. Where Christ achieves some mention, it is only incidental. Thus, the *Bref discours* provides a benchmark from which it is possible to measure out the spirituality of Pierre de Bérulle.[16]

In 1599, the newly ordained Bérulle addressed himself in *Traité des Énergumènes* to the nature of diabolical possession, an issue of raging controversy as that century drew to its close. Diabolical possession, he maintained, was a caricature of the mystical states—ligature, rapture, and ecstasy turned inside out. At its basis lay the profound diabolical hostility to the Incarnation. Through possession, Satan attempts to ape God, "to unite himself to that same nature by a possession which is the shadow and the suggestion [*l'idée*] of that singular possession which God has taken of our humanity in Jesus Christ" (*Traité des Énergumènes* III. 850). Through the Incarnation, Bérulle could understand diabolic states. In a few years, the Incarnation would form the optic through which he understood everything.

In 1602, Bérulle made the *Spiritual Exercises* at the Jesuit House in Verdun. His notes from those weeks disclose many of the themes that will thread their way throughout his life and work, and here they achieve their unity in the person of Christ, the Incarnate Word: "Jesus Christ alone is both *end* and means on the cross and in the Eucharist. There we ought to *bind ourselves to him* as to our end and to make use of him as a means. Our salvation and our perfection consists principally in being such, towards the end and towards the means, as God desires" (*Retraite de Verdun,* Art. ii, 1290). "As the *Incarnation* is the foundation of our salvation, I have also considered very deeply how great should be the *annihilation of myself*" (Art. v, 1294). "I feel a separation from the world and a great *conversion*" (Art. vi, 1295). The Incarnation was beginning to assume a centrality in Bérulle that his *Bref discours* had denied it. Incarnation, annihilation, forgetfulness of self, condition or states, and adherence—the entire subsequent history of Bérulle's contribution to French spirituality could be charted with these topics as coordinates. The development of Bérulle from these weeks at Verdun lay not in the addition of new components to the spiritual life, but in the revolution he worked within their mutual order. Verdun signaled this revolution in a single recognition by Bérulle: "God cannot have any other purpose [*fin*] except himself."[17] The amplification of this insight, its realization in the Incarnation of the Word, and the inclusion of the human race within it through the Incarnate Word will turn Bérulle's spirituality to the theocentrism which constitutes its major characteristic, a theocentrism which his great exponents date from his contact with the *Exercises,* however differently they read its properties and contours.

The next years were rich in their accomplishments, and these deeds contributed substantially to the formation and nature of the literary heritage which is Bérulle's. His doctrine is inseparable from his life. The circle around Madame Acarie, under the immediate leadership of Jean de Quintanadoine and Pierre de Bérulle, had succeeded in bringing to Paris six Spanish Carmelites. Among these were numbered Anne of St. Bartholomew and Anne of Jesus, the first the constant companion of Teresa of Jesus, the other the great prioress whom Teresa called "my daughter and my crown." The nuns arrived to find Carmelite postulants awaiting them, trained by Madame Acarie and living their conventual life in her home (to the dismay of her husband). The first monastery was founded on the rue Saint-Jacques, and the institutionalization of Teresian spirituality into the life of Paris was begun. Whatever tendencies Bérulle might ever have had toward the more abstract spirituality of the Rhine and Flemish masters, a tendency to "bypass" the humanity of Christ in a union with God above imagination and concept, received a further—and final?—blow from these women trained by Teresa herself. Anne of Jesus, to whom John of the Cross dedicated the *Spiritual Canticle,* would have none of it. She wrote of her formation of the first generation of French Carmelites:

> I am careful that they meditate on and imitate Our Lord Jesus Christ, for He is often forgotten here. All devotion is concentrated upon the abstract idea of God: I do not know how it is done. . . . It is a strange affair. I can as little comprehend it as the language in which they seek to explain it; nay, I am unable even to read it.[18]

For all of the self-deprecation in this flash of Leonese irony, the course of the Carmelites is set, and its influence upon its superior seems to have been as profound as it was upon the entire nation. Within only forty years, there would be fifty-five Carmels in France, one of which was to be critically important in the formation of the other genius of Salesian piety, Jeanne Françoise de Chantal, while the Carmel of Bordeaux would figure in the development of Jean-Joseph Surin.[19] They gave institutional form to a spirituality that was irrevocably fixed within the humanity of Christ.

Near the Parisian Carmel and only a few years after its foundation, Bérulle with a number of confrères founded a new society of priests, the French Oratory, begun in 1611 and dedicated to the renewal of the secular priesthood in France, whether that renewal meant reform or sanctification. They adapted the Italian Oratory from Philip Neri to the needs of a reawakening France, as John Henry Cardinal Newman would do some two hundred years later for England. The Oratorians were themselves secular priests, living in common and dedicated to that perfection of charity which denominated the religious orders, but without the vows of the regulars. Bérulle took this form of the life from St. Philip, but gave sharper apostolic emphasis to the revival of the ideals of the priesthood. Once more, what Bérulle had begun took flame. Within eighteen years, some forty-four houses of the Oratory graced France. Other such societies of priests sprang up, formed in the Oratory and consecrated to the same purposes which had given Bérulle's its mission and its importance: Jean-Jacques Olier and the Society of Saint Sulpice, John Eudes and the Congregation of Jesus and Mary, and Vincent de Paul and the Congregation of the Mission. All of these looked to Bérulle not only for the structures that marked their common life and the mission that gave it purpose, but for the spirituality which through them was to become the common inheritance of the French church and the inerradicable feature of the centuries of priests trained in this rich tradition.

As Carmel and the Oratory were taking their beginnings, so a new series of Bérulle's writings was taking shape, conferences and tractates at the service of the communities which their author was calling into being. The titles of these works themselves tell the story of his development since that young student essay, the *Bref discours: Élévation à Jésus sur ses principaux états et mystères; Élévation à la très sainte Trinité sur le mystère de l'Incarnation; Élévation à Dieu en l'honneur de la part qu'il a voulu donner à Marie dans le mystère de l'Incarnation, l'opérant en elle et par elle*. And finally, his greatest work and the one by which Berullian spirituality will always be known: *Discours de l'état et des grandeurs de Jésus* (1623). There is more than an inconsequential shift in titles here. The conversion of perspective which his retreat notes adumbrated now reached its unique completion. The principal focus of Bérulle's spirituality moved from the individual drama of the soul's ascension into God to the Incarnation of the divine Word, that is, from the sanctification of a particular human person to the assumption of the human by the divine. Henri Bremond sees this shift as a profound assertion of a theocentric, as opposed to an anthropocentric, spirituality. Bérulle himself saw it—so long before Kant!—as a Copernican revolution, and he drew the lines of this homology himself to underscore the transformation worked in spirituality by this new system of the world:

An excellent mind of this century has wished to maintain that the sun is at the center of the world and not the earth; that the sun is immobile and that the earth, proportional to its round shape, is moving relative to the sun: by this contrary position, satisfying all the appearances which obliged our senses to believe that the sun is in continual movement around the earth. This novel opinion, very little followed in the science of the stars, is useful and ought to be followed in the science of salvation. For Jesus is the sun, immobile in his grandeur and moving all things. Jesus is like his Father, and being seated at God's right hand is immobile just as God and the cause of the movement of all things. Jesus is the true center of the world, and the world ought to be in continual movement towards him. Jesus is the sun of our souls, from whom they receive all graces, lights, and influence. And the earth of our hearts ought to be in a continual movement towards Him, in order to receive in all its powers and parts, the favorable aspects and the benign influence of that great star. Let us then bring into action the movements and the affections of our souls towards Jesus. Let us give ourselves in eagerness to the praises of God, on the subject of His only Son and of the mystery of the Incarnation. (*Discours de l'état et des grandeurs de Jésus* II. 26–27)[20]

It is not just that the name of Nicolaus Copernicus is found in the margins edging this paragraph. Like Copernicus, Bérulle was searching for the real, objective constitution of the universe: How is the universe one rather than many? For this new unity of the universe and of all creation, one needs a principle, a single internal subject whose own uniqueness can situate the manifold of other subjects. God has established three orders, none of which possesses this kind of integrity: the order of nature, the order of grace, and the order of glory. Each of these could be predicated of a plurality of creatures; none of them can function as a source of unity for everything. If spirituality was to possess a unity comparable to that elaborated in the Copernican solar system, God must form a fourth order, one predicated of only one subject which would draw all other things into a structure around it. This new order was the greatest of God's works: the hypostatic union, the single subject who was both God and human, the God-Man. In the Incarnation, God becomes for the first time the internal focus of his own world (*Discours de l'état et des grandeurs de Jésus* I. 17–20).

Theology and spirituality must reflect that unity if they are to assimilate reality. Reality does not center on the growth in grace or on the movement toward glory of the redeemed sinner, of the adopted child of God—graceful as this is. Reality does center on the Incarnate Word, "the Mystery so surpassing that it contains and comprehends both God and the world within itself" (*Discours* I. 2). In Jesus alone, the universe of things and persons, of actions, movements, and passions, of reflection and discourse achieves its true structure, harmony, and system. There is no human act that can bring the manifold of Bérullian spirituality into unity. Only God constitutes the unity of all things—now an internal principle because now incarnate. Bérulle's is most profoundly a spirituality of the Incarnate Word.

When Francis de Sales would speak of unity, he spoke of love. When Pierre de Bérulle would speak of unity, he spoke of the Incarnate Word. One would have to go back to Bonaventure to find the centrality of Jesus so insistently urged: the medium of all the sciences, the *radix intelligentiae omnium*, and the integral subject of all theology. Bonaventure, like Bérulle

2. Nicholas Poussin, *The Assumption of the Virgin*, c. 1626.

after him, found this centrality best metaphorized by the sun and its dependent plurality: "Just as there is one sun, but it emits many rays, so from the
one Teacher alone, Christ, the spiritual sun, multiform and distinct rivulets
come forth as from the one fountain."[21] Christ in Bonaventure is the one
Teacher, and the profound spiritual unity which joins his affective theology
with that of Bérulle lies not only in the Christocentricity of their focus but
in the identity which their common Augustinianism cast between theology
and spirituality. Introducing his commentary on the *Sentences* of Peter
Lombard, Bonaventure described this unified knowledge in its uniqueness
and in a manner squarely within the heritage he left to Bérulle:

> This knowledge aids faith, and faith is in the intellect in such a way that by
> its very nature it is oriented to move affectivity. And this is obvious: For the
> knowledge that Christ has died for us and similar knowledge moves a human
> being to love, unless he is immovable in his sins. This is not knowledge like
> that other, namely that the diameter is incommensurate with a side.[22]

It would be wrong to look to Bérulle for the speculative advance of the
theology of the Incarnation. What inquiries he initiated ran to traditional
and even increasingly Thomistic conclusions: There would have been no
Incarnation if the human race had not sinned, and the Incarnation could
have been accomplished by any of the persons of the Trinity, however
appropriate it be to the Son. "There is only one person who became incarnate, but the Father and the Holy Spirit were equally capable [*puissants*] of
achieving a like communication of their divine subsistence" (*Discours* I. 15).
Bérulle did not make the original contributions to the theses of theology
that in the same century his countryman Denis Petau would make. His
achievement, certainly as great, is the recapture of an order which Bonaventure before him had formulated and which Bérulle recast within the context
and modes of expression of his own times: the integration of theology and
spirituality, and the coincidence of this integrated knowledge around the
Word Incarnate. "For it is in this mystery that heaven is open and earth is
sanctified and God is adored—and this by an adoration that is new, an
ineffable adoration unknown before on earth and in heaven itself. Before
this, heaven had adoring spirits and a God adored, but it did not yet have
a God adoring" (*Discours* I. 3). The Incarnate Word becomes not only the
internal unity of all things, but the embodiment of the profoundest reaches
of human spirituality in adoration.

Adoration, then, is the critical experience, the human response to the God
who is Incarnate Word. Jesus is at the same time the one who is adored, the
means of adoration, and the paradigm of what it is to adore. One might
paraphrase a standard comment to make this point sharper: Francis de Sales

had restored devotion as vital to Christian spirituality; it remained for Bérulle to restore adoration as the radical experience of Christianity. And it was restored not by an analysis of its conditions and moral effects, but by a spirituality that centered on the experience of God adoring God. The experience out of which his spirituality issued was not an individual moment in Bérulle's life. No special period of darkness or of illumination seems to lie behind his growth into Christocentrism. The experience that is central was not his at all; it was the experience of the Incarnate Word before God. Into this experience, the believer is plunged. In the Incarnate Word, the Christian adores God. What is this experience?

> To adore is to have a very high idea of that which we would adore, and a will surrendered, submissive, and abased before the excellence and dignity which we believe or know to be in that object. Such highest esteem of mind and consent of will wholly surrendered to that supreme dignity . . . constitute adoration; for it demands not only thought, but also affection, subordinating the adorer to the adored, by the use and correspondence to the double faculties of the soul, the understanding and the will, equally employed towards the object that we will . . . to adore. (*De l'adoration de Dieu* #3,1210)[23]

The vocabulary is a bit leaden, but the experience toward which it points is the fundamental movement of the human spirit toward God: the recognition in faith of the grandeur that is God and the surrender of oneself to the greatness of God in *l'anéantissement*—a word almost impossible to translate into English, but which catches up the experience of being nothing before the infinite and eternal being of God.

The expression of such an experience is praise: "We believe that we are obliged to raise ourselves to God [*élever à Dieu*] and to praise Him in His unique work, entrusting to further consideration the states and the grandeurs of Jesus, and to penetrate the secrets and the profundity of this most high mystery." Praise, for Bérulle as for Augustine before him, was the perfect expression of adoration, the surrender to the mystery of God and the utter forgetfulness of self. Praise moves beyond the professions of obedience and of love, both of which speak of the self and of the movements of the soul: "I obey you," or "I love you," both involve references to the human subject. But praise, "How great you are," has lost this reference and is totally focused on the greatness and the grandeur of the one obeyed or loved. Praise is essentially ecstatic, the final linguistic expression of selfless adoration, of the movement that is *nous élever à Dieu* (*Discours* II. 21, 22).

From this expression came a characteristic of Bérulle, the *élévation*. The titles of the books of his maturity indicate the contribution he was making to French literature: adoration found its expression in the epideictic. It is a rhetoric whose function is praise and whose temporal concentration is upon the present, the state of things existing at the present time, though it often recalls the past and suggests the future.[24] The epideictic lends itself thus to an elevation to the Eternal, the changeless now, and the amplifications which have been criticized in Bérulle are the line of argument most suitable for the epideictic. As the poetry of John of the Cross was the expression most cognate to his longing for union with God, so epideictic rhetoric was the form most appropriate to a spirituality whose experience was adoration and whose fulfillment was praise. The *élévation* was the genre that this rhetoric created: through praise to enter into the reality of God. Some have charged that the *élévation* was antimystical. Exactly the opposite is the case; whatever its vocabulary of scholasticism, the *élévation* rests in God as now. The mystery in all its history was eternally present, but in still contemplation and even in a paradoxical silence (*Discours* I. 5–7).

Adoration and praise—both were in function of a spirituality whose internal center was the Incarnate Word. Most important, however, it is through the Incarnate Word that Bérullian spirituality approaches the Triune God. For as Jesus is the inherent focus of this spirituality, so one is not only through him and with him, but most critically within him. In his history, the Incarnate Word embodies a series of "states" in which those who adhere to him can participate. An individual episode from this life happened once and for all, but the dispositions which they incarnate are eternal. "They are past in their execution, but they are present in their virtue: and neither will this virtue ever pass nor the love with which they were fulfilled. Therefore the spirit, the state [*état*], the virtue, the merit of the mystery remain present always" (*De la perpétuité des mystères de Jésus Christ* #1,1053). Thus George Tavard can justly say:

> The contemplation of the states of Jesus belongs to the very heart of Christian life. The faithful are called to participate in the mysteries of the incarnation, not as these were visible in the earthly life of Jesus, but as they are eternalized in his ever-present states. . . . The faithful share the states of Jesus, experiencing in themselves the same interior attitudes in which Jesus lived his mysteries. In this sense the whole of life should be Christ-centered.[25]

But Christ is not only the object of this spirituality; he is its subject. In him and in his adoration, human beings adore the Trinity that is God:

> Jesus has been sent into the world in order that he render homage to the divine essence and to the divine persons and a homage worthy of God. . . .For all the homage of creatures, since they are finite and limited, is not worthy of God and is always infinitely distant from His excellence. We ought to honor Jesus in His capacity as the special adorer and servant of the Holy Trinity and the divine essence. (*De l'adoration à la trés-sainte Trinité* #5–6,1201)

The theological explanation of a spirituality of the Incarnate Word lies with the unities that Jesus embodies: Jesus is one with the Father in his essence, one with humanity in his person, and one with the Eucharist in his body. Three distinct communications of Jesus form the heart of this theology, and it interprets the act, the possibility, and the value of his adoration: of his essence in the Trinity, of his person in the Incarnation, and of his body in the Eucharist (*Discours* VII. 268–69). The return to the internality of God is through these communications: the Eucharist points to the Incarnate Word, and the Incarnate Word to the eternal Trinity.

> The unity, the fecundity, and the unspeakable communion which is in the Holy Trinity, is the object which the same Trinity is contemplating, honoring, and imitating in the Word of the Incarnation. . . . For God is the cause and examplar of all that which proceeds from Himself . . . and the more sublime and excellent these realities are in themselves, the more they mirror something very rare and particular in God to whom they are related and from whom they draw their source and their origin. (*Discours* VII. 282)

The temporal communication of the Word mirrors and draws all creation back to the eternal communication with the life of the Trinity itself. Everything in Bérullian theology is finally through Christ and in Christ to return to this trinitarian life.

And what is the human being to be caught up in Christ? Bérulle shares much of the muted tones of his Augustinian heritage, the sense of sin and the vastness of the dangers of damnation. But his own adherence to the Council of Trent, the Council he did so much to advocate in France, balanced out his readings from Augustine; and, in a lyric definition of the human, he approached Sophocles and Shakespeare and Pascal: "The human being is an angel and an animal, a thing of nought, a miracle, a center, a world, a god, a thing of nought enthroned by God, lacking God, yet capable of God, and if he or she so desires, filled with God" (*De la création de l'homme* 1137). The strong theocentric tendencies of Bérulle were not complemented or filled in with an extensive anthropology, or rather his anthropology was more dynamic, more functional. The human person was a tendency toward God, and the reflections of Bérulle were much more concentrated on the state which evoked adoration from the human being than what the human being abstracted from adoration and praise might be.

All of the other features of Bérullian spirituality now take their origin and their theological meaning within this perspective. The human person becomes *in him* through the grace of baptism and by the voluntary acceptance of that grace through "adherence," a critically important term and one which contains everything which the early Bérulle once wrote about abnegation and annihilation but now integrated into the Incarnation. "Adherence" means more than exterior imitation or even access to God. Cognet has framed its significance quite well: "By adherence, Jesus becomes our life and our all, the way but also the goal. But we must note that in Bérulle's view, the soul, without bypassing Christ, attains divinity itself in him, and is united to it, and we could say that by adherence the soul participates, in a way, in the hypostatic union."[26] Indeed, the hypostatic union is itself the perfection of adherence. The humanity of Christ has no meaning or concentration other than in its assumption by the eternal Word. So the human being that is united with God in Christ is to be detached from any other center or interest. This stricture is not arbitrary. One is only capable of assumption into Christ to the degree that one has not fastened the meaning and the support of one's life on something other than him.

Adherence, then, becomes the principal counsel of Bérulle: the active offering of oneself—in the daily choices and actions of life as well as in moments of formal prayer—to the most subtle influence of God and to the union between the human and the divine that this bespeaks. Adherence is adoration as continuous offertory. Passively, it is the willing acceptance of whatever actions of God are worked within the life or the soul of the human being, as the Trinity moves to draw the person into a perfect assimilation into Christ. As in John of the Cross and Benoît de Canfeld, this movement of adherence is both active and passive. There is that which a person under the drawing of grace can initiate; there are those diminishments and movements toward union that only God can initiate in the soul at a depth opaque to human introspection or obdurately impervious to human intervention. These active and passive moments of the interior life form a rhythm that is the common heritage of many spiritualities. What Bérulle contributes is the integration of these into the reality in which they are perfectly realized, the Incarnate Word. As the humanity of Christ, so the soul must finally abandon itself to purification and also to the glory of its assumption (cf. *De la manière profonde et intime d'honorer Dieu par l'être* 1190–92).

Through adherence, adoration becomes no longer a series of discrete moments, but a state (*état*), no longer a succession of acts, but a constancy of being in a depth of adherence that can only be effected by God.[27] The hypostatic union is both the archetype and the perfection of human destiny, a destiny that all other human beings share in various degrees of imperfect realization.

One will look in vain throughout Bérulle's *Oeuvres complètes* for psychological and phenomenological studies of the various reaches of prayer. It was not that he set himself against such descriptive analyses. His admiration for Teresa of Jesus was unbounded; but his system is elsewhere, in the unity of the humanity and divinity of Jesus, the center internal to creation.

It was within this mystery that he lodged the surpassing grandeur of Mary. Just as the Incarnation introduced the human person into the inner life of God, so it underlined the critical position of Mary in the continual history of human sanctification: "Do not separate in your devotions what God has joined together in a manner so holy, so divinely, and so exalted in the order of grace" (De l'obligation 1285). From her relation to Jesus in the Incarnation, Mary remains the Mother of Jesus and continues in the present to possess "the special power of giving Jesus to souls."[28] The sovereignty of Mary comes from this relation with Jesus, the one mediator between God and human beings. Mary is not to be separated from Jesus in the mystery of the Incarnation, and since that mystery is the optic through which God is revealed and human beings understood, she remains continually with him—just as Jesus is not to be separated from his Father and the Spirit. All are contained within this mystery, and the subsequent history of Jesus spells out its unfolding meaning. Mary was and remains what every human being is called to: "a pure capacity for Jesus, filled with Jesus" (Vie de Jésus xxix, 501).

For this reason, Bérulle composed and tried to persuade the Carmelites of the "vow of servitude to Jesus and Mary." Rather than a blessing, it turned into a battle occasioned both by doubts about its theological value and by a reaction to its successes. The Carmelite friars ranged against the cardinal, and theologians alternated praise and condemnation. Bérulle and Madame Acarie, now a Carmelite lay sister, met for the last time and parted in irreconcilable disagreement, and Bérulle, like Newman later, would write his masterwork in answer to his critics: Discours de l'état et des grandeurs de Jésus. Here was the work that brought into magnificent synthesis both the devotion of his life and the historical significance of his thought. All was finally to be interpreted through the Incarnate Word. And Madame Acarie, perhaps the greatest of the influences on the development of French spirituality in its initiation, even in her final differences with Bérulle, was to be known and eventually beatified as a Carmelite under the religious name Mary of the Incarnation! "Of the Incarnation" was the signature of the spirituality of Pierre de Bérulle.

Louis Lallemant

When Louis Cognet sketched in broad outline the revival of mysticism in seventeenth-century France, he collected these new and promising beginnings under four major headings: the abstract school with Benoît de

Canfeld, Francis de Sales and his first disciples, Pierre Cardinal de Bérulle, and finally the Society of Jesus. This last cannot but excite puzzlement. The French Jesuits of those decades are associated in the popular imagination with "devout humanism." They supplied the confessors of Henry IV and Louis XIII—Pierre Coton, Nicolas Caussin, and Jean Suffren. Coton might write *Intérieure occupation d'une âme dévote,* a book that would anticipate the *Introduction* of his friend Francis de Sales; and Caussin might compose his own three-volume *Cour sainte* on the life of holiness possible even for those whose careers swirled within the Louvre and Tuilleries; and finally Suffren labored to produce the massive four quarto volumes, *L'année chrétienne,* which integrated into the liturgical year instructions for prayer, mortification, confession, and an annual retreat. Nevertheless, their names recalled the court, and the court of neither monarch evoked memories of the gospel. Moralists, educators, savants, Molinists, and, yes, missionaries. Such is the accepted constellation of the French Jesuits of the period, one dipped in blood through the martyrdoms of North America and in poison through the devastating satire of Pascal. But Cognet, like Bremond before him, adds another category: mystic.

To the fifth volume of his *Histoire littéraire du sentiment religieux en France* Bremond appends this first paragraph:

> More integral, more original, twenty times more sublime and twenty times more austere, more demanding than Port-Royal, the school which we are going to study has made little noise. Its contemporaries scarcely suspected that it existed; Sainte-Beuve did not speak of it; and for the most part, the Catholics of today know nothing about it except its name. Its founder, the Jesuit Louis Lallemant died in 1635 without having written anything. Among the disciples of that great man, only one, Father Surin, has achieved recognition [*gloire*], but a recognition that was contested, for a long time suspect, and one of infinite sorrow.[29]

Amid the brilliant achievements of so many of their renowned confreres, Lallemant and Surin were hidden men, but they gathered into France the mystical genius of their founder and such Spanish masters of their order as Balthasar Alvarez, the great confessor of Teresa of Avila, and Luis de la Puente.

Unlike the complex biographies traced out by the lives of Francis de Sales and Pierre de Bérulle, Lallemant's years can easily be summarized in a paragraph. Born in 1587, he entered the Society of Jesus in 1605. His life after tertianship—a third year of novitiate for Jesuits after ordination—was to be spelled Rouen. There at the Jesuit college, he was appointed spiritual father of the house, numbering the missionary and martyr Jean de Brébeuf among those he guided. In 1622, he assumed the office of rector and master of novices, among whom were Isaac Jogues and Antoine Daniel, both destined to die as would Brébeuf among the Indians of North America. These years were in their turn succeeded by the three in which he was tertianmaster (1628–1631); he was soon replaced when his health, never robust, finally proved unequal to the task. Lallemant was sent to Bourges to recover his health, but he died there on 5 April 1635.[30]

A simple life and one that should have easily passed from memory. But his tertians had kept their notes from the instructions delivered by the master.[31] Jean Rigoleuc left his to Vincent Huby. Before his death in 1693, Huby bequeathed them to Pierre Champion, and the next year Champion brought them out in their first publication under the title *La vie et la doctrine spirituelle du Père Louis Lallemant.*

Each of these names adds something to the conundrum of authorship. The great simplicity of the life of Louis Lallemant is equalled only by the complexity of the literary conjectures which this work has evoked. How much of this is the voice of Lallemant, how much the reception and understanding of Rigoleuc, how much the reverent reworkings of Champion?[32] François Courel in the Christus edition of the *Doctrine spirituelle* notes various hypotheses to respond to these questions and then "reproduces purely and simply the *editio princeps* of 1694."[33] Courel's decision has much to recommend it. For it is this work, whatever its troubled authorship, that is immortal.

The *Doctrine spirituelle* complements the masterpieces of Francis de Sales and Pierre de Bérulle, and nowhere does this complementarity manifest itself more than in the centrality Lallemant gives to the Holy Spirit. For if the focal consciousness of the divine in Francis de Sales evolved from the divine majesty of the *Introduction*—to include the maternal metaphor which governs so much of the *Traité*—and if the governing sense of God in Bérulle lies with his great emphasis on the Incarnate Word, Lallemant is primarily occupied with the Holy Spirit, the indwelling presence and gifts of the Spirit of God and the correlative human responses of contemplation and discernment. Of course, each of the persons of the Trinity suffuses the writings of all these authors. The Trinity stands as their common Christian heritage; but it is remarkable that the mysticism of France offers to the newly awakened religious sensibilities of the seventeenth century such various modalities in which Christian spirituality can be concentrated, concentrations whose principal complementarities rest with different persons of the Triune God. The Holy Spirit is the key to Lallemant's instructions.

Henri Bremond has left students of Lallemant eternally in his debt both by the brilliant revival which he sponsored of the *Doctrine spirituelle* and also for his characterization of this doctrine under four headings: the second conversion, the critique of action, the guard over the heart, and the guidance of the Holy Spirit. Aloys Pottier reproaches Bremond for his isolation of atomic elements in so complex a teaching and makes the synthetic principle of all of Lallemant's *Doctrine* the idea of perfection. François Courel finds Pottier's reconstruction artificial and draws attention to the audience of these instructions, the young priests of the Society of Jesus in their third year of novitiate ("tertianship"), following prior years of novitiate and studies and preparatory to their total engagement in ministry. Here the "second conversion" takes on its profound significance and also allows what is central in the *Doctrine* to emerge:

> At the heart of the *Doctrine,* in order to work that radical reform, there is the spiritual discernment which commands all of the thought of Lallemant, as it commands all the advance of the Exercises. . . . One is not able to comprehend Lallemant, we believe, if one does not place at the center of every interpretation this discernment, this "guidance of the Spirit," which leads to the "service of Christ." (*Doc.* 24–25)

Understood in this way, the *Doctrine* is not a list of seven principles, more or less arbitrarily selected, itemized, and examined one after the other. The *Doctrine* charts a journey, one that begins with the experience of human emptiness and terminates with union with God in Christ—and all under the direction of the Holy Spirit.

While Francis de Sales details a steady ascent of the human person toward devotion and toward that prayer and that indifference which are the highest embodiments of the love of God and Pierre de Bérulle traces the movement of the descent of the divine Word into flesh, Eucharist, and church, Louis Lallemant initiates the dialectic inherent in the movement of the *Doctrine spirituelle* with the internal contradiction between human autonomy and the asymmetrical, dynamic orientation of the human toward God. The *Doctrine* opens with this relationship between human emptiness and the divine plenitude, which will define everything in human life: "We have in our hearts a void which all creatures are not able to fill. It can be filled only by God, who is our source [*principe*] and our end. The possession of God fills this void and makes us happy. The privation of God leaves us in that void and this renders us wretched" (*Doc.* I.1. #1, 77). The spirituality of Lallemant opens with an antithetical dynamic contrast. It is not that of contradiction but of privation and its fulfillment, and the seven principles by which his doctrine has been ordered mark a progress between them, from emptiness to plenitude, from the void in the human heart to the God who calls human beings to himself through this void, through this insufficiency of ourselves and of all things.

An emptiness for God, that is what a human being is. Anything that would disguise this radical relationality of the human is illusion, a series of deceptions that human beings will recognize only when they have passed into the crisis of death (*Doc.* II.1.1.2. #3, 90). The emptiness is ontological, constitutive of the human, and the religious call to *la parfaite nudité d'esprit* is only a summons to the integral expression of what the human person is in essence. Only when one has passed beyond the deception, the *tromperie* which the thousand distractions of the culture and of the world press as reality, can one stand in this profoundly simple self-understanding before God: emptiness and fullness, tendency and fulfillment. The paradoxes in such a beginning are numberless: *l'amour-propre* which promises so much is disclosed as self-contradiction, an emptiness attempting to find fulfillment in emptiness; great achievements and the credit of a great name are finally *si petites et si basses* when measured out against the infinite plenitude of God and against the human emptiness that lie beneath them all and which responds only to God. The initial lines of Lallemant fix a horizon by which human values are revolutionized or transvalued, and they form the context in which he calls his tertians to a "second conversion." God's offer of himself to human emptiness constitutes the source of his hope; the goodness of God constitutes the source of his love. All of the *Doctrine spirituelle* is counsel how to respond, how to live *la vie spirituelle*.

Bremond has simplified Lallemant's teaching to four principles, but, centuries before, Lallemant himself had simplified this doctrine still further, dividing it again into a dynamic asymmetrical relationship between the human and the divine:

> The two elements of the spiritual life are the purification of the heart and the direction of the Holy Spirit. These are the two poles of all spirituality. Through these two ways, one comes to perfection: according to the degree of purity which one has acquired and in proportion to the fidelity with which one has cooperated with the movement of the Holy Spirit and has followed his guidance." (*Doc.* IV.2.1. #1, 176)

Into these two "elements" he transposes his prior religious anthropology: emptiness of the heart becomes purity of heart; the plenitude of God becomes the indwelling and directing Spirit. Lallemant's spiritual writings are neither a map of the spiritual life, the gradual and progressive development of the soul into the state of perfect union, nor an epideictic assimilation of the glory of the Incarnation—though the components of both of these spiritualities will find their place within his own. Lallemant has but one purpose: to aid the soul to become sensitive to the influence of the Spirit of God. The Spirit above all and within all is to be the guide of the soul. The soul will move toward union as the Spirit directs it and will assimilate the wonder of God in the love of Christ as the Spirit configures it to the Incarnate Word. The premier religious care of the soul is to be open to this guidance through purity of heart and to be sensitive to this guidance through discernment.

Purity of heart: ancient and laconic as this phrase is, it bespeaks a struggle that engages all the forces of history, culture, nature, and grace—the liberation from adherence to false ideas, erroneous judgments, disordered affectivity, hidden and malicious passions, and the deceptions of Satan. This latter is the most subtle and the most corrupting of all. Under the appearance of good, unsuspected motivations drive the "religious" person toward those deeds which have become in this intentionality only another realization of *l'amour propre*. La Rochefoucauld himself was not more keenly aware of this constant possibility of profound self-deception and hidden self-interest. Diabolic deception can allow us

> to do some exterior actions of virtue, even to accuse ourselves publicly of our faults, to serve in the kitchen, to visit hospitals and prisons because we will content ourselves with this and so flatter ourselves that we inhibit the interior remonstrances of conscience; but it can never allow us to turn our eyes in upon our heart, so that by examination of the disorders that are there we might give ourselves to its correction. (*Doc.* III.1.2. #4, 141)

When one speaks of Lallemant's critique of action or when Lallemant himself gives strong, sometimes even hyperbolic, expression to the danger of activity whose motivation is unconscious, it is this that must be kept in mind. Religious activity and generous service can also be a dodge, a subtle justification through works which obviate the realistic assessment of purpose and of motive and excise the soul from the need common to other Christians to examine one's conscience. The *Doctrine spirituelle* schematizes the order through which such a guard of the heart must move: from sin through the discerned movements of the heart to the final recognition of the inspirations that come from God. Even this growth in purity of heart, for all its struggles at honest self-evaluation and a sober assessment of where our treasure is, can itself become deceptive unless done *doucement* and with a care whose focus is a deep "devotion to Our Lord, a devotion which includes a high knowledge of his grandeurs, a profound respect for his person and for all that he touches, his love and his imitation" (*Doc.* III.1.3. #1, 142). Lallemant never sounded more like Bérulle—though the influence is Ignatius and the common Christian tradition to which they all are heir. This calls to a life of penance, of mortification and the realization of

Christian virtues, of the sacraments and the grace which they offer, and supremely of union with God, who alone can finally bring the soul to the purity which is the vocation of one whom God has called. Purity of heart is finally God's work, and through the purification of motivation God can finally bring a person to such an integrity that God becomes the all of motivation and of consciousness: The soul has such a government "over her imaginations and over her powers that these only obtain their exercise in the service of God. She will not be able to wish nor to remember nor to think of anything nor to understand anything except in its relationship to God" (*Doc.* III.1.3. #2, 143). This progressive purity of heart becomes the finding of God in all things and of all things in God, and it is the progressive emergent of a graced life that moves through conversion, virtue, and sacraments to union.

Docility to the guidance of the Holy Spirit: "When a soul abandons herself to the guidance of the Holy Spirit, he raises her little by little and governs her" (*Doc.* IV.1.1. #1, 171). The figure for this guidance is classic in Christian spirituality: the pillar of fire which led Israel through the desert— by day a column of darkness and, at night, a column of fire. "They followed the movement of that column and they stopped when it stopped; they did not advance beyond it, they only followed it, and they never separated themselves from it. This is the way that we should act and behave with respect to the Holy Spirit" (*Doc.* IV.1.1. #2, 171). As purity of heart involved a particularized form of life, so this docility engages a progressive development through obedience, purity of intention, prayer for enlightenment, and that sensitive recognition of the diverse movements in the human soul that is Christian discretion or discernment. One grows in this gradually, aided by the steady practice of the examination of conscience: first, by fidelity to the light of the Spirit as it is offered; second, by the purification from sins and imperfection which inhibit this light; third, by not allowing themselves to be governed by sensuality—thus "God will open for them the interior senses"; fourth, by an integrity with their interior life so that they do not allow themselves to be dissociated from it or unaware of the movements of diverse spirits within themselves; finally, by the consistent use of spiritual direction, "the complete disclosure of one's heart to the superior or to a spiritual Father." A soul who has that frankness and that simplicity never goes without the favor of the direction of the Holy Spirit" (*Doc.* IV.1.3. #5, 175). Much of Lallemant's advice and analysis is concentrated on this fivefold way in which the human person allows the guidance of the Spirit to deepen in human choice and history. In a parallel fashion, so much of Lallemant's theology lies with an understanding of the gifts of the Holy Spirit and the beatitudes to which they correspond.

There are four kinds of "lights" which can guide human action: reason, which remains utterly inadequate unless informed by faith; the faith that attaches human beings to the truth of God; supernatural prudence, which indicates the appropriate means that respond to faith; and, fourth, "the gifts of the Holy Spirit which, by principles more transcendent, without discourse and without ambivalence, disclose what is the best, making us see this in the light of God with more or less evidence according to the degree that we possess these gifts" (*Doc.* IV.3.2. #1, 188). As purity of heart deals with motivation and the guidance of the Spirit offers the enlightenment and support to awareness and choice, so one can trace in Lallemant a series of considerations not unlike those of John of the Cross's night of the senses, dealing with motivation, and night of the spirit, dealing with faith as the single situation of religious support. Such a transposition would not be false, but it remains a transposition. For Lallemant is focused on the apostolic life, the life in union with God given over to ministry in Christ. That is why the gifts and the leadership they enable take on such an enormous importance in his spirituality. In the apostolic life, it is critically important that one not only seek God in all things, but be able to follow his direction in the manifold options and decisions that are presented daily, that one be able to read events as well as hearts for the indwelling spirit of God. The two "elements" of the spiritual theology of Lallemant compose a life given over in apostolic service, service whose undeviating determination is toward God as motive and in union with the Spirit as configuring guide.

To live such a life is increasingly to be placed with Christ, to be assimilated to that which governs his life and his presence in the world, to live a life in union with him. Here Lallemant takes up as the sixth principle of the *Doctrine spirituelle* the knowledge, the love, and the imitation of Christ. *Pace* Bremond, the very division bespeaks the continual petition of the *Exercises* of Ignatius. Five times a day through the second week of the *Spiritual Exercises,* a week programmed for twelve days, the exercitant prays for the very realities which structure the reflections of Lallemant: "an internal knowledge of the Lord, who for me has become a human being, that I may the more love Him and follow Him."[34] Both Ignatius and Bérulle celebrate the Incarnation—it is the most elaborate of all of the contemplations of the *Exercises* and the one to which the exercitant is continually returned. This concentration is peculiar to neither, but a central part of the heritage common to all Christians, for "it is in the Incarnation that God works the greatest marvel of his power" (*Doc.* VI.1.1.1. #2, 171). There is no competition between Lallemant's Ignatian heritage and the spirit of the *École française,* however different their immediate purposes and ministries.

Contemplation itself is caught up into this apostolic vision. "Contemplation is an awareness and presence [*vue*] of God and of things divine which is simple, free, penetrating, certain and proceeds from love and tends to love" (*Doc.* VII.4.5. #1, 348). Each of these words carries a critically important content, and contemplation itself grows under the influence of the Spirit of God. Not only does contemplation not inhibit apostolic activity, but it is a necessity for a life completely given to zeal for souls. Only a contemplative vision allows one to appreciate how "incomparably more precious is a single soul than the heavens and the earth with all of their grandeurs and richness" (*Doc.* VII.4.4. #1, 347). To live a life of contemplation is to enter into the vision of God, to see the human race for which the Son of God died and to grasp something of the eternal worth or horror of a life which is graced or which has rejected grace. The stages of contemplation, however they move into their own highest degrees of development, do not remove one from this care for those whom God has eternally loved, and so the perfection of contemplation is found in such a habitual union with God that all the practices of activity and contemplation remain constantly united with God even in works that are pressing in their exterior demands (*Doc.* VII.4.9. #3, 363).

If the experience of the compassion of God gives origin to the spirituality of Francis de Sales, the experience of apostolic urgency underlies that of Louis Lallemant. How paradoxical that seems, how contradictory to the battles that have been waged around this figure and his doctrine! Yet mission is the experience that all of his teaching presupposes. The careful manner in which he assesses the finality of human desire and the inspiration by which a person lives in intelligible only if measured against this experience of an almost overwhelming ministerial determination.

None of the seven principles into which the *Doctrine spirituelle* is divided is that of apostolic mission, but all of the seven principles are finally understood and justified in terms of it. The guard of the heart and the criticism of activity, the call to perfection and the need for infused contemplation are placed so strongly as to invite what has been historically a steady unease with his teaching: the charge that he lacks a governing sense of apostolic consecration. His disciples number some of the greatest apostles of France and the New World, and within his doctrine there are those insistent places where even the highest contemplation is evaluated by its contribution to the religious needs of others. How, then, explain this paradox if apostolic mission does not lie as the unspoken but pervasive experience of the *Doctrine,* so obvious in its urgency as not to need the reinforcements of its own tractate, so urgent as to require the reminders that Ignatius himself places in his *Constitutions:* that the means which unite the "human instrument with

God and so dispose it that it may be wielded dexterously by His divine hand are more effective than those which equip it in relationship to human beings." Lallemant's lists read not unlike that of Ignatius: goodness and virtue, a purity of mind in the divine service, familiarity with God our Lord in the spiritual exercises of devotion, and a sincere zeal for souls. Like Ignatius, the *Doctrine* emphasized those "interior gifts which make those exterior means effective towards the end which is sought."[35] The seeming contradictions in the *Doctrine*, either within the text itself or with the tradition of Jesuit spirituality out of which it comes, can be resolved if the apostolic energies of the Jesuits to whom it was directed are accurately assessed. Michel de Certeau has pointed out that the rapid expansion of the Jesuit colleges throughout the newly pacified nation seriously threatened in their demand for apostolic activity the interior life which should have energized this activity. At the same time, some Jesuits—even by way of reaction—were moving toward forms of prayer that threatened ministerial kenosis.[36] This tension would not be eliminated by further exhortations to the apostolate; the French Society was filled with such language and with the generosity of lives spilled out in its consequences. What was needed was to presuppose the apostolic experience, the call out of which such lives came, and to sustain this charism carefully into a spirituality which would encourage the most profound purity of intention and which would place all of this activity and prayer under the guidance of the Spirit discerned in his manifold inspiration and movements within the heart of each of these very different servants of God. Presuppose the dominant experience behind the *Doctrine spirituelle* to be that of apostolic call, and the rest of Lallemant falls easily into an integrity.

The dialectical tension lodged within the *Doctrine spirituelle* is not the contradiction between two opposite and irreconcilable spiritualities, one focused on action and the other on contemplation. The dialectic is one of a synthetic movement between moments only superficially in contradiction; at the heart of each of these moments lies the generation of its contrasting factor. One moves from the recognition of the emptiness of the human void to the fullness of God, from the singleminded concentration on God in purity of heart to the engagement with all things under the guidance of the Spirit, even to union between apostolic activity and infused contemplation. The "second conversion" urged by Lallemant's teaching is a life in which these divergent moments reach their own fullness in a common unity. The progress in this developmental synthesis demands its own time and the expenditure of human energies, and the reflective appropriation of its movement may not have reached its completion in Louis Lallemant. But these are the lines along which his spirituality lay, possibly somewhat misleading if one fails to appreciate the concrete problems he was addressing. But what he instructed his tertians, he can teach to all his readers through the centuries that followed:

> A worker in the Society ought to say with our Lord "I have not come to be served, but to serve and to give my life for the redemption of the many." He ought to serve God and his neighbor, to attend to God in the depths of his interiority and to expend his works and his life up to his last breath to bring about the salvation and the perfection of his neighbor. (*Doc.* V.3.2. #5, 265)

Legacy

These three figures from French spirituality of the seventeenth century do not in any way summarize the century, but they initiate many of the things that were fine within it. Louis Lallemant gave way to his tertian Jean-Joseph Surin and the tragic exorcism of Loudon, to the twenty-five subsequent years in which Surin believed himself possessed and the intervals of balance or sanity—whatever they were—in which he wrote one of the greatest classics on detachment, contemplation, and the movements of the Holy Spirit, *Le catéchisme spirituel*. Through this work and others that came from within the agony that was so much of his life, the influence of Surin and Lallemant came into the eighteenth century to shape the spirituality of Jean-Pierre de Caussade, into the nineteenth century with Jean Grou, and finally into the twentieth century with the "decisive effect" worked by *Le catéchisme spirituel* on the dawning desires for contemplation of Raissa and Jacques Maritain. Raissa Maritain celebrated the discovery of the work in the bookstore of Peguy in her autobiography: "The scattered notions regarding contemplation which we had found in Plotinus, in Pascal, and in Leon Bloy here had their centre of fulness and efficacy. This charter of sanctity, grasped for the first time, seemed to us really alive and human in our spirit as well as in all our acts."[37]

If the influence of Lallemant was a river that flowed through his disciples, that of the great Pierre Cardinal de Bérulle was a cascade. The communities of priests that trace their origin from him and the centuries of French clerics brought under his influence by the dedicated education of the Sulpicians, the Vincentians, and the Eudists have been mentioned. Bérulle began not just a community or even a series of communities; he began a school. The debt of Vincent de Paul and of John Eudes to Bérulle is beyond question, but Molien maintains that it was Jean-Jacques Olier who "in his numerous works has explained with the greatest perfection the doctrine of the *école française*." Olier followed Bérulle in distinguishing the "mysteries" of the

Incarnate Word from the "states." The mysteries were the events of Christ, accomplished once and for all; the states were "the dispositions and sentiments which Our Lord had in accomplishing these."[38] The states were what were incarnate in the mysteries, what made them intrinsically salvific and the endless focus of contemplative prayer, and they gave to both liturgy and asceticism a mystical identification with Christ. They offered to every Christian the graceful possibility for adhering to Christ, as Bérulle had so often taught.

And finally Francis de Sales. He began no school, and only the enclosed community of the Visitandines looked to him as their founder. Not until John Bosco would an active religious group take his name and his spirituality explicitly as their own. Yet his influence was everywhere. His books spoke to a greater public than either the hidden Lallemant or the commanding Bérulle, and perhaps more than both of them he influenced a lay piety which would develop in the centuries in which the laity began to assume their own call to holiness within the church. Perhaps the major contribution of Francis lies here, not in a particular doctrine or in a particular group of disciples, but in making available to every form of human life a devotion and a charity that bespeak Christianity in holiness and in depth.

Mystics and missionaries, spiritual authors, pulpit orators, confessors, and religious leaders would come in plenty over the decades of this great century of French spirituality as the nation gathered strength through the establishment of massive religious foundations and the government of the distinguished men and women. Much of this would waste itself in the fratricidal struggles over Gallicanism, Jansenism, and Quietism, in the irony of religious figures and movements tearing one another to pieces over the most effective way to live the gospel. But even here, in the horrors of religious polemics, there was a greatness that abided, a tradition of contemplation and of Christian service, of wisdom and of charity which has enriched the church for all the centuries that followed. And representative of this greatness and of this promise stand these three figures: Francis de Sales, Pierre de Bérulle, and Louis Lallemant.

Notes

1. Louis Cognet, *La spiritualité moderne* (Paris: Aubier, 1966) 239–41. This classic work constitutes the third volume in the series *Histoire de la spiritualité chrétienne,* edited by Louis Bouyer, Jean Leclercq, François Vandenbroucke, and Louis Cognet. Much of this material is available in an English translation of an earlier work (*A History of Christian Spirituality* [3 vols.; New York: Seabury, 1982]). See also Louis Cognet, *Post-Reformation Spirituality,* trans. P. Hepburne Scott (New York: Hawthorn Books, 1959);

Jacques LeBrun, "France: Le grand siècle de la spiritualité française et ses lendemains," in *Dict. Sp.* 5, cols. 917–54.

2. Henri Bremond, *A Literary History of Religious Thought in France*, trans. K. L. Montgomery (New York: Macmillan, 1930) 2:119. This volume is one of the three translated from the eleven-volume study by Bremond, *Histoire littéraire du sentiment religieux en France* (Paris: Libraire Armand Colin, 1916–1936).

3. As cited and analyzed in Paul Mommaers, "Benôit de Canfeld: Sa terminologie, 'essentielle,'" *Revue d'histoire de la spiritualité (Rev. Asc. Myst.)* 47 (1971) 422. Mommaers is citing from the third part of Benôit's *Règle de la perfection* III, 1, p. 278.

4. H. Bremond, *Literary History*, 2:115.

5. L. Cognet, *La spiritualité moderne*, 242.

6. Important concepts in the thought of Francis de Sales include the following:

Complacence and benevolence: Two states of love. Complacence is the affective affirmation and the rejoicing in the good of the other; benevolence is the desire of the good for the other. God's love for creation begins with benevolence and issues in complacence in the good created; human love for God begins with complacence in God's supreme goodness and then moves to benevolence by glorifying God in creation.

Contemplation: The loving, pure, permanent attention to God or the things of God, in contrast to the discursive movement of meditation. Meditation is the origin of love, but contemplation is its realization and furtherance.

Devotion: A great ardor and readiness in charity, differing only from charity in the manner that a flame differs from its fire.

Indifference: A habitual union and conformity with God's will that goes beyond the acquiescence of resignation and loves all things only as they are caught up and exist within the divine will.

7. Jean Marie Prat, *Recherches historique et critiques sur la Compagnie de Jésus en France du temps du Père Coton* (Lyon, 1876) 3:760; cf. Bremond, *Literary History*, 2:55.

8. For an analysis of the *Treatise* and the *Introduction* of Francis de Sales as well as a synthesis of Salesian spirituality, see Pierre Serouet, "Françoise de Sales," in *Dict. Sp.* 5, cols. 1057–97.

9. *St. Francis de Sales: A Testimony by St. Chantal*, translated and edited with an introduction by Elizabeth Stopp (Hyattsville, MD: Institute of Salesian Studies, 1967) 44–45. This work is the testimony given by Jeanne Françoise de Chantal at the first canonization inquiries for the cause of Francis de Sales at Annecy in 1627.

10. Jacques Maritain, "Foreword," to *The Spirit of Love*, by C. F. Kelly (New York: Harper & Brothers, 1951) ix–x.

11. Leonard Lessius's *De gratia efficaci decretis divinis liberatate arbitrii et praescientia Dei condicionate*, which taught that God gratuitously predestined salvation *post praevisa merita*, had been censured by the then Jesuit General, fearful that its theology so similar to that of Francis would resurrect the conflict with the Dominican *de auxiliis* only recently laid to rest by Pope Paul V. But Lessius believed what Francis believed, and it was to the beleaguered Jesuit that Francis wrote in 1618: "In the Jesuit library at Lyons, I saw your *Traite de la predestination* and although I had but time to glance hastily over it, observed that you hold and maintain the view of predestination to glory according to the prevision of merits, a view with so many titles to honour . . . for it is as ancient as it is comforting. . . . This is a great joy for me; for I have always considered this doctrine the truest, most lovely, and most conformed to the compassion and grace of God, as in my own poor way I have endeavoured to show in my *Traité de l'amour de Dieu*" (Bremond, *Literary History*, 1:72).

12. Bremond, *Literary History*, 1:69.

13. Cf. Joseph B. Wall, *The Providence of God in the Letters of Saint Ignatius* (San Jose, CA: Smith-McKay, 1958) 1–2.

14. Cognet, *Post-Reformation Spirituality,* 66.

15. Important concepts in the thought of Pierre de Bérulle include the following:
Adherence: Interior communion and configuration to God or Christ in conscious awareness, affectivity, and in human existence itself, a bonding to God that grows from initial moments of piety to passive transformation and union.
Anéantissement: A theocentric or Christocentric self-transcendence into the mystery of God, a kenotic movement of consciousness or of affectivity in which one realizes God as the truth of one's being.
Elevation: A kind of prayer whose inner form is adoration and whose native expression is praise, which develops from initial acts of the honor of God to a habitual state of absorption in the mystery of God.
State: In distinction from actions, the habitual dispositions of a person which both define the depths or the quality of this person and lie at the source of every action.

16. Unless otherwise noted, the edition of Bérulle cited is that of François Bourgoing, *Oeuvres complètes de Pierre Cardinal de Bérulle* of Paris published in 1644 by Antoine Estiene and Sebastien Huré, with the final reference for each citation made according to the columns in the Migne edition of 1856. In the reedition of 1960, the Migne columns are noted in the margin. This study of Pierre de Bérulle lies under a heavy debt to the following works: Paul Cochois, *Bérulle et l'École française;* Michel Dupuy, *Bérulle: Une spiritualité de l'adoration;* A. Molien, "Bérulle," in *Dict. Sp.* 1, cols. 1549–81; and the more general studies of seventeenth-century French spirituality previously noted.

17. Taken from a series of unedited meditations of Bérulle; see Dupuy, *Bérulle,* 44.

18. Bremond, *Literary History,* 2:229.

19. Ibid., 230.

20. The edition of this work is that of 1866 (Paris: Siffre fils) 26–27.

21. Bonaventure, Sermo i, Dominica xxii post Pentecostem, "Magister, scimus quia verax es et viam Dei in veritate doces," *Opera omnia* (Ad Clara Aquas [Quaracchi]: Ex Topographia Collegii S. Bonaventurae, 1882–1902) 9:442a. Cf. Bonaventure's inaugural lecture, "Christus, unus omnium magister," 7–9, *Opera omnia,* 5:569a–b.

22. Bonaventure, *In I. Sent.,* Proemium, *Opera omnia,*1:136; cf. *De reductione artium ad theologiam* 26, *Opera omnia,* 5:325b.

23. Bremond, *Literary History,* 3:99–100.

24. Cf. Aristotle *Rhetoric* i.3.1358b16–20.

25. George H. Tavard, "The Christology of the Mystics," *Theological Studies* 42 (1981) 575.

26. Cognet, *Post-Reformation Spirituality,* 73.

27. P. Cochois, *Bérulle et l'École française,* 76.

28. Bérulle à la Mere Prieure et aux Religieuses carmélites de Toulouse (January 16, 1623) *Correspondance du Cardinal Pierre de Bérulle,* ed. Jean Dagens (Paris: Desclée de Brouwer, 1937) 2:345; cf. P. Cochois, *Bérulle et l'École française,* 108.

29. H. Bremond, *Histoire littéraire,* 5:4.

30. Important concepts in the thought of Louis Lallemant include the following:
Contemplation: A presence or awareness (*vue*) of God which is simple, free, penetrating, certain, one which issues from love and which moves toward love. Contemplation is to be distinguished from the discursive prayer that is meditation and from that prayer which centers more on the affectivity which is touched by the considerations of the actions of God.
Gifts of the Holy Spirit: Permanent disposition which God works in the soul together

with the indwelling of the Holy Spirit and the infused virtues, in order to strengthen the natural powers and to render them sensitive to the movements and directions of the Spirit.

Purity of Heart: So comprehensive an orientation of intentionality and affectivity toward God that his will becomes the criteria of all human choices. An undeviating determination toward God.

31. Unfortunately, L. Cognet, so long after the research of Dudon, repeats the error that the then Jesuit General "censured Fr. Lallemant's spirituality as contrary to the spirit of the Society" (*Post-Reformation Spirituality,* 85)—one more legend about the Jesuits that dies hard. The truth of the matter is that Vitelleschi did inquire on 5 April 1629 into the tertianmaster's doctrine and, once informed, gave unstinted praise to Lallemant's teaching, insisting that he remain in office as long as his wretched health would permit and only admitting a temporary replacement when this proved impossible. See Joseph de Guibert, *The Jesuits: Their Spirituality and Doctrine,* trans. William J. Young (St. Louis: The Institute of Jesuit Sources, 1972) 357. See also *Dict. Sp.* 9:133. Cognet corrects the mistake in his earlier work with *La spiritualité moderne,* 439–40.

32. This redoubtable redactor, responsible as well for editing the writings of Rigoleuc and Surin, appended the notes of Jean-Joseph Surin to those of Rigoleuc in his edition of Lallemant and, in an attempt to reassure, actually raises the level of anxiety about authenticity, soothing the reader with the remark that Rigoleuc's fidelity to Lallemant's words "far from taking away any of its power or unction, has actually made additions to them." After three centuries, Michel de Certeau maintains an important position for the editor in the content of the *Doctrine spirituelle.* Georges Bottereau credits Rigoleuc with introducing a somber note into the work and excising from the manuscript three or four small sections to enrich his own writings. The critical edition of Aloys Pottier attempts to restore these to their putative previous positions. For this history together with the text of the *Doctrine spirituelle* used in this study, see François Courel, *La vie et la doctrine spirituelle du Père Louis Lallemant* (nouvelle ed., Collection Christus 3; Paris: Desclée de Brouwer, 1979). The citations from this edition will be by principle, section, chapter, article, paragraph number, and page.

33. P. Cochois, *Bérulle et l'École française,* 13.

34. Ignatius of Loyola, *Spiritual Exercises,* Third preamble to the Contemplation on the Incarnation, #104, *Obras Completas de San Ignacio de Loyola,* ed. Ignacio Iparraguirre (Madrid: Biblioteca de Autores Cristianos, 1963) 221. See also the analysis of Lallemant's doctrine and its sources in Georges Bottereau's "Lallemant," in *Dict. Sp.* 9, cols. 125ff.

35. Ignatius of Loyola, *Constitutions of the Society of Jesus,* part X, #813, *Obras Completas,* 591.

36. Michel de Certeau, "Crise sociale et réformisme spirituel au début du 17ᵉ siècle: Une 'nouvelle spiritualité' chez les jesuites français," *Revue d'ascetique et de mystique* 41 (1965) 339–86.

37. Raissa Maritain, *We Have Been Friends Together,* trans. Julie Kernan (New York: Longmans, Green, 1943) 153.

38. A. Molien, "Bérulle," in *Dict. Sp.* 1, cols. 1574–75.

Bibliography

Sources

Bérulle, Pierre de. *Les Oeuvres de l'éminentissime et révérendissime P. Cardinal de Bérulle.* Introduction by François Bourgoing. Paris: Antoine Estiene et Sabastien Huré. This edition was reedited with different pagination by J. P. Migne in 1856 with some additions. This initial edition was reproduced with the Migne pagination given in the columns: in 1960 by La Maison d'Institution de L'Oratoire, villa Béthanie, Montsoult, S & O. The Migne edition is the one most commonly used.

Dagen, J., ed. *Correspondance du Cardinal Pierre de Bérulle.* 3 vols. Paris: Desclée de Brouwer; Louvain: Bureaux de la Revue, 1937–1939.

Francis de Sales. *Introduction to the Devout Life.* Translated and edited by John K. Ryan. 3rd ed. New York: Harper, 1966.

——. *Library of St. Francis de Sales.* Translated and edited by H. B. Mackey. 7 vols. London: Burns & Oates, 1883–1910.

——. *Oeuvres de François de Sales.* Par les soins des Religieuses de la Visitation du Premier Monastère d'Annecy. Edited by H. B. Mackey and J.-J. Navatel. 26 vols. Annecy: J. Niérat, 1892–1932.

——. *Treatise on the Love of God.* Translated with an introduction and notes by John K. Ryan. 2 vols. Rockford, IL: Tan Books, 1975.

Lallemant, Louis. *The Spiritual Doctrine of Father Louis Lallemant of the Society of Jesus, preceded by an account of his life by Father Champion.* Edited by Alan McDougall. Westminster, MD: Newman Book Shop, 1946.

——. *La vie et la doctrine spirituelle du Père Louis Lallemant de la Compagnie de Jésus.* Introduction and notes by François Courel. 3rd ed. Paris: Desclée de Brouwer, 1979.

Studies

The general studies and articles from the *Dictionnaire de spiritualité* cited in the notes will provide extensive bibliographies of each of the three principal figures discussed in this chapter. The following works, however, can be singled out for special notation. The best secondary material on Lallemant is contained in the more general studies by Louis Cognet (*La spiritualité moderne*) and Joseph de Guibert (*The Spirituality of the Society of Jesus*), in F. Courel's introduction to his edition of the *Doctrine spirituelle,* and in Georges Bottereau's article in *Dictionnaire de spiritualité.*

Bedoyere, Michael de la. *François de Sales.* New York: Harper, 1960.

Cochois, Paul. *Bérulle et l'École française.* Paris: Seuil, 1963.

Dupuy, Michel. *Bérulle: Une spiritualité de l'adoration.* Tournai: Desclee, 1964.

Houssaye, Michel. *Le Cardinal de Bérulle et le Cardinal de Richelieu, 1625-1629.* Paris: H. Plon, 1875.

——. *M. de Bérulle et les Carmélites de France, 1575–1611.* Paris: H. Plon, 1872.

——. *Le P. de Bérulle et l'Oratoire de Jésus, 1611–1625.* Paris: H. Plon, 1874.

Trochu, F. *Saint François de Sales.* 2 vols. Paris: E. Vitte, 1941, 1942.

3

Spanish Sixteenth Century: Carmel and Surrounding Movements

KIERAN KAVANAUGH

The Renewal of Spanish Spirituality

Religious Reform

A T THE BEGINNING of the sixteenth century there began in Spain what could be called, to use the general term applied to that century, a golden age of spirituality. The product of a vast movement of religious reform and renewal that was initiated some time before the Council of Trent, it affected not only religious and clergy but laity as well. Its roots, however, lay in the efforts to reform religious life through a return to the observance of the rule. Those communities practicing the observance were known as the observants, whereas the former communities, which had been forced to relax the rule during the time of the black plague, were known as the conventuals. Within the Dominican order the conventuals became observants; within the Franciscan order there was a separation into two branches. Although practiced by the conventuals, prayer and the spiritual life were considered essential to the observant movement and were clearly correlated, so that development in the spiritual life was measured in terms of development in prayer.

In the preceding century there had already begun to exist in the various religious orders houses of prayer or of recollection, deserts, or places of retreat. These houses were then institutionalized, and their methods of prayer spread to other Christians. In addition, the newly founded printing presses facilitated the dissemination of teaching about prayer, providing people with abundant literature on the interior life.

First there were paths of methodic prayer clearly formulated by spiritual writers, including García de Cisneros in his *Ejercitatorio de la vida espiritual,* published in Montserrat in 1500; Alonso de Madrid in his *Arte para Servir a Dios,* published in Seville in 1521; and St. Ignatius of Loyola, who in 1522 wrote the more important meditations of his *Ejercicios espirituales.* Then a different path of prayer, given the name "recollection," was explained by spiritual writers such as Francisco de Osuna, in his *Tercera parte del libro llamado Abecedario Espiritual,* published in Toledo in 1527; Bernardino de Laredo in his *Subida del Monte Sion,* published in Seville in 1535; and Bernabé de Palma in his *Libro llamado Via Spiritus,* published in Salamanca in 1541. The traditional ascetical teaching on the practice of virtue and the uprooting of vices was usually taken care of in catechisms and moral treatises. The ways of prayer, however, were to lead to love, and some of them, as in the case of those expounded by Osuna, Palma, and Laredo, to pure love.

The most distinctive trait of the Spanish spirituality of this time was the passage from an objective spirituality based on vocal prayer and external works to another vital and subjective one based on personal experience. This transition to a living spirituality did not take place suddenly. One person could pass through different traditional methods before discovering recollection, and the authors of books on prayer recommended only what they had exerienced.

The movement of interiorization (mental prayer, recollection, enlightenment) preceded, was independent of, and was much more profound than the evangelical Christianity of Erasmus, which, though it emphasized the inward aspects of religion at the expense of forms and ceremonies, stopped outside the doors of friendship and love.

Methodic Mental Prayer

García de Cisneros and St. Ignatius of Loyola did not initiate the technique of meditation, yet they developed its inner discipline through concentration of the exterior and interior senses, especially the imagination; through intellectual attention; and through movement toward colloquy and good proposals. The meditation ought not to end in some merely vague desire for action. The images and ideas should lead to a decision for personal action.

This methodic meditation responded to the needs of the time. The inner discipline of the monastery could not benefit one who had to travel to the Indies or throughout Europe or live in Renaissance society. Such an individual needed solid personal convictions acquired through the repeated exercise of going to God. Out of this method developed the practice of imaginative contemplation by which the scenes of the life, passion, and death of Jesus were relived interiorly. In this contemplation one would see, hear, and attend to all the details.[1]

The Way of Recollection

The way called "recollection" produced the first great mystics of the golden age. Characteristic of many Franciscan houses of prayer, or recollection, it began to develop in these houses around 1480. The way comprised three parts: self-knowledge, the imitation of Christ, and union with God. Its essential characteristic was the union with or transformation in God—not by way of intellect but through love. This spirituality found its nourishment in Sacred Scripture and many other classic spiritual works by authors such as Augustine, Gregory the Great, Bernard, the Victorines, Bonaventure, Hugh of Balma, and Hendrik Herp. Bonaventure's writings and the *Mística Teología* by Hugh of Balma, which some had thought also to be a work of Bonaventure, were especially influential. Going beyond the previous forms of spirituality that were weighed down with long hours of vocal prayer and exercises directed toward the practice of virtue and the uprooting of vices, it also went beyond the popular, devotional forms of religious practice, which were characterized by many external and sometimes superstitious manifestations.

The principal themes flowing from this mystical movement of recollection, though not exclusively from it, included the following:

God calls all to Christian perfection, for all were created in his image. Thus, the call to perfection was brought out of the monasteries and extended to the laity.

The transformation of the soul in God is the equivalent of becoming one spirit with him. The union between God and the soul is comparable to that in which two distinct fires become one fire, or that in which the drop of water falls into the sea and becomes one with it.

Good works, external acts, rites and ceremonies should be distinguished from the goal, which is union with God.

The encounter with God takes place in the inmost part of the soul, in the center.

The spiritual authors, such as Osuna, Laredo, and Palma, wrote in the light of their own experience and recommended ways with which they themselves were personally acquainted. They compared their experience with Sacred Scripture, with the affirmations of the saints and of theologians, but they did not consider themselves to be the exclusive interpreters of Sacred Scripture and tradition.

These authors valued the way of love, the way along which God leads the simple, humble, and unlettered, both young and old, though they recognized that one could go to God by way of the intellect, which could include the scholastic science. This way of love made the theory of the universal call to perfection more believable and attractive.

Freedom, for them, consisted in the subjection of reason to the law of God and a consequent independence from both the exterior pressures of the world and the human appetite for power, pleasure, and money.

Love removes self-interest and is attentive to and directed entirely to God alone.

It was taught that Christ must be followed exteriorly and interiorly, in his humanity as well as his divinity, for humans are both corporal and spiritual. Emphasis on the following of Christ in his humanity led to an abundant literature on the passion and death of the Redeemer. The passion of Christ was the most frequent subject of meditation, and this has left its mark on the Spanish church and its art.

The strong stress on the contemplative life may have been at the root of the rise of the spirituality of the Society of Jesus. Though the active life was not held in contempt, by itself it would not lead to perfection. The ideal appears to have been a life that was both contemplative and active.

Quiet contemplation stood at the peak of the prayer of recollection. Various formulas were used to express this reality. One of the well known was *no pensar nada*, "think of nothing," the equivalent of attending to the All. The term "annihilation" was used mainly among the practitioners of recollection to express the awareness of one's own nothingness. This leads to truth, humility, and gratitude toward God for his kindly deeds and gifts, not to annihilation in the metaphysical or psychological sense, nor to inactivity. To die to all creatures was to live solely for the Creator. As regards the esteem for human thought, for love, action, and work, the language is frequently imprecise.

They asserted that they loved more than what they knew. Aware of this through experience, they were not concerned about metaphysical or psychological explanations. They held that in unitive love the soul needs no discourse or intellectual meditations. For the sake of giving expression to their loving knowledge they had recourse to images and symbols and to poetry. They were not anxious about avoiding exaggerations or using precise language.

The Way of the Alumbrados

Commingled with this spiritual movement of recollection, yet not precisely distinguished from it because of a certain vagueness of terminology, was a way promoted as being a shortcut. Its followers acquired the name *dejados*

and, later, *Alumbrados*.[2] Their method of procedure consisted in abandonment to the love of God. Vocal prayer, meditation on the passion, fasts,
penances, rites and ceremonies, the use of images, and the religious life were
all considered to be hindrances or useless. Abandonment to the love of God
placed one at the summit of perfection. It was the quickest and safest way
to union with God. Flowing from this practice and these ideas came a certitude and a self-confidence that resulted in an aggressive contempt for tradition. The problem seems to have developed out of a misunderstanding of
the meaning of pure love.

Another aberration to appear at the time was the unrestrained infatuation
with ecstasy and other extraordinary phenomena. These were regarded as
something to be sought. Both the Dominican María de Santo Domingo and
the Poor Clare Magdalena de la Cruz turned out to be frauds after having
fooled many, including bishops. The former was known for her prophecies,
ecstasies, and raptures; and the latter's reputation came from the claim that
she bore the stigmata. These interests stemmed from Savonarola's Florence
with its visionary, apocalyptic character.

When the Franciscan Isabel de la Cruz set about organizing devotional
centers in such towns as Alcalá and Toledo, her followers abandoned the
visionary approach of Savonarola for that mystical passivity known as *dejamiento* (abandonment) and she enlisted as her assistant Pedro Ruiz de
Alcaraz, a layman. Their work soon became a source of concern to the
Inquisition. The rapid spread of Lutheranism in Germany had presented the
Inquisition with a new field for its activities. Having only the most shadowy
ideas about the nature of Lutheranism, the Inquisitors zealously sought to
uncover it in Spain. Turning their attention to the *Alumbrados,* or Illumi-
nists, they arrested, in 1524, both Isabel de la Cruz and Pedro de Alcaraz
for heresy. The arrests were followed in 1525 by the condemnation of forty-
eight Illuminist propositions. In the same year a decree was promulgated by
the Inquisition of Toledo against the heresies of Luther. The Inquisitors suspected that Lutheranism and Illuminism, though fundamentally different,
were closely connected since both movements emphasized internal religion
at the expense of outward ceremony. Even St. Ignatius of Loyola was interrogated for Illuminist practices and forbidden to preach for three years.
Between the years 1556 and the closing of the Council of Trent in 1563,
there was a further tightening up in Spain. In this atmosphere the discovery
was made, in 1557 and 1558, of what were thought to be Protestant communities in Seville and Valladolid but which may very well have been
Alumbrado communities. As a result, the Inquisitor General, Valdes, published in 1559 an extremely severe index of forbidden books. Well-known
spiritual writers had their works placed on the index. They included Tauler,

Hendrik Herp, Francisco de Osuna, Bernabé de Palma, Luis de Granada, St. John of Avila, and St. Francis Borgia. Sometimes the danger of a book was seen to lie in the theological formulations of the spirituality, which could be misunderstood and result in bad practice.

Origins of the Carmelite Movement

Teresa of Avila

It was on the occasion of the publication of Valdes's index that Doña Teresa de Ahumada, known popularly today as Teresa of Avila, heard words from the Lord in the interior of her soul that hinted at a future in which she was to become one of the best-known mystics and spiritual authors in history. She writes in her *Life* that when some of the books that she enjoyed reading were placed on the index and she was feeling very sad about this, the Lord said to her: "Don't be sad for I shall give you a living book" (*Life,* chap. 26, no. 5).[3]

In the history of spirituality, the figure of Teresa of Jesus, the name she herself later took and was known by, is a complex but intensely interesting one. In addition to her writings and the influence that these have had in the field of thought after her death, there are the other fascinating aspects of her human personality: her consciousness as a woman, her feminine style, her presence to the world even in the nonreligious sphere, and the continuing attractiveness of her ageless spirit throughout the four centuries that separate her from our times. But one cannot fully understand Teresa's contribution to spirituality without knowing about her life.

The main sources for her biography are many of her own writings. Born in Avila on 28 March 1515, of deeply Christian parents, she was the fifth in line among nine brothers and two sisters. At the death of her mother, Doña Beatriz de Ahumada, Teresa, only twelve years old, entrusted her life to Our Lady. Shortly afterward she was placed by her father, Don Alonso Sanchez de Cepeda, in a school for girls under the care of Augustinian nuns. Here Teresa began to experience the first inclinations toward a religious vocation. While recuperating from an illness a little later at the country home of her uncle Don Pedro de Cepeda, who, though a layman, was caught up in the spiritual movement spreading through Spain and was dedicating himself to a life of prayer, she was invited to read to him from his many spiritual books. This introduction to spiritual reading had its beneficial effects. It was the *Letters of St. Jerome* that unexpectedly touched Teresa and moved her to make her decision about religious life and enter a monastery of Carmelite nuns.

Shortly after her profession, made on 3 November 1537, Teresa contracted a serious illness that was exacerbated by the bad treatments used on her by a quack in the town of Becedas; this brought her close to death's door. While awaiting the proper time for these treatments, she passed some days with her uncle once more, and this time he gave her a book on the way of recollection by Osuna, *The Third Spiritual Alphabet* (*Tercera Abecedario Espiritual*). Teresa enthusiastically began practicing the prayer of recollection explained in this book and in a short time received the gifts of the passive prayer of quiet and union.

The illness and the years of convalescence that followed interfered with her desire to give herself totally to the practice of this prayer. As she recovered she began to turn once more to recollection but no longer experienced her previous success, at least as she understood it. For years she encountered only difficulty as she herself reports in strong terms: "I don't know what heavy penance could have come to mind that frequently I would not have gladly undertaken rather than recollect myself in the practice of prayer" (*Life*, chap. 8, no. 7). Those years represent a time in which she was unable to integrate her relationship to the world with her relationship to God: "I was living an extremely burdensome life, because in prayer I understood more clearly my faults. On the one hand God was calling me; on the other hand I was following the world" (*Life*, chap. 7, no. 17). At one point in her pain over the whole situation she decided that the more humble thing to do would be to give up the practice of prayer. Although she gave it up for only a short time, she was forever lamenting that mistaken humility. She regarded the error as the worst of her life and understood that it could have had dire consequences.

In 1554, when in her thirty-ninth year, she experienced on two occasions what marked a powerful conversion. This conversion changed her life completely. On the first occasion, she happened to behold a small bust of Christ, in a scene from the passion, called an *ecce homo*. Moved by the love manifested in the representation, she surrendered herself entirely to the Lord, recognizing that she had been trusting up till then, to a certain degree, in her own efforts. On the other occasion, she was reading in the *Confessions* of St. Augustine about how Augustine heard the voice calling him in the garden. It seemed at the same time that she was hearing the Lord calling her from deep within.

A new life began for Teresa, no longer the life she lived but the life that Christ lived in her. Passive contemplative prayer, later divided into two major forms, the prayer of quiet and the prayer of union, became her habitual mode of prayer. A new inundation of spiritual delight and sweetness, after so many years of dryness and difficulty, led to a certain doubt in

Teresa's mind, for she was aware of the tensions that were arising in the Spain of her time over the interior life. With the help of a layman, Don Francisco de Salcedo, she arranged to consult a priest, Gaspar Daza, known in Avila for his great holiness. But Daza's response to Teresa's story was a demanding one and only resulted in frightening her. Teresa tempered her fears by continuing to speak about her spiritual life with Don Francisco de Salcedo, whom she found less disturbing. He, also as a layman, had entered into the Spanish spiritual renewal movement and had been practicing mental prayer for about forty years. He helped Teresa deal with some of her defects, but soon began to have doubts about her.

At this time, the Carmelite nun realized that she had another problem seriously hampering her efforts to get help. It was her inability to put her experiences into words. Ultimately she found a solution to her difficulty by turning to a book for help. It was Bernardino de Laredo's *The Ascent of Mount Sion*. After having underlined the passages that seemed to describe best her own situation and then having provided some additional information through a written statement of her own, she gave the two documents to her friend Don Francisco. He in turn went to consult Maestro Daza. These two devout consultants concluded that Teresa's experiences were from the devil, a sad and stunning blow to Teresa. They did leave her with a ray of hope, however, by suggesting that she consult a Jesuit.

Jesuits at the time were included among those called *espirituales,* that is, men more experienced in prayer than the average priest or friar. Diego de Cetina, an understanding man and the first Jesuit whom Teresa consulted, assured the anxious Carmelite that her prayer was from God. In his counsel he placed stress on the love of God and urged her to try to do things out of love, and he put no more pressures on her. He did, however, advise her to resist the passive recollection and sweetness and direct her thought in prayer to the passion of Christ. This latter piece of advice resulted in an important lesson for Teresa: that her passive experiences were independent of any kind of technique. If at one time she had thought that for passive prayer a great deal of seclusion and bodily quiet was necessary, she now found that in trying to resist the passive recollection and distract herself from it, she was enveloped all the more "in that sweetness and glory."

A little later when St. Francis Borgia, the former Duke of Gandia, who had entered the Society of Jesus, came to Avila, Diego de Cetina and Don Francisco arranged that Teresa speak with him. He added some qualifications to the instructions of his brother Jesuit. He advised her to begin her prayer with an episode from the passion of Jesus but not to resist when drawn into the passive prayer she was experiencing.

To the ancient Catholic practice of manifesting one's state of soul to a spiritual father, director, or confessor, we owe the outstanding records we possess of Teresa's spiritual life. The penitent believed that God will keep from deception the one who exercises such docility to another member of the church. As she progressed, Teresa derived a sense of inner confirmation from consulting men who were qualified to judge whether or not her spirit was in accord with the teachings of Scripture.

The illuminations coming from her infused prayer made Teresa aware of some further changes that needed to be made in her life. She felt, however, incapable of making them. Speaking of this with her confessor, then the Jesuit Father Prádanos, she was advised to pray over the matter and to recite the *Veni Creator Spiritus,* a vocal prayer to the Holy Spirit. One day in 1555 while reciting this prayer, she experienced her first rapture and heard these words: "No longer do I want you to converse with men but with angels" (*Life,* chap. 24, no. 8). With those words Teresa felt liberated from her attachments to others, from the many bonds from which, with all her efforts, she had been for years unable to disentangle herself.

After this moment, the hearing of words spoken by the Lord, often called "locutions" in spiritual literature, became a common experience in Teresa's life. She submitted this new phenomenon to her confessor. He consulted others. In fact, a group of five or six men gathered to discuss Teresa's spiritual state. Their unanimous decision was that her experiences were caused by the devil, that she should not receive communion as often as she had been doing, that she should distract herself and avoid being alone. Deep inside, Teresa could not feel agreement with their conclusions, but this only added to her fears, and she forced herself to comply. At one point, in a state of confusion and fear over all that was happening, she heard these words: "Do not fear, daughter, for I am, and I will not abandon you; do not fear" (*Life,* chap. 25, no. 18). With these words, in an instant, her fears were taken away, and a wave of courage and inner quietude came over her.

The locutions she received at the time of the publication of Valdes's index marked the beginning of another mystical grace, in which the Lord began to be her living book. This new grace she refers to as the intellectual vision or what is also known as mystical understanding: "Afterward, within only a few days I understood very clearly, because I received so much to think about and such recollection in the presence of what I saw, and the Lord showed so much love for me by teaching me in many ways, that I have very little or almost no need for books. His Majesty had become the true book in which I saw the truths" (*Life,* chap. 26, no. 5).

While her confessors were urging her to pray and get others to pray that God would lead her by a path other than that of these locutions and other experiences, Teresa had her first intellectual vision of Christ. In this vision she understood without image or idea that Christ was present. In the prayer of union and of quiet she knew of the divine presence only through its effects; in this vision she saw Christ's presence clearly and not merely through effects.

God can teach, then, without words, without concepts. "The Lord puts what He wants the soul to know very deeply within it, and there He makes this known without image or explicit words" (*Life*, chap. 27, no. 6). Thus Teresa received understanding of God's desires and of his incomprehensible truths and mysteries. This understanding was accompanied by love powerful enough to convert a person entirely to good. And as love increases, "the soul becomes obsessed with serving the Lord." Teresa's vehement desires to serve the Lord led, among other things, to her founding of seventeen small communities of contemplative nuns in which the rule of Carmel could be lived with greater fidelity.

But with regard to this new mode of understanding, Teresa tasted many of the deep mysteries of the faith, especially those that had most to do with the interior life: the indwelling presence of the Blessed Trinity and of Jesus Christ in his humanity as well as his divinity, grace, sin, the church, the sacraments, especially the Blessed Sacrament, and the communion of saints.

The intellectual visions were soon followed by another kind of vision called the imaginative vision, in which Teresa now beheld Christ not only in a spiritual way but, within her imagination or fantasy, in a corporeal fashion as well. In a word, she beheld the divine beauty, majesty, glory, and splendor of Christ's risen body and experienced its powerful effects. Teresa's visions brought further doubts to the minds of her confessors and stirred up their former fears. Of this she wrote: "The opposition of good men to a little woman, wretched, weak, and fearful like myself, seems to be nothing when described in so few words; yet among the very severe trials I suffered in my life, this was one of the most severe" (*Life*, chap. 28, no. 18).

It was the Franciscan saint Peter of Alcantara who this time came to Teresa's aid. Through his own mystical experiences he was able to explain many things to her and also took it upon himself to go to those who had become fearful of Teresa and explain why they need not doubt or disturb her any further. When after these vicissitudes at the request of the Dominican García de Toledo Teresa wrote the account of her spiritual life and experiences, she received new and special gifts for the task. She describes it thus: "For it is one grace to receive the Lord's favor; another, to understand which favor and grace it is; and a third, to know how to describe it" (*Life*, chap. 17, no. 5).

After some time Teresa entered the highest stage of her spiritual development, what she calls the seventh dwelling place of the interior castle (the symbol she adopts to explain the interior journey to God). Led to this dwelling place by Christ, she entered it through an intellectual vision of the Blessed Trinity that took place in the deepest part of her being. Here, too, the grace of perfect union, which she calls "spiritual marriage," was given her in 1572 through an intellectual and imaginative vision of Christ in his sacred humanity. Through this grace Teresa became inseparable from Christ, "as when a little stream enters the sea" (*The Interior Castle*, VII, chap. 2, no. 4).[4]

On account of her difficulties with spiritual directors, Teresa did more in her writing, especially her *Life*, than simply present a spiritual account of her soul. With impressive tact, she engaged in teaching and took extraordinary pains to analyze and describe in detail the many possible experiences of the mystical life so that she might spare others some of the troubles she had to go through herself.

Insisting on the interior life, illumination from God, and passivity as requisites for spiritual growth, she prevented some of the antimystical reactions, inspired by fear of Illuminism and Lutheranism, from spoiling the spiritual renewal in Spain. Furthermore, her entire life and teaching demonstrate that the loving remembrance of Jesus Christ's human experiences and earthly mysteries is no obstacle to the highest mystical life and prayer. On the contrary, Christ remained the way and the goal for Teresa. "This method of keeping Christ present with us is beneficial in all stages and is a very safe means of advancing in the first degree of prayer, or reaching in a short time the second degree, and of walking secure against the dangers the devil can set up in the last degrees" (*Life*, chap. 2, no. 4). The church, the sacraments, authority, sacramentals, religious life, vocal prayer, properly understood, presented no impediment to the development of a most sublime mystical life. Her submission to the judgment of spiritual directors brought her much suffering but no permanent spiritual loss. Finally, though she definitely benefited by the extraordinary mystical favors that she received, she did not see them as essential for spiritual growth. "The highest perfection obviously does not consist in interior delights or in great raptures or in visions or in the spirit of prophecy but in having our will so much in conformity with God's will that there is nothing we know He wills that we do not want with all our desire, and in accepting the bitter as happily as we do the delightful when we know that His Majesty desires it" (*The Foundations*, chap. 5, no. 10).[5]

In a time when spiritual books were removed from circulation, Teresa wrote new books out of her own living experience for those who sought guidance from her. Her testimony to God's work in her soul, her enthusiastic teaching, profound wisdom, and practical sense aided the church in finding its way through the mystical renewal of the modern age. Teresa's most noted works are *The Life, The Way of Perfection,* and *The Interior Castle.* The first edition of her writings was published in Salamanca in 1588, six years after her death. She was beatified in 1614 and canonized in 1622. In 1970, Pope Paul VI declared her the first woman Doctor of the Church.

St. John of the Cross

If Teresa in her writings is so noticeably a part of her culture and the problems and tensions of her times, St. John of the Cross in his writings seems almost abstracted from them, as though his work could have been written in any age. Born in 1542 in Fontiveros, Spain, he entered the Carmelite monastery in Medina del Campo at the age of twenty-one and studied for the priesthood at the University of Salamanca. After meeting Teresa in 1567, he joined her in inaugurating her contemplative mode of life among the Carmelite friars.

Because of conflicts in jurisdiction over the new segment within the order, his confraters incarcerated him at their monastery in Toledo. There, to pass the time, he wrote some of the greatest lyric poetry of the Spanish language. As expressions of his mystical experience, his poems led later to his profound commentaries, doctrinal treatises written at the request of others about the way leading to union with God and the life itself of that divine union. After escaping from his prison in Toledo, he spent most of the remainder of his life in Andalusia as a superior and spiritual director. He did the greater part of his writing in Granada. He died in 1491, at the age of forty-nine. He was beatified in 1675 and canonized in 1726. In 1926, Pope Pius XI declared him a Doctor of the Church.

Not until four centuries after John of the Cross wrote his works (first printed in 1618) did they begin to attract the attention of scholars and students of spirituality on a wider scale. The twentieth century, it seems, detected an affinity with his fundamental experience.

In poetry John found the least unacceptable way of expressing the mystery of God to which he had access through faith, Scripture, and his own experience. One of his most important and recognized symbols is that of the "dark night."[6] The lyrical language for which he opted created difficulties for theologians and a lack of trust in his writings. In works on spirituality and theology symbolic language was normally employed for inspirational and devotional purposes while only conceptual language was used for theoretical treatises. John's mixing of the two languages formed until the beginning of the twentieth century a serious obstacle in the appreciation of his philosophical and theological doctrine.

His doctrine describes the soul in search of God, in movement toward

3. El Greco, *Fifth Seal of the Apocalypse [The Vision of St. John]*, 1608-1614.

union with him, and in struggle against the obstacles to this goal. But John presents this journey as one who is looking back on it, and he evaluates it in the light of biblical, theological, and philosophical principles. As a consequence of this knowledge, he then also becomes a guide.

John speaks of living persons (God, Christ, the human person or soul) and of living realities more than of themes. The trinitarian God communes with human persons, transforms them, and assumes them into his divine personal life. The union, goal of the spiritual life, is a union of love. This is brought about through a long process of interiorization and purification of all the activities of the human faculties. In this process, through the theological virtues, the soul becomes like, or equal to, God. The union of love is a union of likeness or equality.

The mystery of God's transcendence and immanence forms a pattern of darkness and light. The Friend is felt sometimes as near, sometimes as far. Because God is the transcendent and incomprehensible Good, he must be sought, in John's words, as "hidden."

> You do very well, O soul, to seek Him ever as one hidden, for you exalt God immensely and approach very near Him when you consider Him higher and deeper than anything you can reach. Hence, pay no attention, neither partially nor entirely, to anything which your faculties understand about God, but to what you do not understand about Him. Never stop with loving and delighting in your understanding and experience of God, but love and delight in what is neither understandable nor perceptible of Him. (*Spiritual Canticle*, st. 1, no. 12)[7]

In his major works John shows how the path of searching for the Beloved who is hidden (*The Spiritual Canticle*), or of ascending to the summit of the mountain (*The Ascent of Mount Carmel*), or of escaping at night to meet the Beloved (*The Dark Night*) involves a process that is gradual with its alternating periods of apparent progression and regression until the soul is completely transformed into God as the log of wood is transformed when placed in the fire (*The Living Flame of Love*).

The map of this journey could be a very large one, allowing for the intervals and the sometimes almost imperceptible steps forward. John has chosen, however, to condense it into three very characteristic moments, a conscious simplification. Each phase represents a particular way of living and responding to the entire reality of God's self-communication. The first phase is life in the senses. In the initial responses to the call to set out on the spiritual path, the love of Christ is felt with sensible fervor and helps the beginner to take the first solid steps forward. This is followed by dark night and negation, a decisive phase in John's outline which leads to a more sober and genuine relationship with God. In his works John analyzes in detail the characteristic experiences and phenomena, the theological and psychological causes, the motivating principles, and the fruits of this night. He deals with an experience of great breadth in that it unfolds gradually in an active and passive manner in both the sensory and spiritual parts of a person's makeup. The third phase is full union, or likeness of love. This is the goal and fruit of the previous phases. This union with God is habitual, but there are moments when it becomes more actual, experiential, or alive, through the work of the Holy Spirit. The difference between the transformation in love and the flame of love is like the difference between the wood that is on fire and the flame that leaps up from it. The flame of love is the Holy Spirit. In the actual union "the soul feels Him within itself not only as a fire that has consumed and transformed it, but as a fire that burns and flares within it" (*Living Flame of Love,* st. 1, no. 3).

The soul must seek God in faith and love, that is, without desire for the satisfaction, taste, or understanding of any other thing than what you ought to know" (*Spiritual Canticle,* st. 1, no. 11). But this seeking, prompted by love, is mutual. If the soul is seeking God, God is seeking it much more. God in fact is the "principal lover, who, in the omnipotence of His fathomless love, absorbs the soul in Himself more efficaciously and forcibly than a torrent of fire would devour the drop of morning dew" (*Spiritual Canticle,* st. 31, no. 2). In the doctrine of John of the Cross, God, despite his transcendence, does not remain aloof; he communicates his friendship and love and reveals his secrets. This he does chiefly in giving his Word, his Son, Jesus Christ, whom we receive in faith. "Fasten your eyes on Him alone, because in Him I have spoken and revealed all, and in Him you shall discover even more than you ask for and desire" (*Ascent of Mount Carmel,* II, chap. 22, no. 5).

God, then, gives himself in faith and love, in revelations and manifestations of goodness. The theological virtues, being divine works before becoming human tendencies, constitute the immediate means to union with God. So much does John insist on their value that it at times appears he is denying every other means. God may use persons, realities, or actions in order to commune with us. As such they can be helpful to us in our attempts to respond to him. These means, though, must not be absolutized. "The means are good and necessary for the attainment of the end, as are images for reminding us of God and the saints. But when a person uses and dwells upon the means more than he ought, his excessive use of them becomes as much an impediment as anything else" (*Ascent of Mount Carmel,* III, chap. 15, no. 2).

The mediating value of the theological virtues comes from their identification with Christ, who is both the principle and content of faith, hope, and love. Jesus Christ, in being both God and man, mediates in a way that at the same time unites. Thus the theological virtues constitute the union itself, as well as the means to it. They demand a negation of all that is contrary to the union of love, reaching their high point in contemplation, the general loving attention to God in which one is open to receive the general (obscure, mystical) loving knowledge, or communication, of God.

The Carmelite School

The First Followers

Influenced and enlightened by the teachings and experiences of Teresa and John, those Carmelites who were their first spiritual followers taught that mental prayer was essential to any spiritual growth and effective ministry. For the sake of alerting souls to the obstacles that could get in the way of growth in prayer they offered some guidelines: Those practicing prayer were to avoid too much speculative thinking and be sure to make room for feelings and love and for the conversion of the will to good. They were to avoid excessive activity. Passivity, listening in silence for what God might say, was an important part of prayer. God, it was pointed out, speaks to the soul in that divine silence through illuminations, commonly called inspirations. Since one could be deceived, these inspirations were to be tested against the teachings of Scripture and discussed with confessors or other learned or spiritual persons. The words used in prayer should not be many, but few and simple. In prayer they must not seek delight and favors for themselves but conformity with the will of God. They must shun the tendency to measure progress by the satisfaction found in prayer. Christ's prayer in the garden was most perfect, but yet it was experienced in anguish and agony, so great that those feelings overflowed into the body. Prayer was likened to food, containing both substance and taste. The primary element is that which nourishes and sustains life; the secondary element, that which motivates one to take the nourishment. Just as the more nourishing food may be less pleasing to the taste, so it is with prayer. Thus, spiritual consolations must not be sought as an end, but should be gratefully and humbly accepted, when given, as a means to the perfection of love.

The classic steps of mental prayer common at the time were well described by the Dominican Luis de Granada in his book *Libro de la oración y meditación*. The early Carmelites, though recognizing the value of these steps (preparation, reading, meditation, thanksgiving, offering, and petition), thought that individuals because of their diversity could not be bound to one method. But on account of the wide use of these steps and the emphasis the Carmelites gave in their teaching to passivity, simplicity, and love, they added contemplation as another step following meditation. Traced back to the novitiates in Pastrana and Granada, where St. John of the Cross had resided and left his influence, this addition derives perhaps from him. At least it is certain that, in his capacity as general definitor, he approved the first instruction for novices that was published in 1591. Prepared by a team of three, this work, *Instrucción de novicios descalzos de la Virgen del Monte Carmelo,* is of special importance as a source for understanding the earliest teachings among Teresa's followers, and it includes contemplation as one of the steps of mental prayer.

In another early work, *Tratado de oración,* written in 1587 and attributed to Juan de Jesús María Aravalles, one of those on the team that prepared the above instruction for novices, the author adds contemplation to Granada's six steps, declaring that he considers contemplation to be the goal of meditation and the soul of mental prayer. Stating that he learned this in his novitiate (Pastrana), he clarifies further by saying that actual meditation need not always precede contemplation since one who has the habit of the truths arrived at through meditation enters easily into contemplation.

María de San José, Teresa's intimate friend and confidante, in writing on prayer in her *Libro de recreaciones* shows that also among Teresa's nuns contemplation was added to Granada's steps of mental prayer.

The First Systematizers

The Carmelite writers that followed added to the initial, practical concerns about giving instruction a certain systematic standard, but without producing scholastic treatises in the strict sense. The best known of these are Jerónimo Gracián and Juan de Jesús María Calagurritano.

Jerónimo Gracián (1545–1614), the close friend and spiritual director of Teresa, left a large number of writings, some three hundred, a great many of which have not yet been found. He was the first of the Carmelites to present the development of the spiritual life along lines parallel with those of the different degrees of divine illumination. He never quotes John of the Cross, but turns frequently to Teresa of Jesus. Yet one finds little help from him when looking for clarifications of her doctrine. Rather, in his baroque, erudite style he sets up his own divisions and tends to complicate matters. Using the term "supernatural" in a way different from Teresa and John, he places under that term all that arises from grace and the theological virtues. He then divides this supernatural life into acquired and infused. The acquired comes about through our own efforts presupposing faith, as in meditation. The infused is a gift from heaven. The supernatural infused is further divided into ordinary and extraordinary (ecstasies and raptures). He speaks, then, of an acquired contemplation, which is exercised with the general gifts of grace, and of an infused prayer. Theologically, the infused prayer may be explained by the theory of the gifts of the Holy Spirit or, when extraordinary, by that of graces *gratis datae*. He thought this extraordinary prayer to be the highest since the graces *gratis datae* were considered superior to the gifts of the Holy Spirit. But he opposed any striving for extraordinary experiences and considered them unnecessary for perfection.

Juan de Jesús María Calagurritano (1564–1615) had for his novice master a former disciple of John of the Cross. Sent to Italy, where he finished his theology, he played an important role in establishing the Teresian Carmel there. Writing in both Latin and Italian, he published a good number of works during his lifetime. Taking Teresa as an example, he joined the apostolic life to the contemplative life and urged his Carmelites to aid bishops in their work. He also promoted missions in foreign lands.

In his writings on spiritual theology he sought to work out a system that would integrate the different traditional currents (Pseudo-Denys, Bonaventure, Gerson, and Hendrik Herp) with the elements and stages of the spiritual life as presented by St. Teresa. Though Juan de Jesús María Calagurritano was much influenced by Teresa, it is doubted whether he ever read John of the Cross. In his instruction for novices, he abandoned the addition of contemplation to the steps of mental prayer claiming that beginners would waste their time by trying to contemplate and would lose the benefit of ordinary prayer.

In his *Theologia mystica,* he speaks of contemplation as an act of the intellect by which one receives an intuition of the truth, which in its turn affects the will. He then divides contemplation into natural, supernatural, and divine. The first attains to God, the Creator and foundation of the natural truths of the universe, by the natural light of reason. The second has for its object God as the author of both grace and the supernatural mysteries of salvation and also natural truths attained through the supernatural light of faith. The third has the same object as the second but proceeds from the gift of wisdom.

In the experience of mystical theology the will is drawn to union with God; the intellect follows and finds itself immersed in darkness, which constitutes a mode of knowing beyond the ordinary. The spirit receives a knowledge that is negative yet more perfect than the affirmative knowledge that characterizes the three kinds of contemplation (natural, supernatural, and divine). In a section entitled *Epistolae anagogicae,* which comes at the end of the *Theologia mystica,* Juan speaks about acts of union in which love goes beyond what can be grasped by either the imagination or the intellect. This he calls unitive wisdom.

Further Speculations

A second category of authors corresponds to a further step toward the theoretical sytematization of the inherited spiritual doctrine. While expressing their desire to be faithful to the doctrine of their founders, these authors never actually undertook a critical analysis of the founders' works. In fact, they attempted a theological interpretation that remains strictly within a Thomist framework. They are representative because in matters pertaining to contemplation they took positions that became standard for the Carmelite school.

José de Jesús María Quiroga (1562–1628), an important author in this category, was born in Spain and entered Carmel after his ordination. Appointed general historian of the order in 1596, he became very familiar, in this capacity, with the life and teaching of St. John of the Cross and published the first biography of this saint. Two of his more important spiritual writings are *Subida del alma a Dios* and *Don que tuvo San Juan de la Cruz para guiar almas a Dios*.

He taught that through the repetition of acts of meditation a habit is formed. Contemplation requires this habit, which provides both intellectual and affective drive with a natural content on the basis of which divine illumination proper may take place. It is to the latter that Quiroga reserves the name contemplation. This illumination, made possible through the gifts of the Holy Spirit, has two forms. In one, the illumination comes about in a human mode and is referred to as "contemplation of faith," "simple" or "common" contemplation. Thus, for Quiroga, the gifts work also in a human mode. In the other, the illumination lifts one above the natural mode of acting and is referred to as infused. There is a still higher degree of illumination which, according to Quiroga, calls for a knowledge of God through "infused expressed likenesses of the divinity."

Tomás de Jesús (1564–1627), born in Baeza, Spain, is the most well known of the Carmelite authors in this category. Making his profession as a discalced Carmelite in the hands of Jerónimo Gracián in Valladolid, he was called to Rome by Pope Paul V in 1607 and from that time lived outside Spain. In addition to his many mystical writings, he wrote a well-known treatise on missiology, *De procuranda salute omnium gentium*. Some of his important spiritual treatises are *Tratado de oración mental, De contemplatione acquisita,* and *De oratione divina seu a Deo infusa*.

Tomás de Jesús became the great promoter of the distinction between two principal kinds of contemplation, to which he gave the names "acquired" and "infused." The former can be achieved through one's own efforts with the help of grace; the latter is passive and proceeds only from supernatural inspiration or grace. In theological terms, he elaborated: acquired contemplation proceeds from the infused virtues, different in their mode of operating from the gifts; infused contemplation proceeds from the gifts, which operate in a superhuman mode and act as the principle from which this contemplation is elicited. But Tomás de Jesús finds the means to explain this infused contemplation in the gift of understanding rather than in the gift of wisdom. Like other Carmelites, he speaks as well of another, higher contemplation that proceeds from a principle superior to the gifts. This he calls angelic, seraphic, or supereminent contemplation. In this contemplation we find the highest degree of mystical theology, directly communicated in a passing way, a grace *gratis data*.

The Scholastic Treatises

The unfolding of Carmelite spirituality culminates in the scholastics of the second half of the seventeenth century. These were the Carmelite authors of *summae* on mystical theology who used with full strictness the scholastic method then in vogue.

The Portuguese José del Espíritu Santo (1609–1674) earned a place in the Carmelite school with his *Cadena mystica Carmelitana* and *Enucleatio mysticae theologiae*. In the *Cadena* he attempts a systematization and synthesis of Carmelite positions and expounds the opinions of some thirty of the best of them. The second work is a commentary on Pseudo-Denys.

With regard to contemplation, he explains that the act of contemplation arises in three degrees of ascending perfection: acquired contemplation, a simple gaze of faith, also called acquired mystical theology; infused contemplation, proceeding from a superior illumination of the gifts, in divine darkness; and ultimate or supreme contemplation, the taste and fruition of God, mystical theology strictly speaking. But then he reminds his readers that God does not depend on human systems and that no law obliges him to follow any arrangement that humans set up. In regard to the gifts, he points out that in the instance of the contemplation whose immediate principle is the gifts, the Carmelite authors do not agree whether to attribute this infused prayer to the gift of wisdom or of understanding.

The Frenchman, Philippe de la Trinité (1603–1671) was sent by his Carmelite superiors to Persia and then India, where he taught philosophy and theology. After some ten years in these mission lands, he returned to France as professor of theology and there began his writing. His *Summa theologiae mysticae* in three volumes is the first *summa* to treat of the spiritual life in its entirety.

Following John of the Cross, he tries to bring him into harmony with Teresa, also making use of the Victorines, Bernard and Bonaventure. He upholds the distinction, by then traditional among the Carmelites, between acquired and infused contemplation and appeals to the theory of the gifts to explain this difference. He thinks that infused contemplation may be elicited at different times through different gifts, of either knowledge, understanding, or wisdom. He also admits a higher contemplation that would proceed from a principle more elevated than the gifts.

The Andalusian José del Espíritu Santo (1667–1736) worked twenty years on his *Cursus theologiae mystico-scholasticae*. Consisting of six large volumes, the work remains incomplete, requiring probably two more volumes for completion. Contemplation is the pivoting point of the whole work. An ardent Thomist, José del Espíritu Santo maintains that contemplation is essentially and constitutively an act of the intellect and only by way of complement an act of the will. Nevertheless, these two faculties work together as inseparable twins because evangelical contemplation (as he terms it) in its meeting with philosophical contemplation attains truth in view of love, God as an object of love and fruition.

Following the threefold division of contemplation into acquired, infused, and supereminent, he finds the principle for the first two of these respectively in faith and in the gifts of the Holy Spirit. The supereminent contemplation demands another light similar to the light of glory, and thus he opposes those who explain this contemplation as a grace *gratis data*.

In answering a question in regard to the need for an impressed species and recourse to the fantasy, he explains that when faith is illumined by the gifts, the species need not be entitatively supernatural. As for supereminent contemplation, the species must be entitatively supernatural.

Some other points in his teaching give further indication of the kinds of speculation that were engaged in at the time. The remembrance of Christ in his humanity, who is the Way, does not hinder rest in the term Christ in his divinity. A face-to-face vision of God on this earth is possible but would at the same time be miraculous. This vision seems to have been granted to the Blessed Virgin, St. Joseph, St. Paul, Elijah, and Moses. Perfection lies in charity, the conformity of one's will with God's. But contemplation anticipates the heavenly beatitude, the possession of God through knowledge. The moral aspect of perfection is found in charity; the physical aspect, in contemplation (a formal participation in what is proper and essential to heavenly beatitude). Contemplation is normal in the spiritual life, and one may ask for infused contemplation even though it comes from

God's free gift and is not necessary for perfection. Finally, the spiritual life may be divided into contemplative (concentration entirely on contemplation and love), active (concentration on works of charity), and mixed (contemplation overflowing into works of charity).

The editor of the first edition of the works of St. John of the Cross, which was published in 1618, suppressed and added passages as a safeguard against misinterpretations or accusations of Illuminism. These changes remained, except for some slight corrections, in the later editions until the critical editions that appeared in this century. But even with these early editorial precautions, John of the Cross's writings were at times accused of Illuminism and the works denounced to the Inquisition. Neither John's beatification nor his canonization freed him totally from charges of Illuminism or later of quietism. His followers also underwent suspicions of Illuminism and Quietism. But these Carmelite authors, though they had to be exceptionally careful in the way they expressed themselves—especially when speaking about acquired contemplation, the purification and nakedness of the spiritual faculties, or passive abandonment to the motion of the Holy Spirit—did not relent in their teaching and wrote accomplished apologies of the positions of the Carmelite school. None of the works of St. John of the Cross nor any of those by these other Carmelites was ever, in the end, actually placed on the Index.

In the political and social upheavals of the nineteenth century, many monasteries were forced to close and the friars had to abandon their community life. Not until the twentieth century was the order able to revive and resume the scholarly life. Theologians were again raising questions about acquired contemplation as distinct from infused contemplation and about the role of infused contemplation in the development of the spiritual life. The debate stirred Carmelites of the twentieth century to return to the sources, to critical analyses of their founders' works. The baroque style and sometimes decadent scholasticism of the order's writers in the seventeenth and eighteenth centuries make their writings less appealing today; moreover, these authors now are not considered to be reliable commentators of their founders' works, since they showed no concern about correct methods of exegesis. Nevertheless, the appeal of Teresa of Jesus and John of the Cross remains, perhaps because, in addition to their doctrine, they still have a special power to communicate something of the divine mystery they experienced and lived.

Notes

1. In terms of the Spanish spirituality of the sixteenth century, contemplation can be defined as a form of knowing characterized by a simple act of intuition of the truth

or of tranquil repose in the object known. It can be of the aesthetical, philosophical, or religious order. In its religious sense within Christianity, contemplation in general is a higher form of knowing through faith: an intuition of the revealed truth reached through a faith influenced by charity. This truth is personal in content, God in his own life, perceived as the mystery of salvation, the center of which is Christ, in his death and resurrection, who sheds his radiance on the church and offers his trinitarian life in the depths of one's being.

Contemplation is bounded on one side by meditation, all one's inner acts by which faith expresses itself in reference to God; on the other side, by the beatific vision, in which it culminates outside the realm of obscurity and faith. In meditation, the acts of faith and love may become simpler, taking on a more contemplative bent: active or *acquired contemplation. Infused contemplation,* as the experience of a passive, or infused, secret, or dark, loving knowledge of God, implies through the word "infused" the intervention of another, a gift of God, who is working from within; and, through the word "secret," infused contemplation implies the presence of faith and the ineffable character of the content. Infused contemplation includes two main forms: imperfect and perfect. In *imperfect contemplation* the passivity is intermittent and less pronounced, the presence of God more vague, and the forces of the spirit (mind, will, affectivity) disconnected in their operations. In *perfect contemplation,* in its final form, the spirit now sensitized in its deepest roots by the loving knowledge and made permanently open to God is held habitually by his loving presence, even in the midst of outward activities. Mystical authors have called this contemplative union between the human person and the divine person, with its admirable virtuous effects, the spiritual marriage.

2. *Alumbrados,* also called *dejados,* were those in Spain who, while taking part in the spiritual movement of recollection, chose as a method of procedure an abandonment to the love of God that excluded such things as vocal prayer, meditation on the passion, images, fasts, ritual, and the religious life, all of which were looked upon as either hindrances to spiritual progress or useless. Often included under the term were those who became infatuated with ecstasies, visions, and other extraordinary phenomena, considering them as something to be sought.

3. *The Collected Works of St. Teresa of Avila,* vol. 1, trans. K. Kavanaugh and O. Rodriguez.

4. *The Collected Works of St. Teresa of Avila,* vol. 2.

5. *The Collected Works of St. Teresa of Avila, vol. 3.*

6. The "Dark Night," a symbol with roots in biblical and patristic literature, is used in a mystical poem written by St. John of the Cross referring to the entire life of faith: at first faith is experienced as darkness and privation; then it is present as a valuable guide and means to union; finally, in containing the object of the search, the subject of communion, faith is itself the person of the Beloved. More specifically, the term "dark night" is used to refer to the recurring crisis along the spiritual path in which one finds no satisfaction in the things of God or those of the world, has no inclination to work with the imagination and other powers in prayer, and feels anxious concern about falling back on the road and not serving God. This crisis, brought on by infused contemplation, or also by other difficult situations, can be of a greater or lesser degree in depth and intensity. In its more intense form, one feels irremediably abandoned by God. If the night is to purify, and so be an authentic "dark night," the subject must respond in this crisis with perseverance, continuing to live faithfully with the help of the light of faith and strength of love that God infuses.

7. *The Collected Works of St. John of the Cross,* trans. K. Kavanaugh and O. Rodriguez.

Bibliography

Sources

The Collected Works of St. John of the Cross. Translated by K. Kavanaugh and O. Rodriguez, with introductions by K. Kavanaugh. 2nd ed. Washington: ICS Publications, 1979.

The Collected Works of St. Teresa of Avila. Translated by K. Kavanaugh and O Rodriguez. 3 vols. Washington: ICS Publications, 1976 (vol. 1), 1980 (vol. 2), vol. 3 (forthcoming).

The Complete Works of St. John of the Cross. Translated by E. Allison Peers. 3 vols. Westminster, MD: Newman Press, 1953.

The Complete Works of St. Teresa of Jesus. Translated by E. Allison Peers. 3 vols. London: Sheed & Ward, 1972.

Obras de San Juan de la Cruz. Edited with notes by Silverio de Santa Teresa. 5 vols. Burgos: Editorial El Monte Carmelo, 1929–1931.

Obras de Santa Teresa de Jesús. Edited with notes by P. Silverio de Santa Teresa. 12 vols. Burgos: Editorial Monte Carmelo, 1915–1924.

San Juan de la Cruz: Obras Completas. Textual revision, introductions, and notes to the text by José Vicente Rodríguez and doctrinal introductions and notes by Federico Ruiz Salvador. Madrid: Editorial de Espiritualidad, 1980.

Teresa de Jesús: Obras Completas. Text revised and annotated by Tomás Alvarez. Burgos: Editorial Monte Carmelo, 1977.

Studies

Adolfo de la M. de Dios. "Espagne: L'Age d'or." In *Dict. Sp.,* 4, cols. 1127–78.

Andres, Melquiades. *La Teología española en el siglo XVI.* 2 vols. Madrid: Biblioteca Autores Cristianos, 1976, 1977.

Auclair, Marcelle. *Teresa of Avila.* Translated by K. Pond. New York: Pantheon, 1953.

Baruzi, Jean. *Saint Jean de la Croix et le problème de l'expérience mystique.* Paris: Felix Alcan, 1924.

Clissold, Stephen. *St. Teresa of Avila.* New York: Seabury, 1982.

Crisogono de Jesus Sacramentado. *The Life of St. John of the Cross.* Translated by K. Pond. London: Longmans, Green, 1958.

Dicken, E. W. Trueman. *The Crucible of Love: A Study of the Mysticism of St. Teresa of Jesus and St. John of the Cross.* New York: Sheed & Ward, 1963.

Pacho, Eulogio de la Virgen del Carmen. "Illumination dans l'école carmelitaine." In *Dict. Sp.,* 7, cols. 1346–67.

Peers, E. Allison. *Studies of the Spanish Mystics.* 3 vols. Vols. 1–2, London: Sheldon Press, 1927–1930. Vol. 3, London: SPCK, 1960.

Thompson, Colin P. *The Poet and the Mystic: A Study of the Cantico Espiritual of San Juan de la Cruz.* Oxford: Oxford University Press, 1977.

4

The Counter-Reformation and Popular Spirituality

KEITH P. LURIA

THE REVIVAL AND RENEWAL of Catholicism during the Counter-Reformation changed the religious lives of people at all levels of society. We generally associate the Counter-Reformation with the achievements of great figures: mystics like Teresa of Avila, ecclesiastical reformers like Charles Borromeo, founders of charitable institutions like Vincent de Paul, or theologians like Pierre de Bérulle. Their lives, dedicated to prayer, good works, and the propagation of the faith, became models for the constant search for holiness and perfection. But Catholic reformers sought to extend a new conception of religion far beyond these heroes of the faith. They wanted to alter the entire nature of the spirituality of all Catholics.

The form of piety they introduced contrasted strongly with its traditional predecessor.[1] Late-medieval popular spirituality was characterized by devotion to certain saints and relics, confraternities, periodic festivals, processions and pilgrimages, as well as the sacraments of the church. The religion of the people was often public, emotional, and organized around groups, such as the confraternities, which the church did not entirely control. The spirituality of the Counter-Reformation, on the other hand, centered not on groups but on individuals. The Catholic reformers emphasized a piety in which each person was to engage in frequent examination of his or her own conscience. Religious feeling would be interiorized; therefore, collective and public expressions would occur less frequently. When they did occur, it would be within the parish network of the church. Traditional piety had responded to the thirst people had for miracles. Divine intervention, mediated through saints, helped ease the difficulties of lives lived in a harsh world. Miracles could happen anywhere. And they happened quite often outside the official ecclesiastical structures of the church, not in parishes under the watchful eyes of the clergy but in chapels or out-of-the-way places where the presence of church authority was weak. Catholic reformers sought to establish control over spiritual manifestations by restricting, as far as possible, all religious activity to parishes, where it could be supervised by priests responsible to their bishops. In part, they did so in reaction to their Protestant critics, but they also needed to establish control over all religious life in order to introduce the new, more decorous form of spirituality. Reformers could no longer permit Catholicism to retain its traditional diverse character, in which the people of each region pursued their own customs, practiced their own observances, and worshiped their own saints. If religion was to be centralized and controlled, it would have to be made more uniform. The local symbols of piety would have to be replaced by universal symbols of the church. The customs, observances, and devotions which had represented diversity and popular beliefs would give way to those which represented unity and approved doctrine.

The reformers achieved some notable successes. They first remade the Catholic clergy. Bishops, prior to the Counter-Reformation, were not always diligent in the administration of their dioceses or the religious lives of their flocks. Parish priests were often illiterate and poorly trained. Religious orders were frequently in a state of disarray. The Counter-Reformation church established new orders and reformed old ones. The decrees of the Council of Trent insisted that prelates reside in their dioceses and visit each of their parishes regularly. In fact, bishops were to be the primary agents of the Counter-Reformation. They started by producing a new corps of parish priests who were well trained and imbued with the spirit of the Catholic Reform. The priests were educated in newly established seminaries, and their dedication was constantly reinforced through synods, retreats, and the frequent visits of bishops to parishes.

The reformers also succeeded in promoting their program among the Catholic elite. Devout noblemen and noblewomen and the urban bourgeois avidly read the books of mystics and spiritual advisors such as Francis de Sales. Like Jeanne de Chantal, they founded new orders or established charitable institutions—Monti di Pieta in Italy or hôpitaux généraux in France. They adopted new observances by joining approved Holy Sacrament or Rosary confraternities and worshiping Counter-Reformation saints. Furthermore, they supported the efforts of reformers to carry the new spirituality to people at other levels of society.

It was this part of the reformers' task that represented the greatest challenge. The members of the lay elite were literate and eager to associate themselves with Counter-Reformation spirituality. To change the piety of the lower orders, Catholic reformers had to embark on a vast program of education, which was geared to people whose culture was largely oral. In a sense, the ideas had to be translated into a language that would speak directly to the people's religious experience. The reformers relied on methods of pastoral work which were not necessarily new but which the Counter-Reformation had reemphasized. Preaching, missions, and catechisms were all well suited to accomplishing what the reformers saw as the main goal—the conquering of ignorance and superstition.

To understand the impact of the Counter-Reformation on popular spirituality, we must first look at the way the reformers carried their message to the people through the pastoral program of education. Second, we must assess the extent to which Catholics adopted the new concept of spirituality by examining the spread of the devotions and observances of the Catholic Reform and the disappearance of the old forms of worship.

Methods in the Pastoral Program

Preaching

Preaching can usefully introduce the other methods of Counter-Reformation pastoral work because it played a role in each. Good preachers could instruct, inspire, and enthrall whole communities at once. Their influence was direct, immediate, and very effective. Listeners who would garner little or nothing from books could respond quickly to the stirring orations of the epoch's famous preachers. If we can believe the accounts written of their performances, preachers such as Leonardo a Porto Maurizio and Alfonso Liguori in Italy or Vincent de Paul and Honoré de Cannes in France turned huge audiences of indifferent or ignorant listeners into fervent and well-instructed believers ready to discard sinful habits and superstitions in order to adopt proper doctrine and spiritual attitudes. Such accounts are undoubtedly exaggerated; nonetheless, the popularity of the great preachers cannot be denied. The desire for good preaching kept the star preachers on constant tours from locality to locality. The demand for them from towns, villages, municipal and ecclesiastical authorities, and people of all social levels was unceasing and indicates that preaching was indeed the most direct way to the hearts and minds of the faithful.

The reformers of the Council of Trent had seen the success which Protestant preachers enjoyed. In order to counter it, they recalled all "bishops, archbishops, primates, and others in charge of the conduct of churches" to their "principal" duty of preaching the gospel. Those who failed to fulfill their obligation would risk a "rigorous chastisement." In addition, archpriests, parish priests, and all others in possession of parish churches had, at least on Sundays and holy days, to provide for the "spiritual nourishment" of their people "according to their talent and the capacity of their listeners."[2] The Council insisted that proper sermons should have three characteristics. They should be instructive, teaching people "that which was necessary for all Christians to know in order to be saved." Second, they should be an invitation to personal conversion by pointing out to listeners the vices to avoid and the virtues to practice. Finally, in order to be effective, the sermons should be adapted to the abilities of listeners and should use only terms that were easy to understand.[3] Beautiful words were treated with suspicion. Vincent de Paul ordered Lazarist preachers to instruct the faithful in a simple style with no displays of vanity and to avoid complex theological disputes with Protestant pastors. Simplicity along with compassion and humility would protect his priests from vanity. Alfonso Liguori, founder of the Redemptorists, required his missionaries to preach with short sentences, easy words, and concrete ideas. This method was best for communicating gospel truths and inculcating moral duties.

The reformers had accurately gauged the desire of Catholics for "nourishing" and comprehensible sermons, but providing them was a complicated matter. The greatest problem was that many priests before the middle of the seventeenth century simply were not capable of good preaching. They often did not have even a rudimentary education or a sound knowledge of doctrine. Rural areas suffered the most. The sermon in country parishes often consisted of a reading of news, ordinances, and perhaps the explanation of a few points of religion. Sometimes bishops would instruct parish priests to translate parts of the Mass into the vernacular for use as a sermon (if they were capable of it), or else they might provide their priests with model sermons to use. As improved catechisms became available, preachers extracted sermon material from them, summarizing a chapter each Sunday as a means of providing adult religious education.

Nonetheless, the improvement in preaching by parish priests should not be exaggerated. Progress was slow. For that reason, bishops often turned to members of orders to ensure effective preaching; they were generally better trained than secular priests, and some new orders devoted themselves specifically to preaching as part of missionary work. Municipal authorities had for a long time invited friars to preach during Lent, but rural areas had rarely benefited from the stirring sermons of important preachers. In the seventeenth century, however, itinerant preachers began to find their way into the countryside as well. They did so as part of the most spectacular aspect of the Counter-Reformation's pastoral program—internal missions.

Missions

The missionary effort of the Counter-Reformation church extended around the world. Missionaries worked not only among Catholics and Protestants in Europe but also among non-Christians in Asia, Africa, and America. However, the missions discussed here are "internal"; they were organized not to convert non-Catholics to the Roman church but instead to educate Catholics, renew their faith, and bring them to an acceptance of Counter-Reformation spirituality.

In missions, the Catholic Reform's pastoral work was tuned to its highest pitch. Missionary preachers and the confessors who accompanied them spent only a few weeks or months in each place before moving on. In order for their efforts to have a lasting effect, they needed to make the strongest possible impact in the shortest possible time. The great theoreticians of missions such as Vincent de Paul in France or Alfonso Liguori in Italy (to name only two) devoted a great deal of thought and writing to exactly what sort of impression they wanted their missionaries to make. They ensured that the desired impression would be made by dictating in detail the schedule of activities to be followed in each locality. The plans varied from order to order but ran through the entire gamut of pastoral techniques: preaching, catechizing, Masses, processions, organizing religious groups, planting crosses, even theatrical demonstrations. Rural parishes and entire cities threw themselves into intense enthusiastic religious activities. A vicar-general witnessing a mission in Lyon in 1680 wrote that it was as if his city was being consumed by flames.[4]

Organizers of missions could refer to a long history stretching back to the apostles. The church was quite conscious of this tradition. Counter-Reformation missionaries borrowed the title of the church founders; Francis Xavier, "Apostle of the Indies," was perhaps the most notable. But the strongest impetus behind the European missions of the seventeenth and eighteenth centuries came from the church's efforts in Asia, Africa, and America in the sixteenth. In its attempt to spread the faith and to confine the growth of Protestantism to Europe, Catholicism "called in new worlds to redress the balance of the old."[5] The foreign missions were much on the minds of Catholic reformers as they set to work in the seventeenth century. Bishops Henry Arnauld of Angers and Etienne Le Camus of Grenoble both compared their dioceses to foreign lands when summoning missionaries.

During the early seventeenth century, French missions concentrated on Protestants. But in some regions missionaries also began to work among Catholics. Adrien Bourdoise founded the religious community of Saint-Nicolas du Chardonnet in 1613, and two years later his priests started performing missions in the villages of the Paris region, an undertaking that lasted until 1640. In the succeeding years, numerous orders and religious communities took up the burden of internal missions. In Italy intensive rural missionary activity was a later phenomenon. Southern Italy did not receive many missions until Alfonso Liguori organized campaigns there in the 1740s.

The groups that devoted themselves either exclusively or in part to the tasks of missions were mostly the orders and congregations born out of the Catholic Reform. They included Capuchins, Barnabites, Jesuits, Oratorians, Lazarists, Sulpicians, Eudists, and Josephists. In the eighteenth century, Redemptorists and Montfortains joined their ranks. The list is by no means exhaustive, but it does indicate the vast array of troops the Counter-Reformation church could now call upon to participate in its missionary campaigns. Although there was much that was similar in all their efforts, each order or congregation had its own approach to missions, its own techniques, and its own attitude. Only a few can be described here, but these examples suggest the variety of means which missionaries used to achieve their common goals.

Vincent de Paul, one of the earliest of the new promoters of missions, erected his congregation in 1625. The Lazarist missionaries followed de Paul's *petite méthode,* which stressed simplicity in explanation of doctrine, mass exhortations, and catechizing, all of which would lead the faithful to a general confession and communion. The missionaries' daily schedule included a sermon at the morning Mass followed by the teaching of the *petit catéchisme* to children in the afternoon and the *grand catéchisme* to adults in the evening. The Lazarists stressed the obligation of each of their listeners to examine his or her conscience, and they helped appease discord in the community.[6]

Capuchin missionaries relied on a more spectacular and theatrical approach to convey their teachings. Their emotional sermons were designed to appeal not to their listeners' intellects but rather to their doubts about salvation. Capuchins also moved through rural areas healing the sick and dispensing medicines. They left behind them new confraternities as well as charitable organizations and offices to arbitrate lawsuits and encourage reconciliations. The theatrical and charitable effects of these campaigns made Capuchins the most popular of seventeenth-century missionaries.[7]

Many of the methods which the seventeenth-century French missionaries developed found an echo in the Italian campaigns of the eighteenth century, but Italian missions also employed a baroque sensibility more in keeping with the spirituality of the Mediterranean region. Certain preachers, like Pietro Ansalone, moved their audiences with acts of self-flagellation and

sometimes urged their listeners to follow their example. A Maltese missionary who worked in Civita Vecchia around 1710 arrived with a supply of
scourges to distribute to the congregation. During his stay, he organized five
public processions of flagellants. When the well-known Franciscan preacher,
Leonardo a Porto Maurizio came to Rome in 1749, he led a procession in
which friars carried crosses, banners, skulls, and bones. Leonardo marched
wearing heavy chains and a crown of thorns. Redemptorist missionaries,
preaching in the diocese of Naples, scourged themselves, cursed sinners, rang
bells to wake them up, and some pushed listeners to repent for their loose
tongues by licking the floors of churches, a practice that was much criticized.

The more flamboyant aspects of baroque spirituality had played a long
and important role in the religious lives of Mediterranean people. Confraternities, since the thirteenth century, had practiced the ritual of flagella-
tion as a means of emphasizing penance and personal conversion.[8] The
flagellants who followed the lead of their missionary preachers were abasing
themselves before God and before those against whom they had sinned.
Similarly, the skulls and chains reminded them of the need to seek penance
through humiliation in order to restore a sense of personal and communal
religious equilibrium. However, in the wake of the Counter-Reformation
(and, even more so, under the impact of Enlightenment attitudes), such
flamboyance seemed increasingly out of place. It smacked too much of the
traditional, "superstitious" piety which the Catholic reformers wanted to
supplant. Jesuits who undertook missionary work in northern Italy disapproved of the tactics used in Redemptorist campaigns. One Jesuit wrote:
"From such missions the devil draws innumerable sacrileges and renews his
hold upon miserable sinners, who go from their howlings without any
inward penitence of the soul." Parish priests who witnessed Liguori's
missions criticized the way in which they terrorized parishioners, which led
Liguori to complain, "My God, what do we do it for!"[9]

Italian missions, such as those performed by the Redemptorists, combined
two forms of spirituality. On the one hand, they had firm roots in traditional devotional practices with their emphasis on collective activities and
very vivid displays of emotional piety. Yet on the other hand, they incorporated methods learned from the orders which practiced a more restrained
spirituality. For instance, Redemptorist missionaries promoted the use of
the *esercizio devoto* or the *vita devota*. (French Capuchin missionaries referred to a similar practice as the *oraison mentale*.) The observance bore a
close relationship to the systematic prayer of Loyola's *Spiritual Exercises* or
de Sales's *Introduction to the Devout Life*, but it was intended for a wider and
less literate audience. The exercise consisted of a meditation on some
devotional subject such as the passion or the sorrows of the Virgin. The

meditation was an individual act performed in a communal setting during the mission, though families could also do it at home. Before the meditation, preachers would instruct the congregation in the method to be used and encourage them by insisting on the ability of all Christians, whatever their station in life, to practice it.

As was the case with other spiritual activities of the Catholic Reform, missionaries employed the exercise in order to prompt conversions and a renewal of faith. The meditation embodied the austerity and individualized nature appropriate to the Counter-Reformation, and its frequent practice would remind people of the teachings of the mission. Despite the fact that the meditation was designed to be an individual act which would affect the consciences of its practitioners, the Redemptorists continued to combine it with more traditional, collective spiritual activities. While some orders suggested that each person meditating should hold a crucifix, Redemptorists placed a madonna dressed in mourning clothes before the congregation. Liguori wanted people to make the act of contrition, which ended the exercise, before an image of an *ecce homo*. He also thought that the meditation might be preceded or followed by the singing of a canticle. Redemptorists had a good deal of success in spreading the *esercizio devoto*, and it is likely that it was the combination of traditional and new, collective and individual forms of spirituality, which made it so popular.[10]

Reformers hoped that missions would draw people away from "profane" occupations, such as participating in Carnival or spending Sundays in taverns. When the Capuchin Honoré de Cannes preached at Moulins during Carnival in 1678, his sermons had the effect of turning Carnival "into Lent."[11] After a Redemptorist mission at Sarno, the taverns supposedly remained empty for ten years. In place of these activities, missionaries hoped to substitute new devotional observances. Cardinal Spinelli welcomed the Redemptorists and the *esercizio devoto* in the diocese of Naples. A number of other dioceses adopted the practice as well. Francis de Sales established the eucharistic devotion of the "Forty Hours" (to be discussed later) at Thonon and Annemasse in the Chablais. Most missionary orders had specific devotions which they promoted: Oratorians favored that of the Infant Jesus, Jesuits that of the Perpetual Adoration, and Eudists that of the Sacred Heart, to mention only a few. Missionaries also sought to leave a permanent mark on the communities they had visited by founding new confraternities, charitable organizations, processions, and the like.

For the prelates who were introducing the Catholic Reform into their dioceses, missionaries proved to be a very effective tool. Increasingly in the seventeenth and eighteenth centuries, however, bishops developed other means more directly under their control for introducing a new spirituality

to their people. The two most notable of these methods were the catechisms, which the better-trained parish clergy would use to instruct the
faithful, and the episcopal visits, through which the bishops would
personally try to transform religious life.

Catechisms

Catholic reformers thought that a conscientious use of new catechisms
would firmly fix the religious reforms in the minds of the faithful. In 1546,
the Council of Trent ordered the production of such a catechism. However,
the commission that prepared the work could not complete its task until
the Council had finished its deliberations, so the *Catechismus ex decreto con-
cilii Tridentini ad parochas* (also known as the Roman catechism) was not
published until 1566. The new manual would not gain a large readership
among the laity, nor was it intended to do so. Expert theologians had
composed it to serve the needs of parish clergy or bishops writing diocesan
catechisms.[12]

From 1560, German Catholics had been using the German version of the
Jesuit Peter Canisius's catechism. Its questions and responses were illustrated
with woodcuts to help explain points of doctrine, and it also contained a
calendar. These additions helped ensure its widespread appeal. It went
through two hundred editions in the sixteenth century alone.[13]

The church's success in catechizing the faithful came more slowly elsewhere, in part because of the lack of manuals and in part because of the
poorly trained clergy. Some Italian dioceses had improved by the end of the
sixteenth century, but French dioceses showed little change before the
second half of the seventeenth century. Even as late as 1672, only 34 of the
139 rural parishes in the Paris region had regular catechism instruction.

The church developed new institutions in order to compensate for the
failings of the parish clergy. In 1560, Cardinal Cesar Baronius founded the
Confraternity of Christian Doctrine in Rome. Members of the confraternity dedicated themselves to catechizing children. Charles Borromeo supported a similar organization in Milan. In France at the end of the sixteenth
century, César de Bus formed a society of priests, the Congregation of
Christian Doctrine, who devoted themselves to catechism instruction. Congregations of missionaries, such as the priests of Saint-Nicolas du Chardonnet or the Lazarists, worked at catechizing those areas they visited on
mission.[14]

In the late seventeenth century, the production of catechisms boomed.[15]
The authors of the new catechisms realized the necessity of making their
works accessible to the laity. With a largely illiterate population, priests

would continue to play the major role in reading and teaching the new catechisms. But Catholic reformers felt that they had to challenge the Protestant emphasis on literacy and the reading of religious works. Books accessible to laypeople would help increase literacy and direct reading into proper doctrinal paths. Catechisms were directed at certain age groups, simplified "small" catechisms for children and more complicated "grand" catechisms for adults. Specialized manuals—for servants, for the elderly, or for beggars—also appeared. Catholic authorities realized that in order to obtain a wide readership, they had to produce catechisms in languages people knew: hence the appearance in France, for instance, of catechisms in Provençal, Occitan, and Breton.[16]

Catechisms sought to stamp out beliefs no longer in keeping with the Counter-Reformation doctrine. For example, stories about saints of whom the church no longer approved tended to disappear from the pages of the new manuals,[17] but some catechism authors realized that they would not be able to go as far as they would have liked in uprooting old beliefs. The catechism of the diocese of Meaux during Bossuet's tenure reflected a certain ambivalence about "superstitions" such as bonfires on the festival of Saint John. The response to the question, "Does the church take part in such fires?" was "Yes, in several dioceses, including this one, some parishes build a fire which is called ecclesiastical." The next question asked for the reason behind these ecclesiastical bonfires. "In order to banish the superstitions practiced around the fire of Saint John." Finally, the student had to enumerate these "superstitions," which included dancing around the fire, singing "dishonest" songs, throwing herbs onto the fire, and keeping the coals from it.[18] The Catholic reformers of Meaux could not hope to abolish the main "superstition," the fire itself; instead they tried to use it to get rid of traditional customs associated with the fire. In theory, catechisms had appeared as excellent tools for instilling Counter-Reformation spirituality. In actual practice, they embodied the compromises which the Counter-Reformation had to make with popular religion.

The Changes in Popular Spirituality

Catholic reformers hoped that the educational campaign carried on through the pastoral work of preaching, missions, pastoral visits, and catechism would achieve a considerable transformation in religious practice and attitudes. The church wished to exert greater episcopal authority. In order to attain this goal, the reformers stressed uniformity in practice, obedience to the central hierarchy, and proper decorum. They would strip religious

4. Giulio Cesare Procaccini, *Madonna and Child with Sts. Francis, Dominic and Angels (Institution of the Rosary)*, c. 1613.

observances of local customs and, instead, would favor practices that would be the same everywhere. Old, autonomous confraternities would give way to new associations dedicated strictly to prayer, charitable work, or the conversion of others. Processions and pilgrimages to far-off shrines would meet with condemnation; reformers now preferred those closer to home, which priests could more easily control. The wide range of traditional celebrations—festivals, fairs, Carnival—would begin to feel the wrath of a clergy now eager to push the faithful into more "pious" occupations.

Educating the faithful into a new form of religion meant more than changing the outward manifestations of piety; reformers also wanted to instill new inward spiritual attitudes. To do so, they had to direct the attention of Catholics away from the symbols of the old spirituality toward the symbols of the new. The old saints' devotions, prayers, songs, and rituals had inspired a spirituality with collective and public religious expressions. Traditionally when people worshiped together, they expressed their participation in the universal church but more directly their sense of belonging to particular communities, kinship groups, or religious organizations. The older spirituality often centered on the desire to propitiate saints (who were often only locally known) in order to manipulate a harsh environment. People were prepared to engage in long rituals and penances not only to absolve themselves of a deep sense of sin and to gain salvation in the next world but also to obtain an immediate and materialistic return in this one.

The reformers felt that these spiritual beliefs were indecent. The urge to use religion to fulfill earthly needs smacked of superstition. Public festivities—processions, saints' festivals, confraternity banquets, Carnival celebrations—led to improper behavior, gluttony, drunkenness, and illicit sexual activity. Protestants ridiculed these popular customs, but church authorities too abhorred them. The religious symbols which they invoked would promote order, obedience, and unity. Spiritual feelings which people had formerly expressed in public demonstrations would now be redirected toward an examination of each individual's conscience, and an inward sense of piety would now be the goal of a proper religious life.

The interiorization of spirituality did not mean that religion was to become a purely individual affair. Indeed, reformers insisted that the parish church was to be the focus of religious life; all important ceremonies were to take place there, where the priest could ensure that they went on in the proper manner. Other sacred places, such as confraternity chapels or pilgrimage shrines, where the clergy could not always control observances, would decline in importance.

Baroque Piety

Austere, interiorized spirituality was not the only type of religious life to grow out of the Catholic Reform. A concern with exhibiting the church as triumphant in the face of the Protestant challenge, combined with the more traditional desire of the faithful to publicly display their piety, had led in Mediterranean areas to the development of a more flamboyant style of observance. Expressions of this baroque spirituality included rich church decoration, numerous penitential confraternities, whose hooded members frequently paraded through the streets of Italian and southern French towns, and large public outpourings of devotion toward saints, but especially toward Mary or the Eucharist.

Baroque piety continued to exert a strong influence on the faithful well into the eighteenth century, but religious reformers felt uncomfortable with what they saw as its excesses. It was too ostentatious and too independent of clerical control. Richly ornamented churches were fine, but they should not contain "profane" statues or an extraordinary number of candles. The wealthy could not be denied their expensive funerals; however, sounding bells in churches throughout a city, accompanying the cortege with music, decorating the church with coats of arms, and filling it with candles all seemed excessive. Moreover, the large numbers of requiem Masses could strain the personnel resources of the local clergy. Penitential confraternities, dedicated to approved devotions such as the Holy Sacrament or the Rosary, performed useful charitable work, but the clergy could not easily control them; and reformers disliked their nocturnal processions as well as the fact that their ceremonies often interfered with the parish Mass. Therefore, baroque piety held an ambiguous place within the Counter-Reformation. A spirituality that was to encourage "fervor, veneration, silence, and order" had little room from the noise, color, and public emotion of baroque piety.[19]

Regulated Activities, Customs, and Devotions

This is not to say that the new spirituality led people to turn their backs on the world, for it also emphasized the social responsibilities of lay and clerical elites and encouraged charitable activity. Charity had traditionally been the obligation of individuals, confraternities, and religious houses. The wealthy ordered the distribution of alms in their wills; confraternities hired poor men to accompany the corpses of confraternal brothers in funeral marches; and monks gave away bread at monastery doors. Now charity was to be strictly regulated by offering the poor loans through well-organized pawnshops—the *Monti de Pieta*, or by putting them in hospitals run by governments and religious orders, where they could be taught the value of hard work, self control, and obedience. The treatment of the poor had been a mirror of the public and collective nature of traditional religious observance. In the seventeenth and eighteenth centuries, the poor became a symbol of the new spirituality—obedient, reverent, and orderly.

In order for their program to succeed, the Catholic reformers also had to undermine the festivity of medieval religiosity. Chief among the old festivals was the pre-Lenten celebration of Carnival. Reformers abhorred what they saw as the profanity and licentiousness of Carnival. So, too, they attacked many other practices of popular religion. Saints and their festivals came in for particular scrutiny. The cults of those saints who healed people or protected livestock and crops often contained elements which the reformers detested. Saints' festivals gave villagers the opportunity to hold fairs or to travel to neighboring parishes, where they feasted, drank, and courted. The faithful propitiated saints by all sorts of means: going on processions or pilgrimages to shrines, making offerings, saying special prayers, rubbing holy stones, touching relics, lighting bonfires, shooting guns, dancing. Diocesan authorities forbade all these customs and more.

But the reformers' efforts extended beyond the saints' cults to the saints themselves. Many saints had a purely local reputation; they were unknown or drew little attention outside of specific regions. In the interests of promoting a more uniform religion, the Counter-Reformation wished to deemphasize these local saints in favor of those who could more suitably serve as symbols of the universal church. Historical investigations destroyed the legends of many saints and questioned the validity of their relics, and sometimes even their existence. For instance, one such historian, Girolamo Tartarotti, proved that a St. Adalpreto, worshiped in the Trent valley of the Tyrol, had never been the martyr his legend made him out to be, but was instead quite possibly a schismatic. However, the fact that reformers had proved a saint or relic to be a fabrication did not mean that people's beliefs changed. The inhabitants of the Trent valley thought that Tartarotti, not Adalpreto, was the heretic.

Historical criticism and concerns about superstitious customs or indecent images fueled the reformers' efforts to strip calendars and expurgate breviaries and missals of older saints' festivals. They wanted to direct the attention of the faithful to the saints and devotions of the Counter-Reformation. In the diocese of Grenoble, Bishop Le Camus did away with the festivals of Sts. Mathias, James, Philip, Christopher, Bartholomew, Matthew, Simon, Jude, and Thomas. Certainly these saints were not just local, but they no longer served the purposes of the church. Ironically, near the end of his episcopate, he felt the need to reestablish these festivals in order to assure his flock's devotion. In 1693, the diocese of Autun reduced the number of festivals on which people were obliged to abstain from work (not all of which were saints' festivals) from ninety to seventy-seven. In the same year Bishop Le Peletier of Angers removed twenty-four such observances from the ceremonial calendar of his diocese. In Paris, ecclesiastical authorities threw forty saints' legends out of the breviary between 1676 and 1686. In the eighteenth century, Pope Benedict XIV put his papal authority behind the campaign by encouraging bishops throughout Europe to reduce the number of festivals in their dioceses.

Some saints fell out of public favor even without the urging of ecclesiastical authorities. St. Anthony of Padua, for example, was very popular in seventeenth-century Italy; he protected lovers, mountaineers, pigs, and donkeys, among other things. Many people observed his festival as a day without work, although the church did not require them to do so. By the mid-eighteenth century, fewer people, outside of Padua at any rate, were willing to honor him by giving up a day's earnings. He did not disappear; he aided the Spanish fleet to free Alicante from Algerian corsairs, but no longer received the same devotion as before. Reverence for St. Christopher declined as well. He protected travelers from unexpected death and his picture could be found over many Italian church porches. By the mid-eighteenth century, such pictures were rarer. These saints fell from favor as a result of a continuous process by which people lost interest in old saints and adopted new ones whose power to work miracles seemed stronger. This process of replacing old saints with new ones operated outside of the Counter-Reformation attack on saints who had no historical validity or whose cults were considered to be superstitious. Many of the saints who suffered the denunciation of church authorities continued to play an important role in the lives of the faithful.

Marian Devotion

One of the most important Counter-Reformation persons of devotion was the Virgin Mary. The cult of the Virgin was hardly new; people had venerated Mary under a variety of vocables or titles. The Counter-Reformation sought to promote certain of these vocables, the most important of which was the Rosary. Pope Alexander VI gave his approval to the Rosary devotion in 1495, although there were Rosary confraternities before this date. A century later Pope Pius V published a bull encouraging the Rosary's use. By that time the devotion was already well known in Italy. It became so popular that in many dioceses almost every parish had a Rosary chapel or confraternity. Although the confraternities had both men and women members, women often joined first. For the faithful, the Rosary provided a new and approved way to show their devotion to their closest divine friend and patron. Reformers appreciated the Rosary for the sort of spirituality it inspired. Those devoted to it did not engage in confraternal banquets or long processions; instead they occupied themselves with strictly organized, methodical, meditative prayers and instruction.

The church also found newer devotions, such as the Immaculate Conception, to express its devotion to Mary. The controversy surrounding the purity of Mary's conception was not new in early-modern Europe, and it continued well beyond this period. During the Counter-Reformation, the idea of the Virgin's immaculate origins gained some powerful supporters. The Jesuits vigorously promoted the devotion as a challenge to Protestant attacks on the church's Marian beliefs. Spanish painters like Zurbaran, Ribera, and Murillo frequently depicted the subject of the Virgin untainted by sin. Jean Eudes helped spread the observance in France, and he defended it in his writings by declaring that Mary "was an exact counterpart to Jesus: He (God), would give the Virgin Mother to us. And as the son is the figure of his substance . . . and the perfect image of the Divinity . . . so also Mary should bear a perfect resemblance to him."[20] Pope Clement IX, in 1708, gave approval to the growing cult and ordered all Catholics to observe the feast of the Immaculate Conception. He did not, however, give the doctrine a clear theological definition; nor did Rome carefully explain the doctrine behind another popular Marian devotion—the Assumption. But this lack did not prevent it too from growing. In France, for example, processions on the feast of the Assumption multiplied rapidly, especially afier Louis XIII consecrated his kingdom to Mary in 1638.

Popular Marian devotion did not go unchallenged. The Dominicans, rivals of the Jesuits, opposed the cult of the Immaculate Conception. In eighteenth-century Italy, Muratori criticized the excesses of devotion to Mary in his *On a Well-Ordered Devotion*. In France, the decline of interest in Mary among theologians and Jansenist-influenced laypeople was marked from the end of the seventeenth century. Only half as many devotional books dedicated to Mary were published in the second half of the century as had been in the first. Nonetheless, popular Marian fervor remained strong, and Rosary confraternities and chapels continued to spread under the title of the Assumption or the Immaculate Conception.

Spirituality concerning the Saints

In its attempt to remold popular spirituality, the church not only promoted new Marian devotions but also promoted new saints. The church sometimes legitimized popular religious figures by officially recognizing them as saints, but it also canonized and promoted devotion to its own heroes and heroines in order to shape Catholic piety. During the Reformation, new cults helped provide a bulwark against Protestant attacks on the veneration of saints. As was the case with other aspects of religious observance, the definition of new saints was now brought more firmly under the control of ecclesiastical authorities. Catholic reformers were suspicious of manifestations of piety that did not emanate from the clergy. In the sixteenth and seventeenth centuries, the church instituted new rules of canonization in which physicians were required to attest to the miraculous nature of healings and witnesses to the miracles were carefully interrogated. In the eighteenth century, Pope Benedict XIV argued for even tougher rules in his work *De canonizatione*.

Given these strictures, new saints still represented the variety inherent in the Catholic reform. Some of them had been bishops, such as Charles Borromeo and Francis de Sales. The canonization of prelates who had been tireless reformers helped promote the church's effort to bring all religious activity under the control of the hierarchy. It glorified the episcopal office and reminded those who honored these saints of the power of ecclesiastical authorities.

Other new saints were missionaries. The canonization of figures such as Francis Xavier or Vincent de Paul recognized both their value to the church and their popular appeal as preachers, teachers, and healers. Founders of orders and congregations, such as Ignatius of Loyola, Louise de Marillac, Jeanne de Chantal, and Philip Neri were also made saints. New orders strongly advocated the elevation of their founders to sainthood, but the canonization of these saints also reflected the fact that much of the reforming impulse in Catholicism came from the new organizations. Mystic saints like Teresa of Avila or John of the Cross represented a less widespread element of the reform but one that nonetheless harked back to a long spiritual tradition which the interiorized spirituality of the Counter-Reformation continued to nourish.

The church's interest in these particular types of saints emerges quite clearly in the study by Owen Chadwick of the eighteenth-century canonizations. The church officially recognized twenty-nine people as saints during the century. Twenty-seven of them belonged to orders: eleven to branches of the Franciscan order, three to the Dominicans, three to the Jesuits, and one to the Carmelites. The founders of the Piarists, Somaschi, Lazarists, Servite nuns, and Camillans were also included. Only seven of the new saints were women, and a number of the saints were in the equally small (seven) group of mystical visionaries. Margareta of Cortona and John of the Cross were the most notable of the mystics. Most of the men had been engaged in hospital work, missionary activities, and the founding of orders; among them were Turibio of Peru, Vincent de Paul, and Camillus de Lellis. Jeanne de Chantal also belonged to this group. Some, like Turibio of Peru, Stanislaus Kostka of Poland, or John Nepomuk of Czechoslovakia, became state patrons. Finally, the canonizations also reveal how important the Mediterranean region was to the Catholic revival. Sixteen of the new saints were Italian, five Spanish, and three French. The rest included three Poles, one Czech, and one German.[21]

It must be noted that many new saints had little popular appeal; their cults did not spread widely, and, therefore, they had little impact on popular spirituality. Mystics and bishops owed their canonization more to their orders or the needs of the church than to the feelings of the faithful. In Spain, for example, few of the new saints replaced the traditional miracle workers. John of the Cross, mystic and poet, represented a spirituality that was too austere and intellectual to gain much popular attention. In Italy, Borromeo's speedy elevation to sainthood (he was canonized in 1584, only twenty-six years after his death) resulted from the efforts of church authorities rather than a widespread veneration. His advocates even had trouble finding evidence of miracles, and those people who did honor Borromeo often considered him not a model Counter-Reformation reformer but a plague saint, like Sebastian, because of his work among the sick during an outbreak of the plague in Milan. In France, Francis de Sales had an enormous impact on elite spirituality, but he did not inspire the dedication of many chapels or shrines.

In general, popular saints were those who had been closer to the people. Their spirituality was more traditional, or else they formed a bridge between new and old modes of religious observance. Such was Felix of Cantalice (died in 1587, canonized in 1712), an illiterate cowherd from southern Italy who became a Capuchin laybrother. Felix lived a true mendicant's life by begging in Rome. He remained close to the poor of the city, and they, in turn, received miracles of healing at his tomb. The people of Palermo had the same experience after the death of a local monk, Don Gaetano. Before his death Gaetano confessed that at each consecration of the Host, he had a vision of the Lord opening his arms to him and embracing him. He died while kneeling before the Holy Sacrament. The confessor reported the visions to the parishioners and also claimed that Gaetano could work miracles. People flocked to the church to view and touch the corpse and tear away pieces of clothing for relics. Some received healings. Gaetano was a miracle worker, part of a long tradition of such saints, but his death and his visions had associated his miracles with the Holy Sacrament, the center of Counter-Reformation spirituality.

Benedict-Joseph Labre (lived from 1748 to 1783, but was not canonized until 1881) was another such saint. He was born into a shopkeeper's family near Boulogne, and as a boy he developed, perhaps under the teaching of Jansenist preaching, an overpowering sense of sin, for which he desired to atone through suffering. A number of religious houses rejected this troubled youth, and so he became an itinerant, a pilgrim wandering to shrines in France, Italy, Spain, and Germany. In 1774 he landed in Rome, where he spent the rest of his life begging during the days and sleeping at night in the Colosseum. He could always be found at churches which were celebrating the Forty Hours devotion, associating his traditional mendicant spirituality with the newer christological observance. His death caused such a commotion in the city that an observer compared the tumult to "an earthquake in a people's soul."[22] Romans came to the church of the Madonna dei Monti, where his body was kept, to tear off pieces of clothing and hair for relics. Healings began to occur immediately. The crowds were so great, on Easter Sunday especially, that troops had to be called out to close the church. Ecclesiastical authorities considered Labre a tramp, but Romans thought of him as a new St. Francis.

Even the new orders produced saints who embodied an older form of religiosity, for example, the Redemptorist laybrother Gerardo Maiella (died in 1755, but not canonized until 1904). Maiella spent his life traveling and preaching in the rural areas of southern Italy. His official biographies always emphasize his strict obedience and submission to his superiors. But it is likely that the church was concerned with stressing this aspect of his character because his spirituality escaped its total control. Like the other popular saints mentioned here, Maiella was a miracle worker, and his miracles responded directly to the material needs of everyday peasant life. His career started with the vision of the Infant Jesus offering him white bread. A vision of Jesus offering bread resonates with eucharistic symbolism. But the accounts of the miracle insist also on the fine quality of the white bread, which was rare in the impoverished world of the Mezzogiorno. Much of Maiella's work was concerned with easing the precarious nature of subsistence. He frequently distributed bread or grain to the poor during his travels. His miracles, especially during periods of shortage, performed similar useful functions. He would miraculously produce bread for the poor when all local supplies had run out; or he would see to it that monastic granaries were refilled after the monks had given up their grain as charity; or he would rid fields of hordes of rats. He devoted his life to the people of the rural world, while they in turn treated him as a holy man, whatever the reservations of church authorities.[23]

Saints such as Benedict-Joseph Labre and Gerardo Maiella harked back to a traditional concept of sainthood not only in their role as miracle workers but also in their itinerancy and in the extreme asceticism of their lives. They were "fools for God." Labre lived as a wandering beggar, always poorly clothed and often ill. Maiella practiced long vigils and fasts, sleeping on thorns, and subjecting himself to frequent flagellations. The church of the seventeenth and eighteenth centuries disapproved of such practices and discouraged them, but the harsh lives these saints led—their "madness"—only increased their charisma in the eyes of those who sought their miracles. In fact, madness lent these saints special powers. Maiella could reputedly cure those who were possessed. He followed a long line of other such Christian heroes who could do the same. The Counter-Reformation church was concerned with establishing its control over all manifestations of religion, but it could not exert its authority completely over this form of religious energy. The officials of the eighteenth-century church, increasingly influenced by the rationalistic thought of the Enlightenment, could neither countenance it nor understand it. Figures like Labre and Maiella were first saints of the people and only later saints of the church.

While the Counter-Reformation did not gain much ground in promoting its new saints and could not always fully accept those of the people, it did have more success in reemphasizing the cults of certain older saints. In response to Protestant attacks on the sacrament of penance and the doctrine of the forgiveness of sins, the church affirmed the veneration of those saints who had been redeemed through penance. St. Peter, who had denied Christ and then been forgiven, became a favorite subject for religious paintings. With papal authority severely challenged, there were other reasons for emphasizing St. Peter's importance. Mary of Egypt, a reformed prostitute, received a renewed interest, as did Mary Magdalen. The Magdalen's association with Christ, especially the risen Christ, helped buttress the church's defense of the real presence in the Eucharist.[24]

Other saints associated with the life of Jesus, especially members of his family, also enjoyed both the approbation of the church and an increasing popularity. We have already seen the importance of Mary to early-modern spirituality. Her mother, St. Anne, shared some of this fervor. The church had been promoting her cult for some time before the Counter-Reformation, but its efforts were reinforced in France by apparitions of Anne at Auray during the anti-Protestant campaigns of the 1620s. French Catholics interpreted the visions as a sign of divine favor in their struggle against heresy. Interest in Anne also grew out of the debates over the Immaculate Conception. For the church, Anne was a unifying symbol in whom all Catholics could believe. She was a saint who reflected the importance of her daughter and grandson. Religious art depicted her frequently as a matriarchal figure, but the church no longer approved of the older image of Sts. Joachim and Anne, husband and wife, embracing before the Golden Gate of Jerusalem because of the image's sexual overtones. To the people who venerated St. Anne, her role as a mother was also important, but in a more palpable way. Anne protected pregnant mothers, and prayers to her helped ease the dangers of childbirth. She could also have a purely local significance, as in the Alps, where she protected villagers from avalanches. However, her connection to the experience of motherhood was the strongest.

Joachim did not enjoy any significant growth in popularity but his son-in-law, Joseph, did. In the Middle Ages, Joseph suffered from an ambiguous reputation. Carpenters venerated him as the patron saint of their craft confraternities, but in popular lore he was also a somewhat comical figure, as the archetypal cuckolded husband. With the Counter-Reformation, Joseph took on new importance. In fact, the Joseph of the Catholic reform is an excellent example of how a saint could hold a variety of meanings. In the sixteenth and early seventeenth centuries, Joseph was the favored saint of mystics whose reading of the Pseudo-Dionysius the Areopagite led them to see Joseph as a model, one who had been close to Jesus and yet completely subordinate and self-effacing. Teresa of Avila took Joseph as her patron saint, and over the course of the next two centuries he came to preside over hundreds of Carmelite convents. By the mid-seventeenth century, as a result of theological controversies, the mysticism associated with Joseph was in decline. Joseph's cult, however, continued to grow. In 1621, Pope Gregory XV extended Joseph's feast day to the universal church, and in 1661 it became an obligatory *fête chômée* in France.

Joseph's cult benefited, as did Mary's and Anne's, from the new interest in the states of Jesus' life. Artists no longer depicted Joseph in the manner of their medieval predecessors, as an elderly patriarch. Instead he was now a young father, the protector of Mary and the Child Jesus. In the seventeenth and eighteenth centuries, as Catholic theologians and writers of confessors' manuals came to see marriage and the raising of children as good and useful spiritual occupations, Joseph took on the role of patron saint of Christian families. His family became a sort of earthly Trinity. The promotion of Joseph also helped the church avoid the uncomfortable suggestion of theogamy, a relationship between Jesus and his mother. Joseph was an active husband and father. At Mary's entry into heaven, as Alfonso Liguori describes it, she was met not by her son but by her joyful husband.[25] In paintings such as those by Velázquez and El Greco, it is the Trinity, not Jesus who crowns Mary. If marriage is suggested, the bridegroom is not Christ but Joseph.

It is difficult to know to what extent popular spirituality adopted the new conception of Joseph, but it is certain that his cult spread widely. The number of his chapels and confraternities grew tremendously during the seventeenth and eighteenth centuries. Joseph's position as a husband and a father, especially his role as protector of the Infant Jesus, undoubtedly held much meaning for people. His iconography in chapels and the type of confraternities founded under his name suggest that he was important for other reasons as well. Carpenters still honored Joseph as their saint, and he also incurred a more generalized responsibility as the patron of all manual workers. Joseph was most widely known as the patron of the good death and of the "Agonisants" confraternities. Outbreaks of the plague continued in southern France until the early eighteenth century, and "Agonisants" confraternities were numerous there. People sought a companion who could guide them peacefully through the last rite of passage. Joseph had died in an exemplary manner, attended by the other members of his family while he humbly awaited and accepted the divine will. He is frequently depicted this way in the paintings hung in confraternity chapels; otherwise he is shown being visited on his deathbed by Christ or being welcomed into heaven by his Son. His peaceful death and reception into paradise could offer comfort to those about to face the same fate.

Christological and Eucharistic Devotions

The honor paid to Joseph as well as that paid to Anne and Mary always derived from that paid to Christ. It was in promoting christological devotion that the Counter-Reformation church had its greatest impact on popular spirituality. The most effective way for the Catholic reformers to turn the piety of the faithful away from local cults and superstitious observances was to turn it toward the central devotional figure of Christianity. Christ's position as a universal and unifying symbol of the church was greater than that of any saint. His glory would reinforce the majesty of the church's authority structure. His importance was hardly new, but the Protestant attack on transubstantiation lent a new impetus to the church's efforts to embellish the eucharistic cult. By promoting new forms of Christocentric devotions, the church could defend the centrality of transubstantiation in Catholic worship, and it could attempt to subordinate all non-Christocentric forms of devotion. Furthermore, concentrating the piety of the faithful on the Eucharist and Christ would remind them of their responsibilities in communion and confession and would help them interiorize the teachings of the Counter-Reformation.

The most popular of christological devotions were those concerned directly with the Eucharist; confraternities dedicated to the Holy Sacrament spread widely. Twenty-four were founded in Italian towns over the course of the sixteenth and early seventeenth centuries. They continued their phenomenal growth in France during the seventeenth century. Studies of French dioceses have shown them, along with Rosary confraternities, to be the most common of religious associations. The brethren of the sacramental companies concentrated their devotional practices on the adoration of the Eucharist. They marched in processions with the Host on Corpus Christi, held special Masses, and urged their members to take frequent communion. They sometimes fought with parish priests for the right to display the Host on their confraternal chapel altars. In France strong devotion to the Holy Sacrament not only shaped the spirituality of the Catholic brethren, but was also a weapon in the campaign against the Huguenots. The combination of sacramentalism and anti-Protestantism was most evident in the Company of the Holy Sacrament, not a confraternity but a secret organization of Catholic *dévots* with branches in a number of French cities. The members of the Company grouped themselves under the Sacrament not only to express their own piety but to carry out aggressive attempts to convert Protestants, to put pressure on Catholic clergy to reform themselves, and to provide rural parishes with priests, teachers, and ornaments. The monarchy, which was suspicious of the secret association, eventually suppressed it.

Other forms of eucharistic devotion involved whole communities, not just specific groups. Most notable of these new observances was the Forty Hours devotion. The practice consisted of a vigil held before the Host, which was exposed on a church altar during three days. It started in Milan in 1520 as a series of expiatory prayers. By 1537 the church had carefully defined the rite and granted indulgences to it. Philip Neri brought it to Rome in the 1550s. Jesuits organized the first Forty Hours devotion in Paris in 1574, but Capuchins were mostly responsible for spreading the practice through France.

The original purpose of the devotion was to petition for divine aid in periods of war or epidemics. The French Capuchins used it in other ways: they theatricalized the rite, despite the misgivings of papal authorities and the French episcopate, by preparing elaborate altar decorations which resembled small theaters with the Host at center stage bathed in hidden lights enveloped by veils or drapery. The presentation served to dramatize the presence of the Host and to ensure the success of Capuchin missions. Capuchins used the observance to proclaim the eucharistic cult and to combat Protestantism. They often performed it at the same place and the same time as a Protestant synod. Catholic reformers also employed it in the campaign against popular religious traditions; Forty Hours devotions were organized at the same time as Carnivals, though this happened more in Italy than in France. By the late seventeenth century, church authorities were insisting that the vigil be held only during the day and not at night in order to prevent any possible "indecencies." The interruption helped contribute to the eventual decline of the devotion.

Another eucharistic observance, the Perpetual Adoration of the Holy Sacrament, grew out of the Forty Hours devotion but occurred periodically in a series of churches rather than on extraordinary occasions. The dramatic nature of both observances helped them gain wide popularity; however, they inculcated the new individualized form of spirituality, not the collective traditional type. During the rite, people knelt, two by two, in private prayer before the Host. All attention was focused on it. Older forms of observance, such as processions which expressed group piety and solidarity, no longer had a place in these new eucharistic devotions.

The Christocentrism of Counter-Reformation spirituality did not stop at the cult of the Eucharist. Interest in the stages of Christ's life, as emphasized by Bérulle, spawned a variety of devotions. The passion had attracted intense attention since at least the fifteenth century, as is evident from church decorations and other artwork of the time. The concern with it continued in later rites such as the processions of the seventeenth- and eighteenth-century penitential confraternities, in which the brethren carried the instruments of the passion. So, too, devotion to the cross in Holy Cross confraternities was a survival of late-medieval piety.

Other observances were newer or received a new impetus from the Counter-Reformation. The interest in the infancy of Christ derived from two currents of thought. One, from Bérulle, was relatively austere. It regarded the infant Jesus' life as a spiritual ideal because it epitomized obedience, innocence, and self-effacement. These ideas had a great influence on orders like the Carmelites. The Oratorians, associated with Bérulle, propagated the devotion through their missions. They held processions, such as one in the Avignon area in 1682, which depicted the triumph of the infant Jesus. Men carried the son of a local *seigneur* dressed as an angel on a litter decorated with the image of the Holy Child. Other children followed the litter chanting verses and litanies. Bérulle's influence on popular spirituality, however, was very limited. More widespread was the impact of Italian and northern European humanism, which had a livelier view of the child and which led Italian artists to produce the *bambini* which decorate churches such as the Aracoeli in Rome.

The Aracoeli Holy Child is in a manger, another form of devotion to the infant Jesus that became very popular during the seventeenth and eighteenth centuries. The origin of representing Christ in nativity scenes is uncertain, but it has often been attributed to the Franciscans. In the early eighteenth century, Gaetano da Thiene, founder of the Theatine order, built a crib in his cell after having a vision in Santa Maria Maggiore. A number of orders took up the idea and helped spread it throughout Italy, Austria, and Germany. In the hands of master artisans and wealthy patrons, the cribs became mechanical wonders. This development did nothing to endear the manger scenes to Catholic authorities, who felt that the devotion was unbecoming and too closely associated with puppet theater. Generally, all they could do in the face of the cribs' growing popularity was demand simpler cribs which would lead viewers to reflect on the life of the Holy Child rather than on the ingeniousness of the builders.

The manger scenes did not take hold in France, but the same impulse could be found in Christmas songs and prayers. Despite the impact of Christocentric piety on both popular and elite spirituality, Christ still remained a remote figure for many. People could more easily develop an attachment to the child. He became a protector of the oppressed. The people of Niort in the Poitou, for example, sang on Christmas, "Mon megnon, tirez-nou de la misere / De la taille et de la sau" (Adorable child, save us from misery / from the land tax and the salt tax.).[26]

In the late seventeenth century, the Sacred Heart began to gain ground first in France and then in Italy. The Sacred Heart was a christological devotion and was therefore in keeping with the type of spirituality the church wished to promote. However, the history of its development suggests, once again, that the cult owed much of its success in part to its more traditional spiritual elements. Bérulle described the heart as not just the seat of affectivity but also the source of human action and the meeting place between a person and God. The heart was a symbol which expressed Christ's divine humanity and emphasized the importance of inspiration over reason. A number of reformers, Francis de Sales, Fénelon, and most of all Jean Eudes, propagated the devotion, but it flourished only within certain orders or religious brotherhoods. Then in 1673 a nun, Marguerite-Marie Alacocque, at Paray-le-Monial had the first of a series of visions of flames, bright light, the crown of thorns, and of Christ asking her to be the apostle of the Sacred Heart. The Jesuits adopted it, influenced by the Jesuit Père Croiset's book on the devotion.

The cult also took on monarchical implications. In 1689 Alacocque insisted that Louis XIV have the Sacred Heart painted on his army's standards. The revelation which prompted the demand came as a welcome sign of divine favor during a difficult period for Louis' forces. The exiled James II adopted the devotion as did Stanislas Leszczynski, and in 1792 Louis XVI.

However, the Sacred Heart did not go unopposed. Jansenists in France disliked its emotional, mystical elements. The church refused to sanction it in the 1680s and again in 1729 despite the support of Queen Marie of France. Cardinal Prospero Lambertini argued that the cult suggested that the heart was the center of feeling and since this assertion was doubtful, then the devotion was as well.

Nonetheless, the misgivings of church authorities could not prevent the devotion from spreading. In part the cult's popularity stemmed from Alacocque's visions, but the Sacred Heart worked other miracles as well. In Marseilles, people attributed the end of the 1720 epidemic to their devotion to the Sacred Heart. From Marseilles, it conquered other parts of Provence and then moved into Italy. Paul Danco and the order he founded, the Passionists, used a symbol of a white heart, which might have been associated with the Sacred Heart cult. The Scolopist Domenico Pirrotti promoted a Heart of Jesus cult in the Papal States. By the second half of the eighteenth century, Sacred Heart confraternities existed in Rome, Venice, and Tuscany and in 1765, Pope Clement XIII, who had founded such brotherhoods in the north, granted the Sacred Heart an official feast day.

Conclusion

The Sacred Heart devotion reflects in a specific way the general impact of the Counter-Reformation on popular spirituality. The Catholic reformers wanted to erase the traditional, localized medieval piety and replace it with a spirituality over which they would have more control. They wanted to undermine the old "indecent" or "superstitious" forms of worship and replace them with new devotions represented by symbols understood by all Catholics. In this way worship would become more centralized and uniform. New observances would encourage a faith that was individualized, interiorized, and austere rather than collective, public, and emotional. In part this concern for a new spirituality stemmed from a need to combat Protestant criticism, but the church hierarchy and the elite of the society it served also felt a deeply rooted desire for reform and control.

To an extent the reformers were successful. The Catholic people of Europe did adopt new devotions, especially christological and Marian devotions, but we cannot assume that they derived the same meaning from them that the church intended. The example of the Sacred Heart or of St. Joseph suggests that each element of piety could have multiple meanings. Furthermore, people often returned to their old saints or else looked to new ones like Gerardo Maiella, who were traditional miracle workers. New methods of prayer, such as the *esercizio devoto* may have helped promote the constant examination of conscience which characterized the new spirituality, but the *esercizio devoto* probably had more impact on the elite than on the Catholic population as a whole. People needed a spirituality that responded to the exigencies of their lives. An austere, abstract, interiorized faith might have little meaning for those who still wished to affirm the unity of corporate groups, the efficacy of public displays of emotional piety, and the frequent manifestation of divine power in the world. The Catholic reformers succeeded in winning over the Catholic elite, in reforming the clergy, and in instituting a more decorous and controlled religion. However, the battle to introduce a new spirituality for all Catholics would continue to be waged.

Notes

1. For a classic analysis of the effects of the Counter-Reformation on religious life, see John Bossy, "The Counter Reformation and the People of Catholic Europe," *Past and Present* 47 (May 1970) 51–70.

2. Decrees of the Council of Trent quoted in Jean Delumeau, *Le catholicisme entre Luther et Voltaire*, 62.

3. Decrees cited in Bernard Dompnier, "Le missionaire et son public," in *Journées Bossuet: La prédication au XVIIe siècle* (Actes du colloque Dijon 2-4 décembre; Paris: Librairie A. G. Nizet, 1980) 106.

4. Raoul de Sceaux, "Le Père Honoré de Cannes, capucin missionaire," *XVIIe siècle* No.41, 4 (1958) 355.

5. The phrase is from H. Outram Evenett, *The Spirit of the Counter-Reformation* (Notre Dame, IN: University of Notre Dame Press, 1975) 122.

6. On Vincent de Paul and Lazarist missions, see G. Chalumeau, "Saint Vincent de Paul et les missions en France," *XVIIe siècle* No. 41, 4 (1958) 317–27; F. Lebrun, "Une mission à Brissac en 1707," *Annales de Bretagne et des pays de l'Ouest* 81 (1974) 517–29; B. Dompnier, "Le missionaire et son public," 105–28; Delumeau, *Le catholicisme*, 289–90.

7. R. de Sceaux, "Le Père Honoré de Cannes, capucin missionaire," *XVIIe siècle* No. 41, 4 (1958) 349–74; B. Dompnier, "Activités et méthodes pastorales des capucins au XVIIe siècle, l'exemple grenoblois," *Cahiers d'histoire* 12 (1977) 235–54.

8. Ronald F. E. Weissman, *Ritual Brotherhood in Renaissance Florence* (New York: Academic Press, 1982) 50–58.

9. Quotes in O. Chadwick, *The Popes and European Revolution*, 161.

10. Maurice de Meulemeester, "La *vita devota* des missions napolitaines au XVIIe siècle," *Revue d'ascétique et de mystique* 25 (1949) 457–64.

11. R. de Sceaux, "Le Père Honoré de Cannes, capucin missionaire," *XVIIe siècle* No. 41, 4 (1958) 354.

12. René Taveneaux, *Le catholicisme dans la France classique, 1610–1715*, 166–67; Herman Tüchle, C. A. Bouman, and Jacques LeBrun, *Nouvelle Histoire de l'Eglise*, 3:191.

13. Tüchle, *Nouvelle Histoire,* 202.

14. Eugène Mangenot, "Catéchisme," in *Dictionnaire de Théologie Catholique* (Paris: Letouzey et Ané, 1932) 2:1895–1965; Taveneaux, *Le catholicisme,* 168.

15. Jean-Claude Dhôtel, *Les origines du catéchisme moderne d'après les premiers manuels imprimés en France* (Paris: Aubier Montaigne, 1967).

16. See Roger Chartier, Dominique Julia, Marie-Madeleine Compère, *L'éducation en France du XVIe au XVIIIe siècle* (Paris: S.E.D.E.S., 1976) 7–8.

17. R. Taveneaux, *Le catholicisme,* 172.

18. Quoted in Delumeau, *Le catholicisme,* 269–70.

19. Bishop Fléchier of Nîmes, writing in 1707; quoted in R. Sauzet, "Miracle et Contre-Réforme en Bas-Languedoc sous Louis XIV," *Revue d'histoire de la spiritualité* 48 (1972) 179–92.

20. Quoted in Marina Warner, *Alone of All Her Sex,* 249.

21. O. Chadwick, *The Popes and European Revolution,* 25–27.

22. Ibid, 23.

23. Gabriele de Rosa, "Santeté, clergé, et peuple dans le Mezzogiorno italien au milieu du XVIIIeme siècle," *Revue d'histoire de la spiritualité* 52 (1976) 245–64.

24. On saints redeemed through penance, see M. Warner, *Alone of All Her Sex,* 234.

25. Ibid., 132.

26. Quoted in M. L. Fracard, *La fin de l'Ancien Régime à Niort: Essai de sociologie religieuse* (Paris: Desclée de Brouwer, 1956) 240.

Bibliography

Annales de Bretagne et des pays de l'Ouest 81 (1974). Special issue on missions.

Bossy, John. "The Counter Reformation and the People of Catholic Europe." *Past and Present* 47 (May 1970) 51–70.

Chadwick, O. *The Popes and European Revolution.* Oxford: Oxford University Press, 1981.

Delumeau, Jean. *Le catholicisme entre Luther et Voltaire.* Paris: Presses universitaires de France, 1979.

XVIIe siècle. No. 41, 4 (1958). Numéro speciale: Missionaires catholiques a l'interieur de la France pendant le XVIIe siècle.

Evenett, H. Outram. *The Spirit of the Counter-Reformation.* Notre Dame, IN: University of Notre Dame Press, 1975.

Perouas, Louis. *Le diocèse de La Rochelle de 1648 à 1724: Sociologie et pastorale.* Paris: S.E.V.P.E.N., 1964.

Taveneaux, René. *Le catholicisme dans la France classique, 1610–1715.* 2 vols. Paris: S.E.D.E.S., 1980.

Tüchle, H., C. A. Bouman, and J. LeBrun, *Nouvelle Histoire de l'Eglise,* vol. 3. Paris: Seuil, 1968.

Warner, Marina. *Alone of All Her Sex: The Myth and the Cult of the Virgin Mary.* New York: Vintage Books, 1976.

5

Jansenism and Quietism

LOUIS DUPRÉ

JANSENISM AND QUIETISM have generally not fared well with students of spiritual life. Many hold them to be little more than the stagnant backwaters of an ill-guided Christian piety that gradually asphyxiated what little life they may have contained in the beginning. Yet considered in their own light rather than in the rear view mirror of their historical outcome, they appear quite different. Their inspired representatives retrieved some essential spiritual principles from centuries of neglect. I therefore regard both movements more as pertaining to the Catholic tradition than as deviating from it. They are "traditional" also in another, narrower sense which their later development into separatist sects has equally obscured. Unlike the Reformation they did not oppose themselves in revolutionary fashion against the immediate past, but saw themselves as continuing and intensifying current spiritual trends that were solidly anchored in Catholic orthodoxy. Both movements received much of their insight and inspiration from the leading schools of seventeenth-century France, the so-called *École française* of Jean-Jacques Olier, Pierre de Bérulle, and the *Humanisme dévot* of Francis de Sales. At times one hardly notices the transition. Who would be able to distinguish such works as Pierre Nicole's *Traité de l'oraison* and Jean-Pierre de Caussade's *Le divin abandon* from the best of seventeenth- and eighteenth-century mainstream piety in France?

Jansenism

Origins

If we focus only on spiritual life, we may well wonder whether "Jansenism" and "Quietism" warrant their separate names. Of course, they eventually became sects half separated from the main body of the church. This was particularly the case with Jansenism; but Jansenism as a *sect* is not the subject of this essay. The more spiritual members of the movement found themselves in constant conflict with the mentality of pride and self-righteousness that resulted in sectarian separateness. Jansenism would merit no place in a history of spirituality if it had been nothing more than the theological controversy it was at the start or nothing more than the quarrelsome, elitist party it became in the end. Yet between its arid beginnings and its controversial end lies a movement of spiritual reform that left an indelible mark on the religious life of France and the Low Countries. Even after its organized existence had practically collapsed, it continued to exercise its influence as an undercurrent of religious austerity within the Catholic Church of these areas. As late as the twentieth century Jansenism was still able to inspire such writers as Mauriac, Montherlant, Julien Green, even as it once had inspired Pascal, Racine, and Boileau.

First a word about the movement's theological origins. In 1640 a voluminous, rather abstruse Latin study, *Augustinus,* appeared as the posthumous work of Cornelius Jansen, a former theology professor of Louvain who had spent the last months of his life as bishop of Ieper (Ypres) in West Flanders. Jansen himself had undergone the influence of the theories of his older colleague at Louvain, Michel du Bay (Baius), yet another link in the seemingly endless chain of debates on nature and grace that began with the Reformation. Reacting against the Protestant idea of a "totally corrupt" nature, Catholic theologians of the Counter-Reformation had ever more tended to divide a virtually independent and basically unchanged order of nature from a "supernatural" order, destroyed by sin and restored by grace. Such an extrinsic synthesis which "adds" grace to nature inadequately presented the respective effects of sin and redemption. For Baius the original state of justice was not a supernatural gift which God gratuitously added to the natural condition of humans. It is the natural state of humans in the divine plan. Since sin deprived humanity of a good that it *ought to* possess, Baius concluded that it has, indeed, substantially corrupted human nature. True, humans remain free from external compulsion but not from the necessary drive toward evil. Even virtues, in this sinful disposition, are, as Augustine called the moral qualities of the pagans, splendid vices. Redemption restores the ability to do good, but only as a gratuitous grace, granted to some, withheld from others—not as a natural disposition.

Baius's ideas were condemned and he submitted. Yet the admiring Jansenius felt that more than a little of the controversial theory deserved saving. For all the complexity of his own theology, Jansenius impresses us as a man guided by a simple idea. As a result of some intellectual conversion he became convinced that henceforth only the mystery of redemption through divine grace merited his theoretical and practical attention. His solid acquaintance with the fathers led him to conclude that all that was worth saying on the topic had been written by St. Augustine. In his *Augustinus* he left posterity the fruit of a lifetime of meditation and research. The book caused an immediate and violent reaction. The Jesuits saw their own theology of grace directly attacked. Moreover, the publication violated the ban imposed by Pope Paul V in 1607 on the endless public discussions of grace and free will. In these discussions the Jesuits under Molina's guidance had emphasized the importance of free cooperation, while the Dominicans (with Banez) had opted for a predestinationist view of efficacious grace. Their disputes had rocked the Catholic theological world and, until the Pope's intervention, seriously threatened a doctrinal peace badly needed after the trauma of the Reformation. *Augustinus* had the rare distinction of being condemned several times over, first in 1642 on grounds of its appearance without the previous approval required for publications on grace. In 1653, five specific propositions culled from Jansenius's book as representative of this theory were declared heretical; among them were that Christ had not died for all people, but only for some, and that interior grace is irresistible. Then, in one of the most curious episodes in the history of dogma, Antoine Arnauld and Nicole (the same men who had first selected the five controverted propositions) recognized Rome's sentence in principle (*de droit*), but denied the fact (*de fait*) that the five propositions were actually contained in *Augustinus*. Alexander VII attempted to settle the matter once and for all by formally declaring that the propositions were indeed to be found in *Augustinus*. This was by no means the end of the story. In 1690 Rome promulgated a further list of "errors" and in 1719 yet another bull attacked Jansenius's theology as presented by the Oratorian Pasquier Quesnel. As late as 1794 we still hear anti-Jansenist rumblings in Rome's formal rejection of the Pistoia Synod.

According to Jansenius's interpretation, the human person was created in an original state of justice required by human nature itself. Through the fall humanity lost its original justice. Redemptive grace restored the human condition in all believers (here Jansenius differs from Baius), but this universal grace was no longer sufficient for salvation. Beyond the general offer of grace our fallen nature needs a special grace in order to overcome *efficaciously* its otherwise irresistible inclination toward evil. God does not grant this efficacious grace to all, but only to those whom he predestined in the death of Christ. Much in Jansenius's doctrine appears close to Calvin's theory of predestination. Yet, contrary to Calvin, Jansenius teaches that, in the predestined, faith alone does not suffice for justification; active cooperation through good works (assured through God's efficacious grace) is required as a separate condition.

Personalities and Ethos

One wonders how such an abstract theory on a subject of which the church had declared itself to be profoundly weary could once again spark a century of heated controversies. The reasons undoubtedly lie in part outside the field of theology. In the Jansenist controversy personalities played at least as important a role as doctrine. The "movement" started with an exceptional group of literate, intelligent, and morally concerned persons, worthy representatives of the new *noblesse de robe* in France. But they tended toward legalism and, with a rather enhanced sense of personal dignity, insisted on privileges. Above all, they courted controversy. Yet these social predispositions might have resulted in nothing more than a "Gallican" movement in the French church with an emphasis on national and class rights, had it not been for the more profound impact of a powerful spiritual undertow. This spiritual current was by no means unique to the "Jansenists," but they, being more articulate, succeeded in channeling it theologically and morally.

Much of its initial momentum Jansenism received from two imposing figures: Saint-Cyran and Arnauld. The person who gave it its lasting influence, Pascal, entered the movement after the two pioneers had disappeared from the French scene. I shall focus the discussion on the three main figures. Jean Duvergier de Hauranne, later appointed Abbé de Saint-Cyran, had known Jansenius during his student days in Louvain. Ever since, they had maintained an intensive correspondence, punctuated by occasional, prolonged visits in France or in Louvain. Their letters have a secretive, almost conspiratorial tone with code names for Augustine, the Jesuit order, and all persons with whom they felt involved. "St. Cyran adopted—it was part of his pose—an air of mystery; he went round saying rather ordinary things about the decadence of the Church and then imploring you not to repeat them; if you did, he would deny having said them."[1] Yet Ronald Knox, the author of this unflattering portrait, also stressed that Saint-Cyran was an exceptional spiritual director. He possessed other qualities as well. Richelieu, who later had him arrested, called him the most learned man in Europe. His contemporaries knew him as a sober, ascetic man. Yet all about him had that unpleasant air of introverted self-consciousness which made Henri Bremond exclaim, "Even at his most solemn, most holy moments, he retains a morbid quality, something devious and slightly ridiculous."[2] Nevertheless, it was Saint-Cyran who set the convent of Port-Royal on its definitive spiritual course.

Port-Royal, a relaxed Cistercian convent situated a few miles from Paris, was in full process of spiritual reform when Saint-Cyran became appointed as its director. The reform-minded young abbess, Angélique Arnauld, blindly devoted to the chaplain, took care to implement his ideas in her entire convent. They would soon spread over the wider circle of the nuns' relatives and numerous acquaintances. Eventually, as several intellectuals followed them into their "solitude," the convent became the center of Jansenist theology and of religious reform. Once Saint-Cyran was in jail (he died shortly after his release, in 1643), Antoine Arnauld, Mère Angélique's younger brother, became the leader of the movement. Endowed with a sharp, logical mind and an argumentative disposition, Arnauld zestfully threw himself into the polemics provoked by the group's constant controversy with the Jesuits and its intolerant assertion of Jansenist rigorism. Arnauld established his authority with a learned work, *The Frequent Communion* (1643). In the laxist climate of seventeenth-century France, sanctioned, he believed, by Jesuit casuistry, Arnauld argued that believers should not receive communion without confession and that their confessors should impose extended periods of preparation. The work enjoyed a success hard to imagine for anyone who attempts to read it today. Religious people abstained from communion for months, sometimes for years. In regions affected by Jansenism its influence lasted well into the twentieth century. The book defines the constrictive, least desirable qualities of the Jansenist mind: elitist, quarrelsome, sectarian. They inspired Bremond's devastating judgment:

> The first manifesto of the party, the book which, in one form or another, they will do over and over, making it worse each time, *The Frequent Communion,* is like a pamphlet. They write, think, live always against someone. Their theology is one of civil war. In one word, to repeat M. Olier's terrible verdict, 'they devour the heart of charity by which the Church lives.'' ... Before penetrating into the depth of the mind, it ruins the peace, condition of all true religion. Before making converts it makes partisans, sectarians, whom it fatally severs from the mystical currents of their time.[3]

As we shall see soon, on the movement as a whole this verdict is unfair; on Arnauld it is severe but not incorrect. Particularly with his next book, *Apologies for Jansenius,* Arnauld changed Port-Royal from the nucleus of a reform movement into a hotbed of theological controversy. Jansenism was slowly turning into a "party" that commanded the support of some bishops and religious superiors, and of many intellectuals and aristocrats. Even in Louis XIV's court, which eventually would destroy it, it had its loyal, though unavowed, followers, who were constantly plotting and scheming to protect and enhance it. But then, at the height of his power, Arnauld overplayed his hand. His brutal attack on the Sulpicians for attempting to enforce Rome's ruling on the "factual" presence of the five condemned propositions was condemned by the Sorbonne, which threatened to withdraw his doctorate in theology unless he submitted. Arnauld went into hiding for twelve years, thus adding yet another martyr to the movement's rapidly growing pantheon.

At that moment the third great figure entered upon the Jansenist scene, the only one whose writings would survive the centuries—Blaise Pascal. His debut hardly suggested that he would contribute more than some comic relief (at the expense of charity) to a wearisome, unending controversy. Pascal's first "letters to a man living in the province" appeared anonymously, but they remained anything but unnoticed. Unlike most of the earlier, heavily erudite, polemical writings, Pascal's sharp satire of Jesuit morality bit through all the subtleties of distinction and learning, leaving everyone wondering why it had taken so long to bring a simple matter to an obvious conclusion. The problem is that Pascal himself knew the issues to be complex and did not hesitate to contradict himself in order to make them *appear* simple. We still wonder how an author driven by such an irresponsible desire to win an argument at the very cost of elementary fairness would ever come to write the deeply spiritual *Pensées*. If anything is lacking in the theological disputes of the *Provinciales*, it is a sense of the spiritual. Did fear for his troubled cause temporarily obscure the cause itself? Fortunately, the purpose of this essay allows me to neglect this unspiritual product of *esprit* and to turn directly to the marvelous *Pensées*, the movement's finest achievement.[4]

Spiritual Jansenists

Its reading begins by conveying an impression of unqualified pessimism about human nature, that stands in stark contrast to the exuberant, triumphalist mood of the Counter-Reformation. The theme of human "vileness" keeps returning. Suffering and humiliating misery constitute the human condition. That condition is not alleviated by Christ's redemption, for redemption itself occurs *within* suffering. Even now Jesus remains present in his suffering, as much as in the triumph of his resurrection. "[He] will be in agony until the end of the world" (*Pensées* #919, p. 313). Nor does that suffering reach him from without: it originates in the very union of a divine nature with a conflicting human nature. "In his agony he suffers the torments which he inflicts upon himself" (#919, p. 312). In his person our corrupt nature painfully undergoes the full impact of God's holiness. The union of our nature with Christ's divinity holds no general assurance of redemption. Some are chosen, some rejected. Nevertheless, Pascal's opposition to Calvin's somber view of predestination remains firm and unambiguous. Those whom God chooses are intrinsically redeemed. Calvin's theory of a forensic, external justification sets inappropriate boundaries to divine Providence.

Incredible that God should unite himself to us. This consideration derives solely from realizing our own vileness, but if you sincerely believe it, follow it out as far as I do and recognize that we are in fact so vile that, left to ourselves, we are incapable of knowing whether his mercy may not make us capable of reaching him. For I would like to know by what right the animal, which recognizes his own weakness, measures God's mercy and keeps it within limits suggested by his own fancies. He has so little knowledge of what God is that he does not know what he is himself. (#149, p. 78)

Pascal's pessimism is balanced by a growing awareness of the total transcendence of the God who reaches us. His rejection of both the Jesuit theory of a universally sufficient grace and the Calvinist exclusion of a divine immanence derives from that same sense of divine transcendence. Only from God himself (in faith) can one learn about a total, intrinsic redemption that sanctifies one's attitude and grants merit to one's works. Yet the object of faith itself, the "mystery of Jesus," is such that it blinds some while enlightening others. Only with "the eyes of faith," granted to the elect, can we see the true reality of this mystery. Those who "resist" (for lack of efficacious grace) are like "the carnal Jews [who] understood neither the greatness nor the lowliness of the Messiah foretold in their prophecies" (#256, p. 105). Pascal distinguishes spiritual Christians *and* Jews from carnal Jews *and* Christians. "Jesus Christ, according to carnal Christians, came to dispense us from loving God and to give us sacraments which are fully efficacious without our help: neither of these is the Jewish or Christian religion" (#287, p. 120).

The distinction between spiritual and carnal, essential to Jansenist doctrine, has contributed to its more questionable features—elitism and, in some instances, a self-righteous mentality inclined to pride and subordination. Yet in the later Pascal, as in so many now forgotten members of the Port-Royal movement, it was carried by the humble awareness of an unmerited union with God. Port-Royal was originally, and always remained for its finest members, a center of piety more than of controversy. Its devotion book, the *Exercises,* reveals its spirit far more than Arnauld's noisy polemics. In the *Pensées* we find that piety reflected in the passages on the knowledge of the heart.

While ordinary knowledge, even philosophical knowledge, results in scepticism as its natural conclusion, the knowledge of the heart, the unified center of inner life is the instinct that carries us upward. Through this natural instinct God touches his elect; without it religion remains an uncertain struggle.

Those to whom God has given religious faith by moving their hearts are very fortunate, and feel quite legitimately convinced, but to those who do not have it we can only give such faith through reason, until God gives it by moving

their heart, without which faith is only human and useless for salvation.
(#110, p. 58)

And again: "It is the heart that perceives God and not the reason" (#424,
p. 154). But the heart is unable to reach this understanding of faith through
itself. All knowledge of God must be infused by God. To reason, God
remains "a hidden God" (#228, p. 101). He does not reveal himself so plainly
that "the blindest will see Him"; but neither does he remain "so hidden that
He could not be recognized by those who sincerely sought Him" (#149, pp.
79–80). "There is enough light to enlighten the elect . . . enough obscurity
to blind the reprobate" (#236, p. 102). To seek him is itself a grace that
already contains finding him. "You would not seek me, if you had not found
me" (#919, p. 314). The grace of seeking is granted only to those who will
be allowed to find.

Here we approach the deeper, spiritual meaning of the "election." The
grace of faith alone gives us the vision required to read the signs of the
hidden God. Both Scripture and nature are written in a secret language
which only the continuous enlightenment of faith allows us to decipher. As
Pascal wrote to his sister: "These sacred characters cannot be perceived
without a supernatural light; for as all things speak of God to those who
know Him, and because they reveal Him to all those who love Him, these
same things hide Him from those who do not know Him."[5] The bad reputation that Jansenism has acquired among students of Christian spirituality
stems from its unfortunate tendency to polemicize and its critical stance,
taken especially by Nicole, toward all forms of passive prayer. But these
failures have unfortunately eclipsed the very real spiritual quality of its
devotion. Pascal's famous *Mémorial* presents only one instance.

> The Year of Grace 1654
> Monday Nov. 23 day of St. Clement pope and martyr
> and others in the martyrology.
> Vigil of St. Chrysogonus martyr and others
> From about half past ten in the evening
> to about half past midnight.
> Fire
> God of Abraham, God of Isaac, God of Jacob,
> not of the philosophers and the scientists
> Certitude, Certitude. Emotion. Joy. Peace.
> God of Jesus Christ.[6]

Here Pascal describes a direct "seeing" with the eyes of faith, an indubitable
awareness of God's presence which contains a certain sign of election.
Henceforth he can rest assured of his love. God could not deceive him by
rejecting him after first having buried him under his grace.

Thus by the same way which approaches him to the devout humanists [the school of Francis de Sales] Pascal also rejoins his true brothers, the mystics. This heart which feels God and which also enables us to know "the first principles" must touch, at least in its ultimate boundaries, this "highest point of the spirit," that profound area where God and the soul meet. Thus in a soul fully alive life itself completes, corrects and exceeds the all too narrow formulas by which we thought to rule it.[7]

In this intensive, mystical experience culminates a continuous sense of God's presence. For Pascal, grace consists in an ever-new encounter with that presence.

The same grace which alone can give the first glimpse of it must continue it and make it ever present by ceaselessly retracing it in the heart of the faithful to keep it ever alive, as God constantly renews their beatitude in the blessed, which is in effect a consequence of grace, as also the Church holds that the Father continually produces the Son and maintains the eternity of His essence through an effusion of His substance which is uninterrupted as well as unending. The continuation of the justice of the faithful is thus nothing else than the continuation of the infusion of grace.[8]

Pascal stands out as a "spiritual" Jansenist. He may have been the most eloquent, but he was surrounded by a host of others, many without any of the unpleasant characteristics with which we so readily identify Port-Royal. There was Agnès Arnauld, who had joined her older sister at Port-Royal and would succeed her as abbess. Her *Secret Rosary,* once such a source of controversy, now impresses us as a bouquet of wilted flowers that makes us wonder what the fuss was all about. She herself was a woman of tender piety and affection whose spiritual life remained marked by the early influence of that gentlest of all ascetic masters, Francis de Sales. Her letters aroused the enthusiasm of the staid Sainte-Beuve. Bremond describes her as "meditative, égale, paisible, cloîtrée de coeur, d'esprit et de goût, attentive uniquement aux choses de l'âme."[9] There was Nicole, a natural friend of peace whose sharp, legal mind drew him constantly, but reluctantly, into controversy. The author of the famous distinction between *droit* and *fait* in the dispute over the condemned propositions as well as of the *Letters on the Imaginary Heresy,* he soon withdrew from the battle and remained the spiritual director of extraordinary insight and piety he had always been. True, he had a blind spot for passive contemplation. His attacks on all forms of "modern" mysticism in *Les Visionnaires* earned the entire movement an antimystical reputation. But even this "anti-mystique Nicole" wrote a work of solid and deep piety, the *Treatise on Prayer,* related to the Ignatian method of meditation. It is all the more regrettable that at the end of his life he was, once again, dragged into the anti-Quietist controversy. There was Le Nain de Tillemont, a learned "solitaire" of exceptional virtue and of a contemplative bent of mind. There was Dr. Hamon, Port-Royal's humble and saintly physician whom Sainte-Beuve calls "un des grands spirituels du XVIIᵉ-siecle."[10] But no one realized the full potential of Saint-Cyran's spiritual principles more fully than his nephew, Martin de Barcos. He saw the contemplative life as most congruous with the Augustinian doctrine of grace. Nicole admitted that he had had Barcos in mind in one of his attacks on Quietism. And, indeed, he forms a natural link between the movements. Despite its different mood and antagonistic attitude, Jansenism displays a pronounced "Quietist" undercurrent. In her beautiful letters, Agnès Arnauld never desists repeating that we should not run ahead of the invitation of God's grace and cautions against all violence done to nature. Barcos went further and laid the entire weight of spiritual life upon the obedient passivity nourished in tranquil contemplation. In judging Port-Royal, at least the Port-Royal of the early period, we should constantly remind ourselves that this is not a heretical conclave, but a group of deeply committed Christians, members of traditional religious orders who are concerned with remaining within the tradition of the church and of their own congregations, and whose main innovation consisted in a more radical attempt to return to the pure sources of that pure tradition without sacrificing the bond with the present community.

During its final period as a formal movement Jansenism degenerated into a disputatious sect. This spiritually unrewarding chapter in the ecclesiastical history of France offers little to inspire us today. Jansenist writers of recent times had to look for spiritual nourishment in the earlier period. The unhappy alliance of a major religious reform movement with the Gallican theories which it had fought in the beginning, the wily politics of the dim-witted Cardinal de Noailles of Paris, the opportunist maneuvers of the last writer of stature, the Oratorian Pasquier Quesnel—all this must be forgotten by those who look for edification in Jansenism. Yet none of it justifies the cruel measures taken by its adversaries: the prohibition against accepting new novices and, in the end, the total destruction of Port-Royal itself by Louis XIV's guard. What neither sectarian abuse nor external violence could destroy, however, is the voice of piety that continues to speak to us across the centuries.

Quietism

Origins

Quietism appears to stand at the opposite end of the spiritual spectrum. Jansenists played a prominent role in the Quietist controversy that eventually

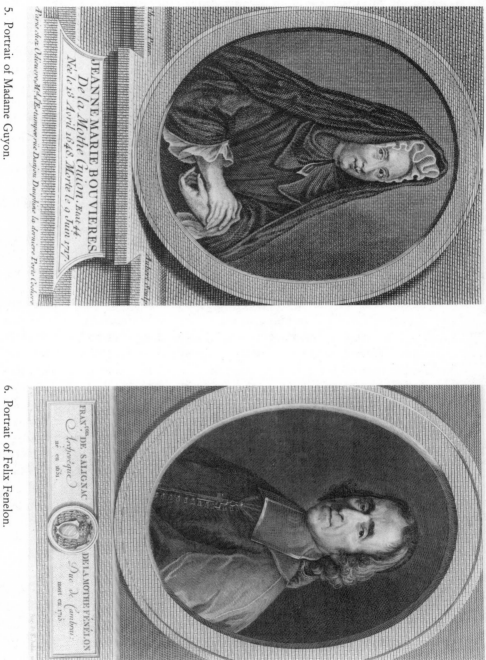

5. Portrait of Madame Guyon.

6. Portrait of Felix Fenelon.

led to the condemnation of Fénelon. In return Fénelon contributed to the
elimination of Jansenism as an organized movement in France. It would be
simplistic to attribute this hostility to a conflict of personalities. We are
dealing with two different religious styles. Jansenism, suspicious of contemplative harmony, stressed moral seriousness and personal effort. Quietism,
distrustful of human initiative in the order of grace, preached passivity and
nonresistance. Yet in France the two movements were intimately connected.
Both started from the same pessimistic concept of human nature which
Bérulle and the masters of the French school had solidly instilled in the
French mind. But the same pessimism led to opposite conclusions. Jansenists concluded that, in earnest cooperation with grace, we must work out
our salvation in fear and trembling. Quietists, stressing the exclusive efficacy
of grace in a corrupt nature, advocated total abandon.

At the same time, the best representatives of both movements remained
heavily indebted to the other school, the "devout humanism" of Francis de
Sales. We clearly detect his influence in the sisters Arnauld and even in Saint-
Cyran. Among Quietists, the bishop of Genève's impact is universal. His
advice not to worry about one's progress in spiritual life became the guiding
principle of the entire movement in France. One might trace the influence
much further, since Francis de Sales himself had merely given new emphasis
and fresh articulation to an idea that went back to the desert fathers and that
appears in schools as far apart as the Rhineland mystics and the Spanish
Carmelites. Unless we keep this long and venerable lineage in mind, we may
be tempted to view Quietism through the narrowing lenses of the polemics
it provoked as a marginal current of thought, a spiritual dead end. In addition to transmitting this remote tradition, the French school introduced a
key concept into the Quietist vocabulary, namely, the idea of *pure love*. At
times, indeed, most of the time, it becomes difficult to distinguish the best
so-called Quietists from their great predecessors. Would "Quietism" ever
have acquired a proper name without the adverse publicity created by a few
immoderate statements and the reactions it provoked in the Holy Office?
It is true, though, if we may believe one of their enemies, that at least in
Naples, the followers of Molinos took for themselves the name of "Quietists."

Those who speak of "precedents" of Quietism usually refer to *controversial*
movements that emphasize contemplative quiet and passivity over discursive meditation and active virtue. One of the names most frequently mentioned is that of the Spanish *Alumbrados*. What little information we have
about them is mostly derived from hostile sources and extorted confessions.
It appears to be neither reliable nor even coherent, but indications are that
it was more a spiritual movement than a single sect and that it may have
had several degrees of "perfection." The Inquisition appears to have been
mostly concerned about the group's alleged contempt for the active pursuit

of moral virtue as a way to perfection. The key term, which also appears in Erasmus's *Enchiridion Militis Christiani* and in Ignatius's *Spiritual Exercises,* was sacred *indifference (dejamiento).* Shortly after the condemnation of Sevilla of 1621, similar tendencies developed in France, but no clear evidence links the French "spirituels" to Spanish Illuminism.

Molinos

Indeed, the first movement clearly identifiable as "Quietism" emerged in Italy, first in the still orthodox form of the *Breve compendio intorno alla perfezione cristiana* (circulating before 1596, published 1611), written by Achille Gagliardi, a Milan Jesuit, under the influence of his penitent Isabella Bellinzaga. The book was translated repeatedly, paraphrased by Camus and the young Bérulle, and recommended by a number of trustworthy spiritual directors, among whom was Surin. The controversy that would later surround the work was occasioned by the subsequent emergence of a real "Quietist" movement. Much of the credit or blame for the latter goes to Molinos. Miguel de Molinos, born in 1628 near Saragossa and a doctor in theology of the University of Coimbra, rapidly gained a reputation as a young preacher and confessor in Valencia. His fellow citizens sent him to Rome to promote the canonization of another Valencian. Nothing came of the case, but Molinos stayed in Rome and soon became known as a great spiritual leader. In 1675 he published a short tract on frequent communion diametrically opposed to Arnauld's position. Yet the book did not attract nearly the attention that his *Spiritual Guide* (in Spanish and Italian) did. It asserted that only contemplative, that is, purely passive, prayer leads to spiritual perfection. To attain it the Christian should avoid all strenuous ascetic efforts and, instead, concentrate entirely on inner quiet and abandon. Once again the Jesuits were first to attack what they considered a threat to their own practice of meditation. But Molinos's reputation was so solidly established that immediately several cardinals came to his rescue and saw to it that his critics were themselves condemned. Still, gradually the effects of his work aroused suspicion and the same Pope Innocent XI who had first protected him eventually had him arrested. Why? Even today we do not know with certainty. His writings, including some twelve thousand letters, were scrutinized by the Holy Office and, after a long and turbulent trial, he was sentenced to lifelong imprisonment, narrowly escaping capital punishment. Molinos was proclaimed guilty of immoral conduct as well as of doctrinal errors. A strange accusation for a man who was known for his exemplary life and venerated by his own household. Was he really the exhibitionist he was accused of being? Or had he been imprudent in his relations with others? Or did his theory of nonresistance to evil even in one's own body suggest a general attitude of moral laxity? The evidence for the verdict which continues to puzzle historians lies buried in the letters—many of them to women—which are still kept under seal at the Vatican. The fact that Molinos admitted his guilt on all the sixty-eight charges proves only his willingness to practice the nonresistance he preached, even in the face of death. Nor does his further life bear out the charges of moral turpitude. After having spent nine years in a Roman jail, a model of goodness and piety to all who approached him, he died a saintly death.

It is difficult to derive the condemned propositions from the *Spiritual Guide*. One recognizes proposition 12, that a person who has given his entire freedom to God should worry neither about hell nor heaven. He should have no desire for his own perfection, for his own sanctity, or his own salvation—even the hope of which he should extinguish. That a person is not morally responsible for physical acts committed by the devil in his body without his consensus (prop. 41) and should not resist them (47), may be dangerous as a general principle, but as specific advice given to particular persons, perhaps of scrupulous disposition, it cannot be judged without its directional context—which we do not possess. At the trial, Molinos insisted that an internal, God-given light enabled him to detect when a penitent's action came from the devil. This prophetic attitude, combined with a strange air of exaltation, has caused some to question his mental balance. Ronald Knox mentions a "disordered psychology" which led him to believe himself to be a prophet and thereby superior to considerations of ordinary moral prudence. The theory is plausible enough, but the supporting evidence (possibly contained in the letters) remains scanty. His published writings, however, suggest a suspiciously one-sided attitude. One point in particular raises questions. Molinos's *Guide* blurs the distinction so clearly stated by St. Teresa, between actively acquired contemplation and infused, purely passive quiet. With it goes a certain contempt for traditional ways of prayer. We seem to have here a mysticism à *volonté* or perhaps an assumption that mysticism is readily granted to all as the only mode of spiritual protection. As Knox succinctly puts it:

> Molinos . . . professes to be writing about a stage of active contemplation, before passive prayer has started. If, then, he uses (and exaggerates) the language used by St. John of the Cross about the purification which the soul must be prepared to meet in its course, he is using language which does not apply to his subject.[11]

But even this point is far from clear. In his *Letters to a Spaniard* (1676) Molinos explicitly declares that he never intended to attack meditation, but merely to provide *another* way to perfection. All he says is that a spiritual person must abandon meditation once God invites him or her to do so.

Hardly irresponsible advice! The question of infused contemplation receives a satisfactory explanation when, in his correspondence with Fr. Oliva, Superior General of the Society of Jesus, he declares it to depend exclusively on God's grace and hence to be beyond our reach altogether. Even "acquired contemplation" is not for everyone, but only for select souls. Still, in the end for Molinos there is only *one* form of perfection: the union with God through infused contemplation. I am not sure, however, that a similar thesis is not implied in John of the Cross and a number of other orthodox writers.

The real problem, as Leszek Kolakowski has well perceived, appears to be that a divine love thus exclusively affirmed, in the end destroys itself.

> The desire of God for his own sake must reach a degree of such purity and intensity as to render the mystic totally indifferent to his own well-being, even to the grace with which God acquaints him. Nevertheless precisely in the experience of these graces do we experience the God who chooses to remain in the empty soul of the contemplative. To become indifferent to these graces, then, is to become indifferent to the contact with God himself, to the mystical union, to all the values which God offers to his servant. Thus in the end the ideal of the mystic is to desire God so vividly that one does not desire him anymore at all.[12]

Madame Guyon

No such ambiguities surround Jeanne-Marie Guyon. With her all is wide-open and feelings are expressed as soon as they are felt, perhaps before. Yet Madame Guyon's readiness to commit unrelated and sometimes unreflected experience to verbal expression creates problems of its own. With her the question is not how much she held back, but how much she overstated her case. For clearly she was prone to being carried away, not only by her emotions but, even more, by her words. Her mental balance remains a subject of controversy. Psychologists have made much of the emotional frustration caused by her mother's neglect and, worse, of her unhappy marriage to an older, morose cousin, of her frequent ill-defined illnesses, of the pain following the loss of her two children and the deformation of a third one by a smallpox epidemic. On the basis of this many have dismissed her as "hysterical." Yet such a facile categorization altogether fails to do justice to her work. Françoise Mallet-Joris in her beautiful biography rebuffs the charges of hysteria as a "vocable commode et mal défini sous lequel on classe tout ce qu'on veut discréditer chez la femme."[13]

The evaluation of this perceptive, spiritual person has clearly suffered the negative impact of the almost universal prejudice against granting a relatively uneducated woman any spiritual authority at all. That Jeanne Guyon suffered more deeply than most is due not to a hysterical disposition but to the particular conditions of her life—not least the subordinate position of women, which caused her to remain uneducated in childhood, to be married against her will to a totally unsuitable man, to be placed under the supervision of a hostile mother-in-law, and to be refused permission to remove her children when the smallpox epidemic broke out. The skill with which she discharged herself of her material duties, including the administration of her estate, conveys an impression of good practical sense. Her judgment may occasionally have been less than perfect, especially in her totally innocent relation with her unbalanced spiritual mentor, the Barnabite Father Lacombe. In judging Jeanne Guyon we must indeed take into account the vicissitudes of her life. But they do not explain her extraordinary spiritual sensitivity. Few modern commentators resist the temptation of ridiculing this easy target, but in doing so they fail to explain the profound impact she had on some of the most discerning masters of her time. Her highly reputed spiritual powers were real and, for all their uncritical exaggerations, her writings impressively authenticate an exceptional mind's itinerary to God. Did she ever undergo the influence of Molinos's theories? She denies it, but her confessor, Father Lacombe, later confessed to have held Molinist doctrines and to have acted in accordance with their more questionable moral principles.

Her *Moyen court et facile de faire oraison* (1685) (*Short Method of Prayer*) defends the prayer of quiet as both the easiest and the most productive. She appears to consider all Christians fit for contemplative prayer, but in her later *Torrens spirituels* she reserves her message for the initiated. This combination of hazardous generalization and spiritual elitism seems characteristic of the entire quietist movement. Impatience with different approaches easily mixes with a kind of spiritual *gnosis*. (Interestingly enough, Fénelon wrote an admiring study, *Le Gnostique de St. Clément d'Alexandrie*). Still, there was never any question that Guyon, Malaval, and Fénelon sincerely wished to remain within the limits of Catholic orthodoxy. Each one of them was at some point censured, and each immediately submitted. Before being published, the *Moyen court* had widely circulated without encountering any serious doctrinal opposition. In vain one looks for a rash judgment or a questionable principle—at most, the one-sidedness of the position tends to oversimplify the course of spiritual development. It remains a useful guide for a particular form of piety which may not appeal to all readers and, I suspect, today less so than when it first appeared.

In the *Torrens* Mme. Guyon distinguishes three stages of spiritual life. Its real beginning occurs when the soul has learned how to become passive. The will and the senses gradually lose their distinct impact in a unified state of affection. Is this condition of quiet acquired or infused? Mme. Guyon mentions "special graces" which will be withdrawn in the next stage. Still she distinguishes the ordinary achievements of this state from those of the third stage which totally surpass a person's innate or acquired capacity. Even the first one, though, changes the normal pattern of conduct, perhaps a liberation of the unconscious that may result in extraordinary psychic phenomena. At a certain point, however, the soul becomes aware of its attachment to the condition rather than to its cause. She recognizes a tendency to appropriate the divine for its own purposes and to take the pleasure of God's presence for God himself. This recognition provokes a new attitude, in which the soul becomes deprived of all taste in prayer and even of its ability to "practice" (actively) virtue. In the new state of aridity and desolation she perceives no more signs of God's love and merely faces her own total inadequacy. This emptiness prepares the final stage, in which God takes total possession of the soul, elevating her to his own level. A stable, supersensible feeling of joy, quite different from the intermittent exaltation of the first state, accompanies the new condition. We are reminded of St. Teresa's description of the spiritual marriage. While her personal capacities remain no longer at the soul's disposal, her whole activity comes to be controlled by God himself as an instrument of his grace.

In Mme. Guyon's case this "transfer" led to automatic writing and speaking: the words no longer seemed to come from herself, but from a deeper source within her. She was not clear about the true significance (and limitations) of this condition, and her unsophisticated interpretation of it led to a number of unnecessary difficulties. Fénelon himself cautioned her against taking for the inspired word of God what might have come from herself. Here perhaps lies the source of that most controversial aspect of the Quietist movement—the counsel, occasionally given, not to resist motions that appear to escape personal control. Henri Delacroix plausibly attributes this intriguing phenomenon to the state of utter passivity in which the mystic's unconscious totally overcomes the normal inhibitions and manifests itself in various, involuntary ways. The ascetic attitude characteristic of the spiritual person gives way to unrestrained expression whether it occurs in perception of voices and visions or in bodily motion. In a visually oriented person such as St. Teresa this may evoke visions—some of which she ascribes to the devil. Precisely because of the absence of a clearly discerning judgment in these involuntary expressions of a liberated unconscious, St. John of the Cross advises the spiritual person not to attach definitive importance to visions and voices of any kind. In others it may have led to involuntary action. Delacroix writes about Mme. Guyon's state of mind:

> Through patient interior work and through the fundamental richness of her creative unconscious Mme. Guyon replaced discursive thinking by an inexpressible intuition which filled almost her entire mind. And since we must *act* to remain in accordance with God, she substituted to voluntary and

personal action an involuntary and impersonal one—which she calls passivity and which appears to her as a creative infinity. Yet this passivity expresses itself not in confused and uncoordinated movements. It is coherent and intelligent; it displays unity and finality.[14]

One cannot but be struck by the basic concordance between Mme. Guyon's theory and that of less controverted mystics. The similarity between the three stages and the upper, properly mystical "mansions" of St. Teresa's *Spiritual Castle* is obvious. It is in the expression more than in the content that Jeanne Guyon's theory becomes occasionally questionable. This is not too surprising in an author who had little formal education in theology and, until the end of her writing career (when it was too late), little occasion to consult with theologians. The salient points of her doctrine seem to be sound and entirely compatible with the Christian tradition. (1) Spiritual life consists in a process of disappropriation, a growing detachment that allows God gradually to take possession of the soul. Almost all Christian mystics, from Eckhart to Ignatius and John of the Cross, shared this ideal in some form or other. (2) Spiritual life is a teleological process that moves from lower to higher stages. Here again we find ourselves on well-trodden Western territory. Less universal (but not unique) is Jeanne Guyon's tendency to equate the phases of her own, somewhat special development with the stages of spiritual life as such. In her case, more than in most, the autobiography is the key to her thought. Her ready identification of life with doctrine accounts for the occasionally apodictic tone of her words and writings, which ruffled more clerical feathers than the content itself. Jeanne came to regard herself as a woman with a divine mission who, through many trials, was to introduce a new era of redemption. Bossuet raked her cruelly over the coals of his heavy sarcasm for this prophetic attitude. What particularly attracted hostility was her naïve way of treating her own single idea as if no history had preceded it and no complications could obscure it. But this same narrow vision also enabled her to forget pain and adversity as soon as they were behind her and to act confidently upon the inspiration of the moment, uninhibited by doubt or memory. The French quip, "une innocente," expresses both her qualities and defects.

Fénelon

Yet Mme. Guyon's impact on a person as exceptionally talented and solidly religious as Fénelon by itself excludes the possibility of her being a "spiritual imposter" or merely a "hysterical woman." Her influence completely transformed the future bishop's style of living and writing. It caused him numerous humiliations: the painful controversy with the acerbic Bossuet, who even questioned the moral integrity of his fellow bishop and favorite pupil; his removal from a prestigious post at Mme. de Maintenon's aristocratic school, St. Cyr, as well as from his court position as the Dauphin's instructor; and, finally, the formal condemnation by Pope Innocent XI of his *Maximes des saints*. Yet Jeanne Guyon's impact survived them all, and until his death he continued to live in the spirit of humble "abandon" which he had learned from his spiritual mentor. We may regret that the learned prelate did not more judiciously sift the content from the form of her counsel and that he took the principle of spiritual childhood rather literally. He thereby exposed himself to ridicule, partly deserved, and to the wholly undeserved suggestions about the nature of his relation with Mme. Guyon.

When they met, after Fr. Lacombe had been removed from her, Jeanne had already established her reputation as a controversial *dévote,* and he that of a seriously religious priest gifted with a brilliant mind and connected with the highest circles. At first he was curious, but reticent. Once "converted" to the life of quiet, his surrender became unreserved. Mme. Guyon became his guide, but also his theological pupil. He moderated her in her all-too-spontaneous expression and provided her with some much-needed patristic and scholastic support. In addition to giving the Quietist movement a theological foundation, he shifted its focus from a particular mode of prayer to a particular mode of love—*l'amour pur.*

The idea of "pure love" had already had a distinguished history in France. Its origins lie in St. Francis de Sales's *Treatise of Divine Love.* In 1640 Francis's disciple, bishop Jean-Pierre Camus, had published his slightly controversial *Défense du pur amour.* In the Quietist movement, pure love had always occupied an important place. But only with Fénelon did it become the center. The flavor of the theory exudes from Fénelon's many spontaneous yet so beautifully written letters. But the doctrinal principles of *l'amour pur* should be studied in the systematic *Explication sur les maximes des saints* (1697). In it he attempts to give a favorable interpretation to the thirty-four articles issued by the committee consisting of Bishops de Noailles, Bossuet, and the superior of Saint-Sulpice after a lengthy investigation of Jeanne Guyon's doctrine. Fénelon had exercised sufficient influence on the committee to avoid precise formulations. Now he was anxious to improve his position by writing a somewhat Quietist commentary on the articles. Meanwhile Bossuet had hardened his resistance and had proceeded to express it in his *Instruction sur les états d'oraison.* Fénelon (or his followers?) rushed the *Maximes* to the printer before Bossuet's book could appear. This circumstance is characteristic of the polemical climate in which the book was written. Each of the articles lists a "true" and a "false" version of the thesis on pure love.

In the introduction Fénelon assumes the defense of "les mystiques" (the term as applied nonpejoratively to living individuals appears first in Guyon and Fénelon) by showing their solid roots in the theological tradition. Next he equates "quiet" contemplation with the exercise of the pure love of God. Meditation, which Fénelon describes as consisting of discursive and distinct acts, is appropriate for that "imperfect love," that is, love mixed with motives of hope and fear, and operating by clearly marked, reflective acts. Contemplation, on the contrary, consists of acts so simple, so direct, and so "quiet," that the soul has no way of distinguishing them from one another. It practices the pure love of God (Art. 21). What does Fénelon understand by "pure" love? He distinguishes concupiscent love, which loves God only because of his benefits, from the love implied in hope (*mostly* because of his future benefits) and from that of charity (*mostly* because of himself). If purified until it loves God only because of himself, charity becomes *pure* love. To these distinctions Fénelon, with doubtful success, attaches a number of current spiritual concepts. Thus, hope marks the beginning of the way of purgation, charity of illumination, and pure love of union. With St. Francis de Sales, the most frequently cited authority, Fénelon distinguishes the "holy resignation" of hope and charity from the "holy indifference" of pure love. The resigned person loves God equally in pain and in suffering but retains his private desires. In indifference the soul has freed itself from all preference (Art. 5). Through trials indifference grows to abandonment, and this leads to the ideal state of passivity. Passivity, Fénelon explains, consists not in the absence of work or of active virtue, but of that restive attitude whereby the soul out of fear of not doing enough runs ahead of the impulse of grace. It marks the disposition of one who leaves all initiative in the order of grace to God.

In the state of pure love the higher portion of the soul appears to become separated from the lower at least to this extent, that sense and imagination have no more part in the simple peace and communication of grace (Art. 14). Christ continued to enjoy the beatific vision even while suffering his agony on the cross. Fénelon's description of the two parts of the soul is clumsy and his reference to Christ inappropriate, as the Holy Office was quick to point out. But he does not claim that the inferior part of the soul is left to its animal desires. Indeed, what he asserts belongs to the mainstream of the Christian mystical tradition, which has always taught that God's direct communication occurs in the *fundus animae*, beyond reflective intelligence and deliberate will. St. John of the Cross speaks of the "substance" of the soul, Tauler of the "little spark" of the soul. Fénelon, adopting St. Francis de Sales's vocabulary, refers to "la pointe de l'esprit ou la cime de l'âme" (Art. 9). Pure love abandons only the methodic pursuit of distinct virtue, but the ground of virtue remains, and enriches the "direct" acts of love. In the ultimate stage of "disappropriation" the soul surrenders all active control over the process of its spiritual self-realization.

Rome's condemnation of the *Maximes* oversimplifies Fénelon's intentions and, by taking them out of context, even his expressions. Its series of dogmatic "theses" fails to capture the subtle, psychological description of states of mind which the unfortunate controversy forced him to condense into theoretical maxims. Does the condemnation represent that exclusive concern for conformity which tolerates no spiritual excellence? Certainly the manner in which the censure was obtained reveals more political shrewdness—and a not always "golden" mediocrity—than a deep concern for spiritual truth. And yet, one cannot escape a certain discomfort in reading theories in which everything is "pure" and the imperfect but commonly attainable is barely granted a right to exist. In the end, the "heresy" of Quietism may have consisted in nothing more than the all-too-deliberate decision to leave the ordinary. It is a heresy which it shares with its natural adversary, Jansenism, but one which has prevented neither movement from training some of the most spiritual minds of the seventeenth and eighteenth centuries. Jansenism and Quietism should be seen as attempts to perpetuate the Christian spiritual tradition in a culture that was breaking away from the basis of that tradition, rather than as separatist drives. What made them "different," perhaps unacceptably so to the mass of believers, stems more from the conceptual matrices established by the new culture—matrices which they both accepted and resisted—than from personal pride and deliberate elitism.

Notes

1. Ronald Knox, *Enthusiasm,* 184.
2. Henri Bremond, *Histoire littéraire,* 4:45–46.
3. Ibid., 306–7.
4. Trans. A. J. Krailsheimer (Baltimore: Penguin Books, 1966, 1973).
5. Letter to Mme. Périer, 1 April 1648, trans. in Jean Mesnard, *Pascal,* trans. Claude and Marcia Abraham, 129.
6. Ibid., 116–17.
7. H. Bremond, *Histoire littéraire,* 462.
8. Letter to Mme. Périer, Nov. 5, 1648, Mesnard, p. 128.
9. H. Bremond, *Histoire littéraire,* 4:2, 177. See also, Sainte-Beuve, *Causeries du lundi* (5th ed.; Paris: Garnier, n.d.) 14:148–62.
10. Sainte-Beuve, *Port-Royal,* 2:755.
11. R. Knox, *Enthusiasm,* 292.
12. Leszek Kolakowski, *Chrétiens sans église,* 518.
13. F. Mallet-Joris, *Jeanne Guyon,* 140.
14. H. Delacroix, *Les grands mystiques chrétiens,* 219.

Bibliography

Jansenism

Pascal, Blaise. *Pensées*. Translated by A. J. Krailshaimer. Baltimore, MD: Penguin Books, 1966.

———. *The Provincial Letters*. Translated by A. J. Krailshaimer. Baltimore, MD: Penguin Books, 1967.

Balthasar, Hans Urs von. *The Glory of the Lord*, 3:172–238. San Francisco: Ignatius Press, 1986.

Bremond, Henri. *Histoire littéraire du sentiment religieux en France*. Paris, 1911–1933. Republished 1968.

Guardini, Romano. *Pascal For Our Time*. Translated by Brian Thompson. New York: Herder, 1966.

Hazelton, Roger. *Pascal: The Genius of His Thought*. Philadelphia: Westminster, 1974.

Mesnard, Jean. *Pascal*. Translated by Claude and Marcia Abraham. University, AL: University of Alabama Press, 1969.

Sainte-Beuve, Charles A. *Port-Royal*. 1889. Paris: La Pléiade, 1953.

Quietism (General)

Armogathe, Jean Robert. *Le Quietisme: Que sais-je?* Paris: Presses universitaires de France, 1973.

Knox, Roland. *Enthusiasm: A Chapter in the History of Religion*. New York: Oxford University Press, 1950.

Kolakowski, Leszek. *Chrétiens sans église*, 492–566. Paris: Gallimard, 1969.

Molinos

Molinos, Miguel de. *Guida spirituale*. Rome, 1675. *Spiritual Guide*. Translated by Kathleen Lyttleton. London, 1906. Incomplete.

Dudon, Paul. *Le quiétiste espagnol Michel Molinos*. Paris, 1921.

Menendez, Pelayo. *Historia de los heterodoxos españoles*, 4:253–74. Madrid, 1947.

Guyon

Guyon, Jeanne-Marie de la Mothe. *Oeuvres*. Edited by P. Poiret. Cologne, 1713–1732.

———. *A Short Method of Prayer* and *Spiritual Torrents*. Translated by A. W. Marston. London, 1875.

Cognet, Louis. "Guyon." In *Dict. Sp.*

Delacroix, Henri. *Les grands mystiques chrétiens*, 108–307. Paris, 1938.

Mallet-Joris, Françoise. *Jeanne Guyon*. Paris: Flammarion, 1978.

Fénelon

Bremond, Henri. *Apologie pour Fénelon*. Paris, 1910.

Gouhier, Henry. *Fénelon philosophe*. Paris: Presses universitaires de France, 1977.

Bedoyere, Michael de la. *The Archbishop and the Lady. The Story of Fénelon and Madame Guyon*. New York: Pantheon, 1956.

6

Recent Catholic Spirituality: Unity amid Diversity

DAVID TRACY

IT IS IMPOSSIBLE, in so short a space, to articulate all the diverse forms of Catholic spirituality in the nineteenth and twentieth centuries. One can, however, study certain common characteristics and representative figures. Accordingly, the first section will examine two influential and representatively Catholic figures: John Henry Cardinal Newman and Baron Friedrich von Hügel. In their work and spirit, one can find the marks of a Catholic spirituality—especially that which found expression in the Second Vatican Council. In a second section, we will analyze certain theologians and philosophers both in their relationship to selected spiritual resources of the Catholic tradition and in their different interpretations of the modern world. The study will be of representative thinkers: theologians Bernard Lonergan, Karl Rahner, and Hans Urs von Balthasar; and religious philosophers such as Pierre Teilhard de Chardin, Edith Stein, and Louis Dupré. The last two sections will study the development, especially in Latin American theologies of liberation and in such North American figures as Dorothy Day and Thomas Merton, of a new trend (or series of trends) in Catholic spirituality since the paradigm set down by Newman and von Hügel: a mystico-political spirituality for a world church which unites political justice concerns to more traditional Catholic emphases.

Even such representative movements and figures, however, cannot do justice to the full range of Catholic spirituality in the modern period. Brief attention will be given to those forms of traditional spirituality which continue to thrive.

The Foundations of Modern Catholic Spirituality: Newman and von Hügel

If one assumes *caritas* as the leitmotif throughout the history of Catholic spirituality, one can further specify Catholic spirituality in the modern period by recalling the reflections of John Henry Cardinal Newman and Baron Friedrich von Hügel. Newman's thought and spirituality have been deeply influential on modern Catholic thought to the point where the spirit of the Second Vatican Council is not unjustly labeled "Newman's spirit." One of the thinkers Newman most influenced was his much younger contemporary Baron von Hügel. Von Hügel himself was deeply involved in the disquietudes of the late nineteenth and early twentieth century over the relationships of Catholic tradition and modern thought—especially science, personalist philosophy, and historical consciousness. Both figures, moreover, were ecumenical in spirit and tone: for Newman ecumenicity came naturally, as his own evangelical and Anglican heritages always remained strong (as seen in his *Apologia pro vita sua*); for von Hügel, this openness to other traditions came from his sensed vocation to recover the Catholic tradition in all its plurality by allowing it to dialogue with modern thought and with other Christian and non-Christian traditions. In one sense, as we shall see below, von Hügel built upon and developed further the theological foundations for a Catholic spirituality articulated by Newman. In another sense, the Second Vatican Council ratified the catholicity of Newman's basic approach in a manner that dispelled the hold of the Ultramontane spirituality which Newman and von Hügel, in their distinct but unrelated ways, both resisted.

Several aspects of Newman's thought and spirituality are characteristically Catholic. First, there is his insistence on doctrine as a necessary component of any religion grounded in revealed truth. An emphasis on "personal experience" in Newman was equally strong, as shown in his justly famous insistence on the "illative sense" and on "real" as distinct from "notional" assent, or his magisterial defense of the faith of the ordinary Catholic for whom faith is a matter of deep personal assent to the truth of revelation. Newman's insistence, moreover, that "conscience" (as the "voice of God") must never be violated was united to his equally emphatic concern that the individual conscience of the Christian be formed in the community of the church through its teachings and disciplines.

The explicitly "personalist" position of Newman yielded both a sensitive psychology of religion and a theological and spiritual defense of "personalism" that had profound resonances with the later philosophies of Maurice Blondel, Max Scheler, and Emmanuel Mounier as well as with the emphasis on "religious experience" of the Catholic Modernists, George Tyrell and Alfred Loisy.

Most striking, however, in Newman's own "personalism" and in his emphasis on personal experience, was its Catholic character. His insistence on revelation as a *truth* and on true doctrine amply indicated this Catholic sensibility. For, however important personal religious experience undoubtedly was for Newman, he never allowed that experience to deny its responsive character to the truth of a Word of revelation. For Newman, the classic doctrines of the Catholic tradition developed out of Scripture and constituted an extension of the acts, images, and symbols of the biblical Word of revelation. In philosophical terms, Newman might be called a "phenomenologist" *avant la lettre*. His interest in religious experience was never only in its autonomous character or in feelings or emotions but in its intentionality. Personal religious experience was always, for Newman, an experience of God mediated through the revealed Word in the words of both the Bible and the tradition.

Newman consistently stressed the objective truth of doctrine as received, in real assent, by the believing person. Indeed, he both credited his first evangelical conversion at fifteen with this affirmation of the doctrinal principle in the famous words in the *Apologia:* "When I was fifteen (in the autumn of 1816), a great change of thought took place in me. I fell under the influence of a definite Creed, and received into my intellect impressions of dogma, which through God's mercy, have never been effaced or obscured."[1] This same fidelity helps to clarify Newman's famous antiliberalism statement upon becoming a Cardinal: "For 30, 40, 50 years I have resisted to the best of my powers the spirit of liberalism in religion."[2] What "liberalism" meant for Newman was not a generalized "liberal spirit" or demand for personal experience (both of which he defended). Liberalism in its exact meaning for Newman was an antidoctrinal spirit. Here one can see the importance of doctrine for modern Catholic spirituality from Newman through Karl Rahner and Dorothy Day. For the Catholic, doctrine as a fitting, developed meaning from the scriptural images and symbols is grounded in the truth of the revealed word of God. As such, doctrine becomes not a hindrance to personal religious experience but a trustworthy guide to all Catholic spirituality.

This same insistence on the unbreakable link between the objectivity of doctrine and the personal appropriation of its spiritual meaning led Newman to his retrieval of the patristic (especially Alexandrian) notions of symbol, sacrament, and Incarnation. Because of God's Incarnation in the Word of Jesus Christ, the Christian can discern objective, revealed truth in the sacraments and in the classic symbols of the tradition. That discernment is likely to lead any individual Christian in her/his own way to understand and practice the faith: hence the emergence of a variety of Catholic spiritualities and theologies. But all these richly different ways will, as Catholic, find their grounding in the objective truth of the Word as the divine reality mediated through the objective means of sacrament, symbol, and doctrine.

This equal stress on both unity and diversity finds ample articulation in Newman's insistence that there must be many "ways," where there are so many kinds of individuals in such different cultures and classes, with such different temperaments and with such different levels of intellectual, moral, and religious development. At the same time, all these ways are grounded in and spiritually responsible to the one way of God's revelation in the Word as that Word is mediated to us in the great tradition of Scripture, doctrine, symbol, and sacrament. This Catholic sense for spiritual diversity amid spiritual unity finds further expression in Newman's reflections on and defenses of these central objective realities in all Catholic spirituality: a sense of tradition, a sense of the wider community, a firm affirmation of doctrine as objective, a sacramental envisionment of all reality by understanding the full significance of the sacraments. These fundamental Catholic affirmations, moreover, led Newman to insist that the modern emphasis on "personal experience" was fully at home in Catholic spirituality. For precisely doctrine, community, tradition, and sacrament do not impoverish but enrich the personal religious experience of every spirituality by providing a secure ground which helps the believer to focus, now on inner-Christian grounds, on the great dilemmas of a spiritual life: the meaning of conscience, the vagaries of emotion and feeling, and, above all, the gradual accumulation of probabilities into firm certitude that one can, after all, be spiritually certain that the way is founded in objective-as-revealed truth. English devotional practices, Newman insisted in the height of the Ultramontane period, are unlikely to be the same as Italian religious practices. They are no less Catholic for that, as both are equally firmly grounded in doctrine, sacrament, tradition, and community.

Newman's reflections of the reality of the church also bear a distinctly Catholic mark. When Newman appealed to the "idea" of the church, he understood "idea" as one's deepest sense of the concrete whole and its constituent parts at once. Like so many in his age, "idea," for him, meant not an abstraction from reality but the reality itself as spiritually sensed and partially but never fully understood. Christianity itself in his *Essay on the Development of Doctrine* was such an organic idea: sensed, felt, understood, and yielding itself to partial, incomplete, but true understanding as it developed through the centuries. The church, as an idea, was the objective reality of the Body of Christ, constituted by the Spirit of Christ. That is why only the truly spiritual could understand the church and why the Christian experienced and understood Christ and the Spirit in and through the church.

The idea of the church was never for Newman a mere idea but the polity which is the church existing here and now: the one Catholics live in, whose gifted reality, as well as human faults and need for self-reform, is always there. It is a part, therefore, of Catholic spirituality to sense and understand the church in its unity and in its distinct parts—parts that can never efface the antecedent divinely graced unity. It is also part of Catholic spirituality to struggle to discern what part of the church now needs strengthening, or development, or correction of excesses by reform. The temptation of the prophetical teaching office (theology) is rationalism; that of the ruling office is power; that of the sacred ministry and piety is superstition. Each temptation needs to be discerned and healed, and the danger of each part thinking itself the whole church needs to be avoided. Thus could Newman appeal to history when, in the fourth century, most of the bishops abandoned the true christological doctrine in the Arian controversy and the church depended on the laity to maintain its true identity. This example impelled Newman to insist on the need to consult the laity and to defend the *sensus fidelium* as a truly ecclesial sense.

In sum, for Newman doctrine, sacrament, tradition, community, and, above all, church as Body of Christ comprising three equally indispensable functions form the spirituality of Catholics in all cultures. This formation allows a great diversity of spiritual ways while uniting them in the central reality of the Spirit's indwelling presence to the individual soul in communion with church as the spiritual presence of Christ. Newman's exceptional sensitivity to the need for diversity and powers of discernment in the ever-shifting historical and theological reality of the church made his spirituality influential for many modern Catholics as both unmistakably Catholic and clearly modern. That same spiritual sense pervades the openness to the good in other religious traditions and to the best of modernity in the major decrees of the Second Vatican Council.

One major example of the influence of Newman on his younger contemporaries may be found in the thought of Baron Friedrich von Hügel. Although perhaps mostly remembered for his complex role in the Modernist crises of the early twentieth century, Baron von Hügel's contribution to modern Catholic spirituality is found in his classic work, *The Mystical Element of Religion as Studied in Saint Catherine of Genoa and Her Friends*. Here, as in his other works, one witnesses the "modern" side of Catholic spirituality that first erupted in the Modernist crisis and returned, after that early suppression by church authorities, in more substantively Catholic form in the great reform movements of early twentieth-century Catholicism that culminated in the Second Vatican Council. The strengths of the Catholic Modernist movement are all present in von Hügel: his insistence on historical consciousness and the use of historical-critical methods for biblical studies and church history; his development of a philosophy of personalism that highlights the existential character of religious truth; his openness to the findings of modern science and indeed to the genuine accomplishments of the modern period; his inner-Christian ecumenical spirit united to his respect for the insights and spiritual ways of the other great religious traditions.

He defended the use of historical-critical methods by Alfred Loisy and the emphasis on personal experience by George Tyrell. He resisted, in his writing, voluminous correspondence, and actions, the triumphant style of the then powerful Ultramontane Roman Catholicism. He honored the institutional reality of the Catholic Church while insisting that it was ever in danger of overcentralization, clericalism, and bureaucratization. And yet, however open to modernity and however critical of the institutional church reality of his day, von Hügel maintained what might be called a Catholic sense of the need for a balance and harmony of elements. Precisely that Catholic sense of balance led him to develop a position that, however sympathetic to the historical contributions of Loisy and the brilliant experiential insights of Tyrell, was less like theirs and more like Newman's and Blondel's. In Newman's case, this balance was struck time and time again — perhaps most tellingly in his reflections on the triple office of the church and the need for constant spiritual discernment of the relative strengths and weaknesses of each element in any particular time in history.

Von Hügel's own work may be viewed as a genuinely modern development of Newman's insight into Catholic spiritual diversity-in-unity. Von Hügel applied that Newmanian insight not solely to the reality of the church but to the reality of religion itself. But von Hügel was far less theological than Newman and less concerned, therefore, with showing the theological reality of the church as the presence of Christ's indwelling Spirit. His principal concern was to develop a philosophy of religion that could show the actuality of the concrete person as a unity-in-diversity and thereby the actuality of religion itself as having the character of a concrete person with both great multiplicity and real unity.

Philosophically, von Hügel (in harmony with the radical empiricism and personalism of his period) developed a personalist philosophy that argued for the presence of emotional, intellectual, and volitional elements acting in harmony in every person. He believed, as did Coleridge and Newman before him, that a prior unity is given to any concrete personal reality. That reality can be sensed and lived but never fully analyzed. One can, however, note the need for the complex development of each person for the full development and harmonization of the emotional, intellectual, and volitional elements.

This personalist model deeply informs von Hügel's discussion of religion in *The Mystical Element of Religion*. There he attempts to show, on the occasion of a historical study of the action-in-the-everyday spirituality of St. Catherine of Genoa, that every living religion bears its clearest analogue in the living person. The believer knows and trusts the concrete reality of God disclosed in the religion. As with a person, the living unity and trust are concretely realized before analysis and criticism are forthcoming. Analogous to the emotional, intellectual, and volitional elements in the person, religion exercises three principal functions. It continuously needs to develop each element and its interrelationships to the other elements to achieve the balance and harmony of an authentic personality.

This personalist analogy led von Hügel to his promising suggestion for understanding the three major elements comprising a historical religion. He employed various phrases for this distinction. One of them insists that every concrete religion comprises three elements: (1) "the external, authoritative, historical, traditional and institutional element" (analogous to the volitional element in the person); (2) "the critical-historical and synthetic-philosophical element" (analogous to the intellectual); and (3) "the mystical and directly operative element of religion" (analogous to the emotional).

Von Hügel attempted, above all, to be faithful to the complexity of Catholic Christianity while also attending to some peculiarly modern intellectual needs. Examples of von Hügel's combination of Catholic balance and modernity are seen in the following: (1) the "institutional" element is real and to be affirmed, but only as related to the necessary fullness of this "external" element more fully described as authoritative, historical, and traditional; (2) the "intellectual" element is crucial and now, in the modern period, must include not only the philosophical-synthetic (as in the classic scholastic theologies and their less happy—for von Hügel—neo-scholastic successors) but also the critical-historical (as in biblical and doctrinal studies); (3) the "mystical" element is not merely passive, but includes a note of action as well—as the spirituality of Catherine of Genoa shows; as, indeed, for von Hügel the most representatively Catholic mystical spiritualities (as incarnational) are also action-oriented in principle.

What Newman attempted to show under the theological rubric of church, von Hügel addressed under the philosophical rubric of "religion." Both can be considered classic modern Catholic spiritualities. Both insist that God's reality is mediated in the concrete historical form of church (Newman) and religion (von Hügel). Only attention to that concreteness as sensed by the believer assures both the personalism and the objectivity essential in

Catholic spirituality. Both acknowledge that this unity occurred in great spiritual diversity: a diversity occasioned by different temperaments, cultures, and historical periods and a diversity grounded in the triple office of the church (Newman) or the threefold elements of concrete religion (von Hügel). Both insisted that in Catholic spirituality this sense of God's reality is mediated to us in Jesus Christ and the church. Both also insisted on the constant spiritual need for Catholics to discern critically corrections and developments of these three functions as well as the contributions and promise of modernity for Catholic self-understanding.

Modern Catholic Spiritualities in Theology and Philosophy

Every theology and religious philosophy includes a particular spirituality. Where the "intellectual" element of Catholic Christianity functions freely and fruitfully, there are likely to be a number of orthodox theologies and spiritualities. The realistic character of Thomas Aquinas's theology also discloses his deeply Dominican spirituality. The cosmic and nature orientation of Bonaventure's emanationist theology also reveals his fidelity to Franciscan spirituality. In the modern period, the sacramental character of Catholic spirituality, which Newman rendered so well, is found in highly different ways in modern Catholic theologies and philosophies. A brief study of six such positions will indicate both how similar and how diverse Catholic thought and spirituality have become in the modern period. In all one may see some of the diversity-in-unity, the Catholic spiritual striving for harmony and balance, which we already witnessed in Newman and von Hügel.

Karl Rahner, S.J.

There can be little doubt that the German Jesuit theologian Karl Rahner has proved to be the most influential Catholic theologian of the twentieth century. His range of interests, his extraordinary output of essays, articles, books, even encyclopedias render him one of the great theologians of the entire tradition. Rahner's theology is characteristically both modern and Catholic. As modern, Rahner takes the "turn to the subject" of modern thought in order to develop a "transcendental" theology. In his earliest works, *Spirit in the World* and *Hearers of the Word*, Rahner argued that a transcendental condition of every act of knowledge, freedom, and love by human beings (as spirit-in-the-world) was the necessary coaffirmation of God as the Absolute Mystery.[3] Human being, as the peculiar being it is, cannot but ask the question of God. For human being is nothing other than a hearer of a possible word of revelation. No one can presume that God must give that self-revelation. And yet, in Jesus Christ, that revelation, as the self-communication of God as Love, has occurred. All, thereby, is changed. The human drive for transcendence is not merely filled but is surpassed by this decisive manifestation of who God is and who human beings are now empowered to become—those who love the neighbor and the self-communicating God of Jesus Christ.

Theological, as distinct from philosophical, reflection is necessary for human beings to understand themselves in the presence of God's self-communication in Jesus Christ. It is characteristically Catholic for Rahner to give so central a role to dogma in all theological reflection. For the great doctrines—especially, for Rahner, the christological doctrines of Nicaea and Chalcedon—remain a firm ground for the ecclesial understanding of God's revelation in Jesus Christ. As much as did Newman, Rahner found doctrine the necessary implication of that revelation of the Word as true.

As Rahner's own theological reflections unfold, it becomes clear how fruitful, both intellectually and spiritually, his peculiar form of transcendental reflection is for Christian thought and practice. Rahner's thought managed to break the hold of the neo-scholastic manuals in theology by its firm grasp of God's reality as mystery, theology of participatory symbol, and Christocentric anthropology. The spirituality present in his theology is profoundly Ignatian, insofar as the kataphatic elements (images, symbols, doctrines, narratives) of this incarnational vision refer to the everyday and the ordinary. He insists that Christian spirituality is not to be found only in extraordinary experiences but in action-in-the-world for the neighbor and in our most ordinary actions—sitting, walking, eating, conversing—as disclosures of the reality of God. On the other hand, clearly apophatic elements became more prominent in Rahner's later "mystagogical theology." He shows how all theology is, at its best, a "reduction to mystery" and how even our most comprehensible theological reflections must ultimately yield to the radical incomprehensibility of God and of our own selves.

This distinctive union of kataphatic and apophatic elements renders Rahner's transcendental theology singularly modern and Catholic. His theology and spirituality remain radically incarnational and hence kataphatic, while his "turn-to-the-subject" increased rather than decreased the spiritual sense of mystery with each intellectual advance, rendering them profoundly apophatic. Nor was Rahner concerned with having all Catholic theology take his particular route. Rather, he encouraged the development of the mystico-political theology of J. B. Metz and the liberation theology of Gustavo Gutierrez. He not merely welcomed but insisted that the most important feature of contemporary Catholic Christianity is its shift from a Eurocentric church to a truly world church.

Bernard Lonergan, S.J.

In the English-speaking world, the greatest theologian since Newman is undoubtedly the Canadian Jesuit Bernard Lonergan. Like Newman (whose *Grammar of Assent* deeply influenced Lonergan's major philosophical work, *Insight*), Lonergan's thought and spirituality bear a distinctly empirical cast.[4] Although he, like Rahner, would take the turn-to-the-subject of modern thought, his formulation of transcendental method is more accurately described as a "generalized empirical method." Again, like Newman, Lonergan's thought had both an empirical and a historical character. He insisted, in *Method and Theology*, that the major task of theology was to mediate the meaning and value of a religion for a culture.

He argued that the modern period had witnessed a crisis of culture and had misinterpreted that crisis as a crisis of faith. Modern consciousness had moved past classical culture and its certainty in its own cultural norms as definitive for all culture to a historically-minded culture where a plurality of cultures should be acknowledged. There was need, therefore, for a new mediation of the same faith to the new historically-minded culture and, in principle, to all other cultures. There was no need—indeed, no place—for a new faith. Lonergan's defense of and respect for doctrine again resembles Newman's insistence on the necessarily doctrinal character of an objective revelation of God in Jesus Christ.

For Lonergan, the question of God was both implied and demanded by a fidelity to the dynamism of human conscious intentionality. For human consciousness, from scientific inquiry through theological inquiry, from Western classical culture to all cultures, was driven by its need to be faithful to the transcultural—indeed, transcendental—imperatives: "Be attentive, be intelligent, be reasonable, be responsible, be loving and, if necessary, change."[5] Human being, in fidelity to those imperatives at the heart of what it means to be human, may find itself called not merely to develop further but to transform itself radically by finding a new orientation for all its thoughts and actions.

Beyond, therefore, the need for the intellectual and moral radical transformations (or conversions) which Lonergan explicated in *Insight*, he showed the need for and the character of religious conversion for the authentically modern (i.e., both empirically- and historically-minded) inquirer. In harmony with the Catholic *caritas* tradition, Lonergan insisted that, in religious conversion, love must precede knowledge. Religious conversion is

constituted by a "being-in-love-without-restriction." Religious conversion
provides the human being with a new horizon and thereby a new orientation that profoundly affects all knowledge and action. In that sense, faith
is nothing other than a "knowledge-born-of-love." We all recognize that
sense, in however muted a form, is a vector, an undertow, of a "dreaded call
to holiness."[6]

In that sense, moreover, religious conversion provides the foundational
horizon within which the Christian discerns the meaning of doctrines (as
true judgments of fact and value) and initiates the intellectual journey of
theology—a journey which, as converted intellectually, morally, and
religiously, is also a spiritual journey.

In sum, Bernard Lonergan produced a methodology that showed how the
human inquirer in the modern period, by fidelity to the transcendental
imperatives of inquiry itself, could acknowledge the reality of the spiritual.
His work—open to modern historical consciousness and modern science—
was rooted in the Catholic sense of the need for unity-amid-increasing-
diversity. By his argument for the needed shift from classical to historical
consciousness, Lonergan showed theology a way to welcome that diversity.
By his empirical attention to the reality of religious conversion as a being-in-
love-without-restriction, he opened a new spiritual horizon for appropriating spiritually and theologically the classic doctrines of the tradition.

Lonergan, like Newman, freed Catholic spirituality from an overconcern
with conceptualities and provided a new way to discern the subtle distinctions and functional relationships in a life of Catholic spirituality. By
centering spirituality and theology on the reality of God's love, Lonergan
provided a modern way to formulate the traditional insistence on the
indwelling presence of the Spirit as the heart of the Catholic understanding
of church, doctrine, tradition, and community. His theology, like his
spirituality, was equally modern and Catholic. It provides a major empirical
and historically conscious model for a study of the unity-in-diversity of all
Catholic spiritualities.

Pierre Teilhard de Chardin, S.J.

In Teilhard de Chardin, the French Jesuit scientist, philosopher, poet, and
mystic, one major aspect of modernity receives a profoundly Catholic interpretation. At the same time, traditional Catholic spirituality receives a
peculiarly modern reading. To read Teilhard de Chardin is less like reading
a philosopher or theologian or scientist (though he was all three) than it is
like reading a great visionary, at once a poet and a mystic. It is the vision,
above all, that counts. It counts by disclosing a new envisionment of both

traditional Catholic spirituality and scientific modernity in a manner that illuminates and transforms both. In one sense, Teilhard gives a Catholic religious interpretation of evolutionary theory. In another sense, he gives an evolutionary reading of certain central motifs (creation, Incarnation, sacrament, love, a personal God, the cosmic Christ of Paul and John) of Catholic theology and spirituality. He does both simultaneously so that it is often difficult to see where the religious vision begins and the scientific theory ends—and vice versa.

After Teilhard's work, it became difficult for Catholic spirituality to retreat to a merely otherworldly or an anti-matter and anti-action stance. For Teilhard, the Christian's affirmation of the Incarnation freed one to make a religious affirmation of matter and earth. That same affirmation, reinterpreted in an evolutionary perspective, freed Catholic spirituality to recover the great "Cosmic Christ," the *Pantocrator* of the Greek church and of the Johannine and later Pauline (Ephesians and Colossians) traditions. That same incarnational affirmation allowed a construal of the whole cosmos as the diaphanous sacrament of God's loving immanence and the return of the half-forgotten image mysticism in new and modern form.

Teilhard believed that Christians should acknowledge their communion with God through the earth by reflecting anew on their central belief in Incarnation in an evolutionary perspective. That perspective allowed one to see how all creation drives toward new differentiations, greater complexity, and ever-greater convergence of ever-new unity-in-differentiation. That drive, moreover, must be understood spiritually. The drive to convergence is none other, in this spirituality, than the drive from matter to spirit to person to Christ.

The ultimate meaning of the evolutionary process can only be understood Christically. Because of the Incarnation, death, and resurrection of this Jesus of Nazareth who is the Christ, the whole struggle of the universe toward convergence becomes clear. The release of Christ's power upon humanity, history, and the cosmos in the original creation and the new creation of this Jesus as the Christ have made clear what scientists, in practice if not in theory, sense: the whole universe is the sacrament of God. And that sacrament is, through God's own evolutionary process, driven by the power of Christ's love and driven to spirit and the ultimate differentiation-in-unity, the love of God in and for the human in its fullness. For God *is* love, and human beings are those beings driven by matter and mind to acknowledge that love is the convergence, the unity-in-difference, toward which the whole of history and the whole cosmos move. Teilhard united Catholic love mysticism with image mysticism in a Christocentric and evolutionary movement toward the ultimate convergence of all-in-love-with God.

At the same time, Teilhard de Chardin's evolutionary perspective is one of the strongest affirmations of Catholic incarnationalism in the whole tradition. In his spirituality action-in-the-world is as important as suffering. This spirituality, although grounded in the otherworldly, supernatural revelation of the Incarnation, results in a this-worldly spirituality for all Christians who profess their faith in the creation and the Incarnation, death, and physical resurrection of Christ.

The immanence of God in all creation has rarely been portrayed with such spiritual power. However relatively muted Teilhard's sense of God's transcendence may have been and however "impersonal" and even "statistical" his understanding of the human dilemma of sin appears to be, it is difficult to deny the spiritual power of his vision. Too often Catholic spirituality in practice and sometimes in theory seemed to encourage a contempt of matter, of the body and earth, and to demand a flight from this world and from one's responsibility for intelligence (science) and action (the struggle for justice and peace and the harmony of cultures and peoples) in this world.

On these counts alone, the spirituality of Teilhard de Chardin does not rest in the philosophical controversies over his understanding of evolution or the theological controversies on his sometimes excessive optimism on the world. His spirituality rests, instead, in a firm grounding in the creation and Incarnation and, perhaps, above all in the physical resurrection of Christ and what those objective realities demand of the spiritual way for the Christian: a spirituality both otherworldly and this-worldly; a spirituality that affirms both spirit and matter, both cosmos and earth; a creation spirituality that acknowledges love as the clearest understanding we have of God, of ourselves, of history, and the cosmos. However "modern" these spiritual emphases may seem to some Catholics, they represent—as Teilhard's work shows despite its other problems—central aspects of any Catholic incarnational spirituality. For Catholics, the whole cosmos is God's sacrament, for, as Teilhard de Chardin shows, the whole of reality is none other than "the divine milieu."

Hans Urs von Balthasar

This remarkable Swiss theologian has, through his many works, especially his multivolume *The Glory of the Lord,* retrieved much-neglected thematics of the classical Catholic tradition for contemporary spirituality and theology. Although he has written on many aspects of "modernity," von Balthasar is far less interested in "correlating" the Catholic tradition with some aspect of modernity than in retrieving the classic resources of the Catholic tradition for what he views as the bleak landscape of modernity.

Unlike Teilhard de Chardin or even Karl Rahner and Bernard Lonergan, von Balthasar views modernity in fundamentally negative terms. He does not deny the genuine achievements of the Enlightenment, but he prefers Herder's and Goethe's versions to Kant's. He holds that the turn-to-the-subject has had profoundly ambiguous effects: it has overemphasized the subjective element in faith and revelation and has fragmented the earlier tradition's link to the natural order and not merely to human nature. While arid rationalism and excessive abstraction of the "manuals" of much neo-scholastic theology receive as strong a condemnation from von Balthasar as from Rahner and Lonergan, von Balthasar's critique of both modern and traditional theology and spirituality has a different source: both have lost the full importance of the *form* for Christian thought. Here von Balthasar's achievement is fully constructive. Through work which is at once historical and systematic, he shows how Jesus Christ is the visible form of God's own inner-trinitarian self. Hence, an authentic Christian theology and spirituality must concentrate not only on spirit but on body, sense, and nature.

In a brilliant series of studies of the visible form in the great patristic and medieval theologians (especially Bonaventure and Dante), von Balthasar develops a constructive theological aesthetics that bears important consequences for spirituality as well as theology. His insistence on the importance of the visible form of Jesus Christ as the expressive form of God's inner-trinitarian self directs spiritual and theological attention to the radically incarnational and sacramental nature of objective revelation and Catholic faith. His emphasis on the role of beauty (as the shining forth of truth *in* the visible form) returns Catholic spirituality to a firmer sense of the importance of ritual, drama, icon, image, symbol, and word itself as visible form.

More than any other Catholic theologian in modernity, von Balthasar recovers the kataphatic tradition for an incarnational Catholic sensibility. He shows the creative continuity of traditional symbols with the form of forms, the Word of God, Jesus Christ, thus providing a careful corrective of the Platonic element in Catholic spirituality.

Unlike Plato, but with Dante, von Balthasar insists that the love of God is to be found *in* the visible form—including the visible forms of the many saints who show the reality of the super-form of forms, God's own true form, Jesus Christ. This deeply incarnational vision, with its concentration on the objective reality of the revealed visible form, helps Catholic spirituality to be in-formed and trans-formed anew through attention to all true forms: the analogies of beauty in the cosmos (as in Gerard Manley

7. Georges Rouault, *Head of Christ*, 1905.

Hopkins), the narratives of the saints, the visibility of the Scriptures, the rituals, the Eucharist, the sacraments—and all the great Christian artists (from Dante to Claudel) who understood the importance of the visible form. The form of Incarnation is at the same time, for von Balthasar, the form of the cross. His theology pays equal attention to the sufferings, conflicts, and tragedies of human existence and to the joy of creation and resurrection.

Von Balthasar's concern and ability to conserve a tradition that could be lost in modern culture, especially the reality of visible form and the importance of beauty-in-the-form of Jesus Christ, constitute a major contribution to a modern spirituality, subject to the danger of being form-less.

Catholic Philosophy and Spirituality

Some recent philosophers have also contributed greatly to the retrieval of classic Catholic spiritualities as they face the dilemmas of modernity. Representative works here include the important study of mysticism by the great neo-Thomist philosopher Jacques Maritain in *Degrees of Knowledge,* and the philosophico-psychological study of mysticism by the transcendental Thomist Joseph Marechal, S.J., in *The Psychology of the Mystics.*[7] The phenomenological tradition in Catholic philosophy, moreover, has been especially productive of works reflective on spirituality: witness the work of Max Scheler (in his Catholic period), Edith Stein, and Romano Guardini.

The German philosopher Edith Stein applied the phenomenological method to the study of Catholic spirituality, and, as E. Husserl's assistant, produced a fine study of empathy. After her conversion from Judaism to Catholicism, Stein wrote several illuminating studies on the relationship between phenomenology and Thomist philosophy. Substantive as these philosophical and cultural contributions are, the importance of Edith Stein for the expression and development of modern Catholic spirituality lies in her work on Carmelite mystics, written after she entered the Carmelite order and adopted the name of Sister Benedicta. Her works of that period culminated in her penetrating *Ways of Knowing God* and her tribute to her Carmelite spirituality in *The Science of the Cross.*

She showed how the tradition of love mysticism of the great Carmelite doctors of the church, Teresa of Avila and John of the Cross, may revitalize the idea of "soul" as that interior life to which God is present. Not knowledge but love constitutes the essence of the soul. This thesis—taught with such power by Teresa and John—became for the philosopher Stein the signal truth of her own thinking. If God is love, then the trinitarian reality of God is less a question for philosophical and theological speculation than an existential response to the reality of God's love-in-love.

Her study of John of the Cross in her major work, *The Science of the Cross,* captures the power of the earlier Carmelite's love mysticism and theology of the cross for a Europe devastated by the horrors of the years 1914–1945: years which included her own murder as a Jew by the Nazis at Auschwitz in 1942. Her fidelity to the "Science of the Cross" and God's love at the heart of all reality and at the core of every human soul discloses the entire meaning of her life and, indeed, the message to the modern struggle to recover the life of the Spirit:

> We are a spiritually impoverished generation; we search in all places the Spirit ever flowed in the hope of finding water. For if the spirit is living and never dies, the Spirit must still be present wherever the Spirit once was active forming human life and the work of human hands. Not in a trail of monuments, however—in a secret, mysterious life. The Spirit is like a small but carefully tended spark, ready to flare, glow and burst into flame the moment the spirit feels the first enkindling breath.[8]

In the same direction, the contemporary philosopher Louis Dupré has stressed the peculiarly modern intellectual's need to mediate the spiritual life through a speculative (philosophical-spiritual) rereading of the classic mystic texts of the tradition. His own rethinking of Ruusbroec's trinitarian mysticism presents an example of this kind of a philosophical mediation of the classic mystical texts in and for a modern spirituality. Similar exercises show the philosophical significance of the great image mystics and, especially, the turn to the "earthy" and "common" realities highlighted by the stress on the humanity of Christ in Teresa of Avila and other Christian love mystics.

In sum, philosophical reflection on the classic mystical texts illuminates both the philosophical and spiritual issues at stake in modernity. Philosophically our alternatives need to be limited by the individualism inherent in the modern model of the purely autonomous self; nor the "death of the subject" of much post-modern thought; nor the vain attempt to move to a pre-modern understanding of self-in-community of much neo-conservative thought. Rather, a phenomenological reading of the classic mystical texts can mediate to modern intellectuals the apophatic sense of spiritual emptiness and of the spiritual need for our negation of all our names for God and soul. A similar retrieval of the classic spiritual resources in the image mystics, the trinitarian mystics, and the love mystics could lead to a deeper spiritual sense of the goodness of creation and a spiritual affirmation of finitude-even-in-its-imperfection for the modern intellectual. The return to activity in its most common and earthy senses so classically portrayed in the post-apophatic mystical theology of Jan van Ruusbroec receives here a new mediation, both spiritual and philosophical, for the modern intellectual Christian.

Beginnings of the Mystico-Prophetic Approach: Merton and Day

Thomas Merton

Thomas Merton, a Trappist monk with the religious name Father Louis, has been one of the most influential proponents of the spiritual life in the twentieth century. A study of the thirty books and numerous poems and articles of this prodigious writer and poet reveals the reasons for his influence. Although Merton provided little that could be considered purely original, his achievement is remarkable in its fully representative nature. In book after book, he rethought in contemporary terms the rich variety of the entire mystical tradition. Few writers have made so deliberate an effort to recover the full range of the mystical traditions in the two-thousand-year history of Catholic spirituality—from the image mysticism of Gregory of Nyssa, Origen, and the great Eastern tradition through the trinitarian mysticism of Merton's own Cistercian tradition and the apophatic radicality of Meister Eckhart to the great love mystics from Bernard of Clairvaux to John of the Cross and Teresa of Avila; from the speculative heights of an Origen or an Eckhart through the autobiographical genius of a Teresa of Avila to the commonsensical simplicity and beauty of the English mystics.

To read Thomas Merton is to find all these often-conflicting Catholic spiritualities, sometimes singly, sometimes together, rendered into plausible spiritual options for contemporary life. The full secret of Merton's representativeness, however, lies not in his analysis of the mystical tradition (although he was always informed by good scholarship) but in its contemporary, literary presentation.

His life, his person, his lifelong rethinking of his own spirituality bear a typically twentieth-century character. At peace, yet never at peace, Merton struggled to find in both the rich Catholic tradition and the ever-shifting contours of the contemporary world a spirituality that was believably Catholic (in its very pluralism and universality) and plausibly modern (in its very restlessness and not-at-homeness in the bleak spiritual landscape of modernity).

Like many modern persons in quest of the life of the spirit, Merton found himself most at home in the tradition of darkness so congruous to those intellectually alive to the spiritual emptiness of our time. It induced him to explore not only the apophatic elements in John of the Cross, Julian of Norwich, and Meister Eckhart but also the theology of Paul Tillich and much existentialist philosophy. In his later years, he studied the understanding of reality as *sunyata* (emptiness) in Zen thought and Tibetan Buddhism. His attraction to a life of radical solitude—as in his troubled commitment to both a monastic community and an eremitical life as a monk—reflects this same apophatic spirituality.

At the same time, Merton, precisely as a monk in community and in the Cistercian tradition, effected ever-new readings of the image mysticism of his monastic heritage. Ever anew he asserted how each person is an image, in Christ, of God's own self. That vision of the image of God in all humans enabled Merton to articulate for his contemporaries suffering from the devastating effects of modern individualism how to recover the "true self" (the image of God) even in their distorted and estranged present selves. Thus, Merton proved a reliable guide to many who longed to partake of the great monastic traditions, even while remaining in the world.

In his final years, he embarked upon a yet more radical spiritual quest. His apophatic spirituality opened him to dialogues with Zen and Tibetan Buddhists. Here in the profoundly apophatic nature of Zen, Merton found a spirituality that had the potential for strengthening Christian spirituality as well. This ecumenicity occurred for Merton at the same time that he committed himself to a mystico-prophetic spirituality. Merton's commitment, as a monk grounded in the mystical tradition, became more and more a prophetic spirituality of action for peace and justice. This is manifest in his 1960s works, especially *Conjectures of a Guilty Bystander*. The Christian, even the monk, he insisted, is freed from the world *for* the world and is obliged, in whatever manner possible, to speak, write, and act in behalf of the oppressed and for a nonviolent Christian ministry of peace and justice. This rare combination of spiritual openness to the traditions of the East and of insistence, on inner-mystical grounds, on prophetic witness and action made Merton's writings and actions in his final years truly representative of the radical turn in Catholic spirituality itself to a world church of genuine ecumenicity and to a prophetic ministry of nonviolence for peace and justice. As the writings on his work increase exponentially, it seems clear that the influence of this Catholic monk-writer will continue. As embedded in the mystical, intellectual, and institutional realities of Catholicism, Merton's own quest saw the need to open that rich tradition more and more to its own mystico-prophetic spirituality of witness for peace and justice and to its own deepest catholicity as a radical openness to other spiritual traditions.

Dorothy Day

Few persons have been as influential in actualizing a new Catholic spirituality for the modern industrial and technological world as the remarkable

writer, spiritual leader, and social-justice activist Dorothy Day. Like her
Russian spiritual mentors Dostoevsky and Berdyaev, and her French
cofounder of the Catholic Worker movement, Peter Maurin, Day believed
that the life of the spirit was the secret to all history and that this life could
only be a life of spirit-in-community. This communitarian Christian personalism insisted on the dignity of every human individual as actual or
potential members of the Mystical Body of Christ.

Unlike other forms of Catholic spirituality, however, Day held that a life
of the spirit in commuity need not withdraw from the economic-social-
cultural world of action for the oppressed. The mystical character of her
profoundly personalist Christian spirituality was rendered into prophetic
action for justice. Her spirituality is misconstrued if it is interpreted as
simply that of a social activitist who came to acknowledge the truth of the
spirit. It is more accurate to say that, after her conversion to Catholicism
following her deep involvement in radical social politics in the American
setting of the early twentieth century, Day developed a Catholic spirituality
wherein the prophetic call to social justice must be understood as at the
heart of the Christian spiritual life.

Her spiritual theology was articulated in her contribution to her advocacy
newspaper, *The Catholic Worker,* and in her many writings. Dorothy Day
also founded the Houses of Hospitality for the poorest of the poor in the
industrial cities of North America, as well as farm communes, in the course
of her constant, deliberate, and unyielding actions on behalf of peace and
social justice. The central characteristics of that theology, as she insisted in
her autobiography, *The Long Loneliness,* was its belief that "all is grace" and
that love in action was the central way to bring the reality of God to life.

She often referred to a passage in Dostoevsky's *The Brothers Karamazov*
as the key to the meaning of the Catholic Worker movement.

> Love in action is a harsh and dreadful thing compared with love in dreams.
> Love in dreams is greedy for immediate action, rapidly performed and in the
> sight of all. Men will even give their lives if only the ordeal does not last long
> but is soon over, with all onlooking and applauding as though on the stage.
> But love is labor and fortitude. . . . Just when you see with horror that in
> spite of all your efforts you are getting further from your goal instead of
> nearer to it—at that very moment . . . you will reach it and behold clearly the
> miraculous power of the Lord who has been all the time loving and
> mysteriously guiding you.[9]

This spirituality of a "harsh and dreadful love in action" became in
Dorothy Day's work both a lifelong series of actions and, in keeping with
her role as an organic intellectual, an intellectual defense and development
in her writings. Intellectually and practically, Day's spirituality comprised

the following seven themes: (1) Despite its great scientific achievements, the industrial and technological modern world is spirit-bereft. The bourgeois spirit levels the demands and possibilities of the spirit into mere private ecstasies and marginalized utopian dreams. Only the reality of the spirit in action can hope to challenge so deadening and enveloping an environment. (2) Each individual has a special inviolable worth and each has equal responsibility for all others. (3) This responsibility of the spirit, in this spirit-less environment, is best met by living in community with the poor and all those others who join in the struggle for the spirit. (4) If that struggle is to be real, then action for the poor must be forthcoming. That action demands responsibility for caring and feeding the poor in the cities of the modern world. (Here Day's spirituality parallels the equally remarkable spirituality of *caritas*-in-action of her mutual admirer, Mother Teresa of Calcutta.) (5) That action also demands a commitment to the struggle for social justice wherever it occurs and the struggle for peace. (Here Day's spirituality parallels the social-justice spirituality of love-in-action of her other great mutual admirer, Dom Helder Camara of Recife, Brazil.) (6) The proper spirituality for this struggle should include a voluntary poverty for a life of religious nonviolence. (Here Day's spirituality parallels the classic nonviolence positions of Mahatma Gandhi and Martin Luther King, Jr.) (7) The aim for society is to find a "third way" between the two dehumanizing and despiritualizing systems of Marxism and capitalism. For Day, in harmony with one strand of the Catholic social-justice tradition of the papal encyclicals and in harmony with the personalist movement in France of Emmanuel Mounier and her cofounder, Peter Maurin, this "third way" societal model was communitarian. It was based on the personalist belief that only by a conversion of the individual could society ultimately be changed, but that such a conversion must be in and for the community of the poor and oppressed. This was, for her, the hope of the spirit that may aid the eventual development of a decentralized, simpler society based on cooperative, personalist sharing of goods in accord with Christian principles of love and justice.

Like her contemporary Simone Weil, Dorothy Day believed that the rootless, spirit-bereft character of our modern bourgeois world demands the development of a new kind of mystic-prophetic spirituality and even a new kind of saintliness-in-the-world struggling for justice and peace. In both action and thought, Dorothy Day rendered present the reality of that new Catholic spiritual vision. Its influence has been strong in all the great mystico-political movements of action and thought across the Catholic world in the late twentieth century. Its impact is both practical and intellectual. Both, in her case, are rooted in the reality of spirit and appeal to all who sense that reality at all: as she wrote in *The Long Loneliness,* "We have all known the long loneliness and we have learned that the only solution is love and that love comes with community. . . . It all happened while we sat there talking, and it is still going on."[10]

Recent Developments in the Mystical-Prophetic Strands of Catholic Spirituality

We have seen how the main elements of modern Catholic spirituality were initially elaborated by Newman and von Hügel. Each element (the institutional, the intellectual, and the mystical) received distinct new forms in the modern era. Especially through the institutional, theological, and religious changes of the watershed event of modern Catholicism, the Second Vatican Council (1961–1965), new forms of Catholic spirituality emerged throughout the Catholic world. As Karl Rahner argued, the Second Vatican Council may be viewed theologically as the affirmation of the emergence of a post-Eurocentric, global church. A series of new Catholic spiritualities across the globe has led to several fresh emphases. Central to all these spiritualities, we shall suggest below, is the articulation, in several forms, of a new paradigm for Catholic spirituality: a mystico-prophetic model. Three issues may help to clarify some of the different forms this model is taking in our period: the liberation theologies with their emphasis on justice; the new creation-centered spiritualities with their recovery of nature and cosmos; and the new openness to the spiritual riches of the other great spiritual traditions as clarified by inner-Christian ecumenical dialogue and wider interreligious dialogue.

Before studying these new forms of modern Catholic spirituality, however, it is equally important to emphasize the continuing integrity and even new forms of more traditional Catholic spiritualities in the modern period. To be sure, certain traditional practices of piety have shown some decline: novenas, the recitation of the Rosary, and Benediction. Even so, one can still observe the continuing strength and import of these traditional forms of Catholic spirituality for millions of modern Catholics: witness the continuing import of Marian piety in such different settings as Lourdes, Fatima, Guadalupe, and Czestochowa.

At the same time, the classic traditions of Catholic spirituality live in ever-new forms in our period: the Benedictine, Carthusian, Dominican, Franciscan, Carmelite, and Jesuit types of spirituality along with the development of new religious orders and secular institutes both maintain the classic Catholic traditions and find new ways to allow these traditions to live in the modern world. Three figures are outstanding representatives of new ways in which the centrality to the spiritual life of the Catholic emphasis on *caritas* finds expression: St. Thérèse of Lisieux, Charles de Foucauld, and Mother Teresa of Calcutta. Each of these exceptional spiritual persons helped to articulate new ways to actualize Catholic *caritas* in the modern world. Thérèse of Lisieux, by her life as a Carmelite sister and her spiritual autobiography, clarified a way of spiritual life both for her fellow Carmelites and for many Catholics in the everyday world. Her "little way" (in contrast to the classic mystical journey of her Carmelite predecessor, Teresa of Avila) enabled many to observe the spirituality of small actions for *caritas* in the everyday world. Her influence continues to grow as more and more Catholics look for better ways to live a believable spiritual life in their ordinary, everyday existence.

Charles de Foucauld and Mother Teresa of Calcutta have helped define new ways for the *caritas* tradition to live amid the poor and marginalized of our world. Both of these spiritual figures have found the way of *caritas* expressed in specific actions of love for the poor, the outcast, and the dying of our age to be *the* way to show the concreteness of the power of love. Both left writings that clarify the vision of *caritas* that had transformed their lives and informed their concrete actions, and both founded or inspired others to found new religious orders to continue their visions: the Little Brothers and Sisters inspired by Charles de Foucauld and the Sisters founded by Mother Teresa of Calcutta.

The ability, in terms of concrete actions and simple prose, to render the reality of *caritas* in the midst of ordinary life (Thérèse of Lisieux) and in the midst of great poverty and suffering (Charles de Foucauld and Mother Teresa of Calcutta) has made all three figures classic expressions of Catholic *caritas*-centered spirituality in our modern period.

Liberation Spirituality

Foremost among emerging forms of Catholic spirituality are the many liberation theologies and spiritualities of the twentieth century. These theologies were initially inspired by the biblical revival (especially its retrieval of eschatology and the prophetic call to justice), the call to involvement in the struggle for social and political justice of the Second Vatican Council and the papal social encyclicals as well as the emergence of European "political theologies." At the same time, the theologies of liberation have brought a new emphasis and complexity to Catholic spirituality. Their primary spiritual insistence is upon the prophetic call to the struggle for justice which they see at the heart of the Christian understanding of total transformation. Their central innovation (like that of Merton and Day before them) is to forge an unbreakable link between the power of love and the struggle for full justice. To rethink the love–justice dialectic of Christian life, these theologians have chosen total spiritual and worldly liberation— personal, economic, cultural, political, and religious—as their central sym- bol for an adequate Catholic spirituality. In institutional terms, the most important declarations of this new liberationist spirituality may be found in the documents of the Latin American bishops at Medellin (1968) and Puebla (1977); in the often-quoted words of the 1971 synod of bishops: "Action on behalf of justice and participation in the transformation of the world fully appear to us as a constitutive dimension of the preaching of the gospel";[11] in the language of "the preferential option for the poor" used by many bishops and by Pope John Paul II himself; in the actions for love and justice of religious and bishops like Dom Helder Camara of Recife, Brazil; and, above all, in the development of new institutional ecclesial realities such as the thousands of "base communities" in Latin America and through- out the Catholic world where common Scripture reading, prayer, liturgy, and spiritual actions inform how these small communities of laypersons and religious attempt to discern the meaning of the gospel call to *metanoia* in their own concrete struggles for justice.

In theological terms, the founding document of this new spirituality and theology is the work of the Peruvian theologian Gustavo Gutierrez, *A Theology of Liberation*. As Gutierrez's own further work and that of many of his colleagues show, liberation theology is grounded in both the spirituality of the people and in many traditional forms of Catholic spirituality: witness the popular piety honored in Gutierrez's *We Drink From Our Own Wells* and Gutierrez's own biblical roots reflected in his theological-spiritual study of Job; the Franciscan sense of community and the call to voluntary poverty and the spiritual awakening of the people in Brazilian Leonardo Boff's theology; and the use of the Ignatian exercises in the theology of Salvadoran Jon Sobrino.

The Latin Americans have led the way for the whole Catholic world in the development of diverse liberation theologies and spiritualities. Nonetheless, new and different forms of a liberationist position may be found in Asian (especially Indian, Korean, and Philippino), African, and in black, Hispanic, and Native American theologies of North America. Moreover, Western European and North American forms of political theology and Eastern European spiritualities (e.g., the Solidarity movement in Poland) share many of the emphases on the importance of justice of their liberationist colleagues.

This same emphasis upon the struggle for justice as being central to Catholic spirituality has led to the development of new Catholic feminist theologies with liberationist themes. Given the role of women throughout the history of Catholic spirituality, these theologies are recovering a too often-forgotten, even repressed history. Witness the study of the role of women in the New Testament by Elisabeth Schüssler Fiorenza, the analysis of the voices of women mystics by many scholars, and the prophetic self-critique of the patriarchal elements in the prophetic tradition itself by theologians like Rosemary Radford Ruether and Anne Carr.

These theologies cast a stern spiritual light of suspicion on the traditional roles of women in all aspects of Catholic institutional, intellectual, and religious life. This new sense of biblical-prophetic justice, moreover, is likely to generate a rereading of the great women spiritual leaders (e.g., Teresa of Avila, Catherine of Siena, Catherine of Genoa, Jeanne Guyon, Dorothy Day), of religious communities (e.g., the beguines), and of the patriarchal prejudices embedded in classic and modern Catholic spiritualities. The future may thus witness a further and yet more radical rereading of Catholic institutional, intellectual, and religious life inspired by the profound spiritual power of both feminist retrieval of often-forgotten spiritual resources and prophetic feminist suspicion of injustice to women in classic spiritualities in the tradition.

Creation-Centered Spirituality: The Recovery of Nature

The prophetic call to the struggle for justice has also helped to impel a new spiritual movement among many modern Catholics. As the full extent of the ecological crisis becomes clear and the threat of nuclear holocaust is more widely appreciated, the call for full justice to all other living forms on our fragile planet becomes a new spiritual journey. For some, the prophetic tradition may suffice to clarify the dilemma of our estrangement from and elimination of nature and to provide sufficient spiritual resources: hence, the recovery in many modern prophetic spiritualities and theologies of the biblical-prophetic sense of human beings as the stewards of all creation.

For others, however, even the prophetic tradition with its powerful critique and its call for justice will not suffice. For these "creation-centered" spiritualities, traditional spirituality may be too anthropocentric—and too oriented to the doctrine of human redemption rather than the doctrine of creation (both the original creation and the new creation proclaimed in Colossians and Ephesians and rearticulated, as we saw above, in Teilhard de Chardin).

Thus, the call to creation-centered spiritualities has led to a study of many neglected elements of Catholic spirituality: the wisdom traditions of both

Testaments with their cosmocentric rather than simply anthropocentric outlook; the Franciscan tradition with its vision of our relationships not only to our fellow human beings but to all living creatures as expressed in the actions and prayers of Francis of Assisi and in the great symbolic and sacramental theology of Bonaventure; the doctrine of Incarnation as implying a far greater respect for our embodied nature and our relationships with nature and the whole cosmos as found in the classic theologies of Eastern Christianity and in many mystics, especially women mystics; the need to rethink the relationships to earlier traditions like the ancient goddess traditions; the traditional Christian disparagement or patronizing of more holistic and nature-oriented traditions like those of Africa or the native traditions of the Americas and Europe; the need to recall "nature" to a central place in the Catholic spiritual tradition, which has often proved too anthropocentric; the need to learn how other religious traditions have maintained the bond to nature and cosmos with greater power than many forms of Catholic spirituality.

Perhaps we can say that just as the more prophetic orientation of liberation theologies has, in recent years, opened to a rethinking of the cosmic and mystical traditions, so too creation-centered spiritualities and theologies are opening to a greater concern with the struggle for human justice as central to their own creation-centered spiritual way. In sum, both are learning new ways to develop a mystico-prophetic spirituality and theology. Part of that search will be a new opening of Catholic spirituality to the other religious traditions.

Ecumenical and Interreligious Dialogue

The biblical, liturgical, and patristic revivals of Catholic Christianity allied to the remarkable openness of Vatican II have encouraged Catholic spirituality toward a new Christian ecumenical attitude and toward serious interreligious dialogue.

Ecumenically considered, Catholic spirituality has rediscovered the Reformed emphasis on the word (as for example in the works of Hans Küng) at the same time as many Reformed traditions have rediscovered their sacramental heritage. The development of both Protestant and Catholic spiritualities in the modern period, therefore, has proved far more ecumenical on both sides: witness the influence of Søren Kierkegaard, Dietrich Bonhoeffer, Dorothea Soelle, and Martin Luther King, Jr., on many Catholics and the influence of Friedrich von Hügel, Edith Stein, Thomas Merton, and Dorothy Day on many Protestants in our period. Moreover, the emergence of prophetically oriented liberation spiritualities as well as the reemergence of great interest in the mystical aspects of the tradition have both stimulated and been stimulated by interconfessional scholarship on the entire history of Christian spirituality. Among both Catholics and Protestants, there is an increased sense of the need for an ecumenically Christian mystico-prophetic spirituality for our times.

Both Catholics and Protestants, moreover, have begun to note not only the power and promise but also the limitations of their own history-oriented Augustinian spiritual heritage. In their need for reflection on our relationships with nature and the cosmos (and not only history), Catholics and Protestants have found themselves learning anew from the great cosmocentric theologies of Orthodoxy. This has occasioned a recovery of the great image mysticism and trinitarian mysticism of Origen, Clement, and Gregory of Nyssa and the discovery of the classic Byzantine spirituality of Gregory Palamas. This same ecumenical sense for cosmocentric-mystical traditions has occasioned, as Gershom Scholem observes in the Jewish case of kabbalistic mysticism, a need to rediscover the archaic heritage of the common tradition. Here the work of Mircea Eliade, the great Romanian Orthodox historian of religions, has furnished new ways to recover the cosmocentric power of the fuller Christian tradition. This Christian ecumenical dialogue has encouraged a search among many Christians for a Christian mystico-prophetic spirituality that could prove responsive to the riches of the full Christian heritage and fruitful for the religious needs, both historical and cosmic, of our day.

Catholic spirituality has also learned new ways to conduct a dialogue with the great tradition of Jewish spirituality. Theologies inspired by Franz Rosenzweig's notion of the "two covenants" as well as the need for a "return to history" by both Jew and Christian in facing the massive horror of the Holocaust (theologically reconstructed as the *Shoah*) have impelled many Catholics to learn in new ways from their Jewish colleagues in both theology and spirituality. The renewed sense of the Jewish insight into the importance of narrative for Christian self-understanding, a firmer grasp of the genius of rabbinic Judaism on the law, and a properly spiritual Christian sense of repentance for the revolting history of Catholic anti-Semitism have opened new possibilities for Catholic–Jewish dialogue on theology and on a mutually transforming spirituality of messianic hope. The Jewish roots of all Christian spirituality have rarely been more apparent, as liberation theologies and all covenantal theologies make clear. The rediscovery of the mystical theologies of Judaism by Scholem and other scholars has reopened, in Judaism as it has in Christianity, the need for a mystico-prophetic option for our times.

The Islamic tradition continues, for both Jew and Christian, to be the third covenantal partner whose rich heritage, at once so different and so similar, needs further honor. The hope for a Jewish–Christian–Islamic dialogue on their common spiritual needs in modernity is in its early stages. Yet that dialogue promises to bear much fruit as these three descendants of Abraham and Sarah learn both to recover their common biblical and medieval heritages and to find modern dialogical ways to aid their common monotheistic spirituality.

All three monotheistic traditions, moreover, have found new ways, in the midst of interreligious dialogue, to discover and learn from the other great spiritual ways. In the Catholic case, these developments are many. In African and Melanesian Catholicism, a new respect has grown for the primal traditions of the African and Melanesian spiritualities. In Latin and North America, there is a rethinking (with an attendant repentance for the past) of the native primal traditions of the Americas: witness the debates on "popular religion" in Latin American Catholicism; the sensed need to learn from the holistic vision of native traditions among many North American Catholics; and the rediscovery of African spiritual roots among many North American, Brazilian, and Caribbean black Christians.

Just at the time when the need in a post-Eurocentric world church for a more global Catholic spirituality was accelerating, Catholic thinkers in Asia were leading the way in serious interreligious dialogue with the great Asian traditions. Again, the examples are many: European and North American theologians of spirituality like Thomas Merton (in Thailand), Bede Griffiths (in India), and William Johnston (in Japan) have risked new ways to incorporate some of the riches of Eastern forms of spirituality (especially Buddhist and Hindu) within a transformed (or, as Merton said, a "self-transcending") Catholic spirituality. Native Asian Catholics, moreover, have found new ways to rethink their Christian heritage in their own spiritual cultures. The dialogues with Muslims in Mindanao, the Christian–Islamic–Hindu dialogue in India, the new forms of spirituality for Catholic Christians in Korea, Japan, and Taiwan encourage the hope that an emerging world church will find new ways to develop a global and dialogical spirituality. Central to that hope will be, for Catholics, the firm foundations laid by Newman and von Hügel for the "three elements" of Catholic Christianity (the institutional, intellectual, and mystical elements). Allied to that hope will be the new elements: the prophetic-liberationist emphasis on the struggle for justice in all Catholic spirituality; the renewed respect for nature in creation-centered spiritualities; and the spiritual openness occasioned by the inner-Catholic sense of the emergence of a world church and by the increasing sense of the Christian need for an ecumenical spirituality and for the mutual transformations afforded by all serious interreligious dialogue.

Perhaps it is not too much to hope that central to all these developments is the paradigm that even Newman and von Hügel did not fully sense: the need, within Catholic Christianity, for a richer unity amid ever greater diversity—for a Catholic, global, mystico-prophetic spirituality.

Notes

1. John Henry Newman, *Apologia pro Vita Sua,* 4.
2. Cited in Wilfrid Ward, *The Life of John Henry Cardinal Newman* (London: Longman, Green, 1912) 2:460.
3. Karl Rahner, *Spirit in the World* (New York: Herder & Herder, 1968); *Hearers of the Word* (New York: Herder & Herder, 1969).
4. John Henry Newman, *An Essay in Aid of a Grammar of Assent* (London: Longman, Green, 1891).
5. Bernard Lonergan, *Method in Theology,* 231.
6. Ibid., 105.
7. Jacques Maritain, *Degrees of Knowledge* (New York: Scribner, 1918); Joseph Marechal, *The Psychology of the Mystics* (London: Burns, Oates, & Washbourne, 1927).
8. Quoted in Waltraud Herbstrith, *Edith Stein* (San Francisco: Harper & Row, 1985) 131.
9. Referred to in Dorothy Day, *The Long Loneliness,* 43, 107.
10. Ibid., 286.
11. "Justice in the World," no. 6, in *The Gospel of Peace and Justice,* ed. Joseph Gremillion.

Bibliography

Sources

Balthasar, Hans Urs von. *The Glory of the Lord.* 3 vols. Edinburgh: T. & T. Clark, 1982–86.

———. *Love Alone: The Way of Revelation.* London: Burns & Oates, 1968.

———. *Thérèse of Lisieux: The Story of a Mission.* London: Sheed & Ward, 1953.

Carr, Anne E. *A Search for Wisdom and Spirit: Thomas Merton's Theology of the Self.* Notre Dame, IN: University of Notre Dame Press, 1988.

———. *Transforming Grade: Christian Tradition and Women's Experience.* San Francisco: Harper & Row, 1987.

de Chardin, Pierre Teilhard. *The Divine Milieu: An Essay on the Interior Life.* New York: Harper & Row, 1960.

———. *The Future of Man.* New York: Harper & Row, 1964.

———. *How I Believe.* New York: Harper & Row, 1969.

———. *The Phenomenon of Man.* New York: Harper & Row, 1959.

Day, Dorothy. *The Long Loneliness.* New York: Image, 1968.

Dupré, Louis. *The Common Life: The Origins of Trinitarian Mysticism and Its Development by Jan Ruusbroec.* New York: Crossroad, 1984.

——. *The Deeper Life: An Introduction to Christian Mysticism.* New York: Crossroad, 1981.

——. *The Other Dimension: A Search for the Meaning of Religious Attitudes.* New York: Doubleday, 1972.

de Foucauld, Charles. *Spiritual Autobiography of Charles de Foucauld.* Edited by J. F. Six. New York: Kennedy, 1964.

Gutierrez, Gustavo. *On Job: God-Talk and the Suffering of the Innocent.* Maryknoll, NY: Orbis, 1987.

——. *A Theology of Liberation.* Maryknoll, NY: Orbis, 1973.

——. *We Drink From Our Own Wells.* Maryknoll, NY: Orbis, 1984.

Hügel, Friedrich von. *The Mystical Element of Religion as Studied in Saint Catherine of Genoa and Her Friends.* 2 vols. London: Dent, 1908.

Lonergan, Bernard. *Insight: A Study of Human Understanding.* New York: Philosophical Society, 1970.

——. *Method in Theology.* New York: Seabury, 1972.

Merton, Thomas. *Conjectures of a Guilty Bystander.* Garden City, NY: Doubleday, 1966.

——. *Contemplative Prayer.* New York: Image, 1970.

——. *Life and Holiness.* New York: Doubleday, 1973.

——. *Mystics and Zen Masters.* New York: Well, 1969.

——. *New Seeds of Contemplation.* New York: New Directions, 1972.

Newman, John Henry. *Apologia pro Vita Sua.* London: Longmans, Roberts & Green, 1864. Reprint, Oxford: Clarendon, 1967.

——. *Essay on the Development of Doctrine.* London: J. Toovey, 1845.

——. *Meditations and Devotions.* London: Burns & Oages, 1964.

——. *Parochial and Plain Sermons.* London: Pickering, 1958.

Rahner, Karl. *Foundations of Christian Faith.* New York: Crossroad, 1978.

Ruether, Rosemary Radford. *Sexism and God-Talk: Toward a Feminist Theology.* Boston: Beacon Press, 1983.

Schüssler Fiorenza, Elisabeth. *In Memory of Her: A Feminist Theological Reconstruction of Christian Origins.* New York: Crossroad, 1983.

Sobrino, Jon. *Spirituality of Liberation: Toward a Political Holiness.* Maryknoll, NY: Orbis, 1988.

Stein, Edith. *The Science of the Cross.* Chicago: Regnery, 1960.

——. *Ways to Know God.* Washington: The Thomist, 1946.

Thérèse of Lisieux, Saint. *The Autobiography of St. Therese of Lisieux.* New York: Image, 1959.

Studies

Bouyer, Louis. *Newman, His Life and Spirituality.* London: Burns & Oates, 1958.

Gremillion, Joseph, ed. *The Gospel of Peace and Justice.* Maryknoll, NY: Orbis, 1976.

Hamilton, E. *The Desert My Dwelling Place: A Study of Charles de Foucauld.* London: Hodder & Stoughton, 1968.

Haughey, John C., ed. *The Faith That Does Justice.* New York: Paulist, 1973.

Herbstrith, Waltraud. *Edith Stein.* San Francisco: Harper & Row, 1985.

de Lubac, Henri. *The Religion of Teilhard de Chardin.* Garden City, NY: Doubleday, 1968.

Miller, William D. *Dorothy Day.* San Francisco: Harper & Row, 1982.

Nédoncelle, Maurice. *Baron Friedrich von Hügel, His Life and Thought.* London: Longmans, 1937.

O'Donovan, Leo, ed. *A World of Grace: An Introduction to the Themes and Foundations of Karl Rahner's Theology.* New York: Crossroad, 1978.

Riches, John, ed. *The Analogy of Beauty: The Theology of Hans Urs von Balthasar.* Edinburgh: T. & T. Clark, 1986.

Tracy, David. *The Achievement of Bernard Lonergan.* New York: Herder & Herder, 1971.

7

Excursus
Reading Holy Writ:
The Locus of Modern Spirituality

DAVID S. PACINI

D EFINING MODERN SPIRITUALITY remains precipitous, even today, for we have had to resign ourselves to the inevitable: we are probably only beginning to discover in what "modernity" consists.[1] Hence, the wariness with which any attempt to chart the course of modern spirituality must proceed may better be understood as symptomatic of the subject matter rather than as a literal conceit.

What we have known about modernity for some time now is that during the second half of the seventeenth century a shift occurred, or was occurring, in the Western conception of language. It was as if language suddenly became opaque. Whereas it had long been understood as a transparent medium through which the divine chain of being shined, language now appeared more as a dense web with a seemingly inscrutable history of its own. When Francis Bacon separated discourse from reason in his revision of the medieval trivium of grammar, logic, and rhetoric, and proposed a comparative philology for the study of the relations among words, things, and reason; when David Ricardo sought to demonstrate the relation of labor conditions to economic production as a touchstone for evaluating social choice; when Georges Cuvier set out to prove that the relation of organic activities to physical and chemical processes is not exemplified by general laws but by characteristics of organic systems; when, in a word, the common locus or great chain of being was eclipsed by competing and perturbing claims about the relationships between language, things, and order, the penumbral effect doomed the knower to a new role.[2] For, once the divinely preestablished correspondence between words and the primitive elements of creation is lost, the lacuna poses for language an unprecedented undertaking: the task of establishing the proper relationship between words and what they signify. Shifting the understanding of language in this way is thus obviously linked to a shift in epistemology, to the role the knower is fated to play. Alexander Pope, in his *Essay on Man*, lent to this epistemological shift an enduring philosophical emblem: "Man is the measure of all things."[3] What Pope surfaced in this dictum was that the modern human being was not only, as before, an object among the panoply of objects in the order of things, but also now a *subject* who posited a relationship between words and what they represent. In *this* subjectivity, the *modern* human being appeared on the scene.

At the very least, this shift in the grammatical position of the human being meant that time was no longer the same. Heretofore, the human being had been placed upon the line of the divine economy in which living, thinking, and suffering were all a carrying out of what had gone before. But as modern subject, the human being comes into being precisely at the same time as does its language, and a new logic flourishes which embalms time in human linguistic practices. Bereft, therefore, of any being preceding or exceeding language, the modern subject charts for itself a course through a field without origin—or at least with no origin but language itself. Thus, the modern subject emerged as the one to whom befell the task of organizing the vacant space of being; yet, paradoxically enough, out of this bankrupt space emerges the idea that the subject in its emptiness could establish, even legitimate, through imposition or decree, limitations of knowledge. Therein the modern subject establishes its own limitations, its own finitude, as the limits and finitude of any possible knowing whatsoever. By this move, the impoverishment of the modern subject becomes the basis of its claimed epistemological sovereignty.

Such, in an event, are some of the shifts that we have long associated with modernity—shifts in the conceptions of language, of the human being, of time, and of knowledge. In view of them, it is probable that the significance of modern spirituality does not reside in a single theological meaning released from a specific set of transparent language practices or even from select lines from the Bible and its Author. Instead the significance of modern spirituality may be derived more probably from a multidimensional configuration of discourses in which are married and contested several thematic trajectories, none of which is original.

More than a different *notion* of language, the shift issuing in the outlook that we are now calling "modern" entailed a certain number of procedures that controlled, selected, and organized the production of new discourses—including those of law, physics, metaphysics, ethics, political science, economics, history, and religion.[4] Notable among these procedures are exclusionary practices, internal rules of classification and ordering, and the social-ritual appropriation of discourses.

These are especially evident in the conception of writing that emerged in the period. Just then, as the conception of language underwent transformation, so also (consequently) did the conception of literary production that owed much of its configuration to the new notion of language. *It is therefore doubtless more accurate to say that I am attempting to locate modern spirituality primarily both in the new understanding of language and in the conception of literary production that grew out of it, and only secondarily in the philosophical and religious themes that conform to and reinforce these practices.* However accustomed we may have become to looking to "consciousness" or the "voice of worship" as principal indices of "spirituality," so also have we in like measure averted our gaze from the formative role of writing and reading practices. But it is precisely these apparently more narrow, yet terribly potent, features of modern life that harbor the distinctive marks of "modern spirituality," as we shall come to see.

The Westminster Confession and the Ploy of the Author

The conception of literary production to which I refer is the identification of writing with *text*—a notion which, despite its familiarity, is notoriously unclear. Perhaps the most prominent, if not most conspicuous, instance of the identification of writing and "text" to be found in the archives of modernity is the Westminster Confession of 1647. Principal among the declarations of the Confession is the claim that Scripture is the sole channel through which the revealed nature and will of God are to be apprehended (I.1).[5] According to this claim, the written record displaces all direct revelation: therein, Scripture and the word of God are explicitly identified. Yet to assign to a writing an Author is to impose a brake on it, and, evidently, for the forgers of the Westminster Confession, to attempt to close it. What blazes forth in the Confession's claim that Scripture is authoritative, because God is its Author, is an implacable dissociation: no external authorities, human traditions, or new revelations of the Spirit have any bearing on the interpretation of Holy Writ (I.4). Hence, the general principles enunciated in Scripture are normative both for its own interpretation and for all decisions in life. Finally, the authoritative versions of Scripture are to be found in the Hebrew of the Old Testament and the Greek of the New Testament. The reasoning behind this claim of the Confession is that Hebrew was the language of the people of Israel and Greek the common language of the time when the New Testament was made matter of revelation (I.2–3).

However novel the Confession's claim that Scripture is identical with the word of God or its stipulation of Hebrew and Greek as the original languages of the writing may have been, its radicality lay in its utter transformation of the meaning of "text" that had been elaborated in the Renaissance and whose thematic origins may be traced in pre-Augustinian theologies. In brief, the (pre-)Renaissance view is that the world was made up of an infinite number of resemblances or similitudes whose vast syntax, tissue, or weaving is the order of the creation. Linked together, as in a great chain, apparently scattered things throughout the universe are drawn to one another without losing their singularity. This vast network of resemblances is "text," whose character becomes evident to human beings only by virtue of God's script(ure) or signature. Holy writing tells us where and how one sees the divine chain of being and by what marks it may be recognized. The power of writing: Holy Writ is in a way an aid to sight, spectacles by which one views God's creation aright, as John Calvin was wont to say.

In sharp contrast with the (pre-)Renaissance view, the Westminster Confession collapses the distinction between script and "text": "text" is condensed into script. It is no longer the case that the whole world of ties is *illumined by* writing—still less that such a world of connective tissue has a distinct being. No, now the word is the world, and the words whirled 'round or "text" are fixed within a format of script. Despite its initial functionary role in the context of Westminster (a delimiting role), the word "text" becomes something of a mana-word. The Westminster Confession is, indeed, an explicit prohibition against further additions to Scripture, a foreclosure on the "text," but it is also more: it saturates the finished work with the claim that the script is "the whole counsel of God" (I.6). And it ascribes the closure of the "text" to authoritative versions—Greek and Hebrew—of the script, which henceforth are to be the final power to which interpretive disputes are to be appealed. Because Scripture is now claimed to contain the whole counsel of God, the text is a finished work, bearing the explicit prohibition against further additions. Moreover, the finished or closed character of the text has been in evidence since the authoritative versions of the script appeared in Hebrew and in Greek. So with the closure of the text, the Author-God disappears, or at least remains at a great remove. It is precisely this mysterious distance which permeates Scripture: Scripture is everything and nothing as befits the absent Author-God. Indeed, the Holy Spirit is a mere echo of the Author's voice, no longer enjoying an ongoing (immanent) interpreting role.[6] Here, then, the ploy of the Author: one speaks of the Author-God, as if one could, but only as one fails to acknowledge the metaphorical status of this claim.

Now, the prescribed exclusionary practices pertain not only to the apoc-
ryphal literature but also to the role of the reader. Whereas the Renaissance
role of the reader was that of *commentator*, whose notations were a playing
out of the similitudes of the script thus constituting the marginalia that
came to be affixed to or extensions of manuscripts, the role of the reader
in the Westminster Confession becomes that of potential *critic*, whose task
will be to discover the Author's intent behind (beneath? within?) the
work—hence, the specification of the authoritative versions of Scripture to
which all disputes are to be referred.

Beyond the exclusionary practices of the notion of "text" set out in the
Westminster Confession, there are, as well, internal rules of classification
that govern the ordering and distribution of discourses within the "text."
The principle of the God-Author attributed metaphorically to the Scriptures unifies and introduces coherence into this disparate set of writings.
The Westminster Confession holds that "the infallible rule of interpretation
of scripture is scripture itself" (I.9): the unchanging identity of the Author
limits the hazards of chance interpretation that would alter the significance
of the biblical discourse. At the same time, the Author-principle lends
coherence to and funds the proposition concerning God's eternal decree:
God has freely and unchangeably ordained whatsoever has come to pass, but
in such wise that God is neither the author of sin nor the cause of the loss
of liberty among creatures. Herein is the declaration of the unity of God's
work, of what has been revealed, and of the hidden sense that pervades
God's work, a declaration in keeping with the distance of the Author-God.
A formative part of the Confession's conception of "text," God's eternal
decree is the answer to every reader's query for the real story that gave birth
to the script. The "answer" of the Author implants into the troublesome
language of Scripture a profile which irrupts in the midst of all the words
employed, infusing them with its character.

Still another set of procedures that govern the meaning of "text" but pertain specifically to its readership permeates the Confession. These have to
do with the social-ritual appropriation of discourses. They make explicit the
way in which seemingly theoretical claims function as socially regulative
principles. Once Script(ure) has been determined to include the whole
counsel of God—that nothing is to be added to it—and that there are
authoritative (literally, Author-itative) versions of it, the manner of reading
has been implicitly prescribed: the "text" is to be read "with godly fear," as
the Confession goes on to make explicit. Such reading with "godly fear" is
not tied to any particular location, but the rituals of singing psalms "with
grace in heart," the "administration and worthy receiving of the sacraments,"
and the "conscionable hearing of the Word" are all specified in the Confession,

as is "prayer with thanksgiving" (XXI.3–5). Thus, the functioning of ritual defines the qualifications required of the "reader," laying down the gestures, behaviors, and outlooks that reinforce the supposed significance of the words in the "text" and their intended (or imposed) effect upon the reader.

Taken together, the procedures of exclusion, of internal classification, and of social-ritual appropriation that shape the new (and, presumably "modern") meaning of "text" that appears in the Westminster Confession suggest that with the collapse of the distinction between script and text—or, better still, with the *identification* of script and text and with the ploy of the (absent) Author-God—text becomes *institution*. By institution, I do not mean a technical apparatus, but rather a theme *and* its derivative regulative procedures that initiate certain attitudes, behaviors, and outlooks in a group of persons whose consequent commonality tends to bestow upon them a distinct and determinate identity. Now insofar as this is a viable rendering of the shift in the meaning of "text," it suggests the following thesis: Insofar as modernity was constituted by the "text" as "institution," the forms of spirituality that emerged during the Reign of the Text have to do with the dynamic relationship between theme and regulative procedures in differing social groups.[7]

Construing the conception of "text" in the Westminster Confession as "institution" accords with the proposed aims of the framers of the Confession. However much in the end their efforts faltered, the framers had hoped to achieve ecclesiastical uniformity. Oliver Cromwell's "New Model" army, consisting mostly of dissenters from both episcopacy and presbyterianism, enjoyed a series of successes in 1646 that upended the prospect that Parliament would make the Confession an instrument of new church order in England, but it could scarcely stay the tide of its influence. The grudging approval Parliament granted the new Confession in 1648 may have qualified its political fortunes, but it was its enduring influence on the business of reading that proved decisive. Churchly practices, it is true, were not immediately transformed, remaining more nearly oriented to the more open Westminster Directory of 1644.[8] Reading, however, is always a matter of force, an exercise of power: in the wake of the Westminster Confession and its ploy of "the Author," it would become increasingly clear that in the modern realm of reading, there is no innocence, no safety.

The Leviathan and the Birth of the Critic

The conception of text as institution found a seemingly unlikely advocate in Thomas Hobbes, whose 1651 *Leviathan* turned upon an astute reading of its implications. A student of both Parliament and the Assembly, Hobbes exiled himself to France for the eleven-year period between 1640 and 1651, owing to his fear of parliamentary reprisals against him for the views he was beginning to set out. Hobbes seemed to recognize that the identification of script and text placed the Author in an ontologically distinct realm. The prohibition against tampering with the text therefore follows naturally from the Author-principle, in which the author becomes inaccessible, because the principles that preside over the organization of the "text" and that animate its procedures are beyond the ken of the reader. In consequence of this, no one within the social crucible that text institutes may claim the legitimacy of these principles as their own, or, alternatively, claim to speak from the perspective of the funding locus of the text. Further, the internal rules and classification of the text, though granting to the text its cohesion, are themselves—again, owing to the Author-principle from which they proceed—inexplicable, which gives rise to the (desired) sense that there is only one possible order to the text.

As this order is ever anterior to the reader, the reader can only gesture "toward it," through the ritual appropriation of discourses of the text. Hence, prayer, no longer participation, becomes obeisance to a rule. The power of the text, accordingly, lies precisely in the distancing of the Author and the attendant powerlessness of the reader, who though schooled in the discourses nevertheless lacks cognitive access to the principles that legitimate the text.

Hobbes exploited the distinction between the ontologically distinct Author and the order of the text in the following way. On the one hand, all power resides with(in) the Author; on the other, all readers are equal with respect to their powerlessness. The empire of the Author is precarious in that it both acknowledges the reality of power and maintains its unattainable remoteness. Hobbes moves to stabilize this relation not by the removal of the Author, but by the invention of the mortal or artificial author (the leviathan), who is the composite of all readers. Standing under the Immortal Author, the mortal author "resembles the *fiat* . . . pronounced by God at the Creation."[9] Succeeding the Author, the artificial author occupies a mediating position between the powerless and the realm of power. As an artifice of the powerless, and so *of* the domain of the powerless, the mortal author can be no more than what its artificers bring to its creation. Nevertheless, the mortal author is said to partake in the invisible power of the Immortal Author (God), and to this extent becomes other than or distinct from the domain of the powerless. Thus, in the person of the artificial author, the gap between the domains of the powerless and of power is somehow spanned.

Here is an example of the way in which Hobbes thinks about the passage from the role of reader to the invention of the (artificial) author. Barred from the chambers of the Author, the reader must turn inward instead. *"Nosce teipsum,* read thyself,"[10] counsels Hobbes. What the reader encounters when turning inward is a whirl of passions, senses, and desires. Baffled by the elusiveness of the principle that funds these drives, the reader nevertheless recognizes their play. Indeed, caught within their play, the reader, by an imaginative outburst of value, interprets the whirl as the drive to self-preservation. Reading oneself requires preserving oneself, but, too, preserving oneself requires reading oneself. This amounts to construing self-preservation both as a drive and as a constraining interpretation in which the reader takes its experience to be an instance both of the right of nature (that a being has the liberty to preserve itself) and the law of nature (that a being is constrained from doing anything that is destructive of its life or would take away from its preservation.[11] The outcome of the reader's inward turn, in short, is the transformation of a basic drive into a rational life-form or universal principle of interpretation.

This role of transformation is neither destructive of, nor yet imperious toward, life. It is perhaps, quite simply, the birth of the critic. For the critic must divine something of the principles of the Author, even if this is no more than acknowledging the limits of the critic's powers in its promethean attempt to steal the Author's fire. To say, as does Hobbes's reader, that the right and law of Nature are God-given underscores the limits of interpretation.[12] The reader can in no wise discern the ends toward which the principle of self-preservation points. Thus, the reader can do no other than to introduce an interpretive fiction: "life is a continual relinquishing of one place and acquiring of another"[13] under the criteria of its own authorship.

Apt though this description may be, it is a turning point. It is both an order and a disorder: an order that acknowledges a certain absence of (the Author) meaning. In the midst of this double message, the readers (critics) transform their own limits into a form of epistemological sovereignty. That which lies beyond the ken of the reader is disparaged, and only that which conforms to the standpoint of the reader is deemed intelligible or, for that matter, efficacious. By establishing a system of the paltry, the readers (critics) assert themselves as author: the system is the author's, or, what is the same, the author the reader creates is a mirror of the reader. Now of this fictive, or artificial, author certain requirements may obtain. When reading itself, the author does not see this or that particular individual, but the whole of the race.[14] Moreover, when the author writes, its script is the writing of all readers.[15] In a word, the reader (critic) confers upon the author a sovereign measure, which, owing to its derivation from the reader, the reader is bound to respect. Once we begin to glimpse the complicity of the critic with the (fictive) author, we are led to suspect the critic's power to neutralize, while upholding, the absence of the Author (God). The critic continues to acknowledge the Author, but the critic's role as artificial author becomes sufficiently pervasive by "filling in" the absence to repudiate the sense of the unintelligibility of the Author. So, the role of the critic flourishes, especially as it maintains the illusion of a bridge between the domains of power and powerlessness.

We must recall, before going any further—for here already is a wealth of possibilities—that Hobbes has thus far only spoken of the relation of the reader to the "text," exploiting the senses of the term that Westminster Confession ascribed to it. But everything is here of course for Hobbes's celebrated political anthropology. On the one side is the need of every individual to preserve himself or herself; and, on the other, the requirement that no individual do anything that would be destructive of his or her own life. The satisfaction of these two needs is met in the creation of the sovereign, who is brought on stage, so to speak, as the voice of the people. In this one person, competing claims are reconciled, which establishes the condition for a peaceable society. Because all power comes from the people, all people are bound to respect the sovereign just as they respect themselves.

This doctrine of "popular sovereignty" originated not with Hobbes, but with Parliament in the 1640s to strengthen its hand against Charles I. Supporters of Parliament claimed that the people had surrendered entirely and absolutely their sovereign power to Parliament, in consequence of which the will of the people and the will of Parliament were identical. Cromwell, too, had claimed for his army power in the name of the people. As we see, what passes into this idea of legitimation are variant strategies for its deployment, none of which came to realization as the will of the people: in 1660, Charles II was restored to the English throne and the defenders of popular sovereignty were swept from power.

Yet if it was a social decision of the English to reject the notion of popular sovereignty, it was nonetheless a decision that bore the marks of the altered relation between reader and "text" toward which Hobbes (and before him, Westminster) had turned his thinking. This is the decision that Hobbes exploited: to split society from its founding themes so that in the absence of knowing itself, society cannot change itself by acts of collective will. Let us be clear about this: to know itself, a society must acknowledge its debt to its founding themes, in the same way that a reader who knows a "text," incurs a debt to the author whose profile imbues it with cohesiveness: the reader (critic) resembles the creational *fiat*. To be forgetful of this debt is to render society captive of the illusion that it generates its own meaning—a move upon which Hobbes capitalizes—or to continue the parallelism with the reader and the "text," to hold that the "text" is the production of the author (critic), which "work" is transmitted to the reader.

By generalizing, perhaps abusively, these few remarks on what I have called the modern conception of "text" and the relation of the reader to it, we can suggest something of the first outlines of modern "spirituality." Born of exclusionary practices that divorce the reader from the text, thereby rendering the reader powerless, the modern spirit generates the fiction that the mind of the author is identical with its own. Thereby the modern spirit endows its own limits with a kind of sovereignty; forgetful of its indebtedness to what is other than itself, the modern spirit conceives of itself as the generator of meaning, as the producer of the "work." Yet the discursive practices of the modern spirit oscillate between two poles, according to the respective density of their functions. When the authorial function predominates and the capacity to partake in and channel inaccessible power surfaces, the discourse of the modern spirit inclines toward a metaphoric form (applying terms to objects to which they are literally inapplicable, e.g., "Author"), as in the case of Westminster. When, on the contrary, the critical function predominates, the epistemological limits or powerlessness of the reader comes into view, and the discourse of the modern spirit is inflected toward a metonymic form (it substitutes a part for the whole, e.g., "artificial author" or leviathan), as in the case of Hobbes, who inveighed, as we know, against the "abuses of speech," denouncing metaphor as an "unordained sense of words" whereby speakers "deceive others."[16] A third form of discourse, it is true, exists: one which attempts to reproduce by its structure the antagonism between the metaphoric and the metonymic, while permitting the reasonings to predominate. This might be called a critico-historical discourse, and of it Spinoza is the best example we know.

The Tractatus Theologico-Politicus and the Politics of Philology

Although greatly enamored of Hobbes, Spinoza recognized all too quickly that fictive authors who are the artifice of the critics' self-reading culminate in "endeavoring to hawk about their own commentaries as the Word of God, giving their best efforts, under the guise of religion, to compelling others to think as they do."[17] This is not to say that Spinoza tried to subvert the reign of the author. On the contrary, he labored to consolidate it; and this he did by championing a critical-historical method for the interpretation of Scripture, which would lay bare the intention of its authors.

Let us follow briefly Spinoza's reaasoning.[18] Holding to the letter, if not the spirit, of Westminster and Hobbes, Spinoza admits no principles for the interpretation of Scripture apart from those found in Scripture itself. Such principles are not defined in Scripture but are found operating within various biblical narratives. Hence, a most interesting situation—Scripture must be examined in light of its history. This declared goal makes history initially into philology, for Spinoza conceives of scriptural statements as expressions of languages whose nature, properties, and conversational usages must be known in order to determine the signification of the words in the statement. Not only does Spinoza want to compare every scriptural statement with conversational uses of the language, but also he enjoins us to determine the life, conduct, and pursuits of the author of the scriptural statement as they bear upon the writing. It would seem, if the analysis is to be exhaustive, that the age and occasion of authorship, the audience to which the author addressed the writing, and the possibility of subsequent redactions all must be determined. With such a "historical foundation," the reader is girded for the task of investigating the "history" of Scripture for what is "most universal and common."

Now that which is most universal and common, Spinoza teaches us, serves as the foundation for Scripture. And what is this most universal, this most common, that permeates Scripture? The oneness and power of God, which are the source of true virtue. To Spinoza, the evidence for this principle is so unmistakable that he thinks it affords us a regulated means for a proper reading of this kind of writing. We are to proceed, he suggests, in descending order from the most common to lesser generalities, until arriving at last at particularities. In other words, Spinoza's work seeks to elaborate a system of deduction, deriving the unknown from the known and carrying the premises from the whole to their legitimate conclusions. We may therefore rightly claim that all we read or hear from Scripture envelopes us in the oneness and power of God. But we must be mindful, too, that this balanced mass of words is the vivid imaginings of historical authors, of prophets. The rules taught by Spinoza aim at reestablishing the historical meaning of the writing, not its metaphysical truth; and he repeatedly cautions us against confounding the two.

Hence, better than a metafiction, what Spinoza leaves us with is a metabolism. It is a metabolism of language, philologically uncovered, that, while preserving the antagonism of Author and critic, of metaphor and metonymy, does not let us fall easily under the spell of those who would corrupt the meaning of sentences in a writing for their own gain. Subverting a sentence for power is always possible for an individual, but subverting the signification of words or of language is not, owing to the common parlance and writing of the masses and the learned alike.

As we see, by its very structure and without there being any need to appeal to further details of Spinoza's argument, this plan of interpreting Scripture is essentially an imaginary elaboration. Language is the repertoire of images known to writer and reader, which the writer is bound to deploy within limits; to trespass upon these limits is to elicit a certain measure of distrust from the reader. This marks a shift in ideological emphasis away from Hobbes. Whereas Hobbes accords the reader (critic) power to invent a fictive author, Spinoza accords the reader (critic) power to discern and delimit the historicity of the author, with the attendant consequence that text becomes historical work. Hobbes supposes, one might say, that the written, the outward, is a reflection of the inner life of the author. Hence, with the distancing or inaccessibility of the author, the critic may "fill in" the subject of the writing. But with Spinoza, language, and not the inner workings of the critic's psyche, affords access to the writer, at least as a public figure. The private life of both author and critic remains an entirely personal matter and, as such, is a liberty both to be respected and to be regarded as nontransferable.

In other words, Spinoza drives a wedge between truth and meaning, between the inner life of the author and the languages of speech and writing. It is the same wedge that he drives between a radical inviolable right to free thought and those rights which are transferable to a sovereign in the interest of peaceful public accord. The latter, of course, is the linchpin of his political theory: in order to preserve oneself, an individual transfers to a sovereign certain of its rights for the utility of peaceful accord and well-being among individuals. Obviously reminiscent of Hobbes's political anthropology, Spinoza's has to it a novelty that seems to me to have been underestimated. What may be transferred to a sovereign are what might best be construed as public rights—freedoms pertaining to conduct—but not what, by way of contrast, may be called private rights—liberties pertaining to thought and speech. For it is precisely in the retention of these liberties that humans remain subjects, but in their ceding that they become slaves.[19] Paradoxical as it may seem, Spinoza exploits this distinction between public and private rights in a way that assigns to the sovereign the responsibility for curbing excesses in religious practices. We know just where this strategy comes from: from Spinoza's plan for interpreting Scripture. Insofar as the meaning of Scripture derives from reestablishing the historical significance of words in writing and common parlance, it is a part of the public domain, as are the practices (e.g., worship and prayer) that are based on it. In turn, the liberty for the exercise of these practices is, as a public liberty, transferable to the sovereign, whose duty it becomes to safeguard the state from such encroachments as might arise from these practices. Accordingly, if religious practices trespass upon the private right of free thought and speech, the sovereign is bound to defend the individual against such intrusions, lest the subject become a slave.

Whether it was this or other prescriptions against religious bigotry in the *Tractatus Theologico-Politicus* that fired the angry storm of controversy surrounding its publication in 1670 is not certain. But the prohibition of the book in 1674 by the Netherlands' States-General and its subsequent placement on the Index by the church of Rome were in one sense a continuation of a history of religious sanctions that had been visited upon Spinoza, including attempts upon his life when he defected from his rabbinic studies, Calvinist threats of forceful conversion, and reprisals for his Rijnsburg association with the excommunicated Collegiant sect. If we read Spinoza, we must use this weight of history to understand the significance and zest of his words. For example: "When people declare, as all are ready to do, that the Bible is the Word of God, teaching man true blessedness and the way of salvation, they evidently do not mean what they say."[20] Or again: "Ambition and unscrupulousness have waxed so powerful, that religion is thought to consist, not so much in respecting the writings of the Holy Ghost, as in defending human commentaries, so that religion is no longer identified with charity, but with spreading discord and propagating insensate hatred disguised under the name of zeal for the Lord, and eager ardour."[21] What Spinoza opposes are the exclusionary practices that flow from the metonymous role of the author and culminate in the arrangement of social practices that reinforce the authority of the critic to define the author.

We do not so much read Spinoza today as dissolve him into the generalities of intellectual history. Hence, we are less clear than, say, G. Lessing, J. W. Goethe, I. Kant, J. Fichte, A. and F. Schlegel, G. Hegel, H. Heine, S. T. Coleridge, P. B. Shelley, and George Eliot—all of whom drank deeply from the well of his thought—about the sobering power of his relentless combat against metonymy. By dint of historical accident, Spinoza was granted lenses through which to see the effects of exclusionary politics, which were located at the very heart of his situation as a writer. So he strove to break the custom, to discover the abuse under the rule of reading that had begun to assert itself in Westminster and Hobbes.

If we want to understand how Spinoza's reader is suited for this combat, we must always remember the garb of the Hobbesian reader: it is fictive dress. Though resembling the Author, the fictive author is an invention, an artifice of the reader. Therein the distinction between the real and the apparent becomes blurred, and the granting of real standing to the unreal (fictive) author repositions the reader. Supposing themselves to be gaining access to the text, the readers are co-opted or combined into the "authorial" standpoint. And "author" now signifies both reader and Author, granting the reader an extension beyond what it legitimately can claim. Spurious though this extension may be, it is the result of an ideological connotation of the metonym "author," which masks the constitutive absence of the Author. Hence the reader is positioned in a role of submission to the "authorial" standpoint, subjecting the whole to the part, and to the oppressive practices (e.g., religious bigotry) which must maintain that standpoint.

By way of contrast, Spinoza's reader is clothed in the historical fabric of language. That is, language is not construed as a matter of individual fashioning but as something other than reader and author to which both are indebted. Indeed, it is the common weal of language that puts the reader under obligation to enter into what might be called an ethics of reading. Bound to respect the languages of authorship and the properties of language use that inform the significance of words, the reader is beholden to what is other or alien, to what is not at the reader's disposal. This is why the reader cannot light upon any fragment of writing as finished, but must look further to discover the filiation of the language and connective tissue whose holding power joins the fragments into a work. This is why, too, the reader cannot presume that the author has language at its disposal: the history of a language and its ambiguities of signification is just as much beyond the ken of the individual author as it is of the reader. Hence, the responsibility that befalls the reader to appreciate the sources and consequences of the fragility of language is the same responsibility that prompts Spinoza to signal for us the distinction between meaning and truth in a writing. What the reader may discern are the domains within which the author plies discourses; with a synoptic eye, the reader may be able to delineate the meaning or thought-worthiness of a writing. With respect to the truth of a writing, however, both reader and author are powerless, because the truth of a writing belongs neither to arrangements of power that inform the author's writing practices, nor the arrangements of power that affect the reader's approach to writing. Instead, the truth resides in the power of the mind of the Holy Spirit. To this the reader does not have rational access, but for it the reader may have rational appreciation. Spinoza's practice of ethical reading thus teaches us that our indebtedness to language is a kind of purgatory we must traverse in search of the promised land of truth, the language of the heart.

Here something happens that matters to our understanding of modern spirituality: by invoking allegiance to writing by any subject, the one who writes and the one who reads, Spinoza transports into our thinking an awareness of the ubiquity of the signifier, which draws us to its end and makes for tentativeness of meaning. The meaning of a writing is therefore no more than a cipher of truth, a substitution whose systematic path follows the very structure of language. Hence, the modern spirit, though divorced as reader from the text, is not obliged to regard the text as so utterly alien that it must invent an author, but may instead venture upon a path of philological or critical-historical reflection, of genetic inquiry, to establish a meaning of the text. In this way, the reader may regard the text as historical work while at the same time acknowledging its powerlessness to know the truth. No doubt this legitimates an epistemological forgetfulness of what is other than the reader (truth), but it also forges the basis of a modern political strategy in which that powerlessness is the object of respect (the sovereign must uphold the right of truth-seeking in thought and speech against any encroachments) rather than a target for abuse.

The Athenaeum Fragments and
Auto-Poetic Epiphany

Long before the romantics, readers who adopted the "authorial," "critical," or "philological" stances toward the text experienced the exhaustion of powerlessness and the sad necessity of ploys to mask this ineffectuality. With what may be called the "romantic" stance toward the text—the last of the modern stances to be considered here—the dimension of this agony is altogether different. Powerlessness is almost an expiatory ordeal, purging the illusory modern desire for a sterile text and configuring the character of the modern reader in its own right.

What we shall have to do with here is not the romanticism one ordinarily hears about, fostering, as it does, notions of the fantastical and the sentimental. Instead, our concern will be with a stance that, while owing many of its distinctive bearings to nineteenth-century philosophical considerations, nonetheless derives its impetus from the crisis that the Westminster Confession precipitated. For, as we have seen, once text and script are collapsed into an identity, the question of the relationship between author and reader looms large indeed, as does that of the significance of a writing and the collaborative practices that legitimate it. True, to these problems a frankly epistemological solution may be lent, which purports to distinguish ideological and epistemological reality: this, in the eyes of the romantics was Immanuel Kant's great merit, even if they thought it was a somewhat incomplete merit.

It was, after all, Kant who set for himself the task of scouring reason of its riotous excesses, its imputations of reality to ideas where no reality existed. His critical philosophy sought not only to do away with the errors of the Western tradition of metaphysics and its hopeless field of discourses, but also to understand the origin and rational attraction of metaphysics in the systematic structure of reason itself. Understanding the rational origin of metaphysics permitted him to develop a coherent interpretation of the relationship between scientific and moral reasoning, without detriment to either one. Because these aims accorded with the deepest aspirations of the modern temperament, and because Kant was regarded as having "proved" the rational foundations of freedom, his critical philosophy quickly became the benchmark of modern religious and philosophical inquiry.

Of the numerous intellectual icons that Kant thought begged to be shattered, Spinoza's strategy of reasoning was but one, although Kant attached a peculiar reverence to it. However much it faltered in his view—no less than the Hobbesian strategy had faltered in Spinoza's—the Spinozistic strategy elicited Kant's compassion, because he sensed that Spinoza's reader is hemmed in. Owing to the lack of harmony between the public and private spheres, the noble ideals of the Spinozist's private thought are beset by deceit, violence, and envy in the public domain. As it is only the public domain which admits of intersubjective commerce, no promised land can ever open before Spinoza's reader, but only a "wide grave" engulfing the reader in an "abyss of purposeless matter."[22]

Where Kant thought Spinoza erred, or seemed to have erred, was in his estimate of the reader, of the modern subject. Spinoza accorded reality, substance, to the unknowable private domain. More than falling prey to an illusion, Spinoza falls short, in Kant's estimate, of the devastating conclusions to his own argument. Possessing no knowable private domain, the modern subject is empty, declared Kant.

In Kant's own assessment, the modern subject is no more than a mere form, a logical necessity, perhaps nothing other than a grammatical exigency. Indeed, it is this form of thought, namely, the reflexive awareness of having thoughts as one's own, that introduces continuity to all thinking. And, Kant continues, the form of the subject, "the self," is the form to which all thinking must conform. No substantial "soul" but an empty form of thinking (the "self") lies at the heart of all modern experience.

True, as a moral being, the modern subject may lay claim to a somewhat larger estimate of itself. For as a moral being, the modern subject is aware of a moral imperative that constrains possible courses of conduct. But it is one thing to be aware of a law, of a form of universalizing reasons for conduct, and another to know freedom. Indeed, of the freedom Kant alleges to reside within the moral imperative, the modern subject has no direct awareness. The modern subject's awareness of freedom is indirect, inferred from the negativity, from the constraint, of the moral law. I ought to do something other than what I am proposing; I can do what I ought; I infer that I am free to do what I ought. Hence the modern subject's "knowing" of freedom consists in the justification for the belief in freedom—nothing more. Yet it was precisely this justification that made Kant for many an enchiridion of modern Protestant sensibilities.

The reach of Kant's discerning eye exceeded even his own formidable conceptual powers. Having underscored the strictly unknowable character of human life and of its formative powers, he nonetheless recognized the need for a subject that could recognize itself and its own insight, coming into being—including moral vision. This undoubtedly was the core of Kant's critical explorations; and we know from his notebooks that it persisted in Kant's ruminations as a symptom of a deeper malady in his system of thought.[23] Despite various efforts, Kant never arrived at a satisfactory solution to this problem: its enduring power thus lay not so much in specific philosophical proposals that Kant mounted as in its galvanizing effect upon some among his readers.

To the Schlegel brothers, Friedrich and August (philologists, and founders in 1794 of the literary journal *The Athenaeum* and the Jena Circle), and to F. Schleiermacher and Novalis, all of whom revered Spinoza but were fired by the Fichtean invocation to forge a "Spinozism of Freedom," it seemed that Kant had bared unmistakably before their eyes the predicament of the modern "reader" and "text."[24] Excluded from the "text," the reader is fated to find tradition wholly alien and its own contemporaneity virtually un-depictable. Hence, the reader without tradition is "empty," and tradition without the reader is "blind." Now the reader or Kantian "self," so emptied, may posture as its own principle of continuity, but this posturing already entails the implicit admission of the loss of traditional continuity (the "soul"); for all its posturing, the "self," too, remains dis-contented. So what this predicament issues in is the desire for a "text" without dominations of ideology, on the one hand, and on the other, for a "text" that discloses traces of the formative power of life that fulfills and surpasses tradition, both intellectual and ecclesiastical, in the present formation of character. Something of this compound desire presses itself upon us in the following observation by Friedrich Schlegel: "It has been said of many monarchs that they would have been admirable citizens, only as kings they were failures. Can we say the same of the Bible? Is it also just an admirable everyday book whose only fault is that it should have become the Bible?"[25]

Only such a canny reading of Kant as this could see in the abrupt loss of the subject and the apparent asocial character of writing a strategy to contend with the modern wish for a sterile text. Grasping, as Schlegel did, the incongruity of this desire—that it seeks a production (text) which does not bear the marks of production, of fecundity, or of a cloudy subject—it became possible to bring its subversiveness into view. One could, alternatively, construe this desire as the attempt to discern the way in which a text (pro-duction) is its *own* making or autoproduction, which configures the fractured position of the modern reader in its own right rather than as an extension of a strategy of domination or oppression.

Friedrich Schlegel and his intimate associates (August Schlegel, Caroline Michaelis, Dorothea Mendelsohn-Veit, Schleiermacher, L. Tieck, Novalis, W. Wackenroder, and F. Schelling) pursued this subversive stance, together with its incongruities, through an experiment that inaugurated a new mode of writing. This experiment catches and communicates to the reader a strange condition: the philosophical and theological circumstances that surround the modern problem of writing cannot be separated from its genre: writing is a fragment. Again, an aphorism by Friedrich Schlegel: "Many of the works of ancients have become fragments. Many modern works are fragments as soon as they are written."[26] Here Schlegel plays with the word "fragment," valorizing it, and imbuing it with greater mobility of function. It calls to mind the exclusion of the reader from the "text" and, hence, the way in which ancient writings are no longer accessible but lie in ruins or fragments, citings of what is lost. Yet "fragment" or shard also invokes more than a reminder of what the modern reader lacks (the great work), insofar as it configures the position of the reader as fissured or fragmented (separated from semblances). With both senses of the term "frag-ment" figured in the genre of writing, every act of such writing becomes (1) a quest for the classical, (2) an attempt to effectuate in modernity what antiquity failed to complete of the classical, and (3) a novel production, insofar as it endeavors to link Homer and Goethe, Plato and Kant. Far from devaluing writing by thinking of it as a fragment, the experiment of Schlegel and his intimates accords writing, construed in this way, the highest value—a terrible contemporaneity—the power of autonomy.

Let us see, following the mind of Schlegel, the sense in which this is so. No genre exists, he claimed, that is fragmentary in form *and* content, "simultaneously completely subjective and individual, and completely objective."[27] In other words, the fragmentary is intimated by, but not limited to, the fragment: letters, memoirs, and dialogue are also fragmentary and bespeak the futurity of a genre that is the adequate recapitulation of the organicity of fragmentation. There is a sense in which the Bible, as a system of books—and not as a single book, in the usual sense—most nearly approx-imates this eternally developing plurality, which is, as such, One. The ques-tion of authorship thereby becomes effaced by the organic community of the universal; what matters is not any particular fragment per se, but the "chain or garland of fragments"[28] or what might be called the manifestation in the form of the ideal, the actual infinity of the process of truth. Only with this broader organicity in mind can the proper relation of fragment to the eternally developing plurality be brought into view. The fragment is a microcosm of the Whole: "A fragment, like a miniature work of art, has to be entirely isolated from the surrounding world and be complete in itself like a porcupine."[29] Like a small work of art, the fragment in its individuality must be understood in terms of its obligation to figure or inscribe the outside of the whole that is essential to the whole. Schlegel makes this point in yet another way in his claim that "fragments are . . . marginal glosses to the text of the age." If the whole is to be likened to a work of art, the fragment stands outside as a marginal gloss. The marginal glosses, construed as a garland or chain, surround or demarcate the contours of the Work of Art. The glosses are thus exergual: outside the Work of Art, they are nonetheless essential to the Work as its contours. It follows from this that the Work of Art lives in the gloss or the fragment, which is a putting into form—"a small work of art" of its own silhouette in writing. This amounts to saying both that the fragment is autonomous insofar as it puts into form its own obligation (to be a gloss) and that the fragment is autonomous because it is auto-formation, lying as it does outside the Work of Art.

The term fragment is eroded for us now, but we can still savor some of the power of this word's abstraction. As we now have it, fragment means both the activity of putting into form in writing *and* the gloss by which one knows what that form is, that is, "a miniature work of art." Schlegel quipped that it is simultaneously philosophy and philosophy of philosophy, and if we do not enjoy the historical culture that might come to the aid of our reading of this aphorism, we know well enough the concept of the reflexivity of the text and its correlate, that literature provides its own internal criteria for interpretation. In the terms of Schlegel's own observations, it doubtless suffices to say that the reflective function of critical discourse is a constitutive element of literature as such.

Yet if none of what Schlegel's romanticism consisted of seems particularly subversive, we need only recall that the question of the author and authorial intent is done away with; that the role of the critic is effaced; that fragmentation dislocates established disciplines such as philology, history, and theology, bringing everything into question. Such, of course, is not without its political ramifications. In the midst of profound economic, social, and political crises in the latter years of the eighteenth century, Germany's bourgeoisie enjoyed new-found access to culture but experienced mounting difficulties in securing employment for their children. At the same time, the apparent promise of the French Revolution had become compromised for many by the realities of the French occupation of Germany. The ideas that Schlegel and his intimates entertained, and in part attempted to live out,

The Philosophy

of Jesus of Nazareth—
extracted from the account of
his life and doctrines as given by
Mathew, Mark, Luke, & John.

being an abridgement of
the New Testament
for the use of the Indians
unembarrassed with matters of fact
or faith beyond the level of their
comprehension.

8. Title page of Thomas Jefferson's *Philosophy of Jesus of Nazareth* from a letter of Jefferson to Rush, April 23, 1803.

were to serve as the model for a new style of life. In its germinal state, this model was more akin to what Schlegel called a secret society whose aim was to disseminate ideas that would aid the political struggle during the revolution. Itself a fragment, this society sought to outline the pure contours of the absent ideal and an organic "republican" or Jacobin politics, the imbrication of fragmentation.

Yet, as we have said, Schlegel's romanticism takes aim at the question of the author, at the privileged position of the critic, and at the location of the established disciplines, and in this takes aim at nothing less than the modern strategies of religious ritual practices that devolve from an inaccessible deity. And what is posed in their place is the issue of the work of art creating itself, the question of the formation of form, and the claim that true religion falls within the limits of art alone: religion is art itself; the artist, "the one who perceives the divine within himself."[30]

Let us make no mistake about Schlegel's critical labors: they constitute a kind of upsurge, of historic shock, for modern spirituality. By buttonholing the strategies of the modern spirit to endow its own powerlessness with meaning, Schlegel makes it imperative that the modern spirit confront its failure in coping with an inaccessible deity. It is not that one or another strategy might better succeed in certain circumstances; it is rather that all such strategies are a masquerade. They hide from view the downfall of exclusive domination that ecclesiastical faith once exercised in the definition of knowledge. Hence, whether assuming an Author, or, in the Author's absence, inventing an author, or pursuing a course of genetic inquiry in order to dodge the excesses of such inventions, the modern spirit invokes categories vested with ecclesial interpretation. Yet it is not an ecclesially defined field of knowledge that spurs the modern spirit, but a principle of continuity that is alleged to be Everyone (and so is no one). Consequently, the defining and delimiting role of this anonymous and impoverished principle—"the self"—makes it impossible for the modern spirit to speak of the Author, the critic, or even a style of genetic inquiry in any terms other than those which mirror to itself its own emptiness. This is why the modern spirit can do nothing efficacious with the "text."

Still, while the modern spirit can do nothing with writing, writing can do something with the modern spirit. The modern spirit is "entered" into writing—or better—becomes a participant in the formation of form, which is fragmentary, incomplete, and infinite. Just what happens in writing exceeds the limits of objective analysis, but it seems to be marked by the following characteristic: it is *I* whom it has come to seek, summoning me to receive its expansive ambiguity. The auto-formation of form in writing is thus simultaneously the formation of character, or the production of what characterizes itself as the modern spirit. So for the romantic the forming of the capabilities of character prescind from the *sui generis* activities of an ego, arising instead through the generativity of auto-creativity—the creative act itself, autonomously conceived.

Ecclesial Rituals of Social Appropriation

We have seen that the contours of modern spirituality may be discerned initially at the level of language (its sudden opacity) and of the conception of literary production that followed upon it (the Reign of the Text). Thanks to the identification of script and text in the Westminster Confession and elsewhere, text assumed the significance of institution, and the formation of discourses around this new understanding exhibited certain exclusionary and internal organizational procedures that came to be inflected in diverse ways. Preeminent among these are the metaphoric, the metanomic, the metabolic, and the fragmental. Cast as founding themes for the practices of reading, these appeared as the authorial, the critical, the philological, and the romantic stances toward the text. The crucial moment for demarcating modern spirituality appears concretely in the appropriating social rituals these themes called for—indeed, required—for their formation. Such derivative rituals bestowed specific identities upon those groups of persons whose outlook, attitudes, and behaviors they governed. It is not, perhaps, too much to say that these practices surrounded their themes, thereby enshrining them, and, no less, isolating them.

The "Authorial"

Let us take up each of these stances in turn. First, the authorial, which, not surprisingly, was strongly reflected in the confessional resurgence of both the Lutheran and Reformed traditions, as well as in the early evangelicalism of the Anglican Church. Among the Lutherans, perhaps the most singleminded and vigorous to fight for the uncompromised authority and inerrant character of the Bible was Ernst W. Hengstenberg. In his view, the inerrancy of Scripture was the foundation of all theology and religious practice: to oppose historical criticism was an obligation of faith; to believe in the divine authorship of the Bible, a matter of religious duty. Such "isolation" of biblical words vouchsafed their authentic character. For, naturally enough, God does not act according to the laws or conditions of history, and only the distinct standing of biblical words—that is, as evidences of God's speech in history—prevents distortions of the pure Words of God. Hence, rigorous practices of stricture against "unchurchly" theology (views not conforming to strict confessional interpretation) must be maintained in the life of faith.

Something of this insularity existed in England, as well, during the first third of the nineteenth century. The view most generally accepted within the Church of England—a view that may be called the early isolationist, posed as it was against the influences of the Continent and the impetus toward the Catholic Emancipation Act—was that the Bible is a theological textbook, composed and dictated by Almighty God to inspired writers. Every statement and sentiment of the Bible was thus to be accepted as the undoubted Word of God. W. Van Mildert noted in his 1814 Bampton Lectures that the acceptance of any biblical criticism indicated moral defectiveness, unsoundness of faith, and disloyalty to the church.[31] Dubbed as "bibliolatry" by Coleridge, this outlook on the Bible discouraged any but a literal interpretation, upon which it was supposed that religion would stand or fall.[32]

The variability of reading practices among the Lutheran, Anglican, and Reformed traditions was not sufficiently great, but perhaps nowhere was the metaphoric effort more audacious than in the Reformed tradition's Princeton theology, which Charles Hodge and his followers developed over a fifty-year period. Zealous to defend the tradition of the Westminster Confession, Hodge claimed that the people of God are bound by nothing other than the Word of God. Scripture is both perspicuous and complete. Opposing abstract Christianity, Hodge maintained that just as the Bible was concrete and to be read literally, so also the tenets and forms of Christianity are to be concrete and literal. Hence, Christianity in general was a fiction, and only its particular forms—Presbyterianism, Methodism, Episcopalianism, or Independent—exist. Emerging as the criterion for Reformed orthodoxy, the Princeton theology not only promoted denominational self-consciousness, but also fostered education and the learned tradition, as an antidote to the excesses of revivalist expressivism. To be sure, the facts of religious experience are not overlooked, but regarded as facts. What, however, are facts? Facts are constituted by the Bible, and their due authentication derives from Scripture. Hence, the advances of science do not encroach upon the Bible, for such facts as science unearths are ultimately to be found in and duly authenticated by Scripture. Why? Because Scripture, Hodge tells all, embodies objective authority and infallibility. So the proper business of theology and religious practice is to set forth in a genuinely scientific way what the Bible teaches. And that is why the method of theology and religious practice is inductive, collecting first the "facts" and then deducing from the "facts" principles. Yet owing to the status of the Bible as the "storehouse" of all facts, this amounts to saying that the Bible alone accords the proper principles for the interpretation of life.

The Princeton theology and its practices of learning won wide acceptance as the bastion of embattled conservatism, and in time became a mooring to which the interdenominational cry for a return to fundamentals would be attached: the publication and distribution of three million copies of the series of twelve theological booklets entitled *The Fundamentals*.

The authorial stance toward the text is known for the ritual-social practices of the literal reading of the Bible, reinforced by moral sanctions against those who entertained the thought of diverging from those practices, from which emerged a good share of modern fundamentalism. We are beginning to realize, however, by the reexamination of certain historical publications, that the grand design of the fundamentalist impulse was not at all the repudiation of modernity, but to develop and impose upon the widest possible populace a thoroughly modern discovery: that is, that to achieve uniformity in outlook, the Bible must be regarded as both script and text, which admits of only a learned, literal reading. Severe guardian of the "true" (univocal, canonical) meaning of Holy Writ, this practice has the function of a superego, whose first, denying task is obviously to reject all metaphor and thus to conceal its own metaphorical character. Hence, those who are schooled in this practice become stricken with a mortal disease of language—ametaphoria, which culminates in a number of murderous censorships—which, should the ametaphoric practitioner survive, becomes the unnameable sacrament over which the practitioner presides as high priest.

The "Critical"

In the critical stance, as we know, the right to interpretation is wrested from what appears to be the murderous letter and put in the service of a different truth: the empowering spirit. Its social-ritual practice found expression in various movements of pietism, including the German Lutheran development, the Wesleyan revival in England, and the so-called Great Awakening in America. As we know, the beginnings of this process of signification, of engaging meaning other than in its literality, are to be found in Jacob Spener's *Pia Desideria*. Against the backdrop of the Thirty Years' War, Lutheran scholasticism, and the territorial church system, Spener's program called first and foremost for the "diligent reading of Scripture." By this Spener meant not only the private reading of the Bible, one book after the other, but also a "fraternal" or collegial reading of the Bible in which various understandings of Scripture might be explored "arranged with an eye to the glory of God." Indeed, such exercises of collegial reading supply, in Spener's view, what is lacking in public preaching and private reading: the critical principle that Christianity consists of practice.

How one reads, then, has a great deal to do with how one exercises Christian love. In the first instance, it commends communal consolidation in the "known truth." It also introduces a duty toward those whom Spener designates as "the erring," that is, those who do not read the same way and who are therefore held to be in error. More than in anything else, this duty consists in bringing the errant into the fold, again with an eye to the glory of God. Bringing the errant into the fold involves a salutary correction of a received opinion: it is a waste of time to think that disputation alone will impart holiness of life to the errant. Rather it is the practice of the holiness of life that is efficacious, and, to this end, those who are appointed to instruct others in the Christian faith must conceive of their work as "workshops of the Holy Spirit."[33] Professors are enjoined to conduct themselves in exemplary fashion in order that students might have living practices by which to regulate their lives. Whether in discourse or in study, students are to be led faithfully in the practical discipline of theology, being introduced repeatedly to opportunities to put "the right rule of conduct" into practice. Only in this way may the Word of God penetrate to the heart of the errant and issue in the right foundations for all ensuing conduct.

Hence, pietism was, in its day, a vital force in the formation of spiritual character, a character gained against the appearances of the world and beyond those appearances in the genuine hope of achieving social reformation: the first charitable hospitals and orphanages in Europe were the fruits of pietist labors. It flourished under the guidance of August Hermann Francke in Halle, greatly aided by the protections offered by Frederick III. And when Halle ceased to be hospitable to its cause, pietism resurfaced in Württemberg, shepherded by the efforts of J. A. Bengel, as well as in Herrnhutt, where Hussites fleeing Moravian persecution found asylum and direction from Count Nikolaus Ludwig von Zinzendorf, godson of Spener.

If today we pay little heed to the missionary zeal of the Herrnhutters in Africa, India, the Caribbean, South America, and North America, we nonetheless remain captive of a certain (somewhat fictive) legacy concerning the influence of Moravian pietism upon John Wesley. Indeed, what would become the Wesleyan revival in England was shaped as much by the Great Awakening in New England, Jeremy Taylor's *The Rule and Exercise of Holy Living* and *The Rule and Exercise of Holy Dying,* Thomas à Kempis's *Christian Patterns,* and William Law's *Christian Perfection,* as it was by Wesley's encounter with the Herrnhutters. But the practice of forming "societies," of weekly reading of Scripture, of guided discussions on religious matters, and of social activism (e.g., the inclusion of women in prominent leadership positions) clearly bear the imprint of Spener's classical vision of pietism.

Yet it would be something of an illusion to suppose that the obsession of the critical stance with the inner life was defined solely by Protestant practices. The critical stance was also obsessed by the inscription of the spirit within a systematic space of signs, and this trajectory found its most forceful expression in the pontificate of Pius IX. Deprived of temporal authority, Pius moved swiftly to consolidate his power in matters spiritual. Hence, the 1854 promulgation of the doctrine of the Immaculate Conception of Mary constituted the first move in the establishment of papal infallibility: the move to institute the critic, who in the discharge of his office, defines the meaning of faith or morals to be held by the universal church. The 1870 promulgation of Papal Infallibility at Vatican I granted official standing to the critical stance Pius IX had already adopted on the dogma of the Immaculate Conception and again in the 1864 Syllabus of Errors, which listed eighty propositions that all Catholics were to reject.

If the promulgation of papal infallibility did not cause the stir that might have been expected, it is because the stance toward the text it embodied had long since been etched in the minds of many moderns—the blistering opposition of the Syllabus of Errors to much of modernity notwithstanding. For it was the wholehearted embrace of and engagement in the process of signification, stripping the literal of its finality and posing in its stead a fundamental value.

The "Philological"

The return to the letter—this time, the letter of philology—was a reversal precipitated, as we have already had occasion to learn, by the excesses of the practices that surrounded the critical stance. On the one hand, there was a growing awareness of the importance of doctrine, which had been minimized or abandoned in some forms of pietism and rationalism, as an antidote to the perceived abuses of "antidogmatic liberalism" and "evangelicalism": this was the point of departure for the Oxford Movement and its principal leader, John Henry Newman. On the other hand, historical biblical hermeneutics revealed that the particular character of individual writings disrupted the dogmatically or pietistically founded unity of the canon: this was the insight of Johann August Ernesti and Johann Salomo Semler, forgers of the movement known as the Neologians. The empire of this new philological letter, however much its parties varied (in outlook, the Neologians more nearly resembled the latitudinarians than the Tractarians of the Oxford Movement), might best be described as grounded in the insight that words themselves are not really grasped until the internal principle of the subject matter they express has been brought into view.

For the Oxford Movement, this principle consisted in the "touchstone of canonical scripture itself," a text for "everything claiming to be of apostolic tradition."[34] For Newman, this principle had a distinctive ring, whose resonance we can scarcely imagine, let alone appreciate, apart from some willingness to entertain the questions that pressed so forcefully upon the outlook of the Tractarians. Whether Scripture is self-interpreting or admits of the necessity of comment; whether revelation and document are commensurate, or one outruns the other; whether the document is but partial revelation or its closure—these were the questions that vexed Newman and his associates (John Keble, Edward Pusey, Richard Froude, and Robert Wilberforce) in the Oxford Movement. Wedged, as they were, between the perceived poles of Rome and Protestantism, these questions begged for a mediating way (*via media*): in opposition to Rome, Newman could not yield to a principle of external authoritative comment in the interpretation of Scripture, any more than he could accede, given his opposition to the Protestants, to the notion of biblical literalism. Hence, despite acknowledgment of the incongruities and unschematic character of Holy Writ, Newman embraced the view that there exists a developmental principle running through the whole of the Bible. He based his conviction on the observation that in the exercise of language practices, certain developmental features distinguish themselves by virtue of their capacity to preserve an essential idea, to exhibit a measure of continuity, and to unify a number of otherwise diverse thoughts. But perhaps the most audacious of his claims on behalf of development was that the process seems to manifest a certain perspicacity, anticipating what form a germinal idea ultimately will assume. The practice of reading Scripture is therefore a matter of following the rule or principle upon which development of theological ideas proceeds. So understood, Scripture, or, more rightly, the proper reading of Scripture, is "the medium within which the mind of the Church has emerged and developed."[35]

However much Newman thought that he could demonstrate the truth of his proposed view, his was not a sanguine posture. For he was duly aware that it is one thing to assert such a view, another to practice it. The chasm between what he deemed a "paper view" and institutional practices marked for him a fatal shortcoming of both Protestant and Catholic Christianity. Hence, he and his associates attempted to spiritualize and give depth to the old Laudian, Tory tradition of English church practice. Appointed by Charles I as Archbishop of Canterbury in 1633, Laud opposed both Puritans and Roman Catholics alike, while attempting to restore a hierarchical structure to the church. More reticent than Laud in their expression of piety, the Tractarians adopted him and Charles I as spiritual forebears of their cause, holding before their eyes the importance of religion to the individual soul. Obsessed with the feeling that what is holiest should be hidden, and yearning for a liturgical ethos, the Tractarians singled out the rite of Holy Communion as the fundamental practice which conjoined "the whole of the Bible, written on the principle of development" and "a right state of heart." Herein, bounded by obedience and holiness, faith can be safeguarded; so contoured, the heart bears the twofold truth that salvation comes from God alone and that God's saving action actually penetrates and transforms human life and conduct.

The ingenuity of Newman's approach, mapped out most fully in his *Essay on the Development of Christian Doctrine,* lay in his recognition that religion and revelation force upon us a historical problematic which neither a literal nor a critical reading of Scripture can dissolve. By placing the idea of history squarely within the bounds of linguistic and ideational development, it becomes possible to discover a rule of interpretation that accords wholly with the practices of scriptural writing—a "great number of writings of various persons, living a different time, put together into one"—and that is rightly reinforced through sacramental practice.

It cannot be by chance that Semler, too, moved to consider the meaning of words, not only in their particular historical linguistic context but also with respect to the cultural ethos of the authors and first readers of Scripture. Hence, knowing the Bible's use of language properly and precisely as no mere lexicographical procedure, but extended of necessity to transformations in the spiritual edifications that imbue language use throughout the ages. Indeed, Semler claimed to be able to discern qualitative gradations in the discourses of Scripture and in the delineation of the constant and growing movement of the human spirit toward God. Understood in this way, Scripture defines appropriate practice in religion. This is why, aside from their grace, scriptural discourses enable us to differentiate among levels of religious meaning and truth: some are merely of historical interest, while others are of perduring religious significance.

The turn to the letter of philology and of critical-historical interpretation of Scripture issued, in its institutional practices, in the following effect: One could take the letter and see its secrets deepen through myriad associations in which would be rediscovered everything about the world—its history, one's own, its great symbols or creeds—shaking off the yoke of literalism and staid criticism and its instrumentalist approach to language. For the letter, so cast, both *means* and *means nothing*. At one and the same time, it imitates nothing and symbolizes all, dismissing the alibis of complacent literalism and tyrannical criticism.

The "Romantic"

Yet perhaps more than in anything else, the Modern period bequeathed us a thesaurus of romantic experiments, dreams, and meanings in the labors of its most pervasive religious practices. Two examples must suffice for our purposes: Coleridge and the Broad Church movement and Harnack and Culture Protestantism.

Coleridge's *Confessions of an Inquiring Spirit* teaches us, by way of seven (fragmentary) letters, how to interpret Scripture. We need not reject it; we must even occasionally place it, or pretend to place it, in the forefront. For the proper interpretation of Scripture appears where it is not expected. Scriptural interpretation is fragmented, pluralized, as if the *one* of interpretation were ceaselessly made to divide into two: synthesis is baffled, and interpretation displaced. Nothing, in a word, can be gained by the claim of biblical literalism, of biblical (dogmatic) criticism, or of biblical historicism, because each seeks to establish what the authority of Scripture is, rather than departing from the self-evident authority of the Bible.

Yet the self-evident authority of the Bible is, for Coleridge, its spiritual truth, "the downshine of the True Light."[36] Such truth is not to be confounded with "natural reason" or with the historical exercise of "human understanding." The source of spiritual truth is, in a word, not human but divine. The light of divine reason, dwelling within each individual, confers upon each insight into divine verities; moreover, divine providence aids the individual through its operation in the history of the world—principally through the work of the church. Hence, the self-evident truth and authority of the Word become sensibly evident in the interaction between church and Scripture as attested to in preaching. Neither church nor Scripture is elevated to the detriment of the other, but they stand in reciprocal relation to each other, exergual, as it were, to the Word.

The Bible, considered as an objective body of writings, exhibiting a literal and unqualified infallibility, is an illusion, which confounds revelation by the eternal Word and actuation by the Holy Spirit. If you look at the Bible close up, you see only a collection of ancient writings; if you step back, tranquilly, you no longer see anything but a "treasure house," a "ground covered with mana."[37] Distance and proximity are promoters of meaning, bringing into view a difference of kind, "a chasm" between inspiration and communion with the Spirit. Owing to this chasm, everything signifies and yet everything is surprising in order not to exhaust the creation of meaning under some banner of "evidences."

To the reader, then, is commended the commission of pilgrim, to seek diligently the spirit of the Bible. The spirit is the food needful and fitting for each sojourner, a precious gift from God. Coleridge thus bids readers to approach Scripture with a "free and unboding spirit," "under the conviction of faith . . . whatever the result may be."[38] Each reader is to take what is precious for himself or herself, and to leave as precious for others that Holy Writ which comforts and guides. What such reading etches in the pilgrim are the contours of what is subjective of the Spirit. That is, what the Spirit quickens in the reader is the individual subject, communicated *as* the subject that Spirit alone constitutes. And this, of course, is the need of the modern individual: to be constituted as a subject.

If the fundamental practice urged upon the faithful was free inquiry, it was scarcely welcome to the Tractarians. Dubbed "Broad Church by its friends; Latitudinarian or Indifferent by its enemies"–or so we are told by W. J. Conybeare in his 1853 essay on "Church Parties" –the movement came to number among its adherents Richard Whatley, J. C. Hare, A. P. Stanley, Thomas and Matthew Arnold, Charles Kingley, and Benjamin Jowett. F. D. Maurice and Horace Bushnell shared many of the aims of the movement, although remaining at something of an independent distance from it, and Alfred Lord Tennyson lent to the movement his poetic voice. Opposition to the movement reached its most heated pitch following the 1860 publication of *Essays and Reviews,* a manifesto which had the courage deliberately to place open and honest inquiry of biblical-critical questions at the point of origin of a movement that greatly broadened the range of permissible religious opinions in mid-nineteenth-century England. Jowett's essay on the "Interpretation of Scripture" was perhaps the emblematic of the group, urging a welcoming of critical inquiry in the name of the Christian love of truth and advocating the interpretation of Scripture along the same lines as all other written documents. So great was the shock of this stance to English sensibilities that for a brief while the storm of indignation over the *Essays and Reviews* overshadowed the maelstrom set off by Darwin's *Origin of the Species.*

If there was in Coleridge and his associates a confidence in the reconciling, aesthetic harmony between opposites, that confidence was muted in the views of Harnack and other representatives of what may be broadly designated "Culture Protestantism." Whether it was the motif of art becoming the new religion; or the radical reconceptualization of the literary genre of the Bible (e.g., the reconfiguration of "parable" in the poetic explorations of F. Hölderlin); or even a certain insouciance toward Holy Writ (S. Mallarmé had observed that one might have "to leave the Book behind"); whether, in a word, there was a certain peril associated with some of the overtones of the romantic stance is a question that Harnack and others of his mind-set did not directly answer, substituting for it an apparently marginal question:

the place of metaphysics in historical inquiry. Following Albrecht Ritschl, Harnack maintained an allegedly antimetaphysical bias. From this distance, he thought he could explore the relation of the essence or norm of Christianity to human life and society. Hence, one begins with "Jesus Christ and His Gospel."[39] Yet one cannot stop there, but must go on to include the generation of Jesus' disciples who were associated with him, and from there one must turn to the religious lives of those who have followed him. In this way, Harnack argued, one is able to arrive at "the Gospel in the Gospel," that which perdures "under differing historical forms, and is of permanent validity."[40] However much Harnack may have vested his energies in the question of historical inquiry, and so of historical reading, the ideological repercussions are evident: every effort of historical study tends to constitute a model, in relation to which its product may be defined.

What Harnack chose as his model was the organic metaphor of growth and development. "We cannot," he wrote, "obtain a complete knowledge of a tree, without regarding not only its root and its stem, but also its bark, its branches, and the way it blooms."[41] Finding what is common to all the forms of the Christian idea and life in reference to the life and Gospel of Jesus and its impression upon historic Christianity leads us to the kernel of the Gospel and Christianity: "Eternal life in the midst of time, by the strength and under the eyes of God."[42] This reversal of what Harnack took to be a metaphysical bias obliges us to recognize the marks of Goethe upon Harnack's historical vision. Like Goethe, Harnack was convinced that Christianity stood in no need of philosophy, but has its own spirit that has prevailed in history. Yet the very manner in which Harnack conceived of the oneness of the spirit in all of history—its fragmentation, its displacement by philosophy and creed, and the a-historical character of the Absolute (Gospel)—owed more to the romantic stance than he outwardly, at least, acknowledged.

In this he did not differ greatly from F. C. Baur, Ritschl, Wilhelm Hermann, or, for that matter, the early historical studies of Ernst Troeltsch (the later writings of Troeltsch, of course, must be said to constitute a decidedly different matter): all sought to understand historical process and the nature of its development in the interest of delineating the proper reading of Scripture. In this respect, the so-called historical approach to the study of religion had far-reaching effect: the basic stance of the "social gospel" movement bore marks of its most distinctive fruits. Promoting, as it did, the idea that there is a fundamental and perduring theme of the Gospel—the prophetic demand for justice and the proclamation of the kingdom of God under the law of love—the social gospel movement, under the leadership of Washington Gladden, Richard T. Ely, and Walter Rauschen-busch, shared the optimistic progressivism usually associated with the Culture Protestantism of Harnack.

But perhaps above all else, Harnack's approach to Scripture consisted in the judgment that at bottom it repristinated the centrality of the ethical. Mindful of the seeming incompatibility between ancient formulations of faith and modern sensibilities, he entered an unexamined field in which Scripture and its relation to doctrine, institution, and values could be redistributed according to a new model of Spirit, displacing traditional church history with a social history of Western Christian religion. Manifest within this social history are the reflections and effects of the powerful personality of Jesus, of his life and of his teachings. To read Scripture is thus to enter into the ethos of this life-work, which transcends all oppositions: it is to acquire the consciousness that ". . . all these oppositions are ulti-mately beneath it . . . and that . . . its own place is above them," which is the consciousness "that gives the gospel its sovereignty."[43] In a word, to read as Harnack instructs us is to turn away from what the modern temperament regards as frivolous and to exert all one's moral force in inward conversion, "so that by the Spirit everything might be made new."

Practices such as these, adopted by the Lutheran and evangelical reform communities particularly in and around Berlin issued in a kind of unex-pected persuasion to make new decisions about the relation of ancient dogmas and their value to the modern world in light of historical under-standing. Not dogma, but a special perception of moral faith was what made its effect known in these reading practices.

Modern Spirituality and the Effacement of the "Text"

Such are, briefly and summarily considered, the broad contours of modern spirituality that come into view when regarded from the perspective of the modern conception of language and of the notion of literary production to which it gave rise. Modern discourses of spirituality suppose, one might say, that text is institution, entailing exclusionary procedures and methods of internal classification, as well as social-ritual practices of appropriation. And if this was how the notion of Holy Writ as text appeared, what changed over the years were the habits of reading it. Preeminent among the social-ritual practices of appropriation, the habits of reading functioned in the sphere of the social in a manner quite similar to the operations the inflections of modern discourse enjoyed in the domain of language. Just as the meta-phoric, metanomic, metabolic, and fragmental inflections in modern discourses altered the play of signification in scriptural interpretation, so also did the authorial, the critical, the critico-historical, and the romantic practices of reading transform their object, the "text": it was scarcely the same "institution" for, let us say, the pietists as it was for the Tractarians. Hence, the habits of reading constitute something of a distributional definition of modern spirituality, causing certain links to appear between each society or communal arrangement and the economy of information it learns to assign to biblical literature.

Earlier, in provisional formulations of the character of modern spirituality, we said that the modern spirit, excluded from the text, had been obliged to assume an Author; or, lacking one, to invent an author; or, further, to avoid the excesses of such inventions, to pursue a course of genetic inquiry; or, finally, in the face of the downfall of such approaches, to enter or participate in the incomplete formation of writing—and all of this seemed to consist in so many attempts to endow the powerlessness of the modern spirit with meaning, thereby fortifying its resolve to contend with an inaccessible deity. Now we are in a position to refine this formulation in a somewhat different fashion. By attending to the way in which reading practices assign patterns of associations among words in order to ameliorate the effects of powerlessness that inhere, in some measure, in each of the modern stances toward the text, we can reasonably hope that certain divergences and disturbances will come into view. Since social need engenders social function, we may say that to the experience of powerlessness that surfaces in the Authorial stance toward the text, there corresponds the impetus to uniformity of outlook; to the critical stance, the drive to garner, by way of "bridging," the power to speak; to that of the philological stance, the endeavor to displace truth with "history"; to that of the romantic stance, the dream of empowerment.

Owing to the diversity among these patterns, it follows that the very form of the conception of the "text," and so of the "literary," must be defined, at least in part, as a divergence in the association of words or signs—a divergence that is reinforced and legitimated by the particular habit of reading associated with it. This suggests, in turn, that given the aberrant associations that inform modern spiritual practices, the historical interpreter is confronted with a sum of insoluble cases. Doubtless, such conceptions of the "literary" and their associated practices stand in some relation with (what might be called) history and society, but this relationship is special and does not necessarily coincide with history and a sociology of contents.

Yet if we depart from merely literal associations and take up a position at the level of connotation, we can at least discern the rudiments of a code, whose validity not only pertains to the diverse conceptions of text as institution and the practices of reading associated with them—in a word, to modern spirituality—but also has had lasting effect for well over a century in the West. Perhaps it is time to lend to this code a name: let us call it a modern variant of *docta ignorantia*. We know that in the classic expression of this teaching, deriving from Nicholas of Cusa, the limits of knowing are acknowledged as the threshold of the reality of the unknown. By a subtle shift in syllabic emphasis, the modern variant turned this teaching to very different ends. If the classic form construed this teaching as learned unknowing, the modern form construed it as learn'd unknowing, teaching through its practices forgetfulness, or systemic unawareness. By isolating and separating the themes which have funded them from the habit of their exercise, each of the practices of reading teaches a forgetfulness of the *otherness* of the themes upon which they rely. Thereby, each of the reading practices impedes cognitive access to the conceptions of literature they legitimate. And, as if by a collective gesture, such practices removed from sight the question of whether its conceptions of literature were sufficient or adequate to account for the equivocity and character of Holy Writ. In consequence of this, the modern practices of scriptural reading and the forms of spirituality that they have engendered have turned more upon self-legitimation and self-preservation—the establishment of their own "epistemological empire" — than upon the exploration of the fundamentality of the "text" they proclaim to defend.

Thus we close the paradoxical circle with which we began: The identification of text and script and the emergence of reading strategies, elaborated in the crucible of ecclesial practices, become both text (institution) and proof of text. Hence it will be understood that the effacement (if not the disappearance of the "text" or the "literary" in modern spirituality implies much more than a simple change in outlook: a veritable ideological transformation in which Holy Writ dies because it is not so much real as spiritual practice and its proscribed ways of seeing.

Notes

1. The mounting literature on "modernity" has become so vast that it precludes comprehensive record in this setting. Nonetheless, it is possible to sketch in broad strokes the prominent contours of this concept, which have informed the development of scholarly investigations. We need only invoke the names of Kant, Hegel, Max Weber, Wilhelm Dilthey, Emile Durkheim, and George Herbert Mead to recall the intellectual landscape within which the concept of "modernity" was cultivated.

Following the spirit of Kant's teachings about the intellectually and morally rational subject, Hegel formulated the notion of modernity as an epochal concept in his *Lectures* on the Philosophy of History (New York: Oxford University Press, 1956). Hegel construed "modernity" as a new age oriented toward the future, which, owing to its distinction from past epochs, had to create criteria out of itself for its self-interpretation. Weber discerned in this formulation a subtle, but nevertheless intrinsic, linking of an epochal theme to an epistemological theme—namely, rationalization. From the standpoint of this epistemological theme, Weber argued that the development of modern societies culminates in "secular culture" (Economy and Society [Berkeley: University of California Press, 1978]). Dilthey, pursuing another approach, tempered the austere lines of rationality that lent themselves in Weber's account to an analysis of "money economy" by focusing instead on the historical, indeed classical Stoic, character of the rationality of the modern life-world ("Weltanschauung und Analyse des Menschen seit Renaissance und Reformation," in Gesammelte Schriften [Leipzig: Teubner, 1921–36] vol. 2). And in a kindred manner, Durkheim and Mead looked to the factors of social environment for a clearer indication of the shaping of "modern" rational processes (The Elementary Forms of Religious Life [New York: Free Press, 1965] and Mind, Self, and Society: From the Stand-point of a Social Behaviorist [Chicago: University of Chicago Press, 1962]).

Although much of the subsequent literature has explored variations of these dominant contours of the concept of "modernity," the call to rethink the way in which this concept had been cast was first sounded in Walter Benjamin's 1940 "Theses on the Philosophy of History" (published in 1950) (Illuminations [New York: Schocken Books, 1969]). Maintaining that the "new age" is not future oriented but grounded in an unacknowledged act of remembering, Benjamin anticipated much of what since has begun to appear under the label of "post-modernism." For by interweaving diverse motifs of provenance, Benjamin radicalized the conception of historical consciousness in a way that has since been explored by Foucault, Derrida, Gadamer, Henrich, Koselleck, Blumenberg, Pacini, Peukert, Habermas, and Lyotard. Far from settled, the concept of "modernity" has thus achieved a new openness.

2. Francis Bacon, Trivium (Works of Francis Bacon; 14 vols.; London: Methuen, 1857); Ricardo, Works and Correspondence (Cambridge: Royal Economic Society, 1951–1973); Georges Cuvier, Le règne animal distribué d'après son organisation, pour servir de base à l'histoire naturelle des animaux et d'introduction à l'anatomie comparée (4 vols.; Paris: Deterville, 1817).

3. Alexander Pope, The Twickenham Edition of the Poems of Alexander Pope, III.i (London: Methuen, 1964) 53).

4. For further discussion of this point, see David S. Pacini, The Cunning of Modern Religious Thought (Philadelphia: Fortress, 1987).

5. The Westminster Confession of Faith (Critical edition, ed. Caruthers) (Manchester: R. Aikman & Sons, 1957).

6. The role of the Holy Spirit as portrayed in the Westminster Confession is on first reading ambiguous. Yet this ambiguity gives way with a comparative reading of the various editions of the Confession. Here it is possible to note only that with the parliamentary requirement for proof texts, which accompanied the third edition, certain textual revisions precipitated significant diminutions of the role of the Holy Spirit. The emphasis on inward illumination gave way, by way of subordination, to the

emphasis on the Holy Spirit as Supreme Judge speaking through sentences of Holy Scripture with saving understanding of the Word.

7. Later in the essay, I shall pursue this relation at some length; at present it suffices to introduce the thematic aims of the essay. I am indebted to the work of Samuel Weber, *Institution and Interpretation* (Minneapolis: University of Minnesota Press, 1987) for provocative formulations that have informed my own way of framing the issue.

8. See "The Westminster Directory," in *Liturgies of the Western Church*, ed. Bard Thompson.

9. T. Hobbes, *Leviathan* (Cleveland: Meridian, 1963) Introduction, p. 59.

10. Ibid., 60.

11. Ibid., I.14, pp. 145–46.

12. Ibid.

13. Ibid.

14. Ibid., Introduction, p. 60.

15. Ibid.

16. Ibid., 74f.

17. Spinoza, *Theologico-Political Treatise*, in *Works* (New York: Dover, 1951) preface, p. 3.

18. This sketch is based on Spinoza's *Theologico-Political Treatise*.

19. Ibid., chaps. 17 and 20.

20. Ibid., 98.

21. Ibid.

22. Immanuel Kant, *Critique of Judgment* (Oxford: Oxford University Press, 1969) 303.

23. Kant, *Opus Postumum*, in *Werke* (Wiesbaden: Suhrkamp, 1960).

24. Spinoza's monism was widely regarded as deterministic, but in the wake of the excitement generated by Kant's moral philosophy of freedom, the call for a monistic philosophy of freedom quickened philosophical interests in many circles. Fichte not only spearheaded this drive but also wrote the first so-called Spinozism of freedom—the 1794 *Wissenschaftslehre*—which deeply impressed the philosophical public, who had deemed the undertaking difficult, if not impossible.

25. F. Schlegel, *Lucinde and the Fragments* (Minneapolis: University of Minnesota Press, 1971) #12.

26. Ibid., #24.

27. Ibid., #22.

28. Ibid., #77.

29. Ibid., #206.

30. Ibid. ("Ideas"), #44.

31. William Van Mildert, *An Inquiry into the General Principles of Scripture Interpretation* (Bampton Lectures, 1814; Oxford: Oxford University Press, 1815).

32. S. T. Coleridge, *Confessions of an Inquiring Spirit* (London: George Bell & Sons, 1904).

33. Jacob Spener, *Pia Desideria*, in *Pietists: Selected Writings* (New York: Paulist Press, 1986).

34. John Keble, "Primitive Tradition," in E. R. Fairweather, *The Oxford Movement* (New York: Oxford University Press, 1964) 63–89.

35. John Henry Newman, *Essay on the Development of Christian Doctrine* (New York: Penguin, 1960).

36. Coleridge, *Confessions of an Inquiring Spirit.*

37. Ibid., 332.

38. Ibid., 331.

39. Adolf Harnack, *What is Christianity?* (New York: G. P. Putnam & Sons, 1901) 10.

40. Ibid., 15.

41. Ibid., 12.

42. Ibid., 8.

43. Ibid., 18.

44. Ibid.

Part Two

POST-REFORMATION
PROTESTANT AND
ANGLICAN SPIRITUALITY

8

Protestant Spirituality: Orthodoxy and Piety in Modernity

I. *Second Age of the Reformation: Lutheran and Reformed Spirituality, 1550–1700*

ERIC LUND

The Spirit of Late Sixteenth Century Protestantism

The Intensification of Religious Conflict

IN THE MIDDLE OF THE SIXTEENTH CENTURY, the original leaders of the Lutheran and Reformed churches reached the end of their productive ministries. After the death of Luther in 1546 and Calvin in 1564, the major continental Protestant movements came under the influence of less forceful leaders and soon faced a series of crises which threatened their very survival. Political conflicts and changes in the relationships between rival religious groups created a mood of uncertainty and suspicion that had an enduring impact on the spirit of Post-Reformation Protestant religious life.

For several decades after 1521, Protestantism had expanded while the emperor of Germany and Catholic church leaders were distracted by other concerns. By mid-century, however, Roman Catholicism began to show signs of new spiritual vitality. Lutherans in Germany experienced this resurgence most dramatically in 1547 when Emperor Charles V defeated the Protestant princes in the Schmalkaldic War and implemented a modest program of recatholicization called the Augsburg Interim. These events intensified the confessional consciousness of the Lutherans and eradicated lingering hopes for Catholic–Protestant reconciliation.

In the same period, Calvinism expanded into formerly Catholic and Lutheran territories, producing additional tensions between religious groups. The state church of the Palatinate became an important center of German

Calvinism after 1559, and, to the dismay of the Lutherans, other important states and cities in the empire embraced the Reformed faith in the next few decades. In France and the Low Countries, Reformed Protestantism was especially popular among political dissenters whose resistance to Catholic rulers eventually produced the French Wars of Religion (1562–1598) and the revolt of the Netherlands against Spain (1566–1609). The shifting patterns of religious affiliation in the late sixteenth century enhanced defensive attitudes within the confessional groups and also contributed to the outbreak of internal theological conflicts within the Protestant churches.[1]

The Defense of Pure Doctrine

The threat posed by the Augsburg Interim accentuated the presence within Lutheranism of divergent understandings of doctrine and the nature of the Christian life. Philipp Melanchthon (1497–1560), Luther's longtime colleague and most logical successor as theological leader of the Lutheran churches, accepted the restoration of some Catholic religious rites and customs with hopes of staving off a more violent attack on Lutheranism. Influenced by the spirit of Renaissance humanism, Melanchthon was inclined to view the precise forms of ecclesiastical practices as matters of indifference (adiaphora). Temperamentally irenic and interested especially in the reconciliation of religious differences, Melanchthon also showed a willingness to be flexible about the formulation of some theological assertions. The Philippist party, as Melanchthon and his like-minded associates came to be called, was harshly criticized by the Gnesio-Lutherans, a rival group of religious leaders who feared that compromise in times of persecution on matters of ceremony as well as doctrine would undermine the reform of Christianity which Luther had inaugurated. Tensions between these divergent orientations within the Lutheran tradition continued long after the Interim crisis was resolved by the Truce of Passau in 1552.[2]

The Religious Peace of Augsburg in 1555 insured the survival of Lutheranism by giving German princes the right to determine the religious allegiance of their territories, but the rival parties continued to dispute with each other in several doctrinal controversies which reflected their different religious concerns and attitudes. Memories of Melanchthon's collaborations with the enemies of Lutheranism aggravated suspicions about the heterodoxy of the Philippists. Frequently the conflicts between Philippists and Gnesio-Lutherans were rooted in their divergent fears about the ways in which simple believers in Lutheran parishes might misinterpret the gospel.

As early as 1535, Melanchthon had attempted to combat manifestations of unregenerate behavior among the peasants by stating that good works are "necessary" for salvation. Philippists who shared his ethical concerns and rejected the seemingly antinomian statements of some Lutheran theologians repeated Melanchthon's position in the 1550s. The Gnesio-Lutherans generally saw a greater danger in the persistence of the idea that salvation could be merited. Consequently they accused the Philippists of straying toward the perspective of the Catholic Church. In the midst of this controversy, extreme Gnesio-Lutherans insisted that good works were not only unnecessary but even detrimental to salvation. Such statements were deemed essential to free simple believers once and for all from the influence of the newly resurgent Catholic tradition.[3]

The humanist sympathies of the Philippists were especially evident in another debate about the role of the human will in salvation. Following the lead of Melanchthon, who viewed the assenting will as a third factor in conversion along with the Holy Spirit and the Word, the Philippists sought to encourage holy living by suggesting that believers must cooperate with God at least by not resisting the offer of grace. In response to this qualified synergism, the Gnesio-Lutherans stressed the absolute passivity of the believer in the process of regeneration. Luther had proclaimed the bondage of the will in his debate with the humanist Erasmus; some Gnesio-Lutherans defended this perspective by insisting on the total corruption of human nature. Matthias Flacius Illyricus (1520–1575), the most prominent leader of the Gnesio-Lutherans, viewed Philippist statements about the consenting will as a blatant revival of Pelagian optimism. In defense of the Lutheran doctrine that sinners are justified by grace alone, Flacius argued that humans can cooperate in conversion just as little as a stone can contribute to its transformation into a statue. The controversy about the role of the human will quickly broadened into theological debates about the nature of original sin and predestination.[4]

The confusion and ill will that these and other theological disputes fostered convinced moderate theologians of the need to formulate a new Lutheran confession which rejected the extreme positions advocated by the two parties. This document, the Formula of Concord, was approved by most of the Lutheran territorial churches in 1580 and provided the foundation for a theological consensus in the following years.[5]

Memories of the preceding conflicts, however, were not easily forgotten, and concern for pure doctrine preoccupied the attention of many church leaders for the next century, the so-called Age of Orthodoxy. Theologians produced elaborate systematic treatises demonstrating continuity between the Formula of Concord, the theology of Luther, and the Scriptures. To aid the defense of the tradition, university scholars developed a Protestant form of scholasticism which utilized Aristotelian terminology and logic for the sake of argumentation. The task of refuting theological errors was foremost in the minds of many pastors, and consequently polemical writings and sermons against Catholics and Calvinists proliferated.[6]

The Reformed tradition was spared the internal divisiveness which plagued Lutheranism, but controversies with Lutherans and persecution by Catholics in France and the Netherlands stimulated a similar concern in the Reformed churches for the defense and systematization of theological truth. Calvin's successor in Geneva, Theodore Beza (1519–1605), developed a more precise definition of the mode of Christ's presence in the Lord's Supper in response to Lutheran attacks and elevated the doctrine of predestination to a more prominent position in Reformed dogmatics. Beza's theological method became increasingly scholastic, and Reformed scholars elsewhere rationalized Reformed theology, isolating particular doctrines for analysis to such an extent that the practical religious concerns which unified Calvin's theology sometimes seemed to disappear.[7]

Outside of Switzerland, the influence of humanism on some Calvinists encouraged greater concentration on a practical Christian faith. Ethical interests were especially prominent among French Reformed theologians who resisted the trend toward metaphysical speculation and the use of Aristotelian philosophy. In the Netherlands, which had a rich heritage of mystical theology and humanism, concern for the linking of doctrine to piety remained strong. The development of scholastic Calvinism was criticized most notably in that region by Dirck Coornhert (1522–1590), an advocate of nonconfessional practical mysticism whose influence extended to some theologians within the Dutch Reformed churches by the end of the sixteenth century.[8]

The Supervision of Religious Life

The systematic theological treatises and confessional documents that were produced in the late sixteenth century were far too sophisticated to be understood by the average member of Lutheran or Reformed congregations. The clergy communicated theological truths to simple believers by sermons and by catechetical instruction. Luther's *Small Catechism* focused on the Ten Commandments, the creed, and the Lord's Prayer. Lutheran pastors read it publicly in church, preached series of sermons on it yearly, and supervised weekly sessions in which children committed it to memory. The Lutheran churches retained the practice of private confession and used it as an occasion for examining the doctrinal knowledge of adults. Each of the national Reformed churches also produced its own catechisms and used them just as extensively. When employed according to their original intention, the catechisms helped people relate doctrine to the practice of Christianity in daily life. At times, however, catechetical instruction became abstract or polemical and only remotely related to the practice of piety.[9]

Pastors cared for the spiritual needs of their parishioners primarily by preaching and the administration of the sacraments. In addition to these tasks, the main work of the pastors consisted of the execution of disciplinary duties. The territorial churches gave the pastors considerable power to punish neglect of church practice, heresy, or offenses against the laws of God. In most regions teams of inspectors composed of clergy and lay leaders visited all the parishes of a territorial church to evaluate compliance with the accepted standards of doctrinal orthodoxy and moral behavior. Cases of blasphemy, gross immorality, and neglect of religious duties were punished as civil crimes by fines or imprisonment.[10] This close cooperation between church and state frequently became a focus of criticism by religious dissenters, who pointed to it as evidence that the church had become conformed to the world.

Popular Piety in Protestant Parishes

The disciplinary procedures used by the state churches generally increased regularity of church attendance in Protestant regions of Europe, but visitation records indicate that improvements in churchliness were not always accompanied by a significant growth in personal piety. Despite the concerted efforts of the religious and secular authorities to inculcate knowledge of doctrine and improve the quality of religious and moral life, many Protestants remained uncertain about what they were supposed to believe and lived in ways which the clergy considered unacceptable.[11]

The folk piety of the Middle Ages also persisted to a certain extent in many regions. For example, some nominal Lutherans continued to address prayers to the saints and called for the ringing of church bells to avert the danger of lightning. When hard times beset the Protestant churches, clergy and laity alike perceived signs of diabolical interference. The devil was frequently blamed for the occurrence of misfortune, and belief in witchcraft intensified along with the growth of confessional strife. To overcome the harm done by the devil and his human agents, the common people often trusted in remedies which the Protestant churches officially condemned. Although the clergy viewed the practice of magic as a sin, some of the laity sought help from individuals who used magical anointings and blessings as therapeutic measures against illness and other inexplicable disasters.[12]

The criticisms of moral and spiritual life recorded in the visitation reports have led some historians to conclude that the Reformation failed to have a significant impact on popular piety. Speaking of Germany in the late six-teenth century, Gerald Strauss has argued that "the Reformation aroused no widespread, meaningful, and lasting response to its message."[13] According to this view, inappropriate methods of pedagogy and a lack of compassion for the religious needs of ordinary people doomed Lutheran efforts to trans-form the religious orientation of popular society. This claim has been challenged by other Reformation scholars who have assembled evidence suggesting that at least in some regions clerical complaints about the quality of religious life diminished notably by the end of the century.[14] The most detailed regional studies of the impact of the Reformation indicate that although popular religion was not wholly transformed, some features of Protestant thought began to leave a clear mark on the beliefs and activities of the common people. The picture of God as a fearful judge became less prominent. Popular spirituality developed a more Christocentric focus which encouraged belief that God was merciful and forgiving. An increasing number of people seemed able to bear suffering with patience and face death without fear because they had apparently derived psychological strength from Protestant worship, the reading of the Bible, and the regular practice of family devotions.[15] Bernard Vogler, one of the most prolific investigators of late sixteenth-century religion, distinguishes among three reactions to Lutheranism. The piety of the majority was limited to weekly attendance at a church service. Of the two significant minority groups, one consisted of the deeply religious, often the well-established citizens of the towns; the other was of the religiously indifferent, generally people on the fringes of society.[16] The intensity of religious life varied regionally, but this general pattern was probably common throughout Protestant Europe.

Dissatisfaction with the State of Religious Life

The So-called Lutheran Piety Crisis

According to some historians, the Lutheran churches faced a new crisis soon after they resolved the doctrinal crisis of the period between 1548 and 1580. Winfried Zeller, who introduced this idea twenty-five years ago, claimed that church leaders concerned with the defense of true doctrine allowed a spiri-tual vacuum to develop in the final decades of the sixteenth century by fail-ing to appreciate the critical function of piety in the development of a meaningful theology. The third generation of Lutheran Protestants success-fully established a standard of basic doctrine for the churches, but its leaders, from Zeller's perspective, no longer possessed the deep religious experience of the original reformers. Many of them insufficiently appreciated the fact that "the purity of a theological existence is not determined only by the correct confession of doctrine but also by the depth and inwardness of spiritual life."[17] As evidence of this piety crisis, Zeller notes the sense of alienation expressed by many critics of religion in this period. Other defenders of this thesis perceive in late sixteenth-century church music and the mannerist style of art and architecture, a crisis of style that can be related to a pervasive feeling of diffidence and disquietude. Since these stylistic developments are manifested in several of the confessional traditions, some historians speak of a comprehensive spiritual crisis throughout Europe in this period.[18]

Zeller's specific description of a Lutheran piety crisis and his explanation of its causes remain open to question for several reasons. The evidence of the previously noted visitation records from Lutheran parishes might seem to support Zeller's claims about the state of piety in the late sixteenth century, but the reports of religious uncertainty and lack of refined moral sensibilities are not uniquely characteristic of this period. The problems alluded to by pious social critics were present all along from the first days of the Reformation and well beyond the late sixteenth century. It would be hasty to conclude from these records that the quality of popular piety was getting worse in the third generation of the Reformation. Furthermore, several historians in the twentieth century have drawn attention to the practical and pastoral activities of many dogmaticians and have challenged the previous dominant characterization of the Lutheran theology of this period as a lifeless orthodoxy.[19] Some theologians were dangerously one-sided in their concern for the defense of pure doctrine, but confessionalism did not always exclude dedication to the cultivation of practical piety.

Despite the lack of evidence for a significant decline in the quality of piety and the need to qualify Zeller's conclusions about the causes and pervasiveness of a crisis mentality in this period, Zeller rightly observes that popular writers of practical religious literature in Lutheran Germany believed that a general reform of religious and social life was desperately needed. More than a few declared that the Protestant churches were in the midst of a moral and spiritual decline which God would not allow to go unpunished. Apocalyptically-minded Lutheran clergy interpreted the occurrence of natural disasters such as famine and earthquakes, and the revival of the Turkish menace in 1593, as early signs of an approaching divine judgment. The escalation of conflicts between Protestants and Catholics in the decades immediately prior to the Thirty Years' War may also have contributed to the rise of pessimism, which in turn influenced the evaluation of moral and spiritual life.

Moderate and Radical Critics of Religious Life

Pious critics of society often differed about the causes of the supposed decline in religious life. Some such as Andreas Musculus (1514–1581), an influential church leader in Brandenburg, blamed Satan and the lay people. Throughout his life, Musculus campaigned against the low level of moral and spiritual life in Germany by writing tracts in which he portrayed each vice as the work of a specific devil.[20] Others such as Johann Arndt (1555–1621) suggested that the Lutheran pastors and theologians contributed to the neglect of true Christian living by the way they proclaimed the Christian message. Arndt charged that the clergy were so preoccupied with doctrinal controversies that they failed to communicate the true meaning of repentance and faith to the parishioners they served. Although he agreed that the church must defend itself against heresy, Arndt lamented the harsh tone of polemical writings in his day and implied that some disputes were about insignificant issues.[21]

Most of these critics were loyal members of the Lutheran churches who frequently assumed important leadership roles. Arndt, for example, served as general superintendent of the territorial church of Braunschweig-Lüneburg. There were some, however, who became so pessimistic about the possibilities of altering the direction of Lutheran religious life that they withdrew from active support of the state churches. A notable example of such radical dissent was Valentin Weigel (1533–1588), a Lutheran pastor in Zschopau, Saxony. Weigel never officially withdrew from the Lutheran church, but he disparaged its concern for detailed creeds and the importance of external religious ceremonies. Toward the end of his life, Weigel abandoned his earlier efforts to reform the church and wrote books that looked forward to the gathering of a new community of true believers who would immediately experience the presence of Christ without the mediation of a clerically dominated, state-supported external institution. Like Dirck Coornhert in the Netherlands, Weigel favored a more individualistic, internalized understanding of Christianity. His vision of a New Jerusalem on earth, associated with the dawning of a new age of the Holy Spirit, reveals the influence of medieval mysticism, the prophetic tradition established by Joachim of Fiore, Protestant Spiritualism, and the natural philosophy of Paracelsus.[22]

The Common Focus of the Religious Critics

All of the religious writers mentioned above, including radicals such as Weigel, shared a concern for a reorientation of pastoral guidance and personal religious life. Foremost among the religious deficiencies which they perceived in their parishes was the widespread manifestation of religious complacency or false security. Unlike most of the Protestant leaders of the early Reformation, they concluded that unregenerate behavior and licentiousness were more pervasive problems than false reliance on good works. Without repudiating the forensic view of justification, the orthodox Lutheran idea that salvation is based on the imputed righteousness of Christ, the moderate critics such as Arndt added a new emphasis on the personal holiness that should result from the inner working of Christ in the believer. They claimed that God's grace ought to produce an empirically observable and personally experienced moral and spiritual change in those who have been justified. This growing preoccupation with the process of sanctification is markedly evident in the numerous devotional books that were published in the late sixteenth and early seventeenth centuries.

Spiritual Writers and the Reform of Protestant Piety

Lutheran Edificatory Literature

From the very beginning of the Reformation, the Protestant clergy had recognized the need to provide books of practical religious instruction for their literate church members. Since the abundant Catholic devotional literature produced during the Middle Ages was generally considered unsuitable for use by Christians who shared Luther's theological viewpoint, Lutheran writers supplemented the guidance provided by sermons, hymns, and catechisms by publishing new collections of prayers, confessional manuals, consolatory treatises, simple works of biblical exegesis, and books designed to help Christians prepare for death. Church leaders in the second generation of the Lutheran movement continued to produce practical edificatory literature, but few of them wrote books that had an enduring influence among ordinary lay people. At the very end of the sixteenth century, however, the intensified dissatisfaction with the state of religious life stimulated new interest in the production of popular religious books. Some of the great classics of Lutheran devotional literature date from this period.[23]

The new Lutheran spirituality shaped by these third-generation authors was influenced significantly by sources outside of the Lutheran tradition. Orthodox devotional writers, as well as radicals such as Weigel, looked to the ascetics and mystics of the Middle Ages for guidance in the nurturing of spiritual growth. This interest in mystical spirituality was not without precedence in Lutheranism, for the young Luther himself had been attracted to certain themes in the writings of German mystics such as Johann Tauler. The new authors, however, were reversing a trend away from mystical piety which had begun in Luther's late theology. They were not blind to the synergistic and spiritualistic tendencies of medieval mysticism which the theologians of the Age of Orthodoxy condemned, but they still valued the testimony which the mystics gave to the transforming work of Christ within the soul.[24]

Martin Moller and Stephan Praetorius were among the first Lutherans to draw extensively on these mystical sources. Moller (1547–1606) published a collection of meditations in 1584 consisting primarily of selections from the writings of Augustine, Bernard of Clairvaux, and Johann Tauler. Moller also translated medieval Latin hymns into German for use in Lutheran worship. Praetorius (1536–1604) wrote eighty edifying tracts in his lifetime which were later collected and published as *The Spiritual Treasurechest*. Convinced that salvation was more than a matter of reconciliation with God, he described how Christ actually dwells in the soul, making the true Christian a living temple of God. Praetorius believed that through baptism the believer becomes a partaker of the divine nature (2 Peter 1:4). This treasure of salvation, he repeatedly noted, should make the Christian a new creature possessing the power to live a virtuous life.[25]

The idea of the indwelling of Christ and the description of the Christian as a new creature figure even more prominently in the writings of Philipp Nicolai and Johann Arndt. Nicolai (1556–1608) devoted equal attention to the defense of true doctrine and the encouragement of holy living. He wrote numerous polemical works against the theology of the Catholics and Calvinists but also focused on practical piety in his *Mirror of Joy*, first published in 1599. In order to help simple believers understand the *ordo salutis,* the standard theological description of salvation as a series of distinct stages, Nicolai compared spiritual growth to the process of natural birth and development. He depicted God, the efficient cause of salvation, as the father and the church, the secondary cause, as the mother. According to this metaphor, conception takes place at baptism and the believer grows spiritually throughout earthly life like the child in the womb until he or she is born into eternal life. Nicolai described union with God as a culminating stage in spiritual growth and adopted the nuptial language of the mystics to characterize this experience of God's presence. The bridegroom Christ unites with the bride, the individual Christian, in a perfect bond of love when the human will has been brought into conformity with the will of God by grace. Nicolai also expressed his longing for union with the

Bridegroom poetically in his well-known hymns, "Wake, Awake for Night Is Flying," and "How Brightly Beams the Morning Star."[26]

Unlike Nicolai, Johann Arndt (1555–1621) devoted minimal attention to the exposition of contested theological issues. He concentrated instead on the development of a comprehensive guide to spiritual growth. His *Four Books of True Christianity*, first published in 1605 and subsequently revised and enlarged several times, became the single most influential devotional book in Lutheran history. This work is not a literary masterpiece, but it conveyed the importance of rebirth and renewal in a psychologically effective manner. Arndt sought to nurture the formation of some fundamental religious attitudes which would be a strong internal source of direction for the practice of piety. First of all, he attempted to arouse his readers from complacency and encourage sincere sorrow for sin by contrasting the state of humanity before and after the fall. After inspiring contrition, he consoled them in *True Christianity* with the promises of the gospel. Seeking to motivate as well as console, he went on to portray the work of Christ in a way that would make his readers expect a change in their lives as a result of the gift of grace. According to Arndt, Christ is a doctor who offers medicine to release Christians from the power of sin. Like a disease, the influence of sin, however, does not disappear all at once. Arndt prepared the Christian for a long and hard struggle against sin and encouraged self-scrutiny and self-denial as ways of promoting renewal. To sustain pursuit of spiritual growth, he also affirmed the importance of imitating the life of Christ and offered his readers the promise that they would ultimately experience a joyful union with Christ.

Not all Lutherans approved of the religious sentiments expressed in this new devotional literature. Arndt, especially, found himself on the defensive in the last years of his life against charges of heterodoxy. Some theologians attacked him for reviving the errors of the Philippists, questioned his optimism about the possibilities of spiritual growth, and claimed that the experiential focus of his piety led people toward the dangerous enthusiasm of spiritualists such as Valentin Weigel. Arndt was also vulnerable to the charge that his writings promoted a retrogression toward Catholicism because he frequently paraphrased passages from Catholic writers in his books. In fact, Arndt quoted selectively and consciously excluded phrases from his sources which he considered incompatible with Lutheranism. His reputation gradually improved throughout the seventeenth century because of the qualified support he gained from notable defenders of Lutheran orthodoxy such as Johann Gerhard (1582–1637).[27]

Arminianism in the Netherlands

During the period in which Nicolai and Arndt were attempting to revitalize and reorient Lutheran piety, a major challenge to Calvinist orthodoxy developed within the Dutch Reformed Church. The humanistic religious perspective defended in the late sixteenth century by Dirck Coornhert and Caspar Coolhaes found a new spokesman in the person of Jacob Arminius (1560–1609), professor at the University of Leiden. Although he had studied at Geneva and had returned to the Netherlands with a letter of approval from Theodore Beza, Arminius began to question the orientation of the Reformed confessional tradition. Like the earlier humanists, he found himself unable to defend the supralapsarian interpretation of predestination which most strict Calvinists favored. In his mind, the belief that God had determined before creation to elect a certain number of persons to receive his mercy and had chosen to damn others seemed to make God the author of sin. As a pastor interested in the promotion of Christian holiness, Arminius also feared that this doctrine would encourage a passive attitude detrimental to a serious concern for morality. In opposition to the strict Calvinists, he claimed that God had decreed to save all who believed in Christ and condemned only those who would refuse an offer of saving grace. This belief, similar in some respects to the position defended by various Lutheran Philippists in the Synergistic Controversy, assumed that humans possess at least a limited capacity to cooperate with God in the process of conversion. To Franciscus Gomarus, leader of the strict Calvinist opposition to Arminius, such a view was tantamount to a defense of Pelagianism.[28]

A major controversy erupted after the death of Arminius, when his sympathizers within the Dutch church drew up a petition asking the state for protection from the disciplinary procedures proposed by their opponents. The Remonstrants, as they came to be called, gained the support of Johan van Oldenbarnevelt, the most powerful official in the government of the United Provinces, but the majority of the ministers of the church organized themselves as a Counter-Remonstrant movement. Dutch society became so polarized that civil war seemed imminent. In 1618, however, Maurice, prince of Orange, ousted Oldenbarnevelt from power and allowed the Counter-Remonstrants to enforce adherence to the Reformed doctrine of predestination. A national synod of the Dutch church held at Dort (Dordrecht) in the same year officially condemned the Arminian heresy and forced many Remonstrant leaders into exile. Nevertheless, the new liberal theology still attracted the sympathy of the republican opponents of the prince of Orange and many of the wealthy merchant families of Holland.

9. Albrecht Dürer, *Knight, Death and the Devil,* 1513.

The Remonstrants continued to exist as a religious minority concerned with ethics more than purity of doctrine. This practical theology appealed to intellectuals such as Hugo Grotius, the influential Dutch legal scholar, and other advocates of religious toleration. The flexible theology associated with this humanistic movement also contributed to the growth of rationalism in the Netherlands during the seventeenth century.[29]

Practical Divinity in the Dutch Reformed Church

After the Synod of Dort, the Dutch Reformed Church was widely hailed as a leading force in the preservation of Calvinist orthodoxy. The Arminian controversy had stimulated interest in the clarification of Reformed doctrine, but it also inspired renewed zeal for church discipline. Dutch church leaders prepared a new church order which prohibited unnecessary work and frivolous recreation on the sabbath. A large body of literature also appeared stressing the importance of moral and spiritual renewal. Gotfried Cornelius Udemans (1580–1649), a pastor who had participated in the Synod of Dort, wrote several popular books which encouraged readers to practice Christian virtues and recommended detailed devotional practices. In *Practice*, published in 1612, he combined general reflections on faith, hope, and love with precise advice about how families could nurture piety in their homes. Reformed devotional writers such as Udemans often reflected on the application of biblical law to specific situations and noted the religious duties of specific social groups or classes of people.

Like his Lutheran contemporary Johann Arndt, Willem Tellinck (1579–1629) warned his readers that correct confession of true doctrine was not the only standard to be used in evaluating true Christianity. In books such as his *Necessary Warning Concerning the Sorrowful State of God's People* (1627), he exhorted the Dutch people to show more concern for practical moral reform. Tellinck criticized the Arminians for overemphasizing the role of human effort in the process of conversion, but encouraged his readers to attend more seriously to the eradication of bad habits and the pursuit of spiritual growth. He focused on the need to practice self-denial in order to overcome the sinful inclinations of human nature. The influence of Puritanism is evident in some of Tellinck's writings, especially when he offers precise directions for the external practice of piety. Having lived for a while in England, he came to appreciate the way Puritan writers related the Ten Commandments to daily Christian living. There is also, however, a subjective dimension to Tellinck's piety which may be derived more directly from the strong mystical tradition in the Low Countries. In *The New Jerusalem* and *The Mirror of Devotion,* Tellinck described an experience of oneness with Christ which is a foretaste of eternal bliss.[30]

English Puritanism influenced the Dutch Reformed Church directly through the lifework of William Ames (1576–1633). Forced into exile from England in 1610, Ames settled in the Netherlands, where he had a distinguished career as a university professor and pastor. He sided with the orthodoxy Calvinists in the disputes with the Arminians but differed from many of his Dutch colleagues in his approach to theology. In opposition to the intellectualistic tendencies of Reformed scholasticism, Ames carried on the tradition of practical divinity advocated by his English teacher, William Perkins. He always related doctrine to piety and treated theology primarily as a science offering knowledge about how to live according to God's will. *The Marrow of Divinity,* the textbook Ames prepared for the teaching of theology, was divided into two parts. The first systematically presented the doctrine of the Reformed churches, and the second discussed at length the public and private religious observances which declare and confirm the Christian's faith. In the aforementioned book and in another entitled, *Cases of Conscience,* he outlined a detailed code of ethics, specifying how concern for godliness ought to affect the way a person thinks, acts, speaks, and even dresses. This casuistic approach to piety influenced many Dutch Reformed spiritual writers throughout the seventeenth century.[31]

The Significance of the Thirty Years' War for Religious Life

The Effect of the War on Popular Piety

These notable efforts to improve the quality of religious life in the Protestant churches were offset by the destructive impact of the Thirty Years' War (1618–1648). After several decades of mounting tension, the Catholic and Protestant princes of Germany formed rival military leagues which clashed for the first time in Bohemia. The religious war quickly spread to other parts of the empire and became international when Danish and Swedish troops came to the aid of the German Protestants. While the Catholic forces in Germany advanced under the leadership of the emperor, the king of Spain, another member of the Hapsburg dynasty, attempted to reconquer the Dutch Protestants who had previously freed the northern provinces of the Netherlands from his control. After 1635, the war became even more complicated when the Bourbon dynasty of France, though Catholic, sided with the Protestant cause for political reasons. The style of warfare used by the combatants was extraordinarily destructive, and pestilence or starvation

killed many who managed to escape a violent death. Some historians estimate that the population of the empire decreased by seven or eight million.

The hardship of wartime life caused some to become indifferent to moral
and spiritual ideals. Drunkenness and other forms of self-indulgence became
widespread among those who abandoned hope for the future. When it
became increasingly difficult to view the war as a heroic struggle for a holy
cause, numerous individuals began to question the importance of the differences which divided the confessional groups.[32] As a result, the communal
aspects of religious life deteriorated in many parishes. The disintegration of
society also redirected the religious interests of many pious Protestants. The
prevailing mood of pessimism encouraged retreat from worldly affairs and
stimulated longings for blissful spiritual experiences. In the midst of social
chaos, the introspective piety promoted before the war by authors such as
Arndt and Nicolai gained a new appeal.[33]

Seventeenth-Century Protestant Hymnody

The effect of the war on the orientation of popular piety is clearly evident
in the hymns written during the middle of the seventeenth century. Some
of the greatest hymn writers of European Protestantism were active during
these decades of distress. Having experienced suffering themselves, they
were inspired to offer memorable words of consolation to other Christians.
Melancholy feelings about earthly life frequently appeared in these hymns.
Nevertheless, the hymn writers pointed to a source of hope in the person
of Christ. The Son of God, they noted, participated fully in the anguish and
sorrow of human life but ultimately triumphed over sin and death. Christians who also bear crosses in this life can face the future with confidence
that they too will share in this victory. Such meditations on the passion of
Christ are especially prominent in the Lutheran hymns of Johann Heerman
(1585–1647). Other hymns reflected in deeply emotional language on the
peace and joy that accompany union with Christ. Numerous hymn writers
described this experience as a possibility in earthly life as well as in the life
to come.

Some of the hymns which expressed these themes were highly sentimental. Their focus on individualistic piety is especially evident in the use of
subjective language and the pronoun "I." The best hymn writers, however,
avoided the extreme manifestations of these tendencies. Paul Gerhardt
(1607–1676) is the most noteworthy of the Lutheran poets. His religious
lyrics combined the warm expression of religious feelings with a continuing
emphasis on the central doctrines of his confessional tradition. For example,

he portrayed Christ as both Redeemer and Friend in hymns such as "O Sacred Head Now Wounded." Some of his hymns meditated on the future happiness of eternal life, while others, especially his morning and evening hymns, called to mind the beauty to be found in the created world.[34]

Hymn writers in the Reformed tradition worked under greater constraints during this period because of the belief that congregational singing should be limited to the use of versified scriptural texts. In the early decades after the Thirty Years' War, however, Jodocus van Lodensteyn (1620–1677) in the Netherlands and Joachim Neander (1650–1680) in Germany produced great hymns of praise. These Calvinist poets, like many of their Lutheran counterparts, combined a mystical interest in the experience of Christ's indwelling with a concern for ethical sensitivity and spiritual growth.

Reformorthodoxy

Although the Thirty Years' War inspired many pious Protestants to retreat into a privatized, subjective religious life, this impulse was far from universal. Others responded to the decline of moral and spiritual life by working for a general reformation of church and society. The mystical elements of Johann Arndt's spirituality contributed to the first type of response among Lutherans, but his appeal for ethical renewal was equally significant in providing guidance for the activists. Both university professors and pastors were well represented in this movement usually referred to as "Reformorthodoxy." These Lutherans continued to be uncompromising adversaries of Catholicism and Calvinism, but they also concerned themselves with the problem of relating theology to the practice of piety. The university faculty at Rostock in particular played a prominent role in these efforts to improve church discipline and pastoral care. Arndtian piety was highly regarded by its theologians, who passed on this influence to the most important devotional writers of the mid-seventeenth century.

Joachim Lütkemann (1608–1655), who studied and taught at Rostock toward the end of the war, is remembered primarily as author of *A Foretaste of Divine Goodness*, published in 1643. These meditations comforted Christians by describing the future experience of Christ's presence. In *Apostolic Exhortation*, Lütkemann concentrated more fully on outlining the features of a holy life. Lütkemann's criticisms of "worldly Christians" were developed more extensively by one of his younger colleagues, Heinrich Müller (1631–1675). This prolific devotional writer aroused considerable controversy by claiming that many Christians, both clergy and laity, were really idolaters who worshiped the baptismal font, the pulpit, the confessional bench, and the altar. Müller did not intend to disparage the significance of the sacraments, but he felt that many church members did not use the sacraments properly. They confessed their faith publicly and participated in external rituals yet failed to become true servants of God in their daily activities. One of the continuous themes of Müller's spirituality was the need for heartfelt love of God and neighbor. In books such as *The Heavenly Kiss of Love* and *The Divine Flame of Love,* he described in very colorful language how God's indwelling can revitalize the soul, producing both inner peace and outward renewal. Müller called for diligent examination of the heart's inclinations and perpetual vigilance against the possibility of spiritual backsliding.[35]

Christian Scriver (1629–1693), also educated at Rostock, extended the campaign to intensify both active and contemplative piety into the final decades of the seventeenth century. He was especially creative in developing new ways of expressing the themes stressed by his predecessors. For example, in *Gotthold's Occasional Meditations* (1663–1669), he presented memorable stories and descriptions of natural phenomena which he interpreted symbolically to convey a spiritual message. Although Scriver acknowledged that this emblematic book was inspired by the writings of Joseph Hall, an English bishop with Calvinist theological sympathies, his Lutheran orthodoxy was never seriously questioned. In his comprehensive guide to the Christian life, *The Treasure of the Soul* (1675), Scriver frequently quoted Luther and expressed his concern for rebirth and renewal within a broader survey of the fundamental articles of Lutheran theology. Scriver's daily routine set an example of the kind of piety he favored. He devoted four hours daily to prayer and devotional reading, an hour to the preparation for a holy death, and two hours to edifying activities such as the singing of hymns, godly conversation, and acts of charity.[36]

Pietism in Late Seventeenth-Century Europe

Lutheran Pietism

The spiritual tradition in Lutheranism which began with Johann Arndt and continued to influence many church reformers and devotional writers both during and after the Thirty Years' War has been described by some historians as an early manifestation of a type of religious life known as pietism. Other historians, however, restrict the use of this term to the religious movement initiated by Philip Jacob Spener (1635–1705) while he served as senior pastor of the Lutheran church in Frankfurt. The latter perspective emphasizes the novelty of Spener's theological ideas and piety, whereas the broader use of the concept accentuates the continuity between Spener and the earlier forms of Lutheran spirituality. Since scholars are far from reaching a consensus about the defining characteristics and origins of pietism, it is important to recognize the merits of both points of view.[37]

Spener first gained notoriety as a religious reformer by the publication of *Pia Desideria* in 1675. This book criticized the state of religious life in Germany and offered concrete proposals for the correction of the church's deficiencies. Many of its themes are far from original. Like Arndt, Spener lamented the lack of true Christian piety in each social class and expressed dissatisfaction with the disputational preoccupations of orthodox Lutheran theologians. Like Müller, he charged that most church members had mistaken notions about the efficacy of the sacraments. They participated in church life without ever manifesting true repentance or a living faith. The understanding of true Christianity which Spener advocated in contrast to this superficial piety was also derived primarily from the Arndtian tradition. It emphasized the idea of rebirth and a continuous process of renewal. Spener accented the practical message of the earlier Lutheran writers more than their mystical interests, but he too affirmed the possibility of an experience of Christ's indwelling.

In addition to these similarities between Spener and earlier Lutheran reformers, there are also some significant differences. First of all, Spener's spirituality incorporated a view of eschatology that his predecessors did not share. He expressed great optimism about the possibility of better conditions in the church and looked forward to a thousand-year reign of Christ on earth. These chiliastic expectations were a major motivation of his quest for reform. His specific proposals for the renewal of the church were designed to hasten the conversion of the Jews and the fall of papal Rome, two events which he associated with New Testament prophecies about the millennium. Second, Spener questioned the prevailing assumption that the cooperative reform efforts of civil and religious leaders were the key to the revitalization of popular piety. In *Pia Desideria,* he challenged the "presumptuous monopoly of the clergy" over the laity and called for a new appreciation of Luther's teachings about the priesthood of all believers. Convinced that "all spiritual functions are open to all Christians without exception," he stressed the right and the duty of the laity to teach, comfort, admonish, and edify one another. Spener put this proposal into effect in Frankfurt by organizing *collegia pietatis* or conventicles in which lay people met to read and discuss the Bible or other devotional books. Spener was not the first Protestant to institute conventicles, but he developed this experiment to an unprecedented degree. He continued to affirm the value of an ordained clergy but hoped that lay fellowship groups would assume an increasing role in the supervision of pastoral care. As *ecclesiolae in ecclesia,* they would promote commitment to holy living more effectively than disciplinary measures imposed from above by the clergy or the state.[38]

Some Lutherans viewed Spener's organizational innovations and eschatological views with great suspicion. They used the name "pietist" pejoratively to refer to his followers, who in turn accepted this designation to distinguish themselves from lukewarm or unregenerate church members. Despite considerable opposition, Spener's influence quickly spread into many regions of Germany. The city of Halle in particular became an important center of pietism under the leadership of August Hermann Francke (1663–1727). This younger friend of Spener is most remembered for his work in education and his establishment of numerous charitable institutions. While serving as a professor at the new university of Halle, he implemented Spener's proposals for the reorientation of theological education. The new curriculum he designed stressed Bible study and subordinated the pursuit of scholarly research to the goal of awakening heartfelt piety. To promote the pietist style of religious training, Francke also founded an orphanage, a biblical institute, several schools, a library, and a publishing house. These institutions flourished because of the support Francke got from the ruling family of Prussia. Similarly, the king of Denmark facilitated Francke's efforts to establish Lutheran missionary work overseas.[39]

Elsewhere in Germany, Spener's influence was most evident in Württemberg. His visit to this region in 1662 reinforced the concern for moral and spiritual renewal that had developed during the Thirty Years' War through the efforts of church leaders such as Johann Valentin Andreae (1586–1640). In contrast to northern Germany, where Francke had a strong following among the nobility, pietism in Württemberg appealed primarily to the middle class and the peasants. It also acquired intellectual respectability because of the leadership provided by theologians at the University of Tübingen such as Johann Albrecht Bengel (1687–1752).[40]

Reformed Pietism

Although Arndtian spirituality and Reformed orthodoxy were the major sources contributing to the rise of Lutheran pietism, Spener also acknowledged his indebtedness to the Reformed tradition. He encouraged his followers to read Puritan devotional literature and may have been inspired to organize conventicles by his contact with Jean de Labadie, a controversial French Reformed pastor. This interaction between the two confessional groups has convinced many historians that pietism should be treated as a religious movement developing simultaneously in several branches of Protestantism.

In the decades after the Thirty Years' War, the most prominent theologian in the Dutch Reformed Church was Gisbertus Voetius (1589–1676). Like many of the Lutheran theologians associated with Reformorthodoxy in Germany, he emphasized the importance of both purity of doctrine and purity of life with equal vigor. Voetius used scholastic methods in his dogmatic writings but also made a significant contribution to the development of a practical theology. Following the pattern established by William Ames and other English Puritans, Voetius offered detailed advice for the application of general moral principles to specific situations. He also emphasized the importance of living in complete conformity with the laws of God revealed in the Scriptures. In response to the critics of this "precisionism," he carefully distinguished between the abuse and the proper use of such an approach to the practice of piety.[41]

Jodocus van Lodensteyn (1620–1677), a student of Voetius, is often viewed as a primary example of Reformed pietism. In addition to writing hymns, he frequently preached against lax morality and superficial religiosity in the Reformed churches. In his devotional writings, Lodensteyn focused on the importance of conversion and encouraged his readers to strive for spiritual and moral perfection. Like many of his Lutheran contemporaries, he pointed to the life of Christ as an example to be imitated, noting in particular the need to practice self-denial and brotherly love.

Lodensteyn frequently spoke of the value of systematic contemplation, which he believed would help the Christian experience the illumination of the intellect by the Holy Spirit and an intimate communion with Christ. Concern for religious experience is even more pronounced in the piety of Theodorus à Brakel (1608–1669). This Dutch pastor devoted less attention to the recommendation of specific rules of conduct and focused instead on the affective benefits derived from prayer and meditation. Like the medieval mystics who described three stages of spiritual growth (purgation, illumination, and union with God), à Brakel distinguished three states of godliness in his book *The Steps of the Spiritual Life*. The last step he characterized as a state of joyful communion with God in Christ. Reformed pietism continued to develop during the lifetime of Spener and Francke under the leadership of Willem à Brakel (1635–1711) in the Netherlands and Theodor Untereyck (1635–1693) in Germany.[42]

Radical Pietism

Critics of late seventeenth-century pietists often accused them of promoting enthusiasm and separatism. All of the individuals mentioned above denied such charges and professed allegiance to their confessional traditions. There were others, however, who became so disaffected that they voluntarily withdrew from the established Protestant churches. The roots of these more radical manifestations of pietism can be traced back to the confessional indifference of sixteenth-century rebels such as Valentin Weigel and Dirck Coornhert and before that to the spiritualists of the Reformation. The critical and mystical elements of Johann Arndt's thought also enhanced doubts about the importance of confessional loyalty and directly inspired separatists such as Christian Hohburg (1607–1675) to repudiate the Lutheran tradition.

In Germany, Jacob Böhme (1575–1624), a contemporary of Arndt, added further strength to the currents of radical dissent. This largely self-educated shoemaker attended a conventicle organized by Martin Moller in Silesia in which he acquired a strong interest in mystical piety. Around 1600, Böhme began to experience moments of illumination which increased his discontent with the organized church and inspired him to develop his own independent theology. Beginning with *Aurora* in 1612, he produced a series of prophetic books, influenced by the natural philosophy of Paracelsus as well as the mystics. His speculative solution to the problem of the existence of evil and his criticisms of traditional institutional religion disturbed the Lutheran clergy, who confiscated his books and forbade him to write any more. Later in his life, Böhme turned the focus of this thought to more practical issues. The nine treatises on the spiritual life published in 1624 as *The Way of Christ* guided the reader to the experience of union with Christ or Sophia (Divine Wisdom). Böhme attempted to maintain a connection to the Lutheran church, but many of his followers became separatists.[43]

Johannes Scheffler (1624–1677) and Gottfried Arnold (1666–1714) are the two most notable radicals influenced by Böhme's piety. Scheffler, better known as Angelus Silesius, was originally a Lutheran, but converted to Catholicism in 1653. Although the poetry for which he is most famous emphasized a highly personal, mystical piety, his disenchantment with Protestantism inspired him to become an increasingly devout defender of the authority of the Catholic Church. He expressed his new-found convictions in numerous polemical works such as *The Lutherans' and Calvinists' Idol of Reason*. After Gottfried Arnold, an acquaintance of Spener, came under the influence of Böhme, he concluded that all of the churches were obstacles to the development of true piety. Arnold eventually moderated his criticisms of the Lutheran Church, but his historical and theological writings encouraged the further growth of sectarian pietism in the eighteenth century.[44]

The development of radical pietism in the Reformed churches owed much to influences emanating from France. Jean de Labadie (1610–1674), a

Catholic convert to the Reformed tradition, retained a high regard for many of the features of Jansenist piety. His belief in the importance of withdrawing from all forms of worldliness caused him eventually to sever the ties between the Reformed church and the conventicle groups he had established. The mystical spirituality of the Quietist movement in France also influenced some radical pietists, who renounced their affiliation with the Reformed church. Popularized by the Reformed pastor Pierre Poiret (1666–1719), Quietism had its strongest effect on the piety of Protestant separatists in northwestern Germany such as Gerhard Tersteegen (1697–1769).[45]

* * * *

The more radical expressions of seventeenth-century Protestant spirituality have tended to distort the evaluation historians and theologians make about the general characteristics of religious life in this period. Orthodox theologians, both Lutheran and Reformed, have been charged with failing to produce a significant practical spirituality. Popular writers from Arndt to Spener have been accused of forsaking the fundamental orientation of the theology of Luther by shifting their emphasis to the doctrine of sanctification. The religiosity of the pietists has often been judged excessively individualistic, ascetic, or eudaemonistic. Critics have also disparaged the spiritual writers of the Reformed tradition for fostering the development of a self-preoccupied and oppressive legalistic piety. It cannot be denied that the efforts of the major spiritual reformers to intensify personal religious experience and concern for ethical conduct sometimes produced these results, but a careful analysis of their writings and reform programs often reveals that the more extravagant piety of some of their followers was quite different from what they themselves intended to promote.

By 1720, the development of rationalism in Europe raised doubts about many features of the intense spirituality associated with the seventeenth-century reformers. Pietism lost its appeal especially among the intellectual leadership of the Protestant churches. Nevertheless, interest in the hymns[46] and devotional books of the seventeenth century revived in the nineteenth century and continued to shape the piety of many Lutheran and Reformed Christians even into the twentieth century.

Notes

1. For a more detailed history of the late sixteenth century, see Richard S. Dunn, *The Age of Religious Wars 1559–1598* (New York: W. W. Norton, 1970); J. H. Elliott, *Europe Divided 1559–1598* (New York: Harper & Row, 1968); Ernst Walter Zeeden, *Das Zeitalter der Glaubenskämpfe* (Stuttgart: Ernst Klett, 1970).

2. On the thought and activites of Melanchthon, see A. Sperl, *Melanchthon zwischen Humanismus und Reformation* (Munich: Kaiser, 1959); and Hans Engelland, *Melanchthon, Glauben und Handeln* (Munich: Kaiser, 1931).

3. See the articles by Robert Kolb, "George Major as Controversialist: Polemics in the Late Reformation," *Church History* 45 (1976) 1–14; and "Good Works are Detrimental to Salvation: Amsdorf's Use of Luther's Words in Controversy," *Renaissance and Reformation* 4 (1980) 136–51.

4. Oliver Olson, "Matthias Flacius Illyricus," in *Shapers of Religious Traditions in Germany, Switzerland, and Poland*, ed. Jill Raitt (New Haven: Yale University Press, 1981) 1–17.

5. Robert Kolb, *Andreae and the Formula of Concord* (St. Louis: Concordia, 1977); Ruth Weddige, *Zur Entwicklung der deutsch-lutherischen Lehre von Luthers Tode bis zur Konkordienformel* (Bethel bei Bielefeld: Buchdruckerei der Anstalt Bethel, 1933).

6. Robert Preuss, *The Theology of Post-Reformation Lutheranism;* Carl Heinz Ratschow, *Lutherische Dogmatik zwischen Reformation und Aufklärung* (2 vols.; Gütersloh: Mohn, 1964, 1966); Hans Weber, *Reformation, Orthodoxie, und Rationalismus* (Gütersloh: Mohn, 1940).

7. There is considerable disagreement about whether Beza's theology changed Calvinism into a Reformed scholasticism that abandoned Calvin's theological program. In favor of this thesis, see Walter Kickel, *Vernunft und Offenbarung bei Theodor Beza* (Neukirchen: Neukirchener Verlag, 1967). Opposed to this, see Jill Raitt, *The Eucharistic Theology of Theodore Beza* (American Academy of Religion Studies in Religion 4; Chambersburg, PA: American Academy of Religion, 1972).

8. On France, see Brian Armstrong, *Calvinism and the Amyraut Heresy* (Madison, WI: University of Wisconsin Press, 1969); on the perspective of Coornhert, see Rufus Jones, *Spiritual Reformers of the Sixteenth and Seventeenth Centuries.*

9. Martin Reu, *Dr. Martin Luther's Small Catechism* (Chicago: Wartburg Publishing House, 1929); Gunter Tietz, *Das Erscheinungsbild von Pfarrstand und Pfarrgemeinde des sächsische Kurkreis im Spiegel der Visitationsberichte des 16. Jahrhunderts* (Tübingen, 1971).

10. Paul Drews, *Der evangelische Geistliche in der deutsche Vergangenheit* (Jena: Eugen Diederichs, 1905); Andreas Zieger, *Das religiöse und kirchliche Leben in Preussen und Kurland im Spiegel der evangelischen Kirchenordnungen des 16. Jahrhunderts* (Cologne Graz: Böhlau, 1967).

11. These generalizations are derived from the study of visitation reports. For a bibliography of printed records of this sort, see Ernst Walter Zeeden and Hansgeorg Molitor, *Die Visitation im Dienst der kirchlichen Reform* (Münster: Aschendorff, 1967).

12. Heinrich Nebelsieck, "Pfarrer und Gemeinde in ehemaligen sächsische Kurkreise," *Zeitschrift des Vereins für Kirchengeschichte der Provinz Sachsen* 35 (1939) 5–95; and Julius Bauer, "Kirchliche und sittliche Zustände in der lutherischen Gemeinden Niedersachsens im Reformationsjahrhundert," *Zeitschrift der Gesellschaft für niedersächsische Kirchengeschichte* 12 (1907) 29–72.

13. Gerald Strauss, *Luther's House of Learning*, 307. See also Strauss, "Success and Failure in the German Reformation," *Past and Present* 65 (1975) 30–63.

14. James Kittelson, "Successes and Failures in the German Reformation: The Report from Strasbourg," *Archiv für Reformationsgeschichte* 73 (1982) 153–74.

15. Bernard Vogler, *La vie réligieuse en pays rhenans dans la seconde moitié du XVIe siècle (1555–1619)* (Lille: Service de reproduction des thèses, 1974); Karl Aner, *Das Luthervolk: Geschicht seiner Frömmigkeit* (Tübingen: Mohr, 1917).

16. Bernard Vogler, "Die Entstehung der protestantischen Volksfrömmigkeit in der rheinischen Pfalz zwischen 1555 un 1619," *Archiv für Reformationsgeschichte* 73 (1982) 158–95.

17. Winfried Zeller, *Der Protestantismus des 17. Jahrhunderts*, xiii–xix. The idea of a Lutheran piety crisis has been adopted by historians such as Erich Beyreuther, F. W. Kantzenbach, Franz Lau, and Edmund Weber.

18. Bernd Jaspert, "'Krise' als Kirchengeschichtliche Kategorie," in *Traditio-Krisis-Renovatio aus theologischen Sicht: Festschrift Winfried Zeller*, ed. Bernd Jaspert and Rudolf Mohr (Marburg: Elwert, 1976) 24–40.

19. See Werner Elert, *Morphologie des Luthertums:* Vol. 1, *Theologie und Weltanschauung* (Munich: Beck, 1931); Hans Leube, *Orthodoxie und Pietismus: Gesammelte Studien*, ed. Martin Schmidt and Dietrich Blaufuss (Bielefeld: Luther Verlag, 1975); idem, *Die Reformideen in der deutschen lutherischen Kirche zur Zeit des Orthodoxie* (Leipzig: Döffling & Franke, 1924).

20. Andreas Musculus, *Christliche Trewe Warnung und Vermanung/wider der grewliche und verdamliche Sicherheit der gantzen Welt* (Erfurt: Georg Bawman, 1559); idem, *Von des Teufels Tyranny/Macht und Gewalt/Sonderlich in diesen letzten tagen/Unterdichtung* (1561).

21. Zeller's idea of a Lutheran piety crisis seems to be based primarily on Arndt's analysis of the time period. In every period of history there are some who think they are living in the worst of times. There is no reason to believe that popular critics in that era were any more accurate in their comparisons of past and present than their counterparts are today.

22. Winfried Zeller, *Die Schriften Valentin Weigels* (Berlin: Verlag Dr. Emil Ebering, 1940); Bernard Gorceix, *La mystique de Valentin Weigel (1533–1588) et les origines de la theosophie allemande* (Lille: Université de Lille III, 1972); Steven Ozment, *Mysticism and Dissent*, 203–45.

23. For a survey of Lutheran edificatory literature, see Hermann Beck, *Die Erbauungsliteratur der evangelischen Kirche* (Erlangen, 1883); Constantin Grosse, *Die alter Troster* (Hermannsburg, 1900).

24. Paul Althaus, *Forschungen zur evangelischen Gebetsliteratur* (Gütersloh: Bertelsmann, 1927); Winfried Zeller, "Luthertum und Mystik," in *Theologie und Frömmigkeit: Gesammelte Aufsätze*, ed. Bernd Jaspert (Marburg: Elwert, 1971) 35–54.

25. Winfried Zeller, *Der Protestantismus des 17. Jahrhunderts*, 1–30. Johann Arndt published the collected writings of Praetorius in 1622. They were revised and reissued by Martin Statius in 1625 as *Geistliche Schatzkammer der Gläubigen*. Other writers of this sort include Valerius Herberger (1562–1627).

26. On Nicolai, see Martin Lindström, *Philipp Nicolais Verständnis des Christentums* (Gütersloh: Bertelsmann, 1939).

27. On Arndt, see Wilhelm Koepp, *Johann Arndt: Eine Untersuchung über die Mystik im Luthertum* (Berlin: Trowitzsch & Sohn, 1912); Edmund Weber, *Johann Arndts Vier Bücher vom wahren Christenthum als Beitrag zur protestantischen Irenik de 17. Jahrhunderts* (Marburg: Elwert, 1969); Hans-Joachim Schwager, *Johann Arndt Bemühen um die rechte Gestaltung des neuen Lebens der Gläubigen* (Münster: Max Kramer, 1961); Eric Lund, "Johann Arndt and the Development of a Lutheran Spiritual Tradition" (Diss., Yale University, 1979). See also Christian Braw, *Bücher im Staube: Die Theologie Johann Arndts in ihrem Verhältnis zur Mystik* (Leiden: Brill, 1986).

28. For a sympathetic interpretation of Arminius's theology, see Carl Bangs, *Arminius: A Study in the Dutch Reformation*.

29. J. L. Price, *Culture and Society in the Dutch Republic during the Seventeenth Century* (New York: Scribner, 1974) 29–39; and Peter Geyl, *The Netherlands in the Seventeenth Century 1609–1648* (New York: Barnes & Noble, 1961) 38–83.

30. For a survey of piety in the Dutch Reformed Church, see F. Ernest Stoeffler, *The Rise of Evangelical Pietism* (Leiden: Brill, 1971) 117–33.

31. Keith Sprunger, *The Learned Doctor William Ames. The Marrow of Divinity* was translated from Latin into English in 1638 and Dutch in 1659.

32. There were two notable attempts to promote religious unity in this period. At the University of Helmstedt, Georg Calixtus (1586–1656) endeavored to overcome confessional differences by emphasizing the early Christian creeds which they all accepted. In Württemberg, J. V. Andreae produced several cryptic tracts describing the existence of a secret pansophical society called the Rosicrucians, who were supposedly committed to intellectual and religious reform. Many people who were seeking an alternative to the established churches sought to contact the Rosicrucians, although they probably never really existed in that context or time. Andreae eventually repudiated the myth he had created. See Arnold Schleiff, *Selbstkritik der lutherischen Kirchen im 17. Jahrhundert* (Berlin: Junker & Dünnhaupt, 1937).

33. Karl Holl, "Die Bedeutung der Grossen Kriege für des religiöse und kirchliche Leben innerhalb des deutschen Protestantismus," in *Gesammelte Aufsätze zur Kirchengeschichte III* (Tübingen: Mohr, 1928) 302–84.

34. See Ingeborg Röbbelen, *Theologie und Frömmigkeit im deutschen-lutherischen Gesangbuch des 17. und frühen 18. Jahrhunderts* (Göttingen: Vandenhoeck & Ruprecht, 1957).

35. On Lütkemann, see Heinrich Lütkemann, *Joachim Lütkemann: Sein Leben und Sein Wirken* (Braunschweig: Hellmuth Wollermann, 1902). Müller's critique of the four idols appeared in *Geistliche Erquickstunden* (1664), chap. 152.

36. On Scriver, see Fritz Becker, *Christian Scriver und sein literarisches Werk* (Münster: Buchdruckerei Althoff, 1929); and Martin Schmidt, "Christian Scriver's *Seelenschatz*," in *Wiedergeburt und neuer Mensch* (Witten: Luther Verlag, 1969) 112–28.

37. For a survey of the debate over the definition of pietism, see the articles by Martin Schmidt, Emmanuel Hirsch, Johannes Wallmann, and Hartmut Lehmann in *Zur neuer Pietismusforschung*, ed. Martin Greschat (Darmstadt: Wissenschaftliche Buchgesellschaft, 1977). For histories of pietism, see Erich Beyreuther, *Geschichte des Pietismus* (Stuttgart: J. F. Steinkopf, 1978); Martin Schmidt, *Pietismus* (Stuttgart: Kohlhammer, 1972); and F. Ernest Stoeffler, *The Rise of Evangelical Pietism*.

38. The eschatological theme is prominent in part 2 of *Pia Desideria*. Spener's discussion of the priesthood of all believers is in the second proposal of part 3. These elements are treated as defining characteristics of pietism by Johannes Wallmann, *Philipp Jakob Spener und die Anfänge des Pietismus* (Tübingen: Mohr-Siebeck, 1970); and Martin Greschat, *Zwischen Tradition und neuem Anfang: Valentin Löscher und der Ausgang der lutherischen Orthodoxie* (Witten: Luther Verlag, 1971).

39. Erich Beyreuther, *August Hermann Francke* (1956); Carl Hinrichs, *Preussentum und Pietismus* (Göttingen: Vandenhoeck & Ruprecht, 1971).

40. Martin Brecht, "Philipp Jakob Spener und die Württembergische Kirche," in *Geist und Geschichte der Reformation: Festgabe Hanns Rückert* (Berlin: de Gruyter, 1966) 443ff.; Hartmut Lehmann, *Pietismus und weltliche Ordnung in Württemberg* (Stuttgart: Kohlhammer, 1969).

41. See the introductory comments and selections from Voetius in John Beardslee III, *Reformed Dogmatics*, 3–25, 261–334.

42. F. Ernest Stoeffler, *The Rise of Evangelical Pietism,* 109–79; and Heinrich Heppe, *Geschichte des Pietismus und der Mystik in der Reformierten Kirche* (1879).

43. Will-Erich Peuckert, *Das Leben Jakob Böhmes* (Jena: Fr. Frommanns Verlag, 1961); Alexander Koyre, *La Philosophie de Jacob Boehme* (Paris: Vrin, 1929); Ernst Benz, *Der vollkommene Mensch nach Jakob Böhme* (Stuttgart: Kohlhammer, 1937).

44. On Angelus Silesius, see Jeffrey Sammons, *Angelus Silesius* (New York: Twayne, 1967). On Gottfried Arnold, see Jürgen Büchsel, *Gottfried Arnold: Sein Verständnis von Kirche und Wiedergeburt* (Witten: Luther Verlag, 1970).

45. F. Ernest Stoeffler, *German Pietism during the Eighteenth Century* (Leiden: Brill, 1973) 168–216; Wilhelm Goeters, *Die Vorbereitung des Pietismus in der reformierten Kirche der Niederlande bis zur Labadistischen Krisis 1670* (Leipzig: Hinrichs, 1911).

46. The formative and expressive power of hymns by Philipp Nicolai ("Wachtet auf," und "Wie schön leuchtet") or Martin Rinkhart ("Nun danket," "Now Thank We All Our God") or Paul Gerhardt ("Jesus, Thy Boundless Love to Me") are now part of the hymn repertoire of Christians in every tradition, across ecumenical lines.

Bibliography

Sources

Arndt, Johann. *True Christianity.* Translated by Peter Erb. New York: Paulist Press, 1979.

Boehme, Jacob. *The Way to Christ.* Translated by Peter Erb. New York: Paulist Press, 1978.

Studies

Bangs, Carl. *Arminius: A Study in the Dutch Reformation.* Nashville: Abingdon, 1971.

Beardslee, John, III, (ed.). *Reformed Dogmatics.* New York: Oxford University Press, 1965.

Elert, Werner. *The Structure of Lutheranism.* Translated by Walter Hansen. St. Louis: Concordia, 1962.

Greschat, Martin, ed. *Orthodoxie und Pietismus.* Stuttgart: Kohlhammer, 1985.

Jones, Rufus. *Spiritual Reformers of the Sixteenth and Seventeenth Centuries.* London: Macmillan, 1914.

Kantzenbach, Friedrich Wilhelm. *Orthodoxie und Pietismus.* Gütersloh: Mohn, 1966.

Neveux, J. B. *Vie spirituelle et vie sociale entre Rhin et Baltique au XVIIe siècle.* Paris: Klincksieck, 1967.

Ozment, Steven. *Mysticism and Dissent.* New Haven: Yale University Press, 1973.

Preuss, Robert. *The Theology of Post-Reformation Lutheranism.* St. Louis: Concordia, 1970.

Sprunger, Keith. *Dutch Puritanism: A History of English and Scottish Churches of the Netherlands in the Sixteenth and Seventeenth Centuries.* Leiden: Brill, 1982.

———. *The Learned Doctor William Ames.* Urbana, IL: University of Illinois Press, 1972.

Strauss, Gerald. *Luther's House of Learning.* Baltimore: Johns Hopkins University Press, 1978.

Zeller, Winfried. *Der Protestantismus des 17. Jahrhundert.* Bremen: Carl Schünemann, 1962.

For references on pietism, see the bibliography following section II of this chapter, "Pietism and Enlightenment: Alternatives to Tradition," by Albert Outler.

II. *Pietism and Enlightenment: Alternatives to Tradition*

ALBERT C. OUTLER

NEITHER THE PROTESTANT REFORMATION nor the Roman Catholic Counter-Reformation achieved its spiritual aim. Born in bitterness and hardened by controversy and an ensuing century of wars of religion, they had torn Western Christendom asunder and had reaffirmed the Constantinian doctrine of a necessary reliance of churches upon the civil states in which they dwelled. Indeed, they had written this principle into the emerging body of international law (*cuius regio, eius religio*). The papal church had successfully resisted reform in all matters of doctrine and polity, even as it was experiencing an exciting revival of spirituality and good works in the upsurge of new religious societies, dedicated to education, philanthropy, missions, and pious devotion (e.g., the Barnabites, Theatines, Capuchins, Ursulines—and, of course, the Jesuits). The Protestants had survived (no mean feat, given the hazards) and had maintained their prime principles (*sola fide, sola scriptura*). But they had then found themselves deeply divided on crucial points of doctrine, polity, and praxis. In place of a hierarchical *magisterium*, they had produced numerous new confessions of faith, together with multivolume systems of doctrines (written chiefly by university professors, thus giving an old term a new meaning). The Edict of Nantes, which when issued in 1598 had been notable as the first major concession in legal polity to religious pluralism in civil law, was finally revoked in 1685, sending the Huguenots into a tragic diaspora. This event is as convenient as any to signify the spiritual exhaustion of the great visions that had animated the sixteenth-century reformers. In 1685, in Germany, the young Christian Wolff (1679–1754) was preparing to become the last truly eminent exponent of rationalistic orthodoxy. In Britain, the Church of England was in grave disarray. Jacques Bénigne Bossuet had been a prime mover in the Revocation; and, in self-justification, he had promptly (1688) published a two-volume *Histoire des variations des Églises Protestante*. His familiar thesis was that Protestants are hopelessly divided and thereby discredited; his conclusion was summed up in his episcopal motto: *Semper Eadem* ("Always in the same manner").

None of the sixteenth-century reformations, except in the case of the Protestant Radicals, had broken with the Constantinian heritage. All had held tenaciously to the notion of pure doctrine as a depositum of conceptualized truth. Each tradition had defined its own special heritage, which it was vowed to protect. Ink and blood had been spilled freely in defense of antithetical absolutes. In the midst of this generalized state of spiritual debility (redeemed by occasional, hidden fires of the Spirit flaming up here and there—often in unlikely places), two alternative movements emerged in uneven succession: pietism in the seventeenth century and the Enlightenment in the eighteenth century.

Both looked away from the imperial traditions of Rome and the Holy Roman Empire, from ecclesiastical establishments, from rites and ceremonies, from external authority. Both stood on foundation stones of liberty and persuasion over against the traditions of dogmatism and coerced conscience. Both were ranged alongside the *modernes* in the famous *querelle des anciennes et des modernes*. But pietism had an almost childlike faith in the biblical history of salvation, whereas the Enlightenment had taken its inspirations chiefly from the Greek and Roman classics and from the traditions of Renaissance humanism. Pietism looked inward and upward—in the temper and spirit of *theonomy*. The Enlightenment also looked inward but more directly at the world around—at the human scene and the human prospect—under the rubric of *autonomy*. Both were antipathetic to orthodoxy and to the standing order generally.

Pietism: Participation in Grace

The Origin of Pietism

Pietism, in the seventeenth and eighteenth centuries, was nothing new. It ran back, in a discernible continuity, to the ancient fathers (Macarius, Ephraem Syrus, et al.) and to the *devotio moderna* of the late Middle Ages (Nicholas of Cusa, Tauler, et al.). There was also a linkage between pious Lutherans like Johann Arndt (the so-called Father of German Pietism [1555–1621]) and the Protestant radicals (Hans Denk, Kaspar Schwenckfeld, et al.) in their shared convictions that the magisterial Reformers had fallen short of their own professed goals, being corrupted by the world. Arndt, in turn, was followed by a succession of great and shining lights like Gisbert Voetius (1589–1676), Philip Jacob Spener (1635–1705), August Hermann Francke (1663–1727), J. A. Bengel (1687–1752), and Count Ludwig von Zinzendorf (1700–1760). Equally important were the great pietist hymn writers like Paul Gerhardt (1607–1676) and Charles Wesley (1707–1788). In Britain, with different accents, there was a continuing tradition running back to men and women like Richard Rolle of Hampole, Juliana of

Norwich to Nicholas Ferrar of Little Gidding, Lewis Bayly (*The Practice of Piety*), Thomas Halyburton of St. Andrews (*Memoirs*) and William Law (*A Serious Call to a Devout & Holy Life*).

The term "pietism" has had pejorative overtones in the rhetoric of both orthodox and liberals who have served as our chief arbiters of theological fashions now for four centuries; this is apparent in any standard church history or history of Christian thought. The orthodox found the pietists intolerable because of their indifference to the niceties of pure doctrine. Lutherans, Calvinists, and Romans were equally outraged by the excessive tolerance of men like Gottfried Arnold, whose relatively impartial *Unparteiische Kirchen und Ketzer-Historie* (1699–1700) reconceived Christian history so that "the heretics" were accorded real sympathy in their times and circumstances. (I still remember, in a rather tense ecumenical seminar back in the 1950s—the discussion was about the positive values of doctrinal pluralism—an eminent German theologian growling to his equally eminent Swiss colleague in an audible aside, "Gottfried Arnold, nicht war?")

The pietists were criticized for their stress on good works as proof of saving faith and condemned on account of their indifference to centralized authority manifest in their *collegiae pietatis* and their *ecclesiolae in ecclesia*. With formidable enemies like Johann Benedict Carpzov, Spener was driven from Frankfurt to Dresden, Francke from Leipzig to Halle. Pietists as a group were easily caricatured for their zeal and discipline. Voetius laments "the bitter accusations, calumnies and hostile attacks . . . against the pious and those who desire a true and full reformation of purity." He even lists the epithets aimed at "the pious": for example, "zealots," "hypocrites," "long-noses," "double-reformers," "misanthropes."[1] The Enlightenment philosophers and the liberal Protestant theologians saw in the pietists a backward-looking development that had not really challenged the old order. They were dismissed as "anti-intellectualists," "individualistic," "self-righteous," "holy group" separatists. In common speech to this day, terms like "pious" and "piosity" have a pejorative ring. The consequence has been a wide-ranging underestimation of the contributions of pietism in the transitions from the medieval to the modern world. Now, however, in a world fast becoming *post*-modern, it may be due for a more serious and sympathetic attention.

The pietists, for their part, saw themselves as the vanguard of a *second* Reformation—which would reject the compromises that the established churches had suffered without repudiating the established order. This is reflected typically in Anthony Wilhelm Boehm's preface to his English translation of Johann Arndt's *True Christianity* (1712):

False Christianity hath so much over-run the Christian world that it is hard to find *True Christianity* in the midst of its many counterfeits. . . . And whereas we ought long ago to have rectified [our lapses] by the Original Pattern left us by the Author of Christianity, we are still farther removed from this blessed Original so that, instead of curing our mistakes, we have multiplied them. And this is the reason that the transcripts which the differing denominations of Christendom make of their Original in these days, prove so very lame, mean and imperfect.

Yet there will come a time when the Church of Christ will come up from this wilderness of various sects, parties, nations, languages, forms and ways of worship—nay, of crosses and afflictions—leaning upon her Beloved and, in his power, bidding defiance to all her enemies.[2]

Pietists were generally undismayed by their marginal status; they understood themselves as leaven in church and society and were content with such a role. This sense of a special calling is reflected in the proposed agenda in P. J. Spener's *Pia Desideria* (1675). Here the chief aim is *reformatio vitae*. His practical proposals include a return to biblical study by the laity—to the text itself with minimum help from commentators, confession, or systems of pure doctrine, a clearer recognition of the laity's role in Christian witness and service, a fresh emphasis on Christian morality and on works of love and mercy. Added to these are basic reforms in ministerial education, such as less preoccupation with speculative theology and greater stress on the arts and skills of pastoral theology (preaching, visitation, pastoral care of the faithful, etc.). Spener urges less polemics in theology and more of an irenic temper—what John Wesley would later call "catholic spirit." Finally, there must be a renewal of evangelical preaching, with Christ at the center and with conversion and sanctification as constant ends in view.[3]

August Hermann Francke continued the development of Spener's agenda. He was a central figure in the new university of Halle (pietism's chief academic center); he founded and directed a pietist *Adelspaedagogium* (a secondary school for the nobility). He was also the moving spirit in a network of orphanages, hospitals, and missions. Francke's *Nicodemus or the Fear of Man* (1706) reflects the pietist sense of liberty in the world; his *Pietas Hallensis* (1707) provides a short history of pietism, describing it as a work of God.

Count Nikolaus Ludwig von Zinzendorf (1700–1760) was a pietist leader in a somewhat different style. Educated at Francke's "paedagogium" and at Wittenberg, he became the patron of a cluster of religious communities on his own estate in Saxony and Upper Lusatia. His prime emphasis was on a *theologia cordis*, "a religion of the heart"; the Christian life, in his view, is one of intimate fellowship with Jesus Christ, the "creator, sustainer, redeemer of the world." He was consecrated as bishop in "The Unitas Fratrum" (1737), but was criticized by other pietists as fostering an excessive emotionalism and a cult of personality. Even so, his influence was widespread and lasting—not least of all through the transformation of his thought that was achieved by F. D. E. Schleiermacher.

Characteristics of Pietism

Pietism is ill-understood, however, without an awareness of the extent to which it wove psalms and hymns and spiritual songs into the fabric of the earnest Christian's daily round. Having renounced the pomp of ceremonies —and, of course, the notion of the outward means of grace as efficacious *ex opere*—they turned hymnody into liturgy and sought their corporate elevations in the Spirit in great hymns and chorales provided by men like Johann Crüger and Paul Gerhardt. Crüger's "Praxis Pietatis Melica" (1647) became a classic beyond the bounds of pietism; Gerhardt's best hymns ("Jesu, Thy Boundless Love to Me," "Befiehl du deine Wege," his translation of St. Bernard's "Salve caput cruentatum," "O Sacred Head, Now Wounded") have entered the general treasury of Christian nurture.

Pietists, for all their diversity, understood themselves as raised up by God to an extraordinary ministry within the churches. John Wesley spoke for more than his own movement when he defined their special mission: "to reform the nation and especially the church; and to spread scriptural holiness over the land."[4] Pietist theology was almost always more complex and subtle than its rhetoric. Its focus was soteriological, and its favorite metaphor was the restoration of the ruined image of God in fallen men and women. The fruit of saving faith was "the elevation of the soul to communion with God the Father, through the saving merits of Jesus Christ, the Son, by the converting and sanctifying power of the Holy Spirit." These notions are omnipresent in the pietist literature, beginning with Arndt's *True Christianity* (1st ed., 1606):

> The image of God in man is the conformity of the human soul, understanding, mind, will, (together with all internal and external bodily and spiritual powers) with God and the Holy Trinity and with all divine qualities, virtues, wills and characteristics. . . .

> Man was to know from the image of God that he was united with God and that in this union the highest human rest, peace, joy, life and blessedness consisted; as, on the other hand, the greatest human unrest and unhappiness arose out of nothing other than when he acted against God's image, turned himself from God and was therefore deprived of the highest eternal good.[5]

In a later comment, Arndt defines the distinctively pietistic perspective and temperament in a form frequently echoed thereafter:

A Christian must be a new creature in Christ (2 Cor. 5:17). . . . In this renewal in Christ—in this spiritual, heavenly, godly truth everything is set. This is the end of all theology and the whole of Christianity. This is the union with God (1 Cor. 6:15), the marriage with our heavenly bridegroom, Jesus Christ, the living faith, the new birth, Christ's dwelling in us, Christ's noble life in us, the Holy Spirit's fruit in us, the enlightenment and healing of the kingdom of God in us. This is all one thing, for where true faith is, there is Christ with all his righteousness, holiness, merit, grace, forgiveness of sins, adoption of God, inheritance of life—that is, the new birth that comes out of faith in Christ.[6]

There is no end to the quotations that could be offered in elaboration of these axial themes (an adequately representative anthology of pietism in its variety would be extremely useful). For our purposes three samplings from different contexts may suffice. The first is from Richard Sibbes (1577–1635), a spokesman for early Puritan devotion. In his *Discovery of the Near Union Betwixt Christ and the Church; and Consequently, Between Him and Every Believing Soul* (1639), the Christian life is described in distinctively pietist terms:

A Christian's life should be nothing but a communion with Christ, a walking in the Spirit. He should adorn his profession by a lively performance of all duty and be exemplary to others . . . and do all the good he can wheresoever he comes. He should "keep himself unspotted from the world," go against the stream and be continually in such a temper that it should be the joy of his heart to be dissolved and to be with Christ.[7]

The historical circumstances in Restoration England were very different from the times of the civil war, but the pietist message retains its distinctive accents, as in *Communion With God* (1667) by Samuel Shaw (1635–1696):

True Christianity is not a notion but a nature. That is not religion which is lapped up from books, or laid up in men's brains. It [i.e., *true* Christianity] is laid down in the very constitution of the soul, refining and spiritualizing all the faculties thereof, and rendering them as like to God himself as such a creature can resemble his Creator.[8]

Von Zinzendorf was a disciple and godson of Spener, laying even greater stress on the Christian's "intimacy with Christ":

Therefore by faith and love, we must so enter into the Saviour (in der Heiland so hinein—gläuber, so hinein lieben) that we can no longer see or hear anything else above or beyond him, that he and we remain inseparably together. . . . He knows me so well: he knows my hours and days; he knows my motions and emotions; he knows my abilities and inabilities; he knows my inclinations and fears; he knows my danger and my security. In short, I can be nowhere better than in his arms.[9]

There was, of course, a hearty active side to Pietism—its constant stress on neighborly love and its denotation of "neighbor" as "any and every child of God, whomsoever and wheresoever." Pietism stood for self-emptying philanthropy; pietists were conspicuous for their service to the deprived, neglected, and suffering—"the stranger in distress, the widowed and the fatherless." They were missionaries and peacemakers; they were in the forefront of prison reform; their denunciations of greed, waste, and self-indulgence were a dike against the rampant epicureanism of their time.

Their indifference to speculative theology had often the ring and sometimes the actuality of anti-intellectualism. This arose, in large part, from their horror of theological warfare (the *odium theologorum,* of which Philipp Melanchthon had complained so piteously and with such good cause). They preferred, in Wesley's phrase, "plain truth for plain people."[10] They were accused of separatism, but falsely; actually, they rarely formed churches on their own. They were, more typically, puritan (in the liberal sense of seeking to purge and purify the churches) or, in Voetius's sense, "precisionists," which is to say, advocates of exactness (ἀκριβῶς) in teaching, law, and conscience.

They were allergic both to doctrinal innovation and antinomian ethics; their aim was the restoration of apostolic Christianity (variously defined). They were also fervent biblicists. More than a century before, Thomas Campbell, an Englist pietist like Thomas Brooks (1608–1680), could *recommend* a radically modest hermeneutics: "I dare not be wise above what is written. Where the Scripture is silent, there I love to be silent, and where the Scripture hath no tongue, there I desire to have no ears."[11]

Not many of them proposed an outright separation of church and state. All of them, however, contended for freedom of conscience and rejected coercion in matters of religion. In the Diognetian sense, they were *in* the world but not *of* it. Indeed, Frederick William of Brandenburg ("the Great Elector") was sufficiently convinced that pietists made good citizens that he welcomed and favored them in his domains (which included Halle).

Enlightenment: Liberation from Authority

The Origin of Enlightenment

Thus, as the dominance of Protestant orthodoxy disintegrated and the bonds of feudalism and divine right monarchy (symbols of the standing order on which the magisterial Reformation had depended) began to lose their force, it was the spirit of pietism, more than any other single resource, that managed to conserve the traditions of biblical and patristic Christianity

10. Rembrandt van Rijn, *The Mennonite Minister Claesz. von Anslo and his wife*, 1641.

in and through the transitions that ushered in the "new" Age of Enlightenment. One can see this in Immanuel Kant, notable as a crusader for "enlightenment." Kant had been born and bred a pietist in Königsberg; and, when his fame as a theological "deconstructionist" spread, he is said to have reassured his pious servant, Lampe, that he had only "destroyed dogma in order to make room for faith." His own proposals for "religion within the bounds of unaided reason" may be seen as a pietistic ethic "grounded in the nature of things" rather than derived from revelation. F. D. E. Schleiermacher was more than half serious when he spoke of himself as "a Moravian of a higher order." Albrecht Ritschl hated the pietists, as his history of them shows, but it is not difficult to see a significant linkage between his stress on an immanent kingdom of God ("an organization of mankind, based on the principles of neighborly love") and the typically cheerful eschatology of pietism.

But the Enlightenment was a radically different alternative to the old order from what pietism had been. Its negative side appears as a revolt against authoritarianism in both church and civil society; its chief target was the Christian tradition as it was manifested in Western civilization. Its positive preoccupation was with the human scene: "Know then *thyself*, presume not God to scan; the proper study of mankind is man" (Alexander Pope, *An Essay on Man*, Epistle II, line 1). In England, the new movement was called "deism"; in Diderot's *Encyclopedie*, "Eclaircissement"; in Germany (first by Moses Mendelsohn) "Aufklärung." Its positive aim was to advance the twin causes of critical reason and uncorrupted feeling. Its negative aim was to liberate the human mind from all the delusions of supernaturalism, miracles, and revelation.

Where pietism had preferred an apophatic theology with great modesty in its claims for human *knowledge* "of God and the things of God," in comparison with the kataphatic rationalism of orthodoxy, the philosophers of Enlightenment turned against both orthodoxy and pietism. In the gentle skepticism of Michel Montaigne's *Essays* (1595) one sees the essential prototype of the temper of enlightenment; its first popularizers were the English deists. John Toland's *Christianity Not Mysterious* (1696) set the tone of the debate. Anthony Collins followed with a contention (*A Discourse on Free-Thinking*, 1713) that the biblical records were unreliable and that "free-thinking" offered a better hope of surmounting ignorance and superstition than any version of historical Christianity. The aged Matthew Tindal rounded out the argument with his glorification of "the religion of nature" in *Christianity as Old as Creation* (1730).[12]

The Enlightenment was multifaceted; it was much less a single body of doctrine than a massive reorientation of attitudes—including a general distaste for the Christian heritage and a fresh confidence in the human future. But in all its diversity, there was a central focus and ideal: the autonomous human being. So complex a development cannot possibly be summarized in short compass without egregious oversimplifications. Happily, that is not as grave a problem here as it might be otherwise since the primary sources of the Age of Enlightenment, together with adequate histories and interpretations of it, are more accessible than for any other comparable epoch in Western intellectual history (Peter Gay, Ernst Cassirer, Wilhelm Dilthey, Paul Hazard, Carl Becker, Will Durant, et al.).

Characteristics of the Enlightenment

Diverse as they are, these interpreters are agreed on the Enlightenment's chief characteristics. There was, above all, its love of liberty and its repudiations of tyranny: in religion, politics, and morality. There were its corresponding rejections of the Christian tradition as the philosophers knew it, intertwined as it was with the coercive power of the state (the Roman Catholic Church in France, the Lutheran *Landeskirchen* in Germany, the Church of England in Britain, etc.). What sometimes goes unnoticed, however, is the number of Enlightenment affinities with similar impulses in the pietist tradition. Both were antiestablishment; neither did well when they came to power as in the Puritan Commonwealth or the French Revolution. Both shared a hatred of inhumanity and a love of philanthropy. Both mistrusted external authority. Pietism was unabashedly supernaturalist and mystical; Enlightenment was aggressively secular in orientation (this is the main point of Carl Becker's classic, *The Heavenly City of the Eighteenth-Century Philosophers*). But both ranged themselves with the *modernes* against *les anciens*.

The Enlightenment's main concern was the liberation of human beings of all sorts from involuntary dependence on external and arbitrary authority. This was Kant's main point in his answer to his own question, *Was Ist Aufklärung?* (1784):

> Enlightenment is man's release from his self-incurred tutelage. Tutelage is man's inability to make use of his own understanding without direction from another. This tutelage is self-incurred when its cause lies not in the lack of reason but in a lack of resolution and courage to use it without direction from another. *Sapere aude!* [Dare to judge for yourself]—that is the motto of Enlightenment.[13]

In a sequel, *Orientation in Thinking* (1786), he enlarged his thesis:

> Thinking for one's self means to seek the supreme touchstone of truth in one's self; i.e., in one's own reason—and the following of the maxim of always

thinking for oneself is enlightenment. . . . By this test, one will soon see superstition and fanaticism disappearing even if he is himself far from possessing the knowledge requisite to the refutation of either on objective grounds.[14]

Linked to the notion of autonomy, and reinforcing it, was the burgeoning idea of progress. For men like Giambattista Vico (1668–1744), "progress" was a variation on the classical theme of "providence"; in the men like Anne Robert Jacques Turgot, Bernard Le Bovier de Fontenelle, Marquis de Condorcet, it signified a dynamic force in the unfoldings of nature and especially human history. At the heart of the doctrine was a new confidence in human nature and in its perfectibility—in this life! Carl Becker's once-familiar summary of the Enlightenment's "articles of religion" is still instructive:

1. Man is not natively depraved;
2. The end of life is life itself, the good life on earth instead of the beatific life after death;
3. Man is capable, guided solely by the light of reason and experience, of perfecting the good life on earth; and
4. The first and essential condition of the good life on earth is the freeing of men's minds from the bonds of ignorance and superstition—as also their bodies from the arbitrary oppression of the arbitrary authority of constituted social authorities [civil or ecclesiastical].[15]

A consequence of such a creed was a nontraditional and distinctively secularizing spirituality: of liberation; of the nurturing of generous, humane, and tolerant dispositions—since men and women are "more easily led by persuasion than by force," "natively inclined to virtue and good citizenship,"[16] and are endowed by their creator with "inalienable rights," including "life, liberty and the pursuit of happiness." The hope of happiness undergirded a new eudaemonism.

The philosophers saw science and technology as a new resource for achieving autonomy—and this was different from the physico-theology of the seventeenth-century pioneers like Isaac Newton, John Ray, William Derham, et al. (and not excluding Copernicus, Johannes Kepler, or Galileo). As faith in the old order waned, however, science and technology came to appear as panaceas in their own right; a new secular priesthood arose to preside over human affairs in the new age. In all fields of inquiry and praxis, from astronomy to medicine, autonomous humanity could look to science and invention as the chief agencies of progress; physiocrats and materialists could join hands in expecting an ampler future. Together, the philosophers could join in hauling down "the heavenly kingdom" out of its empyrean and in relocating it here on earth—a vision appearing in figures as different as Blake, Feuerbach, and Bellamy.

The philosophers were also agreed in their rejections of traditional Christianity as it appeared to them. There was never any doubt that Voltaire's target in his oft-repeated battle cry, *Ecrasez l'infame!*, was historic Christianity, Catholic, Protestant, or pietist. In the beginning, he was less interested in reform than in repudiation; he denounced the actual Christian doctrines as vehemently as Christianity's manifest corruptions. One remembers, of course, that Voltaire, grown old, came to second thoughts about his earlier expurgations. He spoke of atheism as almost as abhorrent as supernaturalism; he even argued that a kindly faith in *le bon Dieu* might help simple folk live well—or at least better. He built a chapel at Ferney—with an inscription on its portal: *Deo erexit Voltaire.* He went so far as to propose that if God did not exist, it would be necessary to invent him—for humanity's sake. There was, however, for so minimal a faith no institutional form that he could ever tolerate.

The philosophers were deeply offended by the Christian record of intolerance and oppressions—so deeply that one of the intolerances they allowed themselves was aimed at intolerance itself (with, of course, an occasional persecution thrown in, always, of course, in good causes). This sense that the Christianity of their day was a debasement of its original appears in a vivid passage by Pierre Bayle, in his entry on "Japon" in the *Encyclopedie:*

> [Early Christianity] was a benign, gentle, patient religion. . . . But the Christianity of the sixteenth century [the sort proposed for export to Japan and elsewhere] was no longer that. It was a sanguinary, murderous religion which has been hardened to the shedding of blood for some five or six centuries past. . . . [Thus, it had lost] the blessing Heaven had granted to . . . the Gospel of peace, patience, gentleness.[17]

Allied with the rationalists in their rejection of the old order—while differing from them in many crucial ways—were the new-age romantics like Jean Jacques Rousseau (in Geneva and France) and Johann Georg Hamann in Germany along with Klopstock and others in the self-styled "Circle of the Sensitives." These *lumières* mistrusted reason and agreed with Rousseau that "feeling is all." Most of them were in sympathy with Hamann's stress on intuition. Rousseau's antipathy to Christian orthodoxy appears in his *Du Contrat Social* (1762) and in his preference for a "simple religion," unburdened with dogma. This later is formulated in the "Profession of Faith" of the Savoyard Vicar in *Emile* (1762). It is a gentle faith, allowing for praise and thanksgiving, but not petition. It urges the practice of kindness and charity toward all, worthy and unworthy; it equates virtue and happiness;

it includes the hope of immortality as the eventual triumph of the good; it allows for a nondogmatic observance of ancestral rites. It was an ideal that Rousseau could not himself live by, but it has haunted modernity ever since with a dangerous charm: of benignity—and rootlessness.

In Hamann, the so-called *Sturm und Drang* of romanticism appears most characteristically. Born a pietist, and at Königsberg as Kant had been, Hamann earned the sobriquet "Magus of the North." He understood himself as *Socrates redivivus,* with a mission to rescue the human spirit from the wretched sophistries of rationalism. His sense of mystery was lively and he rejected all efforts to define or encompass the sacred. Only love can reveal the true nature of things; and one cannot love abstractions, which is all that discursive reason has to offer. His first major publication was entitled, somewhat self-consciously, *Sokratische Denkwurdigkeiten* (1759). As he grew older, however, he became more reconciled to classic Christian doctrines such as the Trinity, seeing them as providing fruitful images for human self-understanding (as in *Zweifel und Einfalle,* 1776). In the process he came to prefer Cusa's and Bruno's appeals to the principle of *coincidentia oppositorum* over the idealism of Kant and Fichte. It is hard to read Hamann and not think of Søren Kierkegaard and vice versa. Between the two of them and a preeminently orthodox dogmatician like Martin Chemnitz, there is a great gulf fixed; and any pietist would tilt toward Hamann, with all his eccentricities.

John Wesley: Enlightened Pietism

A contemporary of many of these figures we have noticed, and himself aware of most of them, was the Anglican evangelical John Wesley (1702–1791)—known more widely as the founder of Methodism, but much more interesting generally as a folk theologian who saw no incoherence in his loyalties to both orthodox Christianity and pietism and enlightenment. He lived in the Anglican Church with no great attachment to its "establishment"; he maintained a lively interest in the excitements of the Enlightenment on into his old age—always rejecting its secularized reductions.

Born a Tory Anglican, reared in an atmosphere where a blend of Puritan piety and Catholic mysticism tempered its genteel poverty, trained in the classics and Scripture at Oxford, he was acknowledged as a competent scholar by his election as Fellow of Lincoln College and also as a popular university preacher by his unusually frequent assignments to preach in St. Mary's. From Oxford, he went on to become a missionary, evangelist, spiritual director of a vigorous religious society within the Church of

England, a folk theologian determined to evade what he regarded as the barren disjunctions of either/or formulations.

That he was a pietist is beyond question: in his fifty-volume *Christian Library* (1749–1755) he included extracts from more than a dozen of them (Arndt, for example, appears in volumes 1 and 2; Sibbes in volume 10). He freely imitated Spener's "program" of Christian renewal and Francke's patterns of Christian philanthropy. But if separatism is a characterizing tendency of pietism, Wesley sought to avoid that and nearly succeeded as long as he lived. He stoutly believed that there was ample room for a reforming society within a sacramental church, especially one that was, as he thought, "settled on its lees." He was steeped in the Christian tradition and loved it; he boasted of being *homo unius libri;* that is, the Scripture (thereby reversing Roger Bacon's original intent for that phrase—namely, as a protest against a theological monopoly, which in the thirteenth century meant Peter Lombard's *Sentences*). He was as orthodox as unfeigned faith in the Anglican *Homilies, Articles,* and *Prayerbook* could make a man. But he set no great store by orthodox opinions, since he agreed with Cranmer that the devils may be more orthodox than believers in their intellectual cognizance of what is true; and "yet they be but devils still."[18] He was convinced that "there is no liturgy in the world, either in ancient or modern languages, which breathes more scriptural, rational piety than the Common Prayer of the Church of England."[19] And yet, he felt free to abridge and "correct" that liturgy on his own authority for the use of the Methodists in America. He went so far as to explain that, in his revision, "many Psalms are left out [entirely], and many *parts* of the others, as being highly improper for the mouths of a Christian congregation."[20] And yet he would also insist that "in religion I am for as few innovations as possible. I love the old wine best."[21]

At the same time, he was also fascinated by many of the Enlightenment perspectives, even as he filtered out their autonomous emphases, as if by reflex. On the crucial point of "liberty from involuntary tutelage," Wesley had broken from the old order before Kant; indeed, his two grandfathers had already led that way. He favored a free church in a free state a full half century before the American Revolution. He was at odds with the "national church"; he was wholly unconcerned with personal "preferment," choosing rather to live and work among the British under class—offering them salvation and dignity at the same time and in the same ministry. His stress on *free* grace was a sort of orthodox prototype of many of the Enlightenment notions of liberty.

He was equally interested in contemporary science and technology. He dabbled with electrical experiments; he read the stories of the seventeenth-century "discoverers" with great interest. In these and other ways, he leaned toward the side of *les modernes* in that famous "quarrel." He read Fontenelle: he accepted his arguments for progress while rejecting his obvious natural- ism. He deplored all views that the human future was doomed; he speaks of them as "instances of black ingratitude to God." He argued that former times were *not* better than the present or the future: "Whoever makes a fair and candid inquiry will easily perceive that true religion has in no wise decreased, but greatly increased in the present century."[22] For evidence, he cites the increase of religious toleration and the hopeful prospects of a global outreach of the gospel.

He was, of course, trying to hold too many disparate concerns together, and this helps explain why he left so few successors who were interested in, or capable of, repeating his special achievements. Even so, a useful clue to the vision that integrated these dissonant perspectives may be sought in the ancient theme of *metousia theou*—"participation in the divine life." The result was a pietism centered on a doctrine of the prevenient grace of the Lord Jesus Christ and on the love of God shed abroad in believers' hearts by the immanent activity of the Holy Spirit. Thus, he sought to combine an ancient mysticism, modern psychology, and a prophetic morality in a piety filled with pneumatological images, as the following passage with its references to breath and breathings will show:

> [In "the new birth"] and the life in the Spirit thus begun, the earnest Chris- tian may now properly be said to *live.* God having quickened them by his Spirit, they are alive to God through Jesus Christ. . . .
>
> God is *continually* breathing, as it were, upon the human soul; the faithful soul is breathing into God. Grace is descending into the believer's heart and prayer and praise are ascending up to heaven. And by this intercourse between God and man—this fellowship with the Father and the Son as by a kind of *spiritual respiration*—the life of God in the soul is sustained. . . .
>
> It consists of all heavenly affections and tempers mingled together . . . , such as continual thankful love to God . . . as makes it natural and, in a manner necessary, to love every child of God with kindness, gentleness and long- suffering. It is such a love that . . . enables us to present ourselves, our souls and bodies—all that we are and all that we have, all our thoughts, words and actions—as a continual sacrifice to God, acceptable through Jesus Christ. . . .
>
> Now this holiness can have no existence till we are renewed in the image [of God] in our mind . . . that is, until we are born again. . . . Consequently, the new birth is absolutely necessary in order to happiness in this world or in the world to come.[23]

Here are characteristic emphases of orthodoxy, pietism, and illuminism intertwined, with their good essences conserved—and at least one strand of Protestant liberalism foreshadowed.

Pietism, with its stress on personal participation in God's encompassing grace, and the Enlightenment, with its stress on human liberation from ignominies of all sorts, had actually a common core and need not have come to stand in such stark opposition as actually they did. But for this to have happened, pietism would have to find a place for the positive values of human culture in this world, and the Enlightenment would have had to allow more room for biblical supernaturalism with its "order of salvation" — from sin to sanctification by grace through faith.

And now that both pietism and Enlightenment, in their traditional forms, are fading before the onset of what is being labeled variously as a *"post*-critical," *"post*-modern," or *"post*-liberal" age, radical reorientations are in order—and in process. In such a time of transition, it ought to be possible to reclaim the best of both pietism (the theme of participation) and of Enlightenment (the spirit of responsible freedom) as resources for any truly hopeful human future. And that, in its own special way, would be real progress.

Notes

1. Gisbert Voetius, "Concerning 'Precision' in Interpretation of Questions 94, 113, and 115 of the Catechism," in *Reformed Dogmatics*, ed. John Beardslee III (New York: Oxford University Press, 1965) 325.

2. Johann Arndt, *True Christianity*, trans. Anton Wilhelm Boehm (London: Joseph Downing, 1720).

3. Philip Jacob Spener, *Pia Desideria* (Philadelphia: Fortress, 1964).

4. John Wesley, "Minutes of Several Conversations," in *The Works of the Rev. John Wesley, A.M.*, vol. 8, ed. Thomas J. Jackson (London: Mason, 1828–31) 299.

5. Johann Arndt, *True Christianity*, in *The Pietists*, ed. Peter C. Erb (New York: Paulist, 1983) 29, 32.

6. Ibid., 277–78.

7. Richard Sibbes, *Discovery of the Near Union Betwixt Christ and the Church; and Consequently, Between Him and Every Believing Soul*, in *A Christian Library*, vol. 6, ed. John Wesley (London: T. Cordeux, 1820) 184.

8. Samuel Shaw, *Communion With the Deity*, in *The Works of Rev. Samuel Shaw, M.A.* (Boston: George Clark, 1821) 2:438.

9. Nicholas Ludwig von Zinzendorf, *Nine Public Lectures on Important Subjects in Religion*, trans. George W. Forrell (Iowa City: University of Iowa Press, 1973) 102.

10. John Wesley, "Preface to Sermons on Several Occasions," *The Works of John Wesley*, vol. 1, ed. Albert C. Outler (Nashville: Abingdon, 1984) 104.

11. Thomas Brooks, *The Works of Thomas Brooks*, vol. 4, ed. Alexander B. Grosart (Edinburgh: James Nichol, 1866) 274.

12. For Tolan, Collins, and Tindal, see E. Graham Waring, ed., *Deism and Natural Religion: A Source Book*.

13. Immanuel Kant, *On History,* ed. Lewis White Beck (Indianapolis: Bobbs-Merrill, 1963) 3.

14. Immanuel Kant, "Orientation in Thinking," in *Critique of Practical Reason and Other Writings,* ed. Lewis White Beck (Indianapolis: Bobbs-Merrill, 1963) 146.

15. Carl Becker, *The Heavenly City of the Eighteenth-Century Philosophers,* 102–3.

16. Ibid., 103.

17. In Denis Diderot, *Encyclopedia,* ed. Jean Lerond d'Alembert (Indianapolis: Bobbs-Merrill, 1965).

18. John Wesley, "An Earnest Appeal to Men of Reason and Religion," quoting from the Homily on Salvation, *The Works of John Wesley,* vol. 11, ed. Gerald R. Cragg (Oxford: Oxford University Press, 1975) 68–69.

19. John Wesley, "Preface, the Sunday Service of the Methodists in North America," in *The Works of the Rev. John Wesley, A.M.,* vol. 14, ed. Thomas J. Jackson (London: Mason, 1828–31) 304.

20. Ibid.

21. John Wesley, "Letter to Mr. Walter Churchey" (June 20, 1789), in *The Works of the Rev. John Wesley, A.M.,* vol. 12, ed. Thomas J. Jackson (London: Mason, 1828–31) 438.

22. John Wesley, "Of Former Times," in *The Works of John Wesley,* vol. 3, ed. Albert C. Outler (Nashville: Abingdon, 1986) 451.

23. John Wesley, "The New Birth," in *The Works of John Wesley,* vol. 2, ed. Albert C. Outler (Nashville: Abingdon, 1985) selections from 193–96.

Bibliography

Becker, Carl. *The Heavenly City of the Eighteenth-Century Philosophers.* New Haven: Yale University Press, 1932.

Brown, Dale W. *Understanding Pietism.* Grand Rapids: Eerdmans, 1976.

Cassirer, Ernst. *The Philosophy of Enlightenment.* Princeton: Princeton University Press, 1951.

Cragg, Gerald R. *The Church in the Age of Reason 1648–1789.* New York: Penguin Books, 1960.

——. *Reason and Authority in the Eighteenth Century.* Cambridge: University Press, 1964.

Erb, Peter C., ed. *The Pietists.* New York: Paulist, 1983.

Gay, Peter. The Enlightenment: An Interpretation. 2 vols. New York: Knopf, 1966.

Hazard, Paul. *The European Mind.* London: Hollis & Carter, 1953.

——. *European Thought in the Eighteenth Century.* New Haven: Yale University Press, 1954.

Schmidt, Martin. *Pietismus.* Stuttgart: Kohlhammer, 1972.

Stoeffler, F. E. *German Pietism During the Eighteenth Century.* Leiden: Brill, 1973.

——. *The Rise of Evangelical Pietism.* Leiden: Brill, 1965.

——, ed. *Continental Piety and Early American Christianity.* Grand Rapids: Eerdmans, 1976.

Waring, E. Graham, ed. *Deism and Natural Religion: A Source Book.* New York: Frederick Unger, 1967.

9

Anglican Spirituality

GORDON S. WAKEFIELD

THE PROBLEM IS, When does Anglicanism begin?[1] All forms of Christianity trace their origins back to Christ and the New Testament, if not to the call of Abraham, but that raises questions of authenticity rather than distinctive origins. There have always been those, very jealous for Anglican Christianity, who have wanted to emphasize direct succession from the pre-Reformation church and to claim that English and Anglican spirituality are one and the same. They seek to make Anglicans of the Anglo-Saxons with their devotion to the passion ("rood" comes from the Anglo-Saxon), and to regard Bede—the historian of the early eighth century—and the English mystics of the fourteenth as one with a church which the Reformation freed from alien yoke but did not destroy. Although spiritual affinities and links are not to be disputed, institutionalism cannot be ignored. We shall define *Ecclesia Anglicana* as that branch of the Christian church, rooted in previous ages, but bringing forth its peculiar flower and fruit in consequence of the Protestant Reformation of the sixteenth century. It has existed since as one of the many consequences of that cataclysm, which was both a breach of continuity—in the attempt, so bedevilled by contending interests, to recover true continuity— and a revival of religion. The uniqueness of Anglicanism has been that it retained more of the order of the medieval church than any other of the Reformed churches and has liked to think of itself, in Matthew Parker's phrase, as a "golden mediocrity" and, later, in the minds of some twentieth-century liberal ecumenists, as a "bridge church."

Alongside this we must remember the effects, not least on spirituality, of the fact that since Henry VIII the Church of England has been by law established and that, after some uncertainties and struggles, it emerged from 1662 on as the church to which the English people must conform or else be subject to certain social deprivations. Even within the last twenty-five years there have been English Anglicans who, though they would not see nonconformists penalized, have found it hard to understand why any

Christians of godliness and good learning should not be Anglicans. It was in the 1930s that Herbert Hensley Henson, bishop of Durham, who had in his earlier ministry been a source of controversy because of his liberalism, on meeting T. R. Glover, classical scholar and Public Orator of the University of Cambridge, and author of best-selling books about Jesus, expressed astonishment that so intelligent a man should be a Baptist.

The effect of the establishment on Anglican spirituality must not be disregarded. Most English Christians have been staunch patriots. This was certainly true of the Puritans and of John Wesley and the Methodists. In spite of sufferings and discrimination, they have not, since the settlement of 1689, wished the English church to go under. They have been like a loyal opposition, at times vehement, if not bitter, in protest and controversy, at times with deep friendships across the divide, and with spiritual affinities, not least in the casuistry of the seventeenth century and in devotion to the person of Christ.

Some adherents and lovers of the Anglican spiritual tradition have a bad conscience because so much of its beauty, like that of the arts, is dependent on affluence and privilege. Bishops and deans are on the roll of its teachers; some of its finest writings are from wealthy pens. It has had its martyrs: the Protestants under Mary Tudor and the Royal Martyr himself the next century. Both have been embarrassments to different parties of their coreligionists. W. H. Auden wrote that George Herbert's "is the piety of a gentleman,"[2] though he made the great sacrifice of renouncing the court for the clerisy, regarded as mean and contemptible in comparison. But Lancelot Andrewes was very rich, as was Pusey. W. R. Inge wrote with all the superiority of the Oxbridge educated classes, and T. S. Eliot's characters are all well-to-do. These days there are many, not least Anglicans, who would be inclined to say in the words of Bishop Heber's Epiphany hymn, "Dearer to God are the prayers of the poor." And one must not forget the spirituality of the lower classes, represented in the seventeenth century by John Bunyan, all of whose villains were gentlemen and women, and the wild and extravagant sectaries whose views, totally defeated then, have become in some circles the new orthodoxy, while experience of the black churches of the modern inner cities has led some present-day Anglicans to speak of their own second conversion.

But Anglican spirituality cannot be other than what the love of God in particular historical and social circumstances has made it. The institution that fostered it has been the English church, independent of Continental theologies both Protestant and Catholic, though not uninfluenced by them from the sixteenth century to the twentieth. And it is the church to which those with but a nebulous Christian faith have been assumed to belong and which has decorated their worldliness with some seemly conventions, like baptism and confirmation (their babies and their girls in white), ceremonies far from the radical transfer of Christian beginnings and the early fathers (with language about death, being buried with Christ, and anointed with the Holy Spirit). If "spirituality" means the influences that consciously or unconsciously shape our actions and our personalities, then the inarticulate, occasionally churchgoing English man or woman will have deep in folk memory some vestigial Christianity which will be more of the Anglican pattern than that of any other form of English religion—and this because of the power of the Book of Common Prayer, of the virtual disappearance of which they are probably the harshest critics.

The Prayer Book and Its Spirituality

Anglican spirituality begins with Thomas Cranmer and his two Prayer Books, particularly that of 1552. The earlier book of 1549 has always had its devotees. That was in the vernacular, contained the Litany of 1544, the offices of morning and evening prayer, and the collects and a service of Holy Communion with a lengthy and comprehensive "great prayer" with the traditional elements of the Mass—Greeting, *Sursum Corda, Sanctus,* Intercessions, Institution, *Anamnesis,* Oblation—ending before the heavenly altar. It was totally Protestant and scriptural in its mighty insistence on Christ's "oblation once offered, a full, perfect and sufficient sacrifice, oblation and satisfaction for the sins of the whole world," and in the provision of "table prayers" after the Consecration, so that communicants, at the climax of the service, might receive the sacred species as forgiven sinners and with true humility. Three years later, Cranmer rearranged the service so as to remove all ambiguities as to its Protestantism. He provided a canon that is unlike any other in the whole of Christian liturgy. The *Sanctus,* on the analogy of Isaiah 6, whence it originates, is followed by the Prayer of Humble Access, transferred from the Table Prayers of 1549, where Stephen Gardiner maintained that it could imply belief in transubstantiation with its Johannine language about eating the flesh and drinking the blood of Christ. The very glimpse of heaven and the echo of the angelic hymn make us aware of "the infinite qualitative distance" between God and us and that we are guests at his table only because of his mercy. The prayer then moves into the narrative of institution, which is not called the Prayer of Consecration and which, unlike that of 1549, has no manual acts; nor does the command over the wine with which the prayer ends have an Amen, so that communion of minister and people is still part of the Anaphora. The canon ends with the Lord's Prayer and the Amen which follows that. The *Gloria in Excelsis* is moved to the conclusion of the service in accordance with the words in the Marcan account of the Last Supper, "After they had sung a hymn, they went out to the Mount of Olives" (Mark 14:26).

The 1552 Book of Common Prayer is for many reasons the foundation of Anglican spirituality. (1) Because of it Anglican spirituality is *liturgical.* It is based on a prescribed text, not on spontaneity. Worship is objective, not experiential, determined by the church, not by the feelings of the worshipers. It is also intended to be a means of unity. The same texts should be used everywhere. Cranmer's book is the product of the convictions of his own times, mediating somewhat in controversies, but it also joins the worshipers to the inheritance of the past, with Scripture, ancient hymns, and forms and words derived from the whole of Christendom — Orthodox, Roman, patristic, and medieval. A Protestant liturgy contains the Catholic faith, some of it in a kind of deep freeze to be brought out and thawed in future times, as John Henry Newman realized three centuries later.

(2) The Western Christian year is retained, though pruned of medieval excrescences such as a plethora of saints' days and Corpus Christi. But the apostolic saints are retained, giving a sense, in Charles Wesley's words, of "one Church above, beneath/though now divided by the stream, the narrow stream of death." There is, in liturgy, no such thing as solitary prayer; neither is there ever a small congregation. Even in the tiniest hamlet, the worshipers join "with angels and archangels and the whole company of heaven." Spirituality and history are all one. Worship includes, in Proust's title, "the remembrance of things past" by which they become real as if present before our eyes.

(3) The word is paramount. The offices of morning and evening prayer become services of the word. The Old Testament is read once throughout the year, "except certain bokes and chapiters, which be least edifyeng and might be spared, and therefore be best left unread." The New Testament was read three times — this in contrast to the short chapters of the traditional office. This has embarrassed many Catholic Anglicans, for, on the one hand, it changes the nature of the divine office, and, on the other, it applies, though slightly, a principle of selectivity, a canon within the canon, as with Luther — and the idea of edification lurks in the wings. But the underlying conviction is that faith comes by hearing, and thereby understanding. To echo a memorable phrase of Bernard Shaw, the hope is that the worshiper will do with his ears what he does with his eyes when he stares. This again is suspect to some who fear that the didactic element in worship may encroach upon the kerygmatic and the eucharistic. In the Reformation as a whole there may have been overemphasis on instruction in reaction to what was believed to have been the ignorance and superstition of much

Catholicism. But words are for music as well as intelligibility, and the language of the Prayer Book as well as the later translation of the Scriptures in 1611 cannot be disregarded as an element of Anglican spirituality. In the Eucharist as in the Western tradition as a whole, the words of institution are all-important, even though for Cranmer they were there in obedience to the command and action of Christ rather than as effecting a change in the substance of the bread and wine. In the Anglican tradition, as in Hooker, the Carolines, and John Wesley's extract of Daniel Brevint's *The Christian Sacrament and Sacrifice,* paraphrased in the Wesleys' *Hymns on the Lord's Supper* (1745), there is no theory of the effect of the words, but a devout agnosticism before the mystery. It is encapsulated in a verse attributed to the first Elizabeth:

> He was the Word that spake it
> He took the bread and brake it
> And what his word doth make it
> That I believe and take it.

(4) It is the Book of *Common* Prayer—a book for the laity, for the whole people of God in their daily lives. It is the foundation of family religion, of domestic piety. This is why the offices, by Cranmer's sheer genius, are reduced to two—morning and evening prayer—to be said daily throughout the year, so that ordinary men and women may begin and end the day with devotions that will not depend on moods or circumstances but will enable them to join with the great church in hearing the word of God and offering most worthy praise. For this purpose, Cranmer combined lauds and matins for morning prayer and vespers and compline, his greatest achievement, for the evening. The book has been charged with being too weighted with penitence, and so at first sight it may appear: the penitential introductions to both offices, added in 1552; the Litany, magnificent, yet almost dirge-like, suggesting a direct causal relation between sins and calamities, as do the exhortations before communion. Yet E. C. Hoskyns began a sermon at Cambridge in 1927 by saying that when a Christian man declares that the four-times repeated response in the litany of the English church—"Have mercy upon us miserable sinners!"—has no meaning for him, he proclaims in public either that he has as yet no understanding of the Christian religion or has apostatized from it.[3] Samuel Johnson, steeped in the Prayer Book, would have understood him. "I shall never forget the tremulous earnestness with which he pronounced the awful petition in the Litany 'In the hour of death and in the day of judgement, good Lord deliver us,'" writes Boswell of Johnson in St. Clement Danes' Church on Good Friday.[4] The Prayer Book is for men and women soiled by involvement in the ambiguities and

compromises of the world. As for overmuch penitence, John Norris of Bemerton, considered to be the last of the Cambridge Platonists—though he was an Oxford man—commended the Book at the end of the seventeenth century because it was so redolent of praise through the amount of psalmody; there is more thanksgiving in the communion service than jaundiced eyes behold. We are to feed on Christ in our hearts by faith, *with thanksgiving.* . . .

In evaluating the book as *common* prayer, the collects are of great significance. Superbly translated by Cranmer, they are a link with the Latin church; some of them were composed by Cranmer. With amazing succinctness and economy, they are prayers that can be learned and often have been, sometimes by threat of punishment. For some children in the past they may have been killed forever. For many they have been, like the Psalms, a spiritual reservoir for future years, when the touch of time has turned them to truth.

Set liturgical forms have the advantage of securing unity and objectivity while allowing each individual to make them his or her own. But with regard to liturgy as form and not as word only, what matters to determine the doctrine is the way in which it is done. The 1552 communion service was very different when, as in Cranmer's intention, the table was in the middle of the church or in the chancel and the communicants came forward to stand around it, from Laud's insistence that it be permanently at the east end and railed in to prevent it from desecration by stray dogs and the like.[5] It was very different when, as for Cranmer, the curate was able to take home what remained of the elements for breakfast than when, in 1662, the prayer which followed Humble Access was called the Prayer of Consecration and the manual acts were restored.

In the 1620s there were those Anglicans who felt that the provisions of the Prayer Book were inadequate for a devotion which both expressed the beauty of holiness and made provision as ample as Rome. John Cosin, for instance, in Geoffrey Cuming's words, ". . . with [Matthew] Wren, the most copious contributor to the Prayer Book since Archbishop Cranmer," loved ceremonial and "the ordered past" and was anxious to show that the English had not set up a new church nor abandoned ancient forms of piety. As Master of Peterhouse, Cambridge, he introduced an elaborate ritual with vestments, lights, and incense. He published in 1626 *A Collection of Private Devotions,* which restored the Day Hours, drawing as Cranmer had done on the Primer and the Breviary and providing "an integral and homogeneous *private* complement to the *common* prayer of the Church."[6] *The Durham Book,* the first draft of the revision of the Book of Common Prayer in 1661, is Cosin's proposal. It is of a moderate high churchmanship, which restores Humble Access to the position of a table prayer, places the Prayer of Oblation immediately after the Prayer of Consecration, provides a rubric about the consumption of the consecrated elements, and implies throughout a doctrine of representational sacrifice. But it did not pass convocation.[7] Even so, the 1662 revision made the Book of Common Prayer just a litte more acceptable to high churchmen, though they remained somewhat ill at ease with it and those who were to become nonjurors looked back to 1549 and also eastward to Orthodox liturgy. But the 1552 Book itself remained at the heart of Anglican spirituality. After all, people had suffered for it, while its language lingered on the ear and entered the very soul of England.

Anglican spirituality takes its character from the Book of Common Prayer. It is not essentially *mystical*, though it may, as we shall see, be for some of its practitioners *metaphysical*, which I adopt to mean simply "poetic." There is an intellectual mysticism in the Cambridge Platonists, though, theologically, they are not "prayer book men." The Book contains the seeds of that moralism which is so vital a part of classic Anglicanism, which for a while in the eighteenth century took over and is inseparable from the Caroline and Tractarian longing for holiness. The aim of the Prayer Book is "a godly, righteous and sober life." It does not encourage flights into the spiritual empyrean, and its *terminus ad quem* may be said to be "never further than thy cross." For some it may be the starting point of "a devotion of rapture," but not for most; it does not encourage enthusiasm nor the perfectionism which was so much part of the Christianity of the radicals of 1640–1660 and of John Wesley (though he claimed that his doctrine did not go beyond the teachings of his own church and concluded his *A plain Account of Christian Perfection* with the collect for purity.) It is a book to nurture conformity and submission to the state—the more so after the civil wars with the addition to the litany of the prayer for deliverance from sedition, privy conspiracy, and rebellion. But it became for many lay people a much-thumbed possession, not simply to be taken down from the church rack on Sundays, but a daily companion in the home, a manual of guidance, meditation, family devotions and inspiration for living. In the 1830s John Henry Newman declared that if only "men" would, instead of adopting "all kinds of strange ways," "honour the rubric" and "conform their families" to the *spirit* of the Prayer Book, they "would practically do vastly more good than by trying new religious plans, founding new religious societies, or striking out new religious views."[8]

Jacobans and Carolines

Classic Anglican spirituality belongs to the period from the death of Elizabeth I to the Restoration, when the English church was discovering its identity as between the Puritans, who would have possessed it for a Reformed ecclesiology, and the Roman Catholics, who sought to recover it for papal power. It emerged as committed to the threefold ministry of bishops, priests, and deacons, the liturgy as we have described it, and loyalty to the Sovereign as its supreme governor—the anointed monarch whose authority was consecrated. In the midst of bitter strife, ending in civil war, and its temporary defeat, its particular beauty became manifest, though there was more than a streak of persecuting intolerance and an ugly contempt for its opponents. There was a period in the first quarter of the seventeenth century when episcopacy could appear as a lovely thing, from which, in some of its exemplars, even Puritans did not withhold their praise—the bishop, the eucharistic minister par excellence, sharing his cure with the beneficed priest and opening for all his people windows into heaven.[9] Not least, he was a man of compassion, a reconciler. This vision was glimpsed again in Edward King, bishop of Lincoln (1829–1910), and in the documents and descriptions contributed to twentieth-century unity talks.

Some episcopal devotional writing was likely to find provenance among the Puritans, for instance, *The Practice of Piety* (1610), by Lewis Bayly, bishop of Bangor, which John Bunyan's first wife brought him as part of her modest dowry and which had phenomenal worldwide circulation for more than two hundred years. It is compounded from many sources, a textbook of theological explanation and definition, containing a series of meditations, which are the heart of its spiritual technique, and, in common with many other manuals of the time, it relates the common tasks of daily life and necessities of nature to their awesome ends. The bed is to remind the sleeper of his grave, his rising of the resurrection from the dead. Cockcrow is to recall Peter's denial and penitence; the putting on of clothes, man's primeval innocence and fallen shame. The sun streaming in is to be a sign of the Sun of Righteousness, risen with healing in his wings.[10]

"The practice of piety" is one of the seventeenth-century terms for what today would be called "spirituality." Another is "holy living," the title of a book by Jeremy Taylor (1613–1667) written during the distresses of the Commonwealth, for Frances, Lady Carbery, in whose South Wales home Taylor had taken refuge. It is a masterpiece of English style which proceeds from rigorous self-examination to rules for every aspect of life. In common with the spirituality of the age, it is full of self-abnegation. There must be much consciousness of sin, and the rules have a severity which allures. John Wesley's original dedication of himself to God as a young man of twenty-two was in part due to Taylor, though Coleridge maintained that Taylor on repentance would drive men to despair and said that "the necessary consequence of Taylor's scheme is a conscience worrying, casuistical monkish work-holiness.[11] There is in Taylor a Pelagianism of which his contemporary, Robert Sanderson, accused him, but this is not apparent in the prayers which conclude each section of the work. The aim of the whole is, as Wesley saw, total dedication out of that love for God which is our response to his love for us. Here is "an act of desire" in preparation for receiving the Sacrament:

> Lord Jesus, come quickly; my heart is desirous of Thy presence and would entertain thee, not as a guest, but as an inhabitant, as the Lord of all my faculties. Enter in and take possession, and dwell with me for ever, that I also may dwell in the heart of my dearest Lord, which was opened for me with a spear and love.[12]

Theology, said Taylor, "is rather a divine life than a divine knowledge. In heaven indeed we must first see and then love; but here on earth we must first love and love will open our eyes as well as our hearts; and we shall then see, perceive and understand."[13]

What must not be forgotten is the omnipresence of death in the seventeenth century, ever in the midst of life with no technological screening, likely to come in so many ways, by accident, natural disaster, war, plague, and in childbirth. The ravages of death became apparent by what for us is youthful middle age, even if one got that far: teeth decayed, eyes grew dim, hair fell out, pain could not be relieved, medical treatment was brutal and barbarous. Jeremy Taylor followed up *Holy Living* with *The Rules and Exercises of Holy Dying*.

> [He] urged his readers to notice the daily increments in their progress towards death. Progress towards death could then become the impetus for forming a self that is not, like the body, biodegradable, a self whose strengthened connection to immortality made it capable of abandoning the dying body.[14]

This made a heavenly dimension essential for all spirituality. The world was a vale of tears for all and for most the only sure hope was beyond the grave, which made it a desperate urgency to gain salvation then. Yet there are marvelous passages in many authors about the immortal hope: John Donne's sermon "Death's Duell," for instance, and the words with which Izaak Walton concluded his account of Donne's last days: "that body, which once was a Temple of the Holy Ghost, and is now become a small quantity of Christian dust; But I shall see it re-animated."[15]

Written prayers, as in Taylor, were among the glories of Anglican spirituality in this period. Chief among them are Lancelot Andrewes's *Preces Privatae*. These were never intended for publication and did not appear until 1648, twenty-two years after Andrewes's death. The manuscript was sometimes on scraps of paper "slubbered with his pious hands and watered with his penitential tears." In total contrast to John Bunyan, for instance, Andrewes did not think it seemly to pray in one's own words. He disliked what seemed often to be extempore irreverence and verbosity and felt that one should address God in the language of Scripture or the holy tradition, while he felt that his own prayers must be part of the great chain of catholic prayer throughout the world and throughout the ages. He said his prayers best with a pen in his hand and with nine or ten books on the shelf beside him. He concentrated his mind by writing down the prayer as he prayed.[16] The result is an original mosaic of devotion, of daily prayers, beginning with "The dial," in which every hour is given its scriptural occasion and reference. Then follow Penitence, Confession of Faith, Hope and Charity, Praise, Blessing, Thanksgiving, Deprecation, Comprecation, Intercession, and the Lord's Prayer paraphrased. There is much penitence; the intercessions encircle the earth and omit none.

Andrewes was successively bishop of Chichester, Ely, and Winchester and had ecclesiastical offices in several other places too. He may be claimed by the universities both of Cambridge and Oxford, and he was court preacher to James I. He had a style all his own with puns and plays on words, Latin and Greek as well as English, which, like the illumination of medieval manuscripts, adorned his very biblical and patristic expositions of the truths of faith and could lead to some powerful climaxes. He drew mostly on the Greek fathers, which may be a distinguishing mark of the Anglican spirituality of this period both from the Puritan and the Roman, which were more in the Latin tradition.

George Herbert (1593–1633), courtier turned cleric, the model country parson, in spite of the brevity of his years of cure, has been deemed Calvinist in theology, but Andrew Louth has argued that the Augustinian influences on him were not predestinarian so much as those of the *Confessions*.[17] Herbert was a poet whose verse expresses the deep longing of the heart for God, the sense of unworthiness of the least of his mercies and the reality of redeeming grace, even when we are chastened by affliction. He is altogether Anglican, priest and poet of "the mean," eschewing the painted lady of the seven hills and unadorned Puritanism. Priestly vestments are not the gewgaws of outward show but the signs of the imputed righteousness of Christ.

> Holinesse on the head
> Light and perfections on the breast,
> Harmonious bells below, raising the dead
> To lead them unto life and rest;
> Thus are true Aarons drest.

Profaneness in my head,
Defects and darknesse in my breast,
A noise of passions ringing me for dead
Unto a place where is no rest:
Poore priest thus am I drest.

Onely another head
I have, another heart and breast,
Another musick, making live not dead,
Without whom I could have no rest:
In him I am well drest.

Christ is my onely head,
My alone onely heart and breast,
My onely musick, striking me ev'n dead;
That to the old man I may rest,
And be in him new drest.

So holy in my head,
Perfect and light in my deare breast,
My doctrine tun'd by Christ, (who is not dead,
But lives in me while I do rest)
Come people; Aaron's drest.[18]

Herbert believed in the importance of preaching even when the sermon was dull or without palpable spiritual power; yet its purpose is to lead to prayer.

Resort to sermons, but to prayers most:
Prayings the end of preaching.

Herbert's sonnet on prayer conveys the numinous richness of the subject by a cumulative use of images, mutually incompatible:

Prayer, the Church's banquet, Angel's age,
God's breath in man returning to his birth,
The soul in paraphrase, heart in pilgrimage,
The Christian plummet sounding heaven and earth;
Engine against the Almighty, sinner's tower,
Reverse thunder, Christ-side-piercing spear
The six-days-world transposing in an hour,
A kind of tune which all things hear and fear;
Softness and peace and joy, and love and bliss'
Exalted Manna, gladness of the best,
Heaven in ordinarie, man well-dressed,

> The milky way, the bird of Paradise,
> Church-bells beyond the stars heard, the soul's blood,
> The land of spices, something understood.[19]

Herbert belongs to a group of poets called "metaphysical," a term applied by Samuel Johnson and sometimes used pejoratively to suggest intricate poetry, allusive and demanding strenuous exegesis. It is in fact "the poetry of meditation," to use the title of Louis L. Martz's book of 1954. The natural and biblical revelations are combined, and earthly scenes, whether from nature or from domestic activity or industry, are seen either as types of heaven or transfigured by the radiance of the divine glory. Henry Vaughan (1622–1695), who called himself "the Silurist," after the ancient British tribe of his native Breconshire, acknowledged a debt to Herbert and was also influenced by the Hermetic writings. Wherever he walked, he was conscious of eternity. In one of his best-known poems, he sees it "like a great Ring of pure and endess light." Some would soar up into it, but most would not, to the poet's puzzlement, until

> One whispered thus,
> This Ring the Bridegroom did for none provide
> But for his Bride.[20]

Thomas Traherne (1637–1674), poet and prose writer, has much in common with Vaughan. He has been called "a supreme exponent of the affirmative way whose vivid sense of the Divine glory transfiguring creation is expressed in rich and moving prose."[21]

There was an interesting experiment on religious community life at Little Gidding in Huntingdonshire, founded by Nicholas Ferrar, a friend of George Herbert, in the late 1620s. Condemned by extreme Protestants as "the Arminian nunnery," its rule was hardly monastic and it was a community of men and women, almost a family living by hourly offices, the recitation of the whole of the Psalter each day and the reading of the four Gospels each month. Holy Communion was celebrated only on the first Sunday of each month and on major festivals. (Caroline eucharistic devotion did not always involve weekly, much less daily, celebrations, which came in with the Anglo-Catholic revival, to some extent anticipated by Wesley.) The community engaged in works of charity, in farming and bookbinding. It had its personal difficulties and was ransacked and dispersed in 1646, but lingered on in nostalgic, high church memory.

There is, in spite of penitence and severity, a certain optimism of grace in the Caroline divines, because of an incarnational theology, particularly illustrated in Andrewes's nativity sermons. At its root is the saying of

Athanasius that God became man in order that man might become God. Deification is undoubtedly taught. But, in Andrewes in particular, this is the work of the whole Trinity. Easter is, for Andrewes, Christ's second birth, a second Christmas, and the Holy Spirit, the bond of union between the Father and the Son, brings us through the birth, life, death, and resurrection of Christ into the very life of God, making us partakers of the divine nature.[22]

The Cambridge Platonists

Deification, or *theosis*, is a Greek idea espoused by an interesting group of seventeenth-century divines, wearied of the bitterness of theological controversy, who sought to restore Christianity to "its old loving nurse the Platonick philosophy."[23] The Cambridge Platonists are to some extent the heirs of Cambridge Puritanism. They managed to survive both the Commonwealth and the Restoration and mostly retained their offices throughout the mid-century turmoil, not because they were time-servers but because they were more concerned for inward than outward religion and were wonderfully free of *odium theologicum*. Yet this angered some of their contemporaries and hardened hearts against them because they believed that confessional convictions for which wars were fought and fellow Christians persecuted were mere relative "notions." Religion, they claimed, is not "Divinity methodized"; it is spiritual.

Deification "in a sober sense" is "for a Christian to live wholly to God, to live the life of God, *having his own life hidden with Christ in God*" (John Smith). Deification is ethical; it is not a state of being lost in God but of loving as he loves, being merciful as he is merciful.

Benjamin Whichcote (1609–1683) declared that "nothing in the natural state is base or vile" and that "a great honour was put upon human nature when the *Son of God* came into it." "Theology is a *Divine life* rather than a *Divine science.*" "The only safe entrance into Divine knowledge is true Holiness" (Henry More).

Their favorite text, as all the world knows, was Proverbs 20:27, "The spirit of man is the candle of the Lord." Whichcote added, "Lighted *by* God and lighting us *to* God." This candle though a modest flame was not a pale flicker, incomparable with sun or stars. It was "Divine sagacity," reason as a spiritual faculty, which Plotinus described as "something greater than reason, reason's prior, as far above reason as the very object of thought must be." They deplored enthusiasm and false and furious zeal as much as superstition, and would have said that Christianity was not "mystical." They are certainly not mystics in the sense that the term is used of Teresa and John of the Cross. There are no paroxysms of love or dark nights of sense or soul. Yet union with God is for them the goal both of philosophy and faith, "a union above mind" through the merging of the rational and the spiritual. We may speak, though in a rather different sense from Spinoza, of "the intellectual love of God."

The Platonists will have no sharp dichotomies. There is no incongruity, no contradiction between nature and grace, any more than between the rational and the spiritual. They were aware of the world around them and lovingly observed nature. Ralph Cudworth and the other Platonists have been expounded by the twentieth-century Cambridge Anglican Charles Raven, ornithologist and botanist as well as theologian, desperate for the reconciliation of science and religion.[24] John Ray, whose life Raven wrote, could plead that "to contemplate the works of God is part of the business of a Sabbath-day." Henry More, for instance, was interested in field studies, and the Platonists belong to that long tradition which sees creation and Scripture as the two books of the works of God. Says John Smith: "Thus may a good man walk up and down the World as in a Garden of Spices, and suck a Divine sweetness out of every flower. There is a Twofold meaning in every creature as the Jews speak of their law, a Literal and a Mistical and the one is but the ground of the other."[25]

Cudworth was an able theologian of science with his concept of "Plastic Nature":

> Wherefore since neither all things are produced Fortuitously, or by the Un-guided Mechanism of Matter, nor God himself may reasonably be thought to do all things Immediately and Miraculously; it may well be concluded that there is a Plastick Nature under him, which as an Inferior and Subordinate Instrument, doth Drudgingly Execute that part of his Providence, which con-sists in the Regular and Orderly Motion of matter; yet so as there is also besides this, a Higher Providence to be acknowledged, which presiding over it doth often supply the Defects of it and sometimes Overrule it; forasmuch as this *Plastick Nature* cannot act Electively nor with Discretion.[26]

For the Platonists, the whole of human life should be prayer, since commu-nion with God is the goal of everything. For the good there is an upward progress of the soul from the contemplation of earthly things to the heav-enly "in this visible outward creation, they find God many times, secretly flowing into their souls and leading them out of the court of the Temple into the Holy Place." Thus one attains to a "holy boldness and humble familiarity with God" (John Smith).

Benjamin Whichcote used to lead his congregation at Holy Trinity, Cambridge, into a long prayer before his sermon. It seems to have been invariable. It was full of Scripture, its foundation in the doctrine of our redemption, asking that Christ may become "a complete Saviour to us," that God may consummate his work of grace in our souls, and "naturalise us to heaven." Religion for the Platonists is a joyful thing, at times indeed rapturous.[27] Holiness is happiness, a share in the happiness of God.

> Religion is not like the prophet's roll, sweet as honey when it was in his mouth, but as bitter as gall in his belly. Religion is no sullen *Stoicisme,* no sour *Pharisaisme;* it does not consist in a few Melancholy passions, in some dejected looks or depressions of Mind but it consists in *Freedom, Love, Peace, Life* and *Power:* the more it comes to be digested into, the more sweet and lovely we shall find it to be.[28]

The Moralists

The turbulent, intense, and religiously passionate seventeenth century was succeeded by the Age of Reason and what the Germans in 1864 christened "the Enlightenment." Dissent—particulary among the Presbyterians—slid into Unitarianism, which is why Samuel Wesley and Susanna Annesley, who became his wife, both children of ejected ministers, turned Church of England, Susanna with non-juring sympathies. The loss of the non-jurors assisted the establishment's tendencies toward rationalism, typified in John Toland's *Christianity Not Mysterious* and in the works of Dr. Samuel Clarke, though no more than with the dissenters did affective and sacramental spirituality die out, much of it due to those of a non-juring inclination. If Dissenters had a tradition that reached from Richard Baxter (d. 1691) to Philip Doddridge (d. 1751), Anglicans had Robert Nelson, a layman who wrote *inter alia* on *Fasts and Festivals,* and William Law, who, though in the isolation of King Cliffe, later became captivated by the heterodox mysticism of Jacob Boehme, and had soul-converting power on John Wesley, Samuel Johnson, and the Tractarians, through his *Christian Perfection* and, supremely, *A Serious Call to a Devout and Holy Life.* "The other day," said John Keble to Hurrell Froude once on taking leave of him, "you said that Law's *Serious Call* was a very interesting book. It was as though you had said that the Day of Judgement will be a pretty sight."

But as early as 1657, there was an anonymous work, *The Whole Duty of Man,* which was precursor of a moralistic school and seemed for more than a century to be almost the charter of Anglican spirituality. Its title is taken from Ecclesiastes 12:13, "Fear God and keep his commandments; for this is the whole duty of man"; it was ethical rather than evangelical or catholic, very much encouraging "a godly, righteous and sober life," hot against drunkenness and vice, containing meditations on communion which encourage a penitential realism in contemplation of the Savior's sufferings and our daily crucifying of him afresh, but which lack the sense of the holy mystery found in Hooker or Taylor. Yet this moralistic strain is not to be dismissed either as Pelagianism or dry-as-dust deontology. In the sermons of John Tillotson, archbishop of Canterbury from 1691 to 1694 and an influential preacher for years before that, it provided plain and practical instruction in an age that needed deliverance from the moral chaos and licentiousness of Restoration courts.[29] In Joseph Butler it gave to the mid-eighteenth-century church a moral philosopher of genius, who contributed not a little to the Tractarian search for holiness. A man of undoubted compassion as well as penetrating intellect, Butler feared corporate insanity—with good reason, we may say with the French Revolution and Hitler's enchantment of the German people in our memories—hence, his dislike of the Methodists and his dismissal of John Wesley with the words, "Sir, the pretending to special revelations of the Holy Ghost is a horrid thing, a very horrid thing." For Butler, conscience should be sovereign and probability the guide of life. Religion is analogous to "the constitution and course of nature," not because nature points us directly to a good and omnipotent Creator but because religion, as wonderful as nature, is also as mysterious. As R. W. Church expounded Butler:

> If religion comes to us with apparent contradictions, and seeming to do only half its work, giving us light but only to a certain point, relieving our pains and remedying our sin, but not completely, showing us something of the next world, but little in comparison with what it conceals, answering some of our questions and fulfilling some of our longings, but leaving much unsatisfied—this is only what we have been familiar with from our birth, in the world, which for all that, we believe was given us to dwell in by God who is just and wise and who, in the mercies of grace and redemption, carries on the same system and acts on the same principles as those to which we are accustomed in our daily contact with the laws and realities of nature.[30]

Life indeed is a poor thing, "but it is a practical thing because it is part of something, the greatness of which no thought can fathom and no words express. In his narrow limited condition—how narrow, how limited, how strange, it is almost impossible to overstate—man is yet under the government of God. . . . Religion is a matter for 'awful solicitude,' for it is that on which man's whole interest and being, and the fate of nature depends."[31] On his deathbed the great bishop "expressed it as an awful thing to appear before the Moral Governor of the world."[32] We may think that he did not take sufficient comfort in the merits of a crucified Redeemer. In this he was perhaps not unlike Dr. Johnson.[33] But the solemnity of the words is not only a rebuke to antinomians; it gives Anglican spirituality a moral seriousness

11. William Holman Hunt, *The Light of the World*, 1851-1853.

without which evangelicalism becomes subjective sentimentality and catholicism a ritualistic charade.

The Evangelicals

By the time Butler was dead (1752) the evangelical revival was in full spate, in part the uprising of folk religion which the Age of Reason could not satisfy and the need of salvation from conditions of industrial degradation and poverty and from the fear of damnation, which brief lives in squalor and pressed service at arms and death for sometimes trivial offenses, made very present to the lower classes. The extent to which Anglican spirituality may claim the Wesley brothers may be disputed; both lived and died as clergymen and former Oxford dons at that, and Charles, the younger, condemned John's ordinations for America and any action that would separate the Methodist societies from the Church of England. They were both Prayer Book men and of high church upbringing, which they never repudiated, and the revival of which they were the instruments was sacramental as well as evangelical. The Eucharist was for them the supreme means of grace to be celebrated frequently, if not daily. Their doctrine was Caroline Anglican, and their altars were thronged as were few in the parishes. But the style they evoked—raucous, excited, and in early years productive of paroxysms—was hardly compatible with Anglican restraint and was deplored by the Tractarians in the next century. They created a new system of church order, evangelical as well as pastoral in intent and demanding an itinerancy incompatible with Anglican parochialism. Their principal aim was the holiness which Newman was to preach and the Tractarians to seek, but they seemed to the Oxford men to have sired a coarse and vulgar progeny, profaning the mysteries by too much shouting at street corners, cheapening the sacred. After John Wesley's death, the people called Methodists went their separate way taking their hymns and class meetings with them, the Anglican loyalties of the Wesleyan branch never quite lost but increasingly strained as the nineteenth century wore on.

There was, however, an evangelical revival within the English church contemporary with that of the Wesleys, and at times the paths crossed; but there were signal differences. The Anglican revival tended to be Calvinist in theology, as against the evangelical Arminianism of the Wesleys and their perfectionism. (Some of Charles Wesley's hymns teach *theosis*.)[34] The evangelical clergy were parochial rather than itinerant, identified by the names of their livings, Grimshaw of Haworth, Berridge of Everton. The outstanding leader was Charles Simeon (1759–1836), the least itinerant of all clergymen, since he was vicar of Whichcote's Holy Trinity, Cambridge, from 1783 until his death. Simeon was converted by reading *The Whole Duty of Man*, but the religion he preached was of personal trust in Christ and a gospel to be offered to all. It was to be received with joy but not an unhealthy triumphalism, and he deplored the fashionable deathbed scenes of the day, such, I fear, as that of John Wesley. "While I am here I am a sinner, a forgiven sinner but a sinner still. And as such I would lie here to the last at the foot of the cross, looking unto Jesus and go as such into the presence of my God." Simeon as a preacher attracted far greater crowds than would Newman and trained many men for the ministry. His spirituality is summed up in these words: "The Bible first, the Prayer book second and all other books in subordination to both." The finest sight short of heaven would be a whole congregation using the prayers of the liturgy in the spirit of them."

Evangelicalism had great influence among the wealthy. William Wilberforce wrote a best seller with a characteristically long and revealing title: *A Practical View of the Prevailing System of Professed Christians in the Higher and Middle Classes in this Country contrasted with Real Christianity*. The book is an attack on hereditary Christianity, "the religion of all sensible men" ("no sensible man ever tells"), and a plea for emotion. As with the Methodists, hymn singing was a natural celebration of faith; witness the Olney hymns of William Cowper and John Newton. The characteristics of evangelical spirituality include the following: (1) the centrality of the word in Scripture—in preaching, in personal testimony, and in private conversation; (2) the necessity of conversion, an inward change, in response to the atoning sacrifice of Christ. "Deliverance through a work not our own";[35] (3) a consequent moral responsibility; (4) prayers very much according to the counsels of Lewis Bayly, in private and in family. ("The daily portion" was all-important, and the sabbath day must be kept holy, with a serious joining in the worship of the people of God essential.); (5) world mission from the British imperial base (For this, societies were founded, notably the Church Missionary Society.); (6) philanthropy and social reform. Wilberforce and Shaftesbury are the great names, and their achievement must neither be minimized nor caricatured, though they were persons of wealth, in some sense patronizing the poor; class distinctions had a theological foundation as in Scripture. Not all were as obnoxious as A. E. Housman's stepmother, who said of the poor: "They don't feel as we do." Wilberforce is more typical, of whom it was said: "He carried the poor in his heart"; (7) profound suspicion of Rome (Said Henry Venn of the Church Missionary Society, "It would be better had China not been opened to the Gospel than that the papacy should take possession of it." Yet he wrote *The Missionary Life and Labours of Francis Xavier*, and although he doubted whether his mission resulted in true conversions, he had to concede that "its exercise was blended with so much tenderness of affection and with such expression of personal humility and Christian courtesy as cannot but excite our admiration as to the robust magnanimity of the man." (The word "robust" is significant. "Muscular Christianity" was an ideal, as with Charles Kingsley and many Methodists. In any event rationalism was more to be feared than Rome, and evangelicals found themselves in alliance with Pusey and the Anglo-Catholics in condemning the biblical scholarship of Bishop Colenso.)

Evangelicalism was household religion, typified by associations of families and neighbors like the "Clapham Sect" with the Stephens, Thorntons, and Wilberforces. Cricket was the evangelical game, displayng "the white flannels of a blameless life," played according to strict rules, gentlemanly to outward view and analogous to the Christian life with the contest between batsman and demon bowler, aggressive or wily, the team spirit, the need to be athletic ("muscular"), the divine umpire, and the applause which welcomed the successful player to the pavilion.

The achievement was amazing; the deficiencies obvious. There was no conception of the church as the Mystical Body of Christ. It was rather "the fellowship of kindred minds" within the state organization. Sometimes there seemed to be no understanding of history. True, history by its very nature may sow doubts; church history depresses by its terrible record of evil in the professedly holy; much is not fact but interpretative myth; historians dislike the category of uniqueness because they organize material by classification and comparison. Yet they give weight to cultural difference and change and allow for "context," which the evangelical may not either in Scripture or the book of life. Yet the Bible does have different meanings and it may be important to distinguish between what it meant originally, what it has come to mean through use, and what it means for the individual believer and for the church here and now.

There was an antimetaphysical streak in evangelicalism and a fear of following the argument wherever it led. Doubt was felt to be sinful. Henry Venn wrote to James Stephen, "I knew as a young man all that could be said against Christianity and I put these thoughts aside as temptations of the devil and they have never troubled me since." Evangelical spirituality did not find it easy to cope with the onrush of science. There is a straight road from Clapham to Bloomsbury, for the descendants of the Stephens and the Thorntons were Virginia Woolf and E. M. Forster—agnostics, cultured despisers, debunkers, and contemptuous of, in Forster's phrase, "poor, talkative Christianity." Together with an undue seriousness, a refusal of the pleasures of the world such as opera, theater, and the arts was a censoriousness, a tendency to lecture and improve, to moralize and to look for faults in others.

The Oxford Movement and Beyond

This was a movement to reassert and recover the catholicity of the English church against its being an arm of the state, a pawn of politicians. It sought to counter that evangelicalism, particularly evident among Methodists, which seemed to cheapen the gospel and relied too much on personal experience and feelings of assurance, while it attacked "liberalism," which as represented by German biblical scholarship sought to bring Christian theology into conformity with modern thought, the legacy of the Enlightenment. It was also a holiness movement, inclined to identify heterodoxy with immorality but more positively to seek sanctification through the discipline and ordinances of the church. The Church of England must trace its origins back, far beyond the reformation to the fathers and the apostles. History was all-important, rather romantically conceived, as in the novels of Sir Walter Scott, though John Keble felt that he wrote too freely about holy things, for reverence was the first disposition of the Christian mind and its expression should be more in poetry than in prose. Keble, regarded as the leader of the movement, was Professor of Poetry at Oxford and, before that, in *The Christian Year* had added to the classics of Anglican devotion simple poems that were singable as hymns (which brought upon him the charge that he was tending to Methodism), indebted to Wordsworth. There is a desire to awaken the poetic child in Tractarianism, reminiscent of Wordsworth's "Ode on the Intimations of Immortality in Early Childhood," while there is a Platonism of sorts as in Newman's sermon "The Invisible World" and Keble's hymn "There Is a Book Who Runs May Read," which represents a long tradition going back at least to the Franciscan St. Bonaventure and found in the aberrant, radical reformer Thomas Müntzer:

> Two worlds are ours; 'tis only sin
>   Forbids us to descry
> The mystic heaven and earth within,
>   Plain as the sea and sky.

The Tractarians made much of the doctrine of "reserve" which they discovered in the early fathers, who found it necessary to practice an arcane or secret discipline, whereby the most solemn acts and profoundest truths of Christianity were concealed not only from a hostile and unbelieving world but from those preparing for baptism. The meaning of the sacraments themselves as well as the high doctrines of the faith were not disclosed until after initiation. This also seems to have been true of the ministry of Christ himself, who told many things by parables, not to make them plain or perspicuous by anecdote but to reveal them only to those who would accept and tease them out by faith and action. There is no blinding revelation of truth but "if any man will to do his will he shall know of the doctrine." Jesus kept his messiahship secret and was not anxious during his ministry to have either his mighty works, or the nature of his vocation blazoned abroad. After his resurrection, he showed himself to his disciples and not to the world. The last the world saw of him was when his body was taken down from the cross and sealed in the tomb, and this must be the temper of Christian discipleship.[36] The Tractarians were suspicious of religious excitement and undue emotion. Worship was its remedy and worship was not a search for feeling but a discipline, in awe and reverence and prayer (Keble constructed the pews in the church he built at Hursley as prayer desks). Impetuous, bold language in religion is to be discouraged.

> One secret act of self-denial, one sacrifice of inclination to duty, is worth all the mere good thoughts, warm feelings, passionate prayers in which idle people indulge themselves. It will give us more comfort on our death-bed to reflect on one deed of self-denying mercy, purity, or humility, than to recollect the shedding of many tears, and the recurrence of frequent transports and much spiritual exultation.[37]

Action was the end of the Christian life and that holiness "without which no man shall see the Lord." Religion was given not to satisfy doubts but to make us better people.

Pusey has been called the "doctor mysticus" of Tractarianism, and he writes and preaches at times with contemplative rapture and is ecstatic as Keble and Newman were not.

> His language is more mystical (in the modern rather than the contemporary sense) than the language of any other Tractarian, and in its dwelling upon the participation of the Christian in the divinity of Christ, the union of the soul with its Redeemer, can rise to heights of beauty. . . . He fetched his language not from the French writers of devotion but from the Greek Fathers, and the Christian Platonism which they represented, though its roots went down into the pietism of the Evangelicals.[38]

Pusey writes of the Eucharist with deep devotion. It is the gate of heaven, the gate by which our Lord who was made flesh descends that he may lift us up to be in his real presence and that of the angels and saints in light. Pusey's spirituality may at times be too hostile to "the world" in the Johannine sense, though we are to use the "very things of time and sense whereby others are drawn down into the world, to rise to the things of God." The Incarnation has hallowed them all, but it is only as we look to Jesus that their tinsel glare may be transfigured into God's glory.

The Oxford divines were concerned with spirituality more than ceremonial. They saw in the English rite a buried catholicism which it was their duty to revive. An outward catholicism was bound to follow, partly because the movement broke the bounds of Oxford and the country parishes and went into the slums, where the poor needed a color in their drab lives that eloquent and beautiful words were insufficient to provide, but also because of militant Roman Catholicism consequent upon Catholic emancipation and the restored hierarchy and the Irish immigration. By the end of the nineteenth century, Anglicans could have in their own church after much strife and suffering all that they desired of Rome without being subject to the Pope. Some of them longed for reconciliation, only to be rebuffed by the encyclical pronouncing Anglican orders to be "absolutely null and utterly void." But Anglo-Catholic spirituality went beyond that of the Tractarians and became post-Tridentine rather than Anglican, providing the Mass or the Latin canon muttered *sotto voce* beside 1662 or even itself used openly in English. This was attended by sacramental confession and schemes of self-examination by the use of manuals. There were translations of Continental books of devotion, in which Pusey had led the way. Roman Catholic moral theology prevailed with its categorization of sins, and devotion to the blessed Virgin, *Ave Marias*, and the *Angelus* were prominent. There was desire for reservation of the Blessed Sacrament, pleaded for on grounds not only of sick communicants but on behalf of those like nurses and postmen who worked "unsocial hours." (Consecration was then believed to belong properly to the forenoon.) It was suspected that what was really desired was adoration, exposition, and benediction. As the French Oratorian Louis Bouyer pointed out, it was unfortunate that Anglo-Catholics took over Roman forms just when the liturgical movement was beginning to question them. But the importing of the Mass, often a High Mass with noncommunicating attendance, encouraged not only the beauty of music and gesture but also contemplation. In a valuable distinction of W. H. Vanstone, there was "space" as well as "place" for worship, freedom from restless hubbub, over-brash heartiness and palliness with the deity, even though there may have been praying *at* the Mass rather than praying the Mass, and the corporate dimension was to some extent absent. The clamor for the Eucharist as the principal service of the Lord's Day grew and for Prayer Book revision with a rite more akin to 1549. Alarmed, evangelicals felt that communion devotion was better served by a service which followed the often well-attended Morning Prayer once a month and which separated the nominal and conventional from the truly converted and committed. Bishop E. A. Knox looked back with regret to the days when that was so and communicants were "marked out by the fact of remaining, and to some extent objects of criticism for not following the outgoing throng." There was felt the force of the words of Doddridge's communion hymn, which may well have been sung,

> Why are its dainties all in vain,
> Before unwilling hearts displayed?
> Was not for them the victim slain,
> Are they forbid the children's bread?[39]

The revival of the "religious" life was a consequence of the Oxford Movement—Marion Hughes took private vows in St. Mary's Oxford in 1841—and innumerable orders of Anglican nuns and monks sprang up, the first of women in 1845, the Sisters of Charity. The outstanding founder in the nineteenth century was Richard Meux Benson of the Society of St. John the Evangelist, "the Cowley Fathers." Ascetically severe, Benson thought that contemplation through reading of the Scriptures was the foundation of the life of holiness, which must reach out into the world. The Gospel demands a prophetic witness over against society, at war with systems and without compromise such as has besmirched church history. "It is the contemplative life gazing up to God and doing battle with Satan, which is the essential character of a Christian life." Roman models and rules were followed very closely in some orders, particularly of nuns. The Benedictine life was introduced to the Church of England as well as the Franciscan, while the Community of the Resurrection (founded by an Oxford theologian later to be Bishop Gore) and the Society of the Sacred Mission (founded by Herbert Kelly, a great original) were native to Anglicanism. All contributed to theological scholarship, ministerial training, and work in the empire. Anglican religious houses fostered the retreat movement, which has grown in the course of the twentieth century and has Free Church exponents.

There is no doubt that the Oxford Movement transformed Anglican spirituality and, insofar as it was within the tradition, drew out from it practices and a theology that were not native and would have astonished some of its seventeenth-century defenders. No one could be unaware of it either as friend, foe, or "of the middling sort." There were some who represented the authentic tradition and must not be ignored as spiritual guides. R. W. Church, "reminiscencer"-in-chief of the Oxford Movement, whose biography has the subtitle "The Anglican Response to Newman," was called by two Methodists "the greatest of the Deans of St. Pauls." Church had moral integrity, an unerring judgment of right and wrong, an austere condemnation of scandal and of that curiosity which classic moral theology has condemned. Pascal was a fitting subject for his exposition. "Say what you will there is something astonishing about the Christian religion," as one of the *Pensées* declares, and Church, like Pascal, could plumb those abysses of judgement and mercy on which the foundations of our prayers are laid."[40] Church knew where the heart of Christianity was, in that he chose for his tombstone in the village of Whatley in Somerset, where he had ministered, the verse from the *Dies Irae:*

> Faint and weary thou hast sought me,
> On the cross of suffering bought me,
> Shall such grace be vainly brought me?

The Cambridge trio of biblical scholars, Lightfoot, Westcott, and Hort, should be studied for their spirituality as well as for their commentaries and work on the text of the New Testament. Their scholarly rigor was grounded in faith and devotion. They approached the Scriptures with an awe inspired by the long tradition of reverence to Christ and their own personal piety. There was no great gulf between the asceticism of the study and the ascetism of the cell. Hort, the greatest of the three, pubished work on plants before he was twenty, discovered a new bramble, *rubus imbricatus,* in the Wye Valley in 1857, and examined in the Natural Sciences Tripos in the same year in which he delivered the Hulsean lectures, *The Way, the Truth, the Life.* He was inhibited by nervousness, and his fairly slender output was the result of agonized struggles. But there is no greater Anglican theological writing than his study of the last discourses of Jesus in St. John, with their leading of the disciples toward the risen and ascended presence of Christ taking its character no longer from their circumstances but from his.

Lightfoot and Westcott became successively bishops of Durham and realized the need for a social gospel amid the mining communities. "What a pitman he woud have made," said a Durham miner of Lightfoot. His *Leaders of the Northern Church* is a collection of his episcopal sermons based on northern saints from Bede to Butler. They recover something of the secret of Celtic Christianity, "the power of earnest, simple, self-denying lives, pleading with a force no eloquence of words can command."[41] Those lives were formed by a desperate discipline of prayer and fasting, something in it of the "fey" and a modesty and humility in their conception of high office.

Mention must be made of Frederick Denison Maurice (1805–1872), who although he was not a "spiritual" writer had great influence on subsequent Anglican theology and thereby the spirituality of the Cambridge trio and many in our own century. He ended his career as a professor at Cambridge, having been dismissed from his chair at King's College, London, because of his reservations about the doctrine of eternal punishment. The erstwhile Unitarian became a vigorous protagonist of the doctrine of the Trinity. He was a universalist and believed that Calvary was the world's baptism and that the divine Logos, incarnate in Jesus, was at work even where Christ was not known or denied. He was, in consequence, a paedo-baptist. A founder of the Christian Socialists, he was much involved in the social application of Christianity. He anticipated Karl Barth in his disparagement of "religion," loved liturgy, was a convinced episcopalian, and sought the unity of human-kind in the Triunity of God.

The Twentieth Century

Anglican spirituality has never been so rich as in these terrible years of war, atrocity, technological revolution and the decline of Christianity in the West. It has become ecumenical, reaching back beyond the Reformation, into that period, dark to so many eyes, known as the Midde Ages, and it has continued to break the bounds of its own formularies.

Our century has seen an immense interest in mysticism. This has been partly due to the search for what Aldous Huxley miscalled "the perennial philosophy," the desire to reach the truth underlying all religions and to be free of those differing institutional constraints and dogmatic formulas which have caused so much bitterness and strife—chiefy to a longing for some anchor in ultimate reality which will remain steadfast amid all the vicissitudes of human mortality. This has resulted, in Anglicanism, in the rediscovery of the fourteenth-century men and women known as the English mystics—Richard Rolle, the anonymous author of *The Cloud of Unknowing*, Walter Hilton, Julian of Norwich, and Margery Kempe. Julian has particularly spoken to the latter half of this century—the rationalist Anglicans of two hundred years ago thought her mad—not least through the American poet turned English and Anglican, T. S. Eliot, in the last of his Four Quartets, "Little Gidding." The words of Julian bring hope as he meditates on the seventeenth-century community, its vision and its dissolution amid the ravages of the civil wars and the seeming defeat of the Royalist and Anglican cause: "All shall be well/And all shall be well/And all manner of thing shall be well."

Julian speaks to our time as many past spiritual writers, famed in their day and after, do not. She was an able theologian, reconciling the truth expressed in Bonhoeffer's words, "Only a suffering God can help," with the Christian affirmation of the eternal changelessness and joy of the divine Being, through the doctrine of the Trinity. She is also in the Anselmic tradition of devotion to the motherhood of God and of Christ. *The Cloud of Unknowing*, influenced by Pseudo-Dionysius the Areopagite, and the *via negativa*, the journey through darkness rather than light, ring powerfully true to the experience of many souls overwhelmed by what is happening in the world and lacking any direct consciousness and knowledge of God yet feeling a love for him in their hearts. What is easily forgotten is that the foundation of mystical union is disciplined prayer taught by the desert fathers, the purgative way which precedes the illuminative and unitive.

The most distinguished and prolific interpreter of mysticism was Evelyn Underhill (1875–1941). She published her definitive work on the subject in 1911. Confirmed as an Anglican, she was for many years a free-lance writer with Roman Catholic sympathies and became a practicing member of the Anglican Church only in the last twenty years of her life. She said that she owed the whole of her spiritual life to the Roman Catholic lay theologian Baron von Hügel, friend of the modernists and liberal within his Roman loyalties. He made her spiritually Christocentric, though in the whole of her experience she came to Christ through God rather than to God through Christ. She wrote an interpretation of the life of Christ in terms of the mystic way, which von Hügel pronounced "as impressive as it is unconvincing." She wrote of mysticism as one who practiced it, and some who met her in the last decade of her life testify to "an appearance of light," a perceptible spiritual radiance.[42]

Preceding all of these and outliving them was W. R. Inge (1860–1954), dean of St. Paul's. His Bampton Lectures, *Christian Mysticism*, were published in 1899, and it was he who first made mytics such as Julian of Norwich known. He must not be judged as "the gloomy dean," the pillar of the church who became two columns in Lord Beaverbrook's *The Evening Standard*, where he wrote some silly, snobbish, and reactionary pieces. Nor is it fair to say that, in contrast to Evelyn Underhill, Inge wrote about mysticism as scholar and historian while for her it was a living way. In truth, his mysticism is more genuinely in the Anglican tradition than hers. He is in the succession of the Cambridge Platonists, whom he saw as representing a third school within the church no less legitimate than Catholicism and Protestantism. He represented an intellectual mysticism like theirs. His *magnum opus* was his Gifford Lectures, *The Philosophy of Plotinus* (1917), but of his many smaller books two stand out. *Speculum Animae* (1911) consists of four addresses given to college tutors and public schoolmasters. It is full of *obiter dicta* related to the whole of Christian life, but its thesis is that amid the distressing diversity *about* religion, the saints do not contradict one another.

Christianity has never been divided up there; wherever we find a Christian who truly prays, there we can point to a member of the true universal Church. I am not speaking, you will understand me, of trance or ecstasy; I am simply speaking of prayer—prayer of which the old and true definition is "the elevation of the mind and heart to God.[43]

Personal Religion and the Life of Devotion, of which there are now dozens of copies on the shelves of secondhand booksellers in England, was the bishop of London's lenten book for 1925. It is given poignancy by his account in the last chapter of the dying of his small daughter, Paula, whom he considered with truth to have been one of God's saints. In *Speculum Animae* Inge says that those troubles which come upon us unaccountably and irrationally often have a more purifying and elevating effect upon our characters than those acts of self-denial which we choose for ourselves—a statement of Protestant rather than Catholic asceticism with its mortifications and disciplines. Inge certainly knew suffering in the loss of his daughter and of a son in the Second World War.

There is much fine Anglican teaching on prayer to be found in volumes now gathering dust. A. L. Lilley, an Anglican Catholic Modernist, wrote in 1924 a small book, *Prayer in Christian Theology,* which is a selective history of what he considers authentic Christian prayer—communion with God, the cross planted at its heart. Kenneth E. Kirk (d. 1954) was the outstanding Anglican moral theologian of his day before cases of conscience shifted to social and bioethical questions. His Bampton Lectures, *The Vision of God* (1931), are an immensely learned examination of the *summum bonum* in the Western tradition. He was also a fine preacher, given to allegorize, but some of the sermons in *The Fourth River,* especially that which gives the collection its title, are profound expositions of Christian spirituality. A paper he wrote for the Oxford diocese where he was bishop on prayer in wartime is by no means confined to the ordeal which provoked it, and the illustration of prayer as the attempts of a small boy helping his watchmaker father to repair a broken watch should be better known than it is. Charles Raven, strangely ignored since his death in 1964, was Regius Professor of Divinity at Cambridge from 1933 to 1950, eager to see the reconciliation of science and religion, not a Platonist like Inge and yet in some sense a disciple of that group of Cambridge men. In an appendix to his Gifford Lectures is this paragraph on Intercession:

> The Cambridge Platonists to whom we have been much indebted have given us a metaphor which will explain in the simplest terms the working of the intercessory power. If the soul is, as they declared, the mirror of the Lord, then the first moment of prayer is to lift the mirror until the light of God falls upon it. The act of contrition and confession that follows represents the cleansing from the glass of the stains revealed by the light. In intercession the light reflected from the soul is directed towards those for whom we wish to pray. It is not our light but God's that streams out towards them. Just as in Scripture the prophet reflects and transmits the vision of God and we feel its illuminative and healing power, so in intercession as we lose ourselves in our

consciousness of God and of those for whom we pray, His presence and power become effective in them to fulfil the purpose of God's love.[44]

John Burnaby, Raven's successor but one as Regius Professor, had already given the Hulsean Lectures as a lay theologian in 1938. *Amor Dei* expounds St. Augustine on the love of God, with awareness of the crisis in which it too is written. It is possibly the outstanding work of Anglican spirituality this century. Burnaby was a theologian, open and brave in faith, who knew that "the royal road of universal love" passes over the pit of doubt and despair and that believer and unbeliever alike are subject to sore trials. "Love never forces and therefore there can be no certainty that it will overcome. But there may and there must be an unconquerable hope."[45] Burnaby also wrote an essay entitled "Christian Prayer" in the symposium *Soundings* (1962), which grapples with the perplexities about prayer in the minds of thoughtful people and grounds prayer in the truths of the Gospel. The kingdom of God is promoted in human history by no other power than the power of love and the power of God's love takes effect in human history in no other way than through the wills and actions of people in whom that love has come to dwell. "To pray is to open the heart to the entry of love—to ask God in; and where God is truly wanted he will always come." Contemplation and petition need not be regarded as two different ways of prayer between which we must choose. The aim of all our petitions must be the alignment of our own will with the will of God; and conversely there can be no real union of the soul with God that is not *active*. The "prayer of quiet" can help us in the Christian life only insofar as it strengthens us to work the works of God. And Christian petition must itself be a "practice of the presence of God."

Burnaby goes on to criticize traditional forms of worship, particularly the predominance of the Psalter, because they ill correspond to the essential character of Christian prayer. "But there is at least in the Church's central act of worship, the memorial of the precious death and passion of God's dear Son, a safeguard against misunderstanding or misuse of the act of prayer which no defects in verbal expression can remove."[46]

The eucharistic revisions in which the Anglican communion has shared have, as follows from the first part of this essay, the most serious repercussions for spirituality. The Book of Common Prayer seems destined to be lost from parish life, its haunting phrases obliterated from folk memory. Grievous as this is, the new liturgies are based on a larger liturgical understanding and an ampler eucharistic theology. As a whole, the new service books throughout the Anglican communion should assist the understanding of prayer which Burnaby desired, though on another issue

Reginald H. Fuller maintains that party extremes have, in England, unlike America, resulted in eucharistic prayers which do not affirm with sufficient strength the classical Anglican position that "in the eucharistic prayer the gifts are offered with thanksgiving for Christ's once-for-all sacrifice in order that through them we might receive the saving consequences of that sacrifice."[47]

This century has subscribed to John Wesley's dictum, whether or not it has been known, that "there is no holiness but social holiness"—and this in two senses. First, the Christian religion is *not* as in Whitehead's aphorism "what the individual does with his own solitariness." It is corporate communion. So there has been a renewed emphasis in worship on the congregation, the body of Christ, not on the altar but in the people: hence, the table in the midst, the minister in the westward position, more people taking active part, and the restoration of the kiss of peace. But, second, there has been a renewed emphasis on the second commandment to love our neighbor. In the title of an invaluable little book by V. A. Demant, Christianity is *A Two-Way Religion* and must include a gospel for society as well as for the individual.[48] There must be a political spirituality. Some Anglo-Catholics have been socialists, such as Conrad Noel, flying the red flag from Thaxted Parish Church, while Alan Ecclestone, a profound spiritual writer, has been a member of the communist party. Strongest in the 1930s and 1940s was the Christendom Group, founded by Maurice Reckitt for the study of sociology with Demant as its ablest mind. William Temple, one of the outstanding and most inspirational Anglicans of the century, was not a member of the Labour Party for very long, since he thought party membership incompatible with episcopacy, but as archbishop, both of York and Canterbury, he devoted much thought, especially during the years of the Second World War, to Christianity and the social order, even venturing into fields such as banking. He may be regarded as one of the founders of the welfare state in Britain. He was also in the succession of the devotees of the Fourth Gospel (and of Robert Browning)—Hort, Westcott, Scott Holland, Inge. His *Readings in St. John's Gospel,* critically conservative, devotionally rich, had a market for a quarter of the century. Evangelicals, too, have come to see that individual salvation is not enough, that prayer cannot be divorced from social action.

There have been some Anglicans, convinced of the relation of religion to life, who in order to help the citizens of our world to faith and to be honest to their own convictions, have sought a reconstruction of belief. Charles Gore attempted that much earlier, but he had not to reckon with Wittgenstein, or with the stampede of secularization. Bishop John Robinson in *Honest to God* (1963) felt the impossibility in our age of believing in a God "up there" and "out there" and turned to Paul Tillich's concept of God as the ground of being. This is not so revolutionary as popular reaction imagined. God as the "fund" or bottom of the soul is very much the theme of V. A. Demant's book, while mystics have talked of "the crucifixion of images." St. John of the Cross demands a complete purging of memory, an emptying out of dearly held concepts and previous ideas of God in order that he may be known as he is in himself and not in our ideas of him and loved for himself alone. But all this is not native to Anglican spirituality, which has always sought a firm base in reason. We must beware of numbering John Robinson among the mystical theologians. Archimandrite Rodzianko, in a paper entitled "Honest to God under the Father's Judgement," made his principal criticism that for Robinson the intellectual quest conditions everything, which implicitly rejects the apophatic way of Eastern theology. Insofar as Robinson's spirituality had affinities with mysticism it was because his awareness of Western doubts and his intellectual quest led him toward ways of prayer that coincided with some of the insights of mystical experience, as in the theme of one of his other books, *Exploration into God;* but his approach was different. It is not dissimilar with Don Cupitt. *Taking Leave of God* is a title from Meister Eckhart, the medieval mystic, and for Cupitt spirituality is central to the Christian life. While he denies objective truth, he "offers powerful and stimulating exposition of how the resurrection, the doctrine of God's omnipresence, the doctrine of providence and the practice of prayer may be understood as expressing spiritual values." But his concern is with the autonomy of spiritual values, just as Kant contended for the autonomy of morals. Spirituality cannot depend on external circumstances, not even on God.[49]

The radical approach to Scripture in which Anglican scholars such as R. H. Lightfoot, Dennis Nineham, and Christopher Evans—all from the Catholic wing—have been prominent, has not perhaps had the influence on spirituality that would seem to be a consequence. Stainer's *The Crucifixion,* its libretto by the late Victorian Anglo-Catholic, W. J. Sparrow-Simpson, is still often sung at passiontide. Its narrative of the passion with the seven words from the cross harmonizes the four Gospels in an attempt to give an almost moment-by-moment account of Calvary. It completely misses the distinctive interpretations of the evangelists. Christopher Evans has done notable work on this, which first appeared as a series of addresses at the liturgical Three Hours on Good Friday at St. Margaret's Westminster in the 1950s.[50] On the other hand, we deprive ourselves of spiritual treasure if in the interests of historical understanding we jettison the interpretations of the past. This may be an arrogant assumption that wisdom begins with us rather than that we are the heirs of the ages. It may fail to recognize that we are as much tied to the categories and intellectual fashions of our age as our predecessors were to theirs. It results in spiritual impoverishment. Something of this lies behind Andrew Louth's *Discerning the Mystery.*[51] *Inter alia,* he advocates a return to allegory, which is at odds with the application of the prevailing school of scientific method in theology and is in the tradition of Eastern Orthodoxy. By an interesting and unexpected conscription of Hort, the study unites theology and spirituality with liturgy at the center.

This was the aim of one whom we may regard as the doyen of Anglican spirituality in the last quarter century, representative of the tradition adapted to the needs of our time. Arthur Michael Ramsey (1904–1988) was Archbishop of Canterbury from 1961 to 1974. He always was inclined to distrust liberalism and never found Charles Raven, for instance, a congenial theologian. His Congregationalist background may have made him all the more appreciative of liturgical spirituality, but his Catholic churchmanship took the Reformation seriously. "Catholicism always stands before the Church door at Wittenberg to read the truth by which she is created and by which also she is judged. 'The true treasure of the Church is the Holy Gospel of the glory and the grace of God.'"[52] He was an apostle of unity with a love from his earliest priesthood of Eastern Orthodoxy with its sense in liturgy and prayer of the "interpenetration of earth and heaven."

> The motif always in Michael's mind was glory. No modern ever had a more vivid sense of what glory is. His favourite private feast of the year was 6 August, the Transfiguration, the feast of the glory of the Saviour. Among all the books which he wrote, the book which he was afterwards most glad to have written was the book about the Transfiguration.[53]

Yet, after a disapproving first response to John Robinson's *Honest to God,* Ramsey came to take seriously the insistence on this-worldly holiness. In his Scott Holland Lectures, *Sacred and Secular* (1967), he outlines the paradox that "two worlds are ours," and he seeks its resolution in contemplative prayer, which should not be reserved only for advanced souls but should be open to every man, woman, and child "who is ready to try to be obedient and humble and to want God very much."[54] In his last book, *Be Still and Know* (1981), which Owen Chadwick believes "will last the longest and which is very likely to become a permanent classic," he again seeks to unite Catholics and Protestants, for he sees in the passivity of contemplative prayer a judgment upon salvation by works and a manifestation of "faith alone" and "grace alone." He says also:

> The prayer with beautiful buildings and lovely music must be a prayer also which speaks from places where men and women work, or lack work, and

are sad and hungry, suffer and die. To be near to the love of God is to be near, as Jesus showed, to the darkness of the world. That is "the place of prayer."[55]

What the future mutations of Anglican spirituality will be it is not for this essay to foretell. The *Spiritual Exercises* of Ignatius of Loyola are having renewed and powerful effect far outside the Society of Jesus and, it is said, in the "inner cities." The spiritualities of other faiths are in dialogue if not contention. Feminist theology is challenging the whole tradition, some-times painfully, and—it might seem—to its destruction. But if Anglican spirituality is still to have life it must set those words as a seal upon its heart. Then it may succeed where Tom Mozley, the Tractarian, bemoaned its failure and make saints among the poor.[56]

Notes

1. There are interesting discussions of the term in *The Study of Anglicanism*, ed. Stephen Sykes and John Booty, 424–29 (J. Robert Wright) and pp. 406f. (Paul Avis). Wright says: "If the term is to be used descriptively and not narrowly or prescriptively, it must fully go back conceptually/doctrinally to the New Testament and historically/ geographically to the martyrdom of St. Alban in the patristic period of Anglican Church history" (p. 428). He refers to S. W. Sykes, *The Integrity of Anglicanism* (London: Mowbray, 1978), but the editors of the symposium take the view of this essay that "the de facto distinctiveness of Anglicanism begins in the sixteenth century."

2. *George Herbert*, selected by W. H. Auden, *Poet to Poet* (New York: Penguin Books, 1979).

3. E. C. Hoskyns, *Cambridge Sermons* (London: SPCK, 1970) 40.

4. James Boswell, *Life of Johnson*, 2:204.

5. Stephen Neill maintained that this "transformed what had been the most corporate form of eucharistic worship in Christendom into the most individualistic" (David Martin and Peter Mullen, eds., *No Alternative* [Blackwell, 1981] 2). His point is prob-ably valid, though somewhat exaggerated.

6. P. G. Stanwood, ed., with the assistance of Daniel O'Connor, John Cosin, *A Collec-tion of Private Devotions*, XXIII. See also "The Anglicanism of John Cosin" with a note on "The Text of Cosin's Devotions," in G. J. Cuming, *The Godly Order* (London: Alcuin Club/SPCK, 1983) 123ff.

7. There is an edition of the *Durham Book* by G. J. Cuming (Oxford: Oxford Univer-sity Press, 1961).

8. J. H. Newman, *Parochial Sermons 1834–1842*, 1:179.

9. Cf. Patrick Collinson, *The Religion of Protestants* (Oxford: Oxford University Press, 1982) 39–91.

10. See Gordon S. Wakefield, *Puritan Devotion* (London: Epworth, 1957) *passim;* C. J. Stranks, *Anglican Devotion*, 35–63.

11. S. T. Coleridge, *Notes on English Divines*, ed. Derwent Coleridge (London: E. Moxon, 1853) 2:38. See C. Fitzsimmons Allison, "The Pastoral Cruelty of Jeremy

Taylor's Theology," *The Modern Churchman* 15/2 (January 1972); also Margaret R. Miles, *The Image and Practice of Holiness* (London: SPCK, 1988) 170f.

12. Jeremy Taylor, *Holy Living*, section X, "An Act of Desire"; one of the prayers appended to the section "Of Preparation to the Holy Sacrament of the Lord's Supper."

13. Ibid.

14. Margaret R. Miles, *Image and Practice of Holiness*, 138.

15. Izaak Walton, *Life of John Donne*, prefixed to *John Donne's Sermons* (London, 1640) 60.

16. See Owen Chadwick, "Classical Anglicanism and Lancelot Andrewes" (The Second Southwell Lecture 1986); also F. E. Brightman, *The Preces Privatae of Lancelot Andrewes;* and R. W. Church, *Pascal and Other Sermons* (London: Macmillan, 1896) 54ff.

17. Andrew Louth, "Augustine and George Herbert" (Rome: Institutum Patristicum Augustianum Roma, 1987). For the Calvinist thesis, see A. J. Festugière, *George Herbert, poète, saint anglican* (Paris, 1971); and Joseph Summers, *George Herbert: His Religion and Art* (referred to by David Daiches, *God and the Poets* [Oxford: Oxford University Press, 1984] 76, 215).

18. George Herbert, "Aaron," in *The Works of George Herbert*, ed. F. E. Hutchison (Oxford: Clarendon Press, 1945) 174.

19. George Herbert, "Prayer," in *Works*, ed. Hutchison, 51.

20. Henry Vaughan, "The World," in *The Works of Henry Vaughan*, ed. L. C. Martin (Oxford: Clarendon, 1957).

21. Goeffrey Rowell, in *The Westminster Dictionary of Christian Spirituality*, ed. Gordon S. Wakefield (1983), published in the United Kingdom as *A Dictionary of Christian Spirituality* (London: SCM).

22. Cf. A. M. Allchin, *Participation in God: A Forgotten Strand in Anglican Tradition* (London: Darton, Longman & Todd, 1988). For the subject in general, see the article by Rowan Williams in *The Westminster Dictionary of Christian Spirituality*, ed. Gordon S. Wakefield. A vehement attack on the notion is in the essay by Benjamin Drewery in *Christian Spirituality*, ed. Peter Brooks (London: SCM, 1975).

23. For the Platonists, see C. A. Patrides, ed., *The Cambridge Platonists*. See also my article in *The Westminster Dictionary of Christian Spirituality.*

24. Charles E. Raven, *Natural Religion and Christian Theology* (The Gifford Lectures, 1951: First Series: Science and Religion) 99ff.

25. The Platonists might have agreed with O. C. Quick that there are two unique sacraments, the created universe and the person of Christ (see *The Christian Sacraments* [London: Nisbet, 1927] 84, 85).

26. R. Cudworth, *The Ditression concerning the Plastick Life of Natur, or an Artificial, Orderly and Methodical Natur for the True Intellectual System of the Universe* (1678) Sect. xxxvii, reproduced from *The Cambridge Platonists*, ed. Patrides, 293.

27. For illustrations from the Cambridge Platonists, see E. Gordon Rupp, "A Devotion of Rapture," in *Reformation, Conformity and Dissent*, ed. R. Buick Knox (London: Epworth, 1976).

28. John Smith, *The Excellence and Nobleness of True Religion*, in *The Cambridge Platonists*, ed. Patrides, 199.

29. See Gareth Bennett, *To the Church of England* (Worthing: Churchman, 1988) 75ff.,

for a sensitive study of Tillotson, which deals faithfully with his "liberality" and its inadequacies; see also E. Gordon Rupp, *Religion in England 1688–1791.*

30. R. W. Church, "Bishop Butler," in *Pascal and Other Sermons,* 28.

31. Ibid., 40, 41.

32. Quoted by J. B. Lightfoot, *Leaders of the Northern Church* (London: Macmillan, 1907) 161.

33. Cf. Johnson's conversation with Mrs. Adams at Merton College Oxford not long before his death: "Madam, I do not forget the merits of my Redeemer; but my Redeemer has said that he will set some on his right hand and some on his left" (Boswell's *Life;* also reproduced in *Johnson on Johnson,* ed. John Wain [London: Dent, 1976]).

34. See A. M. Allchin, *Participation in God,* 24ff.

35. The phrase is that of Dora Greenwell, an Anglican devotional writer whom Henry Bett's *Dora Greenwell* (London: Epworth, 1950) has not succeeded in popularizing.

36. This paragraph incorporates some sentences from my *Kindly Light* (London: Epworth, 1984) 28. The book goes on to give some illustration of how this worked out in Tractarian practice. For "reserve" and "hiddenness," see Tracts 87 and 88 by Isaac Williams, his poem "The Cathedral," Newman's sermons, e.g., *Parochial and Plain Sermons,* 6:113; and Pusey, *Sermons during the Season from Advent to Whitsuntide,* 299–305.

37. Newman, *Parochial and Plain Sermons,* 1:188. It is interesting to compare and contrast this sermon on Peter's protestation, Mark 14:31, with Richard Hooker's on pride, which concludes with the statement that Peter's tears were worth all the protestations of his ghostly strength.

38. Owen Chadwick, *The Mind of the Oxford Movement,* 48, 49.

39. E. A. Knox, *Reminiscences of an Octogenarian 1847–1934* (London: Hutchingson, 1935) 60.

40. R. W. Church, *Pascal and Other Sermons,* 20, 18.

41. J. B. Lightfoot, *Leaders of the Northern Church,* 10.

42. See Susan J. Smalley, "Evelyn Underhill and the Mystical Tradition," in *Scripture, Tradition, and Reason,* ed. Benjamin Drewery and Richard Bauckham (Edinburgh: T. & T. Clark, 1988).

43. W. R. Inge, *Speculum Animae* (London: Longmans, 1911) 6.

44. Charles E. Raven, *Natural Religion and Christian Theology:* II, *Experience and Interpretation,* 208.

45. John Burnaby, *Amor Dei,* 302.

46. John Burnaby, "Christian Prayer," in *Soundings,* ed. A. R. Vidler (Cambridge: Cambridge University Press, 1962) 232–37.

47. Reginald H. Fuller, "Scripture, Tradition and Priesthood" Appendix 2, "The Eucharistic Prayer in Anglicanism," in *Scripture, Tradition, and Reason,* ed. Drewery and Bauckham, 113f.

48. V. A. Demant, *A Two-Way Religion* (London: Mowbray, 1957).

49. John A. Harrod, "God and Spirituality: On Taking Leave of Don Cupitt," in *Freedom and Grace,* ed. Ivor H. Jones and Kenneth B. Wilson (London: Epworth, 1988) 48ff.

50. Published in *Good Friday at St. Margaret's,* ed. Charles Smyth (London:

Mowbray, 1957). A more academic but vivid and vigorous treatment is in *Explorations in Theology 2* (London: SCM, 1978) Part I.

51. Oxford: Oxford University Press, 1983.

52. A. M. Ramsey, *The Gospel and the Catholic Church* (London: Longmans, 1936) 180.

53. Owen Chadwick, "Michael Ramsey and the Beatific Vision," address given at the Memorial Service in Westminster Abbey 27 June 1988; see also Gordon S. Wakefield, "Michael Ramsey: A Theological Appraisal," *Theology* (November 1988).

54. Ramsey, *Sacred and Secular*, 45.

55. Ramsey, *Be Still and Know*, 13–14.

56. For Anglican feminist spirituality, see, e.g., Ursula King, *Women and Spirituality* (London: Macmillan, 1989); and Bridget Rees, "Wandering in the Wilderness: A Feminist Reflects on Education in Spirituality," in *Can Spirituality be Taught? Exploratory Essays*, ed. Jill Robson and David Lonsdale (London: Way, 1988) 51–60. Charles Elliott's *Praying the Kingdom* (London: Darton, Longman & Todd, 1985) is an Anglican political theologian's account of how the Ignatian method may be used in prayer in our world.

Bibliography

Sources

Andrewes, Lancelot. *The Preces Privatae of Lancelot Andrewes.* Translated by R. E. Brightman. London: Methuen, 1903.

Brightman, F. E. *The English Rite.* 2 vols. London: 1915, 1921.

Chadwick, Owen, ed. *The Mind of the Oxford Movement.* London: A. & C. Black, 1960.

Cosin, John. *A Collection of Private Devotions.* Edited by P. G. Stanwood with the assistance of Daniel O'Connor. Oxford: Oxford University Press, 1967.

Hort, F. J. A. *The Way, the Truth, the Life.* London: Macmillan, 1893.

Jay, Elisabeth, ed. *The Evangelical and Oxford Movements.* Cambridge English Prose Texts. Cambridge: Cambridge University Press, 1983.

Law, William. *A Serious Call to a Devout and Holy Life* and *The Spirit of Love.* Edited by P. G. Stanwood. Classics of Western Spirituality. New York: Paulist; London: SPCK, 1979.

More, P. E., and F. L. Cross. *Anglicanism.* London: SPCK; Milwaukee: Morehouse, 1935.

Newman, John Henry. *Parochial and Plain Sermons.* 8 vols. London: Rivingtons, 1875.

Patrides, C. A., ed. *The Cambridge Platonists.* Cambridge, MA: Harvard University Press, 1970.

Pusey, E. B. *Parochial Sermons.* London: Walter Smith, 1869.

———. *Parochial and Cathedral Sermons.* London: Walter Smith, 1883.

Ramsey, A. M. *Sacred and Secular.* London: Longmans, 1965.

———. *Be Still and Know.* London: Collins, Fontana, 1981.

Robinson, J. A. T. *Honest to God.* London: SCM, 1963.

———. *Exploration into God.* London: SCM, 1967.

Temple, William. *Readings in St. John's Gospel.* London: Macmillan, 1945.

Studies

Armstrong, C. J. R. *Evelyn Underhill (1875–1941).* London: Mowbrays; Grand Rapids: Eerdmans, 1975.

Butler, Perry, ed. *Pusey Rediscovered.* London: SPCK, 1983.

Cuming, G. J. *A History of Anglican Liturgy.* London: Macmillan, 1982.

Dillistone, F. W. *Charles Raven.* London: Hodder & Stoughton, 1975.

Fox, Adam. *Dean Inge.* London: John Murray, 1960.

Hennell, Michael. *Sons of the Prophets: Evangelical Leaders of the Victorian Church.* London: SPCK, 1979.

Lossky, Nicholas. *Lancelot Andrewes, le Prédicateur (1555–1626).* Aux Sources de la théologie mystique de l'Eglise d'Angleterre. Paris: Cerf, 1986.

Martin, Brian W. *John Keble, Priest, Professor, Poet.* London: Croom Helm, 1976.

Purcell, William. *Anglican Spirituality: A Continuing Tradition.* London: Mowbrays, 1988.

Rowell, Geoffrey. *The Vision Glorious.* Oxford: Oxford University Press, 1983.

———, ed. *Tradition Renewed.* London: Darton, Longman & Todd, 1986.

Rupp, Ernest Gordon. *Religion in England 1688–1791.* Oxford: Oxford University Press, 1986.

Smith, B. A. *Dean Church: The Anglican Response to Newman.* Oxford: Oxford University Press, 1958.

Smith, Martin, S.S.J.E., ed. *Benson of Cowley.* Oxford: Oxford University Press, 1980.

Stranks, C. J. *Anglican Devotion: Studies in the Spiritual Life of the Church of England between the Reformation and the Oxford Movement.* London: SCM, 1961.

Thornton, Martin. *English Spirituality.* London: SPCK, 1963.

The complete works of the Caroline divines were published in the nineteenth century by the Library of Anglo-Catholic Theology.

Reference should also be made to the following:

Jones, Cheslyn, Geoffrey Wainwright, and Edward Yarnold. *The Study of Spirituality.* London: SPCK, 1986.

Sykes, Stephen, and John Booty, eds. *The Study of Anglicanism.* London: SPCK; Philadelphia: Fortress, 1988.

Wakefield, Gordon S., ed. *The Westminster Dictionary of Christian Spirituality,* which originated as *A Dictionary of Christian Spirituality.* London: SCM, 1983.

10

Puritan Spirituality: The Search for a Rightly Reformed Church

I. *The Anatomy of Puritan Piety: English Puritan Devotional Literature, 1600–1640*

RICHARD C. LOVELACE

What infinite Cause hath this Age to acknowledge the unspeakable Mercy of God, in affording us such Plenty of spiritual Tractates, full of divine, necessary and Conscience-searching Truths; yea, precious Soul-comforting, & Soul-improving Truths? such whereby Head, Heart, and Soul-cheating Errors are discovered and prevented, such as soundly Difference true Grace from all seemings and paintings: No Time, no Nation exceeds us herein. . . . (Thomas Shepherd, *Sincere Convert*, 11)

RITING IN 1640, Thomas Shepherd could look back with satisfaction on an amazing number and variety of devotional writings, produced since the reign of Elizabeth by followers of the religious party that was about to accede to power. Even in 1609, Thomas Cooper could already be thankful for the existence of "many excellent treatizes concerning the power of godliness," by such men as Richard Greenham, William Perkins, Richard Rogers, John Downame, and Arthur Dent (Thomas Cooper, *Christian's Daily Sacrifice*, A-5). During the tenures of James and Charles up to the time of the Revolution, these men and their descendants created a literature of piety of unparalleled depth and abundance, in a variety of forms: manuals of godliness, manuals of comfort, spiritual treasuries, combat manuals, martyrologies, allegories, tracts, and prayer manuals. But the numerous types within this uniquely rich devotional literature duplicate and overlap one another; they share a common spirit and a common core of doctrine, and taken together they define a conception of piety that is discernibly different both from its antecedents and from neighboring forms of contemporary piety.

This paper estimates the degree of this difference by examining the structure of Puritan experience as it is displayed in a representative sample of the literature and locates it within the stream of the history of Christian devotion. The first section investigates some clues regarding the heredity of Puritan piety and also certain environmental forces which contributed to its formation. The second is an attempt to abstract the anatomy of Puritan devotion from its exemplars and to test the conclusions of the first section against the real outline of Puritan piety as it is reconstructed from the sources. The concluding remarks discuss the future influence of this phase of Puritanism and assess its normative value for Christian experience. There have been other attempts at anatomizing Puritan devotion, some of them very fine.[1] Yet no work has appeared which adequately grasps Puritan piety both in its distinctiveness and in its relation to medieval piety and to the developing stream of Christian experience after the seventeenth century.

The Origins of Puritan Piety

The Puritan Critique of the Roman Catholic Tradition

One possible exception to the statement just made is the excellent introductory survey by Helen C. White, *English Devotional Literature (Prose), 1600–1640*, published in 1931. White seeks to establish a close connection between English devotional literature of this period and medieval and Catholic sources. She holds that a hunger for mystical literature survived the period of Protestant controversialism in early sixteenth-century England and that, unsatisfied by the thorny Protestant doctrinal literature that had come in from the Continent, it turned for satisfaction to sources in the medieval past, such as Thomas à Kempis, to the current profuse literature of Catholic mysticism, and to smuggled recusant works.[2]

Helen White's thesis is certainly true for much of the literature she examines, especially for those two great figures, Andrewes and Donne. However, her conclusions have somewhat less bearing on our study, since the object of her interest is the whole spectrum of English devotional literature—produced or put forward by at least four distinct factions: Catholic recusants, half-converted Catholics in Anglican dress, conforming Puritans, and separatists, whereas our interest is centered on just a part of the spectrum. Furthermore, White is most sympathetic to the Catholicizing end of the band; she examines some definitely Puritan works but feels a continual urge to turn aside from "these anxious books" with their "forbiddingly theological approach" to the luminous mysteries of mystical religion, both in its Catholic and pre-Christian forms.[3] One would be inclined to expect her to misread a little the paternity of Puritan devotion.

But there are a number of more concrete indications that White's generalizations are not so largely true for the literature produced by the Puritan wing in seventeenth-century England. First, there is the selectivity with which even sixteenth-century Anglican editors handle republished Catholic material. White herself cites three instances of this: Thomas Rogers's gingerly handling of even such a major figure as Augustine; William Crashaw's tentative endorsement of some writings of Bernard; and Bunny's extensive censorship of works by the Jesuit Gasper Loarte and by Edmond Parsons.[4] This gives some evidence of an alert Protestant doctrinal sensitivity both on the part of editors and audience. Second, there are records of marginal citations of authors given as authorities in the more learned Puritan devotional treatises. These lean heavily on patristic sources: Augustine is by far the most cited, followed fairly closely by Chrysostom, Ambrose, the Cappadocians, and Gregory the Great. A large scattering of antique pagan authors is among those cited, chief among them Seneca; but among the schoolmen Bernard is the only one widely appealed to, except for a few stray references to Aquinas.[5] Robert Bolton makes a few citations of scholastic authors, but refers to them as "a rotten generation of mongrel divines" (*Directions*, 150). Of mystical writers (save for Bernard and Augustine), there is no mention. White alludes to the predominance of patristic authors as part of a search to bolster up a Protestant church with Catholic authority,[6] but it is just as likely that the Puritans cited the early fathers because it was with these they felt the deepest spiritual sympathy, next to the Reformers and the apostles.

Third, there are comments within the sources themselves which indicate that among Puritans Catholic piety was regarded as a kind of rust to be scrubbed off the church rather than as furniture for its devotional life. A rather gentle and moderate author of mediating tendencies, Daniel Featley, writes directly concerning piety:

> Now the oyle which feedeth this sacred flame (next to the inspired holy Scriptures) floweth most abundantly in Treatises of Devotion. In which kinde of writings, the Romanists for the most part exceed in bulke, but our Divines in weight. . . . It is Saint Ierom's observation upon the legall sacrifices, that God never appointed hony to bee offered unto him. And the morall truth vailed under that shadow, was that in our spiritual oblations nothing pleaseth God that is onely sweete, and hath not some smacke in it of biting truth. (*Ancilla Pietatis*, To the Reader)

Featley's remarks hint at some of the differences which the Puritans felt separated their devotional writing from that of Rome. A more outspoken example is from the writings of the Puritan controversialist, Henry Burton, who is concerned about an influx of Catholic devotional literature suddenly appearing in the late 1620s and writes particularly against one manual based on the seven canonical hours, which has lately appeared masquerading as legitimate Anglican reading matter:

> The Authour descends to defend his Septiformious Devotion to be MUCH AFTER THE MANNER PUBLISHED BY AUTHORITIE OF QUEENE ELIZABETH, 1560. MUCH AFTER THE MANNER, is indeed a prettie qualification of the matter.... But for your MUCH, Distingue tempors; Distinguish the times.... That Horarie the Authour speakes of, was set out neere the first yeere of her Raigne, when as Poperie was not buried, nor the Gospell out of her Cradle. Many things might be winked at in the infancy of the church, which are not tolerable in her riper age (*Tryall*, C-3-D)

This last comment, incidentally, offers an interesting explanation of the presence of a good deal of Helen White's evidence. Henry Burton goes on to develop some factors which he feels distinguish Catholic from Puritan piety:

> There is as well a Devotion blind and superstitious, breathed from the Bottomlesse-pit by him, who can transforme himself into an Angel of Light: as a Devotion illuminate, and truly religious, like Elias his Sacrifice, inspired and inflamed by Fire from Heaven. Nor doth the Old Serpent either so usually or effectually infuse his poysonous enchantments into mens minds, as when he propineth them in the Golden Cup of demure Devotion.... What rabbles and swarmes of vowed disciples (to omit the Father-Founders of their severall Monasticke Orders) did these two, St Francis, and St Dominicke draw after them, and all by the strong incantations of their deepe Devotion.... (*Tryall*, C-1)

Objecting to the antidoctrinal tendencies of the author of the offending tract, who protests "the continuall and curious disquisition of many unnecessary questions among us . . . ," Burton comments:

> This man would willingly fold his hands, and wrap up all his Devotion.... And how should the lampe of true Devotion flame forth and burne in holy fervency of effectuall prayer, if it be not fedde with the oyle of saving knowledge, being pressed forth more copiously by the ventilation of errours, and dissipation of mysts, which would dampe and extinguish all.... (*Tryall*, E-4)

The strong doctrinal sensitivity in this is reminiscent of the statement of Thomas Shepherd quoted at the beginning of this paper, and it summarizes the flavor of most of the sources: there is something about them which is quite immiscible with Catholic piety in its native state. To be sure, there is a strong medieval hue to many of the works published in this period by Anglican authors near the right side of the spectrum. A collection like Richard Brathwait's *Spiritual Spicerie,* published near the end of our period, contains selections from such authors as Augustine, Luis de Granada, Aquinas, an anonymous Carthusian monk, and some very un-Puritan musings on the Eucharist by Henry Suso; and it embraces also such characteristic notions as the equation of the physical body with the biblical *flesh* and progress toward union with God through asceticism. That this is quite alien to Puritan tastes becomes evident, however, when Brathwait feels compelled to interject *A Reply to a Rigid Precisian, Objecting, that Flowers from Romish Authors Extracted, Became Lesse Wholesome and Divinely Redolent* (*Spiritual Spicerie* 226). This is not to say that the Puritan authors were as far removed from the Middle Ages as they felt themselves to be, of course; we cannot swallow whole the Reformation's sense of its radical novelty. Even such an author as Lewis Bayly, writer of the immensely popular *Practice of Piety,* mixed Thomistic passages with his Reformed theology, and naively clung to a simple body/mind dichotomy as the basis for the biblical separation between flesh and spirit. Yet it is hard to imagine a real Puritan taking kindly to Luis de Granada when the latter lists as a sign of spiritual progress a "quick and fervent desire to afflict and maltreat the body with fastings, hair-shirts, vigils, disciplines, and other bodily severities."[7] And compare Brathwait's *Spicerie* with Rogers's *Garden of Spiritual Flowers;* the latter begins with a rock foundation of Reformed theology, garnished with such comments as the following:

> Our sinfulnesse is such, as it continually defileth all our actions, our thoughts, words and deeds; and the punishment (which is Gods curse) is such as lieth upon us alwaies, and in all places; and . . . we are nothing but a lump of sinne, and under the wrath of God continually. (*Garden,* 2)

The rest of Rogers's *Garden* has similar granitic borders among its flowers, including a very plain and unaromatic statement on the decrees of God.

The Origin of Puritan Devotional Literature

A type of devotional literature which undoubtedly had some role in the heredity of Puritan devotion is the English Primer, which Helen White treats at length in a later book.[8] The name was originally bestowed in the fourteenth century by the laity to the Latin *Book of the Hours of the Blessed Virgin Mary,* a monastic compilation for devotional use both within and without the cloister. Structured on the basis of the canonical hours, the original Primers contained a mixture of edifying treatises, prayers, graces, confessions, the Paternoster, the Decalogue, the creed, litanies, dirges, and prayers specifically to the Virgin.[9] White traces the evolution of the Primers under the reigns of Henry VIII and Edward VI and under the impact of Protestant teaching, as the establishment sought to use them as an instrument of religious change among the laity; she shrewdly observes that a change in tone can be seen gradually permeating the Primers, based on a shift of emphasis away from the human life of Christ (closely connected with the person of his mother) to a focus on his mediatorial, redemptive function.[10] Further winnowed, this kind of devotional collection continues to be a vehicle of semi-Puritan devotional expression throughout our period.

But more germane to the origin of that type of devotion which is specifically Puritan is the foundational work in theology done in the late sixteenth and early seventeenth centuries by William Perkins and his pupil, William Ames. The theology of both was strongly experimental in character, the former stressing the essential connection between godliness and correct theology, defining theology as the science of living well rather than as a merely intellectual discipline; and the latter constructing his whole system around the concept of regeneration. Just why the peculiarly English expression of Reformed theology should develop along this practical bent is an interesting question which has much to do with our subject. The reason given by a number of older authorities alludes to a supposed pragmatic or experimental tendency in the English character, stressing the practical. But the Puritan ideal of practical godliness has taken root in many different climates since the seventeenth century, often starting spontaneously from the seeds of contact with the New Testament, so that this solution may be too facile. More likely this practical emphasis derives from the nearly universal influence, among Protestants, of the method and philosophy of Petrus Ramus, whose strong reaction against scholasticism was a kind of proto-existentialism, at least in that it anticipated the similar reaction of Kierkegaard against Hegel. The great majority of the works treated in this paper contain, at one point or another, the diagrams typical of Ramist logic.[11]

Perhaps the main literary source of the body of strictly Puritan devotional literature during our period is, not surprisingly, the Puritan sermon, built on the theology of Perkins and Ames. The most distinctive Puritan devotional works are not collections, like their Anglican counterparts, but connected treatises developed either from a text or a main topic and often frankly designated as elaborations of sermonic material. The characteristic expression of the Puritan religious spirit was, after all, not the manual for private meditation, but the sermon. This explanation of the main origin of Puritan devotional literature offers also an easy explanation of the rapid proliferation of Puritan works during our peiod. But what forces made the sermonizing of this period generate these books, and why was there such an evident desire to shape this material into a different literary form and to spread it beyond the individual congregation?

A number of environmental factors contributed to the changing of the focus of Puritan interest from matters of controversy, in the fields of doctrine, government, and religious externals, to the devotional implications of the faith and also to the spread of literature expressing this concern. In the first place, the contained ecclesiastical situation of the Puritans may have had something to do with both of these matters. Helen White puts forth the thesis that while continental Calvinism was occupied with the exterior task of establishing a Christian society, English Calvinism of necessity turned to the inner life, to self-conquest.[12] She notes also that dissatisfaction with the Book of Common Prayer may have led to the creation and dissemination of acceptable Puritan substitutes.[13] Then again, there was just enough opposition given to the Puritan movement throughout this period to make it strong and vigorous in counterattack, but not to crush it; and the main weapon for reprisals was the press, as Haller points out.[14] This last, of course, does not explain by itself why in so much of the literature of the period piety is preferred to controversy.

A partial answer to this last question appears when we realize that the Puritans were attacking not only ecclesiastical enemies and doctrinal errors; they were contending with a society, and with a church, which seemed to be ebbing steadily, spiritually and morally. The economic prosperity which Elizabeth had brought in, combined with the weaning away from religion wrought by the tumultuous ecclesiastical situation of the last century and by the late blooming of Renaissance humanism in England, had combined to dissolve the appearance of Christian culture which medieval England had maintained. Writing late in our period, John Andrewes comments that never has a nation had so much truth given to it as England has in his lifetime, and yet it is utterly derelict in spite of this. Another author of about the same period comments:

There onely remaineth in the world a handful of people which serve Jesus Christ in truth and verity, and they can scarce receive breath in this aire which is so contrary to them being here as fishes without water, as the remainder of great Massacres, as pieces of boards scattered after the breaking of a great vessell: And yet neverthelesse amongst those few . . . Corruption doth encrease, as a cancre or ulcer. Quarrels, vanity, superfluity in apparell, avarice, ambition, sumptuousness. . . . For God is ill served in privat families, their almes are colde; they pray seldome; and read never: In briefe a contagion of vices, by conversing with our adversaries, doth infect us, which is the first step to superstition.... If therefore where God is most purely knowne, he be there ill served: How much more amongst the rest of the world?[15]

The Puritan principle that knowledge is in order to godliness—that, as John Dod puts it, "An ignorant heart is alway a sinnfull heart: and a man without knowledge, is a man without grace ..."—would naturally lead to the dissemination of literature for the turning of this tide of national apostasy. The realization that, if no Protestant devotional works were forthcoming, another class of the ignorant and wayward would be attracted by the vast literature of Roman Catholic piety was probably another incentive in the early production of Puritan works in this category.[16]

But of all these explanations perhaps the most simple and plausible is that Puritan devotional concern represents the natural development of a further stage in the Reformation, which had begun by restructuring doctrine and the exterior order of the church, and which was now turning to the development of its own inner life, heeding the clear biblical teaching that all was worthless without this last step. Conditions were particularly favorable in England for this development for the reasons listed above; but it was a movement implicit in the Reformation from the first, because it was implicit in the Scriptures, which formed the motivating principle of the Reformation. There is plentiful evidence in the sources of a feeling among Puritan divines—at least among the conformists, who make up the main body of our authors—that the foundation of the doctrines of grace were sufficiently laid down, and that it had become time to build upon them an edifice of solid piety. As one expressed it:

> I could finde no one part of Divinity more profitable, in these times, for me to spend my strength upon, then that which consisteth more in experience and practice, then in theory and speculation; and more principally tendeth to the sanctification of the heart, then the informing of the judgement and the increasing of knowledge; and to the stirring up of all to the practice of that they know in the duties of a godly life. . . . These discourses of practical Divinity tending to stirre up devotion, and to excite men to the duties of a godly life, are most fit and necessary for these times. First, because the world is already full of such bookes as doe fully handle the Doctrine of Divinity in all the points and parts of it, and also of learned controversies wherein the truth is sufficiently defended, and all errours which does oppose it, refuted and repelled. Secondly, because our long peace and prosperity have much cooled and quenched the fervour of our zeale and devotion, and have caused us (contenting our selves with some cold formalities, and slight profession) to neglect the sincere practice of those substantiall duties which are required to a godly and Christian life. . . . (John Downame, *Guide,* A-2)

The genesis of pietism is here; note, however, that it is a pietism which builds on doctrine and on the authority of Scripture rather than casting these aside. As the writer last quoted continues, we see in him the dawning recognition that bare controversy may not be the most effective means of contending for the faith, that there may be other superior weapons, not carnal but spiritual:

> Those who allow a place for (truth) onely in their heads, and will afford it no roome in their hearts, by loving, imbracing and practizing it, it is just with God to send them strong delusion. . . . How vaine therefore is their practice who spend all their strength in polemicall disputes, to evince errour, and finde out the truth, if when they have found it out, they will not walke in this light, nor let it be the guide of their lives. . . . (*Guide*, 1)

There is here no repudiation of what the Reformation has achieved polemically, but simply a caveat to build on the foundations which have been laid.

If this is indeed the case, if Puritan devotion is really an attempt at the reconstruction of Puritan piety on a Reformed basis, we would expect the completed edifice represented in the innumerable devotional writings of the period to display at every point the lineaments of its inner doctrinal structure; we would expect a type of piety in many respects differing from that common in the Middle Ages. We must now turn to examine the anatomy of Puritan piety, in order to test this hypothesis.

The Anatomy of Puritan Piety

The Marks of True Conversion

One very distinctive feature of all the Puritan manuals of devotion is that, whatever their type, they never discuss the living of the Christian life without taking up first the matter of the way of entrance into that life. There is always a full statement, usually at the beginning, of the necessity of regeneration and the path of life through faith in the doctrines of grace. Time after time the familiar ground is covered: creation, the fall, total depravity, redemption, faith, with particular emphasis on the mediatorship of Christ. Unlike Roman manuals, the Puritan devotional work assumes the presence within the church of the radically unconverted, who need not merely some guides and incentives for the pathway to eternal life, but who need to be placed upon that path for the first time. In the Roman faith, regeneration and the office of the Mediator have been at least partially assimilated to baptism and the other sacramental functions of the church. But it is also true that for the Puritan, as Gordon Wakefield says, "Union with Christ is not the end but the beginning of the Christian Life"; whereas for the Catholic, the pattern of meditation and prayer has become a ladder which must be climbed in order to reach Christ, and which has hence to some degree displaced him as mediator.[17]

As a consequence of this major difference in approach to the pattern of devotion, Puritan devotional works may really be said to flaunt their doctrinal Protestantism.[18] The problem that confronts the Puritans as they look out on their decaying society and their lukewarm church is not simply to dislodge the faithful from the slough of mortal or venial sin, but radically to awaken those who are professing but not actual Christians, who are caught in the trap of carnal security. A good deal of the literature is devoted to exposing states of mind which look like true faith but which actually are not. William Attersall discourses in traditional Continental form on the four kinds of faith (miraculous, historical, temporary, and justifying) (*Physicke Against Famine*, 116), and Richard Rogers gives a long list of acts and qualities that are not necessarily distinguishing signs of grace: knowledge of the gospel, confession of faith, hearing the Word, hearing it with joy, knowing and bewailing one's sins, striving against sin, sorrow for sin, outstanding service within the visible church, an outwardly good life, fluency in public prayer, a good conscience, and a cheerful death in the hope of resurrection (*Garden*, 300). By the time the reader has finished Rogers's "Twelve Steps Useless Without a Thirteenth," he has begun to wonder seriously what the thirteenth step is and whether or not he has really made it. It turns out to be "buying the pearl," a metaphor for the total exchanging of one's life's motives and entire dedication to gospel obedience, which is frequently used by other writers. Here the fulcrum of justification has been made to lie within the individual rather than in the objective work of the atonement; and a type of literature has been initiated that will continue a rather painful, if edifying, course through Thomas Shepherd to its culmination in the great work of Edwards on the religious affections.

Dealing with the subject of conversions which are really genuine, most of the Puritan works seem to imply a standardized progression of experience toward salvation, beginning with legal terrors and proceeding through various stages of humiliation and contrition toward a final application of the promises in behalf of one's own redemption, after having "sold all" in fully yielding one's life to God's rule. The following beautifully portrays the atmosphere of Puritan conversion:

Oh when the spirit of a man is wounded with the sting, and vexed with the smart of sinne, when being strucken with the curse of the Law, it is sicke at the heart, striving and strugling for life with hellish agonyes; How sweet then are his promises, unto our mouth? more than honey unto our taste. Looke as a weary and fainting Traveller, stifled with dust, and melted with heart, is revived with a coole streame, and gentle breath of ayre, so the soule of an humbled sinner tyred and tormented with firey temptations, is wonderfully refreshed with those sweet breathings of the blessed Spirit, and these waters of Life flowing from the Sanctuary. (Phineas Fletcher, *Joy*, 67–68)

While this type of conversion experience undoubtedly produced depth and stature in godliness in those who went through it, it might be questioned whether it was fully as normative as the English Puritans and certain of their successors in America were to make it.

Genuine conversion can be discerned in its possessors by certain signs or effects of faith. Richard Rogers lists a continuing true grief and hungering for grace as one mark, and then adds as a second the performance of works of love (*Garden*, 217–18). The Puritans were by no means as legalistic in the testing of this matter as they are sometimes made out to be; one extremely important factor in the assurance on one's salvation is always the testimony of the Holy Spirit, according to Rom 8:16. The role of Scripture in this testimony is emphasized both as applied by the Spirit and as the test of the Spirit's genuineness (Thomas Rowen, *Markes*, 84); but there is also a certain element of independence in the work of the Spirit, who is known by more subjective criteria, such as the sanctifying effect of his presence, the impulse toward prayer, a spirit of freedom from legal bondage and fear, a spirit of gentle mourning for sin, the infusion of longings to be with Christ, and boldness in coming to God (John Forbes, *How a Christian*, 63ff., 104ff.). This element of experimental subjectivism at the very foundation of the Christian life explains not only the Puritan stress on religious experience, but also perhaps some of the later emphasis on the inner light among the radical wing of the Puritans, including the Quakers.

Two other elements in the Puritan treatment of conversion deserve additional mention because of their importance in later traditions of Christian experience. One is the teaching of preparatory grace, inaugurated in the rather practical and flexible Calvinism of Perkins and Ames. The typical evangelistic appeal in Puritan devotional literature is not so much to *believe* the gospel, but to *wait* upon God to see whether or not he will save you by performing an experimental operation in your life (Nicholas Byfield, *Oracles of God*, 23C). Nearly every Puritan devotional work becomes at some point in its course a tract, and when it does it invariably assures unbelievers that all their efforts to reach God are vain and sinful, but that nevertheless they had better keep trying and that perhaps God will choose arbitrarily to lift them out of these strivings if they persist. This considerable distortion of Calvinism passes through its most vigorous English statement in Thomas Shepherd's work *The Sincere Convert* (pp. 39, 67) into the belief and practices of Edwards in America, later to cause considerable difficulty in the course of American revivalism.

The other element is the sulphurous atmosphere that generally surrounds the gospel offer when it is made, even in devotional writings. Helen White objects to the menacing and admonitory tone characteristic in Puritan works, and she is right in this; the geography and furniture of hell are minutely described by most of our authors. From the Puritans' point of view, of course, this is no sign of failure in evangelical tenderness. Thomas Shepherd flays his fellow ministers who are too squeamish to carry on a ministry of warning:

> There's no faithful Minister, no compassionate Lot, to tell them of Fire and Brimstone from Heaven for their crying Sins. . . . At the best, they shoot off a few Pot guns against gross Sins; or if they do shew Men their Misery, they lick them whole againe with some comfortable, ill-applied Sentences. . . . Or else, they say commonly, thou has sinned, comfort thy self, but Despair not, Christ hath suffered; and thus skin over the Wound, and let it fester within for want of cutting it deeper: I say therefore, because they want a faithful Watchman to cry Fire, Fire, in the sleepy Estate of Sin and Darkness wherein they lie; therefore whole Towns, Parishes, Generations of Men are burnt up, and perish miserable. (*Sincere Convert*, 101)

Examining Shepherd's hyper-refined standards for conversion, one is inclined to agree with Robert Alwyn, another minister evidently not too keen on Puritan evangelism:

> They speake the piercings of swords; their teeth are speares and arrowes, and their lips of knives, nothing but Law and that Louder than Synai, nothing but thundring. . . . Man-slayers of the Soule . . . Bloudy Preachers, that if it were possible would murther Saints themselves with the edge of their wordes, their tongues that are set on fire of hell; that speake nothing but despaire, nothing but death and destruction. . . . (*Oyle of Gladness*, 2, 3)

Alwyn is pointing to some real excesses here. Unfortunately his treatise of comfort, *The Oyle of Gladness*, is so entirely vague in its treatment of the source of Christian joy that it fails even to mention redemption in Christ as the center and prerequisite of comfort. The Puritans were thoroughly medieval in their use of warning as a spur toward godliness, but they differed from the medieval preachers in that by the use of the imagery of hell they always sought to drive their hearers not to the law and to better behavior, but to Christ.

The Life of Godliness

Helen White, who shrinks a little from the Puritans' "zest in the contemplation of things hard" in the handling of conversion, is compelled to

admire their seriousness and earnestness in the standards they set for
godliness among the regenerate.[19] Another writer comments that the
Puritans retained the medieval notion that the Christian life should
embrace all facets of life, and employed casuistry as a means of extending
the life of faith into every possible area.[20] But more distinctive than the
comprehensiveness of Puritan piety are its intensity and its inwardness.
Here is Thomas Shepherd comparing run-of-the-mill piety with his own
ideal:

> This *Form of Religion* is the easiest religion in the World. . . . What an easy
> Matter is it to come to Church? They hear (at least outwardly) very atten-
> tively an Hour and more, and then to turn to a Proof, and to turn down a
> Leaf, here's the Form. But now to spend Saturday-Night, and all the whole
> Sabbath Day-Morning, in trimming the Lamp, and in getting Oil in the Heart
> to meet the Bridegroom the next Day, and so meet him in the Word, and
> there to tremble at the Voice of God, and suck the Breast while it is open,
> and when the Word is done, to go aside privately, and there to chew upon
> the Word, there to lament with Tears all the vain Thoughts in Duties, Dead-
> ness in Hearing, this is hard, because this is the Power of Godliness, and this
> Men will not take up: So for private Praying, what an easy Matter is it for
> a Man to say over a few Prayers out of some devout Book, or to repeat some
> old Prayer got by Heart since a Child, or to have two or three short winded
> Wishes for God's Mercy in the Morning and at Night, this Form is easy: but
> now to prepare the Heart by serious Meditation of God and Man's self before
> he prays, then to come to God with a bleeding, hunger-starved Heartt, not
> only with a Desire, but with a Warrant, I must have such or such a Mercy,
> and there to wrestle with God, although it be an Hour or two together for
> a Blessing, this is too hard: Men think none do thus and therefore they will
> not. . . . (*Sincere Convert*, 96)

Christianity is to be a "universal daily service" (John Downame, *Guide*, 163);
and against those who would object to this rule as too rigorous to be possible, Thomas Cooper replies that even if it *is* impossible we need to be
humbled by striving after perfection; and that, on the other hand, it is certainly possible, at least as a goal, since it is the biblical pattern for the saints'
lives. It can stand with our ordinary callings, he insists, and it does not
exclude lawful comforts (*Daily Sacrifice*, 18, 21).

A structure for the "universal daily service" is laid down in a number of
Puritan devotional manuals, replacing the old Roman pattern of the
canonical hours. Richard Rogers's order is typical, as well as widely influential. A normal weekday for the Puritan believer is to begin with early rising,
followed by meditations on God's mercy which has enabled one to survive
the night, together with other musings on God's attributes and one's own
sin, accompanying ablutions. Later follows Morning Prayer, alone or with

one's family. Then follows employment in one's lawful calling, during which one must take care to be neither *idle* nor *careful,* to watch over the motions of one's heart and tongue, to be scrupulously discreet in the company of others, strict in solitary thought, and humble if business is prospering. Returning home, the believer is to preface the evening meal with a grace, and to follow supper with a period of nightly reading and catechizing of the whole family, including the servants. At the very end of the day there is to be evening prayer, again with the family; and then, in bed, one is to make sure that one meditates on things spiritually profitable, such as the similarity between the sheets one has just entered and the shroud one must eventually wear (*Garden,* 174–76).

This is not an intolerably strict framework, but the Puritan outline for the sabbath's religious duties is notoriously tighter. Richard Bound's *Treatise on the Sabbath,* published in 1595, had almost single-handedly converted Puritanism from the easy moderation of the Reformers to the most stringent care in the observance of Sunday.[21] Easter and other such holy days are certainly abrogated, John Dod observes, but the sabbath is in stronger force than ever (John Dod, *Ten Commandments,* 136). Rogers's *Garden* adds to the daily routine described above a session of private catechizing of the family before the morning service; mental review of the sermon on the way home and conversation about it at the dinner table, consecutive reading of the Scriptures and other devotional books, preceded and followed by applicatory prayer; and, for the rest of the time, various works of mercy within and outside the family (*Garden,* 174–76). In order to live up to this, the head of a Puritan household must have had to be very nearly a minister of the Word of God himself. He must also have had a remarkable spiritual stamina, to live up to John Dod's prescription:

> Many also are to bee reproved that will come to the Church, and for the time of the day will be content to heare the word, and to doe like duties: but as even, when darkness cometh, then come the workes of darkness; and when they be in their bed, then they be plodding and casting about for worldly affaires, and their heads be then as busie, and as full of earthly matters, as any night in the weeke else. But we are to know, that the Sabbath containeth 24 houres, as well as any other day, and therefore the night must be spent in an holy rest also. . . . Now God bids us keepe the whole seventh day: for hee would have us give as long a day to him, as hee hath given unto us. (*Ten Commandments,* 144)

Here is a rule for the laity as rigorous as some in the history of monasticism; yet its sources are obviously not so much in the medieval past as in Puritan biblicism.

Severity for the sake of severity alone is no part of the Puritan code of godliness. Where strictness arises in the Puritan ethos, it does not result from any bias against the body and the pleasures of sense—these are always declared to be good, in moderation (John Downame, *Warfare*, 429)—but instead from a very refined and precise interpretation of the Bible. It is assumed that the Scriptures, in precepts, principles, and examples, provide objective guidance for the godly walk in every area of life. Thus, Nicholas Byfield's massive *Marrow of the Oracles of God* is cast in the form of a compend of Scripture verses sorted out to fit every perplexity either in faith or in life, instantly answering any problem with divine authority. The Decalogue by itself is thought to contain enough positive and negative instruction to handle most of life's moral situations; hence the popularity of a manual such as Dod's pithy *Ten Commandments*. It is customary to refer to this type of piety as legalistic; this is as good a way as any to escape the obligation of imitating it. However, this is not legalism in the Pauline sense of the term, since it clearly distinguishes the functions of Law and Gospel:

> [The Law] must serve to this end, that seeing our owne unrighteousness and insufficiency, wee should bee humbled in our soules, before the judgement seat of Almighty God, & then flie to Christ to be our righteousness and sufficiency. And finally, to make this the rule of our life, and a lanterne to our feats; that though wee cannot attaine to the perfection, which the law requires, yet we may have that uprightness which God accepts in Jesus Christ. For if we have respect to all the Commandments, and labour faithfully to keepe them (though we cannot perfectly fulfil them) then shal wee constantly enjoy al those blessings and graces, which God hath promised to his righteous servants. . . . (John Dod, *Ten Commandments*, 375)

This does not exactly have a Lutheran sound, but it is not really un-Pauline. This is not legalism in the sense of "Pharisaism" either; our best authority on Puritan casuistry distinguishes this from Catholic moral theology in that the latter is characteristically engaged in defining the thresholds of venial and mortal sin in order to ensure the believer's remaining in a state of grace, whereas Puritanism is engaged in a comparatively disinterested search for that which is most pleasing to God, since the Puritan believer rests in the assurance of salvation by grace.[22] This may not be fair to Roman casuistry at its best, but it seems a fair appraisal of Puritanism.

Whether or not we call it legalism, there was *something* about Puritan godliness that made it unpopular in its neighborhood. The usual word for the offensive quality was *precision,* and we find nearly all of our authors defending themselves againt the embarrassment of this accusation. Most of them are unashamed of the singularity referred to by the word. Robert

12. Attributed to the Freake-Gibbs Painter, American active in Massachusetts, 1670, *The Mason Children: David, Joanna, and Abigail,* 1670.

Bolton defines a "morall Puritane" as one who manages simultaneously, to have both a peculiar moral excellence and humility; who abstains from worldly ways and conversation, and from profane sports; and who has a fine conscience for singular religious duties neglected by the rest of men (*Directions*, 2). William Attersall comments that separation from sin is the mark of the truly godly and that such separation is needed *within* the organized church, because of its obviously mixed character (*Physicke Against Famine*, 61, 106). Thomas Shepherd is, as usual, vigorously on the offensive:

> Lord, what Times are we fallen into now! The Image of God, which was once Man's Glory, is not their Shame; and Sin, which was once Men's shame, is not their Glory. The World hath raised up many false Reports of holy Courses, calling it Folly and Preciseness, Pride, Hypocrisy, and that whatsoever shews Men may make, they are as bad as the worst, if their sins were writ in their Foreheads. Hence it cometh to pass, that many a Man, who is almost persuaded to be a new Man and to turn over a new Leaf, dares not, will not, for Shame of the World, enter upon religious Courses. . . . Men are ashamed to refuse to drink Healths, and hence maintain them lawful. Our Gallants are ashamed to stay a Mile behind the Fashion; hence they will defend naked and open Breasts, and strange Apparel as Things comely. O Time-servers! that have some Conscience to desire to be honest, and to be reputed so, yet conform themselves to all Companies; if they hear others Swear, they are ashamed to Reprove them; they are ashamed to enter the Lists of holy Discourse in bad Company, and they will pretend Discretion, and we must not cast Pearls before Swine; but the Bottom of the business is, they are ashamed to be Holy. Oh fearful! Is it a Shame to be like God? O sinful Wretches! It's a Credit to be any thing but Religious, and with many Religion is a shame. (*Sincere Convert*, 20)

This gives us some idea of the exterior behavior concerning which Puritans were "precise." A number of items are condemned because, indirectly, they lead to offense against the seventh commandment. Rogers lists as "forerunners of adultery" certain fashions in clothing, "artificiall painting, costly perfumes, a rowling eye, and an unchast foot" (*Garden*, 207). John Dod condemns special dancing and stage plays for this reason, the latter because they foster the use of mixed apparel (*Ten Commandments*, 297). Bolton draws on Tertullian for support against the theater (*Directions*, 28), and Downame goes back to Cyprian for a warrant against face-painting (*Warfare*, 411). None of this is monastically unbalanced, but there is just a trace of medieval asceticism in Bolton's comment about the pleasure of marriage, that it must be "a moderate, staid, and serious pleasure, mixed with severity," and indulged within careful limits (*Directions*, 243).

Various other items are condemned because they are harmful to life (drugs, tobacco, sack) or wasteful (dicing, and other recreations which are costly, cruel, or time-consuming) (*Directions*, 198, 154). The peculiar Puritan horror of idleness produces a rather straitlaced attitude toward recreation:

> What? say they, will you have a man live without delight? doe you not allow recreation? why the Scripture doth afford a man recreation. . . . But, (vaine man) doth not the Scripture command a vocation, and the recreation as an helpe to further us in it? Now if one may aske you that stand so much for recreation, what is your occupation? what sore travaile is it that weraeth your bodie? what earnest study troubleth your braine, that you must have so much refreshing, and so much recreation? It must be some very painful labour, that needeth so much rest to make you able to performe it. It is a sore labour indeed, for it is the service of lust and the divell; two hard Masters. But this turning of recreation into a vocatio, or a vexation rather, is not allowable by Gods word. . . . (John Dod, *Ten Commandments*, 98)

The Puritans, however, were super-industrious neither to earn nor to prove salvation, but simply to endeavor to bring their vocation under the rule of God at every moment, as Helen White points out.[23]

There is in none of this that attitude toward a set of codified externals which characterizes some forms of later evangelicalism, although the system may be moving in that direction. But more to the point, this exterior precision is matched by an *interior* Puritanism which harmonizes well with the New Testament picture of godliness.

> Apprehend in they minde, and settle in thine heart, a true estimate, and right conceit of the substance and power, marrow, and materials of Christianitie. Which doth not consist, as too many suppose, In outward shewes, profession, talking: in holding strict points, defending precise opinion, contesting against the corruptions of the times: In the worke wrought, externall formes of religious exercises, set-tasks of hearing, reading, conference, and the like: in some solomne outward extraordinarie abstinences and forebearances, censuring others, etc. But, in righteousnesse, peace, joy in the holy Ghost: in meekenesse, tenderheartednesse, love: in patience, humilite, contentednesse: in mortification of sinne, moderation of passion, holy guidance of the tongue: in workes of mercy, justice, and truth: in fidelitie, painefulnesse in our Callings, conscionable conversation with men: in reverence unto superiours, love of our enemies, and open hearted reall fruitfull affectionatenesse, and bounty to Gods people: in heavenly-mindednesse, selfe-deniall, the life of faith: in disesteeme of earthly things, contempt of the world, resolute hatred of sinne: in approving our hearts in Gods presence, a sweete communion with him, comfortable longing for the comming of the Lord Jesus, etc. (Richard Bolton, *Directions*, 57–58)

The principal thrust of Puritan morality is not directed at externals but at the interior mortification of sin. Thus, Rogers instructs us that the Christian's continual task must be to "cherish all good notions," inwardly, and to kill Sinne in the very conception. . . . otherwise it will grow from motion to likeing, . . . to hardnesse of heart, to the height of all Sin. Examine your thoughts well wither they tend, before you fulfill your owne desires; if you find them unprofitable, curious, vaine, or such as you cannot yeeld a sufficient reason to God or man for kill them in the shell, let them not live or breath longer in you. (*Garden*, 23, 282, 147)

Growth in Godliness and the Cunning of Satan

This brings us to the Puritan conception of growth in godliness, that is, to the doctrine of sanctification. Here again we find a thoroughly Reformed basis: sanctification is wrought through the believer's union with Christ and applied sovereignly by the Holy Spirit so as to prompt the believer's strivings, not to cooperate with them (John Downame, *Warfare*, 282, 59). Despite its ideal of moral perfection—or perhaps because of it—Puritan piety has a quality about it quite different from later perfectionism; it finds Romans 7 fully as pertinent to the earnest Christian as Romans 8. Resting on the assurance of salvation by grace, the Puritan is able to view his continuing sinfulness without rose-colored glasses, lamenting it, but finding no necessity of hiding it from himself. John Downame comments:

> By the way wee may note a difference betweene the state of Gods children and the wicked. Both fall into sin very often, both also commit hainous and grievous sins; yea sometimes the child of God falleth into more fearefull and horrible sins, then a meere worldling. (*Warfare*, 56–57)

But there *is* a difference:

> Herein the chiefe difference betweene them consisteth, that the child of God after his fall is vexed and grieved, and laboureth to rise againe. . . . (*Warfare*, 56–57)

Or, viewed from another angle, the godly sin only with partial consent, the ungodly with a full will (Richard Rogers, *Garden*, 211–12). True practical righteousness is ours not so much in reality as in desire, and often the only sign of uprightness within the saint will be a deep longing for rescue from sin, like the injured sheep's cry to the shepherd. "The desire for grace," says Downame, "is accepted for the grace you desire" (*Warfare*, 76–77). But there is a need for us to study our characteristic weaknesses, both so as to be better able to mortify these, and so as to be properly humbled (Paul Haynes, *Brief Directions*, 126, 201). Robert Bolton expresses a common sentiment when he marvels at the heroic humility of the martyr John Bradford; remembering

Blessed Bradfords abasing himselfe, who was one of the worthiest Martyrs, and the Heavenliest minded man that ever breathed out his last in the flames, and ascended to heaven in a fiery chariot, as himselfe spake at the stake: I am as dry as a stone, saith he, as dumbe as a nayle; as farre from praying, as he that never knew any taste of it. He sometime subscribed in this manner to those Letters which were full of spirituall life, divinest straines, and demonstration of the Spirit: The most miserable hard-hearted unthankefull sinner, John Bradford. A very painted Hypocrite, I. B. etc. (*Directions*, 340)

This is rather distant from the conventional picture of the Puritan as a self-righteous Pharisee.

Unfortunately there were evidently a great number of Puritan believers who could not so easily stand up under intense self-scrutiny, and this created for the Puritan ministers a large class of pastoral problems. Despair was a serious and widespread illness, it appears; Shepherd and Downame speak of the prevalence of suicide among troubled believers (*Sincere Convert*, 102; *Warfare*, 76–77), and most of the manuals of comfort published during the period are designed to minister to this class of psychological ailment. Three causes of the difficulty suggest themselves to the modern analyst: the Puritan insistence on inner experimental evidence of regeneration; misfiring of the Puritan preachers' spectacular artillery for the destruction of carnal security in professors; and the doctrine of election, which could cut two ways, either wounding or healing the believer, depending on how one applied it. The Puritans are unitedly convinced that the main factor in the misapplication of the elements listed above is not the depth of the doctrines involved, nor any weakness in the believer's intellect or constitution, but the active efforts of the powers of darkness against the Christian. Phineas Fletcher is a good spokesman:

> Christian Reader: Whosoever thou art who mournst, and art humbled under the sense of spiritual poverty, to thee belong that blessing of the heavenly kingdom, and strong consolations of that great Comforter. But how cunning Satan is to hide this evidence from thy blubbered eyes, will neede no other testimonie than thine owne unquiet and dejected spirit. The height of grace is rejoycing in the Lord: and this is a joy unspeakeable and glorious, and indeede a lesser heaven upon earth. Now, that cursed enemie envies thee that thy future heaven, but is raging mad that thou shouldst even here also enjoy an heaven of joy, in this vale of teares; therefore employes all his policies, and fallacies to hinder thy rejoycing, and to hold downe thy heart in distrustfull feares and sorrowes. . . . (*Joy*, 2)

The devil adopts a twofold policy in afflicting Christians:

> It is a constant practice of Satan, to hold, and rocke a carnall heart in all presumptuous quietnesse, and rejoycing; and, (if he may) to keepe down the beleeving soule in continuall uncheerefulnesse and mourning. (*Joy*, 2)

This explanation of despair and presumption is not new in Christian tradition; it is found in the mystics,[24] and probably in the fathers beyond them. The solution to the problem of despair is beautifully developed in Downame's great treatise: First, the identity of the spiritual enemy must be discerned behind the attack, either by the touchstone of Scripture, or by the quality of the disturbance created in the believer's conscience, which if caused by the devil will be enveloped in despair, but if wrought by the Spirit will consist in "a peaceable and quiet sorrow," leading to hope. Then the believer is instructed to rely for comfort upon the very doctrine which may have been wounding him, that of unconditional election, recognizing that since his ordination to salvation is predetermined on the merits of Christ and has nothing to do with his own righteousness, no degree of dereliction on his part can exempt him from pardon and restitution (*Warfare,* 243ff.). This rather admirable practical application of Calvinism illustrates again the heavily doctrinal character of Puritan experimentalism.

A number of related spiritual problems are also ascribed to the malicious activity of Satan. Downame notes among these scrupulosity concerning adiaphora, compulsive guidance by impulse, and interior suggestions directing the believer to end his life (one is again reminded of Edwards's problems in Northampton). Downame also analyzes the characteristics of both generalized and particularized anxiety, noting that these appear only in a certain physical-psychological constitution, but that they are mainly caused, in believers, by guilt aggravated by diabolic accusation. Mental breakdown he interprets in more or less the same way, commenting that it usually follows indulgence in the sin of pride, as with Nebuchadnezzar (*Warfare,* 38–39, 65–66, 53). We have here an admirably thorough attempt to deal with the knottier problems in pastoral counseling on the basis of Puritan biblicism. How much of it can be ascribed merely to the continuation of superstitions from the Middle Ages? Perhaps not so much as we might expect; there has been some demythologizing here, at least enough to bring the subject back to the discreet clarity of the New Testament:

> This is much to bee lamented, that in time of superstition men were more feared with the devill when they heard of his hornes, clawes, hollow voice, and such like, then now in the Gospell when they heare of his privie working and fighting against mens soules, which is much more dangerous, . . . and yet wee can never beleeve and feele the gracious help of Gods holy Angels, till wee beleeve and feele the hidden assaults of Satan and his Spirits. (Ezechiel Culverwell, *Time Well Spent,* 75–76)

This passage emphasizes a fact which tends to be rather dim to us today, that the activity of hostile spiritual forces was a matter of intense practical reality for the Puritan; it explained a good many things in his universe. When he spoke of the Christian life as a warfare, he was not, as Haller and White imply, merely dramatizing the believer's conflict with sin, in order to hold his audience; he was speaking of real combatants.[25]

The Means of Grace

John Downame advises his readers in moments of spiritual distress to hold steady and to keep to the means of grace (*Warfare*, 250); and this brings before us a subject of great importance to the delineation of Puritan piety. Of the Scripture as a means of grace, little needs to be said; this is so foundational as to be taken for granted. Edward Vaughn, the author of a small manual of directions for the understanding of the Bible, makes plain the fact that personal reading, as well as hearing, of the Word of God was expected of the pious Puritan:

> For Jesus Christ his sake, and for your owne soules sake, you will (sometimes) sequester your selves from your publike affaires, and sometimes from your most private occasions, for the orderly and thorow reading herof. . . . There is nothing so effectuall in all the world to move a regenerate man to solace in sorrow, to mourne in mirth, and to apprehend rightly the use of all good means which God hath left in his Church for the saving of soule and body, as the reading, meditating and contemplating in the holy Booke of God given us by inspiration. . . . (Edward Vaughn, *Method*, Preface)

As for the Lord's Supper, there is significantly little said about this, although it is everywhere mentioned as a means of blessing. Next to the universal emphasis on the Word, the accent falls most heavily on prayer as a means of grace.

Helen White has some harsh things to say about the Puritan concept of prayer. It strikes her as something purely utilitarian, and as too much involved with "the housekeeping of the soul." [26] Part of this reaction is probably traceable to the Puritans' characteristically doctrinal approach to the subject: again the matter of regeneration is always in the foreground, since no one can pray who is not a real Christian by Puritan standards. However, it is true that the Puritan treatment of prayer tends to be somewhat anthropocentric, as can be seen in the following two definitions of prayer:

> It is an expression of holy and good dispositions. (William Narne, *Pearle of Prayer*, 207)

> Prayer is a principall part of Gods service, wherein a true Christian, leaving the earth in his heart and affections, ascending into Heaven in his mind, approaching unto the throne of grace, presenting him selfe before the

glorious God, hee conferreth, and speaketh familiarly with his Creator, hee offereth a spirituall sacrifice unto his Majestie, he wrestleth with the Omnipotent, he giveth a comfortable victorie, hee becommeth the Temple of God, the holy Spirit dwelling in him, and obtaineth every good gift, that is necessarie for him. (John Preston, *Daily Exercies*, 4)

William Narne discourses much on the benefit of prayer to the believer—not so much the subjective benefit as the objective profit of receiving answers. Phineas Fletcher, in his *Joy in Tribulation*, treats prayer mainly from the standpoint of its character as supplication (p. 118); and another writer, Henry Scudder, emphasizes the part prayer plays in carrying forward God's work on earth (*Key to Heaven*, To the Reader). The overall approach really does seem to be utilitarian.

However, this is easily explainable as a one-sided emphasis on one strand of biblical teaching on prayer, most widely represented in the New Testament. The portrayal of prayer displayed in the Psalms has not been so fully grasped here as it has in the beautifully balanced prayers of Andrewes. Yet the element of worship in prayer is treated, and a particularly large place is given to our communion with the Holy Spirit in prayer. The process of prayer is not only the most intimate cooperation with God, according to Preston; it is actually possible to know when one's prayers prove acceptable, and are to be answered, through the subjective experience of the Spirit's leading in prayer (*Daily Exercise*, 15, 100).

Most of our authors adopt a cautious, mediating position on the question of the use of forms in prayer. John Ball nods to the convictions of "our brethren of the separation," but lists scriptural proofs that read prayers are legitimate and useful and remarks that the Lord's Prayer may be used either as a set prayer or as a pattern (*Power of Godliness*, 354, 505–6). Samuel Hieron finds set prayers useful as a kind of trellis on which to train the prayers of those just beginning the devotional life, but he cautions that the *exclusive* use of forms is a dangerous limitation of the Holy Spirit (*Helpe*, n.p.). Of the various manuals on prayer produced during out period, the distinctively Puritan works tend to be detailed commentaries on the Lord's Prayer, whereas the more traditional Anglican works are collections of set prayers written by the minister for the use of the laity.

Love of Neighbor and Communion with God

Two areas remain to be treated in the analysis of the anatomy of Puritan devotion. The first is that of the pious Puritan's concern for others. Intense and introspective as it often is, Puritan devotion is by no means purely vertical in character; the Puritan was acutely aware of the needs of his fellow human beings, and not merely out of a sense of duty. Unlike the twentieth-century revivalism that is its ultimate descendant, Puritan piety was oddly enough just as concerned about the physical welfare of humans as it was about their redemption. Much of this social concern is a carry-over of the medieval feeling for the solidarity of Christian culture; the theory of social amelioration is still basically medieval. John Dod notes that it is the business of the magistrate to care for the poor and to prevent begging but to caution the believer not to omit philanthropy. Social injustice, in Dod's view, is as bad a sin as sodomy (*Ten Commandments*, 244, 256). John Downame, who is uneasy about the effect of wealth on his readers' Christianity, notes that affluence is good for at least one thing: it enables one to relieve the poor (*Warfare*, 453). Much of the Puritan code's rejection of certain worldly item-sis traceable to the fact that these actions waste resources which are needed by the poor (John Downame, *Warfare*, 646; Robert Bolton, *Directions*, 195).

Puritan devotional literature is curiously moderate in its treatment of the witness of the laity to unbelievers: moderate, that is, in comparison with the frantic activity of nineteenth-century revivalism. Robert Bolton limits himself to some observations on bearing the spiritual needs of persons uppermost in one's mind when visiting them, "walking in wisdom toward those that are outside"; but in another place he remarks:

> Thy selfe being vouchsafed the mercy of conversion; never insolently and imperiously insult over those poore soules, who are beside themselves in matter of salvation, who like miserable drudges, damne themselves in the Devils slavery. . . . Alas! our hearts should bleed within us, to behold so many about us, to inbrew their cruell hands in the bloud of their owne soules, by their ignorance, worldlinesse, drunkennesse, lust, lying, etc. . . . And the rather should we pittie, and pray for such an one, who followes the swings of his owne heart, to his owns everlasting perdition, because, as I said before, there went but the sheares betweene the matter whereof we were all made; onely the free mercy, goodnesse and grace of God makes the difference. (*Directions*, 187–92, 17–18, 113, 126)

Then he has some more comments on the duty of the believer to reprove sin in public; this may, he notes, result in the conversion of the offender. (On the other hand, one is to be careful not to develop into a censorious hypocrite with "sublimated eyesight" for the faults of others) (*Directions*, 126).

There is a commendable movement here away from the wholly vertical direction of monastic piety. There is not yet the radical awareness of the church's mission which will come with the ministry of the Wesleys, but there is a certain calm confidence that if believers take care of their relationship with God, their witness will take care of itself.

The final subject to be touched on is the very comprehensive one of the Puritan concept of communion with God. As has been mentioned previously , Helen White criticizes Puritan devotion for what she conceives to be a failure of sensitivity to the mystery of God's nature, and she goes so far as to state that Puritan literature neglects the ministry of the Holy Spirit.[27] There is little support in the sources for either of these criticisms, especially the second.

There is considerable difference between that concept of communion with God which is properly termed *mystical* and the Puritan concept. Medieval mysticism shares with Platonic (and, for that matter, Buddhistic) mysticism a common structure: that of a threefold path to God, consisting of purification, contemplation, and final union.[28] The presupposition of union is "a mind purified and annihilated as to all particular objects of affection."[29] John of the Cross, one of the greatest of the later mystics, defines the "narrow gate" through which the soul must pass to reach God as the gate of sense perception. The path to perfection involves "systematic denial of everything that could give satisfaction to body or soul . . ." (*Dark Night of the Soul*, Introduction). The writer does not mean to suggest that this kind of fusion between asceticism and Christianity is inherently non- or anti-Christian; otherwise we would have to make some embarrassing apologies for Augustine. But it is clear that the Puritans were extremely worried about this sort of amalgam and that they took pains to emphasize the fact that the biblical *sarx* did not mean the body but the totality of sin affecting the personality; that progress in holiness and approach to God were effected by mortification of sin and not of the senses; and that in any case the sole doorway to God was the Mediator (John Downame, *Warfare*, 16). The writings of Elizabethans influenced by mystical piety, such as Francis Rous, are instantly recognizable from Puritan works by their failure to mention Christ in his mediatorial function, although they do speak of his life as a divine pattern, or as a meeting-ground between the human and the divine. On the other hand, the Ignatian type of mysticism, which stresses Christ in his human nature and the pictorial use of the sensory imagination, is also alien to Puritan communion, which would insist on going to God by a route that it would consider more direct and more spiritual.

There is a hesitancy in Puritan works to define the person of God too clearly, except in biblical terms. When the average Puritan begins to try to describe his experience of fellowship with God, he very rapidly ceases to use his own words and begins quoting Scripture—just as the mystic rarely attempts to describe God himself, but instead speaks about the experience of God, which sounds perhaps more interesting than biblical definitions of God's character. But it is not correct to say that there is no sense of the mysterious, of the supernatural, in what the Puritan does say about God. One considerable difference between the mystical and the Puritan portrayals of God is that the former emphasize God's immanence, the latter God's transcendence. Thus, William Narne remarks:

> The fourth worke which must bee done in true prayer is yet more hard and difficill: Namelie, speach with God, a duetifull and familiar conference, or communication with the Almightie. . . . It is an easie thing to speake of a King, but not so easie to speake to him: so is it easie to speake of God, in regard of his eternitie, wisdome, power, and glorie and of thy owne ignorance, unworthinesse, and infirmitie. (*Pearle of Prayer*, 326)

On the other hand, the Puritan does not feel himself at a great distance from God:

> Let thy holy affections bee ever throwly warmed, and ravisht extraordinarily with the love of God. To which, there are infinite inflaming motives and Obligations. He being absolutely considered, is immeasurably lovely. The most attractive objects of insatiable love, and all amiable excellencies, are eminently and transcendently triumphant in him eternally. . . . Or consider Him in relation to thy selfe: and shouldest thou every moment throw an interminable time, lay downe ten thousand lives for His sake, thou couldest never come neere the requitall of the least inch of His infinite love towards thee, which reacheth from everlasting, to everlasting. Hee bore thee in the bosome of this His free love from all eternitie. . . . Hee brought thee out of the abhorred state of being nothing. . . . He brought thee againe, when thou hadst wilfully lost thy selfe, with the hearte-blood of His onely Sonne. . . . If thou hold an holy familiaritie with thy God, and He looke pleasedly upon thee, thou shalt graspe Jesus Christ more sweetely and feelingly in the armes of thy Faith: partake more plentifully of the joyfull freedome, presence, and communication of His comforting Spirit: be garded more strongly and narrowly by His glorious Angels. . . . (Robert Bolton, *Directions*, 61–62)

Note that this passage rapidly becomes human-centered; and yet it is transparently biblical. The love of God is still primarily defined by the Puritans in terms of obedience (John Dod, *Ten Commandments*, 34), and communion is still in order to action (William Pulley, *Christian's Taske*, 349). Yet this is no dry moralism. Helen White is not quite right when she suggests that "the Intellectual and the ethical are the two driving forces of the seventeenth century meditation in England."[30] There is an element of this, but this is not the only spirit that breathes through Puritanism. "Suffer not your heart to be strict, narrow, and uncomfortable in heavenly things," says Rogers; "this draweth way both the breath, bloud and life of true Godliness. . . . The Lord satisfie you with gladnes" (*Garden*, 98–99). Nicholas Byfield says of the Puritan believer:

The Holy Ghost at some time falls upon him, & sets him all on a fire, on a fire I say, both of sudden and violent indignation at sinne, as it is sinne; as also the fire of holy affections, with which from God hee frequently and on a sudden is inflamed, while he stands before the Lord. For besides the affection which a godly man bringeth with him to Gods worship, he doth feele his heart oftentimes on a sudden surprised with strange impressions, sometimes of sorrow, sometimes of feare and awefull dread of God, some times of fervent desires after God; some times of strong resolutions of holy duties to be done by him. . . . He feeles at some times in the use of Gods ordinances a marvellous work of the Holy Ghost, in respect of the certaine perswasion of Gods love, and the infallible beliefe of the truth. . . . (*Oracles of God*, 172–74)

This is a description of experience which is neither intellectual nor emotional nor volitional, but which takes place in a ground of the personality underlying all these faculties. It is an experience which, if it is accepted as real, must be regarded as supernatural. And if it is so regarded and accepted, it places a stamp of peculiar authority on Puritan piety and suggests to us the thought that there may be things here worthy of our emulation.

The Future of Puritan Piety

The task of relating Puritan piety to future movements in the history of Christian experience has been done more or less *en route* in the foregoing. It remains for a few brief comments to be made regarding the thesis and the normative value of Puritan devotion.

As it has appeared here, Puritan piety has been portrayed as having many crucial linkages with the medieval Catholic Church, some of its best features being traceable directly to inheritance from Rome. Yet in many vital areas there has been a paring of Catholic piety to the biblical quick. The Puritans were not as wholly different from Rome as they imagined. Yet to some degree their reconstructed devotional life was a new direction, or perhaps a very old one, in that it sought to reestablish in modern lives the piety of the biblical ages. How biblical, and how normative for us today, was the reformed piety of the Puritans?

Examining the great revival in America in the 1740s, as Jonathan Edwards describes it, we may delineate four areas of revitalization in the souls of those who were particularly affected by the movement. The first area is that of the soul's consciousness of God, of God's holiness and grandeur, and the awareness of communion with God. The second area is correlative to the first, the soul's consciousness of its own impurity against the white light of divine holiness, and its urgent longing for sanctification. The third is an illuminated vision of reality, in which all created beings are seen as symbols or expressions of divine glory and spiritual truth. The fourth is the area of practical endeavor in the spreading of the kingdom of God. In each of these areas, it is evident that in the course of the Awakening, people were gripped by a quality of experience naturally unattainable, imparted directly by the Holy Spirit. We may take these four areas, with this imparted quality, as a normative standard of developed Christian experience—not, to be sure, because these things characterized *our* Awakening, but because they seem to form an apt condensation of the biblical portrayal of normative Christian experience. If this standard is applied to Puritan piety, how does it measure up?

Not too surprisingly—considering the linkage of Edwards with our English Puritans—it measures up very well. There is a somewhat circumscribed conception of the mission of the church, natural perhaps considering the circumstances of the Puritans. There are excrescences, some of them dangerous, which have been noted in the preceding pages. Yet where these excrescences are brushed aside, and one looks on Puritan devotion at its best, it is a thing of great purity and beauty. Reading these treatises is at times like viewing a dynamo covered by a thin veil, for under the veil of seventeenth-century expression burns the urgency and the supernatural light of apostolic devotion. There is room for us to consider how this same energy might be veiled in our own flesh, some three centuries later.

Notes

1. William Haller's *The Rise of Puritanism* has some excellent chapters on the subject, viewing it, however, more from a literary than a theological point of view and focusing more on its movement toward expression in Milton than on its theological antecedents and descendants. Gordon Wakefield's *Puritan Devotion* is praiseworthy in its appreciative depiction of the character of Puritan piety, but without pretense of any historical endeavor beyond that of mere description.

2. Helen C. White, *English Devotional Literature (Prose), 1600–1640*, 78, 89, 98–115, 131ff.

3. Ibid., 165, 168.

4. Ibid., 77–78, 79, 143–45.

5. This is based on a careful survey of Robert Bolton's *Directions for a Comfortable Walking With God* and John Downame's *The Christian's Warfare*, two works representative of their class.

6. H. C. White, *English Devotional Literature*, 157.

7. Quoted in Joseph B. Collins, *Christian Mysticism in the Elizabethan Age* (Baltimore: Johns Hopkins University Press, 1940) 125.

8. Helen C. White, *The Tudor Books of Private Devotion* (Madison: University of Wisconsin Press, 1951).

9. C. C. Butterworth, *The English Primers (1529–1545)* (Philadelphia: University of Pennsylvania Press, 1953) 2.

10. H. C. White, *Tudor Books*, 126–27.

11. Cf. Ralph Bronkema, *The Essence of Puritanism* (Goes, Netherlands: Oosterbaan & Le Cointre, 1929) 89–114. This work is hopelessly unhistorical, being based quite uncritically and exclusively on older secondary writings; but it contains a few interesting hypotheses and much useful summarizing of the principal secondary authorities.

12. H. C. White, *English Devotional Literature*, 56.

13. Ibid., 159.

14. W. Haller, *Rise of Puritanism*, 85.

15. Pierre du Moulin, quoted in Richard Smith, *Munition Against Man's Miserie and Mortalitie*, 89–90. This European voice simply provides an apt statement of the burden of countless jeremiads in the English literature from the turn of the century on.

16. Cf. H. C. White, *English Devotional Literature*, 51, 64.

17. Gordon Wakefield, *Puritan Devotion*, 160. Mr. Paul Pierson recently commented to the writer that the very profusion of Catholic devotional literature may be due perhaps not so much to the richness of the church's devotional tradition, but to the mediatorial function of devotion in common Catholic practice.

18. *Contra* Bronkema and the older authorities he cites (see *The Essence of Puritanism*, 27), Puritan piety is vigorously doctrinal. The theological shortcomings of Haller and White become apparent in dealing with this facet of Puritan piety, when the latter mistakes the term "rebirth" for a borrowing from German mysticism (p. 205), and the former ascribes a highly gnosticized view of the atonement to the Puritans.

19. H. C. White, *English Devotional Literature*, 200, 235.

20. Thomas Wood, *English Casuistical Divinity During the Seventeenth Century* (London: SPCK, 1952) xi, 57.

21. R. Bronkema, *The Essence of Puritanism*, 165.

22. Thomas Wood, *English Casuistical Divinity*, 64.

23. H. C. White, *English Devotional Literature*, 236.

24. E.g., Ignatius Loyola, *Spiritual Exercises* (London: Mowbray, 1955) 141–53.

25. W. Haller, *Rise of Puritanism*, 25; H. C. White, *English Devotional Literature*, 165.

26. H. C. White, *English Devotional Literature*, 175.

27. Ibid., 189–90.

28. J. B. Collins, *Christian Mysticism*, 1–19.

29. John of the Cross, *The Dark Night of the Soul* (London: T. Baker, 1916) 107.

30. H. C. White, *English Devotional Literature*, 179.

Bibliography

Sources

Alwyn, Robert. *The Oyle of Gladness.* London, 1631.

Attersall, William. *Physicke Against Famine: or, a soveraigne preservative . . . .* London, 1632.

Ball, John. *The Power of Godliness.* London, 1657.

Bayly, Lewis. *The Practice of Piety.* 3rd ed. London, 1613.

Bolton, Robert. *Directions for a Comfortable Walking With God.* London, 1626.

Brathwait, Richard. *A Spiritual Spicerie.* London, 1638.

Burton, Henry. *A Tryall of Privat Devotion.* London, 1628.

Byfield, Nicholas. *The Marrow of the Oracles of God.* 7th ed. London, 1630.

Cooper, Thomas. *The Christian's Daily Sacrifice.* London, 1609.

Culverwell, Ezechiel. *Time Well Spent in Sacred Meditations; Divine Observations, Heavenly Exhortations*. London, 1634.

Dod, John. *The Ten Commandments*. London, 1604.

Downame, John. *The Christian's Warfare*. London, 1609.

————. *A Guide to Godlinesse*. London, 1622.

Featley, Daniel. *Ancilla Pietatis*. London, 1626.

Fletcher, Phineas. *Joy in Tribulation*. London, 1632.

Forbes, John. *How a Christian Man May Discerne the Testimonie of Gods Spirit*. London, 1616.

Haynes, Paul. *Brief Directions Unto a Godly Life*. London, 1637.

Hieron, Samuel. *A Helpe Unto Devotion*. London, 1612.

Narne, William. *The Pearle of Prayer*. London, 1630.

Preston, John. *The Saint's Daily Exercise*. London, 1629.

Pulley, William. *The Christian's Taske*. London, 1619.

Rogers, Richard. *A Garden of Spiritual Flowers*. 5th ed. London, 1609.

Rowen, Thomas. *Markes of Salvation*. London, 1637.

Scudder, Henry. *A Key to Heaven*. 2nd ed. London, 1633.

Shepherd, Thomas. *The Sincere Convert*. London, 1640.

Smith, Richard. *Munition Against Man's Miserie and Mortalitie*. London, 1634.

Vaughn, Edward. *A Plaine and Perfect Method for the Easie Understanding of the Whole Bible*. London, 1617.

Studies

Collinson, Patrick. *The Elizabethan Puritan Movement*. London: Cape; Berkeley: University of California Press, 1967.

————. *English Puritanism*. London: Historical Association, 1983.

Cragg, Gerald R. *Puritanism in the Period of the Great Persecution, 1660–88*. Cambridge: University Press, 1957.

Davies, Horton. *The Worship of the English Puritans*. London: Dacre, 1941.

————. *Laudian Worship and Theology in England: from Andrewes to Baxter and Fox 1603–1690*. Princeton: Princeton University Press, 1975.

Haller, William. *The Rise of Puritanism*. New York: Columbia University Press, 1938.

Keeble, N. H. *Richard Baxter, Puritan Man of Letters*. Oxford: Clarendon, 1982.

Nuttall, G. F. *The Holy Spirit in Puritan Faith and Experience*. Oxford: Blackwell, 1946.

————. *Visible Saints: The Congregational Way 1640–1660*. Oxford: Blackwell, 1957.

————. *The Puritan Spirit*. London: Epworth, 1967.

Wakefield, Gordon S. *Puritan Devotion*. London: Epworth, 1987.

Watkins, O. C. *The Puritan Experience*. London: Routledge & Kegan Paul, 1972.

Watts, Michael R. *The Dissenters: From the Reformation to the French Revolution*, vol. 1. Oxford: Clarendon, 1978.

White, Helen C. *English Devotional Literature (Prose), 1600–1640*. Madison : University of Wisconsin Press, 1931.

II. *Baptist and Quaker Spirituality*

E. GLENN HINSON

BAPTIST AND QUAKER spirituality harks back by way of Puritanism to the contemplative tradition of the Middle Ages. By the time the first Baptists, about 1612, and the first Friends, about 1648 came along, they would not have remembered much about "the rock from whence they were hewn" and, if they had, might have tried to deny it. With the first Puritans, however, it was another matter. They self-consciously returned to the medieval contemplative tradition to gather ideas and practices that would help them to achieve the "further reformation" they sought so ardently to effect in England. Baptists and Quakers thus inherited a substantial tradition that they molded and shaped in ways that would accommodate some of their own special perceptions and preferences. Both, reacting vigorously against efforts to impose uniformity in worship through the Book of Common Prayer, manifested a powerful concern for voluntariness in religious matters. For Baptists this concern expressed itself visibly in rejection of baptism of infants and for Quakers in repudiation of sacraments. The key to the devout life, both insisted, lay in sincere, heartfelt responsiveness to the Holy Spirit. They differed sharply, however, regarding the issue of immediacy of experience of the Spirit. Quakers yearned for direct and unmediated revelation, whereas Baptists insisted on squaring all claims in some way with Scripture, a difference of views that generated fierce controversy between the two groups in the late seventeenth century.

Their experience in history, particularly in the United States, where the majority of both groups now reside, has wrought significant changes in both Baptist and Quaker spirituality. The Great Awakening (about 1720–1760) divided Baptists in spirituality as in other ways in the amount of attention given to conversion. "New Light" or "Separate" Baptists, for instance, differed from "Old Light" or "Regular" Baptists in the emphasis they placed on revival methods, "experience" and witness of conversion, exhortations to respond, and other aspects of experiential religion. The frontier revivals of the early nineteenth century (1790–1820) widened further the gap between Baptists who feared and Baptists who favored experiential religion.

Similarly, Quakers took separate paths at an early date. In England Robert Barclay soon introduced a "rational evangelicalism" into George Fox's mystical and prophetic spirituality.[1] In the United States a cleavage among Quakers has occurred on geographical lines—eastern Quakers favoring the more mystical and socially active piety of Fox and midwestern Quakers the more pragmatic approach of Barclay.

What this means is that no one can accurately depict the wide and numerous variations in Baptist or Quaker spirituality. Broadly speaking, both groups have exhibited a preference for a relatively simple and, above all, sincere piety both corporately and privately. Because of their rootage in Puritanism, both display remarkable affinities with late medieval monastic spirituality not only in thought and practice but even in style and language. As I have demonstrated in an article entitled "Southern Baptist and Medieval Spirituality: Surprising Similarities,"[2] historical evolution notwithstanding, Baptists echo many themes of medieval contemplatives such as Bernard of Clairvaux, Richard Rolle, Walter Hilton, Julian of Norwich, and the unknown author of *The Cloud of Unknowing*. Similarly, Rufus Jones sought to establish a direct lineage for Quakers in the mystical tradition of the Middle Ages, particularly groups such as "the Friends of God" and "the Brothers of the Common Life."[3] More than any other Protestant group, the Friends preserved the contemplative approach to prayer in their emphasis on silence.

The Goal

As a consequence of early influences on their thinking, Baptists and Quakers have envisioned the goal of the devout life somewhat differently. John Bunyan spoke for most Puritans on his day as well as Baptists when he envisioned Christian life as a pilgrimage from the "wilderness" of this world to "the heavenly Jerusalem, the innumerable company of Angels, and the Spirits of just men made perfect." Baptist hymnals today preserve nearly four centuries of their forebears' longing for eternal bliss: "a home far away"; "the golden strand, just beyond the river"; "worlds unknown"; "mansions in the sky"; "scenes of glory"; "beautiful life that has no end"; "a home prepared" where we "shall dwell eternally"; "celestial land, where joys immortal flow"; "rest, eternal, sacred, sure"; "ransomed in glory"; "my Father's house above"; "eternal home"; "heaven so bright"; "fairer worlds on high"; "the haven of rest"; "the eternal rest"; "life eternal"; "blessed home above"; and "the peaceful shore."[4]

Although Quakers were cooked up in the same pot as Baptists—one that produced such radicals as the Ranters, the Levellers, the Fifth Monarchy

Men, and other chiliasts—they did something to the goal of Christian life that most Baptists did not do. They harnessed their hopes for a better and fairer world to a social agenda which they called "the Lamb's War." Equipped with spiritual armaments, they battled in this world for a kingdom not of this world. George Fox (1624–1691) experienced a personal and inward transformation which he believed could also transform all of England. As Jesus Christ spoke to Fox's condition, so too could he speak to the condition of society. Christ came to put an end to the old order and to inaugurate a new. Those who obey his teaching can enter the new order just as Fox had.[5]

Voluntary Obedience

Although they had somewhat different goals in view, Baptists and Quakers were essentially in agreement on the key to it all, namely, holy obedience. In *Pilgrim's Progress* John Bunyan remonstrated with those to whom religion was chiefly a matter of words. Like his Puritan forebears and contemporaries, he measured people in terms of their deeds. True believers, Christian reminds Talkative, are known by "an experimental [i.e., experiential] confession of faith" and by "heart-holiness, family-holiness . . . and conversation-holiness in the world."[6] Most Baptists have construed the quest for holiness in personalistic and privatistic terms, often avoiding social and political involvement. Minutes of Baptist churches overflow with accounts of members disciplined for dancing, drinking, gambling, or related offenses. Occasionally they noted actions taken for such things as charging excessive rents, owning slaves, abusing wives and children, or other social wrongs, but these appear far less frequently. When asked to name their saints, therefore, Baptists will regularly point to models of personal piety rather than social reformers. Despite such preferences, however, Baptists can also claim some notable models who combined both personal and social spirituality. William Knibb, a British Baptist missionary, for instance, led the fight against slavery in the West Indies. Walter Rauschenbusch, pastor and seminary professor, was a theorist for the Social Gospel movement. Clarence Jordan founded Koinonia Farm at Americus, Georgia, as an effort to bring blacks and whites together. Martin Luther King, Jr., drew his inspiration for the Civil Rights movement directly out of Ebenezer Baptist Church in Atlanta.

Perhaps more vigorously than Baptists, Quakers too have measured religion in terms of holy obedience. During his early period as a "seeker," Fox was extremely upset about those he called "professors," that is, superficial believers. When, at age nineteen, two companions at a fair asked him to drink a jug of beer with them and then chided him, saying that whoever did not drink all would have to pay for the whole jug, he got up, plunked a groat down on the table, and, after finishing his business at the fair, went home. That night, God spoke to him: "Thou seest how young people go together into vanity, and old people into the earth; thou must forsake all, both young and old, and keep out of all, and be a stranger unto all."[7] Shortly thereafter, Fox broke all bonds, including those with his family. Everywhere he turned, he found signs of superficiality among both clergy and laity. Early in 1646 he experienced several "openings," one of which was that only the regenerate are true believers. He did not find in the churches the kind of obedience to God he thought authentic. Churches were mere "steeple houses." Like saints of other ages, he became convinced that Christ alone could "speak to thy condition." His bold and impetuous messages following worship services landed him and his followers in jail time after time.

Many Quakers look to John Woolman as the model par excellence of holy obedience, which he presented in his *Journal*. Born in 1720 in West Jersey, Woolman developed early in life the sensitivities characteristic of the tradition of Friends. By age seven, he reported, he "began to be acquainted with the operations of Divine love." Reading Revelation 22 later drew his mind "to seek after that pure habitation . . . God had prepared for his servants." Scrutiny of others' lives convinced him that people his age lived with "less steadiness and firmness" than Scripture demanded. At about age twelve or thirteen he committed an act of cruelty which further sensitized him. He killed a mother robin feeding her young; then, lest they starve, he had to kill the babies too. At one period Woolman claimed to veer toward "youthful disobedience" himself, but an illness brought him up short. "At length that word which is as a fire and a hammer broke and dissolved my rebellious heart," he explained. He vowed, then, that, if his health were restored, he would "walk humbly before [God]." Out of these and other youthful struggles, Woolman arrived at the perception that, "true religion consisted in an inward life, wherein the heart doth love and reverence God the Creator, and learns to exercise true justice and goodness, not only toward all men, but also toward the brute creatures. . . ."[8]

Woolman's career gave him ample opportunity to act on this principle. Hired by a Quaker merchant as a kind of clerk at age twenty-one, he had to write a bill of sale for a black woman slave. He did so, he explained, with great pangs of conscience, salved only by the fact that an elderly Quaker bought her. This so weighed on his conscience, however, that he refused ever after to do the same. Although highly successful in merchandising, he decided to learn the trade of a tailor lest his life become restricted by "more outward care and cumber than was required."[9] From 1746 until his death in

1772 he spent about one month out of every year traveling around the American colonies to plead with Quakers to free their slaves. He became what I would call a quiet revolutionary, conscious that he too had a part in causing injustice. He stopped wearing dyed suits because the dye was made from indigo and indigo from slave labor. He stopped using sugar, rum, and molasses made in the West Indies because they were made by slave labor. Yet he worried lest too many follow his example and bring hurt to those he wanted to help. Little by little, he began to discern a pattern behind all kinds of injustice, namely, insensitivity to the way human desire for comforts and conveniences impacts the lives of others. The answer, he argued, lay in Matthew 6:33, "Seek first the Kingdom of God . . . ," and 25:40, "forasmuch as ye did it to the least of these my brethren, ye did it unto me." He did not live to see the end of slavery even among Quakers, but, largely as a result of his efforts, by 1787 no American Quaker owned a slave.[10]

Both Baptists and Quakers learned through their own trials that obedience to God must be voluntary if it is to be authentic. "God alone is Lord of the conscience," ran Baptist logic. "To be authentic and responsible, therefore, faith must be free. Coercion of any kind invalidates obedience." In both old and new England, Baptists wrote strident tractates demanding complete religious liberty. In the American colonies Roger Williams, after being expelled from the Massachusetts Bay Colony, founded Rhode Island in 1636 as a haven "for persons distressed of conscience." Quakers, severely persecuted wherever they went, also had reason to emphasize voluntariness in religion. Not only their claims to direct inspiration but also their activities as "publishers of truth" stirred bitter hostility. Surprisingly, however, they attracted many persons of lofty social position, such as the Fell family, Robert Barclay, and William Penn. In 1682 Penn founded a colony whose "Frame of Government" assured toleration.

Shaping Saints

Baptists and Quakers have diverged most from the medieval tradition and from one another in corporate spirituality, in great part because of their voluntarism. Monastic spirituality is far more intentional than either of these. Both, however, have not lacked concern for spiritual formation.

Although Baptists have not developed an initiation process equal to the early Christian catechumenate or to a monastic novitiate, they have insisted on believers' baptism as the way to achieve a "regenerate church membership," something they thought established churches in Europe and America lacked. Only persons who freely and of their own accord resolved to become Christians, they asserted, were suitable candidates for baptism.

Baptists exercised care to examine confessions of faith of candidates to see whether they could give credible testimonies of authentic conversion. Ability to recite a creed was not enough to validate heart religion. Like the monks of the Middle Ages, Baptists too wanted "conversion of life and manners." In the United States today, Baptists rely largely on Sunday school instruction and public worship services to "form" people. For Baptists in the South, pressures to effect "decisions" have resulted in a dramatic drop in the age of baptism, from twenty years of age in 1900 to about seven or eight years of age in 1988. The net result is diminishment of formation and increase of second or third "conversions" on the part of persons who later discover that their earlier decisions were inadequate. Other Baptist groups, both in the United States and elsewhere, representing tiny minorities not only in general but also in the religious populace, necessarily exercise considerably greater caution. In England youth are seldom baptized before age sixteen. In the Soviet Union, government regulations prevent instruction and baptism before age eighteen.

Quakers would appear to be even less intentional about formation than Baptists. Since they do not observe baptism or Eucharist, they have relied on modeling of spirituality in the family, meetings, or lives of saints. Spiritual development is obviously a complex process which begins in our earliest social environment, the family. John Woolman owed much of his remarkable sensitivity to devout parents who practiced a firm but positive discipline. Once, he recalled, at age twelve, when he sassed his mother during his father's absence, his father simply noted the fact that he had misbehaved and advised him "to be more careful in the future." He never forgot that gentle rebuke, for he could never remember a time when he "spoke unhandsomely to either of my parents, however foolish in some other things."[11] George Fox himself had a magnetic personality through which he could powerfully influence the lives of others. In a preface to Fox's *Journal*, William Penn spoke of his mentor's "clear and wonderful depth"; ability to bring the best out of people and to open to them the insights of Scripture; his "awful, living, reverent frame" in prayer. "For in all things he acquitted himself like a man, yea, a strong man, a new and heavenly-minded man; a divine and a naturalist, and all of God Almighty's making."[12] Others—Penn himself, Isaac Pennington, Robert Barclay, Margaret Fell, John Woolman—also served as models. Fox was imbued with real skills as an organizer, and his system of "meetings" helped the early movement spread rapidly. Subsequent generations, however, have lacked the dynamism he injected into it. The effect has been serious decline, so that some Quakers, especially in the Midwest, have developed more intentional ways of shaping saints.[13] Indeed, midwestern Quakers have developed styles of instruction and worship similar to those used by Baptists. Despite their numerical decline, those who have quaffed deeply from the Quaker tradition of silent meetings and serious "exercising of the heart toward God" have manifested unquestionable signs of deep and mature spirituality. No other religious group has achieved so notable a record of social ministry and action.

Spiritual Care

Quakers have doubtless preserved more of their Puritan forebears' concern for spiritual nurture than Baptists. In the United States at least, many Baptists have often locked themselves into a conversionist frame of thinking and neglected the growth process. This harks back to the effect of the Great Awakening and the frontier revivals which did so much to shape the Baptist ethos.

Baptists have lacked the extensive means of spiritual guidance supplied by oral confession in the Roman Catholic Church, but sensitive pastors have assisted the faithful through sermons, individual counsel, letters, and day-to-day contact. John Gifford, pastor of the Bedford congregation of which Bunyan later became pastor, taught and did what, "by God's grace" Bunyan noted, was "much for my stability." When he learned about Bunyan's spiritual travail, Gifford invited him to his home to meet with others going through similar trials. He knew both how to comfort and how to confront.[14] Following Richard Baxter's model of *The Reformed Pastor,* Baptist ministers have sought to be present in the special moments with a quiet reminder of the working of grace in human life. Other members of congregations have imitated their pastors in this. Not many Baptists would talk about spiritual direction, but they have experienced some in subtle ways nonetheless.

Among Quakers, nurture has depended especially on the family and the meetings, where Friends try to attune themselves to the Light Within, that is, the Holy Spirit or the Christ of the Prologue of John's Gospel. More than any other group, Quakers bear witness to the conviction that spiritual development depends on God and not on human contrivances. This is not to say, however, that they leave spiritual growth to chance. Within communities of Friends certain persons, such as John Woolman, have been recognized as "ministers" who can take the lead and "clerks" who can record and facilitate decision making. Confronted with the problem of declining congregations, as a matter of fact, midwestern Quakers have fashioned more formal training for ministers similar to that received by other Protestants. Quakers have produced some notable spiritual models and guides, both men and women, such as Rufus Jones, Thomas R. Kelly, Douglas V. Steere,

13. Edward Hicks, *The Peaceable Kingdom with Quakers Bearing Banners,* c. 1830.

and Caroline Stephen. Douglas Steere, longtime professor at Haverford College, has enriched not only Quaker but all Christian spirituality by helping Protestants get in touch with outstanding Catholic spiritual guides such as Baron Friedrich von Hügel and with non-Christian spiritualities. His treatise *On Listening to Another* has opened a window on Quaker style of prayer and worship.[15]

Prayer in Baptist and Quaker Modes

Baptists and Quakers diverge in obvious ways in their styles of worship and prayer. The differences are deeply rooted in perceptions about revelation. For Baptists the Bible is "the sole rule of faith and practice," whereas for Quakers the Inner Light is supreme.

It would not be inaccurate to say that the Bible has been the chief Baptist "sacrament," that is, the means through which Baptists expect to experience God's grace. Privately, Baptists have meditated on the Scriptures in a manner closely analogous to the *lectio divina* of medieval monks. Baptist families have read Scriptures at mealtime and spent some time in silence listening to the message in them before eating. The devout have sat in their rocking chairs, Bibles on their laps, reading, then closing their eyes to let the word soak in. They have brought with them the cares of the day, their loved ones, their neighbors, their communities, and their world and asked direction. A sizable number could probably claim to have read the Bible "from cover to cover" numerous times, some as often as once a year. What has happened in private among a select group of Baptists has happened in corporate settings with most of the Baptist constituency. Baptists vary considerably in educational programs using the Bible, but without exception they major in Bible. For every widely known figure such as Martin Luther King, Jr., there will have been hundreds of "ordinary saints" whose exemplary lives have taken shape through praying the Bible.

The Bible has not been unimportant in Quaker spirituality, but it does not dominate as it does in Baptist. Far more important is attentiveness to the Inner Light, source of direct revelation, guidance, and power. Quakers have sought to revive primitive Christianity's vital experience of the Spirit. The question that Fox put to people was: "Art thou a child of Light, and has thou walked in the Light, and what thou speakest, is it inwardly from God?"[16] "The Spirit of God, which inspired the men who wrote the Scriptures," Elton Trueblood has observed, "is still at work, in each human heart, and will be known by all who respond. Worship, therefore, is not the performance of a dead ritual, but genuine waiting on the Lord to hear His voice and to know his power firsthand."[17] Quakers, of course, have recognized the dangers of this doctrine of the Inner Light if it is not kept anchored to Scriptures, but they have not abandoned their basic conviction about it. For Quakers, prayer is, above all, the orienting of one's inner perceptions to the divine presence, in Brother Lawrence's words, "the practice of the presence of God." Or, as Thomas Kelly has expressed so beautifully, "internal practices and habits of the mind, . . . secret habits of unceasing orientation of the deeps of our being about the Inward Light, ways of conducting our inward life so that we are perpetually bowed in worship, while we are also very busy in the world of daily affairs."[18]

Corporate Spirituality

Neither Baptists nor Quakers have shown a lot of appreciation for liturgical spirituality. Reacting against imposed uniformity of worship in England, both have placed the burden of spiritual growth and development on the shoulders of the individual. In neither case has the Eucharist played the role it does in Roman Catholic, Orthodox, or Anglican churches. This is not to say, nevertheless, that the community of faith has not been important in Baptist or Quaker religious life. It has been of great importance.

Baptist worship, like private devotion, has been essentially Bible-centered. Corporate prayers use much biblical phraseology. In its best form, Baptist preaching has represented the biblical message with power. Music has assumed an increasingly important role in Baptist worship and in spiritual formation. The first generation of Baptists, like their Puritan forebears, used only the Psalms in public worship and rejected hymn singing, since it entailed the use of popular songs. After a fierce controversy in the eighteenth century, however, Baptists have not only employed but contributed significantly to church music. Some of the most intimate religious experiences Baptists can account for appear in hymns they have written. "I am thine, O Lord, I have heard thy voice, And it told thy love to me"; Fanny Crosby (1823–1915) sang, "But I long to rise in the arms of faith, And be closer drawn to thee." Many have echoed too her tender plea: "Thou, my everlasting portion, More than friend or life to me; All along my pilgrim journey, Saviour, let me walk with thee." Next to Scriptures, the sermon has held the most important place in the corporate spirituality of Baptists. Like the Puritans, Baptists have viewed sincerity as the key to authentic preaching. All through their history in virtually every country, they have exhibited suspicion of pedantic and intellectual preaching. Sermons must come from the heart. On the frontier a strong anti-intellectual bias spiced this attitude further. "Among no other religious body was the prejudice against an educated and salaried ministry so strong as among the Baptists,"

W. W. Sweet has observed, "and this prejudice prevailed not only among frontier Baptists, but pretty generally throughout the denomination in the early years of the nineteenth century."[19] Sermons have supplied the faithful with much of the spiritual guidance they have received in Baptist churches. Sensitive pastors, keeping in touch with the needs of their constituencies, have encouraged, exhorted, rebuked, and directed the devout up mountains and through valleys and across plains and deserts. Some Baptists, of course, have not left decision making to chance. Conditioned by the revivals in the United States, they have given much attention to public invitations or altar calls. Southern Baptists have made a kind of sacrament out of the invitation, many considering the decision at the end of the service the *raison d'être* of prayers, Bible readings, sermons, and songs.

The Lord's Supper or Eucharist has not had a high level of importance in Baptist churches. Where Calvinist interpretation of it has prevailed, Baptists have observed it more often and treated it with greater solemnity than where Zwinglian interpretation dominates, as it does in much of the United States. In recent years Baptists in both England and the United States have tiptoed into the stream of liturgical renewal which developed in the thirties and forties.[20] Many congregations still hold communion infrequently, sometimes only once a year, but many others have increased the frequency and highlighted the observance.

Traditionally, Quaker worship has been silent, an exercise in waiting on God. Isaac Pennington, one of the early English leaders, articulated the Quaker quest in a letter "To the Women Friends of Armscot":

> In your meetings together to do service for the Lord, be every one of you very careful and diligent in watching to his power, that ye may have the sensible living feeling of it, each of you, in your own hearts, and in the hearts one of another; and that ye may keep within the limits of it, and not think, or speak, or act beyond it. And know, Oh, wait more and more to know, how to keep that silence which is of the power, that, in every one of you, what the power would have silent may be silent.[21]

While the tradition of silent worship has remained strong among eastern Quakers in the United States, in the Midwest it has yielded to more intentional styles similar to Baptist worship, replete with Scripture reading, public prayers, hymn singing, and sermons. Even there, silence still plays a role, though not as central a role as in eastern Quaker worship.

A Rearward Look

Treating Baptist and Quaker spiritualities alongside one another points up some of the deficiencies that have plagued them throughout their history as well as their real contributions. Like other Protestants, both have left responsibility for spiritual growth largely in the hands of the individual believer. In other words, they have been overly "hands off" in their approach. If one would range church groups across a spectrum from individualism and voluntarism, where the Holy Spirit is seen to effect obedience through the individual will, to corporatism and intentionalism, where the Holy Spirit is seen to effect obedience through the corporate will, at the beginning Baptists and Quakers would have occupied the extreme individualist/voluntarist end of the spectrum and Roman Catholics the extreme corporatist/intentionalist end. As nonconformists, whether in England, the American colonies, or elsewhere, both had good reason to react against uniformity as prohibitive of sincerity in religious commitment. Their individualism and voluntarism, however, have often ended up in selfish autonomist rather than theonomism, the rule of God. A study of Baptist and Quaker history will yield embarrassing proof of the point. There ought surely to be a point of balance between the two extremes such as that toward which Roman Catholics have moved since Vatican II.

Baptists have suffered here from an inadequate definition of grace in Protestant theology. The Reformers gave a too-limited definition of grace when they spoke of it as God's unmerited favor and failed to recognize that it also entails God's presence, power, and love through Holy Spirit. Fearful lest their followers lapse into legalism and Pelagianism, Protestants undercut the motive for Christian growth and development. Quakers have rendered an immeasurable service to Protestantism by reminding them again and again that the risen Christ is present to us in all his power, if only we will become attentive to him, the Light Within.

Quakers have paid a high price for their faithfulness here, however. Through three and a half centuries they have lost much of the enthusiasm that powered the movement of George Fox in England in the late seventeenth century. In consequence, today they number only about three hundred thousand worldwide. That many Friends have themselves recognized the problem is evident from the changes midwestern Quakers have introduced in patterns of worship and ministry. Quaker spirituality has had to become more intentional out of concern for survival.

Meanwhile, Baptists have raised some caution flags about going too far the other direction. Because of the impact of the religious revivals in America, some Baptists have placed their accent on conversion and have virtually ignored the growth process which should follow it. All too many persons remain spiritual infants or, at best, adolescents. The stronger Baptists' commitment to winning converts, the weaker their commitment to cultivation of the devout life. Prayer, Scriptures, worship, and other means of communion with God thus become pragmatic instruments for achieving the aims of the evangelistic enterprise.[22]

Although the deficiencies of Baptist and Quaker spirituality are serious and disturbing, there are signs of hope in this ecumenical era. Both Baptists and Quakers have been returning to the mainstream of spirituality to get in touch with their own heritage. Out of this search may come the pull toward center which will recify some of the imbalances of the past. At the same time Baptists and Quakers may share with the worldwide community of communions the insights about voluntariness and responsiveness to the Holy Spirit which brought them into being in the first place.

Notes

1. See D. Elton Trueblood, *Robert Barclay* (New York: Harper & Row, 1968) 241.

2. *Cistercian Studies* 20 (1985) 224–36.

3. Cf. Rufus Jones, *Studies in Mystical Religion* (London: Macmillan, 1906); *Quakerism: A Spiritual Movement,* 119ff. Jones admitted that George Fox would not *consciously* have borrowed from this tradition but argued that it was a part of "the peculiar religious atmosphere" in which Fox and the Quakers developed. Douglas Gwyn has offered a critique (*Apocalypse of the Word,* xiii–xvi).

4. *The Baptism Hymnal* (Nashville: Broadman, 1956). Not all hymns in this hymnal were composed by Baptists, to be sure, but their selection and inclusion confirm Baptist predilections.

5. See especially the summary of Fox's teaching in Gwyn, *Apocalypse of the Word,* 58–64. For Robert Barclay's reinterpretation, see Dean Freiday, *Nothing Without Christ,* 7–11.

6. John Bunyan, *The Pilgrim's Progress,* ed. E. Glenn Hinson (Doubleday Devotional Classics; Garden City, NY: Doubleday, 1978) I:387.

7. *The Journal of George Fox,* ed. E. Glenn Hinson (Doubleday Devotional Classics; Garden City, NY: Doubleday, 1978) II:29.

8. *The Journal of John Woolman,* ed. E. Glenn Hinson (Doubleday Devotional Classics; Garden City, NY: Doubleday, 1978) 213, 214, 216, 217.

9. Ibid., 224.

10. See my introductions to Woolman's *Journal,* ibid., II:197–212; see also E. H. Cady, *John Woolman: The Mind of the Quaker Saint* (New York: Washington Square Press, 1966); and Janet Whitney *John Woolman, American Quaker* (Boston: Little, Brown, 1942).

11. Woolman, *Journal,* 215.

12. *The Journal of George Fox,* ed. E. Glenn Hinson (Doubleday Devotional Classics; Garden City, NY: Doubleday, 1978) II:25.

13. Note especially the work of Elton Trueblood and the Yokefellows movement.

14. John Bunyan, *Grace Abounding* (London: SCM, 1955) 77, 117.

15. This classic has been reprinted with some other essays by Steere in *Gleanings* (Nashville: The Upper Room, 1987).

16. Margaret Fell, quoting Fox in a sermon, in *The Journal of George Fox,* 1694, I:ii; cited by D. Elton Trueblood, *The People Called Quakers,* 66.

17. Ibid., 67.

18. Thomas R. Kelly, *A Testament of Devotion* (New York: Harper & Row, 1941) 31–32.

19. William Warren Sweet, *Religion in the Development of American Culture* (New York: Scribner, 1952) 111; cf. Richard Hofstadter, *Anti-Intellectualism in American Life* (New York: Alfred A. Knopf, 1963) 104–5.

20. For British Baptists, see Neville Clark's *An Approach to the Theology of the Sacraments;* and Stephen F. Winward, *The Reformation of Our Worship.* For American Baptists, see Wayne A. Dalton, "Worship and Baptist Ecclesiology," *Foundations* 12 (1969) 7–18.

21. In *Quaker Spirituality,* ed. Douglas V. Steere (Classics of Western Spirituality; New York: Paulist, 1984) 154.

22. See the study of this problem by William Loyd Allen, "Spirituality among Southern Baptism Clergy as Reflected in Selected Autobiographies" (Ph.D. diss., The Southern Baptist Theological Seminary, 1984) 199–202.

Bibliography

Barbour, Hugh. *The Quakers in Puritan England.* New Haven: Yale University Press, 1964.

———, and A. O. Roberts, eds. *Early Quaker Writings.* Grand Rapids: Eerdmans, 1973.

Braithwaite, William C. *The Beginnings of Quakrism.* London: Macmillan, 1912. 2nd ed., 1970.

———. *The Second Period of Quakerism.* Cambridge: University Press, 1961.

Brayshaw, Alfred N. *The Quakers.* New York: Macmillan, 1927.

Clark, Neville. *An Approach to the Theology of the Sacraments.* Studies in Biblical Theology 17. Chicago: Allenson, 1956.

Dalton, Wayne A. "Worship and Baptism Ecclesiology." *Foundations* 12 (1969) 7–18.

Davies, Horton. *Laudian Worship and Theology in England from Andrewes to Baxter and Fox.* Princeton: Princeton University Press, 1975.

Freiday, Dean. *Nothing Without Christ.* Newberg, OR: Barclay, 1984.

Gwyn, Douglas. *Apocalypse of the Word.* Richmond, IN: Friends United Press, 1984.

Haller, William. *The Rise of Puritanism.* New York: Columbia University Press, 1938.

Hays, Brooks. *The Baptist Way of Life.* Macon, GA: Mercer University Press, 1987.

Hinson, E. Glenn. "Baptists and Spirituality: A Community at Worship." *Review and Expositor* 84 (1988) 649–58.

———. "Reassessing the Puritan Heritage in Worship/Spirituality: A Search for a Method." *Worship* 53 (1979) 318–26.

———. "Southern Baptist and Medieval Spirituality: Surprising Similarities." *Cistercian Studies* 20 (1985) 224–36.

Hudson, Winthrop S. *Baptism Concepts of the Church.* Chicago: Judson, 1959.

Jones, Rufus. *The Faith and Practice of the Quakers.* London: Methuen, 1949.

———. *Quakerism: A Spiritual Movement.* Philadelphia: Yearly Meeting of Friends, 1963.

Nuttall, Geoffrey F. *The Congregational Way.* Oxford: Blackwell, 1957.

———. *The Holy Spirit in Puritan Faith and Experience.* Oxford: Blackwell, 1946.

———. *The Puritan Spirit.* London: Epworth, 1967.

Rouner, Arthur A., Jr. *The Congregational Way of Life.* Englewood Cliffs, NJ: Prentice-Hall, 1960.

Steere, Douglas V., ed. *Quaker Spirituality.* New York: Paulist, 1984.

Trueblood, D. Elton. *The People Called Quakers.* New York: Harper & Row, 1966.

Watkins, O. C. *The Puritan Experience.* London: Routledge & Kegan Paul, 1972.

Watts, Michael R. *The Dissenters: From the Reformation to the French Revolution.* Oxford: Clarendon Press, 1978.

Winward, Stephen. *The Reformation of Our Worship.* London: Carey Kingsgate Press, 1964.

III. *Puritan Spirituality in America*

CHARLES HAMBRICK-STOWE

THE RISE OF PURITANISM in England as a reaction to the perceived formalism of the Church of England and its transmigration to North America beginning in 1620 were events integrally connected with the general revival of spiritual practice and experience in both Protestantism and Catholicism in seventeenth-century Europe. Modern discussion of Puritan spirituality, however, is relatively new, because scholars have overly emphasized the dogmatic theology and the social outlook of the movement. Puritanism was a movement within the Calvinist or Reformed theological tradition. Its spirituality, therefore, was colored by the particular emphases of the Genevan Reformer: the sovereignty of God, human sinfulness, God's free grace in Christ, the response of the saved to live in a godly fashion and transform society according to God's will. Puritans also shared with Anglicans, Lutherans, Roman Catholics, and others in the Reformed tradition a primary interest in the cultivation of personal religious experience within a holy community or church. Far from being a period of dead scholasticism and ecclesiastical institutionalism, the seventeenth century represents a flowering of Western spirituality. American Puritanism must be understood within this religious context.

"Spirituality" as a word is apparently French Catholic in origin, perhaps going back only to the seventeenth century in that language. Although Puritans did not use the word, they most certainly spoke and wrote at great length about that aspect of their religion which the word "spirituality" now denotes in English. In sermons, devotional manuals, diaries, private poetry, autobiographies, letters, and other writings, Puritans described their personal approach to and encounters with God. American Puritans used several terms for this experiential side of their faith: piety, devotion, godly or heavenly conversation, spiritual exercises, pilgrimage of the soul, and spiritual warfare. None of these terms is uniquely Puritan or Reformed; all were rooted firmly in the Bible and in Catholic tradition and were used by all churches and movements in seventeenth-century Christianity. But through the century, the practice of piety acquired some distinctively Puritan and American characteristics.

Saints in the World:
The Goal and Process of Sanctification

Puritan devotionalism exemplifies the dictum of Pierre Pourrat that three branches of theology are interdependent: dogmatic theology, spiritual theology, and moral theology. Doctrine not only provides a language and interpretive framework for spiritual experience; it shapes experience itself. Similarities between Puritan and Catholic encounters with the divine may be explained by the considerable amount of Christian theology they shared. American Puritan diary accounts of self-examination and meditation on sin differ little from the sentiment of the Ignatian *Spiritual Exercises*. Both Teresa of Avila and Cotton Mather recounted angelic visitations and the flight of their souls heavenward. Puritans and Catholics in meditation on the cross or the Sacred Heart experienced the presence of Christ. On the other hand, no Puritan ever reported a vision of the Blessed Virgin Mary. Since she had no place in their theology, she played no role in their devotions.

Dogmatic and spiritual theology further helped shape Puritan moral theology, notably through the idea of the covenant. Puritanism was from the start a personal faith, but never private or mystical if those words suggest the removal of the individual from the world. Covenantal theology, which Puritans developed fully in New England, provided the social and ethical context within which individuals lived and prayed. The believer was a member of a family, a trade, a neighborhood, a town, perhaps a militia company, and a commonwealth. This social covenant not only bound persons together in civil society; it was considered a spiritual bond. Bible reading, preaching, catechism, psalm singing, prayer, and other devotional activities had an important place in the public ritual life of the New England colonies. American Puritans considered the church, above all else, to be not an arm of the state (as with the Church of England) or the domain of a prelate (as with the Roman Catholic Church), but a spiritual covenant established by God and organized ("gathered") by lay believers or saints. Based on the covenant of grace between God and the individual, the church covenant bound believers together for the purposes of worshiping God, converting others to Christ and hence joining them to the church, and enabling the spiritual growth of believers toward the goal of spiritual perfection in heaven. Only within the social and church covenants—within what could be considered moral theology—could the saints make such progress, in a process described theologically as sanctification.

Sanctification was a stage in the extremely detailed Puritan order of salvation worked out by English theologians such as William Perkins and William Ames and American preachers like Richard Mather, Thomas Hooker, Thomas Shepherd, and John Cotton. Each preacher presented his own version of the scheme, but, since most had studied at Cambridge University under the same mentors and since all followed the same biblical patterns, they were unanimous in the basic outline. American Puritan preacher-theologians set forth a two-part order of salvation: preparation for and implantation into Christ. In the preparatory stages the soul was cut off from sin through contrition and humiliation (with subsidiary stages within each). Ministers were emphatic that the unregenerate sinner could do nothing to prepare himself for salvation, because of the entire corruption of the person. Preparation for conversion was *of* a sinner *by* God alone. But as the Holy Spirit began to stir up a heart to contrition God would lead the person to church and begin to open the heart through the means of grace. These means included sermons, Bible reading, and the other elements of public worship. When the penitent sinner had undergone thorough humiliation, often a violent and tortured spiritual experience leading to despair of any hope of salvation, the heart was ready to receive the promise of God's grace in Christ. At this point the person began the second part of the drama, implantation into Christ.

Sainthood in New England's "gathered churches" did not mean that all church members were far progressed toward perfection or that the work of redemption was complete in their souls. A notebook kept by Thomas Shepherd, pastor in Cambridge, Massachusetts, demonstrates that persons admitted to the church covenant were usually at the point of implantation. That is, they spoke of their contrition and repentance for sin, of their humiliation in sin (their knowledge that they were helpless to save themselves), of God's stirring of their heart with the word that Christ died to forgive sin, and of their hope that this gracious salvation could be theirs. Few spoke of one absolute moment of conversion. Most spoke of their sense that they were making progress toward such certainty and their knowledge that Christ died for their justification. All of them testified to continued spiritual trials and vicissitudes as they looked forward hopefully to the stages of implantation in Christ. Implantation began with the believer's vocation of "effectual calling" by God, and continued through "growth in grace" toward full union with God. Vocation awakened a repulsion from sin, a fear of evil and disgust at sinfulness, and an attraction to the good. Hope, desire for Christ, faith in God, love, and joy stirred increasingly in the soul. Sanctification was the biblical term Puritans used to describe the progress of the saint (the one being made holy) toward perfect union in Christ. Perfection awaited the saint only in heaven, in the final stage of the order of salvation, glorification.

Sanctification was a gradual process by which the saint, while living in the world (in contrast to the cloistered monk or nun of Catholicism), experienced God's transforming power within the secular world. Reformed Protestants like the American Puritans modified classic spirituality by applying it to a new worldly setting, while retaining traditional language, methods, and manuals. Puritan contemplatives (the most earnest ministers and laity) and ordinary faithful alike looked to the stuff of daily life as the starting point and catalyst of meditation and prayer. Theirs was a spirituality not of would-be tertiaries who retreated as best they could from the world, but of householders. As husbandmen and housewives, Puritans would not leave behind the people and things they loved, nor did they believe God wanted them to even if they could. There was no spiritual distinction between clergy and laity; all were called to sainthood and all lived and moved and had their being in Christ and, sanctified, in the world. Ministers, therefore, were no spiritual elite. The exercises they practiced were the very ones they directed their flocks to undertake. American Puritanism was a popular, lay spirituality.

Calvin's doctrine of sanctification played a key role in the development of Puritan spirituality. While the Catholic saint often was considered an extraordinarily gifted mystic separated from the world, the Puritan saint was an ordinary believer being sanctified by God living and praying in the world. According to Puritan theologians in England and America, God sanctified people for life in this world, for proper creaturely enjoyment and fulfillment in preparation for the more lasting joys of heaven. Through God's Spirit, things and relationships even became means of grace. Sanctification was the doctrinal vehicle for a spirituality of the householder in which devotion began with the consideration of physical reality.

Yet this world, Puritans knew, was transitory, and love of the creatures led to grief. Earthen vessels, created by God and sanctified for human use, were bound to die and decay. Here is the crisis that underlay Puritan spirituality. Householders were subject to the grief of losing those persons and things with which God blessed their lives. Devotional acts sparked by grief and humility became for Puritans the means of a deeper sanctification. They still did not abandon the things of this world, but humbly offered them up to the transcendent God. Devotional manuals cautioned the Puritan to travel this world as "a stranger and a pilgrim," not to look for ultimate meaning in any created things. Puritanism was thus a spirituality of "weaned affections," rooted always in this world but reaching toward the other world. This world's dynamic matrix of change and challenge was the setting for the life of prayer. Puritan spirituality is characterized by its effort to embrace worldly aspirations, social and political goals, family love, vocational responsibility, and the pain of loss, and to seek in faithful prayer God's eternal word of hope.

Preparation for salvation was a dominant theme in American Puritan spirituality. Preparationism was not limited to the first part of the order of salvation, however. The whole life of the believer after conversion (that is, from implantation and vocation), the process of progressive sanctification, was one of preparation for the full and final union of the soul with Christ in glory. The practice of piety—spirituality—fueled the soul for this life-long journey through a daily and weekly regimen of devotional activity.

The meditations and prayers of American Puritans differed in only subtle ways from their English counterparts, as witness the enormous popularity of English and Continental devotional manuals in New England. Works such as John Bunyan's *The Pilgrim's Progress* were deemed so universal that Boston publishers printed American editions. But certain distinctively American characteristics also emerged on this side of the Atlantic. Chief of these was the centrality of the biblical exodus theme in their interpretation of personal spiritual progress and of the meaning of the New England sociopolitical enterprise. Just as the Hebrew people, cruelly persecuted in Egypt, fled through the Red Sea and the wilderness to freedom in Canaan, the Puritans were persecuted for their beliefs in England, fled across the ocean, and now sojourned in a wilderness. Although some colonists equated America with the Promised Land, spiritual writers more often saw their settlement in the quite real "howling wilderness" as reminiscent of Israel's time of trial in preparation for arrival in Canaan. The Promised Land, therefore, was understood spiritually as either heaven, achieved after death, or the eschatological kingdom of God, which Puritans believed would soon be established. New England Puritans, bound in covenant like Israel, understood themselves as God's new Israel. Some church members testified upon joining the church that they viewed the sea passage as a renunciation of sin and a commitment to a new life of holiness. The ministers insisted that no mere physical removal could change a person's heart, but they nevertheless saw the migration as emblematic of the spiritual change which many were undergoing at God's hand.

The exodus theme was a powerful image in public and private devotional activity for the first generation of colonists. The second generation, with its ministers trained not at Cambridge but at Harvard and with no experience of persecution, longed for the intensity of the founders' experience. Some young Harvard graduates, like Increase Mather, actually migrated to England and taught and preached there for a time in order to taste persecution before sailing back to commence a New England pastoral career. By the third generation, with ministers like Peter Thatcher, the trip to England was simply a post-graduation tourist holiday. New biblical images became necessary to undergird Puritan spirituality in America. The captivity narrative, exemplified by Mary Rowlandson's account of her ordeal among Indian captives (*The Sovereignty and Goodness of God,* 1682), provided such an indigenous theme. Echoing Israel's Babylonian captivity and redemption, the experiences of women like Rowlandson became emblematic of the soul's captivity to sin and redemption by Christ. For every generation of New Englanders through the seventeenth century, therefore, the theme of the wilderness played a key role in their spirituality, although the use of that image shifted over time. The distinctively American integration of the wilderness image also fit perfectly with the more basic order of salvation with its two stages of preparation and implantation.

God's Presence in the Community: The Means of Grace

Puritan devotional practice in New England centered on the use of traditional "means of grace" through which God communicated himself. While radical Puritans, like the "antinomian" Anne Hutchinson, and Quakers believed that God could be experienced directly without any physical aids, orthodoxy held that unrooted spiritualism was not only theologically wrong but that the desire for an "immediate revelation" was unreliable and devotionally dangerous. Puritans denied both the Catholic doctrine of the efficacy of the forms in themselves and the Arminian doctrine of human capability of salvation through self-willed use of forms. But they believed that ordinarily ("in common course") God could most surely be expected to be present in certain prescribed ritual activity. These ecclesiastical "ordinances" included the concept of "the church" itself and all that went on there each sabbath. Among the means of grace were the sacraments of baptism and the Lord's Supper, the ministry of the Word (reading of and preaching from the Bible), public prayer, psalm singing, days of fasting and of thanksgiving (which were proclaimed periodically, usually seasonally), covenant making (as in the gathering of a new church or the joining of new members), and covenant renewal (a particularly important ritual in the second and third generations). The rituals of public worship took place principally on the sabbath, with two three-hour services every week.

Psalm singing was an important activity of both public worship and private devotion. In the New England meetinghouse of the 1630s the psalters of Sternhold and Hopkins (1562) and Henry Ainsworth (1612) were used, but in 1640 the momentous *Bay Psalm Book* (officially titled, *The Whole Booke of Psalmes*) was published at the new press in Cambridge, Massachusetts. This product of American Puritan scholarship achieved a remarkably accurate and literal translation of the psalter in English meter. If its cadences today seem monotonous, it encouraged memorization and easy participation by all. The ministers encouraged the composition and use of nonbiblical "spiritual songs" and accompaniment with musical instruments in private devotions, but in public worship they limited their congregations to the unaccompanied singing of lyrics found in Scripture. Although many in the congregation owned a copy of the psalter, a lay ruling elder "lined out" the psalm orally so all could participate, literate and illiterate, wealthy and poor. Thus, congregational singing was popular singing, and the phrases of the psalms were etched indelibly in the minds of worshipers.

Prayers, like sermons, were about an hour in length and rehearsed again and again the cycle of sin and redemption, repentance and forgiveness, emptying of self and filling with grace. They contained much rational exposition of Scripture and the themes of the order of salvation. In accordance with the Puritan "plain style," New England preachers avoided flowery rhetoric, but they were capable of a forceful and logical eloquence. In both public prayers and in sermons, their sophisticated use of biblical imagery aimed to bring worshipers into the history of salvation, the orb of God's grace. For God's Spirit to move, Puritans believed, the preacher must not be tied to forms of prayer such as those found in the abhorred Book of Common Prayer of the Church of England. Public prayer was to be "free" or "conceived" in the pastor's heart and responsive to the immediate needs of worshipers and the social situation. Ministers prayed specifically for the conversion and growth in grace of those present in the congregation, for the harvest, for current events. Styles of public prayer varied among ministers, but all worked from a common biblical vocabulary and adhered to the general pattern of the order of redemption.

The preaching and hearing of the sermon were the central acts of American Puritan worship. The rhetorical style was "plain" in that sermons were to follow an accepted outine, be clearly understood, powerfully delivered, soundly argued according to orthodox doctrine, and replete with biblical imagery and allusions. Preaching was a primary means of grace, a "converting ordincance," an occasion when God was considered to be

14. Eunice Pinney, *The Cotters Saturday Night*, c. 1815.

especially present and at work. In seventeenth-century New England sermons, following the reading of the Bible, the text was "opened" in exegesis, doctrines were extracted and "propounded," theoretical objections were refuted, and, finally, applications or "uses" were put forth. These included "uses" of comfort, terror, and exhortation. Preachers often concluded with emotionally compelling exhortations, inspiring flights of alliterative and poetic rhetoric, and even a "chanted" style more often associated with radical spiritualistic groups.

The administration of the sacraments of Baptism and Holy Communion constituted "the seals of the covenant" in American Puritan churches. The two sacraments corresponded to the two stages of the redemptive cycle, preparation and growth in grace. Early New Englanders baptized only children at least one of whose parents was in the covenant. With the second and third generations, the problem of baptism for children of outwardly righteous and intellectually faithful but unconverted baptized parents resulted in the gradual adoption in some churches of the "halfway covenant." The ministers' desire to baptize such children was motivated by a devotional concern, that they be as fully involved as possible in the system of Puritan spirituality. Baptists, a small but growing minority through the seventeenth century except in Rhode Island, where they flourished, dealt with the question by restricting the ordinance to converted adults. The Lord's Supper, ideally celebrated monthly but often less frequently, was far more important to American Puritan spirituality than has usually been supposed. Vessels ranged from wooden chargers and plain pewter cups to exquisite silver plates and chalices, with the trend toward finer designs as the century progressed. Sacramental piety infused both public worship and private devotion, with much emphasis placed on the individual's preparation for the sacrament in daily private devotion for a week prior to its administration. Puritans believed in the real spiritual presence of Christ with the elements, not in a shallow memorialism. The devout experienced Christ himself and received again the promises of salvation as they ate and drank in faith.

God's Presence to Believers: Private Devotional Practices

The practice of private devotion lay at the heart of Puritan spirituality. This practice was carried out in a variety of settings, including regular "private meetings" of believers in homes, "family exercises," private counseling and prayer sessions with a trusted mentor, and individual "secret exercises."

Ministers organized private meetings, dividing congregations into neighborhood or occupational groups. Although the minister was often present at these meetings, lay people usually led the exercises, which included Bible reading and exposition, psalm singing, and prayer. Women's groups, led by women themselves, were popular throughout the century. Only when women attempted to teach men or when heterodoxy was suspected, as with the 1636 meetings led by Anne Hutchinson, did the clergy intervene and assert their control. The fragmentary records extant suggest that American Puritan women enjoyed a spiritual subculture parallel to and largely unknown by their husbands and pastors., Women's spirituality, as the poetry of Anne Bradstreet and scattered references in the diaries of men suggest, was nurtured by their separate roles in society, including childbirth and midwifery, domestic and financial management, funeral preparation, and nursing. Diary entries by both clergy and laity testify to the devotional importance to spiritual growth of the home meetings for both men and women. Laity exercised their abilities to pray and counsel one another in this setting.

Puritan spirituality was heavily concentrated on the family. Indeed, the comparison between the Puritan family and the Catholic monastery has merit. In New England society no one lived alone. Single individuals lived with a family, coming under its economic and spiritual care. Children served apprenticeships in families, and vocational and professional training all took place within the family setting. Fathers served as "priests," although mothers and other adults also shared responsibility for leading family worship. Catechetical instruction (many ministers wrote catechisms for both children and adults), psalm singing, devotional reading (of the Bible, devotional manuals, published sermons), and family prayer formed the content of these exercises both morning and evening. Devotions during the day centered on mealtime, with prayers before and after eating. Ministers spent as much time as they could afford monitoring the progress of family devotions in their churches, periodically visiting to offer advice on how best to conduct the sessions.

"Private conferences"—sessions with a mentor or spiritual director—were an expression of the membership of each believer in the covenant. Parents with children, masters with apprentices, teachers and Harvard tutors with students, older women with girls and young women—indeed, every church member— had a responsibility to care for the spiritual welfare of others. Ministers engaged in spiritual counseling as part of their calling, but they also encouraged everyone to find a "spiritual friend" other than a minister with whom to confide and pray. Although one most often sought such a relationship in time of spiritual struggle, crisis, or melancholy, diary entries also attest to high spiritual attainment resulting from intimate sharing and guidance.

Individual devotion among American Puritans consisted of a variety of "secret" exercises. The three major activities were reading, meditation, and prayer, conducted in that order. Reading centered on the Bible. American Puritans continued to use the sixteenth-century Geneva Bible in combination with the *Bay Psalm Book* until late in the seventeenth century when the Authorized Version (1611) gained popularity. Research has shown that New England was highly literate, both in comparison to colonial Virginia and to England. In Europe as a whole, Protestants were more literate than Roman Catholics; Reformed Protestants, including English and American Puritans, achieved the highest literacy rates of all. One reason was the strong emphasis of Puritanism on lay responsibility for its own spiritual progress. Reading was understood as the single most effective way to spread an acceptance of the gospel. Besides firsthand knowledge of the Bible, ministers were concerned that Puritans understand the rudiments of doctrine and participate in approved devotional activity. Collections of sermons and, most significant for spiritual development, devotional manuals poured off Puritan presses in England (imported in large numbers to America) and New England. The classics of the early seventeenth century included Lewis Bayly's *The Practice of Piety,* Arthur Dent's *The Plaine Mans Pathway to Heaven,* and John Downame's *A Guide to Godlynesse.* In 1650 Richard Baxter in England published his enormously influential *Saints Everlasting Rest,* which sparked renewed interest in meditation and prayer in the second half of the century. In New England, ministers like Edward Taylor and Cotton Mather were guided by Baxter's systematic approach to spirituality. Manuals were published in large printings, and ministers made every attempt to assist in their wider distribution.

In Puritan spirituality, meditation built upon the exercise of reading. In meditation the believer applied the text under consideration (the text preached on the previous sabbath or the text of the day in a regular program of Bible reading) to his or her own soul. Formal or "ordinary" meditation involved the successive application of the passage or topic to each of the human faculties: from cognition and memory to conscience, affections, and will. Using a technique similar to the Catholic "composition of place," Puritans aimed to move the object of meditation from the mind to the heart. They engaged in meditation at regular times, morning and evening, with additional "extraordinary" or "occasional" times of meditation for the especially devout or when circumstances warranted.

Meditation often began with self-examination, identification, and consideration of one's sins. This examination of one's conscience particularly characterized nocturnal meditations, as one scrutinized the day before retiring. Since sleep reminded Puritans of death, the bed an emblem of the grave, they earnestly confessed each sin to God in preparation for his judgment. Further, during certain devotional sessions—on a Saturday evening in preparation for the sabbath, a fast day, the new year, or a birthday, for example—self-examination would be the entire focus of activity. On these occasions, Puritans prepared for the last judgment by meditating on the first stage of the order of salvation, repentance and separation from sin. New England Puritans were not trapped in a morbid spirituality of mortification, however, since repentance led to a renewed experience of God's grace and love. Morning meditations, utilizing the symbolism of rising from the bed and greeting the rising sun, were full of joy, expressive of God's promise of abundant and eternal life. In meditation on the sabbath or special days of thanksgiving, the lofty spiritual flights and soul-ravishing experiences associated with Catholic spiritual exercises were shared by American Puritans.

One other meditative technique achieved currency among New Englanders, that of "spiritualizing the creatures." The English spiritual writer John Flavel promoted the activity in England, and his works were imported, while Cotton Mather and others in New England wrote books and preached on it in America. This method, well-suited for occasional and informal meditation, focused attention on some aspect of nature or human experience, seeking out a spiritual meaning (e.g., as the flame rises from the candle, so our thoughts should ascend to God).

Secret prayer was the apex of Puritan spirituality, the culmination of private exercises every evening and morning. Recalling the classic text of Matthew 6:6, Puritans sought regular times of spiritual privacy. It may well be that "closet prayer" was the one opportunity most individuals in seventeenth-century America had to be completely alone. Although ministers eschewed printed or set prayers in public worship, they encouraged their use for private devotion, at least as guides for beginners and models for free prayer as believers progressed spiritually. Some diaries, such as those of Thomas Shepherd and Cotton Mather, and some extant poetry, such as that of Anne Bradstreet and Edward Taylor, are the record of secret exercises in meditation and prayer.

New England Puritans believed in the efficacy of prayer. Confession of sin was the necessary first step in spiritual development: it was to be repeated daily, especially in evening devotions. Only if one sincerely repented in prayer could one expect to experience God's grace. Further, prayer was believed to sway the future. The conversion of a family member, the survival and healing of a sick person, the beneficial outcome of a social crisis all depended on the prayers of the faithful. Finally, prayer was the means of the soul's communion with God. New England Puritans, both clergy and laity, knew what Catholic spiritual writers called unitive states.

Diary accounts and meditative poems describe the experience of the soul's being melted, filled, or "irradiated" by the Holy Spirit, and elevated to the heavens.

Puritans engaged in ejaculatory prayer in ways not unlike Roman Catholics. This practice of spontaneous or constant breathing of short prayers was well-suited to the this-worldly activism of American Puritanism, with its emphasis on the sanctification of everyday life. Ejaculatory prayer was often the outgrowth of occasional meditation with "spiritualizing the creatures." Believers uttered brief prayers—often mere phrases—of thanksgiving, petition, or intercession in the midst of secular activity in immediate response to events or people encountered. Puritans also used ejaculatory prayer at night, in deep spiritual encounters at the end of an evening's session of secret meditation and prayer, perhaps while lying in bed before falling asleep. Spiritual autobiographies, diaries, and poems attest to personal experiences of Christ at these moments and the believer's response in phrases like "He is come!" and "Come, dear bridegroom!"

Aids to Devotion: Manuals, Diaries, Poetry, and Biographies

Having discussed the underlying principles, the physical and temporal settings, and the major devotional acts in the American Puritan practice of piety, we turn finally to the materials commonly used by American Puritans in their spiritual exercises.

The first of these, already mentioned above, is books. American Puritanism created a bibliophile culture in which books were considered to be means of grace, signs of God's desire to reveal himself. The Bible was the premier devotional book of Puritanism, but devotional manuals were a close second. These manuals contained expositions of spiritual theology and collections of model prayers. Believers meditated and prayed, in family devotions and in secret, with these books in their hands. In additional to the text, many devotional manuals also included iconographic title pages, frontispieces, and printer's ornaments at chapter heads. The elaborate title page of John Downame's popular manual, *The Christian Warfare Against the Devill, World, and Flesh* (London, 1634) contains half a dozen symbolic figures depicting the worldly man, Satan, virtue, and the victorious Christian. The title page of Lewis Bayly's *The Practice of Piety* (London, 1620) has exemplars of faith, prayer, and fasting along with traditional medieval emblems of mortality (skull, hourglass, wings), prayer (burning heart on an altar), and spiritual reading (candle and book on stand). A printer's ornament at the head of the first page of Increase Mather's exhortation to covenant renewal ceremonies, *Returning unto God the Great Concernment of a Covenant People* (Boston, 1680) shows a skeleton climbing out of a casket, flanked by trumpet-blowing cherubs. Books, thus, were in themselves objects of meditation, through both the text and the accompanying illustrative material. Diaries and autobiographies reveal that favorite books were reread hundreds and hundreds of times, becoming inscribed as a well-loved icon in the believer's consciousness.

The use of physical objects and pictures as means of meditation is commonly associated with Catholic spirituality, but American Puritans made use of them as well. Ministers like the poet Edward Taylor sat before the communion elements and vessels in meditation on Saturday nights prior to administering Holy Communion. Diaries and private poetry suggest that New Englanders used the traditional *memento mori* (symbols of death) in their devotional mortification, confession of sin, and preparation for death. Puritans meditated before objects such as hourglasses, human skulls, funeral rings engraved with death's heads, caskets of family members, and gravestones. Emblem books such as Francis Quarles's *Emblemes, Divine and Moral* (London, 1635) circulated and inspired imitators among New England poets, funeral broadside printers, and gravestone carvers. Iconography is an aspect of Puritan piety which has only recently come to light but which was very much a part of their spirituality.

As American Puritans were guided in their exercises by devotional manuals, they were themselves eager to record their practices and experiences in writing. Diary or journal keeping was a distinctively, though certainly not uniquely, Puritan phenomenon. New Englanders kept diaries for entirely secular reasons (for financial, weather, or travel records), but many believers did keep a spiritual record. Diaries recorded daily Bible readings, attendance at neighborhood devotional meetings, family prayers, prayers during milestone events such as births and deaths, spiritual crises, ecstatic experiences, periodic full examinations of conscience, and other exercises. Scholars have pointed to the similarity between the Roman Catholic confessional and the Puritan diary. Diary keeping was a spiritual exercise, integrally connected with meditation and prayer, but the diary then became an object of devotion itself. Puritans poured over old diary entries, in an exercise called "reading the evidence," as a way of achieving greater levels of assurance of grace.

The writing of private devotional poetry, similar in its motivation to diary keeping, was an important New England Puritan activity. The remarkable poems of Edward Taylor, unknown until 1937, bear resemblances to those of Anglican George Herbert and European "metaphysical" poets. Taylor's passionate longing for Christ belies the stereotype of

Puritans as grim rationalists. His poems reveal him in the act of meditation on Saturday night in preparation for the sabbath. Anne Bradstreet's private poetry, too, opens a window into her soul. Poetry for her, and for other New Englanders whose more amateurish poetry is extant, was an expression of spirituality. She wrote her prayers out as poems—for her husband's safe return, in grief for a dead grandchild, at the loss of her house to fire, etc.—as she offered them to God. Some of Bradstreet's poems then served her as devotional aids later. She wrote meditative poems in the meter of the psalter, for example, suggesting that she actually sang these poems to God in her secret devotions. Poetic references also indicate that she went back over old poems in meditation, as Puritans also went over old diary entries or gazed on a physical object as a *memento mori*. Poetry was popular among New Englanders and many wrote it, especially to mark an important event such as a funeral. Poems gave expression to meditation and prayer and then became themselves the focus for further spiritual reflection.

Spiritual autobiography was related to diary keeping in that diaries, not memory, formed the basis of an aged believer's autobiography. As with the diary, the act of writing one's spiritual life story was a devotional exercise intended as a means of grace for the writer. Spiritual autobiography was most clearly a way of preparing for death, judgment, and glory. But American Puritans who left autobiographical statements most often did so as a legacy for younger generations. In New England, as in any religious community, the problem of declension with the passing of the founders weighed upon the minds of the elders. Those who recorded their spiritual pilgrimage hoped that it would serve as a kind of devotional manual for children and grandchildren who would then keep the faith of the founders alive. Spiritual autobiographies were revered so much that some, such as the *Memoirs of Capt. Roger Clap* (Boston, 1731) were soon published to achieve a wider readership. Others, such as the scraps of Anne Bradstreet's autobiographical narratives written for her children, circulated within the family.

History and biography became important to New England spirituality for the same reasons as did spiritual autobiography. Although in the early years of settlement, and for English Puritanism generally, John Foxe's *Acts and Monuments*—or *Book of Martyrs*, as it was popularly called (first published London, 1563)—fueled faith and practice, in late seventeenth-century New England the stories of the people and events of the first two generations formed a mythic self-consciousness and a keen sense of a New England spirituality. Although devotional manuals and other religious literature continued to be imported and reprinted in New England, and despite Cotton Mather's correspondence with leading German Pietists, by the end of the century spirituality tended toward parochialism. The experience of Christian faith not only defined persons as individuals, saints, and church members, but as New Englanders. This process was a defensive reaction against the secularization and rising diversity of society; it helped catalyze major eighteenth-century events, notably the Great Awakening and the American Revolution.

Bibliography

Bercovitch, Sacvan. *The Puritan Origins of the American Self.* New Haven: Yale University Press, 1975.

Caldwell, Patricia. *The Puritan Conversion Narrative: The Beginnings of American Expression.* New York: Cambridge University Press, 1983.

Daly, Robert. *God's Altar: The World and the Flesh in Puritan Poetry.* Berkeley and Los Angeles: University of California Press, 1978.

Elliott, Emory. *Power and the Pulpit in Puritan New England.* Princeton: Princeton University Press, 1975.

Hall, David D. *The Faithful Shepherd: A History of the New England Ministry in the Seventeenth Century.* Chapel Hill: University of North Carolina Press, 1972.

Hambrick-Stowe, Charles E. *The Practice of Piety: Puritan Devotional Disciplines in Seventeenth-Century New England.* Chapel Hill: University of North Carolina Press, 1982.

Holifield, E. Brooks. *The Covenant Sealed: The Development of Puritan Sacramental Theology in Old and New England, 1570–1720.* New Haven: Yale University Press, 1974.

Keller, Karl. *The Example of Edward Taylor.* Amherst: University of Massachusetts Press, 1975.

Miller, Perry. *The New England Mind: The Seventeenth Century.* New York: Macmillan, 1939.

———. *The New England Mind: From Colony to Province.* Cambridge, MA: Harvard University Press, 1953.

Morgan, Edmund S. *The Puritan Family: Religion and Domestic Relations in Seventeenth-Century New England.* New York: Harper & Row, 1966.

Silverman, Kenneth. *The Life and Times of Cotton Mather.* New York: Harper & Row, 1984.

Simpson, Alan. *Puritanism in Old and New England.* Chicago: University of Chicago Press, 1955.

Ulrich, Laurel Thatcher. *Good Wives: Image and Reality in the Lives of Women in Northern New England, 1650–1750.* New York: Knopf, 1982.

Ziff, Larzer. *Puritanism in America.* New York: Viking; London: Oxford University Press, 1973.

11

Spiritual Vision and Discipline in the Early Wesleyan Movement

DAVID TRICKETT

ITHIN THE SPECTRUM of the Christian witness, one of the rays of spiritual light that is now coming into clearer focus is a movement known variously as the Methodist movement or the Wesleyan witness. This distinctive witness did not spring into being *sui generis;* it began as something of a reform movement within the Church of England, and it is within the rich Anglican heritage that many of its roots can be found.

John Wesley (1703–1791), *paterfamilias* of the Methodist movement, was reared in a household wherein biblical, Anglican, and Puritan spiritual insights were part of daily life.[1] Over the course of time, his spiritual nourishment included not only the Edwardian homilies and immersion in the Book of Common Prayer but also a number of significant devotional writings.[2] Several of these works seem to stand above the rest: Jeremy Taylor's *Holy Living* (1650) and *Holy Dying* (1651); *The Imitation of Christ,* usually attributed to Thomas à Kempis (and likely written in the first quarter of the fifteenth century); and two works by a contemporary, William Law: *A Practical Treatise Upon Christian Perfection* (1726) and *A Serious Call to a Devout and Holy Life* (1728). About a half century after this rich formative period in his spiritual pilgrimage, Wesley recorded the significance of his discovery of this body of literature:

In the year 1725, being in the twenty-third year of my age, I met with Bishop Taylor's "Rule and Exercises of Holy Living and Dying." In reading several parts of this book, I was exceedingly affected; that part in particular which relates to purity of intention. Instantly I resolved to dedicate all my life to God, all my thoughts, and words, and actions; being thoroughly convinced, there was no medium; but that every part of my life (and not some only) must either be a sacrifice to God, or myself, that is, in effect, to the devil. . . .

In the year 1726, I met with Kempis's "Christian Pattern." The nature and extent of inward religion, the religion of the heart, now appeared to me in a stronger light than ever it had done before. I saw, that giving even all my life to God (supposing it possible to do this, and go no farther) would profit me nothing, unless I gave my heart, yea, all my heart to him.

I saw that "simplicity of intention, and purity of affection," one design in all we speak or do, and one desire ruling all our tempers, are indeed "the wings of the soul," without which she can never ascend to the mount of God.

A year or two after, Mr. Law's "Christian Perfection" and "Serious Call" were put into my hands. These convinced me, more than ever, of the absolute impossibility of being half a Christian; and I determined, through his grace (the absolute necessity of which I was deeply sensible of [sic]) to be all-devoted to God, to give him all my soul, my body, and my substance.[3]

These major writings helped to stir Wesley in such a way that considerations such as vision, intention, sacrifice (and its implicit correlate, discipline), inward experience, and single-mindedness became absolutely crucial early in his life. They were present in the spiritual climate of the "holy club" in Oxford, and they remained important elements in the subsequent Methodist revival.

Another book that contributed to the spiritual formation of Wesley was *The Whole Duty of Man*. This work had appeared anonymously in 1657, and by the time Wesley appeared on the scene it had exerted a profound influence on many parts of the Anglican communion. The work is relatively simple and focuses on what it may mean for people to live the faith they verbally profess. Expounding sections of the Book of Common Prayer and the Decalogue, it attempts to help communicants discern their responsibilities ("duties") to God and their neighbors. It stresses accountability, which is a theme that has a fundamental role within the early Wesleyan witness. This accountability is given significant depth by the book's keeping before its readers the liturgical insight that a person exercises his or her discipleship while communing with God and one's neighbors; one's embodiment of faith is without question lived in the presence of God and a community of fellow human beings. By regular participation in, say, the eucharistic liturgy, men and women are existentially "centered" in such a way that they are empowered by the spirit of God within them to live courageously, to persevere, and to embody authentically their "whole duty."

The web of influential sources that affected John Wesley is considerably complex. Wesley undertook a regular program of such wide-ranging reading that in addition to his own immediate Anglican traditions and certain Puritan sources, he knew quite a number of patristic authors (and, indeed, was especially sensitive to certain major themes from orthodoxy, perhaps the most important of which was the idea of "participation"), something of the continental reformers, and the like. The account given here has had to be selective. Wesley also turned to a significant number of authors who tend to be overlooked by many today. Three from this company are worthy of brief mention here. Robert Nelson helped to form Wesley's sense of the importance of the relationship between liturgy and spiritual disciplines such as fasting and prayer—all viewed from the communal ecclesial perspective.[4] Among other things, William Beveridge taught Wesley to see the power of prayer not only in the high holy festivals of the church but also in all the "common" moments of an individual's and of the community's life—and that the two go together.[5] The third influence is Daniel Brevint, whose understanding of the Eucharist made a tremendous impression on Wesley. Brevint claimed that the service of Holy Communion is a means of grace, a pledge of happiness and glory yet to come in its fullness, a sign of the present divine graces sustaining the pilgrim people of God, and a participatory memorial of the suffering and death of Christ.[6]

Though it took some time for John Wesley's own spiritual journey to lead him through a stage of genuine struggle and let him emerge with a certain kind of resolution, there is no gainsaying that toward the end of 1738 or in the first months of 1739 Wesley's ministry took on a new form. It would appear that Wesley experienced a profound transformation of his own vision and sense of mission (and certain texts of his own authorship tend to confirm this judgment), and this experience (often linked to his evening in Aldersgate Street) led him to seek new ways of communicating to people the transformed understanding of the life of faith that represented for him a new hope for humankind. The rich spiritual heritage that had had a role in shaping his identity was retained, though he appropriated it afresh.[7] The new feature was Wesley's changed perspective; he had been freed from what somewhat loosely can be termed a "works-righteousness" stance toward the embodiment of faith, for he had come to have an inward assurance that God-in-Christ had freed him from himself for a new life of liberty-in-service. Discipleship became for him something slightly different (but the slight difference made a world of difference!) from what it had been earlier in his life; rather than being primarily a "good work" to be done, it became a matter of living doxologically, of seeing that "Christian life is *devotio,* the consecration of the whole man in love to God and neighbor in the full round of life and death."[8] As he traveled the length and breadth of the kingdom with his renewed proclamation of the Christian gospel, Wesley began to have more and more auditors, a significant number of whom also became his followers and supporters. It is to the vision that Wesley shared with these people, those who formed the early Wesleyan movement, and to the spiritual disciplines enjoined upon them, that this discussion now turns.

What is the heart of the "renewed" Wesley's vision? Before responding, one should remember that it stood squarely within the continuous stream of Christian spirituality that spans the entire history (or better, perhaps, histories) of the church. Yet it also represents a distinctive mode of witness that blossomed in eighteenth-century England, a time and place where some think the established church "was not only lax in the ordering of worship and in pastoral oversight. At the higher levels of church government there was little co-ordination of responsibilities; ecclesiastical authority had become an empty show, and spiritual initiative dissipated itself in political manoeuvring."[9] Even if this assessment of the quality of spiritual life in the Anglican Church of Wesley's day is not altogether accurate, it would never-theless seem that the period in which Wesley grew to majority was not itself one of the high-water marks of Anglican spirituality. This may in part account for the rise of religious societies in general, and the explosive growth of the Wesleyan witness in particular, during the period. The so-called evangelical revival met the spiritual hungers of people, especially the common people, in such a way that they were enabled anew to sense the presence of the living God in the world abroad and in their own lives. Two metaphors with a venerable history in the literature of spirituality help to characterize basic dimensions of this whole movement: the revival led men and women to *hear* the divine word of grace-with-judgment that justifies, and also to *see* a path of righteousness that leads to sanctification, to a new mode of participating in the divine life (and hence also in the world). A dis-tinctive combination of proclamation, evangelism, and nurture, of spiritual formation, lay at the center of this evangelical vision of the Christian witness.

Of recent scholars who have addressed this matter, none has stated better that Albert Outler the heart of the Wesleyan focus of this vision:

> Faith is the primary reality in Christian experience but not its totality. It is . . . a *means*—a necessary means—to a still higher end: "Faith . . . is only the handmaid of love. . . ." The goal of the Christian life is holiness, "the *fullness* of faith." This means the consecration of the whole self to God and to the neighbor in love. This, in turn, involves a process of corporate discipline and effort, guided by the motives of "devotion," by which [Wesley] meant the delivering up of one's *whole life* to God. The outcome to be expected in this endeavor is the renewal of the *imago Dei*, mutilated by sin and ruined by way-wardness. But our aspiration to holiness is as truly a function of faith as justi-fication itself is. The faith that justifies bears its fruits in the faith that works by love.[10]

At some point after his return to England from Georgia, Wesley came to see that earlier in his life he had perhaps known all (or at least many of) the right words (the outward "show") but had not yet been given the tune (the inward vivifying assurance) in order most effectively to bear witness to the grace of the divine mystery that brings life from death; from that point on, though, he became an ardent supporter of the view that God's grace undergirds every part of the universe and that it can actually make a difference *firsthand* in the lives of men and women. He claimed that at various stages along life's way, men and women encounter this grace in its several modes: prevenient, justifying, and sanctifying. This grace is not an intervention from a God who is utterly outside the realm of human experience; Wesley took with great seriousness the insight he had gleaned from the biblical witness and elsewhere that grace is cooperative.[11] By thus viewing human life as a response to and cooperation with the activity of God, Wesley mediated two strains of spirituality sometimes thought to be at odds with one another: the "holy living" tradition and the "salvation by (grace through) faith" tradition.

For most of his life Wesley was grasped by the biblical notion that people are to be single-minded in their devotion to God, and those who are will grow in their understanding of the divine mystery. Such single-mindedness required that there be no major confusion of the creator with the creation; in his articulation of this point, Wesley in some ways prefigured certain figures of more recent times who have defended the "Protestant principle." Nevertheless, even as he maintained that it is only *God* who is to be revered as God, his position also included within itself the embrace of what can be termed the principle of catholicity. This dimension of his spiritual vision stressed both the absolute inclusiveness of God's grace and the presence of God in the world (which entailed his belief that creatures participate in the creator's life). [12] What might be identified as a mystical element in Wesley's spiritual sensibility can be seen at this point; it often came to expression most clearly in his reflections on the sacraments, perhaps best of all in his affective attachment to, say, part of the prayer of humble access in the eucharistic liturgy: "that we may evermore dwell in him, and he in us." One can also see bits of it in Wesley's argument for the reality of perfection in love in a person's life.[13]

In order to live so that these manifestations of God's grace can be efficacious in one's life, however, a person must be committed to a life of discipleship. Such discipleship is a gift of God, but it is costly. It requires the transformation on one's life, "a renewal of our minds in the image of God; a recovery of the divine likeness; a still-increasing conformity of heart and life to the pattern of our most holy Redeemer."[14]

To make progress in one's path of discipleship was to make the spiritual journey with other pilgrims. One of the most effective vehicles of spiritual discipline Wesley ever encountered was the small group meeting. Any number of accounts of his early experiments at Oxford are extant, some of them recounting his own memories while others come from different pens. Several years after Wesley's death, John Gambold published a memoir he had written many years earlier, a piece entitled "The Character of Mr. John Wesley." Since having eventually broken with the Methodists, Gambold had also left Anglican orders for the Moravian ministry, eventually exercising episcopal oversight among the Moravians in England. Despite his divergent spiritual trek, Gambold retained real admiration for the vision and spiritual discipline he remembered in Wesley during the early days of their adult-hood. Recalling the vital meetings of the little band in the university com-munity, Gambold told how the group met in one of their member's rooms in college, how they prayed together, how they had a simple meal with one another, how they often sang, and then how they turned to their "chief business," which was "to review what each had done that day, in pursuance of their common design, and to consult what steps were to be taken next." He related how members of the society undertook a variety of social proj-ects, for they saw outreach to the larger community around them to be a basic feature of the faithful life. They fasted regularly, celebrated the Eucha-rist, and participated in regularly set services of worship outside as well as within the university community. Gambold maintained that at least John Wesley "thought prayer to be more his business than anything else . . . ," though of course this practice was to be cultivated by each group member in the course of his daily routine.[15]

Themes later to be crucial—among them the strict adherence to a disciplined pattern of life that would enable one to "redeem time"—were already present in Wesley's Oxford days. According to Gambold, Wesley "earnestly recommended" that all members of the small group adopt a "method and order" in all that they said and did. A plan for daily conduct included morning devotions (usually at an hour before the sun rose for much of the year!), the determination of what use ought be given the various segments of time in the day (no "trifling" employment is counte-nanced), the observation of fasts, the visitation of poor, imprisoned, or ill people, the regular participation in the Eucharist (especially on Sunday), the careful study of the Bible, the transcription of one's daily expenditures of time and energies into a diary, the regular practice of prayer, and the con-tinual meditation upon the riches of the divine mystery.[16] Anyone aware of the subsequent history of the Methodists can sense here adumbrations of the general rules for the united societies. It was not in rules as such, however, that Wesley was interested; what was most important for him was the nur-ture of the experience of living in a genuine community, a *koinōnia*. In the holy club, Wesley experimented with various means of spiritual formation that he believed to be of service to the *ordo salutis*. Seeds were planted;

though it took some time, fruit eventually appeared in the larger Wesleyan revival.

Not long after John Wesley returned from his apparently disastrous (but actually spiritually important) mission to Georgia, he began the extraordinary itinerant ministry for which he is usually remembered. What, though, was the nature of the spiritual identity and discipline found in this early Wesleyan witness? It is one thing to oversee a handful of Oxford friends, and quite another to attempt shepherding thousands of men and women, many of whom had never had much—if any—formal education. How would one attempt to convey the vivifying sense of God's presence in human life when the community with which one was called to work was vastly larger than—and in some respects clearly qualitatively different from—the *koinōnia* within which one's spiritual guidance had thus far been exercised?.

At least in one respect Wesley had no confusion about what he was trying to do; his efforts for the common folk were aimed at helping them participate actively in the fellowship he knew as the Body of Christ, which always remained for him the Church of England. Wesley wanted in no way to start a new church. He took very seriously Article XIX of the Anglican communion's Articles of Religion, which states that "the visible Church of Christ is a congregation of faithful men, in which the pure Word of God is preached, and the Sacraments be duly ministered according to Christ's ordinance in all those things that of necessity are requisite to the same," even though he seems to have treated the last qualifying clause in a way that has raised some eyebrows (Article XIX, "Of the Church," Articles of Religion, Book of Common Prayer). Wesley's hope was that his societies should serve within the Church of England as an "evangelical order defined by their unique *mission:* 'to spread scriptural holiness over these lands.'"[17] In a number of places, Wesley made a case for an understanding of the Methodist movement that places it within its larger ecclesial context, rather like the notion of an *ecclesiola in ecclesia.* He wanted people to sense that fundamental unity can encompass diversity, and in this conviction he revealed a genuinely ecumenical sensitivity. In his sermon "Of the Church," for example, Wesley used Ephesians 4:1–6 as his text, which in part asserts that Christian people who heed their vocation given them by God are to forbear "one another in love; endeavouring to keep the unity of the Spirit in the bond of peace. There is one body, and one Spirit, even as ye are called in one hope of your calling; one Lord, one faith, one baptism, one God and Father of all, who is above all, and through all, and in you all."[18] Wesley argued for the widespread acceptance of the idea "church" that would include his societies within the one, holy, catholic, apostolic body of Christ. In a related

15. Edward William Clay, *Methodist Camp Meeting,* 1837.

sermon entitled "On Schism," he set forth a view of schism that plays upon a distinction between diversity and disunity, with the Methodists clearly not falling into the latter category. One can also note that even within the Methodist societies Wesley went to considerable lengths to encourage his followers to remain in full communion with Canterbury; he formulated preaching services, for example, that were "liturgically insufficient," so that men and women would not begin to think that he somehow approved of any break with the Church of England.[19]

So it was from within a larger ecclesial framework that Wesley exercised his function as spiritual guide, or mentor, of the Methodists. This ecclesial setting for his work encompassed a historical dimension as well; in part because of his strong sense of identity within the universal body of Christ, he was aware of living amid a vast cloud of Christian witnesses whose respective pilgrimages had been completed but who still had a presence that was spiritually instructive for the current generation of faithful persons. Wesley learned from this collective body a vision of ordered discipleship, the aim of which was always to produce holy living—particularly "inward righteousness, attended with the peace of God; and 'joy in the Holy Ghost'"— never separated, of course, from the setting of a community of believers.[20] "Discipline" was the overarching concept Wesley used to characterize the requirements of the spiritual path his people were to follow; he believed that if one were to maintain a properly ordered embodiment of faith (necessarily grounded in divine grace), it would be possible to live a sanctified life. This being the case, the effective employment of various "means of grace," the means by which one carries out disciplined living, became absolutely essential.

In a sermon entitled "The Means of Grace," Wesley attempted to set straight those of his followers who had endorsed a certain Moravian interpretation of "outward observances" as either unnecessary or dangerous in one's spiritual life. He countered the "quietism" of those men and women by developing an idea he based on Malachi 3:7: "Ye are gone away from mine ordinances, and have not kept them." Though it is true, Wesley said, that the observance of outward and visible religious acts ("ordinances") ought never be confused with "religion of the heart," people should see that both are vehicles of divine grace and that they properly go together in the authentic embodiment of faith. Indeed, in contrast to certain evangelical Christian interpretive schemes, Wesley's vision held certain "outward signs, words, or actions" to be ordained by God precisely in order to serve as the *ordinary* channels whereby he might convey to men preventing, justifying, or sanctifying grace." Wesley then specified some of the more significant of these means of grace, and one can see from Wesley's list that there can be no question but that he saw himself to stand within the mainstream of Anglican spiritual tradition: "prayer, whether in secret or with the great congregation; searching the Scriptures (which implies reading, hearing, and meditating thereon) and receiving the Lord's Supper, eating bread and drinking wine in remembrance of him. . . ." These acts of disciplined spiritual life (as well as at least two others—fasting and the close encounter with fellow Christians that Wesley called "Christian conference") are instituted means of grace and are conducive to a person's spiritual nourishment because the living spirit of God is present "in and by them."[21] Even if a person does not have a personal inner assurance of God's saving love, he or she is called to wait patiently for the dawn of that inward sense *while participating in these means of grace.* God's spirit can and will work within people even if they are not clearly aware of it.

As he argued thus against the proponents of spiritual quietism, Wesley had also to protect himself against the charge that he was putting forth a program of "works-righteousness." In a number of his sermons, including some quite early ones, he plainly claimed that human beings are saved only by God's grace, as mediated through faith. "All the blessings which God hath bestowed upon man," he asserted, "are of his mere grace, bounty, or favour: his free, undeserved favour, favour altogether undeserved, man having no claim to the least of his mercies."[22] In fact, though one can employ any number of "outward signs" of a fully faithful life (and should not be discouraged from doing so), if that person has not the awareness that he or she stands justified and free by virtue of the divine grace, then that person can be no more than an "almost Christian." Though there is real hope for persons in this position, they can become utterly pathetic creatures if they do not eventually come genuinely to know that it is God who works within them to bring them to freedom from bondage. A major difficulty arises if a person confuses his or her role with God's in the *ordo salutis,* and this is rather easy to do, for those who earnestly employ certain means of grace tend to reflect in their lives

> a real design to serve God, a hearty desire to do his will. It is necessarily implied that a man have a sincere view of pleasing God in all things: in all his conversation, in all his actions, in all he does or leaves undone. This design, if any man be "almost a Christian," runs through the whole tenor of his life. This is the moving principle both in his doing good, his abstaining from evil, and his using the ordinances of God.[23]

The more zealous one is in working out his or her salvation, the greater the tendency to misperceive his or her real role in the process. What people are to do is straightforwardly sense that it is the divine presence that is the prime agent of salvation; it is God's grace that awakens people and leads them to respond to the divine embrace, not only by serving God but also by showing commitment to neighbors. And the various means of grace are instrumental in helping to guide souls toward this vision and its disciplined embodiment.

These instituted means of grace were intended to help weave together one's spiritual life within both the church and the much smaller and more intimate societies that the Methodists formed. Prayer, for instance, was to be employed by a person in all places where he or she was to be found; if one prayed regularly, both in the strict privacy of one's own devotional moments and in the increasingly more public settings of one's family, society fellowship, and gathered community of the church, one would in some fruitful sense be found by God. Whether in the form of petition, intercession, thanksgiving, or contemplation, prayer was believed to open a person to God in such a way that he or she would be able to discern a reconciling, healing power in his or her life. This presence, God's spirit, could eventually transform one's vision, thereby increasing one's growth in wisdom. As things developed in the early Wesleyan witness, prayer and hymnody were often very closely related to each other; indeed, one of the literary legacies left by the Wesleys and their followers is a large body of hymns, many of which have served as sung group prayers.

In conjunction with prayer, the Methodist people were enjoined to "search" the Scriptures, which meant that they should hear it when rightly proclaimed as well as regularly read the Bible and meditate upon it.[24] No matter what one's status in the *ordo salutis* was, a careful engagement with biblical texts (under the guidance of a right-minded mentor) was deemed to be spiritually enriching. The matter of being guided in one's study was important; in order to prevent aberrant interpretations of the Gospel from popping up, a system of accountability in the context of the small group was established.

The most important of the various instituted means of grace for the early Methodists was the Eucharist. Wesley maintained that "all who desire an increase of the grace of God are to wait for it in partaking of the Lord's Supper." By communicating regularly and by doing it "in remembrance" of Christ in such a way that the *anamnesis* is participatory, a person can become aware of really participating in the divine life, that, as it were, he or she is consciously re-membered into the Body of Christ by being "made conformable to the death of Christ" and the life-giving grace it conveys.[25] This understanding of the Eucharist is evident in this Charles Wesley hymn:

Come, Holy Ghost, thine Influence shed,
  And realize the Sign,
Thy Life infuse into the Bread,
  Thy Power into the Wine.

Effectual let the Tokens prove,
  And made by Heavenly art,
Fit channels to convey thy Love
  To every Faithful Heart.[26]

The theme of divine–human interaction, or cooperation (synergism), which lies at the heart of John Wesley's theological perspective is envisioned in this hymn as mediated in the Lord's Supper. It was in part this understanding of the relationship between God and human beings that led Wesley to see the Eucharist as paradigmatic of all the means of grace, and therefore to urge "constant communion" to his people. Beyond the fact that sharing in the sacrament can lead persons to see afresh their participation in the life of God, its practice also conveys "the forgiveness of our past sins" and "the present strengthening and refreshing of our souls.'" Thus, the "true rule" that is to guide one's spiritual discipline is this: "so often are we to receive [the Eucharist] as God gives us opportunity."[27] If one does anything less, he or she shows an inadequate grasp of the significance of Christ's command regarding the sacrament (cf. Luke 22:19: "Do this in remembrance of me") and of the real communication of grace mediated through the Eucharist.[28]

Wesley saw that it simply would not do merely to tell people they ought to partake of the instituted means of grace. In order for spiritual fruit to appear, men and women must "trust" the means of grace. To trust them was to seek within them the blessing of God, to believe that "if I wait in this way I shall attain what otherwise I should not." Thus, to speak of trusting the instituted means of grace was to raise the question of the "*order* and the *manner*" of their employment.[29] Building on his fundamental conviction that one is ripe for nurture if only one has "a desire to flee from the wrath to come," Wesley saw that a person could be led to trust the means of grace, a step at a time, while undertaking a spiritual pilgrimage within a relatively small group. Other people have a vital role in each person's spiritual development. It is here that Wesley showed his grasp of a profound insight: growth in grace is an intensely personal experience, but it is never truly private. One is to grow toward spiritual maturity within a social setting that does not ignore the individual needs of the persons making up the group, and yet (as he had found earlier in Oxford) a group that is sensitive to its constituent members must also have operating principles and rules that help bring the individuals together into a coherent group. That the early Wesleyan witness was able to hold together the necessarily personal dimension of spiritual direction with sensitivity to the demands of group process is no mean accomplishment.

To provide for this twofold (i.e., individual and social) model of spiritual nourishment, Wesley championed what he called the exercise of prudential means of grace along with the instituted means. It had become clear that different group configurations were needed, for not all people had begun their spiritual journeys at the same existential point, nor had they proceeded at the same pace. Wesley's original "united society," begun in 1739, had been "a company of men having the form and seeking the power of godliness, united in order to pray together, to receive the word of exhortation, and to watch over one another in love, that they may help each other to work out their salvation."[30] But it had been only a short time before the Wesleyan revival had found it crucial to subdivide its organ of mutual trust and accountability into several kinds of bodies: not only were there to be the united societies, but also classes, bands, select societies, and groups known as "the Penitents." Within this network of groups, Wesley set aside some people as representative leaders (while allowing certain others to emerge from the group dynamic), and for each of the several categories of discipleship he set up a system of accountability. Wesley was aware, however, that certain kinds of organizational structure can at best only *aid* spiritual development. God is the one who works in the souls of men and women, so Wesley saw that it is possible for a person to participate for a time within a society and do so without bearing fruit in any obvious way.[31]

Even while holding this view, Wesley believed that the exercise of some of the prudential means of grace (as with the instituted means) cannot help but be of benefit in any person's life—"namely, watching, denying ourselves, taking up our cross, [and the] exercise of the presence of God." Armed with this conviction, Wesley put together series of questions that were to be asked of those persons who participated in the Methodist revival. The aim of the disciplined engagement with this kind of query was to build up each individual's witness to the reality of divine grace in his or her life and to strengthen the collective witness of the group itself. Questions included matters such as these:

> Do you steadily watch against the world, the devil, yourselves, your besetting sin? . . . Do you deny yourself every pleasure of sense, imagination, honour? Are you temperate in all things? . . . Wherein do you "take up your cross daily"? Do you cheerfully bear your cross (whatever is grievous to nature) as a gift of God, and labour to profit thereby? . . . Do you endeavour to set God always before you; as to see his eye continually fixed upon you?[32]

Questions such as these could be asked of any spiritually "awakened" person (being thus "awake" was the criterion for inclusion in the societies). The various societies were divided into classes of about a dozen people each; there, once a week under one of their own who had been appointed to serve as their leader, class members were advised, reproved, comforted, and exhorted in order that "their souls prosper." In addition to asking after the state of each person's soul, the class leader also collected contributions of money which were used for poor relief, and also met with ministers regularly in order adequately to care for their flock. To continue in membership within a class required some evidence of a person's desire of salvation, which not only entailed regular attendance (which before very long was monitored by the issuance of tickets of admission, quarterly examinations, and even trial memberships) but also adherence to three basic rules (illustrated with a number of examples): First, one was to do no harm, and was enjoined to avoid "evil in every kind; especially that which is most generally practised." Second, one was to do good, "by being in every kind merciful after their power; as they have opportunity, doing good of every possible sort, and as far as is possible, to all men. . . ." Third, one was to use the instituted means of grace ("by attending upon all the ordinances of God"), which in this list of rules were identified as "the public worship of God; the ministry of the word, either read or expounded; the Supper of the Lord; private prayer; searching the Scriptures; and fasting, or abstinence."[33] Clearly, the class within the society was a source of mutual nurture, wherein members made covenant with one another and God to build up each other in a way of faith that could transform their lives. Believing that their chief purpose was to bear witness to God's love and be "fellow-labourers" with that mysterious presence, the early Methodists struggled with one another in their class meetings to embody a discipline that would free them from resistance to the efficacy of the means of grace.

Those within the societies who were "supposed to have remission of sins" were grouped into bands. Those others who seemed "to walk in the light of God" were gathered into still smaller groups, the select societies. And those who had "made shipwreck of their faith" were called aside to meet as "penitents."[34] Members of the bands and select societies were to continue in their regular weekly class meetings as part of the societies even as they undertook more rigorous soul-searching in their respectively smaller units. It was expected that as one moved ahead in the pursuit of holy living, demands placed on one would increase.

The chief end of the band meeting was to fulfill the biblical command in James 5:16, namely, "confess your faults to one another, and pray for one another, that he may be healed." Meeting once a week, beginning with prayer or singing, the agenda moved under the guidance of a leader who emerged naturally from within the group. Each person in turn, "freely and plainly," was able to address the "true state" of his or her soul, specifying faults that had been committed ("in thought, word, or deed") and any temptations faced, since the last band meeting. The meetings were rather emotionally intense, for prior to a person's admission to a band he or she was not only given scrutiny about the present state of his or her soul, but also told that in band meetings one must expect probing inquiry into one's awareness of whether he or she had "the forgiveness of sins" and whether "the love of God [is] shed abroad in your heart." More than this, though, persons were asked these questions: "Do you desire to be told of all your faults, and that plain and home?" "Do you desire we should tell you whatsoever we think, whatsoever we fear, whatsoever we hear concerning you . . . [and] that, in doing this, we should cut to the quick, and search your heart to the bottom?"[35] Trust, confidentiality, and mutual accountability were vital to the functioning of the bands.

It was from this body, not from the larger class meeting of the societies, that the "penitents" tended to come. It was believed that a person "on the way," as it were, and not merely "awakened" as a relatively immature spiritual seeker, was much more likely to experience a "shipwreck" of faith. When a person fell, by one or another willful transgression of a command of God, he or she was taken aside for special instruction, advice, and other forms of nurture. As things seemed to turn out, those who "recovered the ground they had lost" were usually much more sensitive to the awareness of human frailty and every person's need for divine grace than they had been previously, so they seemed to work ever more diligently for the experience of the fullness of love in their lives. It was from this group that membership in the select societies tended to be drawn.[36]

The select societies were those groups wherein the Wesleyan vision of sanctified living was most realized in the hearts of their members. In addition to the guidelines that informed the activities of the bands, the select societies had only three others:

> 1. Let nothing spoken in this Society be spoken again; no, not even to the members of it. 2. Every member agrees absolutely to submit to his minister in all indifferent things. 3. Every member, till we can have all things common, will bring once a week, *bona fide*, all he can spare towards a common stock.[37]

The way of holy living and dying, the path toward perfection in love, was most powerfully sought by these, the relatively few members of the select societies.

When viewed as complementary (as they should be), the societies and their classes, the bands, the select societies, and even the groups of penitents worked as parts of the Methodist movement. These groups were instruments, or vehicles, through which the various means of grace could be mediated in a communal setting to pilgrims at various stages of their journeys in disciplined faith. A conviction of the catholicity of God's grace suffused the whole movement, along with the sense that the proper vocation given men and women—by God's grace, in which they participate—was to embody gratitude and benevolence. Gratitude was to be given God and benevolence to their neighbors-in-existence. An epitome of this basic spiritual vision, is found in the 1780 volume, *A Collection of Hymns, For the Use of the People Called Methodists,* and provides a fitting conclusion to this discussion of the sense of God's presence in the eighteenth-century Methodist pilgrimage of faith:

> Love divine, all loves excelling,
>   Joy of heaven, to earth come down,
> Fix in us thy humble dwelling,
>   All thy faithful mercies crown!
> Jesu, thou art all compassion,
>   Pure, unbounded love thou art;
> Visit us with thy salvation!
>   Enter every trembling heart.
>
> .   .   .   .
>
> Finish then thy new creation,
>   Pure and spotless let us be;
> Let us see thy great salvation
>   Perfectly restored in thee;
> Changed from glory into glory,
>   Till in heaven we take our place,
> Till we cast our crowns before thee,
>   Lost in wonder, love, and praise.[38]

Notes

1. For studies of Wesley's earliest years, see, e.g., the first volume of Robert Southey, *Life of Wesley* (London: Longman, Hunt, 1820); volume 1 of Luke Tyerman, *Life and Times of the Rev. John Wesley, M.A.* (New York: Harper & Brothers, 1872); and the first volume of Martin Schmidt, *John Wesley: A Theological Biography.* Though I shall not pursue the Puritan influence on Wesley (especially in connection with the sense of "inward assurance"), it is nonetheless an important informing factor upon his thought; see, e.g., Robert Monk, *John Wesley: His Puritan Heritage.* Other useful pertinent studies

include Albert C. Outler's introductory essay in the new critical edition of *The Works of John Wesley: Volume I, Sermons I: 1-33* (Nashville: Abingdon, 1984) 1–100; Thomas A. Langford, *Practical Divinity: Theology in the Wesleyan Tradition* (Nashville: Abingdon, 1983) *passim;* and David Lowes Watson, "Methodist Spirituality," in *Protestant Spiritual Traditions,* ed. Frank C. Senn (New York: Paulist, 1986) 217–73.

2. For a list of Wesley's reading between 1725 and 1734, see Appendix I in V. H. H. Green, *The Young Mr. Wesley: A Study of John Wesley and Oxford* (New York: St. Martin's Press, 1961) 305–19. Further data are available in the dissertations (at Duke University) of Steve Harper and Richard P. Heitzenrater.

3. *Works of the Rev. John Wesley, M.A.,* ed. Thomas Jackson (1831) 11:366–67.

4. See Robert Nelson, *A Companion for the Festivals and Fasts of the Church of England: With Collects and Prayers for Each Solemnity* (7th ed.; London: W. Bowyer, 1712).

5. William Beveridge, *The Great Necessity and Advantage of Publick Prayer, and Frequent Communion. Designed to Revive Primitive Piety* (London: R. Smith, 1708) 109.

6. Daniel Brevint, *The Christian Sacrament and Sacrifice, By Way of Discourse, Meditation, and Prayer, Upon the Nature, Parts, and Blessings of the Holy Communion* (2nd ed.; Oxford, 1673) *passim.*

7. That Wesley in no way broke from his spiritual rootage is seen both in his own sermons and in his production of *A Christian Library.*

8. Albert C. Outler, ed., *John Wesley,* 7.

9. Frank Baker, *John Wesley and the Church of England* (Nashville: Abingdon, 1970) 3.

10. Albert C. Outler, ed., *John Wesley,* 28.

11. See, e.g., Philippians 2:12–13, and the sermon Wesley preached upon this text: "On Working Out Our Own Salvation."

12. For a recent effort to hold both principles together, see Avery Dulles, *The Catholicity of the Church* (Oxford: Clarendon Press, 1984).

13. See, e.g., Albert Outler's introductory essay in *The Works of John Wesley: Volume I,* 55f.

14. Cited in Richard P. Heitzenrater, *The Elusive Mr. Wesley: Volume One, John Wesley His Own Biographer* (Nashville: Abingdon, 1984) 70.

15. John Gambold, "The Character of Mr. John Wesley," reprinted in Richard P. Heitzenrater, *The Elusive Mr. Wesley: Volume Two, John Wesley as Seen By Contemporaries and Biographers* (Nashville: Abingdon, 1984) 39, 40.

16. Ibid., 41ff.

17. Albert C. Outler, "Do Methodists Have a Doctrine of the Church?" in *The Doctrine of the Church,* ed. Dow Kirkpatrick (Nashville: Abingdon, 1964) 14.

18. John Wesley, "Of the Church," reprinted in Albert C. Outler, ed., *John Wesley,* 308.

19. Albert C. Outler, "Do Methodists Have a Doctrine of the Church?" 13. It is also possible, for example, to grasp the force of the message in Wesley's sermon "On the Duty of Constant Communion" as being pertinent in this connection.

20. John Wesley, "A Plain Account of the People Called Methodists," cited in Gerald O. McCulloh, "The Discipline of Life in Early Methodism Through Preaching and Other Means of Grace," in *The Doctrine of the Church,* ed. Dow Kirkpatrick, 169.

21. John Wesley, "The Means of Grace," in *The Works of John Wesley: Volume I, Sermons I: 1-33,* ed. Albert C. Outler, 378, 381, 382. See also "The Large Minutes," in *The Works of John Wesley: Volume VIII,* 322ff.

22. John Wesley, "Salvation by Faith," in *The Works of John Wesley: Volume I, Sermons I:1–33,* ed. Albert C. Outler, 117. See also Wesley's sermon on "Justification by Faith," in the same volume, pp. 181–99.

23. John Wesley, "The Almost Christian," in *Works: Volume I,* ed. Albert C. Outler, 136.

24. John Wesley, "The Means of Grace," 387.

25. Ibid., 389.

26. "Hymn LXXII," John and Charles Wesley, *Hymns on the Lord's Supper. With a Preface Concerning the Christian Sacrament and Sacrifice, extracted from Doctor Brevint* (Bristol: Felix Farley, 1745) 51.

27. John Wesley, "The Duty of Constant Communion," in *John Wesley,* 336.

28. For a discussion of the role of the Eucharist in the early Wesleyan witness, see John C. Bowmer, *The Sacrament of the Lord's Supper in Early Methodism.* A related treatment is found in John R. Parris, *John Wesley's Doctrine of the Sacraments* (London: Epworth, 1963).

29. John Wesley, "The Means of Grace," 391, 393.

30. "The Rules of the United Societies," in Albert C. Outler, ed., *John Wesley,* 178.

31. "Minutes" of the First Annual Conference, 143.

32. Ibid., 143, 239–40.

33. "The Rules of the United Societies," 178, 179. In this connection, see two volumes by Leslie F. Church: *The Early Methodist People* (London: Epworth, 1948); and *More About the Early Methodist People* (London: Epworth, 1949).

34. "Minutes" of the First Annual Conference, in Albert C. Outler, ed., *John Wesley,* 143.

35. "Rules of the Bands," in Albert C. Outler, ed., *John Wesley,* 180, 181.

36. For a recent discussion of the various patterns of group organization found in the early Wesleyan witness, see David Lowes Watson, *The Early Methodist Class Meeting.* For a treatment of "penitents," see esp. p. 121.

37. "Minutes" of the First Annual Conference, 144.

38. "Hymn 374," *The Works of John Wesley: Volume VII, A Collection of Hymns for the Use of the People Called Methodists,* ed. Franz Hildebrandt and Oliver A. Beckerlegge, with James Dale (Oxford: Clarendon, 1983) 545, 547.

Bibliography

Ayling, Stanley. *John Wesley.* Cleveland: Collins, 1979.

Borgen, Ole E. *John Wesley on the Sacraments.* Nashville: Abingdon, 1972.

Bowmer, John C. *The Sacrament of the Lord's Supper in Early Methodism.* London: Dacre, 1951.

Holland, Bernard. *Baptism in Early Methodism.* London: Epworth, 1970.

Lindstrom, Harold. *Wesley and Sanctification.* Nashville: Abingdon, 1946.

Monk, Robert C. *John Wesley: His Puritan Heritage.* Nashville: Abingdon, 1966.

Naglee, David I. *From Font to Faith: John Wesley on Infant Baptism and the Nurture of Children.* New York: Peter Lang, 1987.

Outler, Albert C., ed. *John Wesley.* New York: Oxford University Press, 1964.

Rattenbury, J. Ernest. *The Eucharistic Hymns of John and Charles Wesley.* London: Epworth, 1948.

Rowe, Kenneth E., ed. *The Place of Wesley in the Christian Tradition.* Metuchen, NJ: Scarecrow, 1979.

Schmidt, Martin. *John Wesley: A Theological Biography.* 3 vols. New York: Abingdon, 1963.

Snyder, Howard A. *The Radical Wesley.* Downers Grove, IL: InterVarsity, 1980.

Wakefield, Gordon S. *Methodist Devotion.* London: Epworth, 1966.

Watson, David Lowes. *The Early Methodist Class Meeting.* Nashville: Discipleship Resources, 1985.

William., Colin. *John Wesley's Theology Today.* Nashville: Abingdon, 1960.

12

The Spirituality of Afro-American Traditions

THEOPHUS H. SMITH

BLACK SPIRITUALITY IN NORTH AMERICA seems at once a type of Western spirituality and yet also strikingly non-Western. In its Christian forms it appears simultaneously conventional—an imitation of, or a gloss on, the major Protestant and evangelical traditions—and also something alien, intransigently different. What accounts for *both* aspects: the commonality on the one hand and the distinctiveness on the other? The answer to this and related questions can be found in the intersection of black America's two master stories—its "mundane story" and its "sacred story."[1] The mundane story comprises unique as well as more commonplace elements in this people's historical experience. It is the cultural narrative of disparate African communities forcibly removed from their homelands and enslaved in the Americas, then emancipated and segregated, and now struggling for parity in the New World. The other story is composed of biblical texts that are shared within Western culture and with Jewish, Christian, and Islamic communities elsewhere. It is the sacred narrative of ancient Israel's divine election and deliverance from bondage, that people's providential possession of a promised land, and their successive dispersals outside that land under Assyrian, Babylonian, and Roman captivity.

Correlating those two stories, with their notable parallels, has engaged the spiritual energies of generations of black Americans. For our part, the effort to show how they achieved their narrative correlations provides an incomparable opportunity to disclose and to display the spirituality itself. This essay undertakes the task of disclosure by examining that spirituality in the three interrelated areas of religion, art, and politics. Beginning with religion we observe (1) the foundations of Afro-American spirituality in ritual transformations found in the black religious phenomena of spirit possession and magical shamanism or conjuration. Next, since artistic expression is a notable conveyor of spiritual energies, we turn also to (2) the aesthetic display of this transformative spirituality in black music, speech, and literary discourse. A final section fulfills these efforts by displaying (3) the spirituality undergirding black freedom movements and political actions that are patterned on biblical models.

Despite the goal of comprehensiveness, however, the following account does not treat *specifically* Afro-Islamic or Afro-Hebraic traditions in North America, nor Afro-American traditions in the Caribbean and South America, nor the various sects and cults combining other traditions. Nonetheless, it does treat common elements in the folk religion of Afro-Americans, and in a way may disclose formative dynamics in extra-Christian traditions as well. In anticipating such disclosures it is appropriate in a preliminary way to query: How is "the black story" composed out of the often inchoate elements of black experience? In turn, how are elements of biblical narrative selected for correlation with that existentially composed cultural narrative? Fully adequate answers to these questions would involve us in matters of narrative theory and philosophical method. For present purposes it is sufficient to offer in this introductory section a concise version of the black story, and in the final section to draw upon the intervening discussion of transformative and aesthetic dynamics in black spirituality.

Seventeenth and Eighteenth Centuries: Formation of a New World People

One way to cast the black story renders it the pilgrimage of a people toward freedom. That construction is readily understandable and has its merits, but it can also absorb the pre-slavery background of African traditions into a liberal democratic ethos peculiar to the American experience (and forecasts the foreseeable future in such terms exclusively). A more inclusive and arguably indigenous approach frames the story as a quest for transcendent community or *communitas,* defined immediately below. As a framework that can include the imperatives of freedom and justice, the quest for transcendence in community is also more continuous with a West African ethos—an ethos that values as preeminent a harmony of one's tribe with the spirit world of gods and ancestors. With this narrative frame in view, the black story may be divided into three periods and roughly by centuries. Although the slave trade to the Americas began as early as 1518,[2] the years from 1600 to 1800 featured the more massive and protracted dislocation of Africans to the New World. They were apprehended from widespread parts of Africa, endured the horrors of "the middle passage" across the Atlantic, and were distributed to points throughout the Americas. The end of those two centuries was marked by the legal termination of the United States slave trade in 1808, although transatlantic trading continued until the mid-nineteenth century. But this period also featured the formation of a new ethnic conglomerate; gradually a people of common identity emerged out of tribal groups as disparate in Africa as the Wolof in the northwest, the Yoruba and Ibo on the central coast, and the Angolans south of the Congo.

The religious character of these groups was also diverse, incorporating Islamic as well as indigenous African traditions. But just as their various languages gave way to an American English common to "slave culture,"[3] so their religious diversity was largely replaced by the denominational diversity of a shared Protestantism. The formation of an Afro-American people out of a heterogeneous population constitutes the first volume in their cultural narrative. It is the mundane and all-too-familiar story of conquest and bondage, of survival and struggle. Yet it is also the story of the bonding of formerly separate African communities, on the one hand with each other and on the other hand with various European American communities. By what spiritual resources have these intra- and inter-group alliances been achieved? An answer follows in the detailed discussion below.

Nineteenth Century: Freedom at the Limits

The nineteenth century featured an intensive application of spiritual energies to the problem of freedom. By the 1800s black spirituality already combined indigenous African and adapted Christian elements. That combination alongside the freedom imperative was "institutionalized"[4] in the single social structure that Afro-Americans created during the previous period: the independent black church. Notable among such independent bodies were single Baptist churches dating from the mid-1770s and a new denomination founded in 1816, the African Methodist Episcopal (A.M.E.) Church. Thus, the institutional achievements of the nineteenth century rested on the more fragmented and incipient developments of the eighteenth century, including a wave of black conversions during the Great Awakening (1730s and 1740s) and the beginning of black political petitioning that employed both biblical ideas and the 1770s Jeffersonian rhetoric of freedom and equality.

After the groundwork of Christian missions to the slaves had been laid in the eighteenth century and consolidated in the early nineteenth century, the real success of those efforts appeared after the Civil War. The great preponderance of black conversions to Christianity did not occur until after Emancipation,[5] which was regarded by numerous freedpersons with all the awe and jubilation that attends a providential act of divine intervention. Then followed the reversal of democratic reforms in the South through the termination of Reconstruction in the late 1870s. However, the dual quest for earthly freedom and prosperity alongside heavenly salvation was subsequently transferred by many to the North, as the freedpersons and their descendants migrated by hundreds and thousands from the rural South to fill the urban industrial centers. Many also filled the new storefront churches and participated in the creation of urban sects and cults presided over by such figures as Daddy Grace and Father Divine. But already by the turn of the century the black quest for a promised land was severely constrained. The limits of freedom were marked in the North by the underdevelopment and ghettoization of black communities, and in the South by Jim Crow laws (legalized segregation) and by epidemics of gratuitous and brutal lynching of black people extending from the 1880s to the 1930s.[6]

Twentieth Century: Challenging the Foundations

In 1903 the great black scholar and activist W. E. B. DuBois, prefaced his *The Souls of Black Folk* with the declaration that "the problem of the Twentieth Century is the problem of the color line." In 1910 he responded to that problem with other black leaders in the Niagara Movement and with liberal white supporters in the founding of the National Association for the Advancement of Colored People (NAACP). Only a decade later in 1920 a Jamaican leader, Marcus Garvey, organized the Universal Negro Improvement Association (UNIA). The white establishment orientation of the NAACP and DuBois's early Pan-Africanism were matched in the 1920s by Garvey's leadership of the largest mass movement of black people in American history, featuring the back-to-Africa effort and the growth of black nationalism. Garvey's failure combined with the Great Depression of the 1930s to create perhaps the lowest point of black morale in the century. Some commentators have located in the period between the two world wars the prevalence of "Uncle Tomism" and black church accommodation to racial discrimination.[7] Also notable was the humiliating return to domestic mistreatment that greeted black soldiers following their loyal participation in each of the world wars.

The tide turned after the mid-century mark. In 1954 the NAACP's legal strategies succeeded in pressuring the Supreme Court to overturn school segregation in the nation. One year later Rosa Parks initiated the Montgomery bus boycott in Alabama and Dr. Martin Luther King, Jr., rose to leadership in the civil rights movement. His nonviolent tactics and Christian oratory were countered by more radical rivals, including Stokely Carmichael of the Student Nonviolent Coordinating Committee, Malcolm X of the Black Muslims, and Eldridge Cleaver and Huey Newton of the Black Panther Party. Here we can see, in the tension between King and the more militant black leaders, the challenge to the foundational synthesis of Christian and liberal democratic principles that had characterized black movements since the abolitionism of the nineteenth century. That challenge remains fundamentally unresolved as the century closes, despite the successes of black America's cultural "revolution," the dramatic increase of black elected officials throughout the nation, the advent of affirmative action, and the rallying of black capitalism. For observers who take seriously the permanence of a black "under class," the continuing levels of unemployment, imprisonment, addiction and health crises, and the actual reversal of black college enrollments and other achievements of the civil rights era, the twentieth-century chapter in the black story displays only a partial and ambiguous realization of black community in North America, with America, and as Americans.

Ritual Transformations in the Story: Past and Future

The task before us is to display how the preceding story, or its variant compositions, has been fused with the biblical story by means of black spirituality. In the following sections, as introduced above, this spirituality is examined in terms of three major dynamics in which the common element is the ritual process.[8] First, the spiritual-*transformative* dynamics of black religion are described. These include the transformations of self and world that are sought in specifically religious processes, beginning traditionally with ecstatic worship or spirit possession and involving prayer traditions, conjuration and its extensions, and ritual healing including communal therapies and corporate shamanism. Second, the spiritual-*aesthetic* dynamics in black culture are treated. These include ritual structures found not only in black music, as has been increasingly recognized, and not only in the ritualized speech of black preaching, but ritualization found also in rhetorical forms of vernacular speech and in black literature.

In the third section spiritual-*political* dynamics are examined. This section largely concerns the biblical hermeneutic of typology or figuralism. Biblical figuralism is an interpretive tradition that represents both personal and social histories in terms of biblical types, figures, or models. The discussion will focus on the way in which rituals of social figuration constitute an

Afro-American repertory of biblically formed political configurations, spanning the colonial and contemporary periods. The concluding discussion also anticipates new developments in this spirituality of narrative transformation—the transformation of a people's cultural narrative through ritual improvisations of biblical narrative. As we will see, a perennial source of emancipatory improvisations is the transformative process described by anthropologist Victor Turner as *communitas:* the ritual transition of a community from social structures marked by class distinctions and conventional constraints, to modes of "antistructure" that dissolve those constraints and liberate persons for egalitarian relationships.[9]

Spiritual-Transformative Dynamics in Black Religion

Spirit Possession and Ecstatic Cultures

Possession in the African tradition was the height of worship—the supreme religious act.

Possession is the supreme religious act, but it is in essence extremely human and related to the basic, everyday concerns of human life, although transposed to a sacred plane.[10]

Spirit possession in Afro-America and in the traditional religions of West Africa has been often noted and well documented by historians, anthropologists, and religion scholars. Whether possession continues to be a central rather than a marginal phenomenon has less importance in the present discussion than its foundational status in black religion and culture. Indeed, irrespective of its prevalence in religious expression today it provides a "root metaphor" (Turner) for ecstatic performances throughout black culture. For example, Henry Mitchell has suggested that possession functions covertly in secular contexts like jazz clubs, where ecstatic behavior appears to be ritually patterned even if nonreligiously expressed. In a related observation ethnomusicologist Morton Marks presents evidence that culturally conditioned listeners experience possession-trance even during commercial (e.g., radio) broadcasts of black popular music—specifically "soul music." Behavior in a black audience, whether religious or secular (e.g., a political rally), can also be analyzed in terms of ecstatic behavior and ritual process.[11]

In this regard anthropologist Shelia Walker has insisted that possession can be a normal cultural phenomenon and that when it does feature pathology in traditional communities it can also function as a therapeutic means of controlling or coping with distressed behaviors. Furthermore, Walker emphasizes the importance of "cultural determinants" in shaping the possession event.[12] So crucial in her view are cultural factors that the question arises of distinguishing African possession traditions from Western or specifically Euro-Christian forms of possession or "Holy Spirit baptism." But in practice such ethnographic precision has proved nearly impossible to achieve.

The *locus classicus* of this issue in black studies is the debate between E. Franklin Frazier and Melville Herskovits about African "survivals" among black North Americans. In his review of that debate the contemporary historian of black religion, Albert J. Raboteau, refers to the prominence of evangelical religion among slave converts and particularly their attraction to baptism by immersion. In the 1950s Herskovits had argued that this attraction was due to cultural continuity between the Baptist practice of immersion, on the one hand, and African water cults in Nigeria and Dahomey, on the other. Though Raboteau supports some of the criticism of Herskovits's theory, he also endorses one of its neglected aspects: that some elements of American evangelical Protestantism were sufficiently similar to the African background of early black converts to allow their indigenous beliefs and practices to continue in modified form. This "commonality" means that it may now be virtually impossible to distinguish the culture of origin for certain elements. As Raboteau acknowledges, both ecstatic possession and magical conjuration are major elements of such commonality.

> That some elements of African religion survived in the United States not as separate enclaves free of white influence but as aspects hidden under or blended with similar European forms is a thesis worth considering in more detail, especially since there are strong arguments for its validity in the areas of music, folklore, and language. There were two areas of commonality between African and European religion where mutual reinterpretation and syncretism possibly occurred: ecstatic behavior and magical folk-belief.[13]

But even if we grant that there are obvious continuities between African traditional and black American possession behaviors, there are many more direct connections to black religion in the Caribbean and South America. African "survivals" among black communities in the rest of the Americas are significantly more observable and demonstrable, a fact often attributed to two factors: the longer duration and larger populations of the slave trade in the South, a factor maintaining indigenous customs by newer arrivals of native-born Africans, combined with the greater pluralism of Catholic, southern cultures in comparison to the Protestant north. In describing this continuity, Raboteau remarks:

> In the central possession cults of the Yoruba and Fon peoples the devotees are possessed by a god—in the cults of Haiti and Brazil, by several gods in

succession—whose personality displaces that of the human medium. . . . It is believed that the possessed "has been invaded by a supernatural being and is thus temporarily beyond self-control, his ego being subordinated to that of the [divine] intruder."

In contrast to such perceived similarities, North American possession seems radically different. Despite their African heritage, as Raboteau claims, black Protestant possession traditions show a more marked Christian character than parallel phenomena in the Catholic south: "The African gods with their myriad characteristics, personalities, and myths do not 'mount' their enthusiasts amid the dances, songs, and drum rhythms of worship in the United States. Instead it is the Holy Spirit who fills the converted sinner with a happiness and power that drive him to shout, sing, and sometimes dance."[14]

Conjuring and Its Prayer Extensions

The missionary could not, in good conscience, depreciate the presence and mysterious work of the Holy Spirit in the life of the believer. This work could readily be interpreted by the slave as identical with conjuration and the Orisha-possession of his ancestral religion.[15]

In Afro-American experience, as in other traditions, we can see how magical beliefs and practices have been transposed from their most primal forms to more reflective and discursive manifestations. To be sure, conjuration in black folk tradition focused predominantly on the use of natural and physical objects as conveyers of mystical effects and influences. But a development or evolution, which Ernst Cassirer claims for Western spirituality in general, can also be observed in the black tradition of conjuring. This is the development

from the belief in a physico-magical power comprised in the Word to a realization of its spiritual power. Indeed, it is the Word, it is language, that really reveals to man that world which is closer to him than any world of natural objects and touches his weal and woe more directly than physical nature. For it is language that makes his existence in a *community* possible.[16]

It was the need to achieve spiritual coexistence in North American Protestant communities—specifically in communities of discourse marked by biblical figuralism (see the discussion of spiritual-political dynamics below)—that impelled Afro-Americans to extend conjure from its magical modes of empowerment to encompass a theological language of empowerment.

Elsewhere the Jewish philosopher Martin Buber, making explicit reference to conjure (as Egyptian), has described a similar transformation. In expounding the biblical story of Hebrew bondage and oppression in ancient

Egypt, he remarked that "the tormented ones will want to discover (thus they have learned from Egypt) how they can powerfully conjure God to appear forthwith and help." But in the course of their religious experience the Hebrew slaves encountered a God who declares, in Buber's words, "You do not need to conjure Me, but you cannot conjure Me either." The realization of such a truth, Buber acknowledges, constitutes a distinctive moment in the religious development of a people. It indicates, "considered in terms of the history of religion, the 'demagicizing' of faith."[17] But "demagicizing," perhaps coextensive in ancient Israel with its gradual conversion to radical monotheism, is not peculiar to Judaism. A theological development of conjure as a dynamic of faith—or, perhaps more precisely, an extending of conjure to encompass the theological demands of biblical faith—has characterized black experience in North America. In this connection we may posit the theological propriety of that expression crafted by Countee Cullen, a poet of the Harlem renaissance and the son of a Methodist minister: "Faith, the canny conjuror."[18]

In this connection it may be possible to derive a specifically Christian development of conjuration from magical attempts in slave religion to conjure slavemasters. As Raboteau reports, such efforts had mixed success depending on whether the whites involved shared similar beliefs. In this connection Wilmore has attempted to reconstruct the transition from magical conjure to Christian practices.

> The maleficent aspect of the lore these [conjure] specialists had mastered could not help but be used against the whites until it was clear, as Genovese believes, that it did not work as it did against blacks. It was by some such process of demonstrated ineptitude and eventual pacification that practitioners of bad magic gradually became or yielded to practitioners of good magic. The end result was the taking on of more and more of the language, ritual trappings, and symbolization of Christianity until the old African religions were over-powered and the first Christian exhorters began to emerge as confidants and assistants of the itinerant white preachers.[19]

For black Christianity the moral nature of the biblical God highlights by contrast the morally ambivalent nature of conjuration. Thus black church orthodoxy censures the conjurational tendency toward evil magic or "malign occultism." Characteristic in the practice of conjuring in slave religion was the use of charms and counter-charms to harm or avenge harm. "The variety of illnesses, injuries, and misfortunes blamed on conjure was endless," observes Raboteau. Other commentators like Newbell Niles Puckett have observed a moral indifference both in the conjuror's art (in so-called witchcraft) and in African pantheons of spirits: "The same spirit can be persuaded to work indifferently good or evil . . . the same power being turned to different ends, just as fire may be used for warmth and protection or for burning a neighbor's barn."[20] In the slavery period the use of conjure against white people in particular featured moral ambiguities. The motives for conjuring slavemasters and other white people ranged between acts of revenge or sheer malice, on the one hand, and justifiable efforts to escape abuse or to achieve freedom, on the other—as in the slave revolts to be discussed.

At the same time the distinction became blurred between prayers that seek divine help by summoning or "incanting" the deity—conjuring God—and prayers that more obviously importune or supplicate God. In the history of religions the latter type of prayer has been sharply distinguished from magical manipulations of the deity, by which the practitioner expects mechanically to extract or even compel divine favor and benefits. In black religion, by hypothesis, two kinds of conjuring have become operative: folk conjure in its traditional or magical forms and, by extension, conjuring that has been influenced by the approved biblical style of supplication. But just as with spirit possession in the preceding section, a middle ground of ambivalence occurs when a spirituality is in transition to new modes of expression.

Amalgamations or "syncretisms" arise in which religious forms, neither wholly of one tradition nor the other, attempt to convey both. An example of syncretism in the area of spirit possession was the gradually suppressed "ring shout" in which worshiping slaves formed a circle and, clapping their hands and stamping their feet, danced or rocked their bodies while singing— all under the tenacious conviction that "sinners won't get converted unless there is a ring." In reporting this conviction Raboteau stresses the Christian elements in the ritual. In "the 'running spirituals' or ring shout," he observes, "the names and words of the African gods were replaced by Biblical figures and Christian imagery." Other commentators, on the other hand, emphasize the African ambience of the ring as a ritual circle.[21]

New Orleans voodoo, through its obvious Roman Catholic elements, provides the most overt case in North America of influence by Euro-Christian folklore. Voodoo was originally an Afro-Haitian cult and a complete religious organization incorporating both worship and magic, best distinguished by the name Vodun. "But gradually," Raboteau notes, "voodoo as an institutionalized cult of ritual worship disintegrated, while its tradition of 'root work' persisted in folk beliefs widespread among slaves and their descendants down to the present day." Thus the term has been used also to refer to conjure or "hoodoo" as practiced by the folk population of black people throughout the United States.[22] In any case all these traditions, as New World phenomena, share the mixture of European and African magical-religious traditions.

In a similar manner, conjuration illustrates what Raboteau describes in his history of slave religion on southern plantations as a "complementarity" between two overlapping traditions. "The conflict between Christianity and conjure," he claims, "was more theoretical than actual. . . . Christian tradition itself has always been attuned to special gifts (charisms) of the Spirit as they are manifested in prophecy, healing, and miracles. As a result, Christianity and conjure were not so much antithetical as complementary."[23] Here Raboteau highlights two areas of conjurational complementarity with Christianity—prophecy and healing—the latter of which we address in the next section.

Gayraud Wilmore also corroborates this connection, and in a manner that leads to the final topic of this section: the dynamic of conjuring God for freedom. For Wilmore claims that the fusion of African spirituality and biblical religion also undergirds early black *social prophetism*.[24] Whereas social-political prophetism in black experience may be distinguished from the kind of supernatural prophecy that constitutes a Christian "charism," it does not necessarily occur separably from it. Indeed, the experiential inseparability of Afro-Christian supernaturalism and social-political activism is a recurrent feature in the historical relationship of black religion and black radicalism. Perhaps the most celebrated instance of this spiritual-political ethos was the Haitian revolution of 1791, when Toussaint L'Ouverture led a slave revolt that successfully overthrew the French. That victory featured the prominent use of Vodun to secure supernatural invincibility for the Haitian combatants. It even led, following the revolution, to attempts to establish Vodun as Haiti's state religion. Moreover, the "conjuror's doctrine of invincibility"[25] was a distinctive feature of slave revolts in the United States as well, notably the betrayed 1822 conspiracy of Denmark Vesey in Charleston, South Carolina. Vesey preached from the Bible and espoused a radical Christianity, on the one hand, but also relied solidly on the conjurational practices of his coconspirator, Gullah Jack.

Furthermore we should recall the failed 1831 revolt and massacre of fifty-seven whites led by Nat Turner in Southampton County, Virginia, regarded by many as the bloodiest slave revolt in United States history. Turner, demonstrably and more self-consciously Christian than his fellow slaves, also eschewed the common, magical folk practices of conjuring as sub-Christian. "I always spoke of such things with contempt," his interviewer records in Turner's *Confessions*. Nonetheless, the evidence represents him as a seer and prophet, given to mystical or shamanic visions and dreams. Turner's mystical experiences gave rise to explicitly Christian symbolic interpretations (e.g., blood found on corn in the fields was Christ's blood "returning to earth again in the form of dew"), and also supported his convictions of divine retribution against slavery: "he had a remarkable vision in which white and black spirits were engaged in a great battle with blood flowing in streams."[26] Unusual as a literate slave, Turner like Vesey was a compelling Bible preacher. Together they represent two stages in the black religious tradition of conjuring God for freedom. Stage one, represented by Vesey, features magical conjurational practices alongside or in concert with the use of biblical and Christian theological elements. Stage two, represented by Turner, features ostensibly the repression of magical conjure but (precisely thereby) the return of conjurational impulses via Christian symbology and theological discourse. (This hypothesis applies Freud's concept of "the return of the repressed" to psychospiritual phenomena.)

The discussion of spiritual-political dynamics below describes the results of generations of black religionists practicing Vesey's and Turner's facility of *conjuring with Scripture* and *conjuring God for freedom.* (Such practices may be represented by the formula: "conjuring God with Scripture for freedom.") In that discussion it will be important to detail the major symbol systems and theological formations that now constitute a tradition of such practices. In this section we have been more concerned with showing the extending of conjure from its folk roots as "magical shamanism" (Joyner) to a mode of faith and prayer. Of course, the specifically religious or faith domain is not the only context in which such an extension has been evident. The transformative dimension of healing and therapy, as I discuss next, and also the aesthetic domain give evidence of this extension—the extension from "physico-magical power" (Cassirer) to theological and psychosocial modes of spiritual empowerment.

Ritual Healing, Communal Therapies, and Corporate Shamanism

[As] a symbolic means of addressing psychological and social conflict . . . the shaman's own body is the locus of symbol production and this aspect of shamanism distinguishes it from other types of religious activity that symbolically address psychological and social problems, such as prophecy and priestly activity.[27]

The embodied nature of Afro-American spirituality has been acknowledged in recent works by theologians James W. McClendon, Jr., and Archie Smith, Jr. That embodiment displays both therapeutic and ethical aspects. Most observers tend to focus on one or the other of these aspects. But it should be understood that "body ethics" (McClendon) and communal healing are integral in folk spirituality. That view is implied by Smith in his singular effort to "think ethics and therapy together" in the context of black church traditions. Smith acknowledges on the one hand the ancestral, "African character" of combining moral action and therapeutic practice. But he also finds one of its primary manifestations in the ongoing revival tradition of the black church. "Revivals *were* social and psychological therapy for the participants. It *is* a form of psychic release and healing, social cohesion, and a sense of communion with the Divine . . . [linking] therapeutic expressions with the moral life." Furthermore, Smith continues, the personal link between therapy and morality in the folk tradition has been the black preacher.[28]

Thus Smith represents the preacher as a folk "therapist" who is not only concerned with the psychological and spiritual wholeness of his congregation. Traditionally the black preacher has also been charged with securing the moral integrity and social-political freedom of the community. These composite tasks have united in one person the role of a "liberation" practitioner as well as a therapeutic agent for the community. The therapeutic benefits of revival preaching, and ecstatic worship generally, are stressed also by Henry Mitchell and Shelia Walker. Mitchell indicates both religious and secular contexts for the ecstasy which he regards as an instrument of psychic healing. In black worship the fact that both God and community accept the individual's unrestrained personal expression is experienced as a radical affirmation of "the usually concealed real person who . . . must be hidden almost everywhere else."[29]

But a more cogent parallel to the role of the black preacher or the musical performer than the therapist is the "shaman." In an illuminating discussion Amanda Porterfield examines the shamanic character of revival preachers in North America. Of course, the preaching event itself, since the frontier revivals of the eighteenth and nineteenth centuries in the United States, has been vividly documented as a type of ecstatic performance. What Porterfield attempts in a "psychosocial definition" is to distinguish effectively the shamanic element in such preaching from its prophetic or moral dimension. Especially notable is her insistence on the embodied nature of the preaching. As Porterfield observes, revival preaching

> often combines the prophetic activity of making moral pronouncements with the shamanic activity of representing human dilemmas in bodily gesture. Some preachers go into trances that enable them to act out the intense pain and hope that is represented by their symbols of sin and redemption. . . . The compelling power of these preachers is in large part the result of their ability to dramatically embody the emotional problems and social tensions besetting their patrons.[30]

In Porterfield's view, shamanism is personally *embodied* symbol production for the purpose of psychological and social *conflict resolution*. With reference to psychic conflicts it is instructive to note that shamans have often been the subject of their own curative abilities. To repeat Porterfield's emphasis we may say that the shaman personally embodies his or her own therapy. Studies of the shaman as a neurotic, and of shamanic insight as analogous to schizophrenia, have stressed the pathological aspect of the shamanic personality. But balanced observers also stress the curative dimension: "As Eliade puts it, the shaman is not merely a sick man [*sic*] but a sick man who has been cured and has become an agency of curative powers."[31]

Yet in Afro-America one observes not only singular individuals but also family groups and larger networks that function as deliberate agencies of psychosocial cure. Here we may refer particularly to the cure of disorders generated by the oppression of racism. Such effects are experienced by any "target group" in its prolonged mistreatment by a more dominant contact group. Deteriorating self-esteem, internalized feelings of inferiority, and intergroup mistrust are among the demonstrable results of such mistreatment. But to stress those negatives without also affirming the recuperative effect of "revitalization movements"[32] that occur in the history of most oppressed cultures is to reduce the real complexity of their experience. Moreover such exclusive emphasis prevents our recognition of a "corporate shamanism" that often serves to obviate the worst effects of oppression and of oppressive social conditioning.

Corporate shamanism in black culture is especially evident in mass revitalization movements, like the 1960s freedom movement in the United States, that promote communal therapy as well as social-political reform. Thus, Archie Smith describes as a "therapeutic relationship . . . a change in oppressive relational patterns which relieves the suffering of the oppressed and may result in constructive and supportive relations in society." Such relationships in black experience, he indicates, have been found in contexts ranging from one-to-one settings, family systems, small groups like churches and self-help groups, and neighborhood and other community agencies, to large group settings and mass social movements like bus boycotts, labor strikes, organized demonstrations, and other forms of protest and revolutionary struggle. Many participants in the civil rights and antiwar movements, for example, experienced social change as a context for self-examination and personal reintegration. Such matters can be intrinsically correlated to issues of oppression and overcoming oppression through solidarity with others. Occasions for singing together, marching together, and reevaluating together have created "action–reflection" models that address not only issues of social change but also matters of personal transformation.[33]

Furthermore, these movements can be described as shamanic when their social and political visions display incantatory dynamics. The incantatory factor in such visions, to use the formulation that Kenneth Burke borrowed from John Crowe Ransom, consists in their "function as a device for inviting us to 'make ourselves over in the image of the imagery.'"[34] Black communities have performed incantations in this manner by corporately embodying biblical symbols of suffering and redemption, of captivity and freedom, of judgment and forgiveness. They have harnessed these symbols to their own socially despised skin color and bodily features in order, like the shaman, to perform a psychosocial transformation. Perhaps the most striking instance of this sort is the Afro-American embodiment of the biblical figure, the Suffering Servant (Isaiah 53:1–3). As Gayraud Wilmore observes,

> Black people have been struck not only with the similarity of what seemed to be their inexorable fate as a race and the Messianic vocation of suffering, but also with the profound, if not exact correspondence between their experience of blackness in Western civilization and the description of the Messiah. "He had no form or comeliness that we should look at him, and no beauty that we should desire him. He was despised and rejected by men; a man of sorrows, and acquainted with grief. . . . And we esteemed him not."[35]

That experience or "vocation" of suffering has been theologically articulated as "redemptive suffering": the Christian spiritual principle that suffering *for* Christ, *in* Christ, *with* Christ, or *as* Christ, possesses peculiarly transcendent power for transforming the world.

This theology has fallen under much censure from black radicals, as a kind of religious docility or even masochism, since the Black Power movement eclipsed King's explicitly Christian vision. Certainly there are forms of internalized oppression in which negative self-regard and consequent self-abuse have masqueraded as a spirituality of suffering. But a counterfeit does not cancel the reality of the genuine phenomenon. Giving one's body to be blasted by fire hoses and bitten by police dogs in Sheriff Bull Connor's Birmingham during a civil rights march provided a high opportunity for the authentic, and Dr. Martin Luther King's religious leadership specialized in such social-political opportunities. Moreover, even in Christian traditions an aspect of the shaman's task is required in the "discerning of spirits" (1 Corinthians 12:10)—the task of determining whether an ecstatic or avowedly spiritual performance is authentic or counterfeit. In any case, corporate shamanism in black America has convincingly displayed Christian patterns of redemptive suffering in order to transform both the internal and external worlds of "race hatred."[36]

In his essay on political philosophers as shamans, James M. Glass addresses both of the aspects emphasized in the preceding discussion—both the therapeutic and incantatory elements in effective political visions. "What the shaman does, how he enters into a diseased situation, depends on his capacity to construct 'signs,' to devise an incantation that will reach the unconscious . . . [an ability] as critical to the political vision."[37] The incantatory signs that have functioned most powerfully in North America, at the level of "the unconscious," are biblical symbols. Already we have anticipated the incantatory use of such symbols in Denmark Vesey's and Nat Turner's facility of conjuring God with Scripture for freedom. Since that discussion we have also observed, however, the emergence in black history of communities of practitioners in addition to singular individuals. In the concluding discussion we will examine some of the specific biblical symbols employed in this socially transformative, corporate shamanism.

Spiritual-Aesthetic Dynamics in Black Culture

The fact that none of the instruments we used were invented by us, meant that we had to impose on borrowed instruments an aesthetic convention that we obviously possessed even before we acquired them. This is significant. It indicates that a Black aesthetic existed, and that this aesthetic has always governed what we have produced. . . . These were spiritual things, not physical artifacts. When those Black men began to handle those instruments, they were directly in contact with their gods.[38]

Ritual Structures and Black Music

Ritual and incantatory dynamics can be observed also in black aesthetic productions. Here we must limit our observations to music and discourse; however, it should be understood that Afro-American drama and visual arts can also display the heritage of African spirituality.[39] For illustrative purposes we treat first the following aspects of black music that typically occur as elements in ritual performances: style-switching, call-and-response or antiphony, and improvisation. These musical phenomena in particular disclose the means by which Afro-Americans have become a bicultural or a multicultural people. Indeed, musical expression is so indicative of deep structures in the culture that author James Baldwin declared: "It is only in his music . . . that the Negro in America has been able to tell his story."[40]

As shown in the Introduction, a major feature of that story has been the achievement of a new peoplehood in the Americas. That achievement is peculiarly embedded in a distinctive ritual structure called "style-switching" by the social linguist Morton Marks. Based on his research in ethno-musicology Marks presents evidence of this structure in the music of black cultural groups in both the United States and the Caribbean. The essential feature of style-switching is the alternating of patterned expression from the forms of one cultural system to those of a different system. Marks claims further that this alternation functions to induce trance behavior during sacred as well as secular ritual events. "There is more going on than what is conventionally called 'expressive behavior.' *The change in style is generating a ritual event, namely spirit-possession.*" The key to inducing the trance state is the abrupt shift or switch from one element of the dualism to the other. "What is crucial for the discussion is that switching is always from a 'white' style to a 'black' style, from a European to an African one."[41]

The polarization of styles between two cultural systems, one identified as African and the other as European or American, constitutes the duality. In this manner style-switching may be regarded as a by-product of culture contact. The resulting dual symbolization provides a kind of record or deposit of that contact, as Marks suggests, and creates models for patterning other aesthetic productions. But here we should recall that much in advance of Marks's research, W. E. B. DuBois had articulated a more general theory of *double consciousness.* The term refers to DuBois's view of Afro-Americans as a bicultural people who are both African and American; both "black" and "white." His definitive statement of this perspective is found in the essay called significantly "Of Our Spiritual Strivings." Already in 1903, when that essay was included in his celebrated *The Souls of Black Folk,* DuBois represented Afro-American history as "the history of this strife—this longing to attain self-conscious manhood, to merge his double self into a better and truer self. In this merging he wishes neither of the older selves to be lost."[42]

It is that notion of shifting or alternating between the two worlds of DuBois's double consciousness that leads intrinsically to Marks's concept of style-switching. What Marks's concept adds to previous formulations is a structural basis for demonstrating the concrete operation of this duality in a specific domain of black culture: music. But the duality itself of Afro- and Euro-American cultural expressions operates in black discourse as well, as shown immediately below. Before proceeding it is important, however, to observe other modes of spirituality in black musical expression, besides the "trance-associated features" (Marks) that accompany style-switching. In addition to trance states, the deep structure of cultural duality can also convey what Peter Berger has called "signals of transcendence." Indeed, the black literary critic Ralph Ellison has observed how such signals were a compelling feature of the Afro-American musical tradition from the early to mid-twentieth century. That period featured the creative prominence of musicians who felt impelled to master both American jazz and European classical music.

> Culturally everything was mixed, you see, and beyond all question of conscious choices there was a level where you were claimed by emotion and movement and moods which you couldn't put into words. Often we wanted to share both: the classics and jazz, the Charleston and the Irish reel, spirituals and the blues, the sacred and the profane. . . . There were certain emotions, certain needs for other *forms of transcendence* and identification which I could only associate with classical music. I heard it in Beethoven, I heard it in Schumann.[43]

Here Ellison illustrates quite clearly how black musical expression is uniquely suited for displaying cultural dualism between forms identified as black or African and those identified as white or European. With remarkable insight he then proceeds to specify the nature of the transcendence indicated above: "You got glimpses, very vague glimpses, of a far different world than that assigned by segregation laws, and I was taken very early with a passion to link together all I loved within the Negro community and all those things I felt in the world which lay beyond." The transcending of ethnic segregation and cultural isolation[44] through biculturality provides a typical instance of the factors that have shaped Afro-American spirituality from its beginnings in the New World.

In addition to style-switching and genre correlation, there are two other aspects of black music that convey spiritual dynamics: call-and-response and improvisation. Just as style-switching displays ritual structures, so these other aspects of musical expression can also facilitate ritual processes. Speaking of black gospel music, for example, in which antiphony and improvisation recur, ethnomusicologist Pearl Williams-Jones observes that "the gospel experience is almost ritualistic in its sustained drama and spiritual intensity. People are possessed and overcome in this state of high religious ecstasy." Afro-American antiphony, or call-and-response, arises from the participatory aspect of African social performances. "During the narration of traditional tales by the griots it was considered impolite to listen 'dumbly'. . . . Passive audience attitudes are Western European aesthetic norms."[45]

The notion of a black aesthetic that is distinctive and observably different from Western values and conventions was axiomatic for the Black Arts movement of the 1960s and 1970s.[46] Referring to gospel music as a "crystalization" of that aesthetic, Williams-Jones notes how closely a gospel music concert approximates a black church congregation dynamically interacting with the preacher or the choir. The singer (or preacher) might call out, for example,

>What's wrong with Jesus?

and the expected audience response is shouted back,

>He's alright!

Such patterns can be repeated indefinitely through simple verbal variations.

>Caller: He's food when I'm hungry!
>Response: He's alright!
>Caller: He's water when I'm thirsty!
>Response: He's alright!

Or there may follow improvisational exchanges involving irony or "paradoxical communication" (Marks).

>Caller: Some say Jesus is the white man's god.
>Response: He's *still* alright!

In this manner and in more complex patterns a full musical event would elicit audience responses in combination with the leader's "calls."

In his definitive study of black preaching, Henry Mitchell also notes the concurrence of improvisational dynamics in black music and the preaching event. The subject arises significantly in the context of his observation that black preachers traditionally have not used the Bible in the manner of white Christian fundamentalists: "Black dependence on scripture is not slavish or literal." Then comparing this creative use of the Bible to musical performances, Mitchell acknowledges that "the riff or improvisation on the melody, so characteristic of the Black jazz instrumentalist or vocalist, is Black spontaneity at its best. The same freedom applied to the melodic line in Black gospels or religious Soul music is the very trademark of Black culture."[47] Throughout his book Mitchell richly illustrates this hermeneutic (interpretive) freedom with sermon texts from black preachers.

Yet the participatory and improvisational aspects of black creativity extend not only to preaching and other oratory but also to matters of political theory and practice. Such an instance is provided by Albert Murray with reference to black political activism. Extending Baldwin's focus on the preeminence of music referred to at the beginning of this section, Murray indicates how its improvisational aspect serves as a unique resource for measuring cultural integrity and spiritual authenticity in other domains of Afro-American endeavor.

>Perhaps even the young black radicals will move beyond their present academic reverence for radicalism per se and begin playing improvisations on the gospels of Marx, Mao, Guevara, and Fanon. Perhaps even they will begin

to realize that when great Negro musicians like Armstrong, Basie, Ellington, and Parker play by ear, they do so not because they cannot read the score but because in the very process of mastering it they have found it inadequate for their purposes.[48]

Crucial for black spirituality in its aesthetic manifestations is this "will to transformation." Its intentional character consists in an extreme reluctance to passively transmit previously received instruments, artifacts, cultural practices or cognitive materials. On the one hand, improvisation is an aesthetic convention singularly employed in black culture by the jazz player or the blues singer. On the other hand, it is a principle of ethnic and spiritual authentication operating throughout the culture and its productions, including its speech and literary discourse.

Rituals of Black Discourse

Signifying can be a tactic employed in game activity—verbal dueling ... however, [it] also refers to a way of encoding messages or meanings which involves, in most cases, an element of indirection. . . . Viewed as an alternative message form, selected for its artistic merit, [it] may occur embedded in a variety of discourse . . . [yet] not define the entire speech event.[49]

In his literary theory Kenneth Burke also recognized ritual drama as the primal form of human action. Burke described ritual, appropriately using metaphor, as the "hub" from which all other forms of distinctively human action radiate as if they were the spokes of a wheel. Human discourse, in such a view, is best understood as "symbolic action" which still retains genetic elements of its ritual origins. It thereby conveys primal significations, as if continuing to function within a "ritual cosmos" (Zuesse) irrespective of changing contexts. Of course, some language users are more proficient in utilizing the power of discourse to retrieve and recreate ritual significations: poets and vocalists, preachers and orators, writers and dramatists. Their varied inducements to restore a ritual cosmos are also an invitation to make the figurative efficacious—to participate in symbols not only cognitively, but so as to fulfill them on the scale of group actions and social dramas. "One must learn to enact the world differently," observes one researcher. "One must see every *thing* as *symbol*. It takes constant repetition and dramatization to achieve this ritual vision of life."[50]

In order to disclose this ritual enactment in the dynamics of black discourse we may profitably refer to the work of black literary theorist Henry Louis Gates, Jr. Gates discusses a rhetorical strategy often displayed in Afro-American social rituals called "signifying." He defines it as an indigenous and unique black rhetorical construct occurring in both written and verbal discourse. In "signifyin(g) . . . a second statement or figure repeats, or tropes, or reverses the first." Gates locates the folk roots of the verbal art in African storytelling and particularly in the trickster characterization found in the "Signifying Monkey tales" of black folklore in North America. As a folk hermeneutic, signifying is an interpretive art, a discipline for eliciting meanings beyond the dictionary or lexical signification of the words involved.[51]

Furthermore, manipulating this surplus of meanings involves games of reinterpretation and counterinterpretation, as well as devices for subtly tricking, misleading, or outwitting others. But perhaps most interesting for present purposes is the usefulness of the device for understanding the "intertextual relation" (Gates) between black and white systems of meaning. Two instructive instances of intertextuality in Afro-American literature are provided by the fictional creations of a scholar and a folklorist, W. E. B. DuBois and Zora Neale Hurston. DuBois in his 1911 novel, *The Quest of the Silver Fleece,* interweaves black history with Greco-Roman mythology, whereas Hurston, in her 1939 *Moses: Man of the Mountain,* allegorizes black experience using the exodus story. Using the vernacular term we may say that in his novel DuBois "signifies on" texts of Greek mythology, whereas Hurston signifies on the Bible, and that each Afro-American work exists in intertextual relation to one of the foundational literatures of Western culture.[52]

Under the various modes of signifying, Gates gives a rather technical list of tropes or rhetorical devices "used in the ritual of signifying." He thereby acknowledges the performative contexts in which the device occurs and then catalogues such performances using their vernacular nomenclature: "marking, loud-talking, testifying, calling out (of one's name), sounding, rapping, playing the dozens, and so on." But Gates is not satisfied with such lists and catalogues; he pursues further the trickster impulse operating in ritual performances that employ signifying. Indeed, he proceeds to locate the source of that impulse in an indigenous West African spirituality whose contemporary ambience is Pan-African. This spirituality is focused on the sacred trickster of the Yoruba people, "Esu" or "Eshu-Elegbara," who is also found in the Americas.[53] Indeed, several functional similarities arise between this Pan-African *orisha* (spirit) and the Pan-Hellenic god of interpretation, Hermes. Accordingly, we may observe various parallels between Esu and the deity whose very name figures in the Western philosophy of interpretation, "hermeneutics."

By analogy, Gates declares, as Hermes is to hermeneutics so is Esu to the Afro-American discipline of tropological significations. Moreover, Esu as the *orisha* (spirit) of sacred interpretation has his mundane or "profane" counterpart in the Signifying Monkey, a trickster character who provides

16. Romare Bearden, *The Prevalence of Ritual: Baptism*, 1964.

a model of virtuosity in black discourse. In the Afro-American folktale that bears his name, the monkey succeeds in outwitting the lion by speaking figuratively or symbolically in a code that the lion interprets literally, to his own embarrassment and misfortune. Such "tricks" of discourse (compare conjure "tricks"), which effectively overturn the dominance of an antagonist, were routine in the antebellum South among slaves who practiced verbal deceits called, "puttin' on ol' massa." A form of signifying discourse that often provided a means of survival during escape attempts, or an everyday strategy of self-defense from physical abuse, such deception also operated in the use of signifying black music. Both the spirituals and the blues feature the use of coded discourse. In this connection some slave spirituals, like "Steal Away to Jesus," have been analyzed by Mark Miles Fisher as secret messages for organizing meetings and planning escapes. Another commentator has described a much broader relationship between sacred music and social change in black history and contemporary culture.[54]

In seeking to trace an ancestral, African spirituality for Afro-American signifying, we are clearly in the position of theorizing as cultural "hermeneuts" or philologists rather than as ethnographers. In any case, it is useful to regard signifying as an oral or vernacular version of that more formal, literary intertextuality "by which texts—poems and novels—respond to other texts."[55] From that perspective we turn now to the final interest of this study—what might be designated as rituals of "theological signifying" or as intertextuality between black and white systems of religious meaning. For in black social figuration we find a use of biblical texts that serves to respond to, reverse, and "trope" the conventional "texts" and structures of racial domination operating in American culture. As shown next, in the effort to overturn such structures Afro-Americans have improvised biblical texts. We will also see how they have devised counterstrategies and "antistructures" (Turner), not arbitrarily, but for the purpose of making ritual transitions to an American *communitas*—for the practical realization of such political visions as Dr. Martin Luther King's "beloved community."

Spiritual-Political Dynamics
in Black Religion and Culture

The first theological formulations by Afro-Americans based on biblical texts tried to come to terms with their white owners' view points and their own servitude. Since its inception, black theology has been forced to reduce white deception and distortion of the gospel and make the Christian story meaningful in the light of their oppressive conditions.[56]

In their reflections upon Lincoln's Emancipation Proclamation, Christian freedpersons and their folk theologians realized that an event of biblical narrative could become an occurrence in their own historical experience. Lincoln's presidential order, following upon the cataclysm of the Civil War, showed that the miraculous exodus of Hebrew slaves out of Egyptian bondage could become a mundane reality in contemporary terms. The implications of that lesson reinforced previous perceptions of prophetic fulfillment and presaged future repetitions. The likelihood of ongoing recapitulations of biblical narrative became immediately accessible, even compelling, to the religious apprehension of thousands. Henceforth more than a committed minority of believers and converts would be convinced of the possibility that through prayer and expectation, through acts of obedience and righteousness, black folk could inherit divine promises of prosperity and freedom. Furthermore, an apparent precondition for such bestowals would appear to be their linkage to biblical models. That singular instance, the link between Lincoln's role in the emancipation and Moses' role in the exodus, would distinguish itself as a kind of paradigm. In this manner the ancient tradition of biblical typology or figuralism became implanted in the collective soul of a people.

Typology is the hermeneutic (interpretive) tradition that links biblical types or figures to postbiblical persons, places, and events. Moreover, it is crucial for this hermeneutic that each particular dyad of a biblical "type" and its postbiblical "antitype" should be understood to represent a fulfillment of prophecy.[57] The origins of this tradition go back beyond the medieval period to the Christian Scriptures and the early church. Taken as a whole, the two millennia have witnessed its formation into a uniquely Christian spirituality. Black religious figuralism also participates in that spiritual heritage. Nonetheless, its adoption by Afro-Americans did not arise in a vacuum. Neither is that adoption solely attributable to the pervasive influence of Puritan typology on all immigrant and relocated groups in United States culture. That Puritan influence has been so insistent, it is true, that one commentator has coined the term "typological ethnogenesis" to comprehend it. Admittedly, disparate ethnic communities of whites, Jews, and peoples of color have adopted the Puritan figuration of America. Just as the Puritans configured New England as "God's new Israel," as "Canaan" and as "promised land," in order to create their group identity as a New World "chosen people," so have subsequent ethnic communities adopted and adapted that strategy.[58] Nonetheless, a careful ethnographic investigation would reveal that each of them did so in distinctive ways, accommodating the Puritan hermeneutic to their antecedent traditions of spirituality.

Thus it is best to emphasize the bicultural nature of black religious experience. Maintaining a bicultural perspective insures that the complexity of the phenomena is displayed, rather than reducing black spirituality either to imputed African (ritual) elements or to Christian theological conventions like biblical typology. To complicate matters further one commentator has disclosed ritual elements in American Puritan typology[59] while another, as we saw in the discussion of black discourse, has attempted to locate black figural impulses in an African spirituality. Rather than attempt somehow to resolve these matters with ethnographic precision it is sufficient to acknowledge that Afro-American spirituality features composite phenomena. In the case of black religious figuralism we do so by acknowledging the Puritan typological framework as well as the fact that Afro-Americans have adapted that framework to their own uses. That is, they have *improvised* and *signified upon* Puritan typology.

Biblical Figures and Black Significations

The biblical figures that are recurrently selected to inscribe black sociopolitical experiences are exodus, Ethiopia and Egypt, promised land, captivity (exile) and diaspora. Before reviewing these selections as discrete political *configurations* in a typological repertory, however, it is instructive first to introduce them as biblical *figures*. Following a brief comment on the primary figure of exodus, therefore, we look at two other major figures and their "significations"[60] in black experience: Ethiopia and Egypt.

The Exodus Figure

> Slaves prayed for the future day of deliverance to come, and they kept hope alive by incorporating as part of *their* mythic past the Old Testament exodus of Israel out of slavery. . . . The Christian slaves applied the Exodus story, whose end they knew, to their own experience of slavery, which had not ended. . . . Exodus functioned as an archetypal event for the slaves. The sacred history of God's liberation of his [*sic*] people would be or was being repeated in the American South.[61]

In slave religion the figural vision of the emancipation as a type of biblical "exodus" provides the paradigm for subsequent strategies and acts of political imagination. The exodus figure has informed Afro-American political projects from the post-Reconstruction period to the recent civil rights movement, in which a premier instance is Martin Luther King's final speech, "I've been to the mountaintop!" There King envisioned himself as Moses on Mt. Pisgah who looks over into the promised land and affirms that, while he may not get there, someday his people will.[62] But exodus figuration is not the only phenomenon of its kind in black culture. As we will see, related forms of religious figuralism operate as well in other political projects of the nineteenth and twentieth centuries, including black nationalist projects of revitalization. Those projects were spiritual-political in that they sought to transcend the prevailing structures of social oppression by using religious discourse to render the New World and the Old a locus of *communitas*—of freedom, wholeness, and cultural creativity for black peoples.

Thus, on the one hand, "white Christians had identified the journey across the Atlantic to the New World as the exodus of a new Israel from the bondage of Europe into the promised land of milk and honey." But, on the other hand, "for the black Christian, as Vincent Harding has observed, the imagery was reversed: the Middle Passage had brought his people to Egypt land, where they suffered bondage under Pharaoh. White Christians saw themselves as a new Israel; slaves identified themselves as the old."[63] It is this propensity for not only appropriating but here also reversing or "troping" Euro-Christian symbolism that distinguishes the improvisational element in black culture.

The Ethiopia Figure

It is estimated that the single biblical verse most often quoted in black American religious history is not from the book of Exodus, as might be expected, but from Psalms.[64] Psalm 68:31 reads, "Princes shall come out of Egypt; Ethiopia shall soon stretch out her hands to God" (King James Version). Probably eighteenth-century missionary interpretation bequeathed to black believers the use of Ethiopia as a symbol for all Africa and for black people everywhere. White Christians may also have first interpreted the verse as a prophecy of the mass conversion of black people to the faith. Finally, it also seems to be a product of European chauvinism to claim that God's "providential design" ordained the slave trade in order to bring Christianity to Africa.[65] But gradually Afro-Americans cast the Christian fulfillment of the prophecy in their own perspective.

Generations of interpretation eventually developed into a literary-religious tradition called "Ethiopianism," which spanned the late eighteenth to the early twentieth century and engaged black communities on both the African and American continents. In Ethiopianism, Psalm 68:31 "came to be interpreted as a promise that Africa would 'soon' experience a dramatic political, industrial, and economic renaissance." This notion of African resurgence—particularly in the face of the slave trade and Africa's nineteenth-century humiliation by European colonialism—also looked for the decline of the West. "The rise in the fortunes of Africa and all her scattered children would be accompanied by God's judgement upon Europeans." Indeed, this commentator recognizes that through such interpretations nineteenth- and twentieth-century black nationalists have effectively "conjured" with Psalm 68:31.[66]

The Egypt Figure

It should be observed that Psalm 68:31 features both Egypt and Ethiopia as figures for prophetic fulfillment. The Ethiopia figure is explicitly situated in the conversion theme of the second half of the verse: "Ethiopia shall soon stretch out her hands to God." However, Ethiopianism as a social-political movement has been energized in addition by the first half of the prophecy regarding Egypt: "*Princes* shall come out of Egypt"—not slaves whether Hebrew or African! Here we must observe that the negative valuation of Egypt, which conventionally operates in exodus figuration, is reversed in mature developments of Ethiopianism. For historically informed Ethiopianists, ancient Egypt was equally significant as a civilization of black rulers and as the Bible's prison house of Hebrew slaves. An affirmation and even celebration of Egypt occurred, as Gayraud Wilmore points out, among black abolitionists and preachers of the nineteenth century and among black intellectuals following the First World War.[67] Indeed we may recognize the yearning for a Pan-African *communitas* in their antistructural, counteridentification with Egypt and Ethiopia as the two great monarchies of ancient Africa. In their countercultural figuration, Egypt appears as a focus of ethnic pride and reclaimed heritage instead of (conventionally) the land of bondage and oppression. The celebrated wealth and stature of Egypt as one of the earliest human civilizations emerge in Ethiopianism through the retrieval of black people as leaders of culture and representatives of civilization.

A Ritual Repertory of Political Configurations

> The black experience in America is not the Jewish Christian experience in ancient Palestine. . . . [But] the same hermeneutical process which confronts us with the message from Scripture also suggests those categories by which we can deal creatively with the word being spoken by the Black experience.[68]

In this discussion, a configuration is a distinctive pattern of political arrangements that typify a particular period in black social and economic development. Of course, the term deliberately echoes the biblical "figure" embedded in each configural phase. We should also note that, however providential they might be, configurations are experientially and empirically (verifiably) grounded in the intensive patterning of communities upon biblical models. Accordingly, the exodus figure grounds political patterns and arrangements that are referred to here as exodus configurations, the Ethiopia figure forms Ethiopia configurations, and so on with the promised land figure and other patterns. Together these configurations comprise a kind of catalogue or, better expressed, a repertory. Like a music or drama repertory of selections, they provide repeatable alternatives for social and political performances.

The Exodus Configuration

> Whenever the Judeo-Christian tradition has been accessible to oppressed peoples, this scenario of election, captivity and liberation has captured the imagination. . . .[69]

In the black figural tradition it appears that all corporate liberation efforts are envisioned, in the manner of ritual performances, as dramatic reenactments of exodus, and their leaders as approximate types of Moses. We have already referred to the black freedom movement of the 1960s and Dr. Martin Luther King's "Mosaic" leadership in it. But black liberation during the decade of sixties offers only the latest indication of the force of this figural principle. The earliest instance of the configuration antedates even the emancipation-exodus of the slaves in 1863. For we must recall that there were prior emancipation events of various northern states, as well as the termination of the slave trade in Britain and its New World colonies in 1807. The New York State emancipation of 1827, in which Sojourner Truth was freed, provides a case in point. It should also be recalled that following the Civil War era, there occurred the exodus events of the post-Reconstruction generation, extending through the late 1870s and the 1880s. These were not emancipations but migrations: the beginning of the mass migrations of blacks out of the South that culminated in the great urban and northward migrations of the early twentieth century.

Indeed, participants and contemporary observers alike used the term "exodus" to describe the migrations.[70] But irrespective of the use of the term or its spaciotemporal locus, these varying configural patterns meant liberation. "Few men ever worshipped Freedom with half such unquestioning faith as did the American Negro for two centuries," DuBois wrote in *The Souls of Black Folk* a generation after that period. "Emancipation was the key to a promised land of sweeter beauty than ever stretched before the eyes of wearied Israelites."[71] Further discussion of this primary exodus-emancipation configuration must await a larger work. But before ending here we should observe the remarkable representation by a black woman of the patriarchal figure of Moses. It was Harriet Tubman, of course, who was the woman called during her own lifetime "the Moses of her people." Tubman earned this distinction by her performance as a liberator of three hundred slaves on the underground railroad. This instance shows how a black woman also, mistreated as chattel and still stereotyped as "the mule of the world,"[72] has been transformed into a Moses by the "troping" virtuosity of black political figuration.

The Ethiopia Configuration

> Ethiopianism might have remained merely an escapist myth-system based upon Biblical proof-texts and confined to the circle of Negro church people had not a brilliant black scholar appeared on the scene in the 1870's and 1880's. . . . Their movement sprouted from the seed-bed of folk Ethiopianism. . . . His great contribution was toward the development of African "cultural nationalism."[73]

St. Clair Drake in particular has charted the transition from a specifically religious figuration of Psalm 68:31, to its political employment in black nationalism. Ethiopianism had previously served to motivate black Christians in their own missionary efforts to "redeem" Africa by spreading the gospel and making converts there. As we saw above, the Psalm was regarded as prophecy of Africa and her scattered children "stretching out her hands to God" through mass conversion to Christianity. Ethiopianism therefore initially comprised a religious vision. Then arose a singular thinker who remolded Ethiopianism to promote, first, New World emigration back to Africa. Most radically, however, Edward Wilmot Blyden (1832–1912) extended Ethiopianism to create a post-Christian cultural nationalism. "When shorn of Christian beliefs about [Africa's] 'degeneration' and 'redemption' through conversion to Christ, Ethiopianist thinking leads to a belief that the forces are latent within Africa itself to 'redeem' it."[74]

Interestingly, Edwin S. Redkey has described the emigrationist and black nationalist periods of Ethiopianism as a "Black Exodus." The term applies because of the back-to-Africa motivation of black nationalism—a motivation that operated as late as the Garvey movement of the 1920s (the largest mass movement in black history). But this variation in figural terminology serves only to highlight the improvisational aspects of a configural repertory. In this repertory, as we saw in the preceding section, exodus and Ethiopia figurations have been blended together in order to increase the magnitude and imaginative power of connections between black destiny and biblical narrative. Thus, the "flexibility in the black story"[75] allows for black nationalism to be alternatively configured by both exodus and Ethiopia figuration. Indeed, the same crossing of the Atlantic Ocean by which Africans were transported to the Americas is reversed by emigration. In such a reversal, the intratextual imagination can configure the return to Africa as a crossing of the Red Sea *back to Egypt!* But, as we saw in the section above, in such a configuration the Egypt figure has been revaluated by black cultural nationalists as a positive representation of African greatness and potential destiny. By means of such improvisational creativity a Pan-African exodus can lead out of captivity or exile in the New World.

Inverse Configurations: Promised Land versus Captivity

> The idea that America is the Promised Land is compromised almost beyond repair. Injustice, war, ecological devastation, runaway technology, etc., have served to tarnish the dream, perhaps forever. Finally, few of us today look for miraculous, divine intervention as a solution for man's evil.[76]

Afro-American figuration of the United States as promised land has been called into question since the defeat of democratic reforms in the South following Reconstruction. Already in 1903, in his "Spiritual Strivings" essay in *The Souls of Black Folk*, DuBois depicted with suitable pathos the aging freedpersons' slow realization, decade after decade, that their yearning for a promised land was being met instead by a generation of wilderness wanderings (an applicable figure drawn from Deuteronomy 1:34–40). With respect to that realization, and subsequent realizations like it throughout the first half of this century, we must regard any purported promised land configuration in Afro-American social history with great caution and circumspection. Indeed, to the extent that the socioeconomic requirements of capitalism maintain a permanent poverty class in the United States, a configuration based on that system merits close scrutiny.

Precisely such a scrutiny is evident in the "Message to the Black Church and Community" issued by a conference of black theologians who met in Atlanta, Georgia, in 1977. Speaking with pastoral concern about black middle-class "desperation," the group expressed their concern about

> poverty of soul and spirit. We do not believe that better jobs and bigger houses, color televisions and latest model cars prove that people have attained the abundant life of which Jesus spoke. That abundant life cannot be experienced by a people captive to the idolatry of a sensate and materialistic culture.[77]

Inverting the theme of American prosperity with the theme of captivity to materialism, the conference went on to repudiate "physical gratification as the purpose of life" and the "voidance of the gospel's moral, ethical standards." Such a critique of the promised land configuration as a secularized story of capitalist success, and the corresponding prophetic effort to reconfigure black social experience in egalitarian terms, represents a drive toward *communitas* that is more than liberalism. It is also liberationist. "The identification of black liberation with the material success of a few, physically and mentally severed from the black masses, makes mockery of the unity essential for the salvation of us all."

Accordingly, "captivity" rather than "promised land" may best represent the historical present for the two major groupings in black society: the poor and the more successful. The black poverty class is barred from a fulfilled promised land configuration, in continuity with political and economic forces obtaining since the Reconstruction period. Prosperous Afro-Americans are impelled to identify their success with the capitalist scenario of an American Dream which, in turn, distorts the Puritan's "Canaan" configuration of early America. Certainly, the promised land configuration has existed as a source of hope and visionary inspiration for many. At best it has also become a partial socioeconomic reality in black experience. But the cocaptivity of the poor and of the successful to social structures that maintain their respective economic and spiritual impoverishment indicates the ambiguous, if not entirely vitiated, status of that reality.

The Diaspora Configuration

> The Biblical image which has been at the heart of the Black man's [sic] faith in the eventual appropriation of the American myth must be replaced. . . .
> My own very untested suggestion about a possible new image is that of an African Diaspora based on the Biblical story of the Babylonian Exile and the final Jewish Diaspora. It is to the end of the Biblical history of Israel that Black America must look rather than to the beginning.[78]

In 1973 the black theologian Charles Shelby Rooks proposed to abandon the now "compromised" figuration of promised land, along with its tarnished secular derivative of "the American dream." Rooks's tentative suggestion was to reconfigure contemporary black experience as a recapitulation of the Babylonian captivity and the Jewish diaspora. But what Rooks proposed speculatively at the beginning of the 1970s seems increasingly applicable as the century comes to a close. In contemporary black culture the configurations of captivity and diaspora appear most compelling. One intriguing application of the Babylonian captivity figure was borrowed from the black Muslims by the 1960s militant group from Oakland, California, the Black Panther Party. Panther rhetoric alternated the terms "Babylon" and "Babylon America," in mixed metaphorical fashion, with "white devil America," but their use was essentially a reduction of the figure to mean "a decadent society."[79]

The term "African Diaspora" was also employed during the sixties, perhaps for the first time. However, the figural correspondence between the dispersal of Jewish and black African peoples has been recognized since the early nineteenth century, if not before. The word "diaspora" itself derives from the Greek word for dispersion and was typically applied to the "scattering" (as in Nehemiah 1:8) of the Jews among Gentile nations beginning with the fall of the northern kingdom to Assyria in 721 B.C.E. and the Babylonian Exile in 586 B.C.E. The dispersal of Jews in the Hellenistic world of the Roman Empire sets the scene for the rare appearances of the word in the Christian Scriptures (e.g., John 7:35). But historian George Shepperson reminds us that diaspora has extended applications as well.

> This process of Jewish migration from their homeland into all parts of the world not only created a term which could be applied to any other substantial and significant group of migrants, but also provided a concept which could be used to interpret the experience (ofter very bitter experiences) of other peoples who had been driven out of their native countries by forces similar to those which had dispersed the Jews: in particular, slavery and imperialism.[80]

But, like the other configurations, diaspora inherits certain religious-ethical or spiritual implications, by virtue of its figural embeddedness in biblical narrative. It may seem unlikely that Christian spiritual dynamics are attached to the diaspora figure as it is currently employed in black culture. The term may appear incontrovertibly secular now, because of the ostensible social-science orientation of its usage. Probably more influential is its political utility in providing a post-Ethiopianist conceptual framework for Pan-Africanism, as "the latter-day ideology of the African diaspora" (Shepperson). Nonetheless, the "ethnogenesis" (Sollors) of political configurations is not inconsequential.

Unavoidably, a transcendent dimension adheres to diaspora, not through mystification but because the Jewish and black cultures that employ it remain hermeneutic communities with strong traditions of biblical self-identification. Can it really be coincidental that a biblical figure is increasingly accepted by literate Afro-Americans as a designation for their contemporary experience and realities? Can a compelling symbol emerge rootless in such a culture, severed from its origins in a sacred narrative? On the contrary, as Stephen Crites maintains in his essay on the narrative quality of human experience, "A people's mundane stories are implicit in its sacred story, and every mundane story takes soundings in the sacred story."[81]

Crites's comment applies in a peculiar manner to a diaspora people like Afro-Americans. It is remarkable that, in a characteristically oral and ecstatic culture, a people "of the spirit" has also become a people "of the book." In that process they have incorporated the spirituality of their Jewish, Muslim, and Christian coreligionists, thereby participating in the religions of Abraham. They have adopted and adapted the sacred texts of their diaspora host cultures. Theologian George Lindbeck refers to such developments as *intratextuality*, by which he designates the Bible's hermeneutic efficacy among believing communities to "absorb the universe into the biblical world."[82] Accordingly, this term also indicates the Christian influence on Afro-American communities in their use of biblical figures and narrative to interpret and configure their experience. Intratextuality accounts for the fact that the Bible has come to serve as a surrogate sacred text for an ethnic community lacking (or estranged from?) indigenous literary artifacts. It is a community at the same time distinguished by a rich oral textuality and a brilliant improvisational aesthetic. This "surrogacy" of biblical narrative for Black America means that the culture inscribes its experience in the world of Scripture as an extension of that world—as if the Bible were its own literary record of human participation in divine transcendence.

Conclusion

This essay began by observing the appearance of Western and non-Western aspects in Afro-American spirituality. Many observers have attempted to resolve that ambiguity by stressing the continuity of black religious expression with Christianity. Others emphasize instead the continuity with African traditional religions. David W. Wills provides an instance of the former, in his discussion of black religion during the crucial one hundred years from the American Revolution to the Reconstruction era (1770s–1870s). Wills emphasizes that black religion conveyed Protestant and specifically Puritan influences. He is concerned principally with black missions in this period, and he observes that "black religious leaders participated not only in the missionary activity of American Protestantism, but also in the world of religious ideas that lay behind it." Indeed, Wills continues, many such leaders seemed determined to eradicate all traces of African influence and to replace them with mainstream appearances. But other observers like Lawrence Levine remark that such efforts were ultimately frustrated, since cultural continuities are as much a matter of style as of content. The issue "is not one of [African] survivals but of transformations."[83]

From this latter perspective it is a reductionist error to describe the black religious experience as only a variant of American Protestantism. Certainly there are Calvinist and evangelical traditions that provide major sources for the spiritual formation of Afro-Americans. But new ethnographic research, beginning with the burgeoning of black studies in the 1970s, confounds the "carbon-copy" view of black religion and culture. That view has been parodied by James Cone and Gayraud Wilmore with an alternative metaphor: it renders the Afro-American "nothing but a chocolate-covered White American."[84] By contrast, both black and white scholars have begun to recognize that the encounter between Afro- and Euro-American spiritualities is a major factor in the formation of American Protestantism—indeed, that it is as significant and consequential a factor as the Puritan, Calvinist, and evangelical sources of religion in the United States. In this connection David Wills speaks of a "shared framework" and a genuine religious "pluralism" between blacks and whites despite the inability of earlier historians to recognize the fact. For his part, historian Donald G. Mathews, writing about evangelical Protestantism in the antebellum South, remarks that the period ended

> as many antebellum blacks thought History itself would end, with the envelopment and transformation of the meaning of white Evangelicalism through the unfolding of black Christianity. There may be as much poetry as truth in conceiving of black-white religious interaction in this fashion, but it is much truer to the historical record than is the traditional reluctance to take black religion seriously.[85]

Thus, the new and still-developing perspective shifts the focus to the formative influence of black spirituality on North American culture and indeed, as we conclude below, on world cultures. In a previous generation it took an outside observer like Carl Jung to discern this influence on America. Historian Lerone Bennett reports that Jung was astonished by the black presence during his visit to the United States.

> "The first thing which attracted my attention," he was quoted as saying, "was the influence of the Negro, an obviously psychological influence regardless of any mixture of blood." Jung went on to say that the influence of the Negro was apparent in the walking, laughing, dancing, singing and even the praying of white Americans.[86]

Since the increased ethnic awareness of the 1960s, however, more Americans have also begun to recognize the formative impact of black culture. Sociologist Robert Blauner suggests that in the future, for example, informed observers will more readily acknowledge "the South as neo-African."[87]

This growing multiethnic awareness has its parallel in Protestant churches and in Christian educational communities. The real achievements in ecumenism have also advanced interethnic awareness among various church bodies. In theological education an inattention to black religious experience is increasingly exposed as culturally myopic and academically deficient. Beyond the national culture, however, arises the engaging opportunity for non-Western communities, particularly in Third World cultures, to observe in black experience a model for their own religious and sociopolitical transformations. In the same way that a black aesthetic of improvisation has created jazz fusions between African polyrhythms and classical European music and is continuing to fuse jazz with the music of Asian, Hispanic, and other cultures, so Afro-American spirituality has achieved interreligious fusions in ways that provide an instructive model. In this model the theological expression of a people's spirituality "has legitimated a return to the religious genius of the ancestors who came from places other than Europe." From such a perspective Gayraud Wilmore declares the significance of black theological discourse as a model of bicultural spirituality.

> Black Theology authenticated an apprehension of Jesus of Nazareth in cultural symbols and contexts other than those of White American society. In so doing, it provides an example or model for the indigenization of theology in other societies and cultures. Subsequent developments in the United States within Hispanic, Native American, and Asian-American theologies show that this de-Americanization, de-westernization of Christ opened the way for other ethnic groups to identify with him in the depths of their own historical experience.[88]

How can any culture retain the transformative dynamics of its indigenous religious heritage and yet genuinely embrace Christian spirituality? This question also confronted European communities in their earliest encounters with Christianity and even today warrants a realignment and a new, more wholesome (holy, and holistic) integration of Europe's pre-Christian spiritualities. The spiritual dynamics of Afro-America can provide insight, encouragement, and guidance for all communities engaged in that challenge.

Notes

1. Stephen Crites, "The Narrative Quality of Experience," *Journal of the American Academy of Religion* 39 (1971) 296. On "master stories," see Michael Goldberg, *Jews and Christians: Getting Our Stories Straight* (Nashville: Abingdon, 1985) 13ff.; and James W. Fowler, *Stages of Faith* (San Francisco: Harper and Row, 1981) 277–79, 281f., 295f., 301f.

2. Christopher Frye, "The Dynamics of African Dispersal: The Transatlantic Slave Trade," in *The African Diaspora: Interpretive Essays,* ed. Martin L. Kilson and Robert I. Rotberg (Cambridge, MA, and London: Harvard University Press, 1976) 59. A particularly accessible and sensitive depiction of the "rupture and ordeal" of the slave trade and the middle passage is provided in the first two chapters of Nathan I. Huggins, *Black*

Odyssey: The Afro-American Ordeal in Slavery (New York: Vintage/Random House, 1977).

3. On the cultural sources of slave language and spirituality, see the pioneering new study by Sterling Stuckey, *Slave Culture: Nationalist Theory and the Foundations of Black America* (New York: Oxford University Press, 1987) 3–17ff.

4. Gayraud S. Wilmore, *Black Religion and Black Radicalism*, 3.

5. Albert J. Raboteau, *Slave Religion*, 311. For slave petitions for freedom during the Revolutionary War, see Herbert Aptheker, ed., *A Documentary History of the Negro People in the United States* (New York: Citadel, 1951) 6–9.

6. G. S. Wilmore, *Black Religion*, 143. See Arthur H. Fauset, *Black Gods of the Metropolis: Negro Religious Cults in the Urban North* (Philadelphia: University of Pennsylvania Press, 1944); and Joseph R. Washington, *Black Sects and Cults* (New York: Anchor Books, 1973). On lynchings before 1885 and up to 1933, see William Z. Foster, *The Negro People in American History* (New York: International Publishers, 1954) 361, 392, 420f., 456, 480.

7. G. S. Wilmore, *Black Religion*, 41; and cf. James H. Cone on "The Post-Civil War Black Church," in *Black Theology and Black Power* (New York: Seabury, 1969) 103–15.

8. Victor Turner, *The Ritual Process: Structure and Anti-Structure* (Ithaca, NY: Cornell University Press, 1969).

9. Victor Turner, *Dramas, Fields, and Metaphors*, 274.

10. Henry H. Mitchell, *Black Belief*, 144; and Shelia S. Walker, *Ceremonial Spirit Possession in Africa and Afro-America*, 123.

11. Mitchell, *Black Belief*, 145–46; Morton Marks, "Uncovering Ritual Structures in Afro-American Music," in *Religious Movements in Contemporary America*, ed. Irving I. Zaretsky and Mark P. Leone, 114–15. As Thomas Kochman admits in his introduction to the following article, there are "scant allusions to Black audience dynamics in the literature." This article provides a suggestive beginning, however, and perhaps the literature has developed further since its publication: Annette P. William, "Dynamics of a Black Audience," in *Rappin' and Stylin' Out: Communication in Urban Black America*, ed. Thomas Kochman (Urbana, IL: University of Illinois Press, 1972) 101–6.

12. Walker, *Ceremonial Spirit Possession*, 2.

13. Raboteau, *Slave Religion*, 58–59.

14. Ibid., 64.

15. Wilmore, *Black Religion*, 24.

16. Ernst Cassirer, *Language and Myth*, trans. Susanne K. Langer (New York: Dover, 1946) 61–62.

17. Martin Buber, *Kingship of God*, trans. Richard Scheimann (3rd ed.; New York: Harper & Row, 1967) 105–6.

18. Countee Cullen, "Counter Mood," in *Color* (New York: Harper & Brothers, 1947).

19. Wilmore, *Black Religion*, 26.

20. Norman E. Whitten, Jr., "Contemporary Patterns of Malign Occultism Among Negroes in North Carolina," *Journal of American Folklore* 75 (1962) 311–25. Raboteau, *Slave Religion*, 278. Newbell Niles Puckett, *Folk Beliefs*, 175.

21. Raboteau, *Slave Religion*, 69. Stuckey, *Slave Culture*, 58 *et passim*; Lawrence W. Levine, *Black Culture*, 165–66; Mitchell, *Black Belief*, 43–44; John W. Blassingame, *The Slave Community* (New York: Oxford University Press, 1972) 134–35.

22. Raboteau, *Slave Religion*, 75, 80.

23. Ibid., 287f.

24. "It is possible to see an element of early black religion that nurtured the struggle for freedom: a deep-lying African spirituality, a kind of God-madness, an enthusiasm for dream interpretation, visions, and prophecy. These tendencies were unfettered and enhanced when black men and women . . . [became] oracles against the whites in vindication of their own people" (Wilmore, *Black Religion*, 36).

25. Stuckey, *Slave Culture*, 50. On Vodun as the state religion of Haiti, see Wilmore, *Black Religion*, 23.

26. On Turner's *Confessions* and visions, see Wilson Jeremiah Moses, *Black Messiahs and Uncle Toms*, 64; and Wilmore, *Black Religion*, 67. Cf. William C. Suttles, Jr., "African Religious Survivals as Factors in American Slave Revolts," *Journal of Negro History* 56 (1971) 101–3.

27. Amanda Porterfield, "Shamanism: A Psychosocial Definition," *Journal of the American Academy of Religion* 55 (1987) 725–26.

28. On "body ethics" and specifically "Black religion as embodied ethics," see James W. McClendon, Jr., *Ethics:* Vol. 1, *Systematic Theology* (Nashville: Abingdon, 1986) 78–109; Archie Smith, Jr., *The Relational Self: Ethics and Therapy in a Black Church Perspective* (Nashville: Abingdon, 1982) 76.

29. Mitchell, *Black Belief*, 145.

30. Porterfield, "Shamanism," 728–29. On the celebrated Cane Ridge (Kentucky) revival in 1801, "the greatest outpouring of the Spirit since Pentecost," see the vivid description of bodily behaviors in Sidney Ahlstrom, *A Religious History of the American People* (New Haven: Yale University Press, 1972) 432–35.

31. Hughes, "Shamanism and Christian Faith," *Religious Education* 71 (1976) 395–96. On the pathological aspects of shamanism, see I. H. Boyer, "Remarks on the Personality of the Shaman," in *The Psychoanalytic Study of Society*, ed. by W. Muensterberger and S. Axelrad (New York: International Universities Press, 1962); George Devereaux, "Shamans as Neurotics," *American Anthropologist* 63 (1961) 1088–90; A. L. Kroeber, *Psychosis or Social Sanction: The Nature of Culture* (Chicago: University of Chicago Press, 1952) 310–19; Julian Silverman, "Shamans and Acute Schizophrenia," *American Anthropologist* 69 (1967) 21–31.

32. See Anthony F. C. Wallace, "Revitalization Movements," *American Anthropologist* 58 (1956) 264–81.

33. Smith, *Relational Self*, 75. For a recent and groundbreaking discussion of a praxis combining personal with social transformation, see Erica Sherover-Marcuse's outline of "A Practice of Subjectivity" in her *Emancipation and Consciousness: Dogmatic and Dialectical Perspectives in the Early Marx* (New York: Blackwell 1986) 135–42.

34. Kenneth Burke, *The Philosophy of Literary Form: Studies in Symbolic Action* (New York: Vintage, 1957) 100.

35. Gayraud S. Wilmore, "The Black Messiah: Revising the Color Symbolism of Western Christology," *The Journal of the Interdenominational Theological Seminary* 2 (1974) 13.

36. For example, Timothy L. Smith has observed that "Black converts knew they had a lot to forgive." Forgiveness, followed by awe and ecstasy, was the first element in their personal religious experiences, Smith maintains, and supplied the foundations of their theology as well. "The experience of forgiveness and the doctrine of reconciliation were primary. . . . Considering these first may help to make plain how erroneous it is to call either revolt or acquiescence the central theme of Negro faith in America" ("Slavery and Theology: The Emergence of Black Christian Consciousness in Nineteenth Century America," *Church History* 41 [1972] 498).

On the Christian charism of the "distinguishing" or "discerning of spirits," see 1 Corinthians 12:10. On the crucial role of discernment in the Roman Catholic spirituality of Ignatius, see *The Spiritual Exercises of St. Ignatius,* ed. and trans. Louis J. Puhl, S.J. (Chicago: Loyola University Press and the Newman Press, 1951) 3–4, 141–50. The American Protestant tradition of discernment begins with Jonathan Edwards, "The Distinguishing Marks of a Work of the Spirit of God: A Discourse," (Boston, 1741), in *The Great Awakening,* ed. C. C. Goen (New Haven: Yale University press, 1972) 226–63. For a contemporary discussion, see Morton Kelsey, *Discernment: A Study in Ecstasy and Evil* (New York: Paulist, 1978).

37. James M. Glass, "The Philosopher and the Shaman: The Political Vision as Incantation," *Political Theory* 2 (1974) 186. On ancient Greek philosophy as a "successor" to indigenous forms of shamanism, see F. M. Cornford, *Principium Sapientiae: The Origins of Greek Philosophical Thought* (Cambridge: University Press, 1952) 107ff.

38. Jimmy Stewart, "Introduction to Black Aesthetics in Music," *The Black Aesthetic,* ed. Addison Gayle, Jr. (Garden City, NY: Anchor Books, 1972) 81–82.

39. On Afro-American drama, see E. Quita Craig, "Message from Another Culture," *Black Drama of the Federal Theatre Era* (Amherst: University of Massachusetts Press, 1980) 85–96; and Paul C. Harrison, *The Drama of Nommo* (New York: Grove Press, 1972). On the visual arts, see Robert Farris Thompson, "Siras Bowens of Sunbury, Georgia: A Tidewater Artist in the Afro-American Visual Tradition," in *Chant of Saints: A Gathering of Afro-American Literature, Art, and Scholarship,* ed. Michael Harper and Robert Stepto (Chicago: University of Illinois Press, 1979) 230–40, as well as other illustrated articles in *Chant of Saints.*

40. James Baldwin, "Many Thousands Gone," in *Black Expression,* ed. Addison Gayle, Jr. (New York: Weybright & Talley, 1969) 325. On the preeminence of black music for authentic representations of Afro-American culture, see Lerone Bennett's commentary on Baldwin's dictum: "No writer, so far, has fingered pain and dread with the exquisite agony of a Billie Holiday. No Negro poet, no philosopher or pundit has said as much about the human condition as Charlie Parker or Bessie Smith. . . . Negro philosophy still awaits its Sartre; Negro literature still awaits its Kafka. . . . James Baldwin said once that there has not yet arrived a sensibility sufficiently tough to make the Negro experience articulate" (*The Negro Mood and Other Essays* [Chicago: Johnson Publishing, 1964] 57). Albert Murray applies Baldwin's criterion against Baldwin (but in praise of Ralph Ellison) in his review, "James Baldwin, Protest Fiction, and the Blues Tradition," in *The Omni-Americans: New Perspectives on Black Experience and American Culture* (New York: Outerbridge & Dienstfrey, 1970) 166–67. Cf. n. 46 below.

41. Morton Marks, "Uncovering Ritual Structures in Afro-American Music," in *Religious Movements in Contemporary America,* ed. Irving I. Zaretsky and Mark P. Leone, 63–64.

42. W. E. B. DuBois, *The Souls of Black Folk,* 45.

43. Ralph Ellison, *Shadow and Act,* reprint ed. (New York: Vintage Books, 1972) 9, 11–12; emphasis mine. These themes were especially current during the Harlem Renaissance, and are fictionally represented in James Weldon Johnson, *The Autobiography of an Ex-Colored Man* (1912), reprint ed. (New York: Hill and Wang, 1960). Cf. the manifesto of the Harlem Renaissance, and a precursor to the 1960s Black Aesthetic movement, in Alain Locke's editorial introduction to *The New Negro: An Interpretation* (New York: Albert & Charles Boni, 1925) 3–16. Cf. n. 46 below. On "signals of transcendence" in ordinary experience, see Peter Berger, *A Rumor of Angels* (New York: Doubleday, 1969) 52f.

44. Ellison, *Shadow and Act,* 12. DuBois emphasized the Afro-American's "spiritual striving" to transcend cultural isolation in his declaration that "this, then, is the end of

his striving: to be a co-worker in the kingdom of culture, to escape both death and isolation, to husband and use his best powers and his latent genius" (*Souls,* 46).

45. Pearl Williams-Jones, "Afro-American Gospel Music: A Crystalization of the Black Aesthetic," *Ethnomusicology* 9 (1975) 381, 383.

46. "The guiding assumption of the Black Arts Movement was that if a literary-critical investigator looked to characteristic musical and verbal forms of the masses, he could discover unique aspects of Afro-American creative expression—aspects of both *form and performance*—that lay closest to the verifiable emotional referents and experiential categories of Afro-American culture. The result of such critical investigations, according to Neal and other spokesmen such as Baraka and Addison Gayle, Jr. (to name but three prominent advocates of the Black Arts), would be the discovery of a 'Black Aesthetic'—a distinctive code for the creation and evaluation of black art" (Houston A. Baker, Jr., *Blues Ideology and Afro-American Literature: A Vernacular Theory* [Chicago: University of Chicago Press, 1984] 74; cf. n. 40 above).

47. Henry H. Mitchell, *Black Preaching* (New York: Harper & Row, 1979) 113, 198; cf. also 142f., 202. See also Vincent Wimbush, "Rescue the Perishing: The Importance of Biblical Scholarship in Black Christianity," *Reflection* 80 (1983) 9–11.

48. Murray, *The Omni-Americans,* 93.

49. Claudia Mitchell-Kernan, "Signifying," in *Mother Wit from the Laughing Barrel: Readings in the Interpretation of Afro-American Folklore,* ed. Alan Dundes (New York: Garland, 1981) 311.

50. Evan M. Zuesse, *Ritual Cosmos: The Sanctification of Life in African Religions* (Athens: Ohio University Press, 1979) 7. Kenneth Burke, *The Philosophy of Literary Form: Studies in Symbolic Action* (New York: Vintage Books, 1957) 87.

51. Henry Louis Gates, Jr., *Figures in Black,* 48–49. Mitchell-Kernan, "Signifying," in *Mother Wit,* ed. Alan Dundes, 325.

52. On intertextuality, see Gates, *Figures,* 41, 49. Cf. George E. Kent, *Blackness and the Adventure of Western Culture* (Chicago: Third World Press, 1972). On DuBois's intertextuality, Wilson J. Moses observes that "DuBois' early work struggles to fuse two complementary but substantially different mythological traditions. The first of these is 'Ethiopianism'... the other is the European tradition of interpretive mythology... the medieval practice of examining Greco-Roman mythology with the intention of either discovering within it, or assigning to it, Christian meaning." Thus, in his *The Quest of the Silver Fleece* DuBois "created a universe in which the ideology of progressive socialism and the traditionalism of Christian black nationalism work harmoniously within the framework of a Greek myth" (Wilson Jeremiah Moses, "The Poetics of Ethiopianism: W.E.B. DuBois and Literary Black Nationalism," *American Literature* 47 [1975] 411, 417). Elsewhere Moses also observes an African or conjurational element in this fusion of traditions in commenting that, in his novels, DuBois "reveals a semimystical respect for the black preacher, wizard, and conjure woman, who are always commanding figures of power wielding tremendous authority either to preserve or destroy those who fall within their power" (*Black Messiahs,* 20).

Similarly Hurston interweaves the shamanistic abilities of a conjuror, who explicitly conjures the plagues of Egypt and the parting of the Red Sea, in her representation of Moses as "the finest hoodoo man in the world" (*Moses: Man of the Mountain* [Urbana and Chicago: University of Illinois Press, 1984] 147). Moses the conjuror is an Afro-American signification deriving from the slavery period, in which "Moses was understood to be a snake-controlling magic worker of great power" (Mechal Sobel, *Trabelin' On: The Slave Journey to an Afro-Baptist Faith* [Westport, CT: Greenwood, 1979] 73). Cf. Lawrence W. Levine, *Black Culture and Black Consciousness,* 57. In an engaging study of Hurston in a tradition of black women writers, Marjorie Pryse remarks that "Hurston took conjuring a great leap forward—and with it, transposed the terms of literary authority for black women writers" ("Zora Neale Hurston, Alice Walker, and the 'Ancient Power' of Black Women," in *Conjuring: Black Women, Fiction, and Literary Tradition,* ed. Marjorie Pryse and Hortense J. Spillers [Bloomington: Indiana University Press, 1985] 11).

53. Gates, *Figures in Black,* 236–37. For an extensive "portrait" of Eshu-Elegbara as a major *orisha* or spirit, see Robert Farris Thompson, *Flash of the Spirit: African and Afro-American Art and Philosophy* (New York: Vintage, 1984) 18–33.

54. Lawrence Levine observes that after emancipation there was a decrease in the popularity of trickster tales in black culture, giving way to the celebration of black heroes who confront their oppressors directly without resorting to guile or deception (*Black Culture,* 385f.; on spirituals as coded communication, see p. 52). See Mark Miles Fisher, *Negro Slave Songs in the United States* (New York: Citadel, 1969). Levine asserts that Fisher, as the popularizer of this insight, was correct in perceiving the subtextual meaning of these songs but excessive in reducing them to coded messages at the expense of their religious import. Cf. similar criticism including that of E. Franklin Frazier in Calvin E. Bruce, "Black Spirituality, Language and Faith," *Religious Education* 71 (1976) 374. On narratives of slave deception and escapes, with an excellent introduction, see Gilbert Osofsky, ed., *Puttin' on Ole Massa* (New York: Harper & Row, 1969. On the relation between music and activism, see Wyatt T. Walker, *Somebody's Calling My Name: Black Sacred Music and Social Change* (Valley Forge, PA: Judson, 1979).

55. Gates, *Figures in Black,* 41.

56. Cornel West, *Prophecy Deliverance! An Afro-American Revolutionary Christianity* (Philadelphia: Westminster, 1982) 108f.

57. Puritan theology in early America understood the type–antitype dyad to be prophetically or divinely constituted, "the God who predetermines history having lent it this power" (as quoted by Ursula Brumm, *American Thought and Religious Typology* [New Brunswick, NJ: Rutgers University Press, 1970] 23). On dyads and "figural prophecy," see the definitive study by Erich Auerbach, "Figura," in *Scenes from the Drama of European Literature,* ed. Wald Godzich and Jochen Schulte-Sasse (Minneapolis: University of Minnesota Press, 1984) 29, 56, 72.

58. Sacvan Bercovitch, *The Puritan Origins of the American Self* (New Haven: Yale University Press, 1975); and Conrad Cherry, ed., *God's New Israel: Religious Interpretations of American Destiny* (Englewood Cliffs, NJ: Prentice-Hall, 1971). On "typological ethnogenesis," see Werner Sollors, *Beyond Ethnicity: Consent and Descent in American Culture* (New York: Oxford University Press, 1986) 50, 57.

59. Sacvan Bercovitch, *The American Jeremiad* (Madison: University of Wisconsin Press, 1978) 132–76.

60. On "signifying," power relationships, and cultural significations in black America, see Charles H. Long, *Significations: Signs Symbols, and Images in the Interpretation of Religion* (Philadelphia: Fortress, 1986) esp. 1–9.

61. Albert J. Raboteau, *Slave Religion,* 311.

62. Coretta Scott King, ed., *The Words of Martin Luther King, Jr.* (New York: Newmarket Press, 1983) 94.

63. Raboteau, *Slave Religion,* 251. On Afro-American "symbolic reversals," see Lucius T. Outlaw, "Language and Consciousness: Towards a Hermeneutic of Black Culture," *Cultural Hermeneutics* 1 (1974) 403f.

64. On the prominence of Psalm 68:31 in black religious expression, see Gayraud S. Wilmore, *Black Religion and Black Radicalism,* 121; and Albert J. Raboteau, "The Black

Experience in American Evangelicalism: The Meaning of Slavery," in *The Evangelical Tradition in America,* ed. Leonard I. Sweet (Macon, GA: Mercer University Press, 1984) 197. On "Ethiopianism," see Raboteau, "'Ethiopia Shall Soon Stretch Forth Her Hands': Black Destiny in Nineteenth-Century America," The University Lecture in Religion at Arizona State University (Tempe, Arizona, January 27, 1983); and St. Clair Drake, *The Redemption of Africa and Black Religion.*

65. Drake, *Redemption of Africa,* 41.

66. Wilson Jeremiah Moses, "The Poetics of Ethiopianism: W.E.B. DuBois and Literary Black Nationalism," in *American Literature: A Journal of Literary History Criticism, and Bibliography* 47 (1975) 412, 414; idem, *Black Messiahs and Uncle Toms,* 160.

67. Wilmore, *Black Religion and Black Radicalism,* 121.

68. Robert A. Bennett, "Black Experience and the Bible," *Theology Today* 27 (1971) 423, 433.

69. Wilmore, *Black Religion and Black Radicalism,* 37.

70. Herbert Aptheker, ed., *A Documentary History of the Negro People in the United States:* Vol. 2, *From the Reconstruction Era to 1910* (5th ed.; New York: Citadel, 1951) 713.

71. DuBois, *Souls of Black Folk,* 47.

72. Alice Walker, "In Search of Our Mothers' Gardens," in *Black Theology: A Documentary History 1966-1979,* ed. Gayraud S. Wilmore and James H. Cone (Maryknoll, NY: Orbis, 1979) 438.

73. Drake, *Redemption of Africa,* 54, 61f.

74. Ibid., 71.

75. "Conceptualizing the Black story," Harold Dean Trulear insists, does not mean "that it is plagued by the linear rigidity and teleology of western philosophy of history" ("The Lord Will Make a Way Somehow: Black Worship and the Afro-American Story," *The Journal of the Interdenominational Theological Center* 13 [1985] 101). Cf. also James Cone, "The Story Context of Black Theology," *Theology Today* 32 (1975) 145.

76. Charles Shelby Rooks, "Toward the Promised Land: An Analysis of the Religious Experience of Black America," *The Black Church* 2 (1973) 8.

77. Gayraud S. Wilmore and James H. Cone, eds., *Black Theology,* 347–48.

78. Rooks, "Toward the Promised Land," *The Black Church* 2 (1973) 8.

79. Eldridge Cleaver, *Soul on Fire* (Waco, TX: Word Books, 1978) 92.

80. George Shepperson, Introduction to *The African Diaspora: Interpretive Essays,* ed. M. L. Kilson and R. I. Rotberg (Cambridge, MA, and London: Harvard University Press, 1976) 2–3, 8.

81. Stephen Crites, "The Narrative Quality of Experience," *Journal of the American Academy of Religion* 39 (1971) 296.

82. George A. Lindbeck, *The Nature of Doctrine: Religion and Theology in a Post-Liberal Age* (Philadelphia: Westminster, 1984) 135.

83. David W. Wills, Introduction, *Black Apostles at Home and Abroad: Afro-Americans and the Christian Mission from the Revolution to Reconstruction,* ed. David Wills and Richard Newman (Boston: G. K. Hall, 1982) xixf. Lawrence W. Levine, *Black Culture and Black Consciousness,* 5.

84. Wilmore and Cone, eds., *Black Theology,* 464. On the evangelical sources of black religion, see in addition to previous citations the detailed account beginning in chapter 4 of the study by Donald G. Mathews, *Religion in the Old South* (Chicago: University of Chicago Press, 1977); and also Milton C. Sernett, *Black Religion and American Evangelicalism: White Protestants, Plantation Missions, and the Flowering of Negro Christianity* (Metuchen, NJ: Scarecrow, 1975).

85. Mathews, *Religion in the Old South*, xv. On such religious "pluralism" at the national level, David W. Wills argues that "this encounter [between blacks and whites] has indeed often not been thought of as a central theme in our nation's *religious* history but it surely is" (Wills, ed., *Black Apostles*, xi–xii).

86. Lerone Bennett, Jr., *The Negro Mood and Other Essays* (Chicago: Johnson Publishing, 1964) 62.

87. Robert Blauner, *Racial Oppression in America* (New York: Harper & Row, 1972) 135f. Cf. Robert Stepto's related notion of the South as Afro-American "ritual ground," where social structures and performances represent spatial or topographical expressions of "double consciousness" (DuBois) in a culture that is both African and American (*Behind the Veil: A Study of Afro-American Narrative* [Urbana and Chicago: University of Illinois Press, 1979] 68f.).

88. Gayraud S. Wilmore, "The New Context of Black Theology in the United States," in *Black Theology*, ed. Wilmore and Cone, 604–5. In Wilmore's view black theology has begun to respond to the challenge issued by Vincent Harding in the early 1970s: to examine "our African heritage with at least as much care (and prayer) as we have examined the Hebrew, New Testament, and Reformation histories" (Harding, "The Acts of God and the Children of Africa," *Shalom* [Philadelphia: United Church Press, 1973] 5). On future reconstructions of Christian theology in Third World cultures, see Robert J. Schreiter, *Constructing Local Theologies* (Maryknoll, NY: Orbis, 1985).

Bibliography

Barrett, Leonard. *Soul-Force: African Heritage in Afro-American Religion*. Garden City, NY: Doubleday, Anchor, 1984.

Bennett, Robert A. "Black Experience and the Bible." *Theology Today* 27 (1971) 422–33.

Crites, Stephen. "The Narrative Quality of Experience." *Journal of the American Academy of Religion* 39 (1971) 291–311.

Drake, St. Clair. *The Redemption of Africa and Black Religion*. Chicago: Third World Press, 1970.

DuBois, W. E. B. *The Souls of Black Folk*. New York: New American Library, Signet Classic, 1969.

Gates, Henry Louis, Jr. *Figures in Black: Words, Signs, and the "Racial" Self*. New York: Oxford University Press, 1987.

Gayle, Addison, Jr., ed. *The Black Aesthetic*. Garden City, NY: Doubleday, Anchor, 1972.

Joyner, Charles. *Down By the Riverside: A South Carolina Slave Community* (Urbana: University of Illinois Press, 1984).

Levine, Lawrence W. *Black Culture and Black Consciousness: Afro-American Folk Thought from Slavery to Freedom*. Oxford: Oxford University Press, 1977.

Marks, Morton. "Uncovering Ritual Structures in Afro-American Music." In *Religious Movements in Contemporary America*, 60–117. Edited by Irving I. Zaretsky and Mark P. Leone. Princeton, NJ: Princeton University Press, 1974.

Mitchell, Henry H. *Black Belief: Folk Beliefs of Blacks in America and West Africa*. New York: Harper & Row, 1975.

Mitchell-Kernan, Claudia. "Signifying." In *Mother Wit from the Laughing Barrel: Readings in the Interpretation of Afro-American Folklore*. Edited by Alan Dundes. New York: Garland, 1981.

Moses, Wilson Jeremiah. *Black Messiahs and Uncle Toms: Social and Literary Manipulations of a Religious Myth*. University Park: Pennsylvania State University Press, 1982.

414   THE SPIRITUALITY OF AFRO-AMERICAN TRADITIONS

Porterfield, Amanda. "Shamanism: A Psychosocial Definition." *Journal of the American Academy of Religion* 55 (1987) 721–39.

Puckett, Newbell Niles. *Folk Beliefs of the Southern Negro.* Chapel Hill: University of North Carolina Press, 1926.

Raboteau, Albert J. *Slave Religion: The "Invisible Institution" in the Antebellum South.* New York: Oxford University Press, 1978.

Redkey, Edwin S. *Black Exodus: Black Nationalist and Back to Africa Movements 1890–1910.* New Haven: Yale University Press, 1969.

Rooks, Charles Shelby. "Toward the Promised Land: An Analysis of the Religious Experience of Black America." *The Black Church* 2 (1973) 1–48.

Turner, Victor. *Dramas, Fields, and Metaphors: Symbolic Action in Human Society.* Ithaca, NY: Cornell University Press, 1974.

Walker, Shelia S. *Ceremonial Spirit Possession in Africa and Afro-America: Forms, Meanings, and Functional Significance for Individuals and Social Groups.* Leiden: Brill, 1972.

Wilmore, Gayraud S. *Black Religion and Black Radicalism: An Interpretation of the Religious History of Afro-American People.* Maryknoll, NY: Orbis, 1983.

Part Three
ORTHODOX SPIRITUALITY

13

The Revival of
Hesychast Spirituality

PHILIP SHERRARD

O NE OF THE MOST SIGNIFICANT EVENTS in the intellectual life of the modern Western world has been without doubt the discovery of the whole contemplative tradition of the Orthodox church that goes by the name of hesychasm. This discovery itself has passed through two major stages. It may be said to have taken its start in the rediscovery over the last century of the writings of the Greek fathers or of the Greek patristic tradition. More specifically it may be traced back to the publication and exploration in the first decades of this century of patristic texts relating more or less directly to hesychasm and the hesychast way of life.[1]

Yet positive as this rediscovery has been, it must be said that in at least two vital and interrelated respects it revealed a failure to grasp the true nature of the phenomenon with which it was dealing. First, the approach was one of scholarship and research, the norms of which cannot by definition embrace a spiritual tradition whose hallmark, if one may put it this way, is lived experience and a form of transmission that depends more on personal relationship—on the charisma of spiritual paternity—than on impersonal and so-called objective criteria. Second, it tended to regard hesychasm as a purely historical phenomenon, confined both chronologically and geographically. It did not view it as a permanent manifestation of the inner life of the Orthodox church, as intrinsic to it as the sacraments, constituting as it does a kind of sacramental interiorization of baptismal and eucharistic grace. In other words, there was little attempt to view the hesychast way of life within the context in which its invisible and transhistorical character could have revealed itself more adequately—that is to say, in the part it has played and continues to play in the Orthodox world.

The descholasticization and dehistoricization of the approach to hesychasm, and the corresponding recognition that it is a living tradition permeating every aspect—liturgical, iconographic, personal—of the inner and intimate life of the church, mark the second major stage in its discovery in the modern period. Here one must single out the important part played in this second stage by the translation into western European languages—German (1925), French (1928), English (1930)—of a remarkable document written in Russian by an unknown Russian in the nineteenth century and published in Russia in about 1865. This document, entitled in English *The Way of a Pilgrim*, was remarkable in this respect on two accounts. First, it brought to the attention of Western readers the fact that the practice of the hesychast way of life and above all the practice of the Jesus prayer which lies at its core were not limited either to the past or to a specifically monastic context: their presence is revealed in the heart of the Orthodox Christian, no matter what time or place, no matter what outward circumstances. Second, it brought to the notice of these same readers the existence of a book, regarded by the Russian pilgrim with a reverence usually reserved for the Bible alone, that appeared to explain step by step the stages of the mysterious spiritual journey on which the pilgrim had embarked and to lay down the guidelines as to how these stages were to be traversed. To a West in which the split between abstract theology and individualistic "mysticism," gnosis and eros, knowledge and method, had long since undermined the contemplative tradition and in which many were already beginning to turn to the non-Christian religions of the East for guidance as to how the prophetic way of actual experience could be embraced in the light of doctrine, purifying and liberating the intellect, *The Way of a Pilgrim* came as a revelation. It was perhaps the first intimation of and introduction to a "secret science" (*kryptē meletē*) of prayer and spiritual wisdom communicated in the form of a tradition organically attached to the integral tradition of the Christian church and set forth in a work that the pilgrim could carry in a knapsack.

The work in question went by the title *Philokalia* and consisted of a series of texts that together constitute a manual, guide, and companion to the hesychast prayer of the heart and the following of the hesychast way. In fact, the title itself was a venerable one. *Philokalia* was first applied in the fourth century to a selection of ascetic and mystical texts made by Basil the Great and Gregory of Nazianzus from the works of Origen. At a time when the notion of philosophy, although never denied, was too directly associated with "the wisdom of the world" to describe the Christian aspiration to perfection, the term *philokalia* ("love of the beautiful") was an obvious alternative. Yet it was more than simply an alternative. For if in the Greek context—and especially in the Platonic and Neoplatonic context—Beauty coincides with the Good on the highest level, nevertheless it is Beauty to which the Greek compilers of this anthology wished to give preeminence and which they regarded as the essential. Needless to say, they have in mind less the visible and created appearance of Beauty than its invisible and uncreated presence: that presence in which the Light of Truth, transcendent source of life and desire of desires, is united with divine love in a marriage that gives birth to the inner peace and stillness denoted by the word *hēsychia* itself.

The title *Philokalia* was used to designate several other smaller compilations in later centuries. Instructions on *hēsychia,* intended above all for private use or for the benefit of an intimate group of disciples—one has in mind the compilations of a Theodore of Edessa or of a Nicephorus the Solitary—bear witness to the uninterrupted current of contemplative life present in the depths of the church. In other words, one is confronted by a tradition, a living transmission or *paradosis* that carries this current through history. Yet at the same time one cannot with any real precision trace the itinerary of this tradition, the hesychast tradition, as it follows its historical course, if for no other reason than that those who have enshrined it have renounced the world in order better to serve it and have already in this life disappeared from the stage of history. The hesychasts are God's dead, self-effaced so that they may unveil the countenance of the Invisible from whom they and the world they have renounced receive their new life. One can consequently only read the history of this tradition in the signs it leaves of its presence in various other forms, in icons, in the lives of the saints, in the writing and translation of spiritual texts. Thus it has been possible to attest its convergence on Mount Athos in the final centuries of the Byzantine period and above all in the fourteenth century, when its crucial doctrinal thesis—that although God in his ineffable transcendence is absolute and imparticipable, he nonetheless enters into deifying communion with created being through his uncreated energies—was affirmed with such magisterial authority by Gregory Palamas. And, although in the following centuries there may have been a certain decline, it was on Mount Athos some four centuries later, toward the end of the eighteenth century, that the events decisive for the whole hesychast revival in the modern world were germinated. Among these events pride of place must be given to the compilation of the *Philokalia* in a form that has become classic.

The date, as we said, is the latter half of the eighteenth century. In the thought of the West, that breach between God and the world, grace and nature, soul and body, already implicit in the Augustinian disjunction between the order of salvation and the order of nature and enlarged by the scholastics, has now been more than consolidated by figures like Francis

Bacon, Descartes, and the other *buccinatores novi temporis* who accomplished the scientific revolution of the sixteenth and seventeenth centuries.

One might have thought that the remote tongue of land reaching out into the Aegean from the seaboard of northern Greece, and still entitled the Holy Mountain of Athos, would be immune to the secularizing spirit of enlightenment sweeping across Western Europe and the United States of America. But Greek intellectuals, nourished in the same schools and universities as their Western counterparts, were already seeking ways in which they could propagate the new philosophy in their own country and so prepare for a revolution by means of which their fellow countrymen could achieve a form of national independence established on the basis of the same rationalist ideologies. In fact, one of the most persuasive and progressive of these intellectuals, Eugenios Voulgaris (1716–1806), had secured appointment as director of the Athonite Academy situated on Mount Athos itself. It was his presence and the nature of the ideas that he was trying to instill into his pupils that perhaps more than anything alerted the monastic elders to the threat to their own tradition which these ideas signified and gave them intimations of further depredations to come. At all events it was at this time that they undertook to reaffirm their tradition in a manner which, if it does not constitute a direct response to the thought forms whose ascendance was to determine the future of Western civilization, at least reflects an awareness of them.

At the center of this activity was the monk Nicodemus of the Holy Mountain (1749–1809), and it was largely because of his intensive labor that the revival of hesychast spirituality was set within the context of the whole theological, liturgical, and canonical tradition of the Orthodox church. He wrote, translated, or compiled, singly or with others, some twenty-five large volumes covering virtually every aspect of this tradition. The total number of his published and unpublished works is said to come to over a hundred. He was among the first Greeks, after the fall of Constantinople in 1453, to undertake a systematic investigation of Greek patristic manuscripts, and he prepared for publication unpublished works by both Symeon the New Theologian and Gregory Palamas. Moreover—and this demonstrates a surprising catholicity of mind for the age and circumstances in which he lived—he also translated, adapted, and published *The Spiritual Exercises* of Ignatius Loyola and *The Spiritual Warfare* of Lorenzo Scupoli, thus pointing, already in the eighteenth century, to the continuing presence in the West of a current of spiritual understanding and practice still capable of converging to a certain extent with that of the Orthodox tradition. But in the context with which we are here concerned, it was his compilation, in collaboration with Macarius of Corinth (1751–1805), of a collection of texts written between the fourth and the fifteenth centuries by the spiritual masters of the hesychast tradition that is his masterwork. For it is this anthology—*The Philokalia of the Neptic [Watchful] Saints gathered from our Holy Theophoric Fathers, through which, by means of the philosophy of ascetic practice and contemplation, the intellect is purified, illumined and made perfect*, published in Venice in 1782— that constitutes the major event in the hesychast revival in the modern period.

With this work Nicodemus brings the hesychast tradition into the play of history. He not only stresses in his introduction that the prayer of the heart should be practiced equally by lay people and by monks; he also presents to a modern world increasingly to be dominated by a philosophy of action in and on time the alternative of a contemplative knowledge of human destiny and a way of remembrance whose consummation presupposes a reinsertion into the origin of time itself. Yet although the center of Nicodemus's activity was Mount Athos, the immediate impact of the *Philokalia* both on Athos and in Greece as a whole was less than might have been expected, although a new edition of the work was published in Athens in 1893. It is worth noting, however, that the movement associated with it did spread beyond monastic circles and that its influence may be discerned in the works of the greatest writer of imaginative prose in modern Greece, Alexandros Papadiamantis (1851-1911); for these works, like those of Dostoevsky, receive their power from the fact that they are written with the knowledge that it is only in the mystical light of Mount Tabor, the light of the transfiguration, that human life can be truly perceived and given meaning. Yet it is outside Greece that the revival of which Nicodemus is such a crucial instrument was to bear its most direct fruits.

Here the focus is first of all on the Romanian world and the figure of a remarkable "elder," or *staretz*, Paisii Velichkovskii (1722-1794). Paisii was born in the Ukraine and became a monk at an early age. After serving his spiritual apprenticeship in a hermitage situated on the borders of Moldavia, he departed for Athos, to deepen his knowledge and experience of the hesychast way of life. After sixteen years on the Holy Mountain he returned to Moldavia, first as Abbot of the monastery of Dragomirna, then of that of Seculu and finally of that of Neamtzu. It was at the last monastery that he accomplished the great work of his life, a work that in many ways parallels that of Nicodemus. He reestablished the monastic rule, corrected the church office, organized a printing press, and began to translate and publish the works of the Greek fathers. But above all it was while at Neamtzu that he translated a selection of the texts of the Greek *Philokalia* into Slavonic. It was published, with the title *Dobrotolubiye*, in Moscow in 1793 and reprinted in Moscow in 1822. This was the translation carried by the pilgrim in *The Way of a Pilgrim,* and indeed its influence on the piety and cultural world of Russia in the nineteenth century was immense, as the works of Dostoevsky, to go no further, are there to testify. This flowering of hesychast spirituality in Russia stimulated both by the publication of the *Philokalia* and by the arrival of many of Paisii's own disciples, and associated especially with the *startzy* of the famous monastery of Optino, is the theme of another chapter in this book. Suffice to mention here that a translation of the *Philokalia* into Russian was made by Ignatius Brianchaninov (1807–1867) and published in 1857. A further translation into Russian was made by Bishop Theophan the Recluse (1815–1894), who included several texts not in the original Greek edition and deliberately omitted or paraphrased certain passages in some of the texts in the Greek edition. Bishop Theophan's translation was published in Moscow in five volumes, the first appearing in 1877.

The importance of the entire tradition which these spiritual figures represent was solemnly acknowledged in 1988, as, on the occasion of the millennium of Russian Christianity, Paisii, Ignatius, Theophan and the *staretz* Amvrosy of Optino, as well as more modern hesychast Silouan were canonized.

Like Nicodemus of the Holy Mountain, the staretz Paisii too considered that the practice of the prayer of the heart could also be entrusted to lay people and that even the higher forms of contemplation were not incompatible with a life lived in the world and in the context of a certain degree of cultural activity. Yet perhaps the main feature of his teaching was his emphasis on the idea and practice of spiritual paternity. His purpose here was to safeguard the personalization of the spiritual life, to protect this life from the vagaries of individual interpretation and disposition, and to prevent its dissociation from the liturgical life of the church and the heritage of the Greek fathers. At the same time, fidelity and unquestioning attachment to the institutions and forms of the church did not mean that Paisii and his disciples aspired to salvation through social institutions or identified the victory of the Lamb with the concept of a Christian civilization. By definition the hesychast lives the eschatological mystery of the church, something that presupposes a transcendence of the forms of civilization, whether Christian or non-Christian, and even of time itself. As a hesychast aphorism puts it, his purpose is to circumscribe the incorporeal within the house of his body.

In Romania, the work of Paisii was continued by his disciples, in whom he had instilled a love of the ascetic fathers and a desire to see their writings made available in Romanian. Indeed, the first half of the nineteenth century saw the creation of a veritable patristic library on Romanian soil. It was as

17. Nesterov, *Russian Monks*, 1862.

if Romania stood on the brink of an integral patristic and hesychast revival or, what amounts to the same thing, as if the Orthodox church in Romania was about to manifest the plenitude of its spiritual tradition. If it is possible to say that such a revival and the manifestation of the spiritual plenitude of the Orthodox church amount to the same thing, this is because a condition of the church's being what it is lies in its fidelity to the fathers, whose living heritage does indeed constitute the texture of this church, with all its strengths and weaknesses. In this sense the fathers are always contemporary to the life of the church, integrated to it above all through that magnificent instrument of creative contemplation, the Orthodox liturgy, as well as through its auxiliary forms, the iconography and the hymnography.

In fact, the religious revival of which the signs in Romania in the first half of the nineteenth century were so positive was interrupted in the 1860s and subsequently as Romania became subject to a process of secularization on Western lines similar to that which had already overtaken Greece and Russia. But not all was lost: the tradition of the prayer of the heart was continued in the shadow of certain monasteries; the liturgy was still celebrated; the fathers of the church still remained the supreme criterion of Orthodox theology and practice. And toward the middle decades of the present century, in conditions that might appear even less propitious, the seeds sown in the first half of the nineteenth century and secretly nourished in the interior of the church, entered a new phase of maturation.[2]

In this phase it is once again the *Philokalia* that is to play a central part. In a theological atmosphere in which the historical mentality had blunted the sense and scope of a spiritual theology actually lived and experienced, Dumitru Staniloae (b. 1903), in the years immediately preceding the Second World War, embarked on the task of reaffirming the primacy and indispensability of the hesychast contemplative tradition. To this end he undertook the translation into Romanian of the *Philokalia* of Nicodemus, in the 1893 edition, although he also decided to include additional material and to supply new biographical notes and extensive commentaries on the texts. In effect, the first volume of the Romanian *Philokalia* was published in 1946, and the eighth volume in 1986. The bulk of the new material is devoted to Maximus the Confessor, Symeon the New Theologian, and Gregory Palamas, as well as to the staretz Basil of Poiane Marul and of Cernica, and other contemporary Romanian spiritual teachers.

Moreover, the translation itself of the *Philokalia* into Romanian was carried out not simply in the hope that it would counteract the dominantly historical approach to theology then prevailing; it was carried out also in direct response to a thirst for genuine spiritual values among members of the laity. In other words, it if did not signify simply an act of pious devotion and theological culture but represented a manifestation of the reciprocity between the church and the faithful which is a condition and a sign of authentic spiritual regeneration, this was because it coincided with a parallel renewal of the hesychast way and the life of prayer. That this quest for the prayer of the heart should have meant the recovery of a line of filiation stemming directly from the staretz Paisii is of course not accidental. Nor is it accidental—though this is a theme that lies outside the scope of this chapter—that the Paisiian pattern should have been followed, for just as Paisii's disciples had carried the benediction and teaching of their staretz into Russia, so there is a direct line of filiation between the hesychast renewal in Romania and the resurgence of the hesychast way in certain Orthodox monasteries in the Middle East.

This brief account of the hesychast revival in the Orthodox world of Eastern Europe, of which the *Philokalia* has been the testimony, took its start in a description of the stages through which the non-Orthodox Western world began to discover the hesychast tradition, a discovery associated initially with the work of Roman Catholic scholars. Furthermore, figures like the Cistercian monk Thomas Merton (1915–1968), to mention but a single example, show what great possibilities lie in that direction.[3]

In effect, the Orthodox presence in the West as a decisive spiritual factor, although not to be identified with the great Russian emigration provoked by the communist revolution in Russia, was considerably strengthened by it. This is particularly true with reference to what one might call the preparation of the theological ground for the emergence of an authentic hesychast spirituality. One of the most influential Russian writers in this connection had already settled in Paris prior to the communist takeover. This was Myrrha Lot-Borodine (1882–1957), whose article "La doctrine de la déification dans l'Église grecque jusqu'au XIe siècle," published in the *Revue de l'histoire des religions* in 1932–1933, was the first authoritative presentation of the major doctrinal thesis of the hesychast tradition to be published in the West. She followed this article with a series of other works on themes related directly or indirectly to the hesychast way, culminating in a study of the fourteenth-century hesychast master, Nicholas Cabasilas, published after her death. Apart from her example, the main thrust of the renaissance of an Orthodox patristic consciousness in the West has been promoted above all by figures connected with the Russian diaspora.

In this respect, since it is impossible to mention by name all who have been associated with it, one must single out, first, the writings of Vladimir Lossky (1903–1958), whose *Essai sur la théologie mystique de l'Église d'Orient,* published in Paris in 1944, has virtually become a classic; and, second, the magisterial study of Gregory Palamas and the translation into French of one

of his major hesychast works, *Defence of the Hesychast Saints,* both undertaken by John Meyendorff and both originally published in 1959. Alongside
this purely literary preparation for the emergence in the West of an authentic hesychast spirituality one cannot underestimate the part also played,
again above all as a consequence of the Russian diaspora, by the presence
of the Orthodox liturgy, so deeply impregnated as it is with the theology
of the fathers, as well as by that of one of its integral elements, its iconography. The recognition of the icon as the art form par excellence of the
Christian tradition has not been the least of the factors contributing to the
awakening in the West of a genuine patristic consciousness.

This awakening of consciousness to a theological perspective in which it
is stressed again and again that theological knowledge unaccompanied by
personal experience of spiritual realities through a life of prayer and contemplation is little short of vanity–"Our devotion lies not in words but in
realities," Gregory Palamas was to insist, reformulating the Evagrian
aphorism, "If you are a theologian, you will pray truly. And if you pray
truly, you are a theologian"–could not but lead to increasing demand among
the Orthodox Christians in the West for deeper instruction and guidance
on how such experience could best be attained. In other words, in the context with which we are here concerned, it could not but lead to a demand
for access to the *Philokalia* translated into a contemporary Western
language. The first response to this demand was the publication, in London
in 1951, of *Writings from the Philokalia on Prayer of the Heart,* translations
into English made not from the Greek original but from Theophan the
Recluse's Russian version. This was followed, in 1953, by the *Petite Philocalie
de la Prière du Coeur,* published in Paris, and in 1954 by *Early Fathers from
the Philokalia,* again translated from Theophan's Russian version and
published in London.[4] The reception with which these publications met
and the further demand that they stimulated led in their turn to the initiation, both in France and in England, of a translation from the original
Greek of the entire *Philokalia* of Nicodemus and Macarius. The fruits of
this initiation began to be published in the French and English languages
in the late 1970s, and the work is still in progress. Concurrently a number
of Orthodox monasteries have come into being, both in western Europe
and in America, where the hesychast way of life can be practiced more
intensely.

Thus, into a modern Western world dominated for centuries by an activist
time-bound mentality that is antimetaphysical, anticontemplative, and anti-
symbolic, has been squarely placed the alternative of what we have called
a contemplative knowledge of human destiny rooted in a way of life in
which theory and practice, wisdom and method, are inextricably interlocked

and whose fulfillment requires a surpassing of all worldly categories, social, political, economic—in short, of that whole realm of the temporal to which the frenetic activity of modern humanity is confined. Assuredly, behind this antithesis lies another—namely, that between opposed theological and consequently between opposed anthropological orientations. For at the origin (both metaphysical and chronological) of the activist bias of the modern world lies a system of thought which turns God into a transcendent and unknowable essence that, although responsible for setting the cosmic process in motion, does not interiorly penetrate creation in all its aspects, invisible and visible, incorporeal and corporeal, intelligible and material, but leaves it to follow its own course as though it were a self-subsistent autonomous reality. The corollary of such a conception is that the human mind, equated now with its purely rational function, is itself regarded as something sovereign, cut off from the divine and capable of resolving and determining human destiny on earth independently of revelation and grace.

In radically condemning such a system of thought, hesychasm affirms what one might call the bipolarity of the divine; for if it continues to maintain the idea of God's transcendence, it no less insists on his total and ineradicable presence in humanity and in every other form of created existence. In other words, it affirms that God breaks through the wall of his transcendence in order to make himself both the active source and the true existential subject of everything created, down to the least particle of matter itself: a source and subject who not only can be known by human beings but who must be known by human beings as a condition of humans themselves possessing anything more than a distorted knowledge of their own being and of the world in which they live. Such distorted knowledge, of course, is quite inadequate to serve as a guide to any truly constructive action, whatever the goodwill or humanitarian feeling that may lie behind it.

In this respect hesychasm not only rejects the profane humanism which divinizes the human being as an autonomous being, as well as all those concomitant ideological structures whose aim is to establish the just society in terms of this-worldly categories alone; it also rejects the belief, now so common among Christians themselves, that the Christian life can be reduced to love and service to one's fellow beings, especially in some collective form. This is to say that of Christ's two commandments, love of God and love of neighbor, it gives priority to the first and affirms that the love or service of humanity, or indeed any desirable activity on the level of this world, can be effective, both as a means of salvation and as a truly constructive expression of charity and compassion, only if it springs from a prior love of God actualized in the most literal sense of the word. To act in ignorance of this love and apart from its existential actualization is to divorce what one tries to do from its empowering source and so to fall into a kind of idolatry—the idolatry that consists precisely in valuing things apart from God as if they were self-created and self-subsistent.

Hesychasm by no means scorns or undervalues human love and service. It is emphatically not "otherworldly" as this term is usually understood. On the contrary it insists, as we have seen, that the whole of creation is impregnated with God's own life and being and that consequently there can be no true love of God that does not embrace every aspect of creation, however humble and limited. Its purpose is not to abandon the world to annihilation and self-destruction, but to redeem it.

It is to redeem it by transfiguring it. But for the hesychast this transfiguration presupposes the transformation of human consciousness itself, so that it becomes capable of perceiving the divinity that lies at the heart of every created form, giving each such form its divine purpose and determining its intrinsic vocation and beauty. In other words, hesychasts will consider that the way for them, as for any other person, best to serve, at least initially, fellow humans and all other created beings, will be to bring the love and knowledge of God to birth within themselves; for until that has been achieved, their outward actions, instead of being the necessary expression of this love and knowledge, will be tarnished both with self-love and with the idolatry of which we have spoken. This will make it clear why hesychasm is and must be first of all a way of contemplation. For it is only through the contemplative life in all its aspects—ascetic watchfulness, prayer, meditation, the whole uninterrupted practice of the presence of God to which the *Philokalia* is the guide—that humans can actualize in themselves the personal love and knowledge of God on which depend not only their own authentic existence as human beings but also their capacity to cooperate with God in fulfilling the innermost purposes of creation.

* * * *

What, finally, of Mount Athos itself, from the depths of whose solitudes issued, now over two hundred years ago, the *Philokalia* whose subsequent itinerary, both as a document and in terms of its significance in the intellectual life of the modern Western world, we have been tracing? We noted that during the nineteenth century, although monastic life in its hesychast form continued on Athos without interruption, its presence and radiation as a dynamic force were modest. Although toward the end of the century an enormous influx of monks from Russia added a new impetus, transplanting as it did the inheritance of Paisii Velichkovskii associated with the monastery of Optino and *The Way of a Pilgrim* onto Athonite soil,[5] the effects of this had so diminished by the middle decades of the present century that Athos appeared to be threatened with a decline from which recovery might well prove impossible. Moreover, the theological mentality fostered in Greece by the schools and universities was, if not overtly anti-monastic, at least so historicized and abstract that it failed totally to stimulate any aspiration for the contemplative life.

Yet perhaps partially as a consequence of the renewed interest in the West in the Orthodox, and particularly the hesychast, tradition, Greeks themselves, in the decades following the Second World War, began to take fresh stock of this precious heritage, so much of whose literature was written in the Greek language. During the years 1957–1963 a new edition of the *Philokalia* was published in five volumes in Athens, and this was accompanied by the publication of other related works, including *The Way of a Pilgrim* in a Greek translation. As in Romania some twenty years before, the publication of this literature not only provided an antidote to the hidebound historical approach to theology then prevailing; it also represented both a response to and a further inspiration for a growing desire for genuine spiritual values and for the life of prayer. The consequence of this has been a veritable resurgence of monastic life, of which the Holy Mountain has been the center. Moreover, in this resurgence many Orthodox, often converts, from other parts of the world have joined their Greek brethren, so that Athos is rapidly acquiring, or reacquiring, the pan-Orthodox character that is its birthright. One cannot predict the dimensions that this hesychast revival on the Holy Mountain may assume during the closing decades of the twentieth century and beyond. Yet it may be said that already in this Garden of the Mother of God, sown with the seeds of more than a thousand years of contemplative life, the past is becoming the enriching experience of the future, while from the end of time the light that transfigured Christ on Mount Tabor continues to dawn in the hearts of those whose vocation, now as always, is to be hidden witnesses of Him Who is and Who is not, the Alpha and the Omega, the Origin and the End.

Notes

1. Here mention should above all be made of the Assumptionist fathers of *Échos d'Orient* and the Jesuit fathers of *Orientalia Christiana* and of the *Revue d'ascétique et de mystique,* as well as of the comprehensive publication, initiated in Paris in 1942, of patristic texts under the collective title of *Sources chrétiennes.* Also to be noted are the works of Hans Urs von Balthasar, particularly his study of Maximus the Confessor, first published in German in 1941 with the title *Kosmische Liturgie: Maximus der Bekenner* (Freiburg im Breisgau: Herder).

2. For the hesychast revival in Romania, see "Un Moine de l'Église Orthodoxe de Roumanie, 'L'avènement philokalique dans l'Orthodoxie roumaine,'" *Istina* nos. 3 and 4 (1958) 295–328, 443–74.

3. See Thomas Merton's homage to Mount Athos, "L'Athos, république de la prière," *Contacts* no. 30 (1960) 92–109.

4. The French translation was made by J. Gouillard.

5. Staretz Silouan (1866–1938) was a representative of this inheritance on Athos; see Archimandrite Sofrony, *The Undistorted Image*.

Bibliography

Sources

Early Fathers from the Philokalia. Translated from the Russian text *Dobrotolubiye* by E. Kadloubovsky and G. E. H. Palmer. London: Faber & Faber, 1954.

Gregory Palamas, St. *Defense des Saints Hesychastes.* Introduction, texte critique, traduction et notes par Jean Meyendorff. Louvain: Spicilegium, 1959.

———. *The Triads.* Translated by Nicholas Gendle. New York: Paulist, 1983.

John Climacus, St. *The Ladder of Divine Ascent.* Translated by Colin Luibhead and Norman Russell. New York: Paulist, 1982.

Lossky, Vladimir. *In the Image and Likeness of God.* Crestwood, NY: St. Vladimir's Seminary Press, 1975.

———. *The Mystical Theology of the Eastern Church.* London: James Clarke, 1957.

———. *The Vision of God.* London: Hazell Watson and Viney, 1963.

Lot-Borodine, Myrrha. *Nicolas Cabasilas.* Paris, 1958.

A Monk of the Eastern Church. *On the Invocation of the Name of Jesus.* London: Fellowship of St. Alban and St. Sergius, 1949.

The Philokalia. The complete text compiled by St. Nikodimos of the Holy Mountain and St. Makarios of Corinth. Translated from the Greek and edited by G. E. H. Palmer, Philip Sherrard and Kallistos Ware. 3 vols.; 2 vols. in preparation. London: Faber & Faber, 1979–83.

Scupoli, Lorenzo. *Unseen Warfare: Being the Spiritual Combat and Path to Paradise of Lorenzo Scupoli.* Edited by Nicodemus of the Holy Mountain and revised by Theophan the Recluse. Translated from Theophan's Russian text by E. Kadloubovsky and G. E. H. Palmer. London: Faber & Faber, 1963.

The Way of the Pilgrim. Translated by R. M. Franch. London: SPCK, 1972.

Writings from the Philokalia on Prayer of the Heart. Translated from the Russian text *Dobrotolubiye* by E. Kadloubovsky and G. E. H. Palmer. London: Faber & Faber, 1973.

Studies

Colliander, Tito. *The Way of the Ascetics.* London: Hodder & Stoughton, 1960.

Meyendorff, John. *A Study of Gregory Palamas.* London: Faith Press, 1964.

———. *St. Gregory Palamas and Orthodox Spirituality.* Crestwood, NY: St. Vladimir's Seminary Press, 1974.

Mingana, Alphonse, ed. *Early Christian Mystics.* Woodbrooke Studies 7. Translated by Alphonse Mingana. Cambridge: W. Heffer & Sons, 1934.

Ouspensky, Leonid, and Vladimir Lossky. *The Meaning of Icons.* Olten: Urs Graf, 1952. Revised edition, Crestwood, NY: St. Vladimir's Seminary Press, 1982.

Sherrard, Philip. *Athos, the Holy Mountain.* London: Sidgwick & Jackson, 1982.
Sofrony, Archimandrite. *The Undistorted Image: Staretz Silouan 1866-1938.* London: Faith Press, 1958.
Staniloae, Dumitru. *The Tradition of Life: Romanian Essays in Spirituality and Theology.* London: Fellowship of St. Alban and St. Sergius, 1971.
Symeon Grigoriatis, Hieromonk. *The Holy Mountain Today.* London: Alexandria Press, 1983.
Thunberg, Lars. *Microcosm and Mediator: The Theological Anthropology of Maximus the Confessor.* Lund: Gleerup, 1965.

14

The Impact of Western Spirituality on Eighteenth-Century Orthodoxy: An Introduction

I. *Hesychasm and the Western Impact in Russia: St. Tikhon of Zadonsk (1724–1783)*

Elisabeth Behr-Sigel

THE HISTORIAN GEORGES FLOROVSKY has employed the term *pseudomorphosis* to describe the transformation of Orthodox theology under the impact of influences from the West, particularly in the eighteenth century. In his opinion, these influences served to distort Orthodoxy and obscure its true character. Moreover, some of them became imprinted in Orthodoxy, displacing authentic elements.

There is certainly a measure of truth in this severe judgment. But must it not also be qualified? For if on the one hand servile imitation and lack of discernment led to a real alienation, above all in the realm of theology as taught in the Orthodox schools and manuals, on the other it must be said that Orthodoxy's encounter with Western spirituality was not without some stimulating effects. This was particularly true in Russia, and in Greece as well. Those who were strong spiritually, rooted in the bedrock of the tradition of the church, and free (precisely because of this rootedness) from a fear of "the other," were able to transform this encounter into an opportunity for a fruitful integration of traditions. This essay and the following present two spiritual writers engaged in the positive dimensions of the encounter with the West. Although differing in many respects they share the problematic of Orthodoxy's encounter with the West in the eighteenth century. They did not hesitate to investigate and assimilate, with discernment, certain works of Western spirituality when they discovered in them treasures belonging to the *Una Sancta*. And—paradoxically—it is these Orthodox explorers of Western spirituality who stand at the center of the renewal of contemplative prayer and an authentically ecclesial theology in the Orthodox church.

Saint Tikhon of Zadonsk (1724–1783)

Tikhon of Zadonsk, whose personality fascinated Dostoevsky, was a typical man of eighteenth-century Russia. This was a Russia traumatized by a brutal westernization imposed from above, which, at the same time, having been awakened by this shock, was beginning to have an awareness of itself and its own vocation in the modern world. A man of a new age, open to Western influences which he was able to assimilate creatively, Tikhon remained firmly rooted in the faith of the Orthodox church and the tradition of the fathers. In this respect he points to a synthesis which appears to be the historic task of the Orthodox church again today.

Life and Work

Timothy Sokolov (or Sokolovski), given the name Tikhon in monastic life, was born during the reign of Peter the Great in 1724 at Korotsk, a village in the diocese of Novgorod. Like many of the great men of the Russian church his social origins were very humble. His father, Pavel Sokolov, was a sacristan of the village church. His untimely death plunged the family into dire need. Because he was obliged from an early age to earn his bread by laboring with the peasants, the young Timothy risked growing up illiterate. However, his family managed to obtain a scholarship for him to the diocesan school, and, having acquired the rudiments for further education, he entered the new diocesan seminary in 1740 at the age of sixteen. This seminary was at Novgorod. Under the direction of the bishop and Kievan masters, its curriculum was organized along the lines of a Western Jesuit college. Dogmatics was taught in Latin from a manual with marked Thomistic tendencies by a professor from the Theological Academy of Kiev, Theophylact Lopatinski.

After completing his seminary course, the young Sokolov stayed on and was given responsibility for teaching a class in rhetoric. At this juncture he found himself having to choose between two ways of life: Should he opt for the career of a married priest in a parish (as his family wished), or should he follow the call to the monastic life? After some hesitation the latter call became clearer to him as a result of a profound religious experience. During a sleepless night in spring he left the house and contemplated the starry sky. Much later, as a bishop, he recorded what he saw and felt:

> Standing there I meditated on eternal bliss. Suddenly the skies opened and were filled with a glow and a dazzling light such as mortal tongue is unable to describe: the mind is quite incapable of grasping it. This lasted but a moment, and then the skies regained their ordinary appearance, while I, who had beheld this wonderous vision, conceived an ardent desire to lead a life of solitude. And for a long time afterwards my mind recalled what I had seen, and even now, when I think of it, my heart is filled with joy and happiness.[1]

On 10 April 1754 Timothy Sokolov made his monastic profession and was given the name of Tikhon. In the same year he was ordained to the priesthood. A teaching monk, it appeared that he was destined to a career in education. In 1759 he was named professor of dogmatics at the Tver seminary (of which he was soon after chosen to be Rector). He was not able to remain there long enough to realize the program of reform in theological studies and in the formation of future priests, to which he felt called. In the spring of 1761, his name having been added at the last moment to the list of candidates proposed by the Holy Synod, he was chosen by the draw of lots to be the suffragan of the archbishop of Novgorod, with the title Bishop of Keksholm and Lagoda. Two years later at the express wish of Catherine II he was appointed to the see of Voronezh. The empress-philosopher no doubt saw in him one of the "new men" that she hoped would reform the Russian Orthodox Church in line with her ideas. As a "new man," Tikhon was effective but in a sense which was not foreseen by the authorities!

To all around him he appeared to be weak and sickly. It was during this period that the first signs of a mysterious ailment were manifested in him. These may have been of psychosomatic origin. He suffered from trembling, dizzy spells, and fainting. But the Holy Synod having rejected his application for retirement, he buckled down courageously to his pastoral mandate. This was an unusually heavy task: the diocese was distant from the capital; it had suffered abandonment for some time; and it was prey to both political and religious tensions. On arriving in Voronezh, Tikhon was appalled by the coarseness and low moral standards of an ignorant clergy. They thought little of their dignity and consequently they received little respect. The education of these priests was obviously an urgent task. For their use the bishop drew up a *Rule* and *Instructions*. Over against legalism and ritualism Tikhon affirmed and exhorted the priests to inner conversion, asking that they read the Gospel "where Christ himself spoke to them," that they become filled with the word of God, and that they seek to realize, in all humility, the grandeur of their ministry and the divine significance of the mysteries which they were charged with administering. In particular Tikhon insisted on the renewal of the sacrament of confession which often was diverted from its true aim. The humble yet powerful exhortation which he proposed for his priests to address those preparing themselves for confession remains in use in the Russian church to this day.

The formation of the clergy was not, however, an end in itself. Through it Tikhon aimed at raising all of the faithful to a new spiritual level. Tirelessly preaching in his cathedral and in the churches he visited, he addressed the whole people of God. All persons, all Christians, are called to have a sense of their own dignity as well as that of the least of their brothers. All are bearers of the image of God. Together they are members of the Body of Christ, which is the church. Following the apostle Paul and John Chrysostom, Tikhon insisted on the implications of the vision of the church as the Body of Christ for personal and social ethics: "All men are our brothers because they are created in the image of God, purchased by the blood of Christ, they are called to eternal salvation as members of the one Church."

Faith in this mystery, proclaimed Tikhon, ought to change our life and transform society:

> No longer should our brothers be seen wandering the roads and in the squares, starving and trembling with cold, under the icy north wind, naked members of the Body of Christ. The prisons ought no longer to overflow with poor men imprisoned for debts. There ought to be beggars and destitute persons no longer. All should be equal. (*Works* 2:68–69)

The bishop denounced the common vices: drunkenness, fornication, superstition, but he especially attacked hypocrisy and the arrogant luxury of the rich. Although they provided the donations whereby the churches were built, they neglected the temple of God which is the human person himself or herself, their neighbors. Addressing nobles who exploited their servants, he writes:

> You squander your money in banquets, but you watch the least kopec when you force the unfortunate peasant to sell his last cow in order to pay you his taxes. The dogs are your pastime, and you feed them with your own hands from the table, but your serfs often lack bread. (*Works* 5:153)

This social preaching reached its peak in a call to personal conversion. It is also inseparable from the eschatological hope which transcends history, from the vision of the kingdom of God still to come and yet already mysteriously present and accessible. The conversion called for by Tikhon is essentially an encounter with the personal God who appeals to humans through the Incarnate Word in the Christ of the Gospel: "When you hear the Gospel it is Christ who speaks to you there, it is you who speak to him. O sweet, O amiable dialogue! God speaks to man; the King of Heaven deigns to speak with his mortal servants!"[2] Addressing himself to those scorned and exploited by society, Tikhon urged them to become aware of their dignity as children of God, called to freedom. He did this, admittedly, in the dualistic language of his times, but nonetheless he struck the authentic note of a gospel of liberation. The eschatological vision never accepts or justifies the status quo of society:

> Although you are called serfs, you are free men in Christ. In your bodies you are enslaved to men, but your souls are free from sin. . . . Remember poor Christ! O suffering people and loved by God, do not despair! Here below you suffer with Lazarus, but with him you will rest in the bosom of Abraham.[3]

The spirituality of Tikhon does not avoid concrete responsibility. Dressed as a simple monk he would visit the poor, comforting them and leaving them with money or other gifts.

During his four years of pastoral activity in Voronezh the bishop's health deteriorated steadily. A new request to retire received a favorable response in 1767. Rumor had it that the authorities were please to get rid of a bishop who was so daring. Be that as it may, the Holy Synod gave him an adequate pension and left him free to choose a place of residence.

After some hesitation and a false start, Tikhon came to fix his choice on a monastery situated on a tributary of the river Don, which went under the geographical name of Zadonsk. He was to remain there until his death in 1783. For sixteen years he led the seemingly banal life of a retired bishop in a forgotten provincial monastery. His friend Metropolitan Gabriel (Petrov) of St. Petersburg deplored this inexplicable retreat of a man still young and gifted with many talents. He proposed that Tikhon assume the direction of another monastery near Novgorod where he could promote and guide the revival of contemplative prayer in connection with the spread of the *Philokalia*. This famous collection had recently been translated into Russian by the Ukraino-moldavian *staretz* (elder) Paisii Velichkovskii. Tikhon, who was not feeling all that ill at the time, tentatively accepted the invitation. But after suffering a period of doubt he made the decision to stay at Zadonsk, persuaded that this was the will of God for him. "Even if I were to die of it," he told a close relation, "I will not leave this place." This decision made, peace returned to his troubled soul.

Tikhon occupied a modest maisonette, a kind of peasant *isba,* devoid of comfort. He shared it with the two monks charged with attending him, the brothers Basil Chebotarev and Ivan Efimov, both of whom have left important memoirs of him. He slept on the ground without blankets, wrapped in a small sheepskin. He lived as simply as the most humble of monks. His life was divided between physical and intellectual labors. He was receiving visitors, against whom he had to defend himself sometimes, particularly at the end of his life, so great were their numbers. But, above all, he prayed. He assisted at the offices in the monastic church. He sang in the choir but never celebrated the eucharistic liturgy himself, fearing to impose the complex rites of a hierarchical celebration upon the monks. On the other hand, he received communion frequently—a rare thing at that time. He did this together with the monks each Sunday and on feast days. The reading of Holy Scripture held a privileged place in his life. He had a precise and detailed knowledge of the Old as well as the New Testament, and he was capable of reading them in Hebrew and Greek. He enjoyed commenting on passages while his secretary read to him during meals and in the evening. Private prayer, silent prayer, and the chanting of psalms which he knew by heart took up the greater part of the evenings. Prayer was accompanied by prostrations, and often tears. In his cell Tikhon kept pictures representing the different "stations" of the passion of Christ, a sort of Way of the Cross which he used as an aid to his meditation. Georges Florovsky points this out and sees in it a Western influence.[4] Nevertheless, the stress on the sufferings of the Son of God and their concrete representation are actually less unusual in the Orthodox spiritual tradition (at least in its specifically Russian expression) than one might sometimes think. One calls to mind, for example, St. Boris and St. Gleb, and the tradition of the "passion-bearers." Another Russian saint of the nineteenth century, St. Seraphim of Sarov, meditated on the earthly life of Christ and on the passion in particular and even called places close to his hermitage Golgotha and Gethsemane.

When he came to live in Zadonsk, Tikhon was a sick man both physically and psychologically. Indecisive, tormented by scruples concerning the legitimacy of his retirement, haunted by the idea of the services he might yet render to the church (and perhaps also of the honors he might receive in doing so), he passed through periods of profound despair. In their memoirs Efimov and Chebotarev portray the melancholy of Tikhon, his "hypochondriacal and choleric temperament," almost from the very beginning of his stay at Zadonsk. He would shut himself away for entire days in his cell. He was heard to "come and go there praying and supplicating God out loud." These moods, this feeling of abandonment, went together with an irritability which put to flight even his devoted servants:

> During the first year of his sojourn at Zadonsk monastery, he was extremely strict with his attendants. He had a violent temper, and he punished them

for the slightest fault, imposing on them many genuflections and bows during prayer. As the result of these severities he would sometimes lose those attendants who had served him most zealously but who would in the end leave him out of fear.[5]

He was very given to introspection and "would analyse his thoughts even such as were most salutary, with the attention one would employ in tracing the lines and furrows of a palm." He was altogether conscious of his foibles and suffered deep remorse over them. Feelings of guilt often heightened his distress. Miraculously, this tormented man was able finally to acquire peace which radiated to all those around him.

When peace came, Tikhon received it as a grace, a free gift from God. But it was also the fruit of a spiritual struggle leading into deeper faith. As a monk, he experienced ever anew that the power of God was fulfilled in his own human weakness. In the memoirs of his cell attendants the matter of Tikhon's dreams is raised many times. These were accompanied by visions and voices through which he discerned a "paternal visitation" by God. He also received the strength to follow the spiritual direction vouchsafed to him. One day he dreamt that the infant Jesus came and struck him on the left cheek, recalling him in this way to the evangelical counsel of non-violence (Matthew 5:39). Henceforth his quick temper and arrogance gave way to humility. He often asked forgiveness of all those whom he feared he had offended or led into temptation through anger: a cook whom he had reprimanded over trifles or a nobleman whom he had slapped in the course of a conversation. This last episode must have inspired Dostoevsky when he created the character of Bishop Tikhon in *The Possessed*.

Tikhon sensed divine guidance in the incidents of daily life, in the words of interlocutors, in chance encounters, and above all in his contacts with the poor. His comforter during his hours of affliction was Fr. Theophanes, a simple unlettered peasant who fashioned sandals from birch bark. Tikhon greatly admired his simplicity of heart and fervor in labor.

Work played an important role in Tikhon's asceticism. Together with the solitude from which detachment from the world is born and prayer, Tikhon found work to be the best weapon against *"ennui* and dreariness," the typical temptations for the monk. By work he meant both physical and intellectual labor. "Never remain idle!" This was the counsel he offered in his letters of direction, but he applied the precept first of all to himself. When physical strength would return to him, he would remember his past as a Russian peasant. Hearkening back to his village childhood he remembered how to handle an axe in cutting down a tree, how to saw wood for winter heating, how to cut grass for fodder for the horse given to him by

18. St. Tikhon of Zadonsk, contemporary engraving.

19. St. Paisy Velichkovsky, contemporary engraving.

friends to pull his barouche. He was a Tolstoian before Tolstoy, but he also imitated existing monastic models: like Theodosius of the Kievan cave monastery, he came to aspire to a life much more rustic than was possible at Zadonsk. His dream was "to retire to a very distant monastery, to shed not only the dignity of my office, but also my monastic habit; to work, to carry water, saw wood, sweep, bake bread. . . . What a pity this is not possible in Russia!"[6]

For all this, Tikhon remained an intellectual, devoted to works of the spirit. He also had a great love of nature and was enchanted by the various forms and variety in the cycle of the seasons. Like the apostle Paul, he was sensitive to the sighs of creation, striving for fulfillment in God. He read the beauty of the earthly landscape as a parable of the kingdom of heaven, and he looked with hope for the transfiguration of the entire cosmos:

> In this spring perceived by your senses let your spirit be lifted up by faith toward that springtime of beauty and desire promised by God to us in his Word. That spring in which the bodies of men of faith, entrusted to the earth like seeds from the beginning of time, will arise and shoot up and be arrayed in beauty and glory. . . . Then they will be radiant as a bride. They will blossom like the earth in spring. Their heads will be crowned with eternal joy. . . . In this way, straining in spirit toward the longed for spring, you will sow in joy and hope, with the help of God, the seeds of this blessed harvest, which you will then gather up in the fullness of this same joy.[7]

One sees the contemplation of Tikhon opening up into a call to "sow," to action *here and now.* Among the various good works to be undertaken by the Christian is the proclamation of the Good News. Tikhon himself felt called to this ministry, and in his view of the Christian life it occupied a prominent place. Even though he had retired from his official functions as a pastor of the church, he appeared as a messenger of the Gospel.

It was during his retirement that he composed his most important writings and wrote innumerable letters of spiritual direction. These were addressed to members of the clergy, monks, or lay persons. His enormous correspondence made him, in Louis Bouyer's words, "one of the first spiritual teachers of numberless Christians living in the world."[8] It also places him in the context of the tradition of the great spiritual fathers of ancient Russia, of St. Theodosius of the caves, of St. Sergius of Radonezh, with whom he shared a concern for all the people of Russia. He was able to amplify this concern by means of new and improved means of communication.

Over and above his letters, Tikhon also wrote theological and spiritual works. His major writing, a dogmatic treatise in six volumes entitled *On the True Christianity,* was written at Zadonsk. It borrowed its title from the celebrated work of the same name by Johann Arndt, a German Lutheran pastor. Another important work was a collection of meditations with the title *A Spiritual Treasure Collected from the World*. This is recognized as having been influenced by the *Meditatinculae subitanae* of the Anglican bishop Joseph Hall. The book by Arndt was published in Germany in 1605 and often reprinted. It is considered to be an important source of the pietistic currents which exercised an immense influence on German Protestantism over the course of the eighteenth century. But Arndt, it must be noted, provided his text with the support of a solid and traditional theology as well as the warmth of piety. He was admired by a number of Roman Catholic readers. The Russian translation of his work by Simeon Todorski was published in 1735 and went through many editions. The *Meditations* of Hall were not published in Russian until 1796. Tikhon must therefore have read the latter work in Latin. According to N. Gorodetzky both works were to be found in the modest library of the hermitage at Zadonsk, side by side with the Bible and the works of John Chrysostom. Although she has not made a systematic inventory, it seems undeniable that Arndt and Hall inspired Tikhon. It is immediately apparent, however, that it is not a matter of narrow literary dependence but of a creative assimilation by an original thinker of a current of thought with which he sympathized. In the case of Hall's writings, Tikhon found a method of meditation which was consonant with his own temperament. This was the method of transcending mundane sensations in order to ascend in thought to the divine mysteries, not unlike the way one responds to the parables of Jesus. It must be noted that Tikhon took his point of departure from his own reflections and experiences, and not those of the Anglican bishop. It is now known that Hall, a Puritan, drew upon the work of Jean Mombaer entitled the *Rosetum*. This was also a source used in the *Spiritual Exercises* of Ignatius Loyola. This linkage is significant: it indicates that living spiritual experience transcends confessional borders.

In any case, Tikhon had little in common with the sort of scholar who consciously examines other documents in order to construct his own work. His cell attendants served as his secretaries. They took dictation and wrote down the words which seemed to pour out from his mouth. Often they sat together taking notes on the edge of a well in the summer.

His words flowed so rapidly from his lips that I scarcely had time to write them down. When the Holy Ghost became less active in him and he became lost in thought, he would send me away to my cell; kneeling, sometimes lying, with his arms extended in the form of a cross, he would implore with tears that God should send him the All-Activating One. Then, calling me

back once more, he would begin to utter words in such abundance that I
could scarcely follow him with my pen.[9]

Flowing in a beautiful and harmonious imagistic style, quite unlike that of
the scholastic manuals, Tikhon's writing is a synthesis of diverse influences,
both Eastern and Western, showing no exclusiveness. It was formed under
inspiration in the crucible of personal and ecclesial faith. It is this which
constitutes the major interest of the theological and spiritual writings of
Tikhon of Zadonsk.

Tikhon was not preoccupied with recovering a specifically Eastern ascetic
and spiritual tradition, either Greek or Slavic. In this he may be radically
distinguished from his contemporary Paisii Velichkovskii, the translator of
the *Philokalia*. If he admired the monks of Mount Athos and had contact
with several of them (as appears to be the case) and their aspiration to
restore Sinaite and Athonite techniques of prayer to Russian monasticism,
Tikhon remained, in general, a stranger to Athonite "hesychasm," although
there are doubtless some hidden connections with his work. He prayed and
believed in and with the universal church. He heard the word of the living
God in Scripture, and it touched his heart. He attempted to transmit the
fundamental importance of this experience with the help of the intellectual
tools at his disposal. One part of him was shaped by his Kievan masters,
themselves dependent on Western Roman Catholic and Protestant manuals.
But Tikhon instinctively placed himself in the great, central trinitarian
tradition, in the tradition of the Orthodox faith represented in the persons
of Basil the Great and John Chrysostom (the father whom he preferred
above all others).

Through them he inherited the sacramental realism of Paul and the
apostle's vision of the church as the Mystical Body of Christ, together with
the implication of this vision for social and personal ethics—the indissoluble
connection between asceticism, mysticism, and ethics. In this resides his
Orthodoxy. Little matter, therefore, that here and there he used concepts
borrowed from Western scholasticism; that he distinguished between "form"
and "matter" in his sacramental theology; or that he spoke of "satisfaction"
in his theology of redemption. Highly indicative of his "Westernism" is his
focus on the passion of Christ, his obsessive fear of death, and his recurring
thoughts on the last judgment. One senses in fact something rather
Kierkegaardian in Tikhon. But the "fear" and the "trembling" are always sur-
mounted by a confident hope and faith in communion with the resurrected
Christ. Painful and often tragic in tone, his meditation unfolds into the
hope and desire for the ultimate transfiguration of humanity and the entire
cosmos, characteristic of Eastern spirituality.

One discerns in Tikhon an echo of certain passages from Augustine or the *Imitation of Christ* and of a very Western intimate need for a personal assurance of salvation. Ultimately he received all this in the church, within the context of the specifically Russian stress on *sobornost,* the communion in unity of the whole church. "Since you came into the world for all, O Saviour, therefore you came for me." This was his humble and confident confession of faith.

Like Johann Arndt, the father of Protestant pietism, Tikhon proclaimed the necessity of a *living faith,* one in which intellectual assent to doctrine is fulfilled in the personal appropriation of salvation, in which union with Christ penetrates and transforms the entire being. But this subjectivism never lapsed into obscurantism or sentimentalism: Tikhon never depreciated dogma as the rule of faith. The theological task was important to him. But he noted the sterility of a haughty and arrogant orthodoxy, of polemical theology. "True faith in Christ is humble, patient, merciful, full of good will . . . the work in the heart of the Holy Spirit . . . full of joy . . . a gift of the freedom that comes from the Son."[10]

Describing the principal writings of Tikhon and their importance in the history of Russian theology, Georges Florovsky writes:

> This book is less a dogmatic system than a book of mystical ethics or ascetics, yet it marks the first attempt at a theology based on experience, in contrast and as a counterweight to scholastic erudition which lacks any such experience.[11]

It is precisely this "theology based on experience" which attracted Tikhon to the work of the Lutheran pastor from whom he borrowed the title of his book. With a very sure spiritual instinct, he sensed that the demands of such a theology are essentially those of "mere Christianity."

In the tradition of the desert fathers and the Russian hermits, Tikhon sought solitude, and he spoke very warmly of its benefits. He noted that solitude is rarely given up by people without some loss or risk to their interior integrity. He adds, however: "It is not the sinner who must be abhorred, but the sin" (*Works,* vol. 15, letters). All his life this would-be solitary never ceased to strive for "the heavenly gifts" (1 Corinthians 12:31) of true love for humanity, which is inseparable from love for God. But he realistically recognized that in our actual sinful condition, neither he nor any other person naturally possessed this love. Speaking from experience he noted that to be human is to swing between love and hate, attraction and aversion, for one's fellow humans. As he confided in Chebotarev: "Now I feel myself inclined to kiss and embrace all men; now they fill me with a real revulsion."

With his anxious and tormented temperament, anguished almost to the point of despair, Tikhon certainly did not make an easy companion to live with. Few of those who lived close to him really understood him. Speaking in a general way, but obviously about himself, he observed with dry humor that those who seek above all the kingdom of God are often treated as "hypocrites" or "slightly cracked bigots." He was never so happy as when he found himself in the company of simple, unlettered peasants, and of children. The village youths came to see him regularly. He spoiled them and gave them apples and other sweets. Although his nerves were frayed he ultimately acquired peace, which seemed to have been given to him to transmit to those who suffered as he did.

We have referred to the enormous correspondence which was maintained by Tikhon. Through it he exercised, in a new form, the pastoral ministry which he had abandoned: a ministry of compassion for all those who suffered from material, moral, and spiritual distress. He extended this ministry to all those he met on his path. For him all humans were illumined by the vision of the divine image present in them; the image which had been truly restored by the sacrifice of Christ.

At the very beginning of his sojourn at Zadonsk the former bishop of Voronezh did not receive all that many visitors. But as the rumor of his holy life and his overflowing generosity spread, people began to come. People seeking spiritual counsel and authentic direction; peasants looking for work; true pilgrims as well as vagabonds. All misery of the poor of Russia flowed toward the cell "with its doors always open." Those who had survived fire and crop failure appealed to the inexhaustible charity of Tikhon. Having spent the last ruble of the pension paid to him by the empress in soothing some misfortune, he contracted debts. He was to die in absolute poverty, "leaving nothing behind," as his will said—nothing but the testimony of the action of grace and a life painfully fulfilled in doxology:

> Glory be to God for everything! Glory be to God for having created me in his image and likeness! Glory be to God for having redeemed me, the fallen! Glory be to God for having extended his solicitude to me, the unworthy! Glory be to God for having led me, the sinner, to repentance! Glory be to God for having offered me His holy words, like a lamp in a dark place, thus setting me on the path of righteousness! Glory be to God for having illumined the eyes of my heart! Glory be to God for having made known to me His holy name! Glory be to God for having washed away my sins through the bath of baptism! Glory be to God for showing me the way to eternal bliss! The way is Jesus Christ, Son of God, who says of Himself: I am the way and the truth and the life.[12]

On the feast of the Nativity, 1779, Tikhon went for the last time to the monastery church. He sensed that his end was near, and he made his prepa-rations. He did not leave his cell often after this, but he continued to receive some visitors. Struck in 1782 with a partial paralysis which left his mental faculties intact, he finally fell asleep in the Lord during the night of the 13th or 14th of August 1783.

His veneration began spontaneously on the day of his death. He was offi-cially canonized by the Holy Synod of the Russian church on 13 August 1861. The historic importance of Tikhon lies as much in his personality as in his work. In both is realized a remarkable synthesis of the "old" and the "new" (see Matthew 13:52), of the East and the West, of tradition and modernity.

In Tikhon, as Dostoevsky was to sense, Christian Russia encountered and overcame modern nihilism in an intrepid act of faith. It was not a matter of an external polemic with atheists, but a struggle in the depths of Tikhon's soul, a soul that knew the bite of doubt and all the temptations of the spirit and the flesh. With this modern, "westernized" saint, one clearly recovers the highly diverse streams of old Russian spirituality in all their depth:

> The asceticism of death to the world of the recluses of Pechersk, the folly of a life incomprehensibly humiliated for Christ, the love of Christ boxed in the love of men—particularly the poor and the suffering—and above all the yearn-ing for a world and a life transfigured in the risen Christ.[13]

Rootedness in the ancient Russian Orthodox tradition did not prevent Tikhon from being a man of his times, a man of the Age of Enlightenment, a typical example of the reforming element in the Russian church. Tikhon fought ignorance and ritualism. More than anyone else he labored to instruct the clergy, and he did this without divorcing education of the heart and the deepening of personal faith from intellectual formation. He understood the importance of returning to the biblical sources of the faith, and he longed for a translation of the Scriptures into modern Russian, taken directly from the Hebrew and the Greek texts. In his social teaching he refers constantly to the great themes of the modern vision to Christ. Respect for the dignity of humanity and a just reorganization of society in brotherhood are always seen by Tikhon as the very heart of the gospel. Faithful to the authentic tradition of the church, to that of Basil and John Chrysostom, he cleared the foundations for a true Christian humanism at the dawn of a new age, in the tension between the depths of sin and the premonition of the glory to come, which is already glimpsed here and now.

Translated by Andrew E. Morbey

Notes

1. Vasily Chebotarev, in George P. Fedotov, ed., *A Treasury of Russian Spirituality*, 191.
2. Quoted in N. Gorodetzky, *Saint Tikhon of Zadonsk*, 28.
3. Quoted in ibid., 132.
4. Georges Florovsky, *The Ways of Russian Theology*, 158.
5. Ivan Efimov, in G. P. Fedotov, ed., *Treasury*, 215.
6. V. Chebotarev, quoted in N. Gorodetzky, *Saint Tikhon*, 72.
7. Quoted in N. Gorodetzky, *Saint Tikhon*, 201.
8. Louis Bouyer, *A History of Christian Spirituality* (New York: Seabury, 1965) 3:38.
9. Chebotarev, in G. P. Fedotov, ed., *Treasury*, 206.
10. Quoted in N. Gorodetzky, *Saint Tikhon*, 174.
11. G. Florovsky, *The Ways of Russian Theology*, 159.
12. G. P. Fedotov, ed., *Treasury*, 240.
13. L. Bouyer, *A History of Christian Spirituality*, 3:38.

Bibliography

Sources

The written works of St. Tikhon of Zadonsk were bequeathed to the Holy Synod. They were known in Russia, and in the course of the nineteenth century there were many editions and reeditions issued, notably the Synodal edition of the complete *Works* in 1860 and 1889. A biography by Metropolitan Eugene Bolkhovitinov was added to the *Works,* drawing on contemporary testimony, such as the memoirs of Vasily Chebotarev and Ivan Efimov, who were intimate friends of Tikhon. The citations in this article are from the edition of 1860.

Studies

Behr-Sigel, Elisabeth. *Prière et Saintete dans l'Eglise Russe.* Paris: Cerf, 1950. New edition Diffusion, Editions monastique, 1982.
Bouyer, Louis. *Orthodox Spirituality and Protestant and Anglican Spirituality.* Volume 3 of *A History of Christian Spirituality.* New York: Seabury, 1965.
Fedotov, George P., ed. *A Treasury of Russian Spirituality.* New York: Sheed & Ward, 1948. This work contains the memoirs of Chebotarev and Efimov, along with other texts by Tikhon himself.
Florovsky, Georges. *The Ways of Russian Theology.* Belmont, MA: Nordland, 1979). See especially chap. 4, "The St. Petersburg Revolution."
Gorodetzky, N. *Saint Tikhon of Zadonsk: Inspirer of Dostoyevsky.* Crestwood, NY: St. Vladimir's Seminary Press.

There is an abundant literature on Tikhon, referring particularly to his influence on Dostoevsky (as the prototype of the *staretz* Zosima in *The Brothers Karamazov,* for example, and of Bishop Tikhon in *The Possessed*).

II. *Encounter of Traditions in Greece St. Nicodemus of the Holy Mountain (1749–1809)*

Boris Bobrinskoy

BORN IN 1749 IN NAXOS, Nicholas Kalliboutzes received his early instruction at that island's ecclesiastical school. At this time he was already profoundly marked by a traditional religious education and aware of the spiritual needs of his people. At the Evangelical School of Smyrna, then the high point of Orthodox culture under the Ottoman yoke, he acquired a good grasp of foreign languages—Latin, Italian, French, English—which would contribute greatly to his broad knowledge of Western culture. In all of this he was blessed by an amazing memory.

On returning to Naxos in 1770, he became secretary to the local bishop. Under the influence of Macarius of Corinth and the elderly Sylvester of Caesarea (both were his spiritual directors) the desire for the contemplative life was wakened in him. At the age of twenty-six Nicholas went to Mount Athos, settling first at the monastery of Dionysiou. He soon received the monastic habit there, taking the name of Nicodemus. Two years later (in 1777) his friend Macarius Notaras, the metropolitan of Corinth, arrived on the Holy Mountain. This event marked a decisive turn in the life of Nicodemus. He was put in charge of completing and preparing for publication the manuscript text of Macarius's work: the *Philokalia*, the *Evergetinos*, and *On Frequent Communion*. Thanks to the labors of Nicodemus, these three books were published in Venice in 1782.

The daily routine of Nicodemus was divided between prayer and intense intellectual labor. He examined and copied manuscripts drafting and composing numerous texts. He lived in various hermitages and cells on Athos, always actively participating in the spiritual movements and theological conflicts of his times. He never left the Holy Mountain. He died at the age of sixty, on 14 July 1809, the date chosen by the Patriarchate of Constantinople for the celebration of his feast, at the official canonization in 1955.

His Writings

The spiritual labor of Nicodemus must be situated within the context of the major spiritual currents of his time. The monastic current, heir to thirteenth- and fourteenth-century Athonite hesychasm, was strongly opposed to westernizing tendencies and to the infatuation with European literature and culture characteristic of the world of Greek "enlightened" thinkers of the time. At a very early age, Nicodemus was initiated into the practice of hesychasm, but his contemplative vocation always remained inseparable from active service and witness to the Orthodox tradition. This can be seen in that the whole of his life was dedicated to the immense task of publishing the teachings of the fathers and spiritual teachers of the Orthodox church.

It is significant that the first task undertaken by Nicodemus was a redaction of the *Philokalia,* a monumental work prepared by his friend Macarius of Corinth, which contained numerous texts by highly regarded patristic authors of the fourth to the fourteenth centuries, and which gave instruction on "pure prayer" and the ascetic means to achieve it. The goal of this publication was to make accessible to all the people of the church, for the first time, the treasures of the Orthodox spiritual tradition and to widen the sphere of influence of spirituality beyond the walls of monasteries. It was in this same spirit and with the same concern for spiritual expression that the *Philokalia* would be transplanted to the Balkans and to Russia by those extending the work of Nicodemus, above all the Moldavian elder Paisii Velichkovskii (Slavonic translation of the *Philokalia* in 1793), Bishop Ignatius Brianchaninov (augmented Slavonic translation of the same in 1858), and Bishop Theophan the Recluse (amplified Russian translation in 1876). In our times, a Romanian translation (Dumitru Staniloae), English (Bishop Kallistos Ware), and French (Jacques Touraille) translations are in process of publication.

It is in the light of the *Philokalia* that the immense work of compilation, publication, and synthesis of the Orthodox tradition by Nicodemus must be considered and evaluated. It underlines his indestructible attachment to the spiritual experience and ascetic doctrine of the fathers as transmitted through the channels of Athonite hesychasm.

Alongside the *Philokalia,* and in the same spirit, Nicodemus published another compilation of Metropolitan Macarius, the *Evergetinos,* a collection of inspired words and teachings of "the Holy Godbearing Fathers." He composed a *Manual of Counsels (Encheirideon symbouleutikon)* on the guarding of the five senses, the imagination, the spirit, and the heart. This work contained the main ideas of hesychast anthropological doctrine and the spiritual struggle. He also published the *Catechesis* of Symeon the New Theologian (translated into Modern Greek by Denis Zagoraios), his spiritual *Hymns*, and *The Book of Questions and Answers of Barsanuphios and John of Gaza*. Finally, he prepared a complete edition of the works of Gregory Palamas, archbishop of Thessalonica, the principal spokesman of Athonite hesychasm in the fourteenth century. Unfortunately, this edition was not to see the light of day.

We also mention as a matter of interest: (1) the liturgical, didactic, and hymnographical writings of Nicodemus, which serve to underline the connection in his work between theological learning and the liturgical life. The most important texts are the following: *Neon Theotokarion* (ancient Marian canons); canon for St. John the Theologian; the *Great Euchologion; Neon martyrologion* (biographical notes on the new martyrs); *Neon Eklogion* (lives of the saints); *Troparia* for the "Three day Pascha"; several liturgical offices; *Synaxaristes* (synaxaria for the twelve months of the year); *The Garden of Grace* (a commentary on the nine biblical Odes of Matins); *Heortodromion* (a commentary on the canons of the great feasts of the Lord and the Mother of God); *Nea Klimax* (a commentary on the seventy-five antiphons of the Sunday Octoechos); (2) canonical, penitential, and moral writings: *Exomologitarion* (a manual on confession for use by spiritual directors [one ponders over the possible influences here of a Latin model, perhaps of Rhodinos, or Pinamonti, although the tone is profoundly Eastern and Athonite]); *The Standards of Christian Behaviour* (thirteen sermons); *Pedalion* (a collection of ecclesiastical canons, which became the most popular source for canonical practices in the Greek-speaking Orthodox world).

Also, Nicodemus became involved in the conflict caused by the controversy over the *collyvades* (or *kolyvades*, the partisans of *kolybes*, a pudding of boiled wheat blessed and consumed in the church during the service for the departed). This conflict shattered the Turkish-dominated Greek church for almost a century. Connected initially with the issue of whether prayers for the dead could be said not only on Saturdays (as required by the rubrics) but also on Sundays, the confict became centered on the issue of the frequency of eucharistic communion. In 1777, Macarius of Corinth had published a book entitled *On Frequent Communion*. A new edition appeared in 1783 through the efforts on Nicodemus. It recommended frequent communion with support of biblical and patristic citations and criticized contemporary objections to this practice. For Macarius and Nicodemus an authentic spiritual life was inseparable from regular eucharistic communion together with an indispensable spiritual and ascetic preparation.

It is important to recall just how much the spiritual renewal in eighteenth-century Greek Orthodoxy was connected to the rediscovery of the central place of the Eucharist in the life of the church and in sanctification. Nicodemus was accused by his detractors of succumbing to Western influences, precisely because of his attitude toward the Eucharist. But the Assembly of Athos, and then the Patriarchate of Constantinople, cleared him of all suspicion in this respect.

Encounter with the West

The position of political and cultural inferiority of the Orthodox Greeks under the Ottoman yoke was conducive to the implantation and influence of Western churches and Uniates in Greece and Asia Minor. The excellence of Roman Catholic schools attracted Orthodox youths; other young people went so far as to study in Rome, in Venice, or in other Italian cities.

Around 1750, a school established on Mount Athos under the direction of Eugenios Boulgaris began to allow some Orthodox students to receive a better education in religion and secular matters. However, a stubborn resistance by Athonite monks to all secular, philosophical, and scientific studies, forced Boulgaris to transfer his school, first to Salonica and later to Constantinople. His disciple Cosmas the Aitolian, monk and martyr, was one of the great religious preachers at the end of the Turkish occupation. Canonized in 1961, he became a symbol of Orthodoxy, in which he devoted his life to an unremitting evangelization of the Greek people.

It is within this movement that the spiritual commitment of Nicodemus must be located. One can affirm that, on the level of faith and theological doctrine, Nicodemus always adhered without any compromise to the dogmatic tradition of the Orthodox church as elaborated by the fathers and the ecumenical and Byzantine councils. In conformity with the major theological tendencies of his time, he professed a radical anti-Latinism, as is demonstrated in his letters on the rebaptism of Roman Catholics converting to Orthodoxy.

However, Nicodemus was not unequivocally closed to Western spiritual currents. Catholic works revised in the sixteenth and seventeenth centuries helped to establish (paradoxically, it is true) the continuous popularity of Nicodemus in the Orthodox world. Nicodemus published *Unseen Warfare* in Venice (in 1796), and the *Spiritual Exercises* (*Gymnasmata pneumatika*) are a scarcely amplified adaptation of different texts of the Italian Jesuit, J.-P. Pinamonti (1632–1703), in particular of his *Spiritual Exercises,* put together following the pedagogical methodology of Ignatius Loyola. Nicodemus enriched the original text with notes and abundant references to the Bible and the fathers of the church.

ΕΙΣ ΔΟΞΑΝ ΠΑΤΡΟΣ ΥΙΟΥ
ΚΑΙ ΑΓΙΟΥ ΠΝΕΥΜΑΤΟΣ ΤΟΥ ΕΝΟΣ ΘΕΟΥ.

ΒΙΒΛΟΣ ΤΩΟΝΤΙ ΨΥΧΩΦΕΛΕΣΤΑΤΗ

ΚΑΛΟΥΜΕΝΗ

ΓΥΜΝΑΣΜΑΤΑ ΠΝΕΥΜΑΤΙΚΑ.

ΔΙΑΜΟΙΡΑΣΜΕΝΑ ΕΙΣ ΜΕΛΕΤΑΣ, ΕΞΕΤΑΣΕΙΣ,
ΚΑΙ ΑΝΑΓΝΩΣΕΙΣ.

Ἅπερ προθήκαις ὅτι πλείςαις, καὶ ἀφαιρέσεσι, καὶ ἀλλοιώσεσι
καλλωπισθέντα τε, καὶ μετ᾽ ἐπιμελείας διορθωθέντα, καὶ Σημειώμασι
διαφόροις καταγλαϊσθέντα ὑπὸ τῶ Ὁσιολογιωτάτῳ ἐν Μοναχοῖς

ΚΥΡΙΟΥ ΝΙΚΟΔΗΜΟΥ.

ΝΥΝ ΠΡΩΤΟΝ

Τύποις ἐξεδόθησαν διὰ φιλοτίμου δαπάνης, καὶ σπουδαίας
ἐπιςασίας τῦ τιμιωτάτῳ, καὶ χριςιαμικωτάτῳ

ΚΥΡΙΟΥ ΔΗΜΗΤΡΙΟΥ ΚΑΡΥΤΖΙΩΤΟΥ

ΤΟΥ ΕΚ ΠΕΛΟΠΟΝΝΗΣΟΥ.

Εἰς κοινὴ ἁπάντων τῶ Ὀρθοδόξων Χριςιανῶν ὠφέλειαν,
καὶ σωτηρίαν.

ΕΝΕΤΙΗΣΙΝ, 1800. αω.

ΠΑΡΑ ΝΙΚΟΛΑΩ ΓΛΥΚΕΙ ΤΩ ΕΞ ΙΩΑΝΝΙΝΩΝ.

CON LICENZA DE' SUPERIORI.

20. St. Nicodemus, *The Spiritual Exercises*, 1800.

By 1924 Marcel Viller, S.J., had reconstituted the original text and demonstrated that all the sources of the different parts of the Greek edition were from the work of Pinamonti. Almost without exception the thirty-four *Meditations* as well as the eight *Examinations* are drawn from the *Spiritual Exercises* of Pinamonti. The second *Meditation* ("On the End of Man") is borrowed from the *Religiosa in solitudine* of the same author. The first of three parts in the tenth *Meditation,* the twenty-third *Meditation* ("On the Obedience of Christ"), and the third part of the thirty-first *Meditation* appear to be original. Of eight *Lectures* the first seven are borrowed from the *Via del cielo appianata,* and the eighth from *Religiosa in solitudine.* Finally, in the third edition (Athens, 1895), thirty short *Meditations* in Nicodemus's work are complete translations of Pinamonti's *Meditations on the Four Last Things.*

It seems difficult to support, as does the monk Theoklitos, the idea that the original Italian was subjected to a profound and radical transformation and that what Nicodemus produced is "a major work of eastern spirituality, possessing the essential characteristics of Orthodox spirituality."[1] The monk Theoklitos believes that the work of Nicodemus is a radical amplification of a short work composed by Ignatius Loyola under the same title, with which the composition of Nicodemus has (of course) very little in common. The attribution to Pinamonti of nearly the whole original text reduces to a relatively small amount the personal inspiration of Nicodemus.

It must be noted, however, that this revision of Pinamonti's *Spiritual Exercises* by Nicodemus had a very limited circulation in the Orthodox world. Even translations into the Slavic languages did not make the work popular. This can probably be attributed to the Latin and Ignatian flavor of the work. Nonetheless, it takes nothing away from the spirit of freedom of Nicodemus and his courage in seeking to give to Orthodox readers that which appeared to him to be the best of the spiritual literature of the West. One can quote the following words of Nicodemus drawn from *The Standards of Christian Behaviour,* one of his last works, words that confirm the spiritual discernment of Nicodemus vis-à-vis the West: "We must hate and detest the misbeliefs and unlawful customs of the Latins and others who are Heterodox; but if they have anything sound and confirmed by the Canons of the Holy Synods, this we must not hate."[2]

The *Unseen Warfare* of Nicodemus will hold our attention longer. Published in 1796, it quickly experienced a great boom in popularity. In the Preface, Nicodemus acknowledges having translated and altered the work of an anonymous author, a "wise man" (as he qualifies it). It appears that Marcel Viller was the first to uncover the identity of this anonymous person. It seems to be a matter of Nicodemus's adaptation of two opuscules attributed by Viller to Lorenzo Scupoli, the *Combattimento Spirituale* and the *Sentier du Paradis.* Scupoli (1529–1610) was a Theatine cleric who devoted himself to spiritual direction and who died in the odor of sanctity after having been the object of such calumnies that he had been reduced to lay status.

Although Scupoli's authorship of these works has recently been called into question,[3] generally speaking he is considered to be their author. His *Spiritual Combat* made its first appearance in 1589 in twenty-four chapters, without mention of the author, but the following edition, which was augmented up to sixty-six chapters, carried the name of L. Scupoli. Between 1589 and 1750 one counts over 250 editions of this work. It is well known that Francis de Sales read it daily and thought it equal to the *Imitation of Christ.* The spirituality of Scupoli's *Spiritual Combat,* a veritable ascesis of love, joins in the current of the school of Ignatius Loyola, but extends and goes beyond it. The exhortation to pure love is the terminal point of the Ignatian *Exercises.* Pure love is the point of departure for the *Spiritual Combat* of Scupoli. This work is completely centered on the biblical idea of a mortal struggle between human beings and their passions, between the loftier and the base desires. The image of fencing underlies the book, and Scupoli compares the spiritual struggle to combat with swords.[4]

Louis Bouyer explains Nicodemus's predilection for the writing of Scupoli and for the popularity of his adaptations in the Orthodox world in this way:

> [Scupoli], while dependent on the psychological and systematic spirituality of the post-Renaissance, developed it within a two-fold scheme taken from patristic spirituality and interlaced it with these two basic strands. These were, on the one hand, asceticism understood as a struggle against demonic enslavement, and, on the other, its flowering into a spirituality not of suppression of the activities of the senses or condemnation of creation, but of consecration of the world in a glorification of God by the whole man, body as well as spirit.[5]

H. A. Hodges describes in detail the long and fascinating story of the development of the *Combattimento Spirituale,* first of all as penned by Scupoli and perhaps his successors, then in the hands of the Greek translator Nicodemus, and finally, by the Russian adapter, Bishop Theophan the Recluse in the nineteenth century. We have here a touching example of a text of great spiritual needs of its readers. In this respect it is not unlike the *Philokalia* of Macarius, updated by Nicodemus, which knew and knows an analogous destiny in Russia and Romania in the nineteenth and twentieth centuries.

A practical ascetic treatise in the original creation of Scupoli, it soon was enriched by a chapter on prayer and on meditation, and on eucharistic communion, which became, as it were, the ultimate weapon of spiritual combat. The teaching of Scupoli on prayer is nevertheless limited and is introduced less in itself than as a weapon of ascetic warfare.

The translation by Nicodemus of Scupoli's ascetic treatises respects the general order and contents of the original chapters. These are amplified and accompanied by numerous notes and additions specifically for the use of Orthodox readers. Nicodemus eliminates all references to "the Sacred Heart of Jesus" and purgatory, but is not excessively anti-Latin. It keeps, for example, the concepts of ejaculatory prayer, the merits of Christ, satisfaction, and sufficient grace.

I will not enumerate here in detail all the modifications made at this time or in successive publications. The most important concern the twenty-first and twenty-fourth chapters of the Italian text on the guarding of the senses. According to Scupoli, this was accomplished through constant reference of all sensory impressions and energies to God. Aside from numerous expansions in details, Nicodemus inserted a new chapter, his twenty-fifth, on the correction of the imagination and the memory. This ascesis of the sensory imagination led to a true contemplation of and response in God. Thus, Nicodemus develops in a natural way the theme of the prayer of Jesus, or pure prayer. This is the heart of his contribution to *Unseen Warfare,* which we find detailed in his *Manual of Counsel,* and which constitutes the traditional doctrine of the fathers found in the *Philokalia.*

Nicodemus faithfully reproduces Scupoli's chapters on prayer (Scupoli's chapters 44–52), in which prayer is represented as a weapon of spiritual combat. On top of the standard themes of meditation on the earthly life of the Savior, on the Mother of God and the saints, and particularly on the passion and crucifixion of the Savior, along with eminent examples of virtue, courage, and patience, Scupoli devotes a special chapter (chapter 45) to mental prayer, to the lifting up of the heart toward God by means of short, ejaculatory prayers. It is not so much a question here of Ignatian analytic meditation, but of a traditional method closely related to simple prayer (*monologistos euchē*), from which the doctrine of the Jesus prayer sprang. Nicodemus greatly amplifies this chapter (chapter 46) on mental prayer and its various forms. He defines mental prayer as prayer of the intellect (*noera*) and of the heart (*kardiakē*), unifying in this way in one doctrine and common practice the Evagrian and Macarian traditions of the Jesus prayer. This chapter is a fundamental exposition of the hesychast doctrine inherited from Athonite Palamism, which Nicodemus embraced as his own spirituality and teaching.

Once the spirit is calmed and unified in the prayer of the heart, all the other forms of prayer or spiritual activities can be recovered. Nicodemus does not ignore them. He faithfully retranslated without much modification the last seven chapters of Scupoli on meditation. Hodges had reason to point out that the intention of Nicodemus was "not to substitute Latin methods of devotion for Greek, or Greek for Latin, but to marry the two, giving each its proper place in the scheme of the spiritual life."[6]

One final point concerns the chapters on the eucharistic communion. Following Scupoli, Nicodemus distinguishes between sacramental and spiritual communion. The latter ought to be frequent, indeed constant, realizing the presence of Christ in the soul. Scupoli dealt with this in a limited way in his meditation on the grace of the eucharistic communion. For Nicodemus, spiritual communion culminates in the prayer of the heart and its realization in each moment and place, the heart becoming the temple of the Holy Spirit.

In a note in this same chapter (2.4) of *Unseen Warfare*, Nicodemus opposes the "sick and perverse custom" of spiritual directors of forbidding frequent communion. One knows that the encouragement to frequent communion constituted one of the fundamental features of the program of Nicodemus and of his friends the *collybades*. It was because of this that they were accused of having been influenced by the Latins, only to be later rehabilitated by the Assembly of the Holy Mountain:

> This synthesis between frequent sacramental practice and the inspiration of hesychast prayer is by no means the least interesting of the syntheses we owe to him. Indeed we owe to him the reconciliation of the liturgical current and the wholly inner current of Byzantine spirituality with a spirituality of the eucharistic Christ, which owes much to Nicholas Cabasilas without doubt.[7]

The transformation of the *Combattimento Spirituale* of Lorenzo Scupoli from century to century did not stop with the work of Nicodemus. It was resumed and similarly augmented at the time of the Russian translation of the *Unseen Warfare* of Nicodemus of the Holy Mountain in the nineteenth century by Theophan the Recluse. It is this translation—or, rather, this fairly free adaptation for nineteenth-century Russian readers—which H. A. Hodges has translated into English, and which has become the best-known version of the *Unseen Warfare*. Hodges has put forward in great detail all the numerous modifications made by Theophan to the work of Nicodemus. He finds the text presented by Theophan to be "a genuinely Orthodox work, a worthy modern companion to the *Philokalia*, with which, both in Greece and in Russia, it has shared the same editors."[8]

I cannot help expressing the wish to see published one day, in a Western language, a complete and faithful translation of *Unseen Warfare*, as it was when it left the quill of its first editor, St. Nicodemus of the Holy Mountain.

Conclusion

Assessments of the intrinsic quality of the *Unseen Warfare* of Nicodemus and the merits of Nicodemus as an author, are very diverse. Lev Gillet has called the text a "clumsy mixture, . . . a piece of literary and spiritual piracy." He minimizes the influence of the work among the Orthodox. This radical judgment is generally rejected as excessive by other authors.

By contrast, H. A. Hodges sees in the *Unseen Warfare* one of the great spiritual writings of the Orthodox world. The monk Theoklitos agrees, characterizing it as "a veritable hymn of the mystical spirit of the Orthodox fathers and like a pure mirror of the heart and soul of our Holy Orthodox father Nicodemus."[9]

Neither of these judgments appears fully to do justice to the work and to the intention and vision of St. Nicodemus. It is a remarkable feat to have produced two editions of considerable "Western" works within a fundamentally anti-Latin milieu, and, while respecting the schema and basic contents of them, to have put them in the rediscovered perspective of the experience of prayer, in the most authentic Orthodox tradition. The renown of St. Nicodemus has nothing to fear from the tracing of the original text of his editions back to Roman Catholic writers of the sixteenth and seventeenth centuries. Their own rediscovery of the Eastern fathers, particularly St. John of the Ladder, explains the spiritual sympathy between Nicodemus and Western spiritual authors whose works he desired to communicate to this orthodox brethren.

St. Nicodemus of the Holy Mountain used exceptional spiritual discernment in exposing to the light of the Orthodox tradition several of the spiritual writings then in vogue in the Latin church. When all is said and done, the minor modifications made by him, together with the addition of an original chapter on the prayer of the heart, express both the very traditional Orthodox doctrine and his own very personal spiritual experience. This provides the basis for the spiritual recentering of Scupoli's text. Nothing, or very little, is rejected from this latter's work. Instead it is resituated in a very organic, coherent pedagogical context. The themes of the Italian ascetic and spiritual pedagogy are taken up and at the same time supported by numerous biblical and patristic texts, which serve to bathe it in the renewed yet uninterrupted traditional current of Orthodoxy.

The ascetic publications of Nicodemus are an example of a traditional attitude of openness toward major works of spirituality which transcend and speak beyond the divisions of Christians. The success of *Unseen Warfare* in the Orthodox world, even taking into account the fact that its true author is unknown, confirms the matchless spiritual quality of the original Italian text, and justifies the edition realized by Nicodemus. He sought to immerse Roman Catholic writings in the classical current of Byzantine hesychasm (as brought up to date in the new *Philokalia*). He contributed greatly to this task by his literary works and, above all, by his commitment to monastic life and prayer.

Translated by Andrew E. Morbey

Notes

1. Theoklitos de Dionysiou, *St. Nicodemus the Hagiorite*, 197, 199. In Greek.
2. Cited by Constantine Cavarnos, *St. Nicodemus the Hagiorite*, 31.
3. Cf. L. Gillet, "*Unseen Warfare* by H. A. Hodges," *Sobornost* 3 (1952) 584–86.
4. Etienne Marie Lajeunie, *Introduction au Combat Spiritual*, 13.
5. Louis Bouyer, *Orthodox Spirituality and Protestant and Anglican Spirituality*, 42.
6. H. A. Hodges, *The Unseen Warfare*, Introduction, 54.
7. Bouyer, *Orthodox Spirituality and Protestant and Anglican Spirituality*, 44.
8. Hodges, *The Unseen Warfare*, 67.
9. Theoklitos, *St. Nicodemus the Hagiorite*, 196.

Bibliography

Bebis, George S. "St. Nicodemus the Hagiorite." In *Post-Byzantine Ecclesiastical Personalities*, 1–17. Edited by Constantine Cavarnos. Brookline, MA: Holy Cross Press, 1978.

Bouyer, Louis. *Orthodox Spirituality and Protestant and Anglican Spirituality*. Vol. 3 of *A History of Christian Spirituality*. New York: Seabury, 1965.

Cavarnos, Constantine. *St. Nicodemus the Hagiorite*. Belmont, MA: Institute for Byzantine and Modern Greek Studies, 1974.

Gillet, L. "*Unseen Warfare* by H. A. Hodge." *Sobornost* 3 (1952) 584–86. Book Review.

Grumel, V. "Nicodème l'Hagiorite." In *Dictionnaire de Théologie Catholique*, vol. 11, cols. 486–90. Paris: Letouzey et Ané, 1931.

Hodges, H. A., ed. *The Unseen Warfare*. London: Faber & Faber, 1952.

Lajeunie, Etienne Marie. *Introduction au Combat Spiritual*. Paris, 1966.

Le Guillou, M.-J. "Aux sources des mouvements spirituels de l'Eglise Orthodoxe de Grèce. I. La renaissance spirituelle du XVIIIe S." *Istina* 1 (1960) 95–128.

Papoulides, C. *Nicodemus the Hagiorite*. Athens, 1967. In Greek.

——. "Portée oecumenique du renouveau monastique au XVIIIe s., dans l'Eglise Orthodoxe." *Balkan Studies* 10 (1969) 105–12.

——. "The Relationship of the 'Gymnasmata Pneumatika' of St. Nicodemus the Hagiorite with the Spiritual Exercises of St. Ignatius of Loyola." *Makedonika* 11 (1971) 161–73. In Greek.

——. "The Relationship of the *Unseen Warfare* of St. Nicodemus the Hagiorite with the *Spiritual Combat* of Lorenzo Scupoli." *Makedonika* 10 (1970) 23–24. In Greek.

Stiernon, D. "Nicodème l'Hagiorite." In *Dict. Sp.*, vols. 72–73, cols. 233–250.

Théoklitos de Dionysiou. *St. Nicodèmus the Hagiorite: His Life and Works*. Athens, 1959.

Viller, M. "Nicodème l'Hagiorite et ses emprunts à la littérature spirituelle occidentale. Le *Combat Spirituel* et *Les Exercises* de St. Ignace dans l'Eglise byzantine." *Revue d'Ascétique et de Mystique* 5 (1924) 174–77, 416.

15

Trial and Victory:
The Spiritual Tradition
of Modern Russia

SERGEI HACKEL

IT WAS AN EXILE who made the most significant contribution to the development of Russian spirituality in the second half of the eighteenth century. The westernized sophistication and scholarship of the Ukraine held no attractions for the young Paisii Velichkovskii (1722–1794), and the greater part of his life was to be spent abroad in the monasteries of Athos and Moldavia. It was on Athos that he was to benefit directly from that revival of hesychast prayer which was to bear fruit in, and was to be furthered by, the publication of the *Philokalia* in 1782. Paisii introduced it to the Slavic world. His achievement was recognized as he was formally included among the saints in 1988.

The *Philokalia* was a fresh compilation, the editors of which were Nicodemus of the Holy Mountain (1749–1809) and Macarius, formerly metropolitan of Corinth (1731–1805). The contents of it were classical texts of Orthodox spiritual life, the very gathering of which into one set of volumes gave added potency and currency to each.[1] Their currency was to be increased immensely by the Slavonic translation undertaken by Paisii. Although he seems to have regarded the manuscript principally as a working text for his Slav monastics, Paisii was soon persuaded to have it published. Thus, under the auspices of Gavriil Petrov (1730–1801), metropolitan of St. Petersburg, the first of several editions was to see the light of day in the year before Paisii's death (1793). The name of the translated collection was *Dobrotoliubie*. The Russian hesychast tradition of St. Nil of Sora (1433–1508), which had hitherto survived only in the obscurity of distant hermitages, now gained a new prominence and validation.

The circulation of texts was matched and undergirded by the peregrinations of those who sought to apply their teachings. The changing fortunes of Russian monastic foundations in the reign of Catherine the Great encouraged the mobility of monks. Thousands were cast adrift by this monarch's massive secularization of monastic property (1764)—hence the predominance of displaced Russians among Paisii's pupils in Moldavia.

Nevertheless, succeeding reigns saw greater tolerance, even encouragement of the monastic life, and those who then returned to Russia often came as experienced practitioners of hesychast prayer. They came also with new perspectives in the fiield of pastoral guidance. Their influence, and that of their immediate disciples, was to be remarkably widespread and long-lasting.

Furthermore, this influence was by no means limited to monasteries, for the personal guidance offered by the seasoned elders of such monasteries as Optino, Sarov, or Valaam was eagerly sought by thousands of pilgrims. There were also elders who extended the range of their influence (and unintentionally perpetuated it) by engaging in correspondence with their clients. Among the most significant correspondents must be listed the elder (*staretz*) Makarii Ivanov of Optino (1788–1860), several hundred of whose letters were to be published posthumously.[2] Even more prolific was the recently canonized (1988) recluse bishop Theophan (Feofan) of Vysha (1815–1894). The latter eschewed all personal contact with the outside world for the last two decades of his life. Yet at the same time he produced no fewer than eight volumes of letters,[3] quite apart from other numerous and important works of spiritual instruction.[4]

No more than two or three persons had access to Feofan in the years of his seclusion. Yet he was open to the supplications and the plaints of almost anyone who cared to turn to him. Therein is summarized the paradox of elderdom. Separation from the world was a necessary precondition for it, a separateness that was not established merely by the locking of a door. Indeed, as with Feofan, it could involve years of ascetic endeavor and of inner prayer, the necessary work of any monk. But the fruits of this separateness were yet to be communicated, even though the semblance of separateness might thereby seem to be eroded. The prayerful generation of love must necessarily lead to its expenditure—in the words of Makarii, "Our love of God finds its expression in our love of men."[5]

Thus, while Feofan preserved his outward segregation, Makarii, like his predecessor as elder of Optino, Leonid Nagolkin (1768–1841), and also his successor, Amvrosii Grenkov (1812–1891), made himself daily and immediately accessible to those who sought his spiritual counsel and support.

Within the community itself, the elders advocated a daily and total "revelation of thoughts" as part of the monastic routine. It was on the basis of such a revelation that counsel could best be given. The same implicit trust that prompted such a revelation was expected to involve unquestioning acceptance of consequent advice. The practice (earlier promoted by Paisii) was to survive into the present day. In the case of chance pilgrims and distant correspondents, such close scrutiny of the petitioner's inner life could not be undertaken. Nevertheless, each person was treated as an individual, "My advice to you is fashioned according to your inner and outward circumstances," wrote Makarii to a correspondent. "Hence, it can be right only for you." He asked for it not to be quoted or treated as a general rule of conduct: "It is nothing of the kind."[6]

This being so, he would dissuade some individuals from distributing their worldly goods, from undertaking the monastic life or even from the practice of the Jesus prayer, well though he knew the price and value of each. At other times, he would cautiously commend the practice of the same prayer, but only with due humility was one to embark on this most challenging of activities, he counseled. The diligent quest for self-purification must accompany it throughout, though deviations and temptations on this path are many. An experienced spiritual director is essential.

The practice and the teachings of the Optino elders were closely modeled on the teachings of the Greek fathers, whose writings they also consistently translated, published, and distributed. Feofan the Recluse was to match this activity with his own translations and adaptations; not least of his contributions was an (expanded) translation of Paisii's *Dobrotoliubie* into Russian (1876–1890). At Optino, the scholarly work had an unexpected by-product. Here was a point at which the post-Petrine alienation of the Russian educated classes from the Orthodox church began to be counteracted. A pioneer in this partial yet portentous reintegration—it was to culminate in something of a "Russian Religious Renaissance" by the beginning of the twentieth century[7]—was the former Shellingian Ivan Kireevskii (1806–1856), a neighbor of Optino. His collaboration with the elder Makarii's team of translators involved a personal as well as a professional commitment. The same could be said of other members of the Slavophile intelligentsia, out of whose midst were to arise religious thinkers of a new (nonacademic) type and of some importance. Most notable among them was the lay theologian Aleksei Khomiakov (1804–1860), whose concept of *sobornost* (conciliarity/communality) was to have a lasting impact on Orthodox (and not only Orthodox) ecclesiology in the century to follow.

In later years no one was to provide greater publicity for the Optino fathers than the novelist who spent no more than the inside of three days at their monastery to consult the elder Amvrosii, but who incorporated his impressions in a work that was to reach many millions of readers far beyond the boundaries of Russian, Orthodox, or even Christian culture. The novelist was Fedor Dostoevsky (1821–1881). It was the elder Zosima in his *The Brothers Karamazov* who gave utterance to a mystical teaching which seemingly reflected that of the elders themselves. But that the Optino fathers rejected the teaching of Zosima was by no means merely a sign that they lacked literary sophistication. No doubt they noted that Zosima was little concerned for the spiritual disciplines to which they were themselves committed, however flexible they also showed themselves to be. Furthermore, the divinization (*theosis*) of human nature toward which the hesychast would humbly and assiduously strive could hardly be equated with Zosima's perception of a universe transformed already, itself an earthly paradise. That the optimistic nature mysticism of Zosima rested on the occasional and selective use of Christian imagery was insufficient to provide its justification. Rather might they have argued that it spoke of intrinsic and insidious spiritual dangers and temptations.[8]

If approval was to be given by Optino to a popular work on the spiritual life, the work that was eventually to be known in English translation as *The Way of a Pilgrim* (1884) was more likely to attract it. Certainly, the elder Amvrosii gave it his approval in his correspondence.[9] Furthermore, it was among his papers that additional (manuscript) chapters of the work were to be discovered several years after his death.

The title of the (anonymous) original declares its confessional character. *Otkrovennye razskazy strannika dukhovnomy svoemu ottsu* means "The sincere accounts of a pilgrim to his spiritual father." Even though the narrative shows signs of having been reworked to correspond to the literary tastes of the day, its essential authenticity is not in doubt. The author may or may not have been a simple peasant, as he claims, but his work in any case dramatically demonstrates how hesychast spirituality could find its devoted practitioners in the world far beyond monastic walls.[10] Inevitably, the pilgrim finds monastic elders to assist him, but his unfailing and irreplaceable support is an edition of the *Dobrotoliubie*. Beginning with the disciplined, even mechanical, repetition of the Jesus prayer ("Lord Jesus Christ, have mercy on me") many thousands of times per day, he was in due course able (literally) to incorporate it, to link it in the recommended fashion with his breathing and, ultimately, to filter all his experiences through it. Not only was his inner life conditioned thereby: his perception of creation as a whole was transformed: "People, trees, vegetation, animals, these were all related to me, and in all I found the impress of the name Jesus Christ."[11] As never before he came to understand the meaning of the Gospel words, "The kingdom of God is within you" (Luke 17:21).[12]

The evident sanctity of at least one of the three great Optino elders, Amvrosii, was formally proclaimed by the church in 1988. But the spiritual attainments of another great elder were recognized earlier. Indeed, the canonization of Serafim Moshnin of Sarov in 1903 was a notable event in its own right. Both events involved the somewhat belated acknowledgment of the whole Paisian school of spirituality.

The paradox of that separatedness of elders which ultimately could yet promote and justify their accessibility was rarely so strikingly demonstrated as in the case of St. Serafim (1759–1833). His novitiate at Sarov was hardly completed (1786) before he retired into a nearby hermitage, there to spend the greater part of seventeen years (1793–1810). These included several years of severe ascesis, when he committed himself to stylite-like prayer in a strictly limited location. He would take his stance on one rock by day, another by night, and engage in continual repetition of the publican's prayer, "God be merciful to me, a sinner." This was not the Jesus prayer itself, closely though it was related to it. At other times he was to commend the actual Jesus prayer (in several variants), for "those who have truly decided to serve the Lord God must exercise themselves in the awareness of God and in ceaseless prayer to Jesus Christ. . . ."[13] In any case, whichever the precise prayer that engaged him at any particular stage, he would also adhere normally to the daily *Rule of St. Pachomios the Great*.

Already in the hermitage Serafim came to dedicate himself to several years of silence. These were to be followed by several more years as silentiary and recluse within the walls of the Sarov monastery proper. Only occasionally would he permit modification of his prayerful seclusion—and that only after five years had elapsed (1815). But in 1825 he decided to waive each and every restriction. Thereafter thousands were to see him; at times, several thousand in a single day. They came to him as visionary, healer, guide. Some were to testify to the manifest radiance he had attained. Indeed, there was one visitor, Nikolai Motovilov, who was himself to be drawn into it one wintry Thursday in the penultimate year of Serafim's life. The circumstantial and unaffected account which Motovilov left of his experience on that occasion was to define Serafim's image, message, and spiritual achievement with a vividness that has rarely been matched.

Serafim had been explaining that the aim of life was nothing other than the acquisition of the Holy Spirit. There were many paths to this acquisition, he noted, including any virtue practiced for the sake of Christ. Prayer was the most dependable of all, but were there any signs of such an acquisition? Serafim's bland assurance that the whole thing was simple for those who were endowed with the Spirit still failed to satisfy him.

Then Fr. Serafim took me firmly by the shoulders and said to me, "Both of us, my friend, are now within the Holy Spirit. Why do you not look at me?"

21. Russian faithful at Monastery of S. Sergius.

22. Russian faithful before a closed church.

I answered, "I am not able, father, for there is lightning flashing from your eyes. Your face has grown more radiant than the sun, and my eyes cannot bear the pain." Fr. Serafim said, "Do not be afraid, my good Theophilus, you have also now become as radiant as I. You yourself are now in the fulness of the divine Spirit, otherwise you would not be able to perceive me in the exact same state." And inclining his head towards me, he quietly murmured in my ear, "So thank the Lord for his unspeakable mercy towards you. . . . How should we fail to thank him for his ineffable gift to us both?"[14]

Earlier that day, Serafim had discussed the radiance of Moses on Sinai and of Christ on the mount of the transfiguration. These now seemed to find their counterpart in the effulgence of his own person. As for the peace, sweetness, joy, warmth and fragrance which Motovilov also experienced at this time, these (so he was assured by the serene and ever-benign elder) were naturally to be associated with "the kingdom of God come in power."

The advent of the same kingdom is proclaimed and anticipated in the Eucharist of the Orthodox church. Even in his seclusion as a hermit, Serafim would continue his attendance at his community's Sunday celebration of it. Only when he was incapacitated or strictly segregated as a recluse was this practice discontinued. Even then the sacrament was regularly administered to him in his cell. For his part, Bishop Feofan of Vysha celebrated the Eucharist daily during his eleven final years as a recluse. Even as a young layman, another future bishop, Ignatius Brianchaninov, sought to receive communion weekly; subsequently he was to advocate frequent communion consistently in the writings of his maturity. Such advocacy is likewise to be found in the writings of the elder Makarii, but in every case this ran counter to the standard Russian practice of the day. Four communions a year were then considered normal, certainly for the laity at large. Indeed, the law of the land required even less, a single annual confession and communion.

In the latter part of the nineteenth century no one was to demonstrate more vigorously that such a practice was deficient than the saintly parish priest of Kronstadt, Ioann (John) Sergiev (1829-1909). Ioann gained renown initially for his insistence on charity as the necessary concomitant of piety.[15] His local organization of social work for the outcasts of society was exemplary. Aspects of it, like his temperance movement, were to have repercussions far beyond the limits of his parish or archdiocese (St. Petersburg). Indeed, although he was never to resign his post as Kronstadt's parish priest, he was to become a national figure by the 1880s, the "intercessor of the Russian land"—hence the ample funds with which he could support his charitable work; hence, also, the crowds that flocked to his services.

He chose to start each day with the celebration of the Eucharist. Thus he was to ground his work. For "being vested in . . . Christ by faith and through communion in the sacred mysteries I am as firm as a cliff."[16] By contrast, "I am dead when I fail to celebrate the Liturgy."[17] But such celebrations were never intended to be something like a private Mass. Rather was each the action of the universal church. Bystanders had no place in such an action. The Eucharist involved the penitence, self-offering, and communion of those who came to take part. Since personal confession (required before communion) was out of the question with such numbers as attended, thousands would participate in an unconventional communal confession before proceeding to communion. The management of something that could lead to mass hysteria would have been difficult for someone lacking the authority of Ioann himself, and these particular practices were not to survive him. Nevertheless, a positive reappraisal of the eucharistic element in the life of Orthodox Russians was long overdue, and his contribution to that reappraisal was of exceptional importance. None of this implied any belittling of personal prayer, the ordering of the will or the emotions. Ioann's extensive spiritual "diary" leaves no doubt about this.[18] It was his conviction that the work of the individual member of the church cannot but involve the body as a whole, and that body finds its full expression in eucharistic worship and communion.

The parish priest of Kronstadt was to be buried at the emperor's expense, but the days when the church could expect support or even toleration from the state were coming to an end. As far as monasticism was concerned, it soon became plain that the new Soviet state was not concerned with the preservation even of such monasteries as had once made an outstanding contribution to Russian culture. Optino (closed 1923) or Sarov (closed 1927) were of no more interest to the secular authorities than any other such institution. By the 1930s not a single monastery or convent remained open, and their former inhabitants were scattered far and wide, many of them to the camps. For them, as for all their fellow members of the church, a new post-Constantinian epoch had opened unambiguously and abruptly. Without aforethought, and with untold brutality, the achievements of the past were discounted and, wherever possible, dismantled. For some it seemed as if "the last days have come." It was certainly with these words that a bishop (Sergii Voskresenskii) greeted a monk on the latter's return from arctic exile in 1935.[19]

In any case, it was a time of witness and of martyrdom. The old ways were to be tested as never before, but against the dismal background of the Soviet antireligious campaign were to shine forth an impressive number of spiritually untrammeled guides and exemplars. One of the few activities that was to be permitted to registered religious bodies by the revised legislation of 1929 was "performance of the cult." The worship of the church thus gained an unwonted emphasis. The new context encouraged a fresh perception of that which Ioann of Kronstadt had earlier sought to uncover from the patina of previous centuries. Not that this necessarily involved any reform in the manner or the shape of worship. On the contrary, the very reforms that were attempted by various schismatic movements of the time only served to confirm the average member of the Orthodox church in his or her loyalty to the ancient, well-established ways. These now proclaimed the advent of God's kingdom not only in the few surviving churches but also in countless alternative locations, where secret services were held. When the patriarch of Moscow, in the more favorable conditions of the 1950s, was asked for a brief definition of the Russian Orthodox Church, he was to answer, "the Church which celebrates the divine Liturgy."[20] At the time of the greatest depredations and administrative disorientation, the eucharistic bond could yet ensure the integrity of the church's body and promote its holiness.

Deprivation of the Eucharist was thus a grievous burden for imprisoned clergy, not to mention many millions of others. In 1934 the priest-martyr Anatolii Zhurakovskii (1897–1939) was to write from the camps on the White Sea–Baltic canal, "Lord, how my soul yearns for the Liturgy." Yet even this could be seen as part of a coherent pattern. "The Lord has taken from me my treasured priesthood and sanctuary," he had written two years earlier. "For how long I do not know, yet I do know and acknowledge that this is proper and just." He had added, "Righteous art thou, O Lord, and upright are thy judgments" (Psalm 119:137).[21]

The primitive, and necessarily hushed, celebration of the Eucharist which could still take place occasionally here and there even in the camps was endowed with unprecedented dignity and fervor. The same could be said about any of the secret celebrations in the outside world, where ever fewer churches were available for worship. But the open churches themselves had become beacons of light as perhaps never before.

In the postwar period, with the reopening of many more churches (and even monasteries), something of the acute liturgical awareness generated during earlier decades was to survive. However profound and individual a person's spiritual state might be, the roots and validation were still to be sought in the corporate, liturgical, and sacramental life of the church as a whole. For the church, in the words of a muscovite layman, is "the mystery of loneliness overcome."[22]

Elders were still to be found. The last of the Optino elders, Nektarii Tikhonov (b. 1857), died in 1928, expelled from his monastery, albeit still in freedom. But the dissolution of monasteries did not prevent the emergence of new (in several cases nonmonastic)[23] spiritual guides. Although the testimony of each was indeed new, insofar as it was personal, the stability and continuity of the Orthodox spiritual tradition were to be reaffirmed by almost all who left a record of their teachings. Thus, the elder Zakhariia (1850–1936) could be said to speak in the 1930s for preceding and succeeding generations alike.

> Attain simplicity, which is the exclusive product of perfect humility. No words can explain this, experience alone will cause you to understand it. But it is in humility and simplicity that life in God, life for God, can be lived. By means of humility strive to achieve love. Let that love be holy and perfect, let it prayerfully envelop all. . . . And by your mercy to the weak, the sick, the misunderstood, the unhappy, to those engrossed in sin, emulate your heavenly patrons, the saints.[24]

As if to summarize this teaching, he would say, "When you perform the Jesus Prayer . . . you will be all the nearer to the Lord. And he will grant you heavenly love towards all, even to your foes."[25]

The foes were many, but they were powerless to frustrate or undermine such love. The elder Tavrion Batotskii (1898–1979) spent almost three decades of his life in prison or in penal exile. Yet when he spoke of the worst conditions under which his ministry had still been conducted he could quietly smile and quote the Pauline phrase "the word of God is not bound."[26]

As for the humility advocated by the Zakhariias of the twentieth century, this was never to be confused with passivity. On the contrary, as another recent elder has urged, the individual's will should always be exercised to the full and with due responsibility. "Invoke God's name as often as you can . . . ," wrote Abbot Nikon Vorob'ev (1894–1963). "The Lord expects you now to cleave to him and to his holy commandments, to be guided in your life by them, rather than by the promptings of demons or your own fallen nature, corrupted by sin." He concluded, "The choice is in your hands."[27]

Notes

1. An English translation of this work is in progress: *The Philokalia: The Complete Text* . . . , trans. G. E. H. Palmer, Philip Sherrard, and Kallistos Ware (London: Faber & Faber, 1979–).

2. *Sobranie pisem . . . optinskago startsa ieroskhimonakha Makariia k monashestvuiushchim* (Moscow, 1862–63); *Sobranie pisem . . . optinskago startsa ieroskhimonakha Makariia* (Moscow, 1880). Extracts from the latter have been translated by Iulia de Beausobre as: Macarius of Optino, *Russian Letters of Direction 1834–1860*.

3. *Sobranie pisem sviatitelia Feofana* (Moscow, 1898–99).

4. Several of these were also couched in the form of letters: for instance, *Chto est' dukhovnaia zhizn' i kak na nee nastroitsia* (Odessa, 1891).

5. Macarius, *Russian Letters of Direction,* 52.

6. Ibid., 25.

7. The term is used as a title for a study of the period by Nicolas Zernov, *The Russian Religious Renaissance of the Twentieth Century.* It encompasses the work of such outstanding figures as the priest-martyr Pavel Florenskii (1882–1943), archpriest Sergii Bulgakov (1871–1944), and the priest Aleksandr Elchaninov (1881–1934).

8. The teachings of Zosima are reviewed in Sergei Hackel, "Vision or evasion? Zosima's discourse in *The Brothers Karamazov,*" in *New Essays on Dostoyevsky,* ed. Malcolm V. Jones and Garth M. Terry (Cambridge: University Press, 1982) 139–68.

9. *Sobranie pisem optinskago startsa ieroskhimonakha Amvrosiia k monashest-vuiushchim* (Sergiev posad, 1908–9) i, 119–21.

10. Among those who had urged such diffusion of hesychast prayer life was the influential Bishop Ignatius Brianchaninov (1807–1867), another translator of the *Philokalia/Dobrotoliubie* into Russian (1857).

11. *Otkrovennye rasskazy strannika dukhovnomu svoemu ottsu* (Paris, 1948) 107.

12. Ibid., 52.

13. Quoted in V. N. Il'in, *Prepodobnyi Serafim Sarovskii* (Paris, 1930) 152.

14. Quoted in Il'in, *Prepodobnyi Serafim Sarovskii,* 123–24. The original was published only in 1903; the manuscript had earlier been preserved at Diveevo convent near Sarov.

15. In later years, Mother Maria Skobtsova (1891–1945) was to take this further and, indeed, to insist on the primacy of charity over piety. See Sergei Hackel, *Pearl of Great Price.*

16. Ioann Il'ich Sergiev, *Moia zhizn' vo Khriste* (Paris, 1949) i, 216.

17. Quoted in Aleksandr Semenov-Tian-Shanskii, *Otets Ioann Kronshtadtskii* (New York, 1955) 66.

18. Ioann Sergiev, *Moia zhizn' vo Khriste* is translated by E. E. Goulaeff, *My Life in Christ.* Extracts have been edited by W. Jardine Grisbrooke, *The Spiritual Counsels of Father John of Kronstadt.*

19. Quoted in Dimitry Pospielovsky, *The Russian Church under the Soviet Regime 1917–1982,* i, 190.

20. Quoted in A. Mervyn Stockwood, *I went to Moscow* (London: Epworth, 1955) (translation adapted).

21. *Sviashchennik Anatolii Zhurakovskii: materialy k zhitiiu* (Paris, 1984) 151, 126.

22. S. I. Fudel' (1901–1977), "U sten tserkovnykh," *Nadezhda* 2 (1979) 215.

23. Notable among the early nonmonastic elders was the Moscow parish priest Aleksei Mechev (1860–1923), on whom see *Otets Aleksei Mechev. Vospominaniia. Pis'ma. Propovedi* (Paris, 1970).

24. "Skhiarkhimandrit Zakhariia," *Nadezhda* 4 (1980) 195. A comparable statement (1937) is to be found in the scattered correspondence of Fr. Serafim Batiugov: "Humility is ceaseless prayer, faith, hope and love of the tremulous soul which has commended itself to God. Humility is the door which opens the heart and renders it capable of spiritual experience" (quoted by S. I. Fudel', *Nadezhda* 2 [1979] 326).

25. "Skiarkhimandrit Zakhariia," *Nadezhda* 4 (1980) 195.

26. Archimandrit Tavrion Batotskii, oral statement to the author (1968).

27. Igumen Nikon, *Pis'ma dukhovnym detiam* (Paris, 1979) 87.

Bibliography

Alexander, Bishop. *The Life of Father John of Kronstadt.* Crestwood, NY: St. Vladimir's Seminary Press, 1979.

Bolshakoff, Sergius. *Russian Mystics.* London: Cistercian Publications, 1977.

Brianchaninov, Ignatius. *On the Art of Prayer.* Translated by Lazarus Moore. London: J. M. Watkins, 1952.

Chariton of Valamo, Igumen. *The Art of Prayer: An Orthodox Anthology.* Translated by E. Kadloubousky and E. M. Palmer. London: Faber & Faber, 1966.

Chetverikov, Sergii. *Starets Paisii Velichovskii: His Life, Teachings and Influence on Orthodox Monasticism.* Translated by Vassily Lickwar and Alexander Lisenko. Belmont, MA: Nordland, 1980.

Dunlop, John B. *Staretz Amvrosy: Model for Dostoevsky's Staretz Zossima.* Belmont, MA: Nordland, 1972.

Elchaninov, Alexander. *The Diary of a Russian Priest.* Translated by Helen Iswolsky. London: Faber & Faber, 1967. Reprint, Crestwood, NY: St. Vladimir's Seminary Press.

Fedotov, George P., ed. *A Treasury of Russian Spirituality.* New York: Sheed & Ward, 1948.

Grisbrooke, W. Jardine, ed. *The Spiritual Counsels of Father John of Kronstadt.* London: James Clarke, 1967.

Hackel, Sergei. *Pearl of Great Price: The Life of Mother Maria Skobtsova 1891–1945.* Crestwood, NY: St. Vladimir's Seminary Press, 1981.

Macarius of Optino. *Russian Letters of Direction 1834–1860.* Edited by Iulia de Beausobre. London: Dacre, 1944.

Pospielovsky, Dimitry. *The Russian Church under the Soviet Regime 1917–1982.* Crestwood, NY: St. Vladimir's Seminary Press, 1984.

Sergiev, Ioann. *My Life in Christ.* Translated by E. E. Goulaeff. London: Cassell, 1897. Reprint, Jordanville: Holy Trinity Monastery, 1984.

Zander, Valentina. *St. Seraphim of Sarov.* London: SPCK; Crestwood, NY: St. Vladimir's Seminary Press, 1975.

Zernov, Nicolas. *The Russian Religious Renaissance of the Twentieth Century.* London: Darton, Longman & Todd, 1963.

16

Theosis in the Eastern Christian Tradition

JOHN MEYENDORFF

INASMUCH AS CHRISTIANITY is linked to the rise of the modern Western world, it is inevitable that the spiritual traditions of the Christian West—its genius for building institutions, for embracing the positive achievements of creation, but also its tendency to compartmentalize, to establish borders between knowledge and spiritual experience, between doctrine and mystical vision—are too often identified with Christianity as such. During the first millennium of Christian history, however, intellectual and spiritual leadership belonged to the Eastern half of Christendom at Antioch, "where the disciples were first called Christians" (Acts 11:26), and the Greek-speaking world where Paul preached, which was common to Syrians, Egyptians, and Jews, as well as Greeks, and for which the New Testament writings were originally written. It is there that the major doctrinal controversies were fought and councils met. At those councils delegates from the West were present, mostly as respected, and respectful, observers. The Eastern Christian world met its own temptations: Greek intellectualism, cultural factionalism, the corrupting politics of the emperors. Later, it was somewhat historically marginalized by long series of invasions and catastrophes. Nevertheless, its spiritual message has not only survived these historical trials, but may be acquiring today, as the traditional values which shaped the West are severely challenged, a new and unexpected relevance.

"God Became Man so that Man Might Become God"

This famous sentence of Athanasius (*De Incarnatione* 54), picking up an equivalent one by Irenaeus of Lyons (ca. 130–203), has often been referred to as illustrating the betrayal of a supposedly original, biblical understanding of the Christian faith in favor of a vague platonizing form of pantheism. Nothing is further from the truth. Of course, the term "deification" (*theōsis*, *theopoiēsis*) is adopted from a Neoplatonic religious vocabulary, which became standard in Christian theology and spirituality as soon as it addressed itself to the Hellenistic world. But the *content* of the doctrine of deification reflects the paradoxical Johannine affirmation that the "Word was God" and that it "became flesh" (John 1:1, 14), so that created human beings might not boast in the face of God in their "fleshly" nature, but be "in Christ Jesus" (1 Cor 1:29–30), members of his Body, anticipating the eschatological fulfillment when God will be "all in all" (1 Cor 15:28).

"Deification" is, therefore, a Christocentric and eschatological concept, expressed in Platonic language but basically independent of philosophical speculation. It reflects the experience of Christ's divinity, as expressed in the confession of Peter according to Matthew (Matt 16:16), or, according to John, in the reaction of soldiers, who came to arrest Jesus but fell on the ground, when, in a veiled manner, he pointed to his divine identity by pronouncing the sacred Jewish name of God—Yahweh, "I am" (John 18:5–6).

In Eastern Christian thought and spirituality this divine identity of Jesus is an essentially *soteriological* dimension of the faith. Salvation is an act of divine love, and this love is limitless. If God had used an intermediary to save his creatures, there would be a limit to his love. The Old Testament was such a pedagogically *limited* revelation with God speaking through prophets or through angels, but in the new dispensation God becomes fully accessible (cf. Hebr 1:1-14), and—as Cyril of Alexandria proclaimed so forcefully—the Son of God assumes human mortality itself and dies on the cross in the flesh, so that he may rise again, in his humanity, and thus become the "firstborn from the dead" (Col 1:18).

Salvation is seen essentially as this passage from death to life, and only God could be the "Leader" of salvation (Hebr 2:10), because he "alone has immortality" (1 Tim 6:16). God had to become fully a *mortal* human being in order to make the passage truly and authentically, in a way which would be truly *ours*.

This experience of salvation presupposes a certain understanding of what that "fallen" world is, which needs salvation, and a vision of the ultimate goal of creation.

In the Eastern patristic tradition—and also, indeed, in the liturgical and sacramental experience of Eastern Christianity, the world, outside of Christ, is seen as having fallen under the empire of *Death*. This experience is different from the Western, more legalistic, post-Augustinian, medieval conception of "original sin" which makes every human *guilty* of the sin committed by Adam in paradise. In the East, the consequence of Adam and Eve's transgression is seen as a takeover of God's creation by the one whom the New Testament calls "prince of this world" and who is also the "murderer from the beginning" (John 8:44). It is Satan who controls human beings by imposing death upon them but also by pushing them to constant struggle for existence and temporary survival—a struggle that is, necessarily, at the expense of the neighbor: a struggle for *my* property, *my* security, and *my* interests. This struggle is, in fact, the very substance of *sin*, so that the liturgy of baptism begins with an exorcism of Satan. But Satan, who controls creation through death and sin, is overcome by Christ's *resurrection.* Here lie the hope, the freedom, and the ultimate joy of true and eternal life. This is why—since early Christianity—the real "good news" was that of the resurrection, as brought by its eyewitnesses, the apostles, "Christ is risen!" This announcement and this greeting resound at the center of the liturgical year, on Easter night. There is no way of really experiencing the content of Eastern Christian spirituality without hearing it in the liturgical assembly.

But salvation is not only a liberation from death and sin; it is also the restoration of the original human destiny, which consists in being the "image of God." The full meaning of that expression, found in the Genesis accounts of creation, also becomes clear through the divine identity of Jesus Christ. Being the Logos (John 1:1), he is also the living model according to whom every human being was created. He is, therefore, perfect human *because* he is also perfect God. In him, divinity and humanity—the model and the image—are united in a perfect personal unity ("hypostatic union"), and humanity finds its ultimate destiny in communion with God, that is, in *theosis,* or deification.

The Pauline doctrine of a "recapitulation of all things in Christ" (Eph 1:10), the various forms of sacramental communion described by Nicholas Cabasilas (fourteenth century) as one single "life in Christ," the witness of a Byzantine icon of Jesus "pantokrator" ("all powerful"), the experience of the monks invoking the uninterrupted "prayer of Jesus" have no other goal and no other meaning.

The Spirit of Truth

The debates on the divinity of Christ in the early church have clearly shown that Christ's identity cannot be fully defined or understood independently of the person of the Spirit, the "other Comforter," whose mysterious presence permeates both the ministry of Jesus and the life of the Christian community. Indeed, not only did the Spirit "overshadow" Mary when she conceived a Son (Luke 1:35), descend upon Jesus when he was baptized in the Jordan (Mark 1:10 par.), and appear as tongues of fire on the apostles at Pentecost (Acts 2:3–4), but, as a Byzantine liturgical hymn for the day of Pentecost proclaims: "The Spirit bestows all things: it appoints prophets; it consecrates priests; it gives wisdom to the simple; it turned fishermen into theologians; it gathers together the whole assembly of the Church, . . . consubstantial and co-reigning with the Father and the Son."

23. Andrei Rublev, *The Trinity*, 15th century.

The piety and the spirituality associated with the Spirit are often identified too exclusively with the personal or emotional aspects of the Christian experience. This accent on the personal is indeed justified in the sense that faith in Christ presupposes a free personal experience: "Where the Spirit of the Lord is, there is *freedom*" (2 Cor 3:17). Fallen humanity is enslaved to the fear of death, to the struggle for survival, to the determinism of physical needs (or "passions"). Only the Spirit of God bestows freedom, by reestablishing human beings in their former dignity of "image of God" and making them able to overcome the determinism of the "passions." However, this freedom of the Spirit is not reducible to a psychological, emotional, or individual experience. As the hymn quoted above emphasizes, the Spirit also assembles the church, establishes its order, and accomplishes the sacramental presence of the Body of Christ. It does both—appointing prophets and consecrating priests—and therefore inspires and maintains within the church a necessary interaction between sacramental objectivity and psychological experience, between the institutional and the prophetic ministries.

The Christian East has always known this polarity between spiritual leaders who referred to the conscious "certitude" of knowing God and the authority of the ordained ministry—the episcopate and the priesthood. The entire and very varied world of monasticism (it is sufficient to remember Theodore of Studios, Symeon the New Theologian, the hesychasts of the fourteenth century, or the moral authority of monastic centers in contemporary Orthodoxy) often stood up—even against the bishops—for what it considered, under given circumstances, to be the ethical or doctrinal truth of Christianity. But this tension was not seen as a norm: the *same Spirit* was invoked on both sides, and conflict could arise only if the spirit of error was mistaken for the Spirit of Truth by one side or the other. Christian responsibility—implied by the freedom of all children of God—required an effort of *discernment* by all members of the church who received the Spirit at baptism ("The anointment which you received from Him remains in you, and you do not need that anyone teach you, but His anointment teaches you about all," John 2:27).

The sense of responsibility by all is not an institutional or legal principle, but an actual *spiritual* dimension. It does not contradict or reject the hierarchical structure of the church, but only confronts it with the doctrine of the *charismata* (cf. 1 Cor 12:4–31), all of which ultimately belong to the one Body of the church, whereas any individual carrier of a *charisma* can always become unfaithful to it. The spiritual or ecclesial result is that Eastern Christians, while respecting responsible carriers of truth (bishops, primates, councils, etc.), never attribute to them the function of *ultimate* criteria. This function belongs to the Spirit alone, of which all charismata carriers are servants or instruments. However institutionally unpractical—and often considered ecumenically frustrating by Westerners, because it makes change difficult and leadership sometimes undiscernible—this principle of ecclesiology is the one maintained already in the second century by Irenaeus of Lyons: "Where the Church is, there is the Spirit of God; and where the Spirit of God is, there is the Church . . . , but the Spirit is Truth" (*Adversus haereses* 3.24.1).

The One and the Three

We have just seen that the divine identity of Jesus and the divine presence of the Spirit, although united in a single "dispensation" (*oikonomia*) to save the world and restore the image of God in the human being, were nevertheless distinct personal encounters. Indeed, in the New Testament, besides the teachings of Jesus, there are also personal utterings of the Spirit to Philip (Acts 8:29), to Peter (Acts 10:19; 11:12), to the church of Antioch (Acts 13:12), to the apostolic council of Jerusalem ("it seemed good to the Holy Spirit and to us," Acts 15:25). Furthermore, not only did Jesus speak for the *Father*, who sent him, but the central act of the Christian community—the eucharistic prayer—is a gathering "in Christ" made possible through the invocation of the Spirit, being addressed to the Father.

It has often been noted that this initial experience was the ground for the trinitarian formulations of the Greek fathers of the church in the fourth century, whereas the essential unity of the divine being is that which inspired the theology of Augustine and, after him, that of the entire tradition of the West. The contrast between the two traditions must not, of course, be exaggerated. It is indeed legitimate to contemplate the mystery of the One and of the Three, starting with one end of it or with the other. The Cappadocian fathers of the East had to defend themselves against the accusation of "tritheism," but is it not obvious that so many later developments of Western theology and spirituality dealt with the Trinity only as an afterthought?

The vision of God as both One and Three is, first of all, a vision of living Persons to whom the human being relates, as a person. It makes the Christian experience distinct from the Neoplatonic communion with the One, or from the Buddhist merger of the human person into an impersonal God. Christianity indeed implies monotheism, but this monotheism is not absolute, because God reveals Godself in *relationships of love*. The deification or *theōsis*, of the Greek fathers is an acceptance of human persons within a divine life, which already is itself a fellowship of love between three coeternal Persons, welcoming humanity within their mutuality. Jesus prayed: "As you, Father, are in me and I in you, let them also be in us" (John 17:21). The Johannine definition of God as love thus possesses a concrete meaning within the mutually loving Trinity of divine Persons, and an expanding meaning of a love that includes the whole of creation.

Of course, human participation—in the *eschaton* (the "last day") but also *now* already by anticipation, within the fellowship of the Eucharist—in the life of the Trinity does not mean pantheism. The gulf between the Creator and the creatures remains. It is being bridged by *divine* love (or "grace," or "energy"), not by human "created" achievement or natural merit. It always remains a *gift*, not a merger of essences. Significantly, the same Greek fathers who insisted so much on the reality of deification are also teachers of apophatic (or "negative") theology. The essence of God is absolutely transcendent and can be adequately expressed only by negatives: humanity can only know what God *is not*, not what God is. Furthermore, communion with God does not suppress his transcendence, but on the contrary represents an *experience* of the *otherness* of God: Moses saw God in the cloud, and his vision of God as *darkness*—an image cherished by mystics of all times—was a "knowledge through ignorance" (an expression of Pseudo-Dionysius).

In the Eastern tradition, the need to maintain both the transcendence of divine essence and the reality of communion, or deification of creatures within the mystery of the divine Trinity, expressed itself not only in personalistic trinitarianism, but also in the distinction between God's essence and God's *energies*. Indeed. only a Person (and in God always the Three Persons)—not an impersonal essence—can freely *give*, and since the divine gift is always a gift of perfect and unlimited love, it is a gift of *uncreated* divine life, a gift of God himself communicating himself to creatures, while always remaining what he alone is in his transcendence.

Finally, God as Trinity is also the model and foundation not only of each human person but also of the true human community. Deification maintains human diversity and pluralism. which fulfills itself not in mutual exclusiveness but in complementarity and love. That which is authentic in that diversity remains forever in the communion of God. In God, human persons, human relations, human achievements remain unique and diverse. The Neoplatonic vision of Origen, who described the existence of the souls in God and their ultimate destiny in him as being "spherical"—each soul being identical and interchangeable with another—has been formally rejected. On the contrary, the personal invocation of saints, the eternity of human relations established on earth (including, particularly, marriage), and, therefore, the integrity of the *person*, have been formally affirmed by tradition, practice, and theology. This has been possible because God is not an impersonal, transcendent One, but the Father, the Son, and the Spirit, united without confusion and manifesting to creatures not only an abstraction of love but its only authentic reality. This remains today at the heart of Eastern Christian spirituality.

Part Four

TWENTIETH-CENTURY TRAJECTORIES

17

Pentecostal Spirituality: Living in the Spirit

STEVEN J. LAND

And they were all filled with the Holy Spirit and began to speak with other tongues as the Spirit was giving them utterance . . . but this is what was spoken of through the prophet Joel: "And it shall be in the last days, God says, that I will pour forth of My Spirit upon all flesh; and your sons and your daughters will prophesy, and your young men shall see visions and your old men shall dream dreams. . . ." For the promise is for you and your children, and for all who are far off, as many as the Lord our God shall call to Himself. . . . And they were continually devoting themselves to the apostles' teaching, and to fellowship, to the breaking of bread, and to prayer. (Acts 2:4, 16, 17, 39, 42)[1]

No one ever became holy or received the Holy Spirit, or had the vision of God or experienced His dwelling within himself, or ever had Him dwelling in his heart, without previous repentance and compunction and constant tears ever flowing as from a fountain. Such tears flood and wash out the house of the soul; they moisten and refresh the soul that has been possessed and enflamed by the unapproachable fire (cf. 1 Tim 6:1b). (St. Symeon the New Theologian [949–1022] *The Discourses*, IV.10)[2]

When the work the Father gave the Son to do on earth (cf. Jn. 17:4) was accomplished, the Holy Spirit was sent on the day of Pentecost in order that He might continually sanctify the Church. . . . (Vatican II, "Dogmatic Constitution on the Church" [*Lumen gentium* no. 4])[3]

And now, adorable Spirit, proceeding from the Father and the Son, descend upon all the Churches, renew the Pentecost in this our age, and baptize thy people generally—O, baptize them yet again with tongues of fire! Crown this nineteenth century with a revival of "pure and undefiled religion" greater than that of the last century, greater than that of the first, greater than any "demonstration of the Spirit" even yet vouchsafed to men. (William Arthur, *The Tongue of Fire; or, the True Power of Christianity* [1856])[4]

H OLINESS-PENTECOSTAL SPIRITUALITY flows from the Wesleyan renewal of the eighteenth century and the North American holiness movement of the nineteenth century.[5] It is an eschatological, missionary movement of spiritual transformation which lives in the light of the end and in the presence of God. The Wesleyan tradition is vital for the present understanding and the future development of the movement, since it offers insight into the theological importance of crisis experience in the Christian life and the means to dialogue with the Western and Eastern traditions of monasticism, asceticism, and mysticism in the Roman Catholic and Eastern Orthodox churches.[6]

Pentecostalism was born in the fires of millennial expectation in the late nineteenth century. Pentecostal-like revivals, with attendant tongues-speech occurred throughout the 1800s in several places, including England (the Irvingites), Germany, Wales, India, Russia (Armenians, who later showed up in Los Angeles at the Azusa Street Revival), during several holiness revivals (Finney, Moody, etc.) and finally in Topeka, Kansas (1901) and Los Angeles, California (1906–1909).[7] The last two occurrences are especially significant, since it was from the Bible school of Charles Fox Parham in Topeka that the teaching of baptism in the Holy Spirit, evidenced by speaking in tongues, was said to have originated.[8] If Topeka added this spark of insight, the flame of twentieth-century pentecostalism was kindled and spread through the Azusa Street Mission revival and its leader, the humble, one-eyed, black holiness preacher, William J. Seymour, who was a student of Parham. In the beginning, pentecostalism was a decidedly interracial movement.[9] People came from all over the country to Azusa Street and went out the the world to spread the news of this great "latter days" outpouring of the Spirit. Within twenty years there was a large, diverse movement, which began to disagree and divide over the Trinity (and whether baptism should be only in "the name of Jesus" as in the book of Acts), race, and sanctification.[10]

From the perspective of the participants in the movement, the outpouring of the Spirit accompanied by the attesting gifts and signs was evidence that biblical prophecies of the latter-day rain of the Holy Spirit were being fulfilled. The apostolic church was being restored with the apostolic faith (not man-made creeds), the apostolic authority (based on the Spirit and Word and not human organization) and apostolic power for the proclamation of the gospel and demonstration of God's presence. Doctrines were a focus for spirituality and were evidenced in transformed and gifted lives. The gospel of the kingdom (Matt 24:14) would be proclaimed to the nations, the everlasting gospel (now being fully restored to the church) would be proclaimed to prepare the Bride, and the Bridegroom would come to rapture the church. Jesus, not the Spirit, was at the center of their proclamation and was seen as Savior, Sanctifier, Healer, Baptizer in the Holy Spirit and Coming King. The "full gospel," then, included salvation (new birth, justification), sanctification (cleansing, consecration), divine healing provided in the atonement, the baptism in the Holy Spirit, and the premillennial second coming of Christ.[11] To become a pentecostal Christian was to commit to becoming a Christ-like witness in the power of the Holy Spirit. This revival, like the one in Acts 2, manifested eschatological fervor, spiritual outpouring, tongues, signs and wonders, apostolic teaching and fellowship from house to house and in tarrying services all over the world. It offered the larger body of Christ a pentecostal understanding of the one ("one mind and one accord"), holy ("hearts purified by faith"), apostolic (power, authority, message, and experience), and catholic (in and for the whole world) church. What was a new Babel to some was to others a new Pentecost, which would mean the healing of the divisions in the church and among the nations. At first the pentecostals stayed within their churches, but eventually, like their holiness counterparts, they were ejected, frozen out, or felt that they had to leave to avoid compromising vital truths. With Walter Hollenweger this chapter will assume that the first five to ten years represent not the infancy but the heart of the spirituality.[12] In addition, preference has been given to a consideration of the theological roots and historical precedents for the movement rather than focusing on personalities or attempting to select a founder. There was no Luther, Calvin, or Wesley who spoke for the whole movement. In addition, while appreciating the need for a good critical history as opposed to the often ritualized or romanticized versions of some participants, neither critical-historical nor psycho-social deprivation approaches have proved very helpful in understanding the inner logic of pentecostal spirituality or its dynamics as a movement of social and personal transformation.[13]

If the initial impetus to study the finer details of pentecostalism is due to the extent and size of the movement today, there is also implicit in this interest a search for the depth and inherent logic of pentecostal spirituality, which could explain this sustained and still-growing movement whose twentieth-century significance is equaled only by two other great forces of this era—Marxism and ecumenism.

Classification and Extent

The twentieth-century "Pentecostal/Charismatic Renewal in the Holy Spirit, with its goal of world evangelization," represents a "third force" in

Christianity alongside the Catholic/Eastern Orthodox and Protestant churches. This "third force" has swept through the three waves – pentecostalism, the charismatic movement, and mainstream church renewal.[14]

Pentecostals

Pentecostal denominations or movements teach that all Christians should seek a post-conversion baptism in the Holy Spirit, see the gifts of the Spirit as being restored to the ordinary Christian life and ministry, and believe that glossolalia is an initial physical evidence of Spirit baptism. Speaking in tongues, though it may be counterfeited and occurs outside Christianity, was nevertheless the unique sign of the coming of the Holy Spirit in the early church (the other gifts occurring also from time to time before the Christian era). Tongues as a sign of Spirit baptism not only represents a bridge-burning act of commitment to the movement but also is tangible internal and external evidence of the inbreaking of eschatological power to praise God and to proclaim the gospel in "power and demonstration of the Spirit." In the early years of the movement, this position was considerably hardened in response to charges of demonization and/or mental aberration and also because the book of Acts indicated that Peter and others had noted speaking in tongues as just such an evidence in the effusion of the Spirit upon the household of Cornelius (Acts 10:34–48, esp. v. 46).[15] The force of this "first wave" is reflected in the other two with variations dependent on social-cultural location and theological background. The inner logic of pentecostal spirituality, however, has had and will continue to have a not only renewing but also reforming effect in the churches that have experienced its impact. This is contrary to those who see pentecostalism as "only an experience" or a kind of "general fervor" which may be added to any existing religious community without its affecting anything substantially.[16]

Pentecostalism is largely a Third World movement. The non-white, worldwide, indigenous (that is, begun without outside Western or white missionary support) pentecostals were "estimated in 1970 as 60% (rising by 1985 to 75%) of all members of the over 1,000 non-White/third-world indigenous denominations, which, though not explicitly pentecostal, nevertheless have the main phenomenological hallmarks of pentecostalism." They are members of a 250-year-old movement. In addition there are "Black, non-White, or Third-world Christians in over 800 explicitly pentecostal denominations, indigenous to non-White races in that they were begun without outside Western or White missionary assistance or support."[17]

Charismatics

The rapid expansion of this group occurred during the 1950s among those receiving Spirit baptism and remaining within their respective denominations or churches.[18] They demonstrate any or all of the gifts of the Spirit but tend to see tongues as optional or not as significant as pentecostals believe it to be. Another early name, which has now virtually fallen out of use in the literature, was neo-pentecostal. Since 1965 many independent or schismatic charismatic churches have become a part of this grouping; they now comprise around 14 percent of all charismatics. Charismatics variously understand the baptism in the Spirit as a release of the Spirit given in water baptism, a breakthrough to a new dimension of living, a renewal in the Spirit, or an integrated completion of Christian initiation.[19]

Renewal ("Third-wavers")

These are primarily "evangelicals" (and some others) who have experienced a renewal or energizing of the Spirit but nevertheless do not recognize it as an experience separate from conversion. Tongues may be optional, absent, or seen as unnecessary; but signs and wonders, healings, power encounters, etc., are emphasized. They remain in nonpentecostal denominations and tend not to organize into distinct renewal groups.

The members of all three waves of the Renewal are now found in eleven thousand pentecostal denominations and three thousand independent charismatic denominations and constitute 21 percent of organized global Christianity (1988—332 million affiliated church members: 176 million pentecostal, 123 million charismatic, 28 million third-wavers). All three segments of the movement continue to grow at a current rate of 19 million new members a year or around fifty-four thousand per day (one-third of this is demographic—births minus deaths—and two-thirds are converts/new members). As Barrett notes, "Some 29 percent of all members worldwide are White, 71 percent non-White. Members are more urban than rural, more female than male, more children (under 18) than adults, more Third-world (66%) than Western World (32%), more living in poverty (87%) than affluence (13%), more family-related than individualist."[20] East Asia (China and Korea especially), Africa, and Latin America are becoming increasingly pentecostalized, whereas Europe is more charismatic. Charismatics permeate all state churches and national denominations and around 14 percent of charismatics in mainline churches have "become 'independent' each year since 1970, forming some 100,000 White-led independent charismatic churches across the world, loosely organized into forty or so major networks." The majority of the world's megachurches (over fifty thousand members each) are pentecostal/charismatic. One-fourth of all full-time Christian workers in the world are pentecostal/charismatic. They are active in 80 percent of the thirty-three hundred large metropolitan areas.

Members of this movement are "more harassed, persecuted, suffering, martyred than perhaps any other Christian tradition in recent history."[21] Often seen as supporters of the status quo, they are much more likely to be imprisoned or worse in totalitarian countries and killed, tortured, and otherwise discouraged by both sides in countries under dictatorial regimes which are opposed by "leftist rebels." This is usually because of their "third way" pursuit of peace, which is most often interpreted as support for the status quo.[22]

Rituals and Characteristics

Pentecostal spirituality should be understood through an analysis of its ritual practices and general characteristics.[23] In what follows, practices are discussed in relation to general characteristics. The inner logic of these practices applies not only to pentecostals but to what is distinctive in the spirituality of the charismatic renewal.

Spirit-Body Correspondence

There is a high degree of psychomotor activity—visible, bodily evidence of the Spirit's presence—in pentecostal liturgy. The Spirit-filled congregation moves almost as one spirit-mind-body and responds to the divine Spirit in these ways: raising the hands in praise, clapping to the glory of God, extending the right hand of fellowship, joining hands to pray (this is a more recent practice introduced primarily in charismatic circles but now pervasive throughout all segments of the movement); dancing in the Spirit of heavenly victory, swaying in the "wind" of the Spirit, being "slain in the Spirit" (prostrate on one's back, usually with hands stretched upward, overcome with the awesome, holy presence of God); fasting because of a spiritual hunger to draw near, "feed on the Lord," seek his face, have his mind or petition for a particular need in the church or world; doing the Jericho March (marching around—inside usually—the church until the walls of spiritual opposition/resistance fall down and all experience a victory and new freedom in the life and witness of the church); finally, and perhaps most importantly, divind healing through the laying on of hands (anyone in the body may do this) and the anointing with oil (usually performed by the pastor, who may be either male or female, or the elders). The laying on of hands is not so much to transmit healing virtue as it is a sign of identification of the body of believers with the suffering and need of the one anointed. They are healed together, and they rejoice together. Healing evangelists are also prominent throughout the movement, but there has always been an emphasis on healing as part of the ongoing, ordinary liturgy of the local body.

Oral-Narrative Liturgy and Theology

Pentecostals express the ineffable eschatological presence of God through speaking in tongues, and they narrate their daily walk in the Spirit by means of the testimony service in which individuals rehearse their life and experiences in terms of the biblical-theological categories of their faith. This testimony is theologizing out of the corporate and individual histories in the Spirit and represents an ongoing sanctification and empowerment through conscientization of the body. In concert prayer the congregation becomes a temple of stereophonic praise (though it may seem a cacophony to the uninitiated). Speaking in tongues, dreams, and visions, under the constraints of 1 Corinthians 12–14, "liberate the people of God from dehumanizing cultural, economic and social forces. They create room for an oral theological debate . . . unfreeze liturgical, theological and socio-political formulae and replace imported ideologies (whether of a progressive or a conservative kind does not really matter) by the political literacy of the whole people of God, practiced and learned within the framework of an oral liturgy for which the whole congregation is responsible."[24] This kind of authority, based on speech, narrative, and communication "enters into conflict with authority which is based on status, education, money and judicial power."[25] Anointed preaching, teaching, witnessing, and singing evidence the reality of Spirit-Word and its power to transform, move, and be manifested in gifts (healing, miracles, wisdom, knowledge, tongues, interpretation, prophecy) within the pentecostals' journey of faith.

There is a great variety of music and instrumentation used in pentecostal worship throughout the world. There are traditional hymns which celebrate the attributes and deeds of God, and there are Scripture choruses which are usually repeated several times as the body enjoys the presence of God and celebrates its freedom in simple praise. There are also gospel songs, mostly in the first person and usually telling a story, giving a testimony, or calling to action. This is part of the revivalistic heritage of pentecostalism.[26]

Fusion-Fission Tensions

Fusion refers to those polarities or pairs of concepts which tend in pentecostal spirituality to be seen as equal in importance and fused phenomenologically. Most important for understanding this spirituality is the already–not yet eschatological fusion. In a sense all the other polarities and practices rest upon the pentecostal understanding and experience of this one. It explains how the ecstasy of praise is coupled with the agonized urgency concerning world evangelization. This can be felt in the singing of songs such as "Win the Lost At Any Cost," "Oh I want to See Him," or "I see Jesus (Standing at the Father's Right Hand)."[27] Eschatological fusion also explains the relationship of space and time. In the Spirit of the end there is a prophetic telescoping of here and there, now and then. Fusion in the Spirit joins space and time in such a way that Christ's resurrection and second coming are fused with his coming in pentecostal power; tongues and proclamation, praise and petition are one. The Lord is soon coming (imminent) and draws near as the immanent, transcendent Spirit moves. This also explains why pentecostals, when they are moved most deeply, will laugh and cry simultaneously. This is no Gnostic escape; it is neither cosmic pessimism (dualist) nor cosmic optimism (monist). The world as created and brought to consummation is good, remembered and longed for. The "world" as an interlocking system of forces and structures arrayed in rebellion against Christ the King is not to be befriended. But the mission is here and now in *this* created, fallen, redeemed, and being-consummated world. It is a countervailing view of this world, whose true life, like that of the believer, is hidden with Christ in God. The Spirit groans in bringing this cosmos to completion, and all those in the Spirit groan while rejoicing evermore. In such a situation the believer does not know how to pray, but the Spirit helps with groans, sighs, and "tongues of angels." Finally, the believer *dances* in the light of the day dawning in the court of the king but is *still* before the holy mystery of the incarnation, cross, and resurrection of Christ, whose passion he or she is called upon to "fill up" until he comes.

Fusion also explains the relationship of the individual and community in terms of the traditional idea of the body of Christ. Individual gifts are to build up and to serve. The body cares for the individual and vice-versa. To be in the Spirit is to be in the communion of saints. The Scripture is a Spirit-Word to the church and world and comes in power and demonstration through the foolishness of preaching. Each person must receive and abide in this Spirit-Word in order to be church. Clergy and "laity" are one, and no one is more valued or essential than another. Female and male share equally the responsibility to witness and to manifest the graces, gifts, and power of the Spirit which is poured out on all flesh. For many pentecostals feet washing is a rite of sanctifying servanthood for all members, even as Spirit baptism is unto the "prophethood" of all believers.

24. Ransom Rambo, *Never Too Late*, 20th century.

Contrary to some Reformed ways of thinking, faith and works, the testimony and daily walk ("walk and talk"), love and obedience, law and gospel are fused. Works never justify, but one cannot receive justification without simultaneously declaring for righteousness. Law is the structure of love, and here pentecostals, for the most part, are closer to Calvin than Luther in an appreciation of the "third use" of the law. Forgiveness is not incompatible with restitution of wrongs whenever possible. The objective and subjective are fused in spiritual appropriation: the believer is crucified with Christ and now must "crucify the flesh with its passions and lusts." Those "in Christ" must "put on Christ."

The fruit of the Spirit and the gifts of the Spirit are fused also because being and doing, character and personality are one in God. Therefore they must be one in those who in Christ are conformed to his image. Thus, justification asks for sanctification, which asks for Spirit filling, which asks for worldwide evangelism and mission. Justice, love, power, and purpose are fused in eschatological interrelatedness.

Fission, the other side of the tension, represents elements or dynamics that must be kept separate and are unequal in their value to the believer or, in some instances, mutually exclusive. God and Satan, saint and sinner, light and darkness are all mutually exclusive. In the practice of exorcism, for example, which has been especially prominent among Third World pentecostals, the power of God expels evil spirits, who are the agents of Satan.

Sovereignty-spontaneity is an example of the first type of fission, in which the Spirit is sovereign. Therefore, later attempts by some charismatics to induce or teach tongues, or to "speak out miracles" were especially abhorrent to pentecostals. The pentecostal waits to "let the Lord have his way." In the Spirit there is spontaneity of joy, but there is also waiting in tears; neither is more spiritual than the other.

Revelation and reason, heart and head, and Scripture and "creeds" are examples of fission in which the first item is valued more than the second and takes precedence over it. From the beginning pentecostals funded Bible schools and institutes as places where reason would serve revelation. This was more than "experience seeking understanding." The head was to descend into the heart prayerfully, as in certain ancient monastic traditions. The heart was the place of integration of mind (reason), will, and affections. Out of the heart the mouth speaks and the person acts. Therefore, education in the Spirit always had to give priority to the heart aflame with the purifying love of God to insure that "truths" discovered through reason were known within the larger truth of spiritual cosmic existence.

Scripture takes precedence over "creeds" because Scripture is a Spirit-Word. "Creeds" were often seen as "fixed fortifications" in a battle that required mobility and ongoing reformation. Of course, every pentecostal group developed its own "creed" but called it a statement of truths or declaration of faith. They saw themselves as judicially pronouncing on biblical precedent rather than legislating new laws. As naïve as this was, it was correct insofar as the Spirit was prior to Scripture and church. In other words, only God could interpret God. The existential-spiritual dimension of creeds was often missed as the movement focused on their apparently static, time-bound, and in some instances philosophically abstract nature.

The fission of heart and head can also be seen in "praying with the spirit" and "praying with the understanding" (cf. 1 Corinthians 14). All prayer was held to be in the Spirit, but not all prayer was praying in tongues or "with the spirit," for then the mind or understanding is not fruitful. Praying with the spirit is not better or more spiritual than praying with the understanding. The two belong together, and as the believer matures what is at first necessarily distinct begins to fuse more and more. All prayer at all times is in the Spirit—responsive to and beseeching the presence of God.

The church is organism and organization, but organism is primary. The institution, by its organizational, bureaucratic machinery, must not take away the prophetic, priestly ministry of its members in the church and world. Pentecostals developed congregational, episcopal, and presbyterial polities, but in all instances the authority of administrative office was qualified, limited, and made accountable to the body of believers, who were the spiritual peers of the "clergy." Pentecostals found out quickly and firsthand the dangers of fanaticism and cult figures. Though there are still some strong, "charismatic" leaders, most pentecostals today do not put their faith in them. Indeed, pentecostals have seen enough phonies, charlatans, and counterfeits to qualify as the most skeptical of critics. However, even when the messenger is flawed, the Spirit-Word that goes forth is still efficacious.

Crisis–Development Dialectic

The earliest pentecostals spoke of being saved, sanctified, and filled with the Holy Spirit and in this way signaled their subjectively entering into justification, sanctification, and Spirit baptism. These crisis experiences were not mere isolated episodes. To the contrary, this narrative or testimony spoke of an existential history. The individual is first received into the new order of righteousness and makes a declaration for the same. Next the believer encounters the power of the flesh as internal resistance requiring cleansing and moral integration. Filled with the love of God, he or she declares availability for service and the doing of God's will any place at any time and at any cost. To express love and righteousness in the world requires a power not of this world. The power of the Holy Spirit fills the believer so that the forces of evil may be resisted and confronted with God's demands for righteousness and the gospel of love. These experiences are seen as crises within and with a view toward development. Indeed, the development requires the crisis and the crises are intelligible only within the development. This is more a way of salvation (*via salutis*) than an order of salvation (*ordo salutis*). The most helpful faith analogy is the divine Trinity. In the unity of the Trinity there is consubstantiality and coinherence, and yet in salvation history, though the action of one is the action of all, one of the three is prominent. Biblical salvation history is thus seen as a series of crises (creation, covenant, Christ, Pentecost, consummation, etc.) within and with a view toward a development. The meaning, direction, and nature of this development and its attendant crises are only known from the perspective of the end—the kingdom of God. For the pentecostal this development is for last-days missionary existence in the power and presence of God. Because of the power of the world, the flesh, and the devil, the church and each believer faces opposition within and without. Those definite, crucial, transforming moments of individual salvation experience make plausible and possible the mission and ministry of church and believer.

Spirituality and Theology

Doctrines are the occasions for and the structure of the pentecostal passions. If spirituality is the fundament of doctrine, then doctrine is the focus of spirituality. The inner logic or rhetoric of the pentecostal affections will be discussed under the headings of God as Eschatological Presence, Salvation as Eschatological Transformation, and Church as Eschatological Mission.

God as Eschatological Presence

God as Father, Son, and Holy Spirit is spirit and now must be worshiped in spirit and truth, that is, according to God's nature and will. Humanity made in God's image is made for love and fellowship—participation in the triune life of God. God is Holy Spirit, and what is spoken from God is said through Christ and in the Holy Spirit. Creation, redemption, and consummation may be discussed rationally but can only be truly known in the Spirit.[28] The Scriptures, as the Spirit-Word written, are inspired by the Spirit, who addresses us in ways that transcend analytic-critical reason. Experience is vital in knowing the truth, for truth is not merely propositional—it is personal ("he who does not love does not know God," 1 John

4:8). Bible study is transforming as grammatical-historical and critical tools are used to hear what the Spirit-Word is saying to the church. Therefore, in pentecostal spirituality there is a coming together to hear our testimonies, to hear the testimony of Scripture, to wait for the Spirit's critical call to action-application, and then to yield to his leading. As pentecostals act on the word and walk in the light, they have fellowship and are cleansed from all unrighteousness. As they cleanse themselves "from all defilement of flesh and spirit, perfecting holiness in the fear of God" (2 Cor 7:1), then there is the possibility of further hearing and doing of the truth in dialectical process. For these reasons some pentecostals find fundamentalist battles over inerrancy based on rationalistic standards of error and accuracy to be a peripheral concern, while maintaining the centrality of verbal inspiration.

God as Holy *Spirit* is the divine mystery of the world but also as *Holy* Spirit is the incomparable, majestic One who dwells in unapproachable light but is present in transcendent immanence. The Spirit orders and reorders creation according to righteousness. The Spirit moves and works to become the inner motive and bond of love in all persons, and the Spirit is the power who through the Word upholds all things, working in history to bring all things to their intended goal—the divine *telos*. The Spirit, then, is the Spirit of God, the Spirit of Christ, and the Spirit of truth. Creation is divine order, relationship, and purpose in the Spirit. For the pentecostal there is no salvation outside the Spirit of God.[29]

Salvation as Eschatological Transformation

Pentecostal salvation is transformation in the Spirit. The Spirit convinces of sin, righteousness, and judgment, thus calling for repentance toward God and entry into the new order of righteousness. To be pronounced justified through the new God-given faith relationshp is also at the same time to declare for righteousness, personally and socially. The new social existence of the Christian is the church, ordered by and under God's word. But the law of God is the law for all humanity; and Christians are faithfully to respect and proclaim its limits as they live in the world.

Salvation is also a crucifixion of the "passions and lusts," so that there is a new moral integration a new heart. The law must be written upon the mind and the heart, into the understanding and the affections. Love fulfills the law and only that which is done out of the love which cries "Abba" (Father) profits anything at all. Love is joyous union: in light of the character of God represented in the law and poured out in divine love, the bond of communion in the Holy Trinity becomes the bond between believers and God and within the community. This salvation as sanctification means that there is no known "hold-out" or resistance to God. It is not seen primarily in substantialist but in relational categories. When pentecostals are "praying through" to the baptism in the Spirit, they are struggling with their own selfish desires and motives, their own unavailability for mission and service, their own fear. The perfect love of God by grace through faith brings a wholehearted response. This crisis, like that of justification (new birth), is within and with a view toward a development. It is capable of, indeed demands, constant growth in grace and knowledge. Holiness is characterized by humility in the one who offers himself or herself to God in love for constant searching, purifying, and service.

The baptism in the Holy Spirit is a coming or infilling of the Spirit, who gives power to express the righteousness and love of God in the world. Justification is God's work for the believer; sanctification is God's work in the believer; and Spirit baptism or filling is God's work through the believer. All Christians should manifest the fruit of the Spirit, and all may manifest any of the gifts, as the Spirit sovereignly directs. All are called upon to be witnesses to Christ, proclaimers of the gospel in power and demonstration of the Holy Spirit. This Spirit baptism is authorization (*exousia*) and real strength (*dynamis*) to come against real evil and oppression. If the virtue associated with justification is faith and the virtue associated with sanctification is love, then the virtue associated with Spirit filling is hope. This hope becomes the ground for transformation unto and in the light of the end.

The believer then is resurrected into a new order (kingdom of God), which was inaugurated in the incarnation, ministry, and death of Jesus and was vindicated in his resurrection for our justification. The believer is baptized into the kingdom of God, baptized into the death and resurrection of Christ, and baptized into the Spirit of the age to come. These crises of faith, love, and hope are constant dimensions of life in the Spirit. Justification is evidenced in bringing forth works "meet for repentance." Sanctification is evidenced by walking in the light as he is in the light, loving one another as he loved us and obeying his commands out of love. Spirit baptism is evidenced by words and deeds which praise God, proclaim Christ, and manifest the power of the Holy Spirit in fruit, gifts, and zeal for witness. This self-giving witness is the surest evidence of Spirit baptism. As Christ offered himself by the eternal Spirit to the Father so the believer by the Spirit offers herself or himself through Jesus Christ in the Spirit and thus fills up what remains of the suffering and longing of Christ.

The Church as Eschatological Mission

The church is envisioned in four distinctive images: the people of God called to participate in the mystery of God's ordering presence; the body of Christ with diverse gifts, administrations, and operations of the Spirit, designed to build up, exhort, and benefit all; the missionary communion of the Spirit, constituted at Pentecost; a house of prayer for the healing of the nations. Through the presence and power of the Spirit, members of the church are ordained to the ministry of Christ.

In this eschatological people of God, baptism is the *"sign of starting out,* valid once and for all" and "the regular and constant fellowship at the table of the Lord is the eschatological *sign of being on the way.*"[30] Baptism in water is an answer to a ministerial call; the Lord's Supper is the ongoing expression of and means to love in the body of Christ, and baptism in the Spirit is the commissioning to full missionary service in the world.

The kingdom of God is righteousness, joy, and peace in the Holy Spirit as he works personal, social, and cosmic transformation through Jesus Christ to the glory of God the Father. The church exists within and proclaims this kingdom as coming and present.

Conclusions and Prospects

Pentecost is more than a day; for pentecostals, it is the ongoing eschatological reception of and living out of the fullness of the Spirit. In this century pentecostalism has impacted all churches and nations with an abundant diversity of expressions and yet exhibits an underlying spiritual-theological unity. Pentecostalism is more Arminian than Calvinist (human agency, perseverance), more Calvinist than Lutheran (third use of the law), more Eastern than Western (Eastern spirituality of persons like Gregory of Nyssa, St. Symeon, etc.), more Protestant than Catholic (more emphasis on sanctification-transformation than forensic justification), more Anabaptist than Magisterial Reformation (peace, covenanted believer's church, church discipline), more Holiness-Evangelical than Fundamentalist-Evangelical (a different view of Scripture and reason).

Pentecostal spirituality is demonstrated in its practices of worship, prayer, and mission, and especially in the logic of the passions of righteousness, joy, and peace in the Spirit. Righteousness represents corporate limits: love, corporate motive and unity; and power, corporate purpose. Pentecostal spirituality is the fundament of pentecostal doctrine. It is shaped and directed by the Spirit-Word of Scripture and sustained, questioned, and driven to new insight by ongoing praxis in the world and among the churches.

The future agenda for pentecostal spirituality is threefold: doctrinal, missional, and ecumenical. Doctrinally pentecostals need to show how they display their theology in a systematic way and with a comprehensiveness that has been heretofore lacking. The missionary movement is only about a hundred years old—in terms of its intensive and extensive impact. But it is time to do more than write an evangelical theology with special added sections on Spirit baptism and gifts. The biblical and historical work which has been going on for several decades should continue, but it is time to gather up these results into a more comprehensive proposal.[31]

In terms of a theology of mission, pentecostals have theologized via mission strategizing and contextualization. This work is beginning to be published. But a missionary spirituality that will address the need for liberation and healing for the whole person is still being born in the struggles of Third World pentecostals. Another source for this development is the work of black theologians who are beginning to put the movement in touch with its black roots in North America and the Third world.[32] Spirit movements have usually originated among the poor and then are criticized for being an "opiate of the people." But if they create a counterculture of priestly care and prophetic engagement, these charges are vitiated. Poor people cannot be faulted for mistrusting the world's mechanisms and use of power. Pentecostals are developing alternative structures for personal and social transformation and have an opportunity to address the relation between authentic pentecostal encounter and authentic liberation. Now is the time to work out an alternative to the liberal-conservative bodies versus souls approach from a constructive pentecostal standpoint among the poor.[33] Acts 2 cannot be divorced from Luke 4. The apostolic mission is the mission of Jesus (John 20:21). Romans 13 must be correlated with Revelation 13 lest the state be absolutized and Christians become incapable of confronting the powers.

Ecumenically, pentecostals can engage in a new and responsible polemical irenics in order to confront the changes of elitism, divisiveness, experientialism, and subsequence, which according to critics invalidate or vitiate baptism and Christian initiation. In recent years critics have often failed to take note of or to interact with the exegetical and historical perspectives of pentecostals, in both written and oral sources. It is time for a new and more vigorous dialogue. This has already been happening in the Roman Catholic–Pentecostal dialogues, the National Council of Churches–Pentecostal dialogue, the participation of some pentecostals in the World Council of Churches, and the huge gatherings of all the renewal groups in Kansas City and New Orleans in recent years. But this activity can be intensified and broadened. Through common narrative exchange (testimony), study, prayer, and worship, pentecostal spirituality can be understood, enriched, expanded, corrected, and deepened. It has already brought great renewal in the church and great evangelization among the nations. May it not also bring forth some ripened theological fruit?

Notes

1. All Scripture quotations are taken from the *New American Standard Bible* (La Habra, CA: The Lockman Foundation, 1960–67), used by permission. For an excellent discussion of the importance and use of the Old Testament in Luke-Acts and Luke's perspective for pentecostal theology, see Roger Stronstad, *The Charismatic Theology of St. Luke* (Peabody, MA: Hendrickson, 1984). See also Richard Israel, "Joel 2:28–32 (3:1–5 MT): Prism for Pentecost," in *Charismatic Experiences in History*, ed. Mel Robeck (Peabody, MA: Hendrickson, 1985) 1–14; French Arrington, *The Acts of the Apostles: Introduction, Translation and Commentary* (Peabody, MA: Hendrickson, 1988).

2. Symeon the New Theologian, *The Discourses*, trans. J. de Catanzaro (New York: Paulist, 1980) 82.

3. *Vatican II: The Conciliar and Post-Conciliar Documents*, ed. A. Flannery (Northport, NY: Costello, 1975) 351–52.

4. William Arthur, *The Tongue of Fire; or, the True Power of Christianity* New York: Harper & Brothers, 1856) 354.

5. Grant Wacker has provided the most recent, concise, and thorough bibliographical essay for pentecostal studies; see "Bibliography and Historiography of Pentecostalism," in *Dictionary of Pentecostal and Charismatic Movements*, ed. Stanley M. Burgess and Gary B. McGee, 65–76; see also 169–80, 76–84, 279–81, 406–9. The predominantly Wesleyan heritage of pentecostalism is called into question by William M. Menzies and Edith Lydia Waldvogel; see W. M. Menzies, *Anointed to Serve: The Story of the Assemblies of God* (Springfield, MO: Gospel Publishing House, 1971); and E. L. Waldvogel, "The 'Overcoming Life': A Study in the Reformed Evangelical Origins of Pentecostalism" (Ph.D. diss., Harvard University, 1977). The Wesleyan-origins view is defended by Vinson Synan (*The Holiness-Pentecostal Movement in the United States*), Donald Dayton (*The Theological Roots of Pentecostalism*), and Melvin E. Dieter (*The Holiness Revival of the Nineteenth Century* [Metuchen, NJ, and London: Scarecrow Press, 1980]). Donald Wheelock concludes that "Wesleyan and non-Wesleyan Pentecostals agree that personal holiness precedes Spirit baptism. For the former it is a definite crisis experience in which the 'root' of sin is plucked up, while for the latter it is a matter of victorious consecration which is maintained and deepened by the assistance of the Holy Spirit" ("Spirit Baptism in American Pentecostal Thought" [Ph.D. diss., Emory University, 1983] 210). Wheelock further notes that almost all American pentecostals state the following "conditions" for Spirit baptism: obedience to God through separation from all known sin, a request for prayer in unity with others, a praise-filled worship and a "faith-filled expectation." In his address of 11 November 1988 to the Society for Pentecostal Studies meeting at Asbury College/Seminary in Wilmore, Kentucky, Dr. Melvin Dieter acknowledged the past intense conflict between the holiness churches and pentecostals ("The Wesleyan/Holiness and Pentecostal movements: Commonalities, Confrontation and Dialogue"). This was, to a large extent, a family dispute beween fraternal, if not identical, twins. Dieter concluded that even in the largest and more "baptistic" pentecostal denomination, the Assemblies of God, "the Spiritual dynamic of such movements . . . is at least as equally or even more strongly derived from the historical campmeeting perfectionism as it is by any classical Reformed categories. The theological and experiential wineskins of the Keswick low-church Anglicans and others through whom the higher-life message came back to its American home have, it seems to me, been hard put to contain the holiness wine. To use another metaphor, the dominant genes of the vigorous Christocentric pneumatology residing in our common parent, the holiness revival, have left on all of the progeny such a unified imprint of spirituality

and experience that each of us will be the loser if we fail to recognize. . . . the ultimate charge that Warfield and his friends leveled against the movement [New School revivalism of Finney, Mahan, et al.] was that it was really 'Methodist.'" The holiness connection is important for pentecostals because it carries with it the nineteenth-century concern for abolition, prohibition, women's rights, and the reform of society according to the righteous standards of God. When pentecostalism and the holiness churches were impacted by the aftermath of the Civil War, Reconstruction, the new higher criticism of the Bible, the "liberal" social gospel and the increasing "embourgeoisement" of methodism, they were forced to choose between fundamentalism and modernism. By choosing fundamentalism the Wesleyan agenda for "spreading scriptural holiness throughout the land" was reduced to rescue missions, storefront churches, soup kitchens and other kinds of person-to-person involvement. A further result of this alliance has been the presence of both movements at the founding of the National Association of Evangelicals in the 1940s, in spite of the fact that the word "evangelical" in North America usually excludes or redefines the holiness pentecostal paradigm in favor of the more presbyterian-fundamentalist paradigm. This drew both movements into battles concerning inerrancy and drew them away from the rethinking and further application of their fundamentally transformationalist heritage.

6. For useful historical perspectives on pentecostal-charismatic phenomena, see Stanley Burgess, *The Spirit and the Church: Antiquity* (Peabody, MA: Hendrickson, 1984); Harold D. Hunter, *Spirit-Baptism: A Pentecostal Alternative* (New York: University Press of America, 1983) 117–210; Ronald A. N. Kydd, *Charismatic Gifts in the Early Church: An Exploration Into the Gifts of the Spirit During the First Three Centuries of the Christian Church* (Peabody, MA: Hendrickson, 1984).

7. Paul Pomerville, *The Third Force in Missions;* Grant Wacker, "Bibliography and Historiography of Pentecostalism," in *Dictionary,* ed. S. Burgess and G. McGee, 65–76; C. E. Jones, "Welch Revival," in *Dictionary,* ed. S. Burgess and G. McGee, 881–82.

8. J. R. Goff, Jr., "Parham, Charles Fox," in *Dictionary,* ed. S. Burgess and G. McGee, 660–61.

9. See Walter Hollenweger, "Pentecostals and the Charismatic Movement," in *The Study of Spirituality,* ed. Cheslyn Jones, Geoffrey Wainright, and Edward Yarnold (New York and Oxford: Oxford University Press, 1986) 549–53; Douglas Nelson, "For Such A Time As This: The Story of Bishop William J. Seymour and the Azusa Street Revival" (Ph.D. diss., University of Birmingham, U.K., 1981).

10. *Dictionary,* ed. S. Burgess and G. McGee, 644–51, 585–88, 255–56.

11. William Faupel, "The Function of 'Models' in the Interpretation of Pentecostal Thought," *Pneuma: The Journal of the Society of Pentecostal Studies* 2/1 (Spring 1980) 51–71; *Dictionary,* ed. S. Burgess and G. McGee, 532–34; 632–33.

12. Hollenweger, "Pentecostals," in *The Study of Spirituality,* ed. C. Jones et al., 551: "I take the early pentecostal spirituality as the norm by which I measure its subsequent history."

13. Luther Gerlach, "Pentecostalism: Revolution or Counter-Revolution?" in *Religious Movements in Contemporary America,* ed. I. I. Zaretsky and M. P. Leone (Princeton: University Press, 1974) 669–99; idem, with Virginia Hine, *People, Power, Change: Movements of Social Transformation* (Indianapolis: Bobbs-Merrill, 1970); Virginia Hine, "The Deprivation and Disorganization Theories of Social Movements," in *Religious Movements,* ed. I. Zaretsky and M. Leone, 646–64.

14. This entire section is heavily dependent on the massive and exactingly detailed work of missionary researcher David B. Barrett, *International Bulletin of Missionary Research* 12/3 (July 1988) 119–29. The term "third force" was first used by Leslie

Newbigin in *The Household of God* (New York: Friendship Press, 1954) to stress the importance of pentecostalism to ecumenical dialogue.

15. The literature on tongues speaking in particular and Spirit baptism in general is vast. The following is a good place to begin: Watson Mills, ed. *Speaking in Tongues: A Guide to Research on Glossolalia* (Grand Rapids: Eerdmans, 1986). For vigorous pentecostal defense of Spirit baptism, theologically and exegetically, which counters the often-heard charge that pentecostals simply exegete an experience and are not scripturally concerned, see J. Rodman Williams, *The Pentecostal Reality* (Plainfield, NJ: Logos, 1972); *Dictionary*, ed. S. Burgess and G. McGee, 40–48, 335–41, 455–60; Howard Ervin, *Spirit-Baptism;* idem, *Conversion-Initiation and the Baptism in the Holy Spirit;* Harold Hunter, *Spirit Baptism: A Pentecostal Alternative;* R. Hollis Gause, *Living in the Spirit;* Stanley Horton, *What the Bible Says About the Holy Spirit* (Springfield, MO: Gospel Publishing House, 1976).

16. For the crucial significance of the interrelatedness of spirituality, religious affections, and theology, this chapter is heavily dependent on Don Saliers, *The Soul in Paraphrase: Prayer and the Religious Affections* (New York: Seabury, 1980); idem, "Religious Affections and the Grammar of Prayer," in *The Grammar of the Heart*, ed. Richard Bell (New York: Harper & Row, 1988) 188–205.

17. D. Barrett, *International Bulletin of Missionary Research* 12/3 (July 1988) 7.

18. Ibid.

19. Two of the most interesting recent examples of a charismatic reform and renewal within a theological tradition have come from Larry Christenson (*Welcome, Holy Spirit*, ed. L. Christenson [Minneapolis: Augsburg, 1988]) and J. Rodman Williams (*Renewal Theology: God, The World, And Redemption* [Grand Rapids: Zondervan, 1988]). For a helpful summary of the various charismatic views and the persons associated with them, see Henry Lederle, *Treasures Old and New*. Lederle is a friendly critic of pentecostalism who basically echoes the earlier criticisms of Frederick Dale Bruner (*A Theology of the Holy Spirit* [Grand Rapids: Eerdmans, 1970]). Lutheran and Reformed theologians have been among the most severe theological opponents of the movement; this would seem to lend weight to the initial premise of the Wesleyan roots of pentecostalism.

20. D. Barrett, *International Bulletin of Missionary Research* 12/3 (July 1988) 1.

21. Ibid.

22. Cf. the example of the late Reverend J. F. Rowlands, who in fifty years of Christian service among the Indians of South Africa was noted for his early disavowal of apartheid and his personal advocacy for an inclusive Christian counterculture. See also G. C. Oosthuizen, *Moving to the Waters: 50 Years of Revival in Bethesda, 1925-1975* (Durban, South Africa: Bethesda Publications, 1975).

23. R. P. Spittler, "Spirituality, Pentecostal and Charismatic," in *Dictionary*, ed. S. Burgess and G. McGee, 804–9. The definition of rituals is taken from Louis R. Rambo, "Ritual," in *The Westminster Dictionary of Christian Theology*, ed. Allen Richardson and John Bowden (Philadelphia: Westminster, 1983) 509–10: "Rituals are regular, repetitive, rule-determined patterns of symbolic behavior, performed by one or more people, that utilize any or all of the following components: language, action, visual imagery, personification and characterization, specific objects imbued with meaning, and music. . . . Ritual is apparently a fundamental mode of communication, though the meaning is open to diverse interpretations."

24. W. Hollenweger, "Pentecostals," in *The Study of Spirituality*, ed. C. Jones et al., 553.

25. Ibid., 552. See also Cheryl Johns, "Affective Conscientization: A Pentecostal Re-Interpretation of Paulo Freire," and Jack Johns, "Pedagogy of the Holy Spirit"–both

dissertations submitted in May 1987 to the Southern Baptist Theological Seminary. In addition, note Leonard Lovett, "Black Origins of the Pentecostal Movement," in *Aspects of Pentecostal-Charismatic Origins,* ed. Vinson Synan.

26. Delton Alford, "Pentecostal and Charismatic Music," in *Dictionary,* ed. S. Burgess and G. McGee, 688–95.

27. All songs are taken from the *Church Hymnal* (Cleveland, TN: Tennessee Music and Printing Co., 1951).

28. T. F. Torrance, *The Trinitarian Faith* (Edinburgh: T. & T. Clark, 1988).

29. The most concise and tightly argued presently available pentecostal soteriology is that of R. Hollis Gause, *Living in the Spirit.*

30. Jürgen Moltmann, *The Church in the Power of the Spirit* (New York: Harper & Row, 1977) 243.

31. Perhaps this work can be coordinated through the Society for Pentecostal Studies (*Dictionary,* ed. S. Burgess and G. McGee, 793–94) or through some other organization which would coordinate the work of the many Bible institutes, colleges, and newly formed seminaries (see L. F. Wilson, "Bible Institutes, Colleges, Universities," in *Dictionary,* ed. S. Burgess and G. McGee, 57–65).

32. L. Lovett, "Black Origins," in *Aspects of Pentecostal-Charismatic Origins,* ed. V. Synan; D. Nelson, "For Such A Time As This."

33. Theodore Runyon, ed. "Testing the Spirits," in *What the Spirit is Saying to the Churches* (New York: Hawthorne Books, 1975). See also Jose Comblin, *The Holy Spirit in Liberation* (Maryknoll, NY: Orbis, 1988); Robert McAfee Brown, *Spirituality and Liberation* (Philadelphia: Westminster, 1988); Richard J. Cassidy, *Society and Politics in the Acts of the Apostles* (Maryknoll, NY: Orbis, 1988); Sheila M. Fahey, *Charismatic Social Action* (New York: Paulist, 1977); Frederick Herzog, *God-Walk: Liberation Shaping Dogmatics* (Maryknoll, NY: Orbis, 1988); Steven J. Land, "A Stewardship Manifesto for a Discipling Church," in *The Promise and the Power,* ed. Donald N. Bowdle (Cleveland, TN: Pathway Press, 1980); Jon Sobrino, *Spirituality of Liberation: Toward a Political Holiness* (Maryknoll, NY: Orbis, 1988); Leon Joseph Cardinal Suenens and Dom Helder Camera, *Charismatic Renewal and Social Action* (Ann Arbor, MI: Servant Publications, 1979); and possibly the most immediately useful, Paul Valliere, *Holy War and Pentecostal Peace* (New York: Seabury, 1983).

Bibliography

Boer, Harry R. *Pentecost and Mission.* Grand Rapids: Eerdmans, 1961.

Burgess, Stanley M., and Gary B. McGee, eds. *Dictionary of Pentecostal and Charismatic Movements.* Grand Rapids: Zondervan-Regency, 1988.

Christenson, Larry, ed. *Welcome, Holy Spirit: A Study of Charismatic Renewal in the Church.* Minneapolis: Augsburg, 1988. Lutheran.

Dayton, Donald W. *The Theological Roots of Pentecostalism.* Grand Rapids: Zondervan-Francis Asbury Press, 1987.

Ervin, Howard. *Conversion-Initiation and the Baptism in the Holy Spirit: A Critique of James D. G. Dunn, Baptism in the Holy Spirit.* Peabody, MA: Hendrickson, 1984.

———. *Spirit Baptism: A Biblical Investigation.* Peabody, MA: Hendrickson, 1987.

Gause, R. Hollis. *Living in the Spirit: The Way of Salvation.* Cleveland, TN: Pathway Press, 1980.

Gelpi, Donald L. *Pentecostalism: A Theological Viewpoint.* New York: Paulist, 1971. Roman Catholic.

Hamilton, Michael P., ed. *The Charismatic Movement.* Grand Rapids: Eerdmans, 1974.

Hollenweger, Walter J. *The Pentecostals.* Minneapolis: Augsburg, 1972, 1976. Reprint, Peabody, MA: Hendrickson, 1988.

Hummel, Charles G. *Fire in the Fireplace: Contemporary Charismatic Renewal.* Downers Grove, IL: InterVarsity, 1978.

Lederle, Henry. *Treasures Old and New.* Peabody, MA: Hendrickson, 1987.

McDonnell, Kilian. *Charismatic Renewal and the Churches.* New York: Seabury, 1976. Roman Catholic.

——, ed. *Presence, Power, Praise: Documents on the Charismatic Renewal.* 3 vols. Collegeville, MN: Liturgical Press, 1980.

Nichol, John T. *Pentecostalism.* New York: Harper & Row, 1966.

O'Connor, Edward D. *The Pentecostal Movement in the Catholic Church.* Notre Dame, IN: Ave Maria Press, 1971. Roman Catholic.

Pomerville, Paul A. *The Third Force in Missions: A Pentecostal Contribution to Contemporary Mission Theology.* Peabody, MA: Hendrickson, 1955.

Quebedeaux, Richard. *The New Charismatics II.* San Francisco: Harper & Row, 1983.

Schalzmann, Siegfried. *A Pauline Theology of Charismata.* Peabody, MA: Hendrickson, 1987.

Smail, Thomas A. *Reflected Glory: The Spirit in Christ and Christians.* Grand Rapids: Eerdmans, 1975. Reformed.

Spittler, Russell P., ed. *Perspectives on the New Pentecostalism.* Grand Rapids: Baker, 1976.

Suenens, Leon Joseph Cardinal. *A New Pentecost?* New York: Seabury, 1974. Roman Catholic.

Sullivan, Francis A. *Charisms and Charismatic Renewal: A Biblical and Theological Study.* Ann Arbor, MI: Servant Publications, 1982. Roman Catholic.

Synan, Vinson. *The Holiness-Pentecostal Movement in the United States.* Grand Rapids: Eerdmans, 1971.

——. *The Twentieth-Century Pentecostal Explosion.* Altamont Springs, FL: Creation House, 1987.

——, ed. *Aspects of Pentecostal-Charismatic Origins.* Plainfield, NJ: Logos, 1975.

Tugwell, Simon. *Did You Receive the Spirit?* New York: Paulist, 1972. Roman Catholic.

Williams, J. Rodman. *The Gift of the Holy Spirit Today.* Plainfield, NJ: Logos, 1980. Presbyterian.

18

Christian Feminist Spirituality

SALLY B. PURVIS

FEMINIST CHRISTIAN SPIRITUALITY is challenging and trying to transform patriarchal Christian traditions. The kind and extent and duration of the difference that contemporary feminist spirituality will make in the Christian churches of North America cannot now be assessed, whether that difference is measured in institutional change or in transformed persons and communities. Christian feminist spirituality is an emerging movement that is in process. It is possible, however, to trace a few of its origins, sketch its critical and creative aspects, identify and examine four major foci within its diversity, and make some brief observations on the relationship between contemporary Christian feminist spirituality and some of the structures that it affects.

Describing the Scope

Geographical and Cultural Context

While there are important developments in Christian feminist spirituality worldwide,[1] the general statements I make are directly applicable only to the context of the United States of America and are limited to resources in English. Feminists as a whole have become sensitive to the need to be clear about the interpretive lenses through which they view even their shared experience. As a white, Anglo, upper-middle-class, heterosexual, ordained Protestant minister who teaches at a Jesuit institution, I do not claim to represent the perspective of those whose context and cultural experience are different from mine. This essay can speak about but not for persons with other experiential backgrounds.

Historical Context

Contemporary Christian feminist spirituality has roots, or at least precursors, in near and distant past events and communities. As a historical movement, it is part of the "second wave of feminism" that emerged in the late 1960s and early 1970s. The term "second wave" recognizes a first: the feminist theology and spirituality of the middle to late nineteenth century with which this "wave" claims both continuity and disagreement.[2]

Christian feminist spirituality also claims continuity and disagreement with various spiritual movements and groups in the history of Christianity, many of which have been described in this series of volumes. The process of returning to and reinterpreting the spiritual legacy of Christianity is part of the important and ongoing work of contemporary Christian feminist theologians.

Although we acknowledge the importance of the history of Christian feminist spirituality, our concern is with its contemporary manifestations. That is, this study will not encompass its foremothers nor the sisters of other traditions that are currently using feminist tools to dismantle their own oppressive structures.[3] On the other hand, Christian feminists do not necessarily carve out and preserve sanctified Christian spiritual "territory." Though concerned with group identity, Christian feminists do not share the patriarchal concern, and occasional obsession, with "heresy." Thus, the boundaries between Christian and non-Christian are in many cases more permeable than a patriarchal instantiation of Christianity can tolerate.[4]

Contemporary feminism in general emerged from the era of social change that characterized the late 1960s and early 1970s. The civil rights movement, the burgeoning protests against the Vietnam War, impatience with the prerogatives of "tradition" in numerous institutions signaled a kind of *kairos* of human rights. In the process of working with the movements for human liberation, for ecological awareness, for popular control of public issues, women became sensitized to the systemic oppression of various groups in our society and began to turn the logic of human liberation upon their own condition. Those in the vanguard realized that structures of oppression were in place that denied the full humanity of women of whatever race or cultural context,[5] and they discovered those structures to be as prevalent and powerful in the churches as in any other social institution.

Liberating the Spirit

Critical Turns

1968 saw the publication of Mary Daly's *The Church and the Second Sex*. Building on the work of Simone de Beauvoir, Daly identified the pervasive *patriarchy* of the Christian churches and the degree to which women were marginalized by the very institutions that proclaimed the fundamental dignity of all persons grounded in God's gracious love.[6] She gave voice to experience and insights that were shared by women in different institutional settings and that did not necessarily depend on the degree to which women had access to positions of "power," for example, through ordination.[7] Mary Daly was an early prophet of contemporary Christian feminist spirituality and theology, but her voice was joined by many other women, published or not, famous or not, who were involved in the critical task of exposing the patriarchal nature of the Christian faith as it was taught and practiced by the churches.[8]

The experience of being marginalized was and is formative in Christian feminist spirituality; thus, some explanation of it is in order. In the Scriptures, in traditional formulations of doctrine, in liturgy, in ecclesiastical politics, women were represented, if at all, largely by figures, images, descriptions, and positions that presented them as accessories to males and male images and roles. As long as women accepted the patriarchal understanding of them as accessories, there was no conflict between their self-understanding and their experience of being marginalized. However, the conjunction of the developing feminist consciousness in society and women's experiences of spiritual power, creativity, fruitfulness, and value caused a serious conflict between their own interpretation of their lives and that offered by the patriarchal churches with which they were involved.[9]

Furthermore, women who were nurtured within the Christian tradition also became aware that there was a fundamental contradiction between the gospel of liberation and Jesus' concern for justice on the one hand, and the preaching and practice of the Christian churches on the other. The gospel was being heard by marginalized women as though it applied to them in the fullest sense, and that gospel—understood through women's experience—became part of the critical apparatus of Christian feminism, which was then focused on the patriarchal Christian churches. The gospel is reinterpreted in the light of the good news for women, and the churches are challenged to proclaim and practice the good news for all, including women.

Finally, women, who had been marginalized by the patriarchal institutions of Christianity, experienced empowerment in their involvement with marginalized persons, whether those persons were other women or men and groups who also found themselves on the margins of patriarchal Christianity. Cooperative involvement and interaction with persons in attempts to instantiate the "gospel" outside or on the fringes of patriarchal institutions made possible and nurtured spiritual growth and health. Thus, Christian feminist spirituality does not seek to emulate the patriarchal models from the tradition but rather to experiment and to embrace the robust and inclusive models that are emerging from the experimentation.[10]

Creative Turns

As important as the critical turns have been and continue to be, Christian feminist spirituality is an essentially creative phenomenon. The emphasis on women's experience has literally opened new worlds, cognitively and socially.[11] In Nelle Morton's now classic phrase, women have been "hearing into speech" other women and marginalized persons.[12] Both in the telling and in the hearing, new language and new experiences of divinity and humanity have come into being. The experiences of telling and hearing the truth about their lives, including their relationship to God,[13] of refusing to keep hidden the realities of women or the extent to which those realities involve oppression by patriarchy, of breaking the silence about women in the church, are radically creative.[14]

The critical turn and the creative turns in Christian feminist spirituality are closely related, though they can be distinguished. They are not separate "stages" that lead one to the other in some "developmental pattern." Rather, they interact so that each critical turn clears away a bit more of the patriarchal distortion and opens up creative possibilities that had been blocked. Likewise, each creative turn is likely to expose forms of patriarchal distortion, new ways in which patriarchy shackles persons' vision and lives. For example, as Christian feminists develop liturgies that include women, the denigration of women in traditional liturgies becomes more starkly apparent. That insight may, in turn, lead to the development of liturgies that not only include women but also celebrate femaleness.

A question that will continue to be explored is the extent to which the classical Christian tradition, patriarchal though it is, offers resources for feminist spirituality.[15] Both the critical and creative turns are involved as feminists bring their perspectives and their experiences to the tradition. For example, important work has been done and continues in feminist interpretations of Scripture.[16] In Phyllis Trible's work on the texts of the First Testament[17] she rejects patriarchal interpretation, including translations that embody patriarchal assumptions, and she offers a text that opens up to readings not otherwise accessible.

Elisabeth Schüssler Fiorenza's work on the Second Testament involves a social/historical approach that confronts the patriarchal picture of the role of women in early Christianity that the tradition, including the Scriptures, has perpetuated. Schüssler Fiorenza reconstructs that early history from a feminist perspective.

For all Christian feminists, but particularly for Protestant women whose spirituality is so deeply shaped by scriptural stories and emphases, the pain of encountering the denigration of women in these texts is balanced by the depth of discovery as the encrusted layers of patriarchy are peeled away and a new picture emerges, however faintly. Likewise, there is the pain of repeatedly confronting the deeply embedded patriarchal practices in the churches ("But we've always sung that hymn . . .") and the occasional despair when the change that does seem possible is so small compared to the huge amount of energy required to effect it.[18] Yet that pain, too, is balanced by the possibilities for human community that persons not only envision but also experience, at least in the short run. Being part of a community that is essentially cooperative and not competitive, inclusive and nonhierarchical, is for many an experience of "living the gospel" that the institutional church does not (yet) provide.

Along with hope, pain is part of the creative turn of Christian feminist spirituality. The struggles are not just those of individuals but also involve questions of communal identity and praxis. In the last fifteen years two crises in particular have confronted the feminist community and shall continue to do so in the foreseeable future. One crisis occurred when lesbian feminists challenged their sisters with being heterosexist. If lesbians are included at all in conferences, theologies, liturgical events, their official presence is likely to be a token one, and lesbians continue to feel marginalized even within many feminist communities. In a similar way, women of color and women from non-European cultural backgrounds have charged their white sisters with the same arrogance of the dominant voice that their white brothers have so dramatically exhibited inside the churches and out. As white women speak of their experience as "women's experience," women of color and women from minority cultures in this country see themselves disappearing just as women in general disappear when male experience defines "humanity."[19]

These challenges within the feminist community are both political and spiritual.[20] Can those who continue to experience marginalization even among other feminists find common ground with the majority? Can persons in the majority stretch their spirits sufficiently to include all women in the designation "we," or does inclusivity stop at the boundaries of sexual orientation, race, and culture? The questions continue to arise as persons attempt, and often fail, to accommodate and incarnate their own best insights and most deeply held convictions.

Embracing the Spirit

For all of its diversity, and the diversity of its participants, it is possible to identify certain recurring features and emphases in contemporary Christian feminist spirituality.

Inclusivity: Language and Practice

It is likely that many persons in the churches are first exposed to Christian feminism via the issue of inclusive language. Feminists have identified the importance of language since the beginning of this phase of the movement, and when the language designates the deity and the deity's relationship with persons, its importance is only intensified.

As Mary Daly argued in *Beyond God the Father*, the maleness of the deity reinforces the God-qualities of the male.[21] The constant association of the language of and by the divine with male pronouns and images sends a powerful message to females and males that there is something about maleness that in some unspecified way is more God-like than femaleness. If so, then the potential for female spirituality is diminished in comparison to that of males, and females must struggle to overcome some sort of alienation from the divine being not encountered by males.[22]

Christian feminist theology has rejected the maleness of God on several grounds. First, Christianity has always officially taught that God is neither male nor female but rather infinite, beyond the limitations of sexuality and gender. Yet the consistent and exclusive use of male pronouns and images for God teaches that God *is* male. Therefore, insofar as language about God is patriarchal, it is untrue. Second, the maleness of God and especially the metaphor of "God the father" have so thoroughly shaped persons' images of God that other qualities of God and ways of relating to God are obscured. Patriarchy has created a God in the image of "man."[23] Therefore, insofar as language about God is patriarchal, it is idolatrous. Finally, insofar as patriarchal language about God is both untrue and idolatrous, it distorts and limits persons' relationships with God.

Christianity has always claimed that its God is the God of all persons and that God values all persons equally and wishes all persons well. As Rosemary Ruether writes:

> The critical principle of feminist theology is the promotion of the full humanity of women. Whatever denies, diminishes or distorts the full humanity of women is, therefore, appraised as not redemptive. . . . The uniqueness of feminist theology is not the critical principle, full humanity, but the fact that women claim this principle for themselves.[24]

These insights of feminist theology with regard to "God-talk"[25] are fundamental for feminist spirituality. When women image God as male in an environment where males are the instruments of their oppression, then they must choose between a broken spirit, accepting and colluding in their oppression, or a healthy spirit, which requires a rejection of God.[26] On the other hand, when the "maleness" of God is critiqued and discerned as yet another patriarchal tool, then such use of language can be, and must be, rejected for the sake of humanity and God.

The rejection of patriarchal language goes far beyond the question of which pronoun to use, or whether to use one at all, though that signals a crucial issue. It also includes taking care that women's experiences and women's lives are associated with divine life. Thus, "the God of Abraham, Isaac and Jacob," for example, becomes "the God of Abraham and Sarah and Hagar."[27] Creation is a product not just of the "word" but also of birthing. If God is imaged as "person," then speaking of God as female as well as male is appropriate.[28] The task of eradicating exclusive language from the life of Christian churches is enormous, even at times overwhelming. However, the process is under way, as inclusive resources for worship and other aspects of church life emerge from reflective theological creativity and commitment.[29]

As exclusively patriarchal language makes way for inclusive language and imagery, God ceases to be experienced as oppressor. As God ceases to be experienced as oppressor, many of the other characteristics that have been associated with God either dim or disappear,[30] and the way is clear for new possibilities for imaging and relating to God that create a sense of adventure. When the bonds of patriarchal language and imagery are loosened and severed, new movement is possible; a renewed religious life can stand and stretch. Christian feminists turn to other traditions for insights, and a sense of experimenting with new ways of relating to God is an ongoing feature of contemporary Christian feminist spirituality. At the same time, neglected minority features of the biblical tradition are being recovered.

A commitment to inclusivity includes a commitment to diversity. As in the Christian communities of the first century, the task of feminist Christians today is to forge a genuine unity out of the diversity that is represented, without schism and without marginalizing one another. As Christian feminists continue to share their diverse experiences of divine–human relations and to empower one another to even more diversity of prayer and worship, religious communities are beginning to enact concretely a conviction that the "one spirit" is the source of many gifts and that diversity is really a blessing and not a threat. Persons are enhanced, not diminished, by being exposed to different manifestations of the Spirit of God in lives very different from their own.

Connectedness

In the literature of Christian feminist theology and spirituality and in the prayers and liturgies of contemporary Christian feminists there is a pronounced emphasis on *connectedness*. Feminist Christians neither ignore nor minimize the degree and extent to which alienation marks human life, but Christian feminists are identifying, reclaiming, and celebrating the connections that exist, connections that patriarchy has obscured and to some extent has severed. I shall describe this feature of contemporary Christian feminist spirituality at some length, beginning with the critical turn and moving to the creative.

A patriarchal conception of reality can be imaged as a pyramid, with God on top, males just below God, females below males, then human children and then other living beings classified by their genetic proximity to "man."[31] As one moves down the pyramid, beings have less control, value, and importance. Furthermore, whatever value is ascribed to those below is theirs by virtue of their relationship to the being(s) above them on the pyramid. Likewise, interaction is properly restricted to those immediately above and below, so, for example, women require the intercession of men to deal with God. Careful distinctions, boundary drawing and maintenance, separation and distance, the identification of ordered "stages" characterize the hierarchical pyramid of patriarchy.

Feminism rejects this image. While patriarchal cosmology and ontology[32] proclaim separateness as primary and relationship as the task to be performed, women experience themselves as essentially related. In biological reproduction a woman experiences her body developing and bringing forth new life, and she herself is forever touched by the experience. As a person whose body nurtures another's, a woman sees the effects of her own nutrition in the well-being and growth of her infant, or she sees the effects of her poorly nourished life in the thin limbs and dull eyes of her child. They are strong or weak together. Persons who are nonbiological nurturers quickly discover the degree to which self-care is implicated in care for others. Furthermore, persons' very being is formed by the relationships they have and foster and maintain, and their identity, though distinct from, *is not separate from* those relationships. Likewise, God is not "out there" somewhere, in some "higher" space, remote and reachable only through the male-controlled institutions of religion but rather is "right here" amid the lives of ordinary people doing ordinary, or extraordinary, things. While Christian feminists do not deny the "transcendence" of God, feminist spirituality teaches that transcendence is not God's most prominent characteristic, and that divine transcendence must be reconceived.

The feminist rejection of the patriarchal pyramid, both as a description and as a prescription for human life, is found in all areas of feminist scholarship.[33] In Christian theology, its rejection takes a number of forms.

Rosemary Ruether's work has established the insidious pervasiveness of dualisms that depict reality as separate pieces that have fallen apart rather than as distinctive aspects of reality that are essentially connected.[34] We may be able to separate them *conceptually*, though doing so may have the unfortunate result of obscuring the more fundamental ways in which they are connected, but they are not found separately in human experience. Two dualisms that have been very influential in the history of Christianity are the mind-spirit/body dualism and the male/female dualism. Of Platonic origins, the mind-spirit/body dualism made its way into Christianity primarily through the Stoics. This dualism splits the human self into mind-spirit on the one hand and body on the other. It then pronounces the mind as superior to the body. Human flourishing depends on the "higher" faculty, the mind-spirit, subduing or at least controlling the "lower" part, the body, and human salvation is salvation from the prison of material existence.[35] A human being becomes, then, a collection of "parts," not fully integrated, rather uneasily associated for a while, and arranged in a rigid hierarchy.

Likewise, animal life in general, and human life in particular, is rigidly separated into two kinds of beings: males and females. The tradition is not univocal with regard to the degree of shared humanness it allows between the two genders, but for the most part the gender itself is more determinative of the reality of the person than its membership in the human species.[36] Put another way, the capacities and value of each person have classically depended more on gender than on simple membership in the human race.

The two dualisms are linked as males come to be associated with rationality and spiritual being and females become associated with embodiment and sexuality. Males are "higher" on the patriarchal pyramid than females are, with all the attendant privileges and "responsibilities." Females not only are incapable of the full range of rational and spiritual (and moral) achievements of men; their nature requires that they be under male control.

These are not the only two dualisms humans have created. The tendency to divide and hierarchize is identified as extremely dangerous by feminists and other persons without political and social power. One of the most effective ways to justify oppression is to identify a group as "other" and deficient or inferior. If persons can be so identified, then it is "just" and "in their best interests" to deny them equal treatment and equal access to social goods. Dualisms, then, are not just mistaken philosophical categories; they have been and continue to be dangerous tools of oppression.

Beverly Harrison's work has included a rejection of divisions and a recognition of the connection among various "spheres" of human life.[37] She develops and demonstrates the degree to which personal, political, social, and religious concerns overlap and influence one another. Relegating concerns to the "private" realm is not a descriptive move but rather is itself a political maneuver that trivializes and disempowers those concerns. Dorothy Soelle also lectures and writes extensively about the interconnectedness of various areas of human life, including persons' relationship with God.[38] Likewise, Letty Russell has been developing a "praxis of connectedness" that reveals and embodies in the here and now radically new communities that subvert social, economic, and political divisions. One might characterize her theology as a "this-worldly eschatology," and she claims to be looking not to creation with its fixed forms of human relationships but to the *eschaton*, which promises to break down the "natural" divisions between "Greek and Jew, slave and free, male and female . . ." (Gal 3:28).

All of these approaches make the critical turn, rejecting patriarchal dualisms and their consequences, and they all, in some form, make the creative turn toward connectedness. Rather than imaging reality as a pyramid with its fixed levels, a feminist may image life as a web. The shape and strength and even ongoing existence of a web depends on the strong bonds between each of the strands. Furthermore, each part of the web contributes to and is dependent on the strength of every other part, not just those strands that are closest. It is in the best interest of each part to strengthen every other part; survival depends on cooperation, not competition. A strain on any part will reverberate through the whole. Each part has its being only as part of the whole.

The web is not the only feminist image for reality, since no one image is adequate to include the whole. The major deficiency of the image of "web" is its failure to account for the human experience of autonomy, of separateness and uniqueness, not as distinct from one's relationality, but as a feature of it. Delores Williams has suggested the image of a mosaic. Her image has the advantage of adding color and the possibility that the pieces can move around. However, pieces of a mosaic can be replaced by others and discarded without destroying the mosaic but only changing its composition. Thus, the image of "mosaic" does not represent as clearly as does the web the interdependence of the well-being of the whole and the well-being of each part. The web image and the mosaic image together capture nicely central features of a feminist view of reality.[39]

The connections among persons extend through temporal as well as spatial distances. As Christian feminists are uncovering stories of foremothers that were erased or obscured by patriarchy, they are experiencing a sense of being grounded in a history that does not depend on a male chronicler. Likewise, Christian feminist spirituality respects the connection non-European cultures have had to ancestors as feminists experience apparently similar connections with their "Christian ancestors" of the last century and beyond. Though not entirely in accord with post-Christian feminists who claim spiritual continuity with persons in ancient history and pre-history who worshiped the Goddess, Christian feminists carefully sort through the records of those the tradition has labeled heretical to reclaim potential commonalities. Contemporary Christian feminists will experience stronger ties to those exiled from the community than to those doing the exiling. Although the search for historical roots is common to all Christian feminists, black feminist theology in particular is drawing on the stories of its foremothers as a rich resource for contemporary spiritual growth.[40]

Christian feminist spirituality is rediscovering the intimate connections between persons and other living beings. Human well being, physical-spiritual well being, is inexorably tied to one's relationship with nature. For the most part, feminists are not suggesting a romantic "back-to-nature" movement that leaves behind the political/social/economic institutions they wish to escape. Feminism has exposed not only the irresponsibility but also the sheer impossibility of doing so. Nor does feminist spirituality simply recommend a duty-bound commitment to "ecological issues." Rather, women are finding that their spirits are nurtured, can only be nurtured, as they are more intentionally and spiritually connected with non-human life.[41]

Finally, Christian feminist spirituality speaks almost with one voice about the connectedness with God that women are experiencing. The distance created and maintained by the patriarchal "father God" has been traversed by the variety of images, stories, songs that express women's experience of a personal God as female and nonpersonal ways of symbolizing the God relation.[42] It is at once the simplest and most obvious and at the same time the most remarkable and most powerful discovery of Christian feminist spirituality: God deals directly with females with no maleness present, on either side of the relationship.

Embodiment

Christian feminists reject the mind-spirit/body dualism of patriarchy. Experiences of "the spirit" are at the same time experiences of themselves and other creatures. Christian feminist spirituality is embodied spirituality.[43] This feature of Christian feminist spirituality is enormously complex, and my discussion will focus only on two of its features.

First, feminist Christians are reclaiming the erotic as a feature of spirituality. From a feminist perspective, the (patriarchal) Christian tradi-tion's teaching about human sexuality and its relationship to God is one of its deepest and most convoluted distortions of the gospel. By splitting mind

25. Martha Graham and the Martha Graham Dancers in "Hymn to the Virgin" from *Primitive Mysteries* by Martha Graham.

and body and associating males with rationality and females with the body, including sexuality, the tradition has wrongfully harbored deep suspicion of human sexuality, at the same time that women have been defined in terms of their sexuality.[44] Women's experience does not suggest that sexuality is an overwhelming force that if left to its own devices will run amok, destroying all order and values. Rather, the erotic is a source of power for new life, whether that life is a new human being or new energy for persons already embodied.

The erotic as spiritual energy has been interpreted by Carter Heyward as "passion." Passion is a positive force, the source of our strength to fight injustice as well as our power to find intimacy and union with other persons and with God. It is through "our passion for justice" that we experience the passion *of* God as shared energy.[45] The same source empowers our work and our love, and that source is experienced in human life as erotic. Our sexuality does not separate us from God, as the tradition teaches. Rather, it is the energy that unites us with God and with others. It is the conduit of our connectedness.

Eroticism as experienced and conceptualized in Christian feminist spirituality includes but is not confined to genital sexuality. The erotic, the passionate, is part of everything persons do if they are fully engaged and well grounded. Physical touch, an embrace, is an enacted metaphor of connectedness among us. Lactation and breast-feeding enact human power to provide nourishment of all kinds for other beings. Genital sexual intimacy enacts personal intimacy and union.

Eroticism is the energetic presence of the whole person, in all her or his aspects, in whatever activity one is engaged. An emphasis on eroticism as a fundamental feature of spirituality is able to account for the similarity between an orgasmic experience on the one hand and on the other hand the satisfaction and fulfillment one experiences in the engagement with others in "transcendent" spiritual enterprises. In this respect feminist spirituality retrieves both biblical eroticism (as with the Song of Solomon) and that of medieval mysticism (as with Teresa of Avila). Finally, Christian feminist spirituality openly acknowledges that the power of prayer reaches to every part of the human person; intimacy with God does not leave our sexuality aside.

By embracing embodiment, Christian feminist spirituality is student of and celebrant for those aspects of women's lives that this culture either ignores or refuses to value. For example, menstruation is not a "taboo" but an experience and sign of women's connections with the life cycle. As menstruating women celebrate the Eucharist, patriarchal Christianity's judgment of "unclean" is concretely refuted. Likewise, the image of God in humankind is not seen only in the young. Aging and older women's and men's bodies are seen as valuable and beautiful records of a life lived in joy and sorrow and as promises of much more life to come.

The other feature of the Christian feminists' emphasis on embodiment as an aspect of spirituality is the reinterpretation of power as life-giving and life-enhancing, both for self and for others. In a patriarchal system, power means "power over," the ability to control another in order to achieve one's own ends.[46] Women's embodied experience of power grounds the feminist conviction that power is primarily "power with others." Peak moments of effectiveness emerge when persons receive from others and/or give to others life-enriching affirmation, and the fullest experiences of power come when their own energy, interests, and ends are joined to those of others for the mutual enhancement of all.

Letty Russell characterizes this process as "synergism," a relationship of cooperation or mutual empowerment that increases the amount of energy available for all.[47] In a genuine partnership one plus one make more than two, and the energy of two multiplies beyond what would be available as the sum of the two individuals. Empowerment does not act "over" others but with them.[48]

Power that alienates and isolates persons does not sustain itself but must be refueled by new conquests, new victories. Sustaining power is power that multiplies not by elevating one over others but by expanding the capacities and faculties of all. Grounded in women's embodied experiences of community, Christian feminists are articulating power as the power of life in all dimensions of reality and in ways that they claim resonate deeply with the Christian gospel.

Embodied spirituality does not seek to escape from the body, nor does it reject the ordinary.[49] Resources for Christian sprituality multiply as women learn and share the ways in which their spirituality develops and nurtures others in the "mundane" experiences of women's lives, and potentially men's as well. Neither God nor human spirituality is "out there" but rather is encountered where we are, not demanding the renunciation of embodiment but functioning as the power of concrete life fully lived.

Liberation

Freedom, unpredictability, spontaneity, the element of surprise, unimpeded access to God have been features of spiritual renewal throughout the history of Christian spirituality. Freedom is important in contemporary Christian feminist spirituality as well, and the term "liberation" is used to capture and emphasize the political dimension of freedom.

In Christian feminist spirituality, liberation means liberation *from* patri-archy. That liberation has not ever been experienced fully. No one, no matter how thoroughly fortified with feminist insights, escapes encounters with or the effects of patriarchy. On the other hand, there are moments of vision, proleptic tastes of what a world free of patriarchy would entail. Those moments are deeply inspirational and empowering.

For Christian feminists, liberation is *for* God as richly experienced by persons of both genders, all colors, ages, ethnic origins, languages. It is liber-ation for others in a wide range of affirmation of life. While breaking down or at least peering over as many boundaries as possible, persons begin to discover commonalities and connectedness, sometimes in surprising ways. Thus understood, spiritual life liberates one's self as persons celebrate the gift of life in concrete ways and celebrate all those connections that sustain life. It is liberation for community, sometimes of women alone when male-ness itself seems oppressive and sometimes of women and men who can join together in creative, mutually empowering ways.

For Christian feminist spirituality, liberation from patriarchy remains more a hope than a lived reality. It is, however, a hope that shapes the pres-ent as persons continue to reject bondage for themselves and for others, even when, especially when, that bondage is found within Christianity itself. Experiences of liberation for self, others, and God continue to fuel the energy required to return again and again to groups and institutions and instrumentalities within Christianity that refuse to accept, for now, the full humanity of women and the inclusion of all persons in the embodied con-nections that Christian feminist spirituality holds at the center of Christian community.

Institutional Settings

A focus on commonalities can obscure diversity, and, although a thorough comparison is not possible here, we may note the degree to which the different institutional settings of feminist Christian spirituality affect its development. In Roman Catholicism, the intransigence of the hierarchy's refusal to consider the issue of the ordination of women to the priesthood (as well as virtual exclusion from shaping church policy) both frustrates the impact of feminism on church structures and provides a focal point for organized opposition to patriarchy in the church. Christian feminist spirituality flourishes among Roman Catholic feminists as they are forced to seek spiritual community outside of the institutional structures in inten-tionally feminist communities.

Although women may be freely ordained to ministry in predominantly white Protestant denominations, patriarchy continues to be pervasive though more subtle, as women are not hired by "high steeple" churches or are passed over for senior positions in multistaff churches. Furthermore, since "female" is not equivalent to "feminist," a larger number of female pastors does not by any means guarantee a hospitable environment for feminist spirituality. Women with power in patriarchal structures may diffuse awareness of and opposition to the patriarchy that remains. In predominantly black and racially mixed churches, issues of sexism and racism interact in complex and sometimes competitive ways, as scarce resources and limited human energies must be allocated to fight systemic oppression in several dimensions at once. Firmly grounded in the experiences and identity of the black community, womanist Christian spirituality develops out of struggles and toward visions of liberation and new community that are only partly shared by and available to non-black persons.

Finally, within any major denominational, racial, or ethnic group, there will be enormous differences from parish to parish and congregation to congregation. The spiritual foci of inclusivity, connectedness, embodiment, and liberation are found throughout contemporary Christian feminist spirituality, and these common elements yield a variety of expressions and experiences in persons' lives and in the institutions feminists seek to transform.

Notes

1. See, e.g., *New French Feminists: An Anthology*, ed. Elaine Marks and Isabelle de Courtivron (New York: Schocken Books, 1981). For a good annotated bibliography of "third world" feminist writings, see *Inheriting Our Mothers' Gardens*, ed. Letty M. Russell et al.

2. For an excellent discussion of the racial tensions of the "first wave" and their contemporary counterparts, see Angela Y. Davis, *Women, Race and Class* (New York: Random House, 1981).

3. My language alludes to Audre Lourde's famous essay entitled, "The Master's Tools Will Never Dismantle the Master's House," in Audre Lourde, *Sister Outsider: Essays and Speeches by Audre Lourde*, 110–13.

4. See Rosemary Ruether's discussion of "testing the spirits" in *Women–Church: Theology and Practice of Liturgical Communities*, 35.

5. I am not suggesting that the *experience* of oppression is the same for different races and cultures; it clearly is not. Rather, feminists discovered that no race or class or culture was exempt from the patriarchal denigration of women.

6. Narrowly defined, patriarchy is any system that favors the father. It is also used in a general sense by feminists to indicate any system that advantages males with respect to females.

7. I am not suggesting that the question of the ordination of women is not fundamentally important. However, even traditions that do ordain women, including those that

have done so for a long time, still marginalize women in the ways that I shall outline.

8. In addition to Daly (who has repudiated Christianity as irredeemably sexist) some of the early publications in Christian feminism include Valerie Saiving, "The Human Situation: A Feminine View," *The Journal of Religion* (April, 1960); Nelle Morton's essays now collected in Nelle Morton, *The Journey Is Home;* Rosemary Ruether's early work, especially *New Woman, New Earth: Sexist Ideologies and Human Liberation;* Audre Lourde, *Sister Outsider.* For a good general anthology of early feminist religious writings, see *Womanspirit Rising: A Feminist Reader in Religion,* ed. Carol P. Christ and Judith Plaskow. It is interesting to compare this volume with the one compiled by the same editors ten years later: *Weaving the Visions: New Patterns in Feminist Spirituality.*

9. The phenomenon I am describing is something that sociologists call "cognitive dissonance"; see Leon Festinger, *A Theory of Cognitive Dissonance* (Stanford: Stanford University Press, 1957).

10. It is, of course, often the case that the "spiritual giants" of the Christian tradition have themselves been marginalized. Christian feminist spirituality does not reject *male* models in general, but rather *patriarchal* ones, whether male or female.

11. See Peter Berger and Thomas Luckmann, *The Social Construction of Reality: A Treatise in the Sociology of Knowledge* (Garden City, NY: Doubleday, 1966).

12. Nelle Morton, *The Journey Is Home,* 202–21.

13. Some Christian feminist theologians argue that the term "god" is inescapably associated with male imagery and should be replaced. I choose to use it, at least for now, because it is too important a word to surrender to patriarchy. Also, its use by feminists claims continuity between feminist spirituality and the non-patriarchal elements in the tradition. I am, however, aware of the problems.

14. My language alludes to a collection of essays by Adrienne Rich entitled *On Lies, Secrets and Silence: Selected Prose 1966–1978.* Though not the subject of this essay, a significant number and variety of new feminist spiritual communities have come into being. See Rosemary Radford Ruether, *Women–Church;* and Elisabeth Schüssler Fiorenza, *Bread Not Stone: The Challenge of Feminist Biblical Interpretation* (Boston: Beacon Press, 1984). The Women's Theological Center in Boston is a good resource for current information about ongoing developments in feminist spiritual communities.

15. The issue becomes particularly acute in conversations between Christian and post-Christian feminists, though Christians from different denominations often operate with vastly different sensibilities. For example, many Protestant feminists largely ignore Mary, while she remains a topic of debate among Roman Catholics. See Mary Jo Weaver's discussion of "the Mary's" in *New Catholic Women: A Contemporary Challenge to Traditional Religious Authority,* 201–11.

16. See especially Phyllis Trible, *God and the Rhetoric of Sexuality;* Trible, *Texts of Terror* (Philadelphia: Fortress Press, 1984); and Elisabeth Schüssler Fiorenza, *In Memory of Her: A Feminist Theological Reconstruction of Christian Origins.* For an anthology of discussions about feminist biblical interpretations, see *Feminist Interpretation of the Bible,* ed. Letty M. Russell.

17. My use of the terms "First and Second Testaments" is an attempt to avoid the Christian triumphalism implicit in the terms "Old and New." The term "Hebrew Bible" is anachronistic for Christians since it is part of the "Christian Bible" and few Christians read it in Hebrew. Its use also leaves the problem of what to call the rest of the Bible: "Greek Bible"? (But there is the Septuagint). *My* terminology gives a priority to the early texts that is theologically indefensible, and I eagerly await better options.

18. On the role of pain in Christian feminist spirituality, see Rita Nakashima Brock,

"On Mirrors, Mists and Murmurs," in *Weaving the Visions,* ed. J. Plaskow and C. Christ, 235–43.

19. Alice Walker coined the term "womanist" to distinguish the anti-patriarchal and anti-racist work of black women from the largely white feminist community. She said that "womanist is to feminist as purple is to lavender" (*In Search of Our Mothers' Gardens,* xi–xii). For a discussion of racism in contemporary feminism, see "Roundtable: Racism in the Women's Movement," *Journal of Feminist Studies in Religion* (Spring 1988) 93–114.

20. As I will discuss below, the distinction between the political realm and the spiritual realm is itself suspect from a feminist perspective.

21. Mary Daly, *Beyond God the Father,* 13.

22. See, e.g., Augustine, *The City of God* in *Works of Aurelius Augustine,* trans. Marcus Dods (Edinburgh: T. & T. Clark, 1871) Vol. 1, Bks. XII, XIV; and Thomas Aquinas, *Summa Theologica,* trans. Fathers of the English Dominican Province (London: Washbourne, 1912) Vol. 13, Part 1, Question 92.

23. For a discussion of this process, see Sallie McFague, *Models of God: Theology for an Ecological, Nuclear Age.*

24. Rosemary Ruether, *Sexism and God-Talk: Toward a Feminist Theology,* 18–19.

25. The term is Rosemary Radford Ruether's (*Sexism and God-Talk*).

26. An example is Celie's reaction and Shug's option in Alice Walker, *The Color Purple* (New York: Washington Square Press, 1982) 175–79.

27. It is, of course, not enough to include only Sarah and exclude Hagar, though the "new" liturgies often do so. To omit Hagar is to continue to marginalize the most disadvantaged and the most vulnerable persons in society.

28. The spectrum of acceptable options with regard to male language for God is as wide as the diversity in Christian feminist theology itself. It may be the case that the male language is so dominant that it needs to be eliminated for a while and replaced by female language in order to achieve a genuine balance in the possibilities for relating to God. It may be that personal language is itself so problematic in light of the patriarchal tradition that it needs to be replaced by impersonal images. Some persons argue for using both male and female imagery for God.

29. In addition to the *Inclusive Language Lectionary,* there are many liturgical resources available. One of the early ones is Linda Clark, Marian Ronan, Eleanor Walker, *Image-breaking/Image-building: A Handbook for Creative Worship with Women of Christian Tradition* (New York: Pilgrim Press, 1981). Ruth Duck has edited some widely used volumes, among them *Bread for the Journey: Resources for Worship* (New York: Pilgrim Press, 1981) and *Flames of the Spirit: Resources for Worship* (New York: Pilgrim Press, 1985). A more recent volume is Miriam Therese Winter, *Woman Prayer, Woman Song: Resources for Ritual* (Hartford: Meyer Stone Books, 1987).

30. McFague, *Models of God.*

31. For an excellent introductory description of patriarchy, see Elizabeth Dodson Gray, *Patriarchy As A Conceptual Trap.*

32. I am, of course, speaking of Western cosmology and ontology. Feminist Christians are finding important connections between their insights and Eastern cosmologies and ontologies. See, e.g., Anne Carolyn Klein, "Finding a Self: Buddhist and Feminist Perspectives," in *Shaping New Vision: Gender and Values in American Culture,* ed. Clarissa W. Atkinson, Constance H. Buchanan, and Margaret Miles (Ann Arbor: UMI Research Press, 1987) 191–218.

33. See, e.g., Carol Gilligan, *In A Different Voice: Psychological Theory and Women's Development;* and *Beyond Domination: New Perspectives on Women and Philosophy,* ed. Carol Gould (Totowa, NJ: Rowman & Allanheld, 1983).

34. In addition to works already cited, see *To Change the World: Christology and Cultural Criticism* (New York: Crossroad, 1983).

35. Although orthodox Christianity does not "officially" teach that salvation is *from* the body, that is in fact what the churches teach when the Christian promise is narrated as "the soul living on after death."

36. See *Women and Religion: A Feminist Sourcebook of Christian Thought,* ed. E. Clark and H. Richardson. Also see Pope John Paul II's apostolic letter "Mulieris Dignitatem" reprinted in *Origins* 18/17 (October 6, 1988).

37. Beverly Wildung Harrison, *Our Right to Choose: Toward a New Ethic of Abortion;* and *Making the Connections: Essays in Feminist Social Ethics* (Boston: Beacon Press, 1985).

38. See, e.g., her collection of poetry, *Revolutionary Patience.* Also see her *Strength of the Weak: Toward a Christian Feminist Identity,* trans. Rita and Robert Kimber (Philadelphia: Westminster, 1984) and *Of War and Love,* trans. Rita and Robert Kimber (New York: Orbis Books, 1983). Feminist theologians whose work leads them to emphasize the relationships between private and public, political and personal, social and religious also tend to identify themselves as liberation theologians.

39. I heard Delores Williams use that image at a conference in New York sponsored by Auburn Theological Seminary in October 1987.

40. See Katie Geneva Cannon, "Moral Wisdom in the Black Women's Literary Tradition," in *Weaving the Visions,* ed. J. Plaskow and C. Christ, 281–92. For her development of that tradition see her *Black Womanist Ethics.*

41. The "garden" has become a rich metaphor for women's connections with previous generations of women. Begun by Alice Walker in her volume of essays, *In Search of Our Mothers' Gardens,* it has more recently been developed by an international group of women in the volume entitled *Inheriting Our Mothers' Gardens,* ed. Letty Russell et al.

42. The most famous example of a feminist, or womanist, nonpersonal symbol for God is, of course, the color purple.

43. For an excellent treatment of the complexity of persons as mind and body without slipping into dualism, see Luke Johnson, *Sharing Possessions: Mandate and Symbol of Faith* (Philadelphia: Fortress Press, 1981) 31–43.

44. See Margaret Farley, "Sexual Ethics," in *The Encyclopedia of Bioethics* (New York: Free Press, 1978) for a careful discussion of traditional Christian teaching about sexuality. Also see Elaine Pagels, *Adam, Eve and the Serpent* (New York: Random House, 1988) for an argument that, in the first three centuries of Christian theology, sin and sex were not so closely associated.

45. See Carter Heyward, *Our Passion for Justice: Images of Power, Sexuality and Liberation.*

46. I am following Letty M. Russell's definitions in *Household of Freedom: Authority in Feminist Theology* (Philadelphia: Westminster Press, 1987) 21.

47. Letty M. Russell, *The Future of Partnership.* She used the term "synergism" in a course on Feminist Theology and Ethics (co-taught by Margaret Farley) at Yale Divinity School in the fall of 1984.

48. The Christian feminist interpretation of power based on an affirmation of embodiment deeply resonates with certain strands of the tradition. See especially Paul's emphasis on "building up" the community.

49. For an anthology of spiritual reflections on women's experience, see *Sacred Dimensions of Women's Experience,* ed. E. Dodson Gray.

Bibliography

Cannon, Katie Geneva. *Black Womanist Ethics.* Atlanta: Scholars Press, 1988.

Christ, Carol, and Judith Plaskow, eds. *Womanspirit Rising: A Feminist Reader in Religion.* San Francisco: Harper & Row, 1979.

Conn, Joann Wolski, ed. *Women's Spirituality: Resources for Christian Development.* New York: Paulist Press, 1986.

Daly, Mary. *The Church and the Second Sex.* San Francisco: Harper & Row, 1968.

———. *Beyond God the Father.* Boston: Beacon Press, 1974.

de Beauvoir, Simone. *The Second Sex.* Translated by H. M. Parshley. New York: Random House, 1974.

Gilligan, Carol. *In a Different Voice: Psychological Theory and Women's Development.* Cambridge, MA: Harvard University Press, 1982.

Gray, Elizabeth Dodson. *Patriarchy as a Conceptual Trap.* Wellesley, MA: Roundtable Press, 1982.

———, ed. *Sacred Dimensions of Women's Experience.* Wellesley, MA: Roundtable Press, 1988.

Harrison, Beverly Wildung. *Our Right to Choose: Toward a New Ethic of Abortion.* Boston: Beacon Press, 1983.

Heyward, Carter. *Our Passion for Justice: Images of Power, Sexuality and Liberation.* New York: Pilgrim Press, 1984.

Hooks, Bell. *Ain't I a Woman: Black Women and Feminism.* Boston: South End Press, 1981.

Lourde, Audre. *Sister Outsider: Essays and Speeches by Audre Lourde.* Trumansburg, NY: The Crossing Press, 1984.

McFague, Sallie. *Models of God: Theology for an Ecological, Nuclear Age.* Philadelphia: Fortress, 1987.

Morton, Nelle. *The Journey Is Home.* Boston: Beacon Press, 1985.

Plaskow, Judith, and Carol Christ, eds. *Weaving the Visions: New Patterns in Feminist Spirituality.* San Francisco: Harper & Row, 1989.

Rich, Adrienne. *On Lies, Secrets and Silence: Selected Prose 1966–1978.* New York: Norton, 1979.

Ruether, Rosemary Radford. *New Woman, New Earth: Sexist Idealogies and Human Liberation.* New York: Seabury, 1975.

———. *Sexism and God-Talk: Toward a Feminist Theology.* Boston: Beacon Press, 1983.

———. *Women-Church: Theology and Practice of Liturgical Communities.* San Francisco: Harper & Row, 1985.

Russell, Letty M. *The Future of Partnership.* Philadelphia: Westminster, 1979.

———, ed. *Feminist Interpretation of the Bible.* Philadelphia: Westminster, 1985.

———, et al., eds. *Inheriting Our Mothers' Gardens.* Philadelphia: Westminster, 1988.

Saiving, Valerie. "The Human Situation: A Feminine View." *The Journal of Religion* (April, 1960).

Schüssler Fiorenza, Elisabeth. *In Memory of Her: A Feminist Theological Reconstruction of Christian Origins.* New York: Crossroad, 1983.

Soelle, Dorothee. *Revolutionary Patience.* Translated by Rita and Robert Kimber. New York: Orbis Books, 1977.

Trible, Phyllis. *God and the Rhetoric of Sexuality.* Philadelphia: Fortress, 1978.

Walker, Alice. *In Search of Our Mothers' Gardens: Womanist Prose by Alice Walker.* San Diego: Harcourt Brace Jovanovich, 1983.

Weaver, Mary Jo. *New Catholic Women: A Contemporary Challenge to Traditional Religious Authority.* San Francisco: Harper & Row, 1985.

19

Christian Spirituality
in an Ecumenical Age

DON E. SALIERS

THE TWENTIETH CENTURY IS, by all reckoning, the ecumenical century. Within and among the diverse traditions of Christianity. profound shifts are taking place which are even now reconfiguring the Christian world. How is it that the vision of a few Benedictine monks, beginning with Prosper Gueranger in the nineteenth and Lambert Beauduin and Virgil Michel in the twentieth century, could have changed the liturgical life of much of the Western church, Protestant and Roman Catholic alike? Who could have predicted the impact of the liturgical reforms promulgated a quarter century ago by the Second Vatican Council upon renewed sacramental practice and a common lectionary of Scripture to be read in the Christian assembly across every major ecclesial body? Few could have imagined the recovery of a primary role for the laity in worship and in church life across ecumenical lines. Yet these changes, among many others, characterize the situation now affecting the emerging shape of Christian spirituality.

Because we are presently immersed in the continuing consequences of both the ecumenical and liturgical movements of the past hundred years, it is difficult to gain enough distance to discern the most formative and distinctive forces that are shaping Christian spirituality in the present age. Any such attempt must be from a standpoint that is embedded in its own particularity and incomplete vision. Out of the vast welter of factors and developments, both those in continuity with Reformation, Counter-Reformation, and nineteenth-century traditions of faith and practice as well as those which break with tradition, I have chosen to concentrate especially on four areas: (1) the geographical and cultural diversity of world Christianity which blend heretofore distinctive patterns of spiritual life and discipline; (2) the emergence of an ecumenically shared liturgical spirituality, based on the restoration of a classical balance of word and sacrament and the whole economy of worship and devotional life; (3) the development of house-church and base community spiritualities; (4) the patterns of fundamentalism, evangelicalism, and the charismatic renewal movements. A concluding section will examine the challenges and prospects for the future of Christian spirituality in light of feminist, liberationist, and ecologically oriented developments.

This essay is concerned with emerging spirituality within the Christian churches rather than with developments outside specifically Christian traditions. Larger cultural and social/political shifts have produced genuine alternatives to the inherited ecclesial forms of religion, and the detailed study of Christianity in relation to world religions and the larger cultural forces in the modern world awaits its own separate volume in this series. The impact of secularization and of the dialogue among historical religions is part of the complex background of the developments discussed here. This essay highlights distinctive forms of Christian prayer, liturgical reform and renewal, and the disciplines of life that are part of the emerging Christian tradition. Orthodoxy and the Eastern churches with their resurgence amply described in the previous section of this volume, have also made a distinctive contribution to these emerging streams of spiritual life among the Western churches.

Although we recognize that personal spirituality and the interior life of individual believers can never be divorced from the social ethos of worship and the praxis of ecclesial life, our accent in what follows is upon the latter. There is always a swing of the pendulum between individualistic concern with personal piety and more social liturgical piety in every age of reform and renewal. Surprisingly, nineteenth-century revivalism, which stressed individual conversion, generated a social impulse and missionary fervor which in turn formed a significant vision of Christian unity. The great nineteenth-century missionary movements created the conditions and, in some cases, the ecclesial structures of twentieth-century ecumenism. On the other hand, Christians within more structured liturgical traditions have more recently become involved with charismatic renewal movements stressing personal experience of God and ecstatic states of prayer. Other intentional groups, often crossing over Roman Catholic and Protestant constituencies, have come to speak of the spirituality of the whole of daily life. Still others have begun to explore the liturgical and sacramental implications of their initial faith commitment to social and political engagement. The very term "spirituality" has come to reflect both the earlier Roman Catholic focus on prayer and the interior life with God, and an emerging, more comprehensive sense of the whole of life lived in the concrete world in relation to God and neighbor.[1]

Twentieth-Century World Christianity

The period since 1945 has witnessed unprecedented shifts in the picture of world Christianity which bear directly on current and unfolding patterns of worship, doctrine, and life. There has occurred what Andrew Walls describes as a "much more diffused Christian presence geographically, a much more diverse presence culturally. . . ."[2] The rapid growth of Christian communities in Africa, Asia, and the Pacific basin and the changes in the Latin American churches are shifting the geographical center of the Christian population and vitality toward the southern hemisphere and away from the centuries-old predominance of European and North American types of church life with their associated liturgical, devotional, and common assumptions of church practice. In Latin America, large portions of the Christian population are now pentecostal, while traditional Roman Catholics and Protestant evangelicals of the missionary heritage are growing much more slowly. But even Roman Catholicism itself, with the growth of the "base communities" and the theologies of liberation, is in the process of altering traditional piety and spiritual temperament. In other words, a widespread process of diffusion of Christian patterns of life *within* cultures and nations, rather than *across* them as with the earlier nineteenth- and twentieth-century missionary enterprises, is now shaping a variegated and richly complex Christianity.

The geographical diffusion and cultural diversity have affected nearly every tradition and are generating new forms of Christian worship and engagement with the social/political world. No longer can we assume highly distinctive divisions along expected lines or an easy division of the churches as closed spiritual types into Protestant, Roman Catholic, and Orthodox. Openness to other traditions is part of the story. More specifically, shared theological sources, in-common liturgical reforms, and institutional cooperation have emerged as real forces shaping Christian identity and practice within the last half century. As one commentator has observed:

> In practice, seminal Christian thinkers exercise an influence no longer bounded by their own confessions. The central affirmations and emphases of each tradition now often find echoes in the others. A liturgical movement among Western Protestants emphasizes God's action in the sacraments as in traditional Catholic theology; one among Western Catholics emphasized the simplicity of common participation in the Lord's Supper, as Protestant Reformers had done. . . . Catholic and Protestant consultation and cooperation take place in countless ways which would have been unthinkable even in the 1940's; and in such bodies as the World Council of Churches, Protestant and Orthodox share without inhibition.[3]

All of this must be seen in light of the missionary movements themselves. In the late nineteenth and early twentieth centuries, the evangelization of new churches in Africa, on the Indian subcontinent as well as in the Far East and in Latin America saw a series of international conferences for the promotion of missionary efforts.[4] Out of this grew quite naturally the ecumenical movement itself. Striking examples of new church unions such as the Church of South India developed precisely because the cultural situation was markedly different from that of the missionary source countries. The very energies of the missionary and cooperative ecumenical enterprises created a new discernment of the social and cultural conditions which called for new models of church life and discipline.

> Christianity is developing new local forms shaped by the priorities and conditions of the cultures in which it has more recently taken root; . . . these new forms growing out of the soil of Africa and Asia and Latin America seem to be producing configurations of Christianity as distinct as the Catholicism shaped by southern and the Protestantism shaped by northern Europe.[5]

A brief sketch of some of the emerging regional patterns of Christian communal life will give a concrete sense of the new situation of world Christianity. African Christianity presents us with a remarkable situation as the twenty-first century approaches. Immediately following the Second World War, the Catholic and Protestant forms of piety and church life were quite distinctive. Relatively few Christians belonged to communities outside the mainline denominations. But today an enormous number of African Christians belong to the African Independent Churches, which are much more indigenous in spiritual temperament and their social organization and social sense of the world. In various countries such as Kenya and Zaire, specific churches have emerged that cannot be classified as either Roman Catholic or Protestant—as, for example, with the Aratai (Spirit-church) of the Agikuyu, or the so-called African Orthodox Church, the Sacred Order of the Cherubim and Seraphim, or the Church of the Lord (Aladura). Some of these show highly defined liturgical and symbolic (hierarchical) patterns, while others show more kinship with Western charismatic churches, often based on highly charged prophetic and healing traditions rooted in the indigenous religious sensibility of the region. A much more basic faith and practice of African churches may be emerging, where the religious symbolization and expression are a new combination of antecedent and Christian traditions.[6]

One sees the concern among African-born Christian theologians in their recent work with traditional African religion and patterns of spiritual life. Stress is placed on the continuity in images and experiences of the divine in premissionary Africa and the Christian communities. New indigenous theological work on the interpretation of traditional religion in the African context is reminiscent of the struggles to clarify the meaning of Christian faith and practice in the Hellenistic period of early Christian expansion.

It is not clear, however, whether the indigenous patterns of ancestor worship are in fact being synthesized with Christian practice. Here traditions differ, and the more biblically conservative missionary churches still exhibit great caution concerning the integration of such matters. Still, the conception of God as immediately active in the lives of believers and the conflict between good and evil spiritual powers do give these Christians a distinctively dramatic way of reading the Scriptures. Furthermore, the more ancient manner of employing basic Christian symbols such as the water of baptism or the cross as sources of power against the forces of illness and death is quite evident.

In the realm of liturgical practice, there is often a combination of spontaneity and freedom alongside formulaic prayer and ritual action. The sense of hierarchical authority goes hand in hand with a fully congregational style of participation in the gathered assembly. Thus, the inherited tensions from the Western church concerning ritual form versus freedom or hierarchical authority versus congregational participation are often simply irrelevant to the emerging practices in these churches.[7] Word and sacramental action along with devotion and scriptural discipline shape the Christian life, both collectively and individually. These are principal sources of spiritual formation and expression. African perceptions of reality—historical, natural, and social—are likely to be dominant forces in the next century as African Christianity becomes less dependent on inherited European and North American patterns of church life.

An equally dramatic manifestation of cultural diffusion of Christianity throughout a geographical area is Latin America. Even as late as the 1940s, the Hispanic-speaking churches of Latin America were regarded, and understood themselves, as an extension of European Catholic Christianity with some enclaves of Protestantism. The traditional cultures of native American populations had been taken up into Spanish and Portuguese forms of church life and spirituality. But in the past fifty years a distinctive Latin American Christianity has been reconfiguring itself. A strong influence of Protestant evangelicalism and the powerful emergence of pentecostal and charismatic forms of religious life and expression have, in some cases, nearly superseded the inherited Catholic patterns. As the essay in this volume by Steven Land amply indicates, there is a vigorous and enthusiastic style of worship and social ministry now associated with classical pentecostal missionary efforts. This is also occurring within the mainline Protestant churches such as the Presbyterians, Methodists and Baptists, as well as among Roman Catholic constituencies.

> The steady development of Pentecostal churches elsewhere in the world . . . : the ecstatic features in African Christianity; and the presence of a "charismatic movement" within Western Catholicism and the older churches of Western Protestantism, all suggest that the associated phenomena are becoming more widely associated within Christianity than at any time since its first century.[8]

It is the social situation of poverty and centuries of political oppression, coupled with a new emphasis on the laity and upon direct access to Scripture, which has produced the most revolutionary change. The recovery of a vision of Christian social order distinguished by equality and justice as well as by freedom from political oppression has literally erupted within the framework of the older Catholicism.

The strikingly new role of the laity gathered about the Bible and led by community leaders or priests who take the social teachings of a reformed Catholicism after Vatican II with great urgency marks the pattern of prayer and action in the so-called base communities. The forms of church life emerging into Latin American Catholicism recall the forms of faith and practice of the radical reformation more than anything else within the Western tradition. The "theology of liberation," even with its ambiguous cross-borrowing from Marxist social/political analysis, is clearly charting a new direction for the spiritual energies of the laity among the poor and marginalized peoples.

The older forms of Catholicism continue, but in diminished power to attract and to hold the vast majority of believers. And, although many of the enthusiastic Protestant forms of religious life have not traditionally been engaged in social and political change, there is no doubt that here, too, prayer, Scripture, holiness, and social engagement with oppressive structures are beginning to recombine in a startling manner. These developments within Catholicism and Protestantism in Latin America are not without confusion and ambiguity, but they are changing the face of Christian life in what is now the largest Christian culture area in the world.

In Asian cultures, the impact of twentieth-century Christianity has been far less pronounced. Still, there are vigorous minority communities throughout places such as India and China and, most strikingly, in Korea. The Church of South India represents a significant achievement in ecclesial unity, beginning in 1947. A parallel has since taken place in North India. The spiritual climate there is profoundly affected by the Hindu traditions, which can readily absorb central Christian beliefs about God and Christ without altering basic Hindu dispositions in the world. At the same time, the complexities of Indian society·in the post-1945 period have created changes which Indian Christian theology and life have tried to understand and interpret in ways that traditional Hindu patterns have not. Theologians such as M. M. Thomas, the long-time director of the Christian Institute for the Study of Religion and Society in Bangalore, have made distinctive contributions to the discussion of the meaning of salvation in the Indian context.

Perhaps no Asian voice has influenced Western Christianity in the past fifty years more than has Mahatma Gandhi's. The force of his own personal witness and his impact on American evangelical missionaries such as E. Stanley Jones and especially on Martin Luther King, Jr., have been enormous.[9] The central theme of resistance to evil as nonviolent yet intentional and active is at the heart of King's shaping the American Civil Rights movement in the late 1950s and 1960s in the United States. The kind of liberation that Gandhi envisioned and manifested in his own movements centered on redemptive suffering—a kind of vicariousness that many see at the heart of the Christian message—the praxis of Jesus of Nazareth as the paradigm for the Christian's life. This thematic is still exerting a remarkable influence, even though more politically active modes of liberation theology have emerged to challenge the seeming passivity of Gandhi's patient suffering in the face of social oppression.

The encounter between Christianity and other major faith traditions in Asia is the subject of a subsequent volume in this series. It must suffice here to note that the dialogue between Christian faith and life and Hindu- and Buddhist-permeated cultures is emerging with new vigor. One thinks immediately of Thomas Merton's threshold discoveries in relation to Buddhism in his late *Asian Journals,* for example, or the work of Henri Le Saux (Abhishiktananda) with his exploration of the relations between Christianity's mystical traditions and Hinduism. The appearance of K. Kitamori's *Theology of the Pain of God*[10] manifests the insights of one who took seriously the Christian tradition yet speaks out of a deep interiorization of themes in traditional Japanese religious sensibility.

In Korea one finds the most rapidly growing Christian communities in all of Asia. In particular, the developments of so-called "Minjung" theology, rooted in the ordinary life of popular culture, manifest the emerging synthesis of theological and spiritual discussion. The survival of both Protestant and Catholic communities through persecution and the cultural revolutions of Mao's China is a striking example of countercultural persistence of Christian life. In the Pacific basin, there is also a distinctive Melanesian pattern of Christian faith and life which has developed in the twentieth century. Charles Forman, in his book on South Pacific island churches has observed:

> . . . the Pacific churches had their own character and a distinctive life, which they themselves had created. They had their own understanding of the Christian faith and their own moral codes, which though they were derived from missionary reading were much influenced by local attitudes in the way they were carried out.[11]

We are thus in an unprecedented situation with respect to Christian forms of worship, teaching, and common life when seen from such a global perspective. The period of the last twenty-five years has witnessed the recombination of certain strands within Christian religious tradition and the new social aspirations of oppressed peoples in all of the regions mentioned thus far. In South Africa the political role of the spirituality of a variety of black churches as well as a new awareness growing within Anglican and Dutch Reformed circles is creating a new climate as well as a volatile religious/political environment. Here we note the mutual influences of American theologians such as James Cone and new voices such as Alan Boesak and Bishop Desmond Tutu in South African theological and spiritual writings.

All of this points toward a period of immense flux and mutual interaction between traditions. Nearly every Christian body in the world has been forced by this new situation to raise fundamental questions about the meaning and shape of Christian life in the world today. The drive toward Christian unity which has characterized the work of the World Council of Churches since 1948 is but one dramatic manifestation of the ecumenical era. At the same time, the cultural diversity and the new diffusion of Christianity across geographical and cultural regions is generating new patterns of church life. There can be little doubt that the development of a conciliar pattern of dialogue, consultation and, where possible, consensus among Christians in quite different traditions and areas is awakening a powerful impulse toward mutual recognition not unlike that of the earliest Christian patterns. The spirituality that emerges from a perception of being one people of God, rooted and grounded in the Hebrew Scriptures, worshiping the God of Abraham and Sarah, the Holy One of Israel whom Jesus Christ manifests in human form is marvelously rich in texture. It is source and expression of a Christian identity that is both local and global, both embedded in specific cultural forms and transcending the parochialisms of denominational and regional Christian faith, worship, doctrine, and mission.

Such an account is an ideal vision, seen from the standpoint of all those who work and pray for deeper Christian unity. The twentieth century has indeed witnessed the emergence of organized national and international church structures which pursue the vision of "Christian interchange and the quest for Christian universality."[12] The worldwide Faith and Order movement, from its beginning in 1920, became an ecumenical intellectual center of gravity. Other centers of dialogue and common prayer and work such as those at Iona in Scotland and Taizé in France, as well as intentional groups such as at Dombes (from 1937 on), have contributed to the deepening of the ecumenical vision and its influence on churches throughout the world.

The ambiguities and tensions arising with newly emerging church life are also present as a result of the postwar global situation. Yet there can be little doubt that mutual enrichment across traditions of spiritual life so long divided is taking place in the consciousness and the actual lived practice in a remarkable range of communions. We can speak, therefore, of a genuinely "ecumenical spirituality" which creates new lines of identity and loyalty as well as struggle within and across traditions.[13]

Ecumenism and the Liturgical Movement

The twentieth century has brought an unprecedented era of ecumenical sharing across historical traditions. While many denominations, especially those of a more conservative theology and practice, maintain their distinctive features—as, for example, Anglo-Catholic liturgical style, opposition to women's ordination, or the evangelistic styles of preaching, singing, and free prayer in ranges of Protestantism—there is presently occurring a profound cross-influence of both structure and style among Protestant and Roman Catholic communions. This is due in part to the ecumenical and liturgical movements which affect nearly all major Christian traditions—especially in their established forms emerging from the Reformation and Counter-Reformation in sixteenth-century Europe. At the same time, the cross-influence is a function of twentieth-century social and religious situations just discussed, in which ethnic diversity, cultural pluralism, and the profound dilemmas of contemporary existence raise basic questions about the meaning of being Christian as well as the why and how of worshiping the God of Christian Scriptures. In light of historical, cultural, and theological shifts, the very style and substance of authentic Christian celebration of common prayer require a new kind of perception. Discussions have emphasized the need to recover the whole "canon" of Christian worship if the reform of texts and rites, resulting from the liturgical movements and the impact of Vatican II, is to lead to genuine renewal of worship.

Just as there is a canon of Scripture which is both source and norm of the faith and teaching of the church, so there is a canon of essential elements or structures which have, over the centuries, constituted a *sine qua non* for the integrity of Christian identity and worship. These basic structures, while not always understood and practiced with equal weight in each tradition, are indispensable to a full and pastorally whole pattern of Christian life as the gathered assembly. These four basic structures are: the rites of Christian initiation (known as baptism, "confirmation," and the process of formation and catechesis), the liturgy of Word and Eucharist, the cycles of time (feasts and seasons which unfold the story of God's relation to the world and the significance of Jesus Christ as the revelation of God), and the pattern of daily prayer. We may also speak of a fifth element which flows from the first four: the patterns of gathered worship which ritualize and celebrate passages in human lives: marriage, funeral rites, forms of prayer with the sick and the dying, and the forgiveness of sins and reconciliation of the penitent.

All of the major traditions, along with most of the Third World churches, are in the process of reappropriating this whole canon of Christian worship, but within a new understanding of the indigenous sensibility and appropriate ways of celebrating in the vernacular. The liturgical reforms and renewal of Christian liturgical life, spearheaded by the reforms of the Second Vatican Council, emphasize the common action of the gathered community about the Scriptures, the meal of the Euchairst, and the baptismal font. A wide range of liturgical ministries which belong to the ordering of these common actions and which were evident in the earliest forms of Christianity are being recovered: reading, serving, leading prayer, teaching, to name a few. These are principally ministries to be performed by the laity rather than the clergy. The new reforms accent a new mutuality between clergy and laity.

We could also speak of the twentieth century as the era of the laity, for one of the dominant features of Christian spirituality among Protestant and Roman Catholics alike has been this recovery of corporate worship as the primary act of the whole church. This is, regarded in light of recent history in the European traditions at least, a revolutionary development. It characterizes a distinctive theme which appears in various churches. The rediscovery of common worship as the primary context for forming and expressing spiritual life is itself the result of a long-term intertwining of the ecumenical and liturgical movements of the twentieth century. Certain notes sounded in various traditions in the nineteenth century are clearly at the origins of these movements— especially among the Benedictines, beginning with Dom Prosper Gueranger in France. One might also include the earlier nineteenth-century Tractarian or Oxford Movement in England and among certain Anglicans, though these movements are perhaps best understood as forces unleashed by the Reformation and the Counter-Reformation in the sixteenth-century West.

The liturgical movement, resourced by a century of biblical, historical, and liturgical/pastoral studies, has reached a flowering in the late twentieth century reform and renewal of worship. This has been described by Max Thurian as "a stage in which the liturgical movement no longer has an independent existence; it is part of the life of the whole Church—*theological, sacramental, ecumenical* and *missionary*."[14] A widely shared ecumenical conviction concerning the centrality of the gathered liturgical assembly in the formation and expression of the local congregation's faith and mission has now emerged. In the *Constitution on the Sacred Liturgy* of the Second Vatican Council, this was articulated as liturgy being the "source and the summit" of the Christian life. This conviction is increasingly shared, despite continuing differences over specific theological dimensions of worship, among all Anglican, Episcopalian, and mainline Protestant traditions who have been engaged in liturgical renewal since the 1960s. Concretely this means the restoration of the classical balance of word and sacrament—something desired by all the major reformers—in the worshiping life of the local community.

These developments have generated a new realignment of attitude and sensibility within certain traditions, most especially among so-called Free Church Protestants. In North America, for example, those Methodists, Presbyterians, Disciples of Christ, United Church of Christ, and others who have been formed in the ecumenical sharing of liturgical traditions find themselves more closely aligned with more progressive Roman Catholics, Lutherans, and Episcopalians with respect to sacramentality, liturgical participation, and even the concept of the church as "servant." On the other hand, such liturgical ecumenism has revived and reinforced a more traditionalist mentality as well. The liturgical renewal has therefore brought ambiguity as well as a mutual enrichment of liturgical spirituality. Various kinds of fundamentalism, not only biblical but also ecclesial and liturgical (or anti-liturgical) have emerged in the very churches which have experienced a profound deepening of liturgical life. Many of the differences now exist *within* denominations and *within* local congregations, which in previous generations divided denominations (and Protestants and Roman Catholics) from one another.

The House-Church and Basic Community

An interesting manifestation of the new vigor of the laity may be seen in the remarkable, worldwide rise of the house-church. The global developments

26. Stephen Alcorn, *Dancing Figures,* n.d.

among mainline Western churches are counterpointed by the house-church. Remarkably parallel to the first house-churches of the Christian era founded by St. Paul and other evangelists, the domestic church in its twentieth-century form is an intentional, highly participative grouping of Christian believers, often located in a particular family's home. In addition to the base communities of Latin America and the traditional small independent churches of a Protestant evangelical type, throughout the world today a rapidly increasing number of such house-churches are emerging. They are characterized by Christians who share an intense commitment to common worship, devotional life, mutual care, and often a structure of social ministry. While such familial social groupings show affinities to the units of intentional Christian life found in diverse parts of the Reformation—the "ecclesiolae" of Spener, the Puritan conventicles, or the classes and bands of John Wesley—the twentieth-century domestic churches show an independence of denominationalism.

The households of faith referred to in the New Testament manifested a familial social-political pattern of life.[15] As then, such communities today are experientially intense, demanding a high degree of commitment to a whole discipline of life; in this they resemble monastic communities and the Wesley classes. The process and structure of Christian faith and its formation and expression in worship and service are the responsibility of the entire body. It would be insufficient, however, to regard such new church structures as merely derivative of Protestant Free Church tradition as self-sufficient, local congregations, since many in the Third World share communion with one another and a common ritual and sacramental life and tacit cultural understandings.

While the early households of faith mentioned in the New Testament were certainly not the only social structures of their kind, they gave a unique formative identity and life-shaping power to the actual web of relationships. So today, a common set of ritual practices—prayer, common meals, biblical study, and Eucharist, along with developing rites of initiation and teaching—is creating a much more communal ethos of the spiritual life than is found in most local parishes. The impact of the house-church phenomenon on more traditional parish structures will be increasingly vital as time goes on. Already, in such examples as the Church of the Savior in Washington, D.C., the significance of house meetings and intentional groups has become a model for others across an ecumenical range. Shawn Madigan, in a recent paper, "Liturgical Spirituality, Domestic Spirituality: Possibilities and Perils," has summed up the liturgical spirituality of the early house-churches, which is the explicit aim of many of the domestic churches, especially among Roman Catholics today.

First, the cosmic reconciliation of the world in Christ is experienced in the visible and creative integrity of a community that is one church . . . living one baptismal responsibility. Oneness is not diminished by plurality of structures and practices. Second, the centrality of the Lord's Supper is formative, expressive, and critical of the communion of the new creation and essential to the evangelical essence of the community. Third, the communion manifest in the Lord's Supper extends beyond the celebrating community to an embrace of the (local) situation as well as to the world. Fourth, the freedom of the Spirit to give whatever gifts are necessary for the community is presumed. . . . Fifth, a plurality of structures, of ministries, of use of gifts and of rules or order emerge as a function of cultural and religious differences.[16]

There are presently between eighty thousand and one hundred thousand domestic churches in Brazil alone. A pastoral plan for the guidance of these communities and for the import of their life for the future of the Roman Catholic Church was drawn up by the bishops there in the 1960s. The Medellin Conference of Latin American bishops supported these plans.[17]

Already these pastoral plans, in large measure influenced by the liberation theologies, have generated a new awareness of mutuality and cooperation between the institutional church and these domestic churches. Similar phenomena are found in Africa as well as in the Philippines, where bishops of seventy-five dioceses cited the rise of the domestic church as a top priority for pastoral work. In North America many such Christian house-churches have emerged from lay renewal movements such as Marriage Encounter, Cursillo, Renew, and from charismatic groups within and split off from local parish churches. The ethos of spiritual life in such communities in the North American context seems more sectarian in impulse than does that of the Latin American and African communities, though both emphasize familial relationships and a sense of "extended family."

Fundamentalism: A Counter-Point

Alongside the widespread ecumenical and liturgical developments has emerged a distinctively different stream of Christian thought and church life which exerts a powerful shaping influence upon millions of Christians. Fundamentalism, a set of beliefs and practices based on a literalist reading of the Bible and a desire for absolute certainty in how God rules the world and expects human beings to live, emerged in the early twentieth century as a protest against ecumenical and liberal trends. At its inception, American and English-speaking fundamentalism consisted of a number of late nineteenth-century movements which formed an uneasy alliance in counter-reaction to the growing, perceived threat of theological liberalism. This Protestant phenomenon paralleled the conservative reaction of Vatican I and the Modernist controversy in Roman Catholicism at the turn of the century.

Two of the nineteenth-century movements provided fundamentalism with its distinctive method of interpreting Scripture. Spearheaded by the Princeton theology of Charles Hodge and Benjamin Warfield, fundamentalists understood the Bible to be a divinely inspired deposit of inerrant propositions—revealed data that could be organized into doctrines and applied to Christian piety and conduct. Early fundamentalism was not anti-rational; rather, it was ultra-rational in its defense against historical criticism of the Bible. Because the acknowledgment of a single error would undermine the claim for the inspiration of the truth of all of Scripture, a rational apologetic was developed to convince persons of the reliability of God's truth, which would enable any decision of faith to have a firm grounding. The foundations for such a view were laid much earlier in the seventeenth-century turn described in the essay by David Pacini in this volume.

At the same time, their dispensational eschatology, developed in nineteenth-century England by John Nelson Darby, served as a hermeneutic that was widely popularized by the *Scofield Reference Bible* (still widely distributed today and used for study and devotion). History is divided, in this view, into a series of rigid dispensations, each a result of the supernatural conflict between God and Satan, and each characterized by a different mode of divine activity in the world. To understand properly a verse or a passage of Scripture, readers must place it in its appropriate dispensation. The Sermon on the Mount, for example, is understood not as an ethic for the present age, but for the age to come. In sharp contrast to Protestant liberalism, which sought to interpret Scripture within the larger context of history and historical self-understanding, dispensationalism interpreted history within the context of Scripture as divinely revealed.

Divinely given, inerrant Scripture was thus a counter to ecumenical sensibility, which, in the minds of the fundamentalists, was too ready to sacrifice truth for Christian unity. Only doctrinal truth could be the basis of unity among Christians. In this sense, fundamentalists tended to be radical separatists, fighting error and apostasy in doctrine and morals. Dispensationalism, which predicted such religious apostasy of churches in the last days of human history, simply reinforced these separatist tendencies.

Fundamentalism was also marked by a highly individualistic picture of the Christian life. Revivalists such as D. L. Moody called for individual conversion through personal decision for Christ. Through a second, subsequent decision of faith, believers could receive the "baptism of the Holy Spirit," which enabled them to live a holy, "victorious life" over sin, to obtain peace and joy instead of sorrow and anxiety, and to receive power for Christian witness. The hymns and songs of popular composers such as Fanny Crosby and Ira Sanky reinforced this piety. "Blessed Assurance, Jesus is Mine" sings of a powerful, individual relationship between the believer and the Savior. Not all such evangelical hymnody was confined to fundamentalism. Distinctive marks of fundamentalist belief and spirituality were carried by selective use of songs and hymns that illustrated fundamentalist themes.

Such a concern for individual holiness and salvation was a shift from the radical social piety of the pre–Civil War holiness movement in the United States, which spawned, among other important movements, the abolishment of slavery as a social evil. This shift was encouraged by the dispensational eschatology in which all future events were predetermined and the social order was expected to worsen. With a belief that Christ was coming soon to take the true believers to heaven in the rapture, it was the salvation of individuals that became of paramount concern.

By the 1940s, opposition had developed within various fundamentalist groups to its general lack of social concern. Sometimes called "neo-evangelicals," this group sought to overcome the internal doctrinal divisions by the formation of the National Association of Evangelicals, a moderate alternative to the more militantly fundamentalist American Council of Christ Churches. Billy Graham, a major figure of the moderates, sought cooperation from mainline Protestants and Roman Catholics in his popular evangelistic crusades, drawing criticism from fundamentalists. Evangelistic crusades led by Graham and others produced a broad popular response which could no longer be called fundamentalist, giving evidence in the 1950s and 1960s of a decidedly ecumenical evangelicalism.

Theologian Carl F. H. Henry, in *The Uneasy Conscience of Modern Fundamentalism*, insisted that social concern is essential to Christian faith and life; out of this renewal of evangelical social ministry emerged such organizations as World Vision International. At the same time, the more broad-stream evangelicals turned away from dispensationalism to the older millennial eschatologies, which were more conducive to social ministries.

The earlier fundamentalist withdrawal from intellectual and cultural life in the wider society was criticized by theologians like Henry and E. J. Carnall. Determined to restore evangelical scholarship to the quality that characterized the nineteenth-century Princeton theology, younger evangelicals began to earn degrees from leading liberal universities such as Boston and Harvard, in order to prepare for a more sophisticated apologetics. Radio evangelists Charles E. Fuller established Fuller Theological Seminary as a new center of evangelical scholarly excellence.

By the 1960s many evangeicals were engaged in a thoroughgoing critique of the older fundamentalism, drawing on the deeper historical heritage of the evangelical traditions of the eighteenth and early nineteenth centuries, Puritanism and Reformation themes, as well as a knowledgeable appropriation of the ideals of the early church. A new spiritual vision was emerging from the internal and external critique of fundamentalist constraints. Evangelical social concern surfaced in the reformist politics of Ron Sider and the Evangelicals for Social Action, the countercultural radicalism of Jim Wallis and the Sojourners Community, and evangelical versions of black and liberation theologies.

Alarmed by such trends toward the political left, other evangelicals such as Ronald Nash countered with theological defenses of capitalism. Neofundamentalists began increasingly to embrace American values of free-market capitalism. The rise of groups such as "Moral Majority" in the United States manifests a combination of literalist biblical interpretation, a moralistic piety, and a cultivation of uncritical American social-political loyalty, characteristically grounded in a polemic against "secular humanism."

It is difficult to assess the future of the politically engaged neo-fundamentalism which has shaped lives in a socially conservative political agenda since the 1970s. National issues such as abortion, welfare, prayer and sex education in public schools have seen cooperation between neo-fundamentalists such as Jerry Falwell with like-minded Roman Catholics, Mormons, and others who formerly were avoided by separatist fundamentalists. The complex interaction of revisionist fundamentalism and revitalized evangelical concern across denominational lines has created a new climate, at once volatile and generative of new strands of church life which are shaping and giving expression to Christian spirituality in a multifaceted social context, one which the earlier fundamentalists as well as more classical evangelicals could not have imagined a few decades ago.

The current conflict over Scripture often leads to a picture of evangelicalism simply as another form of rational scholasticism reminiscent of post-Reformation orthodoxy. But the center of gravity in nineteenth-century evangelicalism was elsewhere. Revivalism and the holiness movements, strenuously opposed by the Princeton theologians, dominated the spiritual ethos in the United States. Prior to the Civil War a multitude of inter-denominational social reform movements and benevolent societies had emerged. By the end of the nineteenth century and on into the twentieth, the image of the "higher life" of the Christian and the sanctified life became increasingly privatized and less socially oriented. This turn toward a more inward piety expressed itself in private charities rather than in the earlier anti-slavery and social reformist sensibility. Both the growing influence of dispensationalism and the increasing alienation of evangelicals from modernist intellectual and cultural currents lay behind this shift.

In twentieth-century pentecostalism, which emerged from the more personalist holiness movements, the understanding of Holy Spirit baptism becomes increasingly linked to the empowerment of Christians for witness and action in the world. The baptism of the Holy Spirit, while evidenced by such phenomena as speaking in tongues, was centrally identified with empowerment for service, thus broadening the conception of sanctification. While Steven Land discusses this in detail in his essay, it remains for us to describe a few distinctive features of the spirituality of the charismatic movement with which pentecostalism has much in common.

The charismatic movement which flowered in the 1960s brought pentecostal spirituality into mainline Protestant, Roman Catholic, and even Eastern Orthodox traditions. Suddenly the discovery of freer, more expressive modes of prayer, the experience of healing, and less-mediated access to God brought Christians from quite divergent doctrinal and ecclesial traditions together in a new way: common experience of the working of the Holy Spirit was a newly recognized bond and identity. Yet this experiential ecumenism did not do away with denominational traditions. While charismatics initially tended to adopt pentecostal understandings of their experiences, including the idea of a "Spirit baptism" as a second distinctive work of grace following conversion, eventually charismatics began to reinterpret and integrate such experiences in light of their own tradition. Thus, Roman Catholics and Episcopalians saw charismatic renewal of personal life and the church as sacramentally oriented.

Whereas classical pentecostals exercise spiritual gifts such as prophecy and healing in Sunday worship, charismatics in mainline denominations, where such phenomena are often controversial and even divisive, practice these gifts in prayer and praise meetings. Large covenant communities have formed in various places, with the participants committed in varying degrees to sharing a common life and to accountability to a common discipline. Many of these communities, such as those at Ann Arbor, Michigan, and at Notre Dame, Indiana, are Roman Catholic in origin; most are ecumenical in constituency. In some communities submission to ruling leaders, who can only be men, has led to controversy, especially when such practices have become rigid, abusive, or oppressive of women. But it is clear that such communities also reflect a yearning for some form of domestic monasticism or communitarian life such as has shaped the spiritual cohesiveness and identity of sectarian Protestant communities in the past, especially those coming out of persecution following the Reformation.

Many charismatics are affiliated with independent associations of churches and ministers, some of which may well become new denominations with distinctive teachings and self-styled ways of life. One such teaching is "restorationism," having roots in the Latter Rain movement within pentecostalism in the 1940s. Adherents consider the task of the Christian community to be restoration of New Testament Christianity and God's reign in some pure form. It is now advocated by many independent charismatic communities as well as among the house-church restorationist movement in Great Britain and other English-speaking countries.

Another nondenominational branch of the charismatic movement is "faith confessionalism," or the health and prosperity gospel. Such spirituality has roots in the pentecostal healing revival of the late 1940s and in the New Thought or "mind cure" movement of the late nineteenth century, whose fruit includes Christian Science and the Unity School of Christianity. Instead of the simple power of the mind over physical reality, faith confessionalists speak of the creative power of faith and of the fact that God wishes Christians to have health and prosperity. A positive confession of faith believes God is bringing these things about despite evidence to the contrary. This is "revelation knowledge" and to acknowledge continuing symptoms of illness or financial distress is simply a negative confession based only on a human "sense knowledge."

The connection between Christian spirituality and modern conceptions of health and happiness is a profoundly ambiguous matter, yet it permeates a great range of popular piety well beyond charismatic circles. The "power of positive thinking" has influenced millions of ordinary Christians in America across all denominations. The rise of huge "mega-churches" appeals in part to the prosperity and growth values so indigenously American.

Such a preoccupation with prosperity and personal power stands in sharp contrast to the socially engaged ministry and forms of common worship of other charismatics, many of whom are involved in the inner city ministries (such as the Church of the Redeemer in Houston, Texas). It contradicts the radical social perspectives of the Reba Place Fellowship, the large charismatic contingent in the Sojourners Community, and other Protestant and Catholic communities, especially those emerging in the Third World.

Challenges and Prospects

It has been observed that the most radical thing to affect Protestantism in the twentieth century was the Second Vatican Council, convened in 1963 by Pope John XXIII. The council itself addressed a series of questions which bear directly on the life of the Christian church in the modern world:

liturgy, the mission and unity of the church, economic and social development, and ecumenism, among the chief concerns. Running through all of the debates and documents was an overriding hope: the renewal of the Roman Church and the closer spiritual unity of all Christians. It was truly an ecumenical council, with bishops from the entire world (those from the North Atlantic and traditional centers of church power were actually in the minority), and hosts of observers from non-Roman traditions. It was here that the years of behind-the-scenes ecumenical common prayer and work and the impact of the liturgical movement blossomed, along with the growing sense of conciliar Christianity, which had developed in the World Council of Churches as well.

Now that many of the major liturgical reforms have been made in the Roman Catholic and mainline Protestant churches, we can say that the more complex process of renewal and acculturation of the Christian life in community has begun. There has been a monumental shift in the status and role of the laity in the Christian churches in our era. It is not too strong, I think, to speak of a "second reformation"—one that starts not in a polemic against abuses, but is irenically in search of the more spiritual sources of Christian unity. This "second reformation," first having begun among the Benedictines, centered in monastic communities in France, Belgium, and Germany, extended to the United States, especially at St. John's Abbey in Minnesota. But the question remains what the long-range outcome will be of this massive sea-change so recently begun. The impact on how ordinary believers experience worship, devotional life, and the formative life of the church has been striking but ambiguous. So much liturgical change has come in the context of much religious and social uncertainty. For many Christians, the loss of familiar patterns of worship, such as the Latin Mass or the older prayer book in the case of Anglicans and American Episcopalians has brought disaffection. Ecclesial issues such as the ordination of women and the emerging feminist and liberationist concerns have strained the more conservative traditions—liturgical and evangelical Free Church alike.

Since spirituality refers to the lived religious experience of believers, such changes in liturgical pattern and the challenges of theology in a twentieth-century world of post-holocaust, technologically complex, political and social volatility have a critical impact on Christian spiritual life. The very term "spirituality" in the Christian context is no longer an exclusively Roman Catholic or even Christian term. Yet for the Christian tradition, spirituality still has to do with the struggle to pray, with a sense of holiness and the mystery of life and death, with the challenge of seeking a wholeness to human existence in relation to God and neighbor and the created order. To the intensification of the innermost dimensions of our existence, the demands of the twentieth century have revealed the necessity of linking the interior sphere with the engagement of self and community with the struggle for justice and the restoration of relationship with nature and the larger cosmos. What we see is a wide range of styles of Christian spirituality emerging, often in tension with one another, and all under the haunting question of the possibility of faith in God in a time of the eclipse of the sacred for Western technological societies.

Multiple themes and multiple strategies toward a deeper human life have led to new discourse about feminist, black, creation, liberationist, and even ecumenical "spirituality." It is no longer possible to call upon a culturally homogeneous central tradition of spiritual literature as being normative for all Christians.

A growing awareness of the interdependence of all things and of the vulnerability of the whole earth as an ecosystem is at the heart of "creation spirituality." A view of the world that honors its status as bearer of the divine has much in common with native American perceptions and shows every indication of deepening Christian sacramental understandings of the created order. Such an emerging viewpoint is not to be confused with a general pantheism. Rather, we are witnessing a widespread reappropriation of the doctrine of creation.

Alongside a heightening of basic ecological awareness, a profound shift toward concern for peace and justice on a global scale is becoming increasingly integrated into the prayer life of churches. The word "solidarity" is but one linguistic expression of this. The strikingly new feature of this concern is its linkage with consciousness of worldwide suffering and the necessity for peace in a time of potential nuclear holocaust. It is the global apocalyptic sense which is beginning to mark late twentieth-century religious sensibility across all traditions. In nearly every gathered worshiping community one now hears preaching, the people's prayers and intercessions, and increasingly the hymns Christians sing reflecting these themes. Johann Metz has spoken of Christian prayer itself being an expression of solidarity with the long history of human suffering.[18]

In these movements, the shape of Christian spirituality is at once ecumenical and much more concretely engaged in the concern for environment and for the pressing issues of injustice and the threat of nuclear holocaust. Consequently, the vision of what the spiritual life entails is expanding and shifting our attention to factors beyond the inherited Reformation/Counter-Reformation liturgical and devotional order of things. The preoccupations of individualist piety and the focus on interior life with God are increasingly mixed with active engagement in the social and political structures of the society. Figures such as Thomas Merton and Dorothy Day,

Martin Luther King, Jr., and Mother Teresa have popularized this new configuration of Christian life, combining both activist and contemplative strands from earlier and what often appear to be conflicting sources and traditions.

Yet for all the complexity and plurality, there is also a sense of gain. For within Christianity the convergence of patterns of worship and the increasing power of mutual appreciation and recognition of authentic Christian faith and life across traditions are creating a more comprehensive global Christian identity as well. Plurality in the spiritual life relativizes parochialisms of various kinds—whether scriptural, ecclesial, or social/ethical. The crises of the twentieth century have forced the question of authenticity and integrity as part of the matter of what constitutes the essentials of Christian life in the world.

In such a context, the distinctive features of Christian spirituality may be all the more striking. In a world where millions have little or no food, the symbolism of Eucharist as bread for the world is rendered more powerful than at any time in previous sacramental practice and interpretation. The vision of an eschatological community that encompasses all human divisions and surpasses particular Christian ecclesial concerns is itself a distinctive feature of Christian hope and thought in the present age.

For still it is the case that love of God and neighbor enabled by what is disclosed and illumined by Jesus of Nazareth is the heart of the lived experience of faith. Mystery and suffering and joy must still embrace in the seeking of God, even as the images of life with God and neighbor must change and older parochialisms be challenged. At the same time Dean William Inge's warning must be heard: "The church that marries the spirit of the age will be a widow in the next generation."

There is enough challenge in seeking God and an authentic Christian life in community in our time to keep Christians from presumption, yet enough connection with the depth of the enduring spiritual traditions within Christianity to revitalize authentic faith-life in the emerging social and cultural extremities in our near and distant future. Whether the twentieth century's ecumenical vision and mutual convergence are enough to overcome the fragmenting, world-threatening forces of post-industrial life, or whether the very religious way of being "in but not of the world" which is at the heart of Christian spirituality can be sustained, is an open question.

As the third millennium of Christianity dawns, we can catch only a glimpse of the complex tapestry of spirituality that is the legacy of the traditions and their attendant forms of life discussed in this volume. Lived faith is always embedded and embodied in particular human communities whose contemporary social and cultural circumstances always impinge on their worship, prayer, and life-disciplines. The diversity we have traced since the Reformation period testifies to this. Whatever else may emerge, a simple Roman Catholic/Protestant contrast can no longer be made, nor a simple East/West duality. Yet the intention to live faithfully and responsibly the Christian life in each particular context raises the perennial questions of continuity and discontinuity with the broad central streams of Christian spirituality. New expressions of Christian spiritual life may manifest quite different relationships to confessions and to church structures than in the past. But such expressions, in turn, will be tested in time in light of the fundamental Christian vision of divine reality, the relation of the church to the world and to the eschatological hope of the kingdom of God.

Questions of spirituality, while embodied in church structures, communal practices and related to matters of doctrine, show a generative independence as well. No single pattern of spiritual life can exhaust the fullness of God's self-communication claimed by the larger ecumenical sense of the Christian tradition. Just as no single dogmatic formulation or theological schema can comprehend the truth of God's revelation fully, and no single church structure can claim static and absolute universality without collapsing the distinction between church and eschatological community, so no single spiritual way will hold sovereignty. But each authentic pattern of holiness and each authentic pattern of church life, when in reconciliation and conciliar dialogue, illuminates the faithfulness of the other. Yves Congar, in speaking of the fullness of the mystery of God in Christ, wisely observed that "the church, the body of Christ, contains [that mystery] by the gift of God, in a way that is not exhausted by the manner in which it is expressed."[19]

Ecumenism has brought to life in our time a distinctive awareness which represents a new departure in the search for a plenitude of religious experience, commitment, and identity. It will doubtless coexist in tension with more fundamentalist forces within and between various traditions. Christian spiritual identity as opposition to other forms of being Christian is so deeply embedded in social memory and institutional habits of self-preservation that conversion to an ecumenical spirituality is quite revolutionary. However, if the love of truth and the love of God is also love for those who suffer and struggle toward a vision of the reconciliation of all things in God, then there remains a bright promise. This is the hope for a more inclusive Christian life for the sake of the whole inhabited world.

Notes

1. For an informative account of the widening horizons of Christian spirituality in light of ecumenical contact and its emergence as a distinctive intellectual discipline in

the twentieth century, see Sandra M. Schneiders, I.H.M., "Theology and Spirituality," *Horizons* 13/2 (1986) 253–74.

2. Andrew Walls, "The Christian World," in *Religion in Today's World,* ed. Frank Whaling, 83.

3. Ibid., 87.

4. Perhaps the most important gathering in the early twentieth century was the World Missionary Conference held at Edinburgh, Scotland, in June 1910. John R. Mott, the visionary Methodist layman from the United States and the founder of the World Student Christian Federation in 1895, presided. The twelve hundred delegates from Protestant missions around the world discussed the problems of the importation of Western church divisions on the faith and practice of the mission churches. See *A History of the Ecumenical Movement,* Vol. 1, ed. R. Rouse and S. C. Neill.

5. A. Walls, "The Christian World," 88.

6. For a review of the literature on African Independent Churches, see H. W. Turner, *Bibliography of New Religious Movements:* Vol. 1, *Black Africa;* D. B. Barrett, *Schism and Renewal: An Analysis of Six Thousand Contemporary Religious Movements* (Nairobi: Oxford University Press, 1968); and Inus Daneel, *Quest For Belonging: Introduction to a Study of African Independent Churches* (Gweru, Zimbabwe: Mambo Press, 1987).

7. The African Independent Churches, both of the Ethiopian and Spirit types, show influences of the hierarchical system inherited from traditional society and Anglican missionary influence, yet with a mixture of Presbyterian and Methodist forms of church life. At the same time, the forms of common worship are highly participatory, and prophecy, healings, exorcisms, and enthusiastic singing and free prayer characterize the free style of the ritual. M. L. Daneel observes of the celebration of Holy Communion, for example: ". . . one of the cardinal features of the communion is that it is a *total experience.* Everyone who has legitimately entered the sanctuary—adults, infants, children—*participate together,* singing, speaking in tongues, sharing the renewal in Christ from the mystical experience of God's presence (with the arrival of the principal leader) to the exuberant festive rejoicing (after receiving the sacrament). In the Independent Churches, *this climax is a crucial cohesive factor to counter fragmentation,* and to individual members one of the most inspiring parts of their religious life" (*Quest For Belonging,* 229).

8. A. Walls, "The Christian World," 98.

9. Jones's tribute to the spirituality of Gandhi is vividly expressed in his *Mahatma Gandhi: An Interpretation,* written in 1948 and republished as *Gandhi: Portrayal of a Friend* (Nashville: Abingdon, 1983).

10. Richmond: John Knox, 1965.

11. Charles Forman, *The Island Churches of the South Pacific: Emergence in the Twentieth Century,* 125.

12. Bernhard Lambert, *Ecumenism* (New York: Herder & Herder, 1967) 30.

13. See Geoffrey Wainwright's thoughtful discussion in "Ecumenical Spirituality," in *The Study of Spirituality,* ed. Cheslyn Jones, Geoffrey Wainwright, and Edward Yarnold, S.J. (New York and Oxford: Oxford University Press, 1986).

14. Max Thurian, "The Present Aims of the Liturgical Movement," *Studia Liturgica* 3 (Autumn 1964) 108.

15. For some descriptive accounts, see Acts 16:15, 31ff.; 17:6; 18:1–8; 1 Cor 1:14–16; 11:19; Rom 16:3ff.; and Philemon 2.

16. *Proceedings of the Annual Meeting of the North American Academy of Liturgy* (Valparaiso, IN: Valparaiso University, 1988) 110–11.

17. See "The Present Day Transformation of Latin America in Light of the Council

and Pueblo: Evangelization at Present and in the Future of Latin America"
(Washington, DC: National Conference of Catholic Bishops, 1979).

18. See Johann B. Metz and Karl Rahner, *The Courage to Pray* (New York: Crossroad,
1981).

19. Yves Congar, O.P., *Diversity and Communion*, 170.

Bibliography

Allchin, A. M. *The World Is a Wedding: Exploration in Christian Spirituality.* New York:
Oxford University Press, 1978.

Congar, Yves. *Diversity and Communion.* Translated by John Bowden. Mystic, CT:
Twenty-third Publications, 1985.

Elwood, D. J. *Asian Christian Theology, Emerging Themes.* Philadelphia: Westminster,
1980.

Fey, H. E. *A History of the Ecumenical Movement,* Vol. II. London: SPCK; Philadelphia:
Westminster, 1970.

Forman, Charles. *The Island Churches of the South Pacific: Emergence in the Twentieth
Century.* Maryknoll, NY: Orbis Books, 1982.

Fox, Matthew. *A Spirituality Named Compassion: The Healing of the Global Village,
Humpty-Dumpty, and Us.* Minneapolis: Winston, 1979.

Horgan, Thaddeus D., ed. *Apostolic Faith in America.* Commission on Faith and Order,
NCCOUSA. Grand Rapids: Eerdmans, 1988.

Küng, Hans, ed. *Post-Ecumenical Christianity.* Concilium Volume 54: Ecumenism. New
York: Herder & Herder, 1970.

Leech, Kenneth. *True Prayer.* New York: Harper & Row, 1980.

Marx, Paul. *Virgil Michel and the Liturgical Movement.* Collegeville, MN: Liturgical
Press, 1957.

Merton, Thomas. *Contemplation in a World of Action.* Introduction by Jean Leclercq,
O.S.B. Garden City, NY: Doubleday, Image Books, 1973.

Rahner, Karl. *The Practice of Faith: A Handbook of Contemporary Spirituality.* New
York: Crossroad, 1986.

Rouse, Ruth, and S. C. Neill, eds. *A History of the Ecumenical Movement,* Vol. I. 2nd
ed. London: SPCK; Philadelphia: Westminster, 1968.

Runyon, Theodore, ed. *Sanctification and Liberation.* Nashville: Abingdon, 1981.

Saliers, Don E. *Worship and Spirituality.* Philadelphia: Westminster, 1984.

Schmemann, Alexander. *For the Life of the World.* Rev. ed. Crestwood, NY: St.
Vladimir's Seminary Press, 1974.

Thurian, Max, ed. *Ecumenical Perspectives on Baptism, Eucharist and Ministry.* Faith and
Order Paper No. 116. Geneva: World Council of Churches, 1983.

Torres, S., and J. Eagleson, eds. *The Challenoe of Basic Christian Communities.*
Maryknoll, NY: Orbis Books, 1981.

Turner, H. W. *Bibliography of New Religious Movements.* Vol. 1, *Black Africa.* Boston:
G. K. Hall, 1977.

Wallis, James. *The Call to Conversion.* New York: Harper & Row, 1981.

Whaling, Frank, ed. *Religion in Today's World.* Edinburgh: T. & T. Clark, 1987.

Yong-Bock, K., ed. *Minjung Theology: People as Subjects of History.* Singapore: Christian
Conference of Asia, 1981.

Contributors

Louis Dupré, coeditor of this volume, is T. Lawrason Riggs Professor in the department of Religious Studies at Yale University. His books include *The Other Dimension* (1972, 1979), *A Dubious Heritage* (1977), *The Deeper Life, The Common Life* (1982), *Marx's Social Critique of Culture* (1983).

Don E. Saliers, coeditor of this volume, is Professor of Theology and Liturgics at Emory University, Atlanta, Georgia. Among his publications are *The Soul in Paraphrase: Prayer and the Religious Affections* (1980) and *Worship and Spirituality* (1985).

John Meyendorff, collaborating editor of this volume, is Dean of St. Vladimir's Orthodox Theological Seminary, Crestwood, New York. He is the author of *A Study of Gregory Palamas* (1974), *Christ in Eastern Christian Thought* (1975), *Byzantine Theology* (3d ed., 1987), *Byzantium and the Rise of Russia* (1981), and other books.

Elisabeth Behr-Sigel is the author of a dissertation on Alexandre Bukharev, a Russian theologian (1977) and a challenging book on the role of women in the church, *Le ministère de la femme dans l'Eglise* (1987).

Boris A. Bobrinskoy is Professor of Systematic Theology at the Orthodox Theological Institute (St. Sergius), Paris. He is the author of *Le Mystère de la Trinité* (1986).

Michael J. Buckley, S.J. is Professor of Theology at Notre Dame University. He wrote *Motion and Motion's God* (1971) and *At the Origins of Modern Atheism* (1987).

Sergei Hackel has taught Russian literature at the University of Sussex, England. His books include *The Poet and the Revolution, Aleksandr Blok's "The Twelve"* (1975) and *Pearl of Great Price: The Life of Mother Mary Skobtsova* (1981).

Charles Hambrick-Stowe is Pastor of the Church of the Apostles, UCC, and Adjunct Professor of Church History, Lutheran Theological Seminary, Gettysburg, Pennsylvania. His publications include *The Practice of Piety: Puritan Devotional Discipline in 17th Century New England* (1982), *Early New England Meditative Poetry: Anne Bradstreet and Edward Taylor* (1988).

545

E. GLENN HINSON is the David T. Porter Professor of Church History at The Southern Baptist Theological Seminary, Louisville, Kentucky. His publications include *The Evangelization of the Roman Empire* (1981), *The Reaffirmation of Prayer* (1978), and *Seekers After Mature Faith* (1968, 1978).

KIERAN KAVANAUGH, O.C.D., founder of the Institute of Carmelite Studies, has edited and translated, in collaboration with Otillo Rodriguez, *The Complete Works of St. John of the Cross* and *The Complete Works of St. Teresa of Avila*.

STEVEN J. LAND is Assistant Professor of Theology at the Church of God School of Theology, Cleveland, Tennessee, of which he is one of the founding faculty. He has lectured widely at international pentecostal gatherings. His publications include "The Local Church and the Poor" in *Pentecostal Minister* (1986) and "A Stewardship Manifesto" (1980).

RICHARD C. LOVELACE is Professor of Church History at Gordon-Conwell Theological Seminary, South Hamilton, Massachusetts.

ERIC LUND is Associate Professor of Religion at St. Olaf College, Northfield, Minnesota. His publications include "The Impact of Lutheranism on Popular Religion in Sixteenth-Century Germany" in *Concordia Journal* (1987).

KEITH P. LURIA is Assistant Professor of History at North Carolina State University. He is the author of the forthcoming *Territories of Grace: Cultural Change in the Seventeenth-Century Diocese of Grenoble* and essays and reviews on early-modern European popular culture and religion.

JOHN W. O'MALLEY, S.J., is Professor of Church History at Weston School of Theology, Cambridge, Massachusetts. His publications include *Giles of Viterbo on Church and Reform* (1968), *Praise and Blame in Renaissance Rome* (1979), *Rome and the Renaissance* (1981), *Catholicism in Early Modern History* (1988), *Tradition and Transition* (1989).

ALBERT C. OUTLER taught History of Christian Thought at Duke, Yale, and Southern Methodist universities. His publications include *Psychotherapy and the Christian Message* (1954), *The Christian Tradition and the Unity We Seek* (1957), and the four-volume edition of *The Works of John Wesley: The Sermons,* I–IV (1984–1987).

DAVID S. PACINI is Associate Professor of Christian Thought at Emory University, Atlanta, Georgia. Among his publications is *The Cunning of Modern Religious Thought* (1986).

SALLY B. PURVIS is Assistant Professor of Religious Studies at Fairfield University, Fairfield, Connecticut, and is an ordained minister in the United Church of Christ.

PHILIP SHERRARD, formerly of King's College, London, has been one of the editors of the English edition of the *Philokalia* and has published much on modern Greek literature and contemporary Orthodoxy.

THEOPHUS SMITH is Assistant Professor of Religion, Emory College of Emory University, Atlanta, Georgia. Among his publications is "A Phenomenological Note: Black Religion as Christian Conjuration" (1983).

DAVID TRACY is Distinguished Service Professor at the University of Chicago. He is the author of *Blessed Rage for Order* (1975), *The Analogical Imagination* (1981), and *Plurality and Ambiguity* (1987).

DAVID TRICKETT is Executive Director of the Washington Theological Consortium and Professor of Theology and Ecumenics. Among his publications are "Study of the Life and Thought of H. Richard Niebuhr" and "Study of Christian Responsibility in the Context of Ecological Integrity."

GORDON S. WAKEFIELD, formerly principal of Queen's College, Birmingham, is currently chaplain at Westminster College, Oxford. Among his publications are *Puritan Devotion* (1957) and the *Westminster Dictionary of Christian Spirituality* (1983).

Photographic Credits

1. Scala/Art Resource, New York.
2. National Gallery of Art, Washington, DC. Alisa Mellon Bruce Fund, 1963.
3. The Metropolitan Museum of Art, New York. Rogers Fund, 1956. (56.48).
4. The Metropolitan Museum of Art, New York. Purchase, Enid A. Haupt Gift, 1979. (1979.209).
5. Prints and Plates Collection, Arts of the Book, Yale University Library.
6. Prints and Plates Collection, Arts of the Book, Yale University Library.
7. The Chrysler Museum, Norfolk, Virginia. Gift of Walter P. Chrysler, Jr.
8. The Thomas Jefferson Papers, Manuscript Division, Special Collections Department, University of Virginia Library.
9. National Gallery of Art, Washington, DC. Gift of W. G. Russell Allen.
10. Bildarchiv Foto Marburg/Art Resource, New York.
11. Bildarchiv Foto Marburg/Art Resource, New York.
12. The Fine Arts Museums of San Francisco. Gift of Mr. and Mrs. John D. Rockefeller, 3rd.
13. Courtesy, The Henry Francis du Pont Winterthur Museum.
14. National Gallery of Art, Washington, DC. Edgar William and Bernice Chrysler Garbisch Collection.
15. Courtesy of The New York Historical Society, New York City.
16. Hirshhorn Museum and Sculpture Garden, Smithsonian Institution, Washington, DC. Gift of Joseph H. Hirshhorn, 1966.
17. Courtesy of St. Vladimir's Orthodox Theological Seminary, Crestwood, New York.
18. Courtesy of St. Vladimir's Orthodox Theological Seminary, Crestwood, New York.
19. Courtesy of St. Vladimir's Orthodox Theological Seminary, Crestwood, New York.
20. Courtesy of St. Vladimir's Orthodox Theological Seminary, Crestwood, New York.
21. Courtesy of St. Vladimir's Orthodox Theological Seminary, Crestwood, New York.
22. Photograph credit: Alfred Talchinzky.
23. Sovfoto/Eastfoto.
24. Photograph from Historical Center, United Pentecostal Church International.
25. Photograph © Barbara Morgan.
26. Courtesy of Stephen Alcorn, Cambridge, New York.

Indexes

Subjects

abandonment, spiritual: *Alumbrados* and, 73, 133

absorption, spiritual, 30

accountability: Methodism and, 355, 358–59, 366–68

adherence, spiritual, 51–52

L'Adieu de l'âme devote laissant le corps (Richeome), 28

adoration: Bérulle and, 48–49, 50, 52

aesthetics, theological: of von Balthasar, 156–58

African Christianity, 523–24, 527

Afro-American traditions, 372–406; aesthetic-cultural aspects, 387–94; African "survivals" in Christianity, 378–87; appearance of independent black churches, 374–75; civil rights movement and, 375–76, 396, 399; conjuring and prayer in, 379–83; diaspora configuration in, 402–4; discourse, rituals of, 391–94; Egypt figure in, 398; Ethiopianism and, 397–98, 400–401; exodus theme in, 395, 396–97; healing in, 383–87; mundane story of, 372–76; music and, 387–91; National Association for the Advancement of Colored People and, 375; political aspects, 394–404; promised land vs. captivity themes in, 401–2; prophecy in, 382–83; religious aspects, 377–87; sacred story of, 372, 377–404; shamanism and, 384–87; signifying in, 391–94; slave trade and, 373–74; spirit-possession and, 377–79; suffering and, 386; transcendence in community as goal of, 373; Universal Negro Improvement Association and, 375

Alumbrados, 72–74, 91; Jesuit direction and, 23; Ignatius Loyola and, 15; Mercurian and, 17; Nadal and, 18; Quietism and, 132–33

Amor Dei (John Burnaby), 285

Anglicans, affluence of, 258; on Bible, 196; Book of Common Prayer and, 259–63, 285; Cambridge Platonists and, 269–71, 284–85; Carolines and, 263–69; catholicism of, 277–80; conformity and, 257–58; evangelical revival of, 274–76, 357; Jacobans and, 263–69; John Wesley and, 252–55, 258, 357, 360–63; law and, 257–58; liturgical character of, 260; moralistic school of, 271–74; mysticism and, 263, 269–70, 276, 278, 282–84; origin of, 257–59; Oxford Movement and, 277–82; prayer and, 284–86; Puritans and, 258; social action of, 286; Tractarians and, 277–78; twentieth-century, 282–89; *see also* Catholicism

L'Année chrétienne (Suffren), 54

annihilation, spiritual, 29, 72

anthropology: of Bérulle, 51; of Francis de Sales, 40

Apologia pro vita sua (Newman), 144

Apologies for Jansenius (Antoine Arnauld), 125

Aracoeli Holy Child, 117

Arminianism, 224–26, 268

art: literary fragment as, 192

Arte para Servir a Dios (Alonso de Madrid), 69

Ascent of Mount Carmel (John of the Cross), 83

The Ascent of Mount Sion (Laredo), 76

asceticism: Jesuit, 8, 9, 17; of popular saints, 112

Asian Christianity, 525–27

Athos, Mount: hesychasm and, 419–21, 428–29, 450

Augsburg Interim, 213–14

Augustinianism: Barcos and, 130; Bérulle and, 51; Jansen and, 122, 123

Augustinus (Jansen), 122, 123

authorial Bible interpretation, 195–97

authors: Anglican, 263–69, 271, 280–89; Calvinist, 226–27; John Wesley influenced by, 354–56; Lutheran, 221–23; Reform-orthodoxy, 229–30, *see also* writings

Names

Colophon

Christian Spirituality: Post-Reformation and Modern,
Volume 18 of World Spirituality: An Encyclopedic History of the
Religious Quest, was designed by Maurya P. Horgan and Paul J. Kobelski.
The type is 11-point Garamond Antiqua and was set by
The Scriptorium, Denver, Colorado